Global Environmental Politics

Dilemmas in World Politics

Dilemmas in World Politics offers teachers and students in international relations a series of quality books on critical issues, trends, and regions in international politics. Each text examines a "real world" dilemma and is structured to cover the historical, theoretical, practical, and projected dimensions of its subject.

FIFTH EDITION

Global Environmental Politics

PAMELA S. CHASEK

DAVID L. DOWNIE

JANET WELSH BROWN

WESTVIEW
PRESS

A MEMBER OF THE PERSEUS BOOKS GROUP

Published by Westview Press,
A Member of the Perseus Books Group

Find us on the World Wide Web at www.westviewpress.com.

Every effort has been made to secure required permissions to use all images, maps, and other art included in this volume.

Westview Press books are available at special discounts for bulk purchases in the United States by corporations, institutions, and other organizations. For more information, please contact the Special Markets Department at the Perseus Books Group, 2300 Chestnut Street, Suite 200, Philadelphia, PA 19103, or call (800) 810-4145, ext. 5000, or e-mail special.markets@perseusbooks.com.

Library of Congress Cataloging-in-Publication Data
Chasek, Pamela S., 1961–
    Global environmental politics. — 5th ed. / Pamela S. Chasek, David L. Downie, Janet Welsh Brown.
        p. cm.
    Includes bibliographical references and index.
    ISBN 978-0-8133-4442-3 (alk. paper)
    1. Environmental policy. I. Downie, David Leonard. II. Brown, Janet Welsh. III. Title.
    GE170.C46 2010
    363.7'056—dc22
                                    2009047221
10 9 8 7 6 5 4 3 2

Contents

List of Illustrations

Tables

Figures

Photos

Cartoons

Boxes

Acknowledgments

This book has been made possible by the inspiration, encouragement, and assistance of our colleagues at the *Earth Negotiations Bulletin*, Manhattan College, Columbia University, Fairfield University, and the United Nations. We thank Gareth Porter and Janet Welsh Brown for their contribution to the study of global environmental politics by initiating this book and then entrusting us to carry on. We also want to thank the team at Westview Press, including Anthony Wahl, Meredith Smith, Kelsey Mitchell, Erica Lawrence, and Jennifer Kelland, for their hard work, support, and positive attitude throughout this process.

In addition to all our colleagues who were thanked in earlier editions of this book, we thank Mary Brown, Scott MacKenzie, Alexandra Roem, Charlotte Sida, Sofia Trevino, and Krysten Kenny for their research assistance. We are also grateful to the following colleagues and friends who reviewed portions of the manuscript for accuracy or clarity or provided other valuable assistance, feedback, and moral support: Alexis Terrizzi, Laura Whitman, Tony Fitzgerald, Aaron Cosbey, Mark Halle, and David Rosenberg.

Last, but certainly not least, David Downie thanks his family—Laura Whitman, William Downie, and Lindsey Downie—for making all the good things in his life possible. Pamela Chasek thanks her family—Kimo, Sam, and Kai Goree—for all of their patience, support, and love.

PAMELA CHASEK
DAVID DOWNIE

List of Acronyms

AOSIS	Alliance of Small Island States
APEC	Asia-Pacific Economic Cooperation
BCSC	Business Council on Sustainable Development
CAFE	Corporate Average Fuel Economy Standards (U.S.)
CBD	Convention on Biological Diversity
CDM	Clean Development Mechanism
CFC	chlorofluorocarbon
CITES	Convention on International Trade in Endangered Species of Wild Fauna and Flora
CO_2	carbon dioxide
COFI	Committee on Fisheries (FAO)
COP	Conference of the Parties
CSD	Commission on Sustainable Development
CTE	Committee on Trade and Environment (WTO)
CUE	critical-use exemption
EC	European Community
EEZ	exclusive economic zone
ETM	environmental trade measure
EU	European Union
FAO	Food and Agriculture Organization of the United Nations
FIELD	Foundation for International Environmental Law and Development
FSC	Forest Stewardship Council
FTA	financial and technical assistance
G-77	Group of 77 (developing-country negotiating bloc)
G-8	Group of Eight (international forum for governments of the world's eight largest economies)
GATT	General Agreement on Tariffs and Trade
GDP	gross domestic product
GEF	Global Environment Facility
gha	global hectare
GHG	greenhouse gas
GM	Global Mechanism
GMO	genetically modified organism
GNP	gross national product
GPA	Global Programme of Action for the Protection of the Marine Environment from Land-Based Activities

GRID	Global Resource Information Database
HCFC	hydrochlorofluorocarbon
HFC	hydrofluorocarbon
HIPC	heavily indebted poor countries
IFCS	Intergovernmental Forum on Chemical Safety
IFF	Intergovernmental Forum on Forests
IGO	intergovernmental organization
IISD	International Institute for Sustainable Development
IMF	International Monetary Fund
IMO	International Maritime Organization
INC	Intergovernmental Negotiating Committee
INGO	international nongovernmental organization
IOMC	Inter-Organization Programme for the Sound Management of Chemicals
IPCC	Intergovernmental Panel on Climate Change
IPEN	International POPs Elimination Network
IPF	Intergovernmental Panel on Forests
IPR	intellectual property rights
IUCN	International Union for the Conservation of Nature and Natural Resources/World Conservation Union
IUU	illegal, unreported, and unregulated (fishing)
IWC	International Whaling Commission
JPOI	Johannesburg Plan of Implementation
LMO	living modified organism
LMO-FFP	living modified organism intended for food, feed, and processing
LRTAP	Convention on Long-Range Transboundary Air Pollution
MARPOL	International Convention for the Prevention of Pollution from Ships
MDG	Millennium Development Goal
MEA	multilateral environmental agreement
MMPA	Marine Mammal Protection Act (U.S.)
MOP	Meeting of the Parties
MSC	Marine Stewardship Council
NAFO	Northwest Atlantic Fisheries Organization
NAFTA	North American Free Trade Agreement
NEPAD	New Partnership for Africa's Development
NGO	nongovernmental organization
NIEO	New International Economic Order
NO_x	nitrogen oxide
OAS	Organization of American States
ODA	official development assistance
ODS	ozone-depleting substance(s)
OECD	Organization for Economic Cooperation and Development
PCB	polychlorinated biphenyl
PIC	prior informed consent

POP	persistent organic pollutant
POPRC	Persistent Organic Pollutants Review Committee
PRSP	Poverty-Reduction Strategy Paper
RST	review of significant trade
SO$_2$	sulfur dioxide
SPREP	Pacific Regional Environment Programme
TED	turtle-excluder device
TRAFFIC	Trade Records Analysis of Flora and Fauna in Commerce
UNCCD	United Nations Convention to Combat Desertification
UNCED	United Nations Conference on Environment and Development
UNDP	United Nations Development Programme
UNECE	United Nations Economic Commission for Europe
UNEP	United Nations Environment Programme
UNFCCC	United Nations Framework Convention on Climate Change
UNFF	United Nations Forum on Forests
UNGA	United Nations General Assembly
VOC	volatile organic compound
WCMC	World Conservation Monitoring Center
WHO	World Health Organization
WMO	World Meteorological Organization
WSSD	World Summit on Sustainable Development
WTO	World Trade Organization
WWF	World Wildlife Fund/Worldwide Fund for Nature

Chronology

1800   Atmospheric carbon dioxide (CO_2) and methane concentrations in the atmosphere hover around 270 to 290 parts per million (ppm) and 700 parts per billion (ppb), respectively. Most scientists today use these numbers as a pre–Industrial Revolution baseline for comparison.

1827   Jean-Baptiste Joseph Fourier, a French mathematician and physicist, publishes perhaps the first paper speculating on the existence of what we now call the natural greenhouse effect.

1859   John Tyndall, an Irish physicist, becomes one of the first scientists to study the greenhouse effect as well as the relative radiative forcings of different gases in the atmosphere, including CO_2.

1872   Yellowstone National Park, the first national park in the United States, is created.

1896   Svante Arrhenius, a Swedish scientist, publishes an article that concludes that doubling the amount of CO_2 in the atmosphere would raise temperatures by 5 to 6 degrees Celsius.

1900 CO_2 concentration in the atmosphere reaches 295 ppm.

1902   The Convention for the Protection of Birds Useful to Agriculture is signed.

1903   The first international conservation NGO is formed, the Society for the Preservation of the Wild Fauna of the Empire, in the United Kingdom.

1909   U.S. president Theodore Roosevelt convenes the North American Conservation Conference in Washington, D.C.

1911   The Treaty for the Preservation and Protection of Fur Seals is signed.

1913   The Commission for the International Protection of Nature is founded.

1933   The London Convention on the Preservation of Fauna and Flora in Their Natural State is signed.

1938   G. S. Callendar revisits Arrhenius's 1896 publication and argues that increases in CO_2 concentration could explain recent warming trends.

1940   The Convention on Nature Protection and Wildlife Preservation in the Western Hemisphere is signed.

1945   The United Nations is established.

1946   The International Convention for the Regulation of Whaling is signed; the International Whaling Commission (IWC) is created.

1947   The International Union for the Conservation of Nature (IUCN) is established, becoming first international nongovernmental organization with a global outlook on environmental problems.

1948   The International Maritime Organization (IMO) is created.

1949   The International Convention for the Northwest Atlantic Fisheries is signed.

1950   The World Meteorological Organization (WMO) is created.

  -    The International Convention for the Protection of Birds is signed.

1952   A toxic mix of dense fog and sooty, black coal smoke kills at least 4,000 people, and perhaps as many as 12,000, in the worst of London's "killer fogs."

1954   The International Convention for the Prevention of Pollution of the Sea by Oil is signed.

1956   The European Economic Community is established.

  -    Roger Revelle and Charles David Keeling publish a paper on CO_2, showing the trend of increasing atmospheric concentrations over the past century.

1959   The Antarctic Treaty is signed.

1962   Rachel Carson's *Silent Spring* is published.

1963   The Agreement for the Protection of the Rhine against Pollution is signed.

1967   The supertanker *Torrey Canyon* runs aground in the English Channel, causing a massive oil spill.

1969   The U.S. Congress passes the National Environmental Policy Act (NEPA).

1971   The Ramsar Convention on Wetlands of International Importance is signed.

1972   The United Nations Conference on the Human Environment is convened in Stockholm.

  -    The United Nations Environment Programme (UNEP) is created.

  -    *The Limits to Growth* report for the Club of Rome is published.

  -    The Convention on the Prevention of Marine Pollution by Dumping of Wastes and Other Matter (London Convention) is signed.

  -    The Convention for the Conservation of Antarctic Seals is signed.

1973   The Convention on International Trade in Endangered Species of Wild Fauna and Flora (CITES) is signed.

  -    The International Convention for the Prevention of Pollution from Ships (MARPOL) is signed.

  -    The U.S. Endangered Species Conservation Act banning whaling and whale imports becomes law.

1974   The Declaration on the Establishment of a New International Economic Order (NIEO) is issued by the Sixth Special Session of the United Nations General Assembly (UNGA).

-    M. J. Molina and F. S. Rowland publish their theory that chlorofluorocarbons (CFCs) threaten the ozone layer.

-    The World Population Conference is held in Bucharest, Romania.

-    The World Food Conference is held in Rome, Italy.

1975   The UNEP Regional Seas Programme is created.

1976   The Convention for the Protection of the Mediterranean Sea against Pollution is signed.

-    The United Nations Conference on Human Settlements is held in Vancouver, British Columbia.

-    The UNEP International Register of Potentially Toxic Chemicals is established.

1977   The United Nations Conference on Desertification adopts the Plan of Action to Combat Desertification.

-    The Ad Hoc Conference of Experts convened by UNEP approves the World Plan of Action on the Ozone Layer.

1979   The Convention on the Conservation of Migratory Species (CMS) is signed.

-    The Convention on Long-Range Transboundary Air Pollution (LRTAP) is signed.

-    The First World Climate Conference, convened in Geneva by WMO, UNEP, and the International Council for Science, warns of the danger of global warming.

1980   The Convention on the Conservation of Antarctic Marine Living Resources is signed.

-    The World Conservation Strategy is launched by IUCN and UNEP.

-    The *Global 2000 Report to the President* is published.

1981   The Montevideo Programme on International Environmental Law is launched.

1982   Formal negotiations begin on protection of the ozone layer.

-    The United Nations Convention on the Law of the Sea (UNCLOS) is signed.

-    The phaseout of commercial whaling over a three-year period is passed by the IWC.

1984   The International Tropical Timber Agreement (ITTA) is signed.

-    The Union Carbide disaster occurs in Bhopal, India.

- The Protocol for Long-term Financing of Monitoring and Evaluation of the Long-range Transmission of Air Pollutants in Europe (part of the LRTAP regime) is signed.

1985   The Vienna Convention for Protection of the Ozone Layer is signed.

- The Antarctic ozone-hole discovery is published in *Nature*.

- Canadian scientists discover abnormally high levels of persistent organic pollutants, or POPs, in some Inuit communities in northern Canada, revealing global transport of toxic chemicals.

- The Helsinki Protocol to LRTAP is signed, committing signatories to sulfur dioxide emissions reduction.

- A London Convention Meeting of the Parties votes to ban all further dumping of low-level radioactive wastes in oceans until it is proven safe.

- A conference of climate experts produces consensus on the serious possibility of global warming.

- The Tropical Forestry Action Plan is approved by donor countries at a conference in The Hague.

- The Montreal Guidelines for the Protection of the Marine Environment from Land-Based Sources are signed.

1986   A major explosion at the Soviet nuclear plant in Chernobyl sends a radioactive cloud across western Europe and Japan.

1987   The Montreal Protocol on Substances That Deplete the Ozone Layer is signed.

- The International Tropical Timber Organization holds its first meeting in Yokohama, Japan.

- The Report of the World Commission on Environment and Development (the Brundtland Report) is published as *Our Common Future*.

1988   The world's governments agree to establish the Intergovernmental Panel on Climate Change (IPCC).

- British scientists issue a report on the dramatic decrease in the ozone layer over Antarctica; an Ozone Trends Panel report documents ozone-layer decreases in the Northern Hemisphere.

- The Sofia Protocol to LRTAP is signed, committing the signatories to nitrogen oxide emissions reduction.

- The Convention on the Regulation of Antarctic Mineral Resources Activities is signed in Wellington, New Zealand.

1989   The *Exxon Valdez* spills oil in the Gulf of Alaska.

- A communiqué of the Group of Seven (G-7) heads of industrial democracies focuses on the global environment.

- Twenty-four nations issue The Hague Declaration on the Environment.

- The Basel Convention on the Control of Transboundary Movements of Hazardous Wastes and Their Disposal is signed; the European Community reaches agreement with Africa, Caribbean, and Pacific states to ban hazardous waste exports to countries without the capacity to dispose of them safely.
- The Ministerial Conference on Atmospheric Pollution and Climate Change issues the Noordwijk Declaration in the Netherlands, calling for stabilization of CO_2 emissions by 2000.
- The seventh CITES Conference of the Parties (COP) votes to ban trade in African elephant ivory products.

1990   The second Meeting of the Parties to the Montreal Protocol convenes in London to strengthen the Montreal Protocol and establish the Multilateral Fund.

- The communiqué of the G-7 heads of state summit meeting in Houston calls for negotiation of an international agreement on the world's forests.
- The Bergen Ministerial Declaration on Sustainable Development in the Economic Commission for Europe calls stabilization of CO_2 emissions the first step.
- The Meeting of Antarctic Treaty Consultative Parties in Santiago, Chile, agrees to begin negotiations on a convention for environmental protection of Antarctica.
- The ban on whaling is extended by the IWC.
- The IPCC releases its First Assessment Report, asserting that the average global surface temperature has increased by 0.3 to 0.6 degrees Celsius since 1980.

1991   The Bamako Convention on the Ban of the Import into Africa and the Control of Transboundary Movement and Management of Hazardous Wastes within Africa is signed.

- The Global Environment Facility (GEF) is established.
- The Protocol on Environmental Protection to the Antarctic Treaty is signed.
- The Volatile Organic Compounds Protocol to LRTAP is signed.

1992   The United Nations Conference on Environment and Development is convened in Rio de Janeiro, Brazil.

- The United Nations Framework Convention on Climate Change is signed in Rio de Janeiro.
- The Convention on Biological Diversity is signed in Rio de Janeiro.
- The UNGA establishes the Commission on Sustainable Development.

1993   The United Nations Conference on Straddling and Highly Migratory Fish Stocks is convened.

1994   The United Nations Convention to Combat Desertification is signed.

-      The United Nations Convention on the Law of the Sea enters into force.

-      The General Agreement on Tariffs and Trade (GATT) Uruguay Round concludes negotiations in Marrakech, Morocco.

-      The International Conference on Population and Development is held in Cairo, Egypt.

-      The Global Conference on the Sustainable Development of Small Island Developing States meets in Barbados.

-      The World Conference on Natural Disaster Reduction meets in Yokohama, Japan.

1995   The World Conference on Social Development convenes in Copenhagen, Denmark.

-      The Fourth World Conference on Women convenes in Beijing, China.

-      The Agreement on the Conservation and Management of Straddling Fish Stocks and Highly Migratory Fish Stocks is signed.

-      The World Trade Organization is established.

1996   The IPCC releases its Second Assessment Report, which concludes that there is a discernible human influence on the global climate.

1997   The UNGA Special Session convenes to review the implementation of Agenda 21.

-      The tenth CITES COP votes to reopen the ivory trade in Botswana, Namibia, and Zimbabwe.

-      The Kyoto Protocol to the Framework Convention on Climate Change is signed.

1998   The Protocols on Heavy Metals and Persistent Organic Pollutants to LRTAP are signed.

-      The Rotterdam Convention on the Prior Informed Consent Procedure for Certain Hazardous Chemicals and Pesticides in International Trade is signed.

1999   A UNGA Special Session meets to review the implementation of the Barbados Programme of Action on Small Island Developing States.

-      The Protocol to Abate Acidification, Eutrophication, and Ground-Level Ozone to LRTAP is adopted.

-      The first legal sale of ivory in a decade takes place in Windhoek, Namibia.

-      The Protocol on Liability and Compensation to the Basel Convention on the Control of Transboundary Movements and Hazardous Wastes and Their Disposal is adopted.

2000   The Cartagena Protocol on Biosafety is adopted by the Conference of the Parties to the Convention on Biological Diversity.

-      The United Nations Forum on Forests is established.

- The Millennium Summit is held at United Nations Headquarters in New York.

2001   The Stockholm Convention on Persistent Organic Pollutants is signed.

- The IPCC's Third Assessment Report concludes that the evidence of humanity's influence on the global climate is stronger than ever.

- The Food and Agriculture Organization (FAO) of the United Nations adopts the International Treaty on Plant Genetic Resources for Food and Agriculture.

2002   The International Conference on Financing for Development is held in Monterrey, Mexico.

- The United Nations World Summit on Sustainable Development is held in Johannesburg, South Africa.

2003   The African Ministerial Conference on the Environment adopts the New Partnership for Africa's Development (NEPAD) Environment Action Plan.

- The Cartagena Protocol on Biosafety enters into force.

2004 CO_2 concentration in the atmosphere reaches an unprecedented 379 ppm.

- The Rotterdam Convention enters into force.

- The Stockholm Convention enters into force.

- The Nobel Committee awards the 2004 Nobel Peace Prize to Professor Wangari Maathai, Kenya's assistant minister of environment and natural resources and founder of the Green Belt Movement.

2005   The Kyoto Protocol enters into force.

- The Millennium Ecosystem Assessment is released; 1,300 experts from ninety-five countries provide scientific information concerning the consequences of ecosystem change for human well-being.

- The Mauritius International Meeting on the Implementation of the Barbados Programme of Action on the Sustainable Development of Small Island Developing States is convened.

- The World Conference on Disaster Reduction is held in Kobe-Hyogo, Japan.

- The European Union's Greenhouse Gas Emission Trading Scheme (EU ETS) begins operation as the world's first multicountry, multisector greenhouse gas emission trading scheme.

- Data indicate that 2005 was the warmest year since people began keeping regular records more than a century ago. The years 1998, 2002, 2003, and 2004 stand as the second, third, fourth, and fifth warmest years, respectively.

2006   The ITTA successor agreement (ITTA 2006) is adopted in Geneva.

- UNEP adopts the Strategic Approach to International Chemicals Management.

- The Stern Report makes the convincing economic case that the costs of inaction on climate change will be up to twenty times greater than the costs of measures required to address the issue today.

- NASA reports that recovery of the ozone layer is greater due in part to reduced concentrations of CFCs phased out under the Montreal Protocol.

2007   The IPCC Fourth Assessment Report confirms that climate change is occurring, that the human contribution to this change is unequivocal, and that impacts are already apparent and will increase as temperatures rise.

- The European Parliament adopts a resolution calling for greenhouse gas emissions reductions to limit the rise in global temperature to 2 degrees Celsius by 2100.

- The Nobel Committee awards the 2007 Nobel Peace Prize to the IPCC and former U.S. vice president Albert Gore for their efforts to create and disseminate knowledge about climate change.

- Australia ratifies the Kyoto Protocol, leaving the United States as the only major industrialized country outside the treaty.

- The parties to the climate regime meet in Bali, Indonesia, and agree on a framework for negotiating a successor agreement to the Kyoto Protocol.

2008 CO_2 levels in the atmosphere reach 387 ppm, the highest for at least 650,000 years.

- The European Union announces its intention to cut its greenhouse gas emissions by 20 percent from 1990 levels by 2020 and to require that 20 percent of total energy consumption come from renewable energies.

- The World Glacier Monitoring Service releases data showing that the average rate of melting on thirty glaciers in nine mountain ranges more than doubled between 2004 and 2006.

- A 160-square-mile chunk of ice in western Antarctica, about seven times the size of Manhattan Island in New York City, collapses in March, putting an even greater portion of glacial ice at risk.

2009   The parties to the Stockholm Convention significantly expand the regime, limiting the production and use of nine additional toxic substances.

- A group of 181 investor institutions, which collectively manage more than $13 trillion in assets, issues a statement calling for a new strong and binding global treaty to address climate change.

- The parties to the climate regime meet in Copenhagen to discuss post-2012 greenhouse gas emissions-reduction commitments to succeed the Kyoto Protocol.

1

The Emergence of Global Environmental Politics

Until the 1980s, most governments regarded global environmental problems as minor issues, marginal both to their core national interests and to international politics in general. This situation has changed. The rise of environmental movements in the industrialized countries and the appearance of well-publicized global environmental threats that could profoundly affect the welfare of all humankind—such as the depletion of the **ozone layer**, global **climate change**, and depletion of the world's fisheries—have awarded global environmental issues a much higher status in world politics. Environmental issues are no longer viewed as minor scientific and technical matters but as important issues both in their own right and because they are increasingly intertwined with other significant issues in world politics including economic development, international trade, North-South relations, and even international conflict and national social and political stability.

Growing international concern about the environment is no historical accident. It developed in response to alterations in major components of the **biosphere,** including the atmosphere, the oceans, soil cover, the climate system, and the range of animal and plant species. Many by-products of economic growth—such as the burning of fossil fuels, air and water pollution, release of ozone-destroying chemicals, production of toxic chemicals, increased use of natural resources, and decreasing forest cover—have put cumulative stresses on the physical environment that now threaten human health and economic well-being. The costs of these activities to future generations will be much higher in developing as well as highly industrialized countries than they are to the world's current population.

The past four decades have seen an enormous increase in scientific understanding of global environmental issues. The realization that environmental threats have serious socioeconomic and human costs and that unilateral actions by individual countries cannot solve them has produced increased international cooperation aimed at halting or reversing environmental degradation. This realization has also unleashed a political force, a global environmental movement that undertakes increasingly effective transnational action on various issues. But some states, as well as certain economic interests, have opposed strong international actions to reduce or eliminate particular activities that threaten the global environment.

The result is an intensifying struggle over global environmental issues. As an introduction to global environmental politics, this chapter highlights the economic and environmental trends underlying the emergence of global environmental politics as a major issue area, defines its scope, and outlines some of its major characteristics. The chapter also traces some of the major intellectual currents and political developments that have contributed to the evolution of global environmental politics.

GLOBAL MACROTRENDS

Global economic, demographic, and environmental macrotrends describe key changes that drive global environmental politics. Indeed, the rise of global environmental politics can be understood only within the context of the major changes in the physical environment produced by the explosive growth in economic activity and population during the past sixty-five years.

Humanity's potential stress on the global environment is, in large part, a function of world population multiplied by per capita consumption and waste production. One way to measure this is through a country's "ecological footprint," or "the sum of all the cropland, grazing land, forest and fishing grounds required to produce the food, fiber and timber it consumes, to absorb the wastes emitted when it uses energy, and to provide space for its infrastructure."[1] WWF's measurement of the global ecological footprint assesses humanity's demand on the biosphere in terms of the area of biologically productive land and sea required to provide the resources we use and to absorb our waste. In 2005 the global ecological footprint was 17.5 billion global hectares (gha), or 2.7 gha per person (a global hectare is a hectare [10,000 square meters] with world-average ability to produce resources and absorb wastes). On the supply side, the total productive area, or biocapacity, was 13.6 billion gha, or 2.1 gha per person. This means that in 2005, global demand was 30 percent greater than the supply of the earth's total biocapacity.[2]

For more than fifty years, per capita consumption of natural resources such as wood, energy, fish, and water has been rising much faster than population growth. For example, private consumption expenditures (the amount households spend on goods and services) increased more than fourfold from 1960 to 2000, even though the global population only doubled during this period.[3] Along these lines, humanity's ecological foot-print first exceeded the Earth's total biocapacity in the 1980s. As the developing world pursues the lifestyles of North America and Europe, the future will likely bring ever higher per capita rates of consumption. In China, for instance, the per-person ecological footprint and population both doubled between 1961 and 2005, producing a more than fourfold increase in its total ecological footprint.[4]

But despite increases in the consuming class in places like China and India, the gulf in consumption levels within and between countries continues to draw attention. The 12 percent of the world's population that lives in North America and western Europe accounts for 60 percent of private consumption spending, while the one-third living in South Asia and sub-Saharan Africa accounts for only 3.2 percent. The United States, with less than 5 percent of the global population, uses about a quarter of the world's fossil fuel resources—coal, oil, and natural gas.[5] The United States has had more private cars than licensed drivers since the 1970s, and until the oil-price shock of 2008, gas-guzzling sport utility vehicles were among the best-selling vehicles. The average size of new single-family houses in the United States has grown by about 38 percent since 1950,[6] despite a decrease in the average number of people per household, and larger houses consume more resources, both in their construction and during their operation.

At the other end of the spectrum, 1.4 billion people—one out of five—live on less than $1.25 a day; nearly 1 billion people lack access to safe drinking water; and 2.5 billion people live without basic sanitation.[7] Providing adequate food, clean water, and basic education for the world's poorest could be achieved for less than people spend annually on makeup, ice cream, and pet food[8] (see Table 1.1).

TABLE 1.1 Annual Expenditure on Luxury Items Compared with Funding Needed to Meet Selected Basic Needs

PRODUCT	ANNUAL EXPENDITURE	SOCIAL OR ECONOMIC GOAL	ADDITIONAL ANNUAL INVESTMENT NEEDED TO ACHIEVE GOAL
Makeup	$18 billion	Reproductive health care for all women	$12 billion
Pet food in Europe and the United States	$17 billion	Elimination of hunger and malnutrition	$19 billion
Perfumes	$15 billion	Universal literacy	$5 billion
Ocean cruises	$14 billion	Clean drinking water for all	$10 billion
Ice cream in Europe	$11 billion	Immunizing every child	$1.3 billion

Source: World Watch, *State of the World 2004* (New York: W.W. Norton, 2004), p. 10.

FIGURE 1.1   **World population, 1950–2050 (projected)**

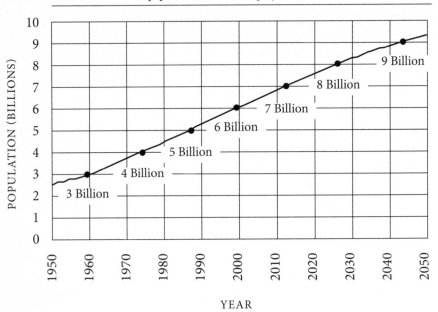

Source: "World Population Information," U.S. Census Bureau, August 7, 2009,
www.census.gov/ipc/www/idb/worldpopinfo.php.

Population growth worldwide also has a major impact on the environment. Global
population doubled between 1950 and 1987 (from 2.5 billion to 5 billion) and reached
the 6-billion mark in October 1999. World population is projected to reach 7 billion
early in 2012, up from the current 6.8 billion, and surpass 9 billion by 2050[9] (see Figure
1.1). World population is currently growing at a rate of 1.2 percent annually, significantly
less than the peak growth rate of 2.04 percent from 1965 to 1970 and less than the rate
of 1.46 percent from 1990 to 1995. These figures imply a net addition of 78 million people per year. The United Nations Population Division estimates that between 2010 and
2050, nine countries will account for half of the world's projected population increase:
India, Pakistan, Nigeria, Ethiopia, the United States, the Democratic Republic of Congo,
the United Republic of Tanzania, China, and Bangladesh.[10] The vast majority of children
born each year, perhaps as many as 90 percent, live in developing countries.

Population-growth and consumption patterns contribute to environmental degradation by increasing stress on both natural resources (such as fresh air and water, arable
land, and fish stocks) and vital natural systems (such as the ozone layer and climate
system). The increasing numbers of people and their needs for refrigeration, transportation, and manufactured goods have far-reaching implications for climate change,

pollution, energy use, and the natural resource base, especially with regard to agricultural land, forests, and fisheries.

In 2005, the single largest demand that human consumption put on the biosphere was its carbon footprint, which grew more than tenfold from 1961 (see Box 1.1). The carbon footprint measures how human activities have a direct impact on the carbon dioxide (CO_2) emitted into the atmosphere, contributing to climate change. Which countries as a whole place the greatest demand on the planet, and how has this changed over time? In 2005, the United States and China had the largest total national footprints, each using 21 percent of the planet's biocapacity. China had a much smaller per-person footprint than the United States but a population more than four times as large. India's footprint was the next largest; it used 7 percent of the earth's total biocapacity but its per-person footprint was even smaller than China's.[11]

Today, the world's richest countries use on average eleven times more energy than the poorest ones; the richest comprise only 15 percent of the world's population, but they use more than half its energy[12] (see Figure 1.2). The average American consumes five times more energy than the average global citizen, six times more than the average Chinese, and twenty times more than the average Indian (and the vast majority of this energy still comes from burning fossil fuels).[13] However, energy consumption in developing countries, especially in Asia, is increasing rapidly, driven by industrial expansion and infrastructure improvement, high population growth and urbanization, and

---

BOX 1.1   WHAT IS A CARBON FOOTPRINT?

A carbon footprint measures the impact our activities have on the environment, particularly on climate change. It relates to the amount of greenhouse gases (GHGs) produced in our day-to-day lives from burning fossil fuels for electricity, heating, transportation, and so forth. The carbon footprint measures all GHGs we individually produce in units of tons (or kilograms) of CO_2 equivalent.

A carbon footprint has two parts. The primary footprint measures our direct emissions of CO_2 from burning fossil fuels, including energy consumption (e.g., household heating and electricity) and transportation (e.g., cars and planes). The secondary footprint measures the indirect CO_2 emissions from the whole life cycle of products we use, that is, the emissions associated with their manufacture and eventual breakdown. To put it very simply, the more we buy, the more emissions will be released on our behalf. We have more control of our primary footprint but less control over the secondary.

"What Is a Carbon Footprint?" Carbon Footprint, Ltd., 2009, www.carbonfootprint.com/carbonfoot print.html.

FIGURE 1.2   Global energy use, 2006

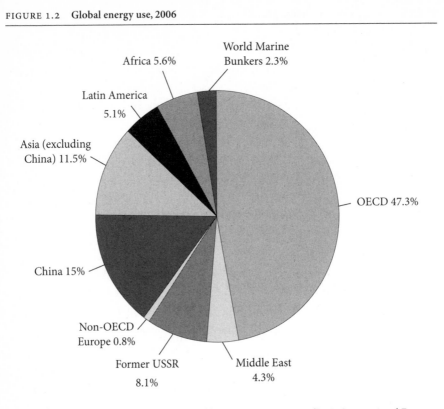

Source: International Energy Agency, *Key World Energy Statistics, 2008* (Paris: International Energy Agency, 2008).

rising incomes, which, in turn, enable families to purchase energy-consuming appliances and cars (see Figure 1.3). In 1980, China and India together accounted for less than 8 percent of the world's total energy consumption; in 2005 their share had grown to 18 percent. Even stronger growth is projected over the next twenty-five years, with their combined energy use more than doubling and their share increasing to one-quarter of world energy consumption in 2030. In contrast, the U.S. share of total world energy consumption is projected to contract from 22 percent in 2005 to about 17 percent in 2030.[14]

If present trends in energy and fossil fuel consumption continue, energy-related emissions of CO_2 are projected to rise from 29 billion metric tons in 2006 to 33.1 billion metric tons in 2015 and 40.4 billion metric tons in 2030—an increase of 39 percent over the projection period. More than two-thirds of the projected increase in emissions will come from developing countries, whose emissions are projected to exceed

FIGURE 1.3   **World energy consumption (quadrillion BTUs)**

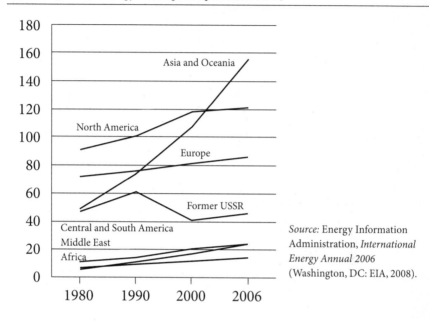

Source: Energy Information Administration, *International Energy Annual 2006* (Washington, DC: EIA, 2008).

industrialized-country emissions by 77 percent by 2030[15] (see Figure 1.4). Developing countries will remain big users of coal, the most carbon-intensive of fuels. Power stations, cars, and trucks will be responsible for most of the increases in energy-related emissions. Since combating climate change requires stabilizing and then reducing greenhouse gas emissions, many policy makers and scientists agree on the importance of avoiding, or at least reducing, emissions increases. Doing so is difficult given current population, energy, and consumption trends, but it may be possible through large increases in the use of renewable energy, further advances in energy efficiency, in both household consumption and production processes, and a shift in general consumption patterns toward inherently less energy- and resource-intensive goods and services.

Almost three out of five people in developing countries—some 3 billion—live in rural areas. But most of the land available to meet current and future food requirements is already in production. Further expansion will involve fragile and marginal lands. As land becomes increasingly scarce, farmers are forced to turn to intensive agriculture; the dramatically higher levels of irrigation and chemicals will, in turn, contribute to soil erosion and **salinization**, deteriorating water quality, and **desertification**. Population growth and development are converting forests into agricultural land and urban areas.

In addition, soaring food prices in recent years have increased the number of people vulnerable to starvation, severe hunger, and malnutrition. The World Bank estimated

FIGURE 1.4   World CO_2 emissions, 2006–2030

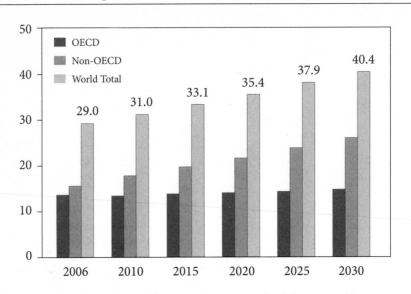

Sources: 2006: Energy Information Administration (EIA), *International Energy Annual 2006* (June–December 2008), www.eia.doe.gov/iea. *Projections:* EIA, World Energy Projections Plus (2009).

that food prices increased 140 percent from January 2002 to February 2008.[16] Escalating prices are driven partly by supply disruptions (below-average harvests in Europe and severe drought in Australia in 2006 and 2007) but mostly by rising demand due to changing diets, economic growth, an expanding world population, urbanization, use of food crops for **biofuels**, and certain agriculture policies, including subsidies in developed countries.

One key factor has been the large increase in biofuel production. Biofuels are liquid renewable fuels such as ethanol (an alcohol fermented from plant materials) and biodiesel (a fuel made from vegetable oils or animal fats) that can substitute for petroleum-based fuels. Biofuels tend to allocate productive resources (e.g., land, water, labor, capital) away from the production of food crops into the production of feedstock for biofuels. For example, in the United States 25 percent of the production of corn goes to ethanol production, and in the European Union (EU), 47 percent of vegetable oil production is used to make biofuel. Without the increase in biofuels, global wheat and corn stocks may not have declined as much, and price increases due to other factors could have been moderate.[17]

A second factor is the increasing cost of food production—more expensive seeds due in part to patents and other **intellectual property rights**, as well as higher costs for fuel (for machinery and vehicles), fertilizers, pesticides, water, land, and labor. The third factor is the increasing demand for meat and fish for the growing numbers of middle-class consumers in countries like China and India. While their consumption of such food is still far below that in Europe, North America, Australia, and New Zealand, the increase has led to a substantial growth in the demand for feed for animals and aquaculture fish. Using food as feed for animals whose meat and milk are then consumed by humans requires nine times as many calories as those required for direct human consumption.[18]

The convergence of population growth, rising demand for lumber and fuelwood, and the conversion of forests to agriculture has also put increasing pressure on the world's forests, especially in developing countries. At the beginning of the twentieth century, the world contained about 5 billion hectares of forested area; now fewer than 4 billion hectares remain.[19] **Deforestation,** in turn, has contributed to the loss of **biodiversity** (the variety of living things), including the extinction of species and the loss of genetic diversity within species. Biodiversity is being lost at a historically unprecedented rate. Scientists began warning in the 1980s that the destruction of tropical forests, which hold an estimated 50 to 90 percent of all species, could result in the loss of one-fourth, or even one-half, of the earth's species within a few decades. However, the earth's biodiversity is not confined to the tropical forests: Human actions have dramatically transformed virtually all of the earth's **ecosystems.** The Millennium Ecosystem Assessment (see Box 1.2) estimated that between 10 and 50 percent of species are currently threatened with extinction, including some 12 percent of bird species, 23 percent of mammals, and 25 percent of conifers (cone bearing trees).[20]

Many of the world's major fisheries are overfished or on the verge of collapse. Because the waters and biological resources of the high seas belong to no nation, it is not surprising that overfishing has become a serious problem. According to the Food and Agriculture Organization of the United Nations (FAO), an estimated 80 percent of major marine fish stocks have been fully exploited, overexploited, or significantly depleted. The Northeast Atlantic and the Mediterranean and Black seas contain stocks with the greatest need for recovery, followed by the Northwest and Southeast Atlantic, Southeast Pacific, and Southern oceans. Seven important species are considered fully exploited or overexploited (anchoveta, Chilean jack mackerel, Alaska pollock, Japanese anchovy, blue whiting, and Atlantic herring).[21] Staples such as tuna, swordfish, Atlantic salmon, and even cod could soon be on the endangered list. This would cripple the industries they support. In addition, inefficient fishing practices waste a high percentage of each year's catch; 20 million metric tons of **bycatch** (unintentionally caught fish, seabirds, sea turtles, marine mammals, and other ocean life) die every year when they are carelessly swept up and discarded by commercial fishing operations.[22]

Marine environments are also under siege from land-based sources of marine pollution, believed to account for nearly 80 percent of the total pollution of the oceans.

BOX 1.2   WHAT IS THE MILLENNIUM ECOSYSTEM ASSESSMENT?

The Millennium Ecosystem Assessment examined the health of the world's ecosystems and the consequences of ecosystem change for human well-being. Sponsored by the United Nations, the World Resources Institute, and other international organizations and initiated in 2001, the assessment involved the work of more than 1,360 experts worldwide who conducted comprehensive reviews of current knowledge, including scientific literature and field data. Their findings, contained in five technical volumes and six synthesis reports, provide a state-of-the-art scientific appraisal of the conditions and trends in the world's ecosystems and the services they provide (such as clean water, food, forest products, flood control, and natural resources), as well as the options for restoring, conserving, or enhancing the sustainable use of ecosystems.

The assessment's core finding, released in 2005, is that human actions are rapidly depleting earth's natural resources and putting such strain on the environment that we can no longer take for granted the ability of the planet's ecosystems to sustain future generations. At the same time, the assessment shows that with appropriate actions it is possible to reverse the degradation of many ecosystem services over the next fifty years, but the changes in policy and practice required are substantial and not currently underway.

The assessment's reports and information on its findings, history, operation, participants, and use by scientists and policy makers can be found on the Millennium Ecosystem Assessment website at www.millenniumassessment.org.

The major land-based pollutants are synthetic organic compounds; excess sedimentation from mining, deforestation, or agriculture; biological contaminants in sewage; and excessive nutrients from fertilizers and sewage.

The world's freshwater resources are also under serious stress. In some regions, water use exceeds the amount of water that is naturally replenished every year. About one-third of the world's population lives in countries with moderate-to-high water stress, defined by the United Nations to be water consumption that exceeds 10 percent of renewable freshwater resources. By this measure, some eighty countries, constituting 40 percent of the world's population, were suffering from water shortages by the mid-1990s.[23] By 2020, water use is expected to increase by 40 percent, and 17 percent more water will be required for food production to meet the needs of the growing population. By 2025, 1.8 billion people could live in regions with absolute water scarcity, and two out of three people in the world could be living under conditions of water stress.[24] Agricultural water use accounts for about 75 percent of total global consumption, mainly through crop irrigation. Industrial use accounts for about 20 percent. The remaining 5 percent is used for domestic purposes[25] (see Figure 1.5).

Environmental quality in urban areas is also a major problem. In 2008, for the first time in history, the world's urban population equaled the rural population. Between 2007 and 2050, the population living in urban areas is projected to grow by 3.1 billion, passing from 3.3 billion in 2007 to 6.4 billion in 2050. Thus, urban areas will likely absorb all the population growth expected over the next four decades while at the same time drawing in some of the rural population. As a result, the world's rural population is projected to start decreasing in about a decade, and 600 million fewer rural inhabitants are expected in 2050 than today. Overall, the world is expected to be 60 percent urban in 2030[26] (see Figure 1.6).

While cities can provide significant economies of scale for environmentally friendly technology and practices, under current conditions in many parts of the world, increasing urbanization implies heavier water and air pollution and a higher rate of natural resource consumption. The number of cities supporting at least 5 million inhabitants is projected to rise from thirty in 2007 to forty-eight in 2025. The number of megacities—cities supporting 10 million inhabitants or more—is expected to increase from nineteen in 2007 to twenty-seven in 2025 (see Table 1.2). Most of these large cities are located in developing countries.[27] The current pace and scale of urbanization often strain the capacity of local and national governments to provide even basic services to urban residents. According to the United Nations Human Settlements Programme, if nothing is done to check the current trend, the number of people living in slums, with little or no access to fresh water, sanitation, or refuse collection, will rise from 1 billion today to some 1.5 billion by 2020.[28] Environmental quality and human health and well-being are so much at risk in these situations that the **Millennium Development Goals'** (time-bound targets to respond to the world's main development challenges) target of significantly improving the lives of at least 100 million slum-dwellers by 2020 will be difficult to achieve.

The major trends in the global environment described in this section are the forces that shape global environmental politics. They have resulted from the intense economic development, rapid population growth, inefficient production, and nonsustainable resource consumption prevalent in many parts of the world during the last sixty years. This is not to say that population and economic development are necessarily harmful. Indeed, most would argue they are not. Rather it is the manner in which much of this economic development occurred, one characterized by high levels of resource consumption and pollution, which produced these troubling changes in the global environment. Thus, with this as a backdrop, it is time to look at the issues and politics surrounding natural resources and the environment.

FIGURE 1.5   Evolution of global water use

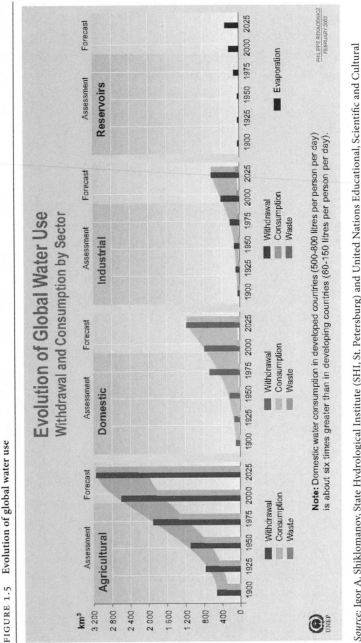

Source: Igor A. Shiklomanov, State Hydrological Institute (SHI, St. Petersburg) and United Nations Educational, Scientific and Cultural Organization (UNESCO, Paris), 1999. Reprinted with permission from UNEP, *Vital Water Graphics—An Overview of the State of the World's Fresh and Marine Waters* (Nairobi: UNEP, 2002).

FIGURE 1.6 Percentage of population residing in urban areas by major areas of the world: 1950, 1975, 2005, and 2030

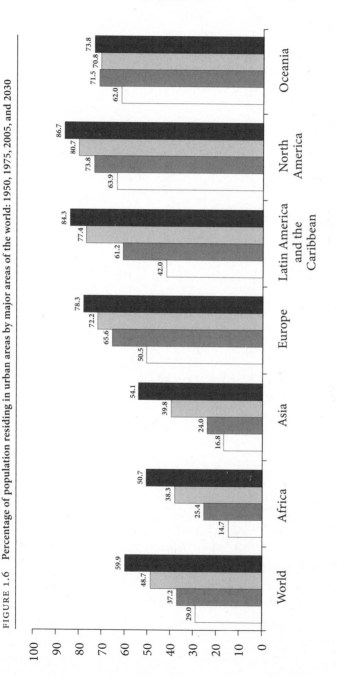

Source: Population Division of the Department of Economic and Social Affairs of the United Nations Secretariat, "World Population Prospects: The 2006 Revision," United Nations, www.un.org/esa/population/publications/wpp2006/wpp2006.htm, and "World Urbanization Prospects: The 2007 Revision," United Nations, http://esa.un.org/unup.

TABLE 1.2   The World's Megacities, 2007

RANK	URBAN AGGLOMERATION	POPULATION
1	Tokyo, Japan	35.7
2	New York-Newark, USA	19.0
3	Ciudad de Mexico (Mexico City), Mexico	19.0
4	Mumbai (Bombay), India	19.0
5	São Paulo, Brazil	18.8
6	Delhi, India	15.9
7	Shanghai, China	15.0
8	Kolkata (Calcutta), India	14.8
9	Dhaka, Bangladesh	13.5
10	Buenos Aires, Argentina	12.8
11	Los Angeles-Long Beach-Santa Ana, USA	12.5
12	Karachi, Pakistan	12.1
13	Al-Qahirah (Cairo), Egypt	11.9
14	Rio de Janeiro, Brazil	11.7
15	Osaka-Kobe, Japan	11.3
16	Beijing, China	11.1
17	Manila, Philippines	11.1
18	Moskva (Moscow), Russian Federation	10.5
19	Istanbul, Turkey	10.1

Source: United Nations Department of Economic and Social
Affairs/Population Division, *World Urbanization Prospects: The 2007
Revision* (New York: United Nations, 2008), 10. Available at
www.un.org/esa/population/publications/wup2007/2007wup.htm.

AN INTRODUCTION TO GLOBAL
ENVIRONMENTAL POLITICS

Environmental problems do not respect national boundaries. Transboundary air pollution, the degradation of shared rivers, and the pollution of oceans and seas are just a few examples of the international dimensions of environmental problems. The cumulative impact that human beings have had on the earth, together with an increased understanding of ecological processes, means that the environment cannot be viewed as a relatively stable background factor; indeed, the interaction between economic development and the complex, often fragile, ecosystems on which that development depends has become a major international political and economic issue.[29]

Environmental politics include at least two important dimensions: the environmental consequences of the economic or other activity in question and the state and nonstate actors involved. If the consequences are global, or they transcend more than one international region, or the actors transcend more than one region, then we consider the activity and its consequences to be a global environmental issue.[30]

Global environmental issues can be analyzed in many ways. From the economist's point of view, global environmental problems result from resource misallocation caused by negative "externalities"—the unintended consequences or side effects of one's actions that are borne by others. Externalities have always existed, but when the use of helpful, but polluting, technologies—such as coal, synthetic fertilizers, pesticides, herbicides, and plastics—expanded rapidly to keep pace with population growth and increased per capita consumption, they became critical.[31]

In this sense, the negative externalities that lead to environmental degradation are similar to the "tragedy of the **commons**." The ecologist Garrett Hardin observed that overgrazing unrestricted common lands, prior to their enclosure, was a metaphor for the overexploitation of the earth's common property: land, air, and water resources.[32] The root cause of overgrazing was the absence of a method for obliging herders to take into account the harmful effects that their own herds' grazing had on the other herders who shared the common land. The solution lay in assigning property rights so that owners could limit the use of the commons. Yet, Hardin recognized that air, water, and many other environmental resources, unlike the traditional commons, could not readily be fenced and parceled out to private owners who would be motivated to preserve them. Without sufficient knowledge or structures to restrain them, people (or states) will logically pursue their interest in utilizing the earth's common resources until they are destroyed, resulting in the tragedy of the commons. How to address externalities and the damage they inflict on environmental resources that, by their very nature, no one can own is a central challenge in global environmental politics.

Oran Young, a political scientist, groups international environmental problems into four broad clusters: commons, shared natural resources, transboundary externalities, and linked issues.[33] Young describes the commons similarly to Hardin, as the natural resources and vital life-support services that belong to all humankind rather than to any one country. These include Antarctica, the high seas, deep seabed minerals, the stratospheric ozone layer, the global climate system, and outer space. They may be geographically limited, as in Antarctica, or global in scope, such as the ozone layer and climate system. Shared natural resources are physical or biological systems that extend into or across the jurisdiction of two or more states. These include nonrenewable resources, such as pools of oil beneath the earth's surface; renewable resources, such as migratory species of animals; and complex ecosystems that transcend national boundaries, such as regional seas and river basins.

Transboundary externalities refer to activities that occur wholly within the jurisdiction of individual states but produce results affecting the environment or people
in other states.[34] Transboundary externalities include the consequences of environmental accidents, such as the 1986 explosion at the Chernobyl nuclear power plant in
the former Soviet Union or the Baia Mare cyanide spill in 2000, when a retaining wall
failed at a gold-processing plant in Romania, releasing cyanide and heavy metals into
a river system, killing fish and contaminating drinking waters in parts of Romania,
Bulgaria, Hungary, and Serbia. Transboundary externalities can also include transnational air pollution or the loss of biological diversity, caused in part by the destruction
of tropical forests, which leads to species extinction as well as reduced potential for
developing new pharmaceuticals. Linked issues refer to cases where efforts to deal
with environmental concerns have unintended consequences affecting other regimes,
and vice versa. The most controversial issue of this type is the link between efforts to
protect the environment and those to promote economic development within countries or trade between countries. For example, does the protection of the stratospheric
ozone layer and the global climate system mean that developing countries must forgo
the use of particular products or resources, such as fossil fuels, that have played key
roles in the development of industrialized societies?[35]

All sectors of the international community are involved in addressing these clusters
of global environmental issues. The policies and actions of various international institutions affecting the environment are an integral part of the issue area. The development-
assistance agencies of large donor countries, UN agencies such as the United Nations
Development Programme (UNDP) and the FAO, multilateral financial institutions
such as the World Bank and International Monetary Fund (IMF), and the World Trade
Organization (WTO) make decisions that have impacts on the environment. These
institutions are the targets of lobbying and pressure not only from states but also from
nonstate actors, including nongovernmental organizations (NGOs) and multinational
corporations.

Different combinations of internal economic and political forces influence states'
policies toward environmental issues. Because the actual costs and risks of environmental degradation are never distributed equally among all states, some governments
are less motivated than others to participate in international efforts to reduce environmental threats. States also often possess different views about what constitutes an
equitable solution to a particular environmental problem. Yet, despite their disparate
interests, states must strive for **consensus,** at least among those that significantly contribute to, and are significantly affected by, a given environmental problem.

An important characteristic of global environmental politics is the significance of
veto power. For every global environmental issue, there exists one state or group of
states whose cooperation is so essential to a successful agreement for coping with the

problem that it has the potential to block strong international action. When these states oppose an agreement or try to weaken it, they become **veto** (or **blocking**) **states** and form **veto coalitions**.

The role of veto coalitions is central to the dynamics of bargaining and negotiation in global environmental politics. On the issue of a whaling moratorium, for example, four states, led by Japan, accounted for three-fourths of the whaling catch worldwide; they could therefore make or break a global regime to save the whales. Similarly, the major grain exporters (Argentina, Australia, Canada, Chile, the United States, and Uruguay) were in position to block consensus on a **biosafety** protocol under the Convention on Biological Diversity in February 1999 for fear that the proposed provisions on trade in genetically modified crops were too stringent and would hamper grain exports.[36]

Veto power is so important that even militarily or economically powerful states are not free to impose a global environmental agreement on much less powerful states if the latter are strongly opposed to it and critical to the agreement's success. For example, industrialized countries could not pressure tropical-forest countries such as Brazil, Indonesia, and Malaysia to accept a binding agreement on the world's forests during the 1992 United Nations Conference on Environment and Development (UNCED), also known as the Earth Summit. Moreover, in global environmental negotiations, weaker states can use their veto power to demand compensation and other forms of favorable treatment. This occurred during the expansion of the ozone-layer regime when India and China led a coalition of developing countries that successfully demanded a financial mechanism that would provide resources to assist them in meeting the higher costs of using new non-ozone-depleting chemicals. Nevertheless, although some developing states can prevent an agreement or bargain for special treatment on some environmental issues, in general the major economic powers wield greater leverage due to their larger role in global production and consumption and their ability to deny funding for a regime they oppose.

A second characteristic of global environmental politics is that the political dynamics of issues often reflect the roles of state actors in the international trade of a particular product. The issue of international hazardous waste trading, for instance, is shaped by the relationship between industrialized countries that are exporting the waste and developing countries that are potential importers. The issue of international trade in endangered species is defined by the roles of the developing countries that export illegal wildlife products and the major economies that import them. And trade relations between tropical timber exporters and consuming nations are critical to the dynamics of tropical deforestation. Sometimes the trade patterns are so significant that they provide the producing-exporting countries or the importing countries with veto power.

PHOTO 1.1   Public opinion can play an
important role in global environmental
politics.
Courtesy IISD/Earth Negotiations Bulletin.

A third characteristic of global environmental politics is that economic power can affect the positions of states and even the outcome of bargaining on international agreements in some circumstances, whereas military power is not useful for influencing such outcomes. A country's ability to give or withhold economic benefits, such as access to markets or economic assistance, can persuade states dependent on those benefits to go along with that power's policy if the benefits are more important than the issue at stake in the negotiations. Thus, Japan and the Republic of Korea accepted international agreements on drift-net fishing and whaling because they feared loss of access to U.S. markets. And Japan succeeded in ensuring the support of some small nonwhaling nations for its pro-whaling position by offering assistance to their fishing industries.

Military power has not affected negotiations on global environmental issues. Global environmental politics do not give rise to a **hegemonic** power in the traditional sense; that is, when a state enjoying superior military power coerces other states into accepting the hegemon's position. No positive correlation exists between dominant military power and leadership on global environmental issues, and there may be a negative correlation between the two in that high levels of military spending divert financial resources from environmental issues. Moreover, it is almost universally accepted that global environmental threats can be successfully addressed only through the active cooperation of the key actors. Using military force to enforce an environmental agreement would be impractical, even if it were politically acceptable.

A fourth characteristic is that, despite the obstacles of veto power and sovereignty, the outcomes of multilateral bargaining processes usually result in cooperative efforts at curbing environmental threats (although not all of these efforts are successful). The international political system within which negotiations on global environmental issues take place is a decentralized system in which sovereign states are free to act on their own definition of national interest. But during the past three decades, ever larger numbers of states have reached agreement in addressing global environmental problems, sometimes giving up freedom of action in the process. The ways in which sovereign states with divergent interests are able to act collectively is one of the major themes of this book.

A fifth characteristic of environmental politics is the importance of public opinion and nonprofit NGOs, especially national and international environmental NGOs. Environmental issues, like human rights issues, have mobilized the active political interest of large numbers of citizens in key countries, inducing shifts in policy that helped turn the tide for various environmental issues. Public opinion, channeled through electoral politics and NGOs into national negotiating positions, has influenced aspects of the global bargaining on whaling, endangered species, hazardous wastes, **persistent organic pollutants** (POPs), and ozone depletion. Public opinion has not played a comparable role in security and economic negotiations. This situation may be changing, however, as indicated by the international action taken to ban land mines and by popular votes rejecting further integration within the European Union.

INTERNATIONAL REGIMES IN ENVIRONMENTAL POLITICS

The Concept of International Regimes

Understanding global environmental politics entails recognizing the importance of **international regimes,** a concept that has been defined in two very different ways. According to the first definition, a regime is a set of norms, rules, or decision-making procedures, whether implicit or explicit, that produces some convergence in the actors' expectations in a particular issue area. In this broad definition, the concept may be applied to a wide range of international arrangements, from the coordination of monetary relations to superpower security relations. This way of conceiving regimes has been strongly criticized for including arrangements that are merely patterned interactions, operational frameworks, and even methods to agree to disagree with no long-term predictability or stability.[37]

According to the second definition, the one used in this book, a regime is a system of principles, norms, rules, operating procedures, and institutions that actors create or accept to regulate and coordinate action in a particular issue area of international relations. Principles are beliefs of fact, causation, and rectitude. Norms are standards of behavior. Rules are specific prescriptions or proscriptions for action. Operating procedures are prevailing practices for work within the regime, including methods for making and implementing collective choice. Institutions are mechanisms and organizations for implementing, operating, evaluating, and expanding the regime and its policy.[38]

Regimes are essentially international-policy, regulatory, and administrative systems. Although states, as the dominant actors in the international system, are the primary and most important creators of international regimes, they are not the only source, and the involvement of other actors often proves critical. A regime usually centers on one or more formal international agreements, but key elements can also include the relevant actions of important international organizations, parts of other interrelated international agreements, and accepted norms of international behavior among actors active in the issue area (which can include governments, international organizations, NGOs, multinational corporations, and others). These elements together form the entire suite of principles, norms, rules, and procedures that govern and guide behavior on the particular issue.

Regimes are found in most areas of international relations, including trade, money, environment, human rights, communications, travel, and even security. As a result, regimes receive a good deal of theoretical and empirical attention from scholars of international relations and are among the most significant offshoots of the long-standing inquiry into international cooperation—especially into how, why, and under what circumstances states attempt to cooperate or create international institutions and what factors influence the success of such attempts.[39]

One important line of progenitor theories is marked by concern for the impact and mitigation of structural anarchy, especially the difficulty of establishing international cooperation (anarchy in this usage does not mean chaos but the absence of hierarchy, specifically the lack of world government or other formal hierarchical structures to govern international politics).[40] A second flows from scholars called constitutionalists, who study treaties and the formal structure of international organizations, and from researchers employing the institutional process approach, which concentrates on how an organization's day-to-day practices, processes, and methods of operation influence its outcomes.[41]

A third line of antecedents starts with the premise that despite structural anarchy, extensive common interests exist among states and their people and that scholars and statesmen must learn how these interests can be realized. Present in eighteenth-century enlightened optimism, nineteenth-century liberalism, and twentieth-century Wilsonian idealism, this view influenced in the 1970s a branch of legal and political scholarship concerned with world order and international law that argued that custom, patterned interaction, and the needs and wants of civilian populations are important sources of international law and require the respect of states.[42]

Functionalism represents a fourth important line of predecessors. Functionalism, often associated with the work of David Mitrany, argues that the scholarly and political focus of international cooperation must center not on formal interstate politics but rather on providing opportunities for technical (nonpolitical) cooperation among specialists and specialized organizations to solve common problems.[43] Functionalists argue that such technical cooperation can begin a process in which increasing interdependence and "spillover" (technical management in one area begetting technical management in another) will present opportunities for organizing more and more government functions internationally and technically rather than nationally and politically—a process that will slowly erode or bypass domestic regulators in favor of peaceful global institutions.

While attractively optimistic, functionalism proved inadequate to explain the totality of actions and outcomes in an international system in which politics is always a factor, states do not want to relinquish control, and technological determinism has not responded automatically to all (or even most) aspects of increasing interdependence. However, functionalist insights did influence several important theoretical approaches, including neofunctionalist integration theory, transnational relations theory, turbulent fields, complex interdependence, and regimes.[44]

Neofunctional integration theory critiqued and extended functionalism, arguing that gradual, regional integration is most important for understanding and creating effective international governance.[45] The approach added politics (including the importance of states and individual political figures) and regional encapsulation to functionalist strategies emphasizing spillover and managed incremental advancements. This approach also lost favor, particularly when Ernst Haas, formerly a leading proponent, argued that focusing exclusively on regional encapsulation had become inadequate for addressing the new, "turbulent" issue areas of international relations characterized by different types of competing interests and high degrees of complexity and interdependence (which we now know include environmental issues). Haas argued that the interplay of knowledge, learning, and politics is critical to understanding and managing turbulent issue areas as well as the conduct and adaptability of international organizations created to address them.[46]

Research on transnational relations, which are nongovernmental interconnections and interactions across national boundaries, argued similarly that interdependence can fracture international politics into distinct issue areas and that states are neither the only important actors in international politics nor even totally "coherent" actors.[47] These insights culminated in "complex interdependence," proposed by Robert Keohane and Joseph Nye as an alternative to realism as a **paradigm** for understanding international relations.[48]

The study of regimes results from these lines of inquiry. If international relations are increasingly interdependent, influenced by new types of actors and interactions, and fractured into issue areas across which power and interests vary, then how actors choose to manage these issue areas—the regimes they create to manage them—becomes important to the conduct and study of international politics. Thus, regimes should be properly defined, examined, and explained.

John Ruggie is often credited with introducing the term *international regime* as a "set of mutual expectations, rules and regulations, plans, organizational energies and financial commitments, which have been accepted by a group of states."[49] Ernst Haas

PHOTO 1.2   In multilateral negotiations, states must believe they will be better off or no agreement will be reached.
Courtesy IISD-*Earth Negotiations Bulletin.*

initially defined regimes as "collective arrangements among nations designed to create or more effectively use scientific and technical capabilities."[50] Robert Keohane and Joseph Nye first defined regimes instrumentally: "By creating or accepting procedures, rules or institutions for certain kinds of activity, governments regulate and control transnational and interstate relations. We refer to these governing arrangements as international regimes." In the same work, they defined a regime as a "network of rules, norms, and procedures that regulate behavior."[51] In 1983, a group of leading scholars working with Stephen Krasner attempted to standardize and extend regime study. Most definitions, including the one used in this volume, are variants of the definition they developed.[52]

States and other actors create regimes through multilateral negotiations. Negotiations take place when at least some states consider the status quo unacceptable. Quite often, states believe very negative consequences and high costs, even a crisis, will result if existing trends continue. Although reaching agreement on how to manage the problem is in a state's best interest, so is gaining as much as possible while giving up as little as possible. Nevertheless, the expected value of the outcome to each state, and hence the total value of the outcome, must be positive (or at least neutral), or else there would be no incentive to negotiate or to accept the outcome. In multilateral negotiations, states will not come to an agreement unless they believe they will be better off than they would be with no agreement.[53]

Most regimes center on a binding agreement or legal instrument. For global environmental problems, the most common kind of legal instrument is a **convention**. A convention may contain all the binding obligations expected to be negotiated or followed by a more detailed legal instrument, often called a **protocol**, which elaborates more specific norms and rules. Since the members of most international regimes are states, regime rules apply to the actions of states. However, actors that engage in the activities addressed by regimes frequently include not only states and international organizations but also private entities, such as multinational corporations, banks, timber companies, and chemical companies. Thus, states participating in international regimes assume responsibility for ensuring that private entities within their jurisdiction comply with the norms and rules of the regime.[54]

If a convention is negotiated in anticipation that parties will negotiate one or more subsequent elaborating texts, it is called a **framework convention**. Framework conventions usually establish a set of general principles, norms, and goals for cooperation on the issue as well how the members of the regimes will meet and make decisions. The latter usually takes the form of a regular **Conference of the Parties,** an annual or otherwise regularly scheduled gathering of all parties to the convention as well as interested observers (observers often include representatives from nonparty states, international organizations, nongovernmental environmental organizations, and industry groups). Framework conventions usually do not impose major binding obligations on the parties. A framework convention is then followed by the negotiation of one or more protocols, which spell out specific obligations on the overall issue in question or on narrower subissues. The negotiation of a framework convention and protocols usually takes several years, as it did for transboundary air pollution, ozone depletion, and climate change.

A nonbinding agreement can form the centerpiece of a regime to the extent that it establishes norms that influence state behavior. This type of agreement is often referred to as **soft law**. Nonbinding agreements, codes of conduct, and guidelines for behavior exist for a number of global environmental problems, including land-based sources of marine pollution and **sustainable forest management**, with varying degrees of effectiveness. Some consider Agenda 21, the plan of action adopted at the 1992 Earth Summit, a soft-law "umbrella regime" for worldwide **sustainable development** because it defines norms of behavior for a wide range of environmental and development issues. Although such nonbinding agreements can influence state behavior to some extent, regimes based on legal instruments are usually more effective. That is why some countries become dissatisfied with a given nonbinding code of conduct or other soft-law agreement and argue that it should be turned into a legally binding agreement.

GLOBAL ENVIRONMENTAL REGIMES

Today, regimes exist on a wide variety of global environmental issues from whale protection to climate change to hazardous wastes. Chapters 3–5 describe in more detail the evolution of, and challenges faced by, eleven prominent regimes. As these chapters demonstrate, global environmental regimes can vary significantly in their history, purpose, rules, strength, and effectiveness.

Environmental regimes also change over time, often expanding and becoming stronger but sometimes weakening or changing in scope. The whaling regime, for example, grew out of the International Convention for the Regulation of Whaling (1946), which was originally intended as a regime for the regulation of commercial whaling but evolved into a ban on whaling in 1985 (see Chapter 5). The regime that seeks to control marine oil pollution began with the 1954 International Convention for the Prevention of Pollution of the Sea by Oil, which established rules only for ships within fifty miles (eighty kilometers) of the nearest coast, allowing for significant and deliberate oil spillage outside this area.[55] This ineffectiveness led states in 1973 to create the International Convention for the Prevention of Pollution from Ships, also known as the MARPOL convention, which limits oil discharges at sea, prohibits them in certain sensitive zones, and sets minimum distances from land for the discharge of other pollutants. However, shipping interests in crucial maritime states opposed the MARPOL convention so strongly that it did not enter into force until a decade later. States also negotiated the Convention on the Prevention of Marine Pollution by Dumping of Wastes and Other Matter, or the London Convention (1972), which prohibited the dumping of specific substances, including high-level radioactive wastes, and required permits for others. It was the first marine-pollution agreement to accept the right of coastal states to enforce prohibitions against pollution and became an important forum for negotiating further controls on ocean dumping.

In another example of regime evolution, until the 1970s virtually all wildlife conservation treaties lacked binding legal commitments and, perhaps consequentially, were ineffective in protecting migratory birds and other species. The first global convention on wildlife conservation that had strong legal commitments and an enforcement mechanism was the 1973 Convention on International Trade in Endangered Species of Wild Fauna and Flora (CITES; see Chapter 5). It set up a system of trade sanctions and a worldwide reporting network to curb the traffic in endangered species and thus, by eliminating the market, to reduce the incentive to capture, kill, or harvest them. While effective in many instances, it also contains loopholes that allow states with interests in a particular species to opt out of the controls on it.

The regime that seeks to reduce hazardous waste, control its trade, and ensure its environmentally sound management and disposal began with negotiations initially aimed largely at preventing the movement (and sometimes outright dumping) of hazardous waste from rich countries where it was produced to poor countries. The regime's first and central agreement, the 1989 Basel Convention on the Control of Transboundary Movements of Hazardous Wastes and Their Disposal, does not prohibit the trade but establishes conditions for it (see Chapter 3). Dissatisfaction with this aspect of the agreement on the part of many developing countries, especially in Africa, resulted in the negotiation of an amendment that would impose a complete ban on waste exports, although this amendment has not yet received enough country ratifications to enter into force. Subsequent negotiations have expanded the regime extensively into developing norms for the management and disposal of hazardous wastes.

As noted above, many regimes are strengthened as efforts shift from creating an initial framework convention to negotiating and implementing specific protocols. For example, the regime controlling cross-border **acid rain** and air pollution in the Northern Hemisphere began with the 1979 Convention on Long-Range Transboundary Air Pollution (see Chapter 3). This framework convention did not commit the signatories to specific emissions reductions. The regime was later strengthened considerably by the addition of eight protocols that financed the monitoring and evaluation of long-range air pollutants in Europe (1984); the reduction of sulfur emissions (1985 and 1994); the control of nitrogen oxides (1988); the control of emissions of **volatile organic compounds** (1991), heavy metals (1998), and POPs (1998); and the abatement of acidification, **eutrophication**, and ground-level ozone (1999). The heavy metal and POPs agreements represented significant expansions of the core mandate established by the original convention.

The ozone regime also began with a framework convention (see Chapter 4). The 1985 Vienna Convention for the Protection of the Ozone Layer did not commit the parties to reducing ozone-depleting chemicals; in fact it did not even mention them by name. The Montreal Protocol (1987) represented the first real step toward protecting the ozone layer by requiring reductions in the consumption of certain chlorofluorocarbons (CFCs). Then, in the late 1980s and 1990s, significant advances in scientific understanding of the threat, the discovery of alternative chemicals, and the use of innovative regime rules that provided for relatively rapid negotiation and implementation of amendments and adjustments to the protocol allowed governments to reach a series of agreements that significantly strengthened the regime. The ozone regime now mandates the complete phaseout of CFCs and almost all other ozone-depleting substances (ODS), and the production and use of CFCs and several other ODS have already been eliminated in the United States, Europe, and other industrialized countries.

The agreement that created the climate regime, the 1992 Framework Convention on Climate Change (UNFCCC; see Chapter 4), also failed to impose binding targets and timetables for emissions of GHGs. It did call on industrialized countries to return emissions to 1990 levels but stated this as a nonbinding goal. With the adoption of the Kyoto Protocol in 1997, however, industrialized country parties agreed to reduce their collective emissions of six GHGs by at least 5 percent below 1990 levels by 2012.

Some treaties and regimes, like the 2001 Stockholm Convention on Persistent Organic Pollutants and the Montreal Protocol, have very clear, binding controls. Others do not, a characteristic that can reflect the nature of the environmental issue or the politics surrounding it (such as the presence of veto states). The 1992 Convention on Biological Diversity (see Chapter 5), for example, does not obligate parties to measurable conservation objectives but instead requires the development of national strategies for the conservation of biodiversity. Similarly, the 1994 Convention to Combat Desertification (see Chapter 5), which established a regime to address the problem of desertification, the desertlike conditions that result from the destruction of formerly productive lands' biological potential, calls for countries to draw up integrated national programs in consultation with local communities.

Some regimes, such as the ozone and CITES regimes, are widely considered successes. These regimes have not completely solved the environmental issues they address, and each contains loopholes, but the situation is far better than it was before they were created. This will likely be the case with the Stockholm Convention as well, at least with respect to the toxic chemicals specifically covered by the treaty.

However, many of the regimes discussed in chapters 3 to 5 have had only mixed successes at best. Nevertheless, negotiation of the central agreement and other aspects of the regime (such as the related activities of international organizations) provide greater opportunities for addressing the environmental issue in question than when no regime exists (either because negotiations failed or none were attempted).[56] Thus, while the biodiversity and climate regimes have not yet come close to solving those problems—in fact each problem continues to accelerate, with potentially disastrous results—the situation would be far worse, and the prospects for future improvements more remote, if the regimes did not exist.

Evidence for this exists in issues that have no extant regimes or for which initial attempts to create a regime have failed. For instance, several efforts to create some type of regime for the protection of coral reefs have failed to gain traction, and coral reefs continue to degrade rapidly around the world. Shark populations continue to fall, largely as a result of sharks killed as bycatch or for their fins (largely for sale to make shark-fin soup). Efforts to initiate global protections for most sharks have failed, although negotiations toward a potential new agreement to protect migratory sharks began in late 2007 under the auspices of the Convention on Migratory Species.[57] Many countries have laws protecting coastal **mangroves**, but many of these same countries also sanction their enclosure or even tearing them down to create ponds for shrimp farms. Without an international regime leading all countries to adjust their behavior simultaneously, this situation is likely to continue, and mangroves (and the ecological and economic value they have) will continue to disappear. In the absence of an international regime preventing overfishing, cod stocks off the coast of Newfoundland suffered a devastating collapse in 1992. Thousands lost their jobs, and the marine ecosystem has not recovered.

Theoretical Approaches to International Regimes

Several major theoretical approaches have been used to explain the concept of international regimes, how they come into existence, and why they change.[58] These include the structural, game-theoretic, institutional-bargaining, and epistemic-community approaches. Each may help explain one or more international regimes, but none individually can account for all the regimes described and analyzed in this book.

The structural, or hegemonic-power, approach holds that the primary factor determining regime formation and change is the relative strength of the state actors involved in a particular issue and that "stronger states in the issue system will dominate the weaker ones and determine the rules of the game."[59] This approach suggests that strong international regimes are a function of a hegemonic state that can exercise leadership over weaker states and that the absence of such a hegemonic state is likely to frustrate regime formation.

The structural approach can be viewed in two ways, one stressing coercive power, the other focusing on "public goods." In the coercive-power variant, regimes are set up by hegemonic states that use their military and economic leverage over other states to bring them into regimes, as the United States did in setting up trade and monetary regimes immediately after World War II.[60] The second variant views the same postwar regimes as the result of a hegemonic power's adopting policies that create public goods, that is, benefits open to all states who want to participate, such as export markets in the United States and the dollar as a stable currency for international payments.

However useful the structural approach has been to explain the post–World War II global economic systems, it cannot explain why global environmental regimes have been negotiated. In the 1970s and 1980s, the United States was not a military hegemon but part of a bipolar system with the Soviet Union. Beginning in the mid-1980s, the United States faced the rise of competing economic powers in Japan and Europe. Moreover, the European Union, whose member states negotiate on global environmental issues as a single bloc, became the economic equal of the United States in the 1990s. Finally, the United States did not pursue many of these environmental regimes. From 1981 to 1993 and from 2001 to 2009, both crucial periods in the creation and expansion of most global environmental regimes, the United States had presidents ideologically hostile toward international environmental regulation; consequently, the

United States did not take many lead positions (as the theory argues a hegemonic state must do). Thus, the successfully negotiated environmental regimes depended on wide consensus among a number of states, not on imposition by the United States.[61]

Another approach to regime creation is based on game theory and utilitarian models of bargaining. In game theory, bargaining is distinguished by the number of parties involved, the nature of the conflict (zero-sum or non-zero-sum), and the assumption that the actors are rational (they will try to pursue outcomes favorable to them) and interconnected in some way; that is, they cannot pursue their own interests independently of the choices of other actors. This approach suggests that small groups of states, or coalitions, are more likely to succeed in negotiating an international regime than a large number because each player can more readily understand the bargaining strategies of other the players. Political scientist Fen Osler Hampson took this approach into account when he analyzed the process of regime creation as an effort by a small coalition of states to form a regime by exercising leadership over a much larger number of national actors.[62]

Due to the importance of veto power in global environmental politics, however, relatively small groups of states are no more likely to form successful regimes than much larger ones. To succeed, an environmental regime must include all the states that have a large impact on the issue, including potential veto states. Veto states follow their own interests (as all states do), so a veto state in a small group will likely be as prone to opposition as it would be in a large group of states. And, if veto states are left outside the small group, they will still be in a position to frustrate regime formation when the regime is enlarged, or they may simply refuse the join the regime, a situation likely to limit the regime's success.

A third approach is the epistemic-communities model, which emphasizes the impact of international learning and transnational networks of experts and bureaucrats, primarily on the basis of scientific research into a given problem, as a factor influencing the evolution of regimes.[63] This approach, advanced initially to explain the creation of, and compliance with, the Mediterranean Action Plan, identifies intraelite shifts within and outside governments as the critical factor in the convergence of state policies in support of a stronger regime. The shifts empowered technical and scientific specialists allied with officials of international organizations. These elites thus formed transnational epistemic communities, that is, communities of experts sharing common values and approaches to policy problems.

The importance of scientific evidence and expertise in the politics of many global environmental issues cannot be ignored. Indeed, a significant degree of scientific understanding and consensus has sometimes been a minimum condition for serious international action on an issue. The 1985 agreement to reduce sulfur dioxide emissions across Europe by 30 percent of 1980 levels was made possible by mounting scientific evidence of their damaging effects on European forests. The impetus for agreement in 1990 that the world should phase out CFCs completely came from incontrovertible scientific evidence that damage to the ozone layer was much greater than previously thought and that CFCs were largely responsible. The Kyoto Protocol was made possible, in part, by the Second Assessment Report of the Intergovernmental Panel on Climate Change (IPCC), which found that the earth's temperature had increased and that there is a "discernible human influence" on climate.

Although scientific elites may play a supportive and enabling role in certain environmental negotiations, on other issues they remain divided or even captured by particular government or private interests. And on some issues, such as the whaling ban, the hazardous waste trade, desertification, the Antarctic, and the ocean dumping of radioactive wastes, scientists have contributed little to regime formation or strengthening. In some of these cases, scientific elites were not particularly influential in policy making, while in others key actors explicitly rejected scientific findings as the basis for decision.[64]

The case studies presented in chapters 3 to 5 also suggest that theoretical approaches based solely on a **unitary actor model** (one suggesting that state actors can be treated as though they are a single entity encompassing one internally consistent set of values and attitudes), ignoring the roles of domestic sociopolitical structures and processes, are likely to form poor bases for analyzing and predicting the outcomes of global environmental bargaining. Negotiating positions usually reflect domestic sociopolitical balances and may change dramatically because of a shift in those balances. For example, after Barack Obama was elected president, the United States dramatically shifted its stance from opposing to supporting global negotiations on a potential new regime to reduce mercury emissions (these negotiations began in 2009). Although the structure of an issue in terms of economic interests may indicate which states are most likely to join a veto coalition, domestic political pressures and bargaining can tip the balance for or against regime creation or strengthening. A fully complete theoretical explanation for global environmental regime formation or change must incorporate the variable of state actors' domestic politics.

A theoretical model of regime formation and strengthening, therefore, should link international political dynamics with domestic politics and view the whole as a "two-level game." While representatives of countries are maneuvering the outcome of bargaining over regime issues, officials must also bargain with interest groups within their domestic political systems. Because the two processes often take place simultaneously, the arenas influence each other and become part of the negotiations at each level.[65]

A theoretical explanation for the formation of global environmental regimes must also leave room for the importance of the rules of the negotiating forum and the linkages between the negotiations on regimes and the wider relationships among the negotiating parties. The legal structure of the negotiating forum—the "rules of the game" regarding who may participate and how authoritative decisions are to be made—becomes particularly important when the negotiations take place within an already established treaty or organization. The whaling case illustrates how these rules can be crucial in determining the outcomes of the negotiations.

Economic and political ties among key state actors can also sway a veto state to compromise or defect. Particularly when the environmental regime under negotiation does not involve issues central to the economy of the states that could block agreement, the potential veto state's concern about how a veto would affect relations with states important for economic or political reasons sometimes makes possible the formation or strengthening of a regime.

Building a theoretical approach that accounts for actual historical patterns of regime formation and strengthening and can predict most outcomes will require advancing a series of testable hypotheses encompassing multiple variables rather than relying on a single-variable approach. Some scholars are engaged in such work. However, because explicit hypotheses have not yet been generated and tested sufficiently, the discussion of regime formation in this book focuses primarily on identifying common patterns through case studies. We use a phased-process approach to analyze the negotiations that result in the establishment of environmental regimes.

PARADIGM SHIFTS AND ENVIRONMENTAL POLITICS

Public policy and regimes are shaped not only by impersonal forces, such as technological innovation and economic growth, but also by people's, governments', and institutions' perception of reality. In times of relative social stability, public policies and systems of behavior flow logically from dominant paradigms, or sets of beliefs, ideas, and values. Every dominant paradigm is ultimately challenged, however, as its anomalies—the contradictions between its assumptions and observed reality—multiply and its usefulness wanes. Finally, it gives way to a new paradigm through a process known as a paradigm shift.[66] The hypothesis that an alternative socioeconomic-development paradigm, one showing more sensitivity to environmental realities, is emerging provides a lens through which to view the issues discussed in the rest of this book.

The Dominant Socioeconomic Paradigm

Because economic and environmental policy are so intertwined, the paradigm that has dominated public understanding of environmental management during the period of rapid global economic growth has been essentially a system of beliefs about economics. It has been referred to as the **exclusionist paradigm** because it excludes human beings from the laws of nature. It has also been called frontier economics, suggesting the sense of unlimited resources characteristic of a society living on an open frontier.[67]

In capitalist societies, this paradigm has rested primarily on two assumptions of **neo-classical economics**: the free market will always maximize social welfare, and there exists an infinite supply of both natural resources and "sinks" for disposing of the wastes that accrue from exploiting those resources—provided that the free market is operating. Humans will not deplete a resource, according to this worldview, as long as technology is given free rein and prices are allowed to fluctuate enough to stimulate the search for substitutes; in this way, absolute scarcity can be postponed indefinitely into the future.[68] Waste disposal is viewed as a problem to be cleaned up after the fact—but not at the cost of interference with market decisions.[69] Because conventional economic theory is concerned with the allocation of scarce resources, and nature is not considered a constraining factor, this paradigm considers the environment largely irrelevant to economics. (Despite a different economic and political ideology, the former Soviet Union and other Communist states also shared this assumption.) The traditional international legal principles of state sovereignty (including control over resources within a state's borders) and unrestricted access to the earth's common resources, such as the oceans and their living resources, buttressed the exclusionist paradigm.

In the early 1960s, the dominant paradigm came under steadily mounting attack. The critique started, surprisingly to some, in the United States and then spread to Europe and other regions. The 1962 publication of Rachel Carson's *Silent Spring* documenting the dangers to human health from synthetic pesticides marked the beginning of an explosion of popular literature in new scientific knowledge about new threats to the environment, including radiation, heavy metal toxic wastes, and chlorinated hydrocarbons in the water. The first mass movement for environmental protection, which focused on domestic issues including air and water pollution, developed in the United States in the late 1960s. Throughout this period, research and writing on environmental issues began to raise awareness that public policies supporting economic activity without concern for the environmental consequences carried high costs to society. Parallel changes in public concern about pollution also occurred in many other non-Communist industrialized countries. The burst of environmental concern in the United States led to the passage of a series of landmark pieces of legislation, including the National Environmental Policy Act of 1969, the 1970 Clean Air Act, the act creating the U.S. Environmental Protection Agency, and new rules to combat water pollution. These new laws and those that built upon them dramatically decreased air, water, and soil pollution in the United States. Looking toward the future, the National Environmental

Policy Act also directed federal agencies to support international cooperation in "anticipating and preventing a decline in the quality of mankind's world environment."[70]

The first global environmental conference in history, the United Nations Conference on the Human Environment, convened in Stockholm in 1972. Sweden, supported by the United States, had made the original proposal for a substantive global conference aimed at concrete results and offered to host the historic meeting. The motto of the Stockholm Conference, "Only One Earth," was a revolutionary concept for its time. The 114 states attending the conference (Soviet bloc states boycotted the meeting as part of the Cold War disputes) approved a landmark declaration containing twenty-six broad principles on the management of the global environment along with an action plan containing 109 recommendations for international environmental cooperation. These recommendations included creating a new international organization, the United Nations Environment Programme (UNEP), to provide a focal point for environmental action and coordination of environmentally related activities within the UN system. Also, in preparation for, or as a result of, Stockholm, environmental ministries and agencies were established in more than one hundred countries; most governments did not have such ministries before 1972. Stockholm also marked the beginning of the explosive increase in nongovernmental and intergovernmental organizations dedicated to environmental preservation, with an estimated 100,000 such organizations formed in the following twenty years.[71]

The Rise of an Alternative Paradigm

The rapid rise of environmental consciousness in the 1960s and early 1970s attacked the dominant paradigm but did not produce a widely accepted set of alternative assumptions about physical and economic realities that could become a competing worldview. The essential assumptions of classical economics remained largely intact. Confronted with evidence that existing patterns of resource exploitation could cause irreversible damage, proponents of classical economics continued to maintain that such exploitation was still economically rational.[72]

During the 1970s and 1980s, however, an alternative paradigm challenging the assumptions of classical economics began to take shape. Two of the intellectual forerunners of this paradigm were the *Limits to Growth* study by the Club of Rome, published in 1972, and the *Global 2000 Report to the President*, released by the U.S. Council of Environmental Quality and the Department of State in 1980.[73] Each study applied global-systems computer modeling to the projected interactions among population, economic growth, and natural resources and concluded that if current trends continued, many ecosystems and natural resources would become seriously and irreversibly degraded and that these environmental developments would then have serious economic consequences. Because each study suggested that economic development and population growth were on a path that would eventually strain the earth's "carrying capacity" (the total amount of resource consumption that the earth's natural systems can support without undergoing degradation), the viewpoint underlying the studies was generally referred to as the limits-to-growth perspective.

Defenders of the dominant paradigm, among them Herman Kahn and Julian Simon, criticized these studies for projecting the depletion of nonrenewable resources without taking into account technological changes and market responses. These critics argued that overpopulation would not become a problem because people are the world's "ultimate resource," and they characterized the authors of studies as "no-growth elitists" who would freeze developing countries out of the benefits of economic growth. They argued that human ingenuity would enable humanity to leap over the alleged limits to growth through new and better technologies.[74]

The development of an alternative paradigm was set back in the United States in the early 1980s when the Reagan administration enthusiastically embraced the exclusionist paradigm. Meanwhile, however, knowledge about ecological principles and their relationship to economic development continued to spread. A global community of practitioners and scholars emerged, allied in the belief that ecologically sound policies must replace economic policies based on the exclusionist paradigm.

By the mid-1980s, sustainable development was emerging as the catchword of an alternative paradigm and was heard with increasing frequency at conferences involving NGOs and government officials in the United States and around the world.[75] An important milestone was the 1987 publication by the World Commission on Environment and Development of *Our Common Future* (better known as the Brundtland Report after the commission's chair, former Norwegian prime minister Gro Harlem Brundtland).[76] The United Nations established the Brundtland Commission to examine the impact of environmental degradation and natural resource depletion on future economic and social development. The commission's report is considered a landmark in global environmental politics in part because it helped to define, legitimize, and popularize the concept of sustainable development. Drawing on and synthesizing the views and research of hundreds of people worldwide, it also codified some of the central beliefs of the emerging sustainable development paradigm, and news coverage of the report gave it greater visibility and momentum.

The Brundtland Commission defined sustainable development as "development that meets the need of the present without compromising the ability of future generations to meet their own needs."[77] The central themes of its report criticized economic and social systems (and the dominant paradigm) for failing to reconcile those needs. It asserted that the earth's natural systems have finite capabilities and resources and that the continuation of existing economic policies carries the risk of irreversible damage to the natural systems on which all life depends.

The sustainable development paradigm emphasizes the need to redefine the term *development*. It posits that economic growth cannot continue at the expense of the earth's natural capital (its stock of renewable and nonrenewable resources) and vital natural support systems such as the ozone layer, biodiversity, and a stable climate. Instead, the world economy must learn to live off the "interest" of the earth's natural capital. That means reducing the amount of resources used per unit of gross national product (GNP), shifting from fossil fuels to renewable energy, and recycling rather than consuming and discarding resources. It implies a transition to sustainable systems of renewable natural resource management, efforts to stabilize world population,[78] and a more measured approach to consumption.

The sustainable development paradigm assumes the need for greater equity not only between wealthy and poor nations but also within societies and between generations (**intergenerational equity**). Highly industrialized countries such as the United States, which use a disproportionate share of the world's environmental resources, are seen as pursuing a type of economic growth that is inherently unsustainable, as are societies in which the distribution of land and other resources is grossly unequal. Sustainable development further holds that future generations have an equal right to use the earth's resources.[79] The paradigm recognizes that developing countries must meet the basic needs of the poor in ways that do not deplete the countries' natural resources, and it also points to a need to reexamine basic attitudes and actions in industrialized countries regarding unnecessary and wasteful aspects of their material abundance.[80]

One of the main anomalies of the classical economic paradigm is its measure of macroeconomic growth, that is, GNP. Advocates of sustainable development note that GNP fails to reflect the real physical capability of an economy to provide material wealth in the future or to take into account the relative well-being of the society in general. Thus, a country could systematically deplete its natural resources, erode its soils, and pollute its waters without that loss of real wealth ever showing up in its income accounts. Moreover, the economic expense of trying to fix these problems would actually add to GNP.

In the second half of the 1980s, some economists began to study how to correct this anomaly in conventional accounting and to advocate for governments and international organizations to use alternatives to GNP—such as "real net national product," "sustainable social net national product," or "index of sustainable economic welfare"— which include changes in environmental resources as well as other indicators that measure human welfare.[81] Of particular importance is the annual UNDP Human Development Report, which uses "human indicators" to rate the quality of life in all countries by other than economic measures, including literacy, life expectancy, and respect for women's rights.[82] The Himalayan kingdom of Bhutan measures well-being not through GNP but through Gross National Happiness, a concept that encompasses economic development, governance, and cultural and environmental preservation.[83] The Environmental Sustainability Index ranks countries on twenty-one elements of sustainability covering natural resource endowments, past and present pollution levels, environmental-management efforts, contributions to the protection of the **global commons**, and capacity to improve its environmental performance over time.[84] The European Commission has developed an extended set of indicators to measure sustainable development within the European Union.[85]

The alternative paradigm points to the general failure of traditional markets to encourage the sustainable use of natural resources. It argues that prices should reflect the real costs to society of producing and consuming a given resource or emitting pollution that harms people or the environment. Conventional free market economic policies, however, systematically underprice or ignore natural resources.[86] Public policies that do not correct for market failure thus encourage overconsumption and more rapid depletion of renewable resources and the degradation of **environmental services** (i.e., the conserving or restorative functions of nature, for example, the conversion of carbon dioxide to oxygen by plants and the cleansing of water by wetlands). Raising the prices of certain processes, such as burning coal, to make them reflect real social and environmental costs is the favored means of showing the rates of consumption of energy and tropical timber. Adjusting the markets to send such price signals and exchanging income taxes for **green taxes** are means of implementing the "polluter pays" principle, endorsed by the 1992 Rio Declaration on Environment and Development (discussed below). Placing an upper limit on consumption is another method.[87]

In the early 1990s, the sustainable development paradigm began to displace the exclusionist paradigm in some sections of the multilateral financial institutions, in some state bureaucracies, and in some parliamentary committees dealing with the environment and development. For instance, publications of the Asian Development Bank, the Inter-American Development Bank, and the Organization of American States as early as 1990 impugned the mistaken unsustainable development paths of the past and recommended new sustainable development strategies.[88] In 1992, Al Gore, a former U.S. senator and vice president of the United States, published *Earth in the Balance*, in which he declared himself a proponent of a paradigm shift and advocated a new kind of "eco-nomics," to reorient economic activity toward environmentally sensitive production and investment in future resources.[89]

The 1992 Earth Summit

The alternative paradigm gained significant credibility through UNCED, also known as the Earth Summit, held in Rio de Janeiro in June 1992. UNCED was preceded by two years of discussions on domestic environmental and poverty problems and global environment issues, especially questions of North-South inequities and responsibility.

PHOTO 1.3   UNCED, Rio, 1992: NGO representatives join hundreds of thousands who signed
the Earth Pledge leading up to the Earth Summit.
Photo by Charles V. Barber, World Resources Institute.

The conference, which drew the participation of 110 heads of state, nearly 10,000 official delegates from 150 countries, and thousands of NGO representatives, was a monumental effort by the international community to reach consensus on principles and a long-term work plan for global sustainable development. Conceptually, its explicit focus on integrating environmental and development policies represented a major step forward from the Stockholm Conference on the Human Environment twenty years earlier.

The major output of UNCED was a nonbinding agreement called Agenda 21 (referring to the twenty-first century), which is a global plan of action for more sustainable societies. Negotiations on Agenda 21 were among the broadest and most complex international talks ever held. The 294-page comprehensive Agenda 21 encompassed every sectoral environmental issue, international policies affecting environment and development, and the full range of domestic social and economic policies, all adding up to 38 chapters and 115 topics. The conference also produced two nonbinding sets of principles—the Rio Declaration on Environment and Development and the Statement of Forest Principles—that helped create norms and expectations.[90] The UNFCCC and Convention on Biological Diversity, negotiated independently of the UNCED process on parallel tracks, were opened for signature at the Earth Summit and are often mentioned as UNCED-related agreements.

Negotiations on Agenda 21 acted as a bellwether for the state of international consensus on the full range of issues affecting the long-run sustainability of human society, including domestic social and economic policies, international economic relations, and cooperation on global commons issues. Among the more important norms agreed on, despite the reluctance of developing countries and some industrialized countries, are provisions calling for the removal or reduction of subsidies inconsistent with sustainable development (such as the sale of U.S. timber from public lands at prices below the full costs of production) and the improvement of price signals through environmental charges or taxes.[91] Agenda 21 also committed countries to expand their national statistical accounts by including environmental factors and unpaid work.[92] Despite these agreements, most countries still have not implemented such policies, at least not systematically.

Delegates in Rio also agreed upon a number of proposals to create new global environmental regimes or strengthen existing ones. Agenda 21 called for negotiations on toxic chemicals, the depletion of the world's fish stocks, land-based sources of marine pollution, desertification, and the unique environmental and development problems faced by small island developing states. Agenda 21 also addressed issues from sustainable human settlements to sustainable agriculture, solid waste and sewage, freshwater resources, air pollution, deforestation, mountains, and radioactive waste. At the insistence of the developing countries, Agenda 21 also elevated the issue of inequitable consumption patterns as a cause of global environmental degradation.[93] Industrialized countries were asked to accept the responsibility to change their "unsustainable lifestyles."

Questions concerning financial resources, **technology transfer** (the transfer of scientific and technological knowledge, patents, or equipment, usually from the most industrialized nations to the less developed ones), education, and capacity building for implementing Agenda 21 and global environmental agreements formed the core of the compact reached at Rio and remain a central issue today. The agreement reached in Rio essentially held that developing countries would try to put into practice more environmentally sound development policies if the industrialized countries agreed to provide the necessary support, that is, "new and additional" financial resources, technology transfer on concessional and preferential terms, and assistance with capacity building, education, and training.

Yet, nearly twenty later, few countries have lived up to their UNCED commitments. National Agenda 21 efforts in various countries in the 1990s led to academic debates,

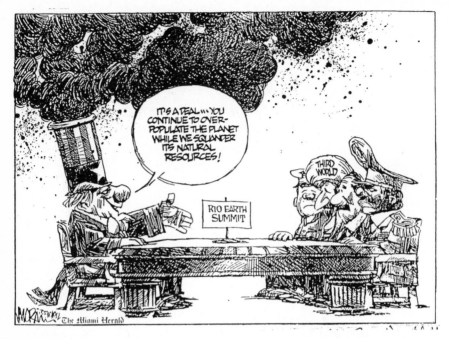

CARTOON 1.1   "It's a deal . . . you continue to overpopulate the planet while we squander its natural resources."
© 1992 by the *Miami Herald*, reprinted with permission.

heightened public awareness, and minor adjustments in the system of national accounts and taxation rules, but they have not fundamentally altered the way we manage and measure our national economy.

Paradigm Shift?

Within most of the powerful institutions in the United States, China, India, and many other countries, a number of elements of the exclusionist paradigm still tend to dominate policy making. Corporations, government ministries dealing with trade and finance, the leaders of some political parties, and some of the top officials of the World Bank and other multilateral institutions have been slow to change. Interest groups dominated by commerce and industry locked on old paradigms continue to determine many national political agendas, while the globalization of industry, finance, technology, and information has gradually eroded certain aspects of the powers held by national authorities and democratic institutions.[94]

Has the sustainable development paradigm failed? Delegates and observers asked themselves this question as they gathered in Johannesburg, South Africa, in September 2002 at the World Summit on Sustainable Development (WSSD) to review the implementation of Agenda 21 and the other agreements adopted at the Earth Summit in 1992 (see Box 1.3). Some argue that the sustainable development paradigm has not failed but that its ascendancy has stalled because of the rise of a variation of the exclusionist paradigm—**globalization**.[95] Globalization has become identified with a number of trends, including a greater international movement of commodities, money, information, and people, as well as the development of technology, organizations, legal systems, and infrastructures to allow this movement. Economic globalization means globe-spanning economic relationships. The interrelationships of markets, finance, goods and services, and the networks created by transnational corporations are particularly important manifestations.

Observers see globalization as different from the sustainable development paradigm. They argue that globalization policies advocate the liberalization of international markets, reducing trade and other national economic barriers, minimizing regulations on the market, especially in highly regulated developing countries, and granting rights to corporations to invest in any country of their choice without restraints or conditions. Governments should not interfere with the free play of the market, and social or developmental concerns (for instance, obtaining grants from developed countries to aid developing countries) should be downgraded.[96]

Some of the main factors in the ascendancy of the globalization paradigm were actions by some of the most powerful countries. Former UNDP administrator James Gustave Speth argues that some U.S. policy makers saw the globalization paradigm as supplanting the need for international assistance and even the sustainable development paradigm. "Trade, not aid" became a Washington mantra during the second Bush administration. Moreover, even among those U.S. policy makers favorable to environmental and development objectives, the priority given to the trade and globalization agenda tended to occupy the available political space and crowd out sustainable development concerns. In the battle for attention, environmental objectives typically lost out.[97] The same argument could be made about key policies in China, India, and Russia, among other large countries.

This said, Speth and others argue that the eclipse of some UNCED commitments has surely resulted from more than the ascendancy of the globalization paradigm. The post–Cold War period, for example, was supposed to bring a peace dividend of financial and political resources that could then be applied to promoting environmental and development objectives. Instead, the United States and others have been enmeshed in a series of military and peacekeeping engagements, including the war on terrorism triggered by the September 11 terrorist attacks, that have consumed much of their available time, energy, and money.[98]

Will the exclusionist or globalization paradigms dominate future political and economic perspectives, or will sustainable development have a chance to be implemented

BOX 1.3   WHAT IS THE WSSD?

The World Summit on Sustainable Development (WSSD) convened in Johannesburg, South Africa, in 2002. Its central goals were to hold a ten-year review of the 1992 Rio Earth Summit that would highlight accomplishments, identify areas requiring further efforts to implement Agenda 21 and other UNCED outcomes, produce tangible and action-oriented decisions, and result in renewed political commitment to achieving sustainable development.

The negotiations leading up to Johannesburg did not provide reason to expect dramatic agreements, and there were none. Although many world leaders attended the WSSD, the United States did not send a high-level delegation. The summit resulted in two main outcome documents. The Johannesburg Declaration on Sustainable Development largely reaffirmed central principles of the Rio Declaration from 1992 and the Millennium Development Goals.[1] The Johannesburg Plan of Implementation was a more action-oriented document that outlines the steps to take in pursuit of these principles.[2] NGOs strongly criticized both the declaration and action plan for not providing real new commitments, binding actions, specific targets, and funding for stated goals or implementation provisions. The WSSD also resulted in calls for a new strategy of partnership initiatives—voluntary and nonbinding action-oriented programs between governments, businesses, or civil society. Analysts saw these initiatives as a means to deliver some results without really committing governments to enacting specific new policies.

1. Johannesburg Declaration on Sustainable Development, A/CONF.199/20, Chapter 1, Resolution 1, Johannesburg, South Africa, September 2002, United Nations Documents, www.un-documents.net/jburgdec.htm, or United Nations, www.un.org/esa/sustdev/documents/WSSD_POI_PD/English/POIToc.htm.

2. Plan of Implementation of the World Summit on Sustainable Development, A/CONF.199/20, Chapter 1, Resolution 2, Johannesburg, South Africa, September 2002, United Nations Documents, www.un-documents.net/jburgpln.htm, and United Nations, www.un.org/esa/sustdev/documents/WSSD_POI_PD/English/POIToc.htm.

comprehensively? Although globalization remains a powerful force, some signs point to sustainable development's having a chance of becoming "mainstreamed" in certain economic and political circles. In June 2006, the European Council adopted a renewed and ambitious "sustainable development strategy" for the European Union. The sustainable development strategy formally recognizes the need for EU states to gradually change unsustainable consumption and production patterns and move toward a better integrated approach to policy making. The policy also reaffirms the need to devise a global approach to sustainable development as well as to work with rapidly developing countries (such as China and India) whose economic choices will significantly impact the global environment.[99] Political rhetoric often exceeds actual policy changes in this area, but many European governments do appear committed to achieving economic growth that is truly sustainable through relying increasingly on alternative energy, eliminating many toxic chemicals, improving energy efficiency, adopting the **precautionary principle** to guide decision making on environment and human-health issues (see discussion later in this chapter), and other measures.

In 2009, the Obama administration took office with a commitment to improving the sustainability and security of the U.S. energy system. Some Chinese leaders have begun to acknowledge that many benefits of their country's unparalleled economic expansion over the last twenty years will be threatened if the accompanying environmental degradation is not controlled and eventually reversed. China's legislature has also approved a resolution on the need to "actively deal with climate change," which, combined with other government initiatives, potentially signals plans to accelerate efforts to address the issue.[100]

Other signs include the tremendous growth in the deployment of proven clean-energy technologies, including wind, solar, geothermal, and tidal energies; increasing government and private sector commitments to energy efficiency; the amount of private investment activity in potential breakthrough technologies such as biofuels made from algae (such biofuels would not use arable land or significant quantities of energy and water to grow); and commitments by some large corporations, including Wal-Mart, General Electric, 3M, Hewlett-Packard, and Iberdrola Renewables, to incorporate sustainability into many important aspects of their operations—in the expectation that this will yield significant economic as well as environmental benefits.

Some argue that a future paradigm shift will not result from changing economic or political interests but rather will require a "revolution of social consciousness and values."[101] Paul Raskin, for example, believes a new sustainability paradigm is possible, but it will "happen only if key sectors of world society come to understand the nature and the gravity of the challenge, and seize the opportunity to revise their agendas."[102] Governments and, more importantly, people do not necessarily change entrenched behaviors when they become aware of the seriousness of a potential threat. Such behavior change sometimes requires a broader societal shift. With increased public debate and education about the importance of sustainable development in conjunction with changes in economic and political power, it is possible that such a paradigm shift will occur.

Environmental Change as a Security Issue

Two other potential new paradigms have emerged that impact global environmental politics. The first holds that environmental degradation and resource depletion can impact national security. The central idea is that environmental degradation and resource scarcity act as threat multipliers that augment other conditions known to cause violence between opposing groups within a state or even between states. As argued by Thomas Homer-Dixon, who helped to pioneer our understanding of this issue, resource scarcity, ecosystem collapse, and other environmental problems can act as tectonic stresses, exacerbating existing political, social, or economic instability to the point that armed conflict occurs.[103] Environmental degradation can help cause or increase the impact of other problems known to contribute to violence within or between states, such as resource disputes, refugee movements, poverty, hunger, and weak governments.

Changing climate conditions contributed to the devastating ethnic conflict in Darfur, Sudan. While long-standing animosity existed between elements of the nomadic Afro-Arab ethnic groups that dominate in the North and the non-Arab farming ethnic groups in the South (the government and several rebel groups have opposed each other for years), severe changes in rainfall patterns and deteriorating soils likely played a significant role in events that led to a full-scale ethnic war. Many farmers had traditionally shared their land and water with the herders. However, increasing drought caused many farmers to block off the remaining fertile land, fearing shared use by the herders would ruin it. Many Arab herders were angry that they were not receiving their share of the land, leading to violent clashes. Environmental factors alone did not cause the violence, but they pushed other factors, including poverty, increasing ethnic and political divisions, and the territorial ambitions of certain groups, past the tipping point into widespread, systematic violence. The results have been horrific. The United Nations estimates that more that 400,000 people have died, and more than 2 million have been displaced, due to the resulting war, governmental efforts to remove some ethnic groups from their land in Darfur, and the increased hunger, poverty, human-rights violations, and worsening social conditions the conflict has spawned.[104]

In North America, the collapse of fisheries in northwestern Mexico contributed to the decision by some fishermen to become involved in drug smuggling and other crimes, which has contributed to the declining security situation in Mexican and U.S. border communities.[105] In Kenya, years of rapid population growth combined with environmental degradation have produced increased scarcity of jobs, fertile land, water, and other resources. This, combined with the government's efforts to exploit this scarcity in support of its allies, produced a huge surge in ethnic violence between 1991 and 1993.[106] Similar conditions exist today with a severe multiyear drought (which some scientists trace to climate change) and land degradation feeding even more intense poverty and increasing violence. In Haiti, massive deforestation (less than 2 percent of the nation remains forested) led to severely eroded hillsides, massive soil erosion and runoff, and declining water quality. This exacerbated the already difficult situation for rural farmers trying to work the country's mountainous terrain. Soil runoff from the mountains also polluted many of the nation's already overfished coastal areas, nearly eliminating fishing as a source of income. With no means to make a living in rural areas, the vast majority of Haitians moved to city slums, most living without clean water or proper sanitation. Rival gangs rule these areas, and severe violence exists throughout parts of many villages and cities. Experts warn that the current levels of poverty and chaos threaten to turn Haiti, already one of the poorest countries in the world, into a completely lawless state.[107]

The United States and European political, military, and intelligence communities have accepted certain aspects of the emerging paradigm that environmental degradation can lead to security concerns.[108] Of particular concern is climate change, which could produce huge numbers of refugees from flooded coastal areas, increase water and food scarcity, spread disease, and weaken economies in parts of the world that are already vulnerable, unstable, or prone to extremism or that suffer significant cultural, ethnic, or economic divisions. Climate change could also potentially contribute to violent conflict and even terrorism in the Middle East and Africa. As a recent study of the issue noted, "Demand for water already outstrips supply; climate models are predicting a hotter, drier and less predictable climate in the Middle East. Climate change threatens to reduce the availability of scarce water resources, increase food insecurity, hinder economic growth and lead to large-scale population movements. This could hold serious implications for peace in the region" and the world.[109] Africa, meanwhile, while "least responsible for greenhouse gas emissions, is almost universally seen as the continent most at risk of climate-induced conflict—a function of the continent's reliance on climate-dependent sectors (such as rain-fed agriculture) and its history of resource, ethnic and political conflict."[110]

Environmental degradation and the mismanagement of natural resources can fuel conflict between and within states and contribute to poverty and state failure. On the flip side, war and other security issues can impact the environment. Military spending absorbs government finances and policy attention that might otherwise be dedicated to environmental protection. Military operations, even in peacetime, can consume huge quantities of natural resources and produce significant pollution. Armed conflict itself produces habitat destruction, overexploitation of natural resources, and pollution. Civil wars in Africa, Asia, and Latin America have destroyed many hectares of forests and wetlands. The oil spill in the Persian Gulf during the 1991 Gulf War, considered the worst oil spill in history, caused considerable harm to wildlife and destroyed habitats. The Kuwaiti oil fires, set by retreating Iraqi forces during the same war, generated considerable air, water, and soil pollution.

Armed conflict also impacts states' and regions' ability to guard protected areas and enforce conservation regulations.[111] This is particularly true during civil war or in very weak states where the breakdown of the rule of law, increased firearms and weapons possession, and disrupted economic and agricultural production all impact environmental protection. In the Congo, for example, armed conflict since 1994 has had a severe impact on many nature reserves, including some designated as World Heritage sites. Governments, international organizations, and NGOs have faced huge obstacles due to the "proliferation of arms and ammunition; displaced people, military, and dissidents; a general breakdown of law and order; uncontrolled exploitation of natural, mineral and land resources by various interest groups; and the increased use of wild areas as refuges and for subsistence."[112] Antipoaching patrols ceased in many areas for different periods, and increased poaching, harvesting of game for food, and habitat destruction seriously affected wildlife populations in some parks. Cross-border impacts can occur as well. The civil war in southern Sudan, the violence in Uganda, and the civil war and devastating genocide in Rwanda affected parks in those countries as well as the Garamba, Kahuzi-Biega, and Virunga border parks in the Congo, all World Heritage sites.[113]

Drug traffickers, either on their own or in alliance with rebel groups, sometimes prevent the enforcement of wildlife conservation, habitat protection, or deforestation laws in Bolivia, Colombia, Peru, and Mexico by essentially controlling access to certain areas or bribing or intimidating inspectors and other officials.[114] The rise of drug smuggling and violence in coastal areas of northwestern Mexico has made it much more difficult to study and protect the endangered sea turtles and marine mammals that live in or pass through that area.[115]

The new environment-and-security paradigm replaces the old line of thinking that environmental degradation is irrelevant to a state's national-security interests. The new paradigm does not imply that the environment is more important than traditional security calculations, but it does argue that an analysis of factors that can negatively impact a state's security must include environmental degradation and resource mismanagement (much as the sustainable development paradigm argues that serious environmental degradation can negatively impact a state's economy). It is not clear, however, that increased awareness of this relationship will lead to new types of actions by developing-country or donor-country governments to ward off resource collapse in vulnerable parts of Africa, Asia, and Latin America and the Caribbean. Nor is it clear that recognition of the very serious regional and even global security problems potentially posed by climate change will lead to increased efforts to reduce GHG emissions.

The Precautionary Principle: A New Paradigm for Environmental Policy

The exclusionist paradigm implies that economic policy calculations need not factor in resource scarcity and environmental degradation. Should resource scarcity begin to occur, the market will respond by raising prices, which will reduce demand and spur the search for substitutes, thereby averting a crisis. Similarly, there is no need to consider or take steps to avoid environmental problems before they occur, as these can be remedied after the fact if the market demands it.

Unfortunately, while these deductions make sense from a purely market perspective, they fail to account accurately for the physical limitations of the earth's biological and physical systems. It is true that prices will rise, and incentives will exist to develop substitutes when scarcity becomes an issue, but for some environmental problems, these market forces will occur too late. Certain environmental impacts simply cannot be remedied once they occur, at least not on timescales relevant to human economic and political systems. If the ozone layer thins significantly, a rainforest gets destroyed, a coral reef dies, the climate system shifts to a different equilibrium, a species becomes extinct, or a human life is shortened by air, water, or toxic pollution, these changes will last, if not forever, then at least for a very, very long time.

In other cases, operating under the exclusionist paradigm might simply represent a poor economic decision. For example, the impacts of the environmental degradation caused by some types of pollution might cost far more than economic benefits accrued from emitting it. Deforestation in Haiti and other areas is an example. For the country as a whole, the economic benefits of using the wood or cleared land are far fewer than the economic costs associated with the harm caused to fisheries, farming, and freshwater resources due to the severe erosion and runoff from hills and mountains that no longer have trees to hold the soil in place. In others cases, such as climate change or ozone depletion, preventing the worst aspects of the problem from occurring costs far less than the impacts.

This argument holds that in many situations, the best policy—from an environmental, human-health, and even economic point of view (and perhaps an ethical one as well)—is to avoid producing certain very serious environmental problems in the first place. The difficulty, of course, is that the complexity of many environmental issues prevents clear calculations of an activity's environmental costs, while its economic benefits are usually quite clear. Thus, the lack of scientific certainty regarding the range, extent, and cost of environmental impacts from particular activities or products can prevent effective policy in the face of strong lobbying by economic interests.

The precautionary principle attempts to resolve this dilemma and provide guidance in the development of national and international environmental policy in the face of scientific uncertainty. The most widely used definition of the precautionary principle was set forth by governments in 1992 at the Earth Summit in Principle 15 of the Rio Declaration: "Where there are threats of serious or irreversible damage, lack of full scientific certainty shall not be used as a reason for postponing cost-effective measures to prevent environmental degradation."[116]

The precautionary principle contains several main policy-relevant ideas:[117]

- the importance and efficacy of taking preventative action, even in the face of uncertainty, when the lack of action might produce essentially irreversible, unwanted impacts on the environment or human health;
- the need to shift the burden of proof from those seeking to protect human health and the environment to those supporting a particular activity or product. Rather than forcing others to prove something is definitely harmful, which has traditionally been the case, now proponents of, for example, using a particular chemical would show it is not harmful;
- the need to explore alternatives to possibly harmful actions in search of more sustainable options;
- the need to keep science and rational arguments central to decision making involving health and environmental issues with the understanding that scientific certainty or unanimity regarding future harm is not required to make policy designed to protect the environment or human health from irreversible damage; and
- the importance of asking why we should risk irreversible or very serious harm for a particular product or activity.[118]

Several important global environmental statements and treaty regimes contain key elements of the precautionary principle either explicitly or implicitly.[119] For example, the Rio Declaration's Principle 15 not only defines the principle but states, "In order to protect the environment, the precautionary approach shall be widely applied by States according to their capabilities."[120] The WSSD endorsed this idea in 2002. Examples within individual regimes include the Ministerial Declaration from the Second International Conference on the Protection of the North Sea (1987), which states, "In order to protect the North Sea from possibly damaging effects of the most dangerous substances, a precautionary approach is necessary which may require action to control inputs of such substances even before a causal link has been established by absolutely clear scientific evidence."[121] Declarations at subsequent meetings in 1990 and 1995 reaffirmed that precaution is the regime's guiding principle.

The landmark 1987 Montreal Protocol on Substances That Deplete the Ozone Layer also endorsed the concept of precautionary policy, stating that parties to the agreement are "determined to protect the ozone layer by taking precautionary measures to control equably total global emissions of substances that deplete it."[122] Moreover, the regime itself is precautionary in that governments negotiated the framework 1985 Vienna Convention almost entirely before discovery of any actual ozone depletion and then created the 1987 Montreal Protocol (which mandates 50 percent cuts in eight ozone-depleting chemicals) before scientists had proved, with certainty, that CFCs and other chemicals were definitely depleting the ozone layer (this confirmation came in 1988 and 1989).

The climate regime includes the concept of precaution as one of its central principles. Article 3 of the UNFCCC, entitled "Principles," states,

> In their actions to achieve the objective of the Convention and to implement its provisions, the Parties shall be guided, *inter alia*, by the following: . . .
>
> The parties should take precautionary measures to anticipate, prevent, or minimize the causes of climate change and mitigate its adverse effects. Where there are threats of serious or irreversible damage, lack of full scientific certainty should not be used as a reason for postponing such measures.[123]

The 2000 Cartagena Protocol on Biosafety expressly allows parties to ban imports of genetically modified organisms, even where there is a "lack of scientific certainty due to insufficient relevant scientific information and knowledge" concerning health or environmental impacts.[124] The 2001 Stockholm Convention on Persistent Organic Pollutants defines the objective of the regime: "Mindful of the precautionary approach as set forth in Principle 15 of the Rio Declaration on Environment and Development, the objective of this Convention is to protect human health and the environment from persistent organic pollutants."[125] In addition, the treaty states that "precaution" should be used when considering additional substances to add to the control measures and that the lack of scientific certainty regarding the precise levels of a substance's toxicity or propensity for long-range transport and bioaccumulation shall not be grounds for failing to consider controlling it under the regime. The International Tribunal for the Law of the Sea cited "prudence and caution" as the basis for its decision that required Japan to cease all efforts in its experimental fishing program that potentially endangered stocks of the migratory tuna species.[126]

Many individual local and national laws in a number of countries have also incorporated the principle. Most important is the EU announcement in 2000 stating that the precautionary principle will guide EU policy decisions on environmental and human-health issues and is also a "a full-fledged and general principle of international law."[127]

Yet, even though there is increasing reference to the precautionary principle in international politics, arguments exist that it should not be accepted as a principle of international law (on par with universally accepted principles such as sovereignty). Some argue that shifting the burden of proof means that decisions will not be based on scientific certainty but rather on "emotional and irrational" factors.[128] Others argue that precautionary actions will cost too much, harming companies and hindering economic development.[129] Some argue that it is essentially impossible to prove that anything in all situations is totally safe.[130] Some believe that too many different definitions and interpretations of the principle exist to make it a clearly defined principle of international law. By one count, at least fourteen different definitions, formulations, and uses of the precautionary principle exist in international policy, plus many more at the national and local levels.[131] Others note that its acceptance by international legal bodies as a guiding point of international law is not universal.[132] For example, during the second Bush administration, the United States argued during several international negotiations that the precautionary principle was not an accepted principle of international law that bound states to certain norms. Under this interpretation, references to precaution in treaties that the United States signed or ratified related only to the particular activity under discussion—not a general international legal principle applicable across all countries and issues.[133]

Other analysts, legal scholars, and policy makers dismiss these arguments. They believe that inclusion of the precautionary principle (or its key elements under another name) in so many international treaties, its status within the EU, and its emergence in local and national laws in countries around the world argue convincingly that "the precautionary principle has evolved from being a 'soft law' 'aspirational' goal to its present status as an authoritative norm recognized by governments and international organizations as a firm guide to activities affecting the environment."[134]

Clearly the precautionary principle has become a major part of international environmental law and policy—having found its way into an increasing number of global regimes, influenced international decision making, and been more and more accepted in debates on national policies in multiple countries. Yet, if the precautionary principle is a new dominant paradigm for environmental policy, then why don't we see greater levels of international commitments with regard to climate change, biodiversity, and rain-forest protection?

Perhaps there is no real dominant paradigm. It appears that multiple paradigms exist today and compete for primacy. Elements of the exclusionist paradigm still influence some global, national, local, and corporate policies but so, too, do elements of the sustainable development paradigm and the precautionary principle.

At the same time, the totality of the evidence supports the thesis that we are likely in a time of paradigm transition—from exclusionist premises to sustainable development and precaution. But the future is far from clear. As economies, populations, cities, energy production, and resource demands continue to grow, the paradigms that influence current and future policy debates could go a long way toward determining what the world will look like in the future.

CONCLUSION

Global environmental politics involve interactions among states and nonstate actors that transcend a given region regarding international decisions that affect the environment and natural resources. The emergence of this issue area in world politics reflects the growing awareness of the cumulative stresses economic activities have put on the earth's resources and life-support systems during the past century.

Much of global environmental politics focuses on efforts to negotiate multilateral agreements for cooperation to protect the environment and natural resources. These agreements constitute global environmental regimes of varying effectiveness that govern state behavior regarding the environmental problem in question.

Legitimate differences in economic, political, and environmental interests make achieving unanimity among states responsible for, or directly affected by, an environmental problem a political and diplomatic challenge. The ability of one or more states to block or weaken multilateral agreements is a primary problem in global environmental politics, and finding ways to overcome such blockage is a major concern. For a regime to form, veto states must be persuaded to abandon their opposition to a proposed regime or at least to compromise with states supporting it.

Another obstacle has been a dominant socioeconomic paradigm that justifies essentially unlimited exploitation of nature. Despite the weakening of that paradigm and the apparent widespread recognition of an alternative sustainable development paradigm, especially in conjunction with the 1992 Earth Summit, the rise of globalization and a resurgence of the traditional paradigm have complicated the shift to this alternative socioeconomic paradigm. Subsequent chapters in this book will discuss the actors involved in global environmental politics and how their interests may either promote the alternative paradigm or retain the traditional paradigm of resource exploitation and what this entails for the future.

Theoretical approaches advanced to explain the formation of international regimes include the structural, game-theoretic, and epistemic-community models. These approaches fail to account for most global environmental regimes. To explain why environmental regimes are formed and strengthened, a theoretical approach must deal with the central problem of veto coalitions and why they are, or are not, overcome in regime negotiations. It will also have to avoid relying solely on the unitary actor model and encompass domestic political forces, the structure of the negotiating forum, the interplay of economic interests, and the role of other international political concerns.

Subsequent chapters in this book will explore these issues. Chapter 2 examines the main actors in global environmental politics. States are the most important actors because they negotiate international legal instruments, create global environmental regimes, and adopt economic, trade, and regulatory policies that directly and indirectly affect the environment. At the same time, nonstate actors also play major roles. International organizations, treaty secretariats, NGOs, and multinational corporations help set the global environmental agenda, initiate and influence the process of regime formation, and carry out actions that directly affect the global environment.

Chapters 3 to 5 look at the development of eleven important global environmental regimes: transboundary air pollution, hazardous chemicals, hazardous waste, ozone depletion, climate change, whaling, endangered species, biodiversity loss, fisheries, desertification, and forests. Each issue is analyzed according to the stages of negotiation and the role of veto coalitions in shaping the outcomes of bargaining.

Chapter 6 looks at obstacles to creating, implementing, and complying with environmental regimes and the means of effective implementation. The first two sections examine factors that make it difficult to create regimes with strong control measures and for states to comply with them. The third section outlines methods to improve compliance and effectiveness. The final section discusses options for increasing the financing available to help implement global environmental regimes. Because the lack of adequate financial and technical resources seriously inhibits the ability of many developing countries to comply with environmental regimes, the question of financial resources has been at the center of global environmental policy for many years and will continue to be for the foreseeable future.

Chapter 7 focuses on the interplay between environmental issues and economic and social development as the three "pillars" of sustainable development. This chapter looks at three elements in this broadening debate: North-South economic relations and the environment, the role of environmental politics in the evolution of global economic and social-development policies, and the clash between the drive for free trade and environmental protection.

Chapter 8 examines the interplay between globalization and the environment, as well as the challenges of global governance, and concludes with some thoughts on the past, present, and future of global environmental politics.

DISCUSSION QUESTIONS

1. Discuss the ways in which population and environmental factors interact. What is the effect on energy? On fisheries? Why is per capita consumption a potentially important issue?
2. Why are global environmental trends an issue? Why were they not an issue before the 1970s? What has changed physically and in people's consciousness?
3. What are veto states? Why are they so important in global environmental politics?
4. What is an international regime?
5. According to the different theoretical approaches described in this chapter, what factors make it easier or more difficult to achieve strong international agreement on a global environmental issue?

6. What method is currently used to measure macroeconomic growth? Why is it an inadequate benchmark? How would alternative methods of measurement overcome the limitations of the present one?

7. What is the exclusionist paradigm? What is the sustainable development paradigm? How do they differ?

8. What is the precautionary principle? Describe why you think this principle should or should not be used by a national government in helping to determine its policy on a global environmental issue.

2

Actors in the Environmental Arena

States are the most important actors in global environmental politics. States adopt the broad economic, regulatory, trade, and development policies that impact the environment. They decide which issues receive formal consideration by the international community directly (through advocacy for international action on a particular issue) and indirectly (through membership in the governing councils of international organizations). States negotiate the international legal instruments that create and implement global environmental regimes. Donor states influence the effectiveness of these regimes and other environmental policies through aid programs and donations to implementation programs and multilateral banks.

But nonstate actors also exert significant and increasing influence on global environmental politics. Intergovernmental organizations (IGOs) help to set the global environmental agenda, initiate and mediate the process of regime formation, and cooperate with developing countries on projects and programs directly affecting the environment. Nongovernmental organizations (NGOs) also participate in setting the agenda, influencing negotiations on regime formation, and shaping the environmental policies of donor agencies toward developing countries. Multinational corporations influence the bargaining over regime creation and carry out actions that directly affect the global environment. In addition, treaty secretariats can have an impact on agenda setting and financing issues that affect global environmental regimes. This chapter examines the roles that these actors play in global environmental politics.

NATION-STATE ACTORS: ROLES AND INTERESTS

Perhaps the most important actions by state actors in global environmental politics concern the creation, implementation, and expansion of international environmental regimes. In regime negotiations, a state may play one of four roles: **lead state, supporting state, swing state,** or **veto** (or **blocking**) **state**. A lead state has a strong commitment to effective international action on the issue, moves the negotiation process forward by proposing its own negotiating formula as the basis for an agreement, and attempts to win the support of other state actors.

A supporting state speaks in favor of a lead state's proposal in negotiations. As the price for its going along with an agreement, a swing state demands a concession to its interests but not one that would significantly weaken the regime. A veto or blocking state either opposes a proposed environmental regime outright or tries to weaken it to the point that it cannot be effective.

States sometimes shift roles. The United States shifted from a veto state in the climate negotiations under President George W. Bush to a swing state under President Barack Obama. Sometimes states play different roles for strategic reasons, such as shifting from a swing to a veto role because threatening a veto is sometimes the best means of enhancing bargaining leverage. For example, during the critical second **Meeting of the Parties** to the Montreal Protocol in London in June 1990, India and China refused to join an agreement that would bind them to phase out chlorofluorocarbons (CFCs) in 2010 until the industrialized countries agreed to provide significant financial and technical assistance to developing countries to assist them in their transition to less harmful, but equally productive, chemicals and more advanced technology.

There may be more than one lead state on a given issue. For example, Sweden and Norway were allied from the beginning in pushing for a long-range transboundary air pollution agreement. Canada and Sweden both played lead roles in initiating action resulting in negotiations on persistent organic pollutants (POPs). Sometimes a state steps forward to advance a policy that puts it clearly in the lead for a particular period, as Germany did with the climate-change issue in 1990 and Canada did with the fisheries issue in 1992. As issues go through several stages, the role of lead state may shift from one state or combination of states to another. In the negotiation of the Vienna Convention for the Protection of the Ozone Layer in 1985, Finland and Sweden took the lead by submitting their own draft convention and heavily influencing the draft put before the conference. In 1986, the United States stepped into the lead role by proposing an eventual 95 percent reduction in CFCs, and by 1989 and 1990, several Organization for Economic Cooperation and Development (OECD) states had become the lead states by working for a CFC phaseout before 2000. In the early 1990s, the European Union (EU) emerged as the lead state in negotiations to phase out other ozone-depleting chemicals such as methyl bromide and hydrochlorofluorocarbons (HCFCs).

Lead states use a wide range of methods for influencing other state actors on a global environmental issue. A lead state may:

- fund, produce, and/or call attention to research that defines the problem and demonstrates its urgency, as when Swedish research showed the serious damage done by acid rain, Canadian research revealed long-range dangers posed by POPs, and U.S.-based research revealed a threat to the earth's protective ozone layer;
- seek to impact public opinion in target states, as Canada did when it supplied U.S. tourists with pamphlets on the acidification of its forests and waters and instructed its Washington, D.C., embassy to cooperate with like-minded U.S. environmental organizations;
- use its diplomatic clout to encourage an international organization to identify the issues as a priority, as when the United States and Canada persuaded the OECD to take up the ozone layer and CFCs, and the African countries persuaded the United Nations to begin negotiations on a treaty to combat desertification;
- rely on the worldwide network of NGOs to support its position in other countries and at international conferences, as the Alliance of Small Island States (AOSIS) did in its proposal to place quantitative limits on greenhouse gas (GHG) emissions in the Kyoto Protocol negotiations;
- make a diplomatic démarche to a state that is threatening a veto role, as the United States did with Japan on African elephant ivory; or
- pledge to commit financial or technical resources to the problem, such as the positive incentives that industrialized countries accepted in the Montreal Protocol and Stockholm Convention, and so gain significant developing-country participation.

Although scientific-technological capabilities and economic power cannot ensure that a lead state will prevail on an environmental issue, they constitute valuable assets for helping to create a regime. When a big power like the United States takes a lead role through scientific research, unilateral action, and diplomatic initiative, as it did on the issue of ozone protection, it helps to sway states that do not otherwise have clearly defined interests in the issue.

States play different roles in different issues. A lead state on one issue may be a potential veto state on another. Whether a state plays a lead, supporting, swing, or veto role in regard to a particular global environmental issue depends primarily on domestic political factors and the relative costs and benefits of the proposed regime. Another variable, which has been important in some issues, is the anticipation of international political consequences, including increased national prestige or damage to the country's image worldwide.

Domestic Political Factors

Both a state's definition of its interests with regard to a particular global environmental issue and its consequential choice of role depend largely on domestic economic and

CARTOON 2.1   "Anti-Norway feeling increases."
By Jeff Danziger. Reproduced with permission from the June 16, 1996 issue of *The Christian Science Monitor* (www.CSMonitor.com). © 1996 *The Christian Science Monitor.*

political interests and ideological currents. Whether a government opposes, supports, or leads on an issue depends first on the relative strength and influence of powerful economic and bureaucratic forces and domestic environmental constituencies. Ideological factors related to broader domestic political themes can also play prominent roles in the definition of interests.

Domestic economic interests are particularly prominent in promoting veto roles. When the Liberal Democratic Party dominated Japanese politics, for example, major trading companies generally received government support for their interests in whaling because of their close ties to the party.[1] Norway's fishing industry, which claims to have suffered declining fish catches because of the international protection of whales, has prevailed on its government to defend Norwegian whaling before the international community. Norway, Japan, and Greece tended to be swing or blocking actors on questions of marine pollution from oil tankers because of the economic importance of their shipping industries. Germany, Italy, the Netherlands, and Sweden, all of which have smaller shipping industries, were more flexible in negotiations on pollution from ships.[2] The United States has been a swing or blocking actor on climate-change and chemicals-related issues because of pressure from domestic oil, gas, automobile, and chemicals manufacturers.

A state's position on a global environmental issue sometimes reflects the interests of dominant socioeconomic elites. Indonesia, for example, allocated control over a large proportion of its forest resources to a relatively small elite of concessionaires. In 1995, twenty Indonesian conglomerates controlled more than 63 percent of the 62 million hectares of the country's timber concessions. These businesses had close ties with the family of former president Suharto, which allowed them to ignore logging concession regulations. A plywood exporters' cartel controlled by a timber baron crony of Suharto's dominated the Suharto regime's forest policy.[3] It is not surprising, therefore, that Indonesia opposed proposals for new international norms on forest management in the early 1990s or that it supported Canada's 1997 proposal for a forest convention that would allow each major timber-exporting country to create its own ecolabeling system.

Government bureaucracies with institutional interests that global action on a particular environmental issue would impact negatively often attempt to influence the adoption of swing or blocking roles. During the negotiation of the Montreal Protocol in the mid-1980s, officials in the U.S. Departments of Commerce, Interior, and Agriculture, together with the Office of Management and Budget, the Office of Science and Technology Policy, and some members of the White House staff, began to reopen basic questions about the scientific evidence and the possible damage to the U.S. economy from imposing additional CFC controls, but they were overruled.[4] The major obstacles to the United Kingdom's agreeing to an acid rain agreement were two public bodies, the National Coal Board and the Central Electricity Generating Board, which did everything possible to avoid having to reduce sulfur dioxide emissions.[5]

Authoritarian political regimes that can simply suppress opposition to their policies enhance the ability of powerful economic or bureaucratic interests to resist restrictions on their despoiling of the environment. The military regime that ruled Brazil from 1964 to 1985 enjoyed virtually unlimited power in determining how natural resources were exploited and permitted no opposition to its campaign to open the Amazonian rain forests to agriculture and other large-scale commercial activities. But under an elected government, which NGOs and media were freer to criticize, Brazil became less hostile toward an international agreement to slow deforestation.

A state's taking a lead role on a global environmental issue becomes far more likely if there is little or no domestic opposition. The United States could easily take the lead role on the issue of whaling, for example, because the U.S. whaling industry had already been eliminated. Similarly, the absence of significant bureaucratic or business interest in opposing a ban on imports of African elephant ivory products made it easy for the United States to assume a lead role on that issue.

The existence of a strong environmental movement can be a decisive factor in a state's definition of its interest on an issue, especially if it is a potential swing vote in parliamentary elections. The sudden emergence of West German and French bids for leadership roles on certain environmental issues in 1989 reflected in large part the upsurge of public support for strong environmental-protection policies in western Europe. The West German Green Party had already won 8.2 percent of the vote in the 1984 European Parliament elections, and by 1985 the Greens, backed by popular environmental sentiment, were already a strong force in the German parliament.[6] Before the 1989 European Parliament election, polls indicated a new surge in environmentalist sentiment in West Germany and France. As a result, in early 1989 both countries became part of a lead coalition of states proposing negotiations on a framework convention on climate change to stabilize carbon dioxide (CO_2) emissions. Germany continues to be a lead state on climate change, in part because of the presence of the Green Party in coalition governments led by the Social Democratic Party and because it has one of the largest and most active environmental movements in Europe.[7] The German environmental movement's clout helped overcome the influence of the powerful German coal industry.

But a strong environmental movement does not guarantee that a state actor will play a lead or supporting role on a particular issue. The U.S. environmental movement is among the largest and best organized in the world, but it has been unable to sway U.S. policy regarding the Kyoto Protocol or ratification of the Biodiversity, Basel, Rotterdam, or Stockholm conventions. Powerful interests that oppose U.S. participation in these treaties and an environmental movement that has been unable to influence the outcomes of congressional or presidential elections are responsible for this failure.[8]

Conversely, the absence of a strong environmental movement makes it more likely that a state will play a swing or blocking role on an international environmental issue. For example, Japanese NGOs are relatively underdeveloped in comparison with those in North America and Europe, and the Japanese political system makes it difficult for interest groups without high-level political links to influence policy. The Japanese government therefore felt little or no domestic pressure to support regimes on African elephants, whaling, and drift-net fishing. In contrast, U.S. wildlife NGOs placed a great deal of domestic pressure on the U.S. government to take strong positions on these issues.

A final domestic political factor that can shape a country's definition of its interest in an environmental regime is the ideology or belief system of the policy maker. Although the United States had exported very little of its hazardous waste, the George H. W. Bush administration led the veto coalition against a ban on hazardous waste exports to developing countries because of its hostility to the intervention of states in national and international markets. The first Bush administration also vetoed a proposal for industrialized states to set targets for per capita energy use because officials saw this as unwarranted state interference in consumer preferences.[9]

Comparative Costs and Benefits of Environmental R

A second group of variables that shape the definition of national in
environmental issue includes the potential risks and costs of an environmental threat
as well as the costs and benefits associated with the proposed regime.[10] Exceptional
vulnerability to the consequences of environmental problems has driven countries to
support, or even take the lead on, strong global action. Thirty-two small island states
especially vulnerable to sea-level rise because of **global warming** formed AOSIS in
November 1990 to speak with one, more influential voice in the climate negotiations.
States with densely populated coastal plains, such as Bangladesh, Egypt, and the
Netherlands, are also likely to face particularly severe disruptions from storm surges,
hurricanes, and typhoons as a result of climate change and have generally supported
efforts to strengthen the United Nations Framework Convention on Climate Change
(UNFCCC).

Sweden and Norway, which led the fight for the Convention on Long-Range Transboundary Air Pollution, have been the major recipients of sulfur dioxide from other
European countries, and their lakes and soils are also acid sensitive. The damage from
acid rain therefore appeared earlier and was more serious in those Nordic countries
than in the United Kingdom or Germany. Similarly, Canada pushed for strong action
on POPs after the discovery that the chemicals tend to bioaccumulate in the Arctic
food chain and disproportionately affect Inuit communities in northern Canada.

The costs of compliance with a given global environmental regime may differ
dramatically from one country to another, and such differences have sometimes
shaped the roles played by states in regime negotiations. The negotiation of the Montreal Protocol provides several examples of states whose roles were linked with economic interests. Former United Nations Environment Programme (UNEP)
executive director Mostafa Tolba is reported to have observed, "The difficulties in
negotiating the Montreal Protocol had nothing to do with whether the environment
was damaged or not. . . . It was all who was going to get the edge over whom."[11] Because of an earlier unilateral ban on aerosols using ozone-depleting chemicals, the
United States was ahead of members of the European Community (EC) and Japan
in finding substitutes for CFCs in aerosol cans; it therefore joined Canada and the
Nordic states in supporting such a ban. Western Europe and Japan rejected a ban
on CFC aerosols in the early 1980s in part because they did not yet have technological alternatives. The Soviet Union, fearful that it would be unable to develop new
technologies to replace CFCs, resisted the idea of significant CFC cuts until 1987.
China and India, who were minor producers at the time but already gearing up for
major production increases, also feared that the transition to ozone-safe chemicals
would be too costly without noncommercial access to alternative technologies.

Moreover, India's chemical industry planned to export half its projected CFC production to the Middle East and Asia.

The anticipated economic costs of compliance were the underlying issue during the negotiations that resulted in the Kyoto Protocol to the UNFCCC. Achieving reductions in GHG emissions is easier and/or cheaper for some countries than others. For example, EU states are generally net importers of fossil fuels and have learned how to reduce energy use without compromising economic growth. Because the EU states saw that their cost of compliance would be comparatively low, they were able to play a lead role in the negotiation of the Kyoto Protocol. In December 2008, the EU agreed to reduce GHG emissions across the EU by 20 percent by 2020 and to increase the share of renewable energy to 20 percent of energy use by 2020.[12] In adopting this "20-20-by-20" policy, the EU took into consideration internal burden sharing, meaning that those countries with the greatest resources or best able to reduce their GHG emissions at the lowest cost would carry the burden for those countries on which reductions would place a greater economic burden.

International Political and Diplomatic Considerations

States also consider potential benefits or costs to broader international interests when considering whether to assume a lead or veto role on a particular global environmental issue. A state may hope to gain international prestige by assuming a lead role, or it may decide against a veto role to avoid international opprobrium or damage to its relations with countries for which the environmental issue is of significantly greater concern.

Concern for national prestige—a state's reputation or status in the international community—was once confined to the issue area of international security. But in the early 1990s, a few states began to regard leadership on the global environment as a means of enhancing their international status. In the early 1990s, the United States and Germany both made bids for leadership on a possible world forest convention, in large part because both anticipated that such leadership would enhance their environmental image around the world. In 1994, then EU environment commissioner Yannis Paleokrassas hailed the prospect of a regionwide carbon tax, which would give the EU a lead role in climate change and result in "the resumption of world environmental and fiscal leadership by the European Union," suggesting that the EU would gain a new kind of international prestige.[13]

At the 1992 Earth Summit, the United States tarnished its image in the eyes of many observers because it stood alone in rejecting the Convention on Biological Diversity (CBD). Germany and Japan, among other countries, shared U.S. unhappiness concerning some provisions in the CBD but shunned a veto role for fear of damaging their prestige. A George H. W. Bush administration official later charged that Germany and

Japan had departed from the U.S. position in part to demonstrate their new status as emerging, independent world powers.[14]

A state's concern about how a veto role might affect its image sometimes focuses on a particular country or group of countries. For international trade in hazardous wastes, for example, the decision by France and the United Kingdom in 1989 to alter their position and not play a veto role stemmed in part from a broader national interest in maintaining close ties with former colonies in Africa. Japan chose not to block efforts to ban trade in African elephant ivory in 1989 largely because it feared damage to its relations with its most important trading partners, the United States and Europe. Canada ratified the Kyoto Protocol in 2002 in part to protect its "environmentally progressive international image," which would be severely damaged if it rejected the protocol.[15]

Subnational Actors

National governments, despite their assertion of exclusive rights to act in international relations, are no longer the only governmental actors in global environmental politics. In recent years, cities, states, and provinces have shown increased interest in adopting their own environmental and energy policies, and these could have a major impact on global environmental problems, especially climate change. Although municipal and state governments are unlikely to usurp national government functions in regime strengthening, they may reinforce and supplement efforts by national governments. Large cities are major producers of GHGs in part because of their heavy consumption of energy, the biggest source of CO_2 emissions. Urban policies, then, if effective, could substantially reduce GHG emissions. With this in mind, in May 2005 a bipartisan group of 132 U.S. mayors, frustrated by the George W. Bush administration's refusal to ratify the Kyoto Protocol, pledged that their cities would try to meet Kyoto's main target—a 7 percent reduction in GHG emissions from 1990 levels in less than ten years. The cities ranged from liberal centers such as Los Angeles, California, to strongholds of conservatism such as Hurst, Texas. By 2009 more than 970 mayors from all fifty states, the District of Columbia, and Puerto Rico, representing a total population of over 84 million, had signed onto the Mayors Climate Protection Agreement.[16]

In some cities, GHG reduction policies are well underway. Seattle, Washington's municipal power utility, Seattle City Light, was the first in the nation to become carbon neutral, with no net GHG emissions.[17] Salt Lake City, Utah's municipal operations have reduced GHG emissions by 31 percent since 2001, well below the targets of the Kyoto Protocol. Over 20 percent of the electricity used at the Salt Lake City County Building is from renewable wind energy.[18] In November 2007, the New York City Council passed Local Law 55, which codifies the goal of reducing citywide GHG emissions by 30 percent below 2005 levels by 2030. The law also requires the city to reduce the carbon footprint of municipal operations much more quickly, by 30 percent by 2017.[19]

There has also been action to reduce GHG emissions at the U.S. state level. By 2009 twenty-nine states plus the District of Columbia had renewable portfolio standards in place. Renewable portfolio standards are policies that require electricity providers to obtain a minimum percentage of their power from non-fossil-fuel energy resources (such as solar, hydropower, geothermal, biomass, and hydropower) by a certain date. Together, these states account for more than half of the electricity sales in the United States. For example, California will derive at least 20 percent of its electricity from renewable sources by 2010, New York will derive 25 percent by 2013, and Illinois and Minnesota will derive 25 percent by 2025.[20]

Both Washington and Oregon require that new power plants offset a certain portion of their anticipated CO_2 emissions, either by undertaking emissions-reduction or through offset projects. Massachusetts, New Hampshire, and some other states have gone even further by requiring CO_2 emissions reductions from existing power plants. The California Public Utilities Commission is developing a GHG cap and trade program for the electric sector.[21]

Ten Northeast and Mid-Atlantic states have agreed to limit GHG emissions through a cooperative effort called the Regional Greenhouse Gas Initiative (RGGI). Connecticut, Delaware, Maine, Maryland, Massachusetts, New Hampshire, New Jersey, New York, Rhode Island, and Vermont will require a 10 percent reduction in GHG emissions from power plants by 2018. The Regional Greenhouse Gas Initiative is the first mandatory, market-based CO_2 emissions-reduction program in the United States. The first auction of CO_2 allowances was held in September 2008, and the first compliance period for each state's linked CO_2 budget trading program began January 1, 2009.[22] A group of six western states and two Canadian provinces launched the Western Climate Initiative in August 2007, and nine Midwestern states and one Canadian province established the Midwestern Regional Greenhouse Gas Reduction Accord in November 2007. Both groups have pledged to set up their own cap-and-trade program to reduce emissions.[23]

The United States is not the only country in which activities are taking place at the state and provincial levels. In May 2008, Australia's most populous state, New South Wales, announced that all government operations, including state-run schools, hospitals, and police stations, will be carbon neutral by 2020. The centerpiece of the state's sustainability plan will aim to curb government GHG emissions by 300,000 tons over the next decade.[24] In British Columbia, Canada, the provincial government has pledged to be carbon neutral by 2010, and all new cars leased or purchased by the provincial government must have hybrid engines.[25] Several large cities in the developing world have begun working with groups of foundations, NGOs, international organizations, and major corporations to reduce their energy use and GHG emissions through energy-efficiency projects and retrofitting old buildings (many of which yield savings for the city government through reduced energy and other operational costs).[26]

INTERGOVERNMENTAL ORGANIZATIONS

The influence of IGOs on global environmental politics has greatly increased since 1972. IGOs are formed by member states either for multiple purposes—for instance, the United Nations and various regional associations such as the Organization of American States (OAS)—or for more specific purposes, examples of which include the Food and Agriculture Organization (FAO) and the World Health Organization (WHO), both specialized agencies of the United Nations. IGOs range in size and resources from the World Bank, which has a staff of more than 10,000 and lends billions of dollars annually, to UNEP, with its annual budget for the 2008–2009 biennium of only $152 million and a professional staff of 342. Although ultimately accountable to governing bodies made up of representatives of their member states, IGO staff can take initiatives and influence outcomes on global issues. The professional skills of these bureaucrats can be an important factor in environmental negotiations. IGO bureaucracies have widely varying degrees of independence. Senior staff at UNEP and the FAO must take their cues from their governing councils in setting agendas, sponsoring negotiations, and implementing development and environment programs. The governing councils comprise large subsets of the governments that participate in the IGO. They usually meet every one to three years to provide formal guidance to the IGO. At the World Bank, which depends on major donor countries for its funds, the staff nevertheless has wide discretion in planning and executing projects.

An IGO may influence the outcomes of global environmental issues in several ways:

- It may help determine which issues the international community will address through its influence on the agenda for global action.
- It may convene and influence negotiations on global environmental regimes.
- It may provide independent and authoritative information on a global environmental issue.
- It may develop norms or codes of conduct (soft law) to guide action in particular environmental issue areas.
- It may influence states' environmental and development policies on issues not under international negotiation but relevant to environmental politics.[27]
- It may affect the implementation of global environmental policies through the provision of funds.

BOX 2.1   PROMINENT IGOs IN GLOBAL
ENVIRONMENTAL POLITICS

Many IGOs play important roles in different aspects of global environmental politics. These include but are not limited to

African Development Bank (AfDB)
Asian Development Bank (ADB)
United Nations Commission on Sustainable Development (CSD)
United Nations Food and Agriculture Organization (FAO)
Global Environment Facility (GEF)
Inter-American Development Bank (IDB)
International Monetary Fund (IMF)
International Maritime Organization (IMO)
Intergovernmental Panel on Climate Change (IPCC)
International Tropical Timber Organization (ITTO)
Organization for Economic Cooperation and Development (OECD)
Organization of the Petroleum Exporting Countries (OPEC)
United Nations Development Programme (UNDP)
United Nations Environment Programme (UNEP)
United Nations Population Fund (UNFPA)
United Nations Human Settlements Programme (UN-HABITAT)
World Bank
World Health Organization (WHO)
World Meteorological Organization (WMO)
World Trade Organization (WTO)

No IGO influences global environmental politics by performing all these functions. IGOs tend to specialize in one or more political functions, although one may indirectly influence another.

Setting Agendas and Influencing Regime Formation

In the past, UNEP dominated the agenda-setting function of global environmental politics because of its unique mandate, growing out of the 1972 Stockholm Conference, to catalyze and coordinate environmental activities and to serve as a focal point for such activities within the UN system (see Box 2.2). Through decisions by its governing council, comprising fifty-eight UN member governments elected by the United Nations General Assembly (UNGA), UNEP identifies critical global environmental threats requiring international cooperation. In 1976, for example, the UNEP Governing Council chose ozone depletion as one of five priority problems, and consequently UNEP convened a meeting of experts in Washington, D.C., that adopted the World Plan of Action on the Ozone Layer in 1977—five years before negotiations on a global agreement began.

UNEP played a similar role in initiating negotiations on climate change. It cosponsored with the Rockefeller Brothers Fund the Villach and Bellagio workshops that helped create scientific consensus and raised worldwide consciousness about the threat of global warming. Along with the World Meteorological Organization (WMO), UNEP sponsored the Intergovernmental Panel on Climate Change (IPCC) to study scientific and policy issues in preparation for negotiations on a global convention on climate change. UNEP convened international negotiations on many of the major environmental conventions of the past two decades: the Vienna Convention for the Protection of the Ozone Layer (1985), the Montreal Protocol on Substances that Deplete the Ozone Layer (1987), the Basel Convention on the Control of Transboundary Movements of Hazardous Wastes and Their Disposal (1989), the Convention on Biological Diversity (1992), and the Stockholm Convention on Persistent Organic Pollutants (2001). In 1995, the UNEP Governing Council decided that UNEP would convene, together with the FAO, an intergovernmental negotiating committee with a mandate to prepare an international legally binding instrument for the application of the **prior informed consent** (PIC) procedure for certain hazardous chemicals in international trade. The Rotterdam Convention on the Prior Informed Consent Procedure for Certain Hazardous Chemicals and Pesticides in international trade was adopted in September 1998.

UNEP also has sought to shape the global environmental agenda by monitoring and assessing the state of the environment and disseminating that information to governments and NGOs. Since its founding in 1972, UNEP has acted as the secretariat for the UN's systemwide Earthwatch and established:

- the Global Environmental Monitoring System/Water Programme (1978) to provide authoritative, scientifically sound information on the state and trends of global inland water quality;
- the Global Resource Information Database (1985), a global network of environmental data centers facilitating the generation and dissemination of key environmental information;
- the IPCC, created in cooperation with the WMO (1988) and at the request of the world's governments, to assess scientific, technical, and socioeconomic information relevant to understanding climate change, its potential impacts, and options for adaptation and mitigation; and
- the UNEP–World Conservation Monitoring Center (2000), as the world biodiversity information and assessment center.

BOX 2.2   WHAT IS UNEP?

The United Nations Environment Programme (UNEP) is the lead UN organization on environmental issues. Founded as a result of the United Nations Conference on the Human Environment in June 1972, UNEP's original mandate was to promote, catalyze, and coordinate the development of environmental policy within the UN system and internationally. UNEP's current mission is "to provide leadership and encourage partnership in caring for the environment by inspiring, informing, and enabling nations and peoples to improve their quality of life without compromising that of future generations."

UNEP assists in the development and implementation of international environmental policy, helps to monitor and raise awareness of environmental issues, assists developing countries in implementing environmentally sound policies, promotes environmental science and information, seeks to coordinate UN environmental activities, and encourages sustainable development at the local, national, regional, and global levels.

Headquartered in Nairobi, Kenya, UNEP maintains offices and units in several other countries (such as the UNEP Chemicals office in Geneva that houses the secretariats for the Basel, Rotterdam, and Stockholm conventions). UNEP has a relatively small staff and budget compared to many UN organizations. This reflects its original mandate to act as a catalyst and coordinator rather than an on-the-ground manager of large programs like United Nations Development Programme (UNDP), UNICEF, or WHO. Nevertheless, UNEP has had notable successes, particularly in assisting with the development, implementation, administration, and expansion of global environmental regimes.

For additional information on UNEP, including current focal areas, see www.unep.org.

UNEP has also undertaken a number of global assessments, including four Global Environmental Outlook assessments (since 1995), six ozone assessments (since 1998), the Global Biodiversity Assessment (1995), the Cultural and Spiritual Values of Biodiversity Assessment (1999), the Global Marine Assessment (since 2001), the Global Mercury Assessment (2002), the Global International Waters Assessment (2003), the

Millennium Ecosystem Assessment (2005), the Global International Waters Assessment (2006), and the International Assessment of Agricultural Knowledge, Science and Technology for Development (2008).

Former UNEP executive director Mostafa Tolba influenced environmental diplomacy through direct participation in the negotiations. In informal talks with the chiefs of EC delegations during the negotiations on the Montreal Protocol, he lobbied hard for a phaseout of CFCs.[28] At the London Conference of the Parties (COP) in 1990, he convened informal meetings with twenty-five environment ministers to work out a compromise on the contentious issue of linking protocol obligations with technology transfer. He also urged a compromise to bridge the gap between U.S. and western European timetables for a CFC phaseout (see Chapter 4). At the final session of the negotiations on the CBD, Tolba took over when there appeared to be gridlock on key issues regarding the financing mechanism, and he virtually forced the acceptance of a compromise text (see Chapter 5).

Tolba sometimes openly championed the developing countries against the highly industrialized countries. During the final round of negotiations that created the Basel Convention, for instance, he fought for a ban on shipping hazardous wastes to or from noncontracting parties and for a requirement that exporters check disposal sites at their own expense. But Tolba and the developing countries lost on both issues because they were opposed by the waste-exporting states (see Chapter 3).

In the 1990s, several factors sharply reduced UNEP's role in agenda setting and convening regime negotiations. Despite his siding with them on the emotional waste-trade issue, the developing countries had begun to lose confidence in Tolba and UNEP by 1990. They thought he was not sufficiently committed to their agenda and that he put too much emphasis on climate change, ozone depletion, and loss of biodiversity, all of which they considered "northern" issues. When UNCED was being organized in the UNGA, the **Group of 77** sought to emphasize environmental problems of primary concern to developing nations, including drinking water and sanitation, urban pollution, desertification, capacity building, and other issues. It succeeded in naming the twentieth anniversary of the Stockholm environmental conference the 1992 United Nations Conference on Environment *and* Development and assigned organizing responsibility to the United Nations Secretariat rather than to UNEP. At the same time, the UNGA took the climate negotiations out of the hands of UNEP and WMO and gave them to an ad hoc UN body, the Intergovernmental Negotiating Committee (INC), which reported directly to the UNGA.

And after UNCED in 1992, the UNGA established the United Nations Commission on Sustainable Development (CSD) to monitor and coordinate the implementation of Agenda 21. The CSD's creation and Tolba's replacement with a new executive director,

Elizabeth Dowdeswell, further reduced UNEP's role in agenda setting for global environmental politics for most of the 1990s. Among other things, Dowdeswell alienated key donor countries by failing to consult them adequately. While UNEP has had its share of successes during this period, it struggled to keep pace with the dramatic changes in international environmental policy making. Chronic financial problems, the absence of a clear focus and mission for the institution, challenges associated with its location in Nairobi, and management difficulties all contributed to the erosion of UNEP's participation in the international environmental policy making process during the 1990s.[29]

In February 1998, Dr. Klaus Töpfer was appointed UNEP's executive director, a position he held until 2006. In a demonstration of renewed faith in the organization, its leadership, and its work program, donor pledges to UNEP's Environment Fund increased. During Töpfer's tenure, UNEP rebounded within the confines of budget and location. Among its accomplishments were the development of the Global Earth Observation System of Systems to achieve comprehensive, coordinated, and sustained earth observations and so improve integrated environmental assessment; the development of the Strategic Approach for International Chemicals Management; improving the scientific base of UNEP; and the creation of the Global Ministerial Environment Forum to keep under review the state of the global environment, to assess environmental challenges continuously, to identify new and emerging issues, and to set assessment priorities.[30]

Achim Steiner became UNEP's fifth executive director in 2006. In 2007, UNEP adopted a new medium-term strategy[31] that further streamlined its operations to focus on six cross-cutting thematic priorities: climate change, disasters and conflicts, ecosystem management, environmental governance, harmful substances and hazardous waste, and resource efficiency (sustainable consumption and production). UNEP also embarked on negotiations to address mercury. Many still argue that UNEP's small budget, small staff, and lack of a strong mandate continue to hinder its effectiveness, but governments have not agreed on serious efforts to strengthen the organization.

The CSD has also had opportunities to play an agenda-setting role in global environmental politics (see Box 2.3). The CSD is responsible for reviewing progress in the implementation of Agenda 21 and the Rio Declaration on Environment and Development, as well as providing policy guidance to follow up the Johannesburg Plan of Implementation (JPOI). It is the high-level forum for sustainable development within the UN system. No other UN institution tries to examine head-on the linkages between the environmental, social, economic, and political arenas at the global scale. The commission has successfully generated greater concern for some issues on the international sustainable development agenda. By creating the Intergovernmental Panel on Forests (IPF) and, subsequently, the Intergovernmental Forum on Forests (IFF), the CSD successfully focused the forest issue and created more understanding that forests are owned by someone and provide a livelihood for many people. Freshwater resources and energy are two issues that did not receive much attention in Rio and have gained more prominence under the CSD's agenda and, through that, at the 2002 World Summit on Sustainable Development (WSSD). Similarly, the CSD's discussions on sustainable production and consumption patterns, sustainability indicators, and the need for technology transfer, education, and capacity building in developing countries have raised the profiles of these issues.

The CSD's record in elaborating policy guidance is far more mixed. Since the commission does not have a mandate to create legally binding agreements, it is limited to passing resolutions that "recommend" and "urge."[32] As noted, the CSD has managed to put some issues on the agenda and to initiate processes that continue into other forums. The main issue areas where the CSD has had some limited success are forests and oceans.[33] On forests, deliberations began in 1995, which led to the establishment of the IPF. This helped focus international dialogue on an issue that had polarized delegates during the 1992 Earth Summit. When the IPF's mandate expired, the CSD continued the dialogue through the IFF and then recommended the establishment of a more permanent intergovernmental body charged with fostering a multilateral process on forests. The UNGA established the United Nations Forum on Forests (UNFF) in 2000. In 2007, the UNFF adopted the Non–Legally Binding Instrument on All Types of Forests (see Chapter 5).

On oceans, at CSD-7 in 1999, delegates stressed the importance of finding ways and means to enhance the annual debate on oceans and the law of the sea. A CSD recommendation to the UNGA resulted in the establishment of the United Nations Open-Ended Informal Consultative Process on Oceans and the Law of the Sea, which has taken place annually since 2000 to improve deliberations on developments in oceanic affairs and strengthen international cooperation on ocean-related issues.[34]

In addition, the CSD has put the issues of mining, sustainable consumption and production, sanitation, transport, freshwater, and tourism on the global agenda and has advanced discussions on finance, but it has been plagued overall by a focus on the past rather than the future. For example, it has renegotiated principles and past agreements and has failed to progress discussions beyond arguments around fundamental principles and toward a more strategic debate on furthering implementation. Even in the WSSD, all governments agreed that they did not want to see a renegotiation of Agenda 21, and yet negotiators often moved the debate backward into the territory of the Rio principles and core objectives. After the WSSD, the commission developed a new work program, with the hope that a two-year cycle, with each cycle focusing on clusters of specific thematic and cross-sectoral issues, would enable it to

BOX 2.3 WHAT IS THE CSD?

The Commission for Sustainable Development (CSD) is the international body principally responsible for reviewing progress in the implementation of Agenda 21 and the Rio Declaration on Environment and Development (agreed to during the 1992 United Earth Summit in Rio) as well as providing policy guidance to follow up the Johannesburg Plan of Implementation (JPOI) approved at the World Summit on Sustainable Development (WSSD). The JPOI reaffirmed that the CSD is the high-level forum for sustainable development within the UN system. Thus, the CSD's mandate is to coordinate the activities of other UN bodies as they relate to issues of sustainable development; to analyze progress at the national, regional, and international levels toward implementing Agenda 21 and the JPOI; and to promote the implementation of Agenda 21 and the JPOI.

Fifty-three countries are elected to sit on the CSD. Other UN member states, IGOs, and major groups may attend as observers. The CSD held its first substantive session in June 1993 and has convened annually since then at UN Headquarters in New York. Following the WSSD, the CSD adopted a multiyear program of work that is organized on the basis of seven two-year cycles. The first year is a "review year," which evaluates progress made in implementing sustainable development goals and identifying obstacles and constraints. The second year is a "policy year," where the commission decides on measures to speed up implementation and mobilize action to overcome these obstacles and constraints. The thematic clusters to be discussed during each cycle, unless changed by the commission, include:

- *2004–2005:* water, sanitation, and human settlements;
- *2006–2007:* energy for sustainable development, industrial development, air pollution, atmosphere, and climate change;
- *2008–2009:* agriculture, rural development, land, drought, desertification, and Africa;
- *2010–2011:* transport, chemicals, waste management, mining, and sustainable consumption and production;
- *2012–2013:* forests, biodiversity, biotechnology, tourism, and mountains;
- *2014–2015:* oceans and seas, marine resources, small island developing states, disaster management, and vulnerability; and
- *2016–2017:* overall appraisal of implementation of Agenda 21, the Program of Further Implementation of Agenda 21, and the JPOI.

United Nations Department of Economic and Social Affairs, Division for Sustainable Development website at www.un.org/esa/dsd/csd/csd_index.shtml.

review implementation issues during the first year and discuss policy issues during the second (see Box 2.3). However, it seems that for over fifteen years, negotiators have struggled with making the shift from abstract debate to strategic implementation.[35]

Providing Independent and Authoritative Information

IGOs can also influence global environmental politics by providing independent and authoritative scientific information to states, other IGOs, the public, and the press. By their very nature, many environmental problems do not lend themselves to precision (see discussion in Chapter 6). The causes and long-term effects of particular environmental problems are not always clear. The internationalization of environmental issues tends to add more uncertainty than it alleviates. In very few cases are all of the scientific issues completely understood and their future implications projected exactly before negotiations begin. Many environmental problems are so complex scientifically, with so many different parameters, interrelations, and correlations that cannot easily be stated as precise causal relationships, that the substance of what is being negotiated, what is an appropriate trade-off, what is a reasonable fallback position, and what are effective outcomes can be difficult to define for many years.[36] At the same time, the probable environmental consequences could be catastrophic. Therefore, states are left in the unenviable position of having to elaborate policies on issues rife with uncertainties.

PHOTO 2.1   Different countries, NGOs, and IGOs use the annual meeting of the CSD to promote best sustainable development practices.
Courtesy IISD/*Earth Negotiations Bulletin.*

The scientific community has always played a role in intergovernmental environmental treaty negotiations, going back to some of the earliest negotiations on oceans. As environmental issues, like climate change, have become more technical and scientific uncertainty about possible long-term effects has grown, we have come to rely on scientists to present the facts and projections, which often set the stage for treaty negotiations. Over the past twenty years, international networks of cooperating scientists and scientific institutions have become actors in global environmental policy. Huge teams of scientists can review each other's work, perform integrated assessments, and generate ideas that far exceed the aggregation of each individual's particular knowledge.[37]

One of the first international bodies of scientists to provide independent and authoritative information to international negotiators was the Ozone Trends Panel. While not an official IGO, as it was organized by the U.S. National Aeronautics and Space Administration, it was a sixteen-month comprehensive scientific exercise involving more than one hundred scientists from ten countries. Released in March 1988, the conclusions of the report of the Ozone Trends Panel made headlines around the world: Ozone-layer depletion was no longer a theory; it was substantiated by hard scientific evidence, and CFCs and halons were implicated beyond a reasonable doubt. Thus, the state of the science had fundamentally changed, bringing pressure for a complete phaseout of CFCs and a strengthening of the Montreal Protocol. Further scientific evidence in the subsequent five years led to the complete phaseout of CFCs and halons, along with phaseouts and reductions in the use of a number of other ozone-depleting chemicals as the ozone regime was strengthened.[38]

The best-known example of an IGO providing authoritative scientific information is the IPCC. Established by the WMO and UNEP in 1988, the IPCC is charged with providing independent scientific advice on the complex issue of climate change. The panel was asked to prepare, based on available scientific information, a report on all aspects relevant to climate change and its impacts and to formulate realistic response strategies. The first assessment report of the IPCC, released in 1990, served as the basis for negotiating the UNFCCC. Since then, the IPCC has released three additional comprehensive assessment reports (1995, 2001, and 2007), as well as numerous other reports on specific topics, and has involved the work of thousands of scientists from around the world. It has had a profound influence on the climate-change negotiations, specifically, and on national discussions on climate-change mitigation and adaptation. Its work has been so essential that in 2007, the IPCC and former U.S. vice president Al Gore were jointly awarded the Nobel Peace Prize for their efforts to build up and disseminate greater knowledge about man-made climate change and to lay the foundations for the measures needed to counteract such change.

There have been several attempts to use the IPCC model to create scientific bodies to serve other conventions. UN Secretary-General Kofi Annan called for the Millennium Ecosystem Assessment in 2000. Initiated in 2001, it aimed to assess the consequences of ecosystem change for human well-being and the scientific basis for action needed to enhance the conservation and sustainable use of those systems and their contribution to human well-being. The assessment was coordinated by UNEP and overseen by representatives of different conventions (Convention on Biological Diversity, Convention to Combat Desertification, Ramsar Convention on Wetlands, and the Convention on Migratory Species) as well as national governments, UN agencies, civil society representatives, and the private sector. More than 1,300 scientists and other experts from ninety-five countries were involved in its work between 2001 and

2005. Like the IPCC, the Millennium Ecosystem Assessment evaluated an immense array of scientific literature, government and IGO reports, and field data, and ultimately published five technical volumes.[39]

Developing countries have proposed the creation of an Intergovernmental Panel on Land Degradation, Desertification and Drought modeled on the work of the IPCC to provide independent scientific information that would guide the work of the United Nations Convention to Combat Desertification (UNCCD).[40] As an interim measure, the UNCCD held a scientific conference at its ninth COP in Buenos Aires in 2009 to bring more scientific expertise into its work.

Developing Nonbinding Norms and Codes of Conduct

International organizations also influence global environmental politics by facilitating the negotiation of common norms or rules of conduct that do not have binding legal effect on the participating states. A variety of creative nontreaty measures, often called soft law, have been developed to influence state behavior on environmental issues. Soft law measures include codes of conduct, declarations of principle, global action plans, and other international agreements that create new norms and expectations without the binding status of treaties.[41]

These nonbinding agreements are negotiated by groups of experts representing their governments, usually in negotiating processes convened by intergovernmental organizations. Most UN agencies have contributed to this process, but UNEP has done the most to promote it. Concerning the management of hazardous waste, for instance, a UNEP ad hoc working group of experts helped draft guidelines in 1984. In 1987, the same process produced guidelines and principles aimed at making the worldwide pesticide trade more responsive to the threats these substances pose to the environment and human health. Other examples include the 1980 International Programme on Chemical Safety and the 1985 Action Plan for Biosphere Reserves, each of which has become the recognized standard in its field.

Since 1963, the Joint FAO/WHO Food Standards Programme (via the Codex Alimentarius Commission) has developed food standards, guidelines, and codes of practice aimed at protecting the health of the consumers and ensuring fair trade. The FAO has drafted guidelines on the environmental criteria for the registration of pesticides (1985) and the International Code of Conduct on the Distribution and Use of Pesticides (1986).

The 1995 FAO Code of Conduct for Responsible Fisheries sets out principles and international standards of behavior for responsible practices with a view to ensuring the effective conservation, management, and development of living aquatic resources. It builds on thirty years of FAO work on the issue (see Box 2.4). The FAO Committee on Fisheries (COFI), consisting of FAO member states, was established in 1965 as a

BOX 2.4   WHAT IS THE FAO?

The Food and Agriculture Organization of the United Nations (FAO) leads international efforts to defeat hunger, advance agricultural productivity, and ensure food safety. It serves both developed and developing countries, acting as a neutral forum where nations meet to discuss issues, negotiate agreements, and create programs. The FAO also serves as a source of information, helping developing countries modernize and improve agriculture, forestry, and fisheries practices and ensure good nutrition for all. FAO's work currently focuses on food security, natural resource management, forestry and fisheries, early warning for food emergencies, disaster recovery, food safety, bioenergy, and other issues. Since its founding in 1945, the FAO has paid special attention to developing rural areas, home to 70 percent of the world's poor and hungry.

Today, FAO has more than 191 member states. Headquartered in Rome, it has an extensive set of regional, subregional, and country offices. The FAO works in partnership with many different institutions—UN agencies, national governments, private foundations, large NGOs, grassroots organizations, companies, professional associations, and others. Some partnerships operate at the national level or in the field; others are regional or global in nature. In 2009, the FAO had about 2,050 field projects in operation with a total value of more than $760 million. Only about 6 percent of these are funded through the main FAO budget (paid by the member states), which also funds salaries and office operation. The remaining 94 percent of field projects are funded by trust funds and other sources supported by certain developed countries, private foundations, corporations, NGOs, and other UN institutions.

Project data comes from "Database of FAO Projects," FAO, www.fao.org/tc/tcom. More information on the FAO can be found on its website at www.fao.org.

subsidiary body of the FAO Council and has remained the primary global forum for the consideration of major issues related to fisheries and aquaculture policy. Until the late 1980s, COFI focused on problems of coastal states in the development of their fisheries, especially after they acquired two-hundred-mile coastal fishing zones in the 1970s. But when the pressures of overfishing on global fish stocks became increasingly difficult to ignore, COFI and the FAO Secretariat began pushing more aggressively for new international norms for sustainable fisheries.

The FAO Secretariat has helped mobilize international support for more sustainable fisheries management by collecting and analyzing data on global fish catch, issuing annual reviews on the state of the world's fisheries, and organizing technical workshops. These efforts helped to focus government and NGO attention on such issues as excess fishing capacity and fisheries subsidies. In 1991, COFI recommended that the FAO should develop the concept of responsible fisheries in the form of a code of conduct, and the FAO Secretariat convened negotiations, which resulted in the adoption of the 1995 Code of Conduct for Responsible Fisheries. The code of conduct is the most comprehensive set of international norms for sustainable fisheries management that currently exists, and despite not being legally binding, it has influenced state and producer practices.

Soft-law agreements are often a good way to avoid the lengthy process of negotiating, signing, and ratifying binding agreements. They do not require enforcement mechanisms and can sometimes depend on the adherence of networks of bureaucrats who share similar views of the problem. But when soft-law regimes are adopted because key parties are unwilling to go beyond nonbinding guidelines, then the norms agreed upon are not usually particularly stringent, and state compliance is likely to be uneven at best. The 1985 Code of Conduct on the Distribution and Use of Pesticides and the 1985 Cairo guidelines on international hazardous waste trade are examples of this pattern.

Soft law may be turned into binding international law in two ways: Principles included in a soft-law agreement may become so widely regarded as the appropriate norms for a problem that they are ultimately absorbed into treaty law, or political pressures may arise from those dissatisfied with spotty adherence to soft-law norms that they successful advocate for international negotiations to turn a nonbinding agreement into a binding one.

Influencing National Development Policies

IGOs affect global environmental politics in a fourth way by influencing the environmental and development policies of individual states outside the context of regime negotiations. National policy decisions on how to manage forests, generate and use energy, increase agricultural production, allocate government resources, regulate pollution, and manage other economic, development, and environment issues determine how sustainable the country will be and the impact it will have on global environmental issues. IGOs can influence such policies, and thus the sustainability of societies, in several ways:

- They provide financing for development projects, as well as advice and technical assistance that help shape the country's development strategy.
- They provide financing for environment-protection projects.

- They provide financing, technical assistance, training, and capacity building to create or improve government agencies.
- They undertake research aimed at persuading state officials to adopt certain policies.
- They provide targeted information to government officials, NGOs, the private sector, and the public.
- They focus normative pressure on states regarding sustainable development policy issues.

The FAO, for example, had a major impact on the policies of the developing world—much of which critics charge has historically been negative—through its promotion of the commercial exploitation of forests and export crops, large-scale irrigation projects, and heavy use of chemical inputs, believing such activities (which followed the exclusionist paradigm) would promote national economic development.[42] In more recent years, the FAO has used research to promote sustainable alternatives to the conventional agricultural-development model. FAO's program on integrated pest control in South and Southeast Asia, launched in the early 1980s, helped spread **integrated pest management** techniques to farmers in several Asian countries. FAO research showing the superiority of natural pest-control strategies over reliance on chemical pesticides helped convince key Indonesian government officials in 1986 to adopt integrated pest management as an alternative to heavy reliance on pesticides and to train Indonesian farmers to make their own informed decisions about pest management.[43]

In the early 1990s, the organization was restructured for the first time for the purpose of integrating sustainability into its programs and activities.[44] In 1993, the FAO received a new mandate from its governing body to focus more on the consequences of the earth's shrinking natural resources, as well as on sustainable agricultural and rural development and food security through the protection of plant, animal, and marine resources. Since 1993, the FAO has focused extensively on the implementation of sustainable agriculture, supported the sustainable forestry initiatives of other international organizations,[45] and cosponsored with UNEP the negotiation of the Rotterdam Convention for the application of the PIC procedure to certain hazardous chemicals in international trade.

The FAO also embarked upon the revision of the 1983 International Undertaking on Plant Genetic Resources to harmonize it with the goals of the CBD, addressing the conservation, exploration, collection, documentation, and sustainable use of plant resources for food and agriculture. Its successor, the International Treaty on Plant Genetic Resources for Food and Agriculture, was adopted in 2001. Similarly, the FAO in 2007 adopted the Global Plan of Action for Animal Genetic Resources to ensure sustainability and preserve the genetic diversity in animal production systems, with a focus on food security and rural development. As noted above, the Code of Conduct

---

BOX 2.5   WHAT IS UNDP?

The United Nations Development Programme (UNDP) is the UN global development organization. Headquartered in New York, UNDP has offices in 166 countries, which work with national governments, IGOs, NGOs, and others to implement programs and build developing countries' capacity to address local, national, and global development challenges. In each country office, the UNDP representative also normally serves as the coordinator of development activities in that country for the UN system as a whole. Through such coordination, UNDP seeks to ensure effective use of UN and international aid resources. UNDP's networks also help to implement, link, and coordinate efforts to achieve the MDGs, including the overarching goal of cutting poverty in half by 2015. UNDP's annual Human Development Report is a widely cited and important resource, containing updated global and national statistics while also focusing attention on key development issues. UNDP is among the largest UN agencies and its administrator is the third-highest-ranking member of the United Nations after the UN secretary-general and deputy secretary-general.

UNDP's website at www.undp.org. For the Human Development Report, see http://hdr.undp.org/en.

---

for Responsible Fisheries, developed under FAO auspices, created a comprehensive set of norms for sustainable fisheries management that have positively influenced state policy and producer practices.

UNDP, with a budget of more than $13.5 billion annually, a staff exceeding 5,000 worldwide, and liaison offices in 166 countries, is a large source of multilateral grant-development assistance (see Box 2.5). Since 2000 and the adoption of the Millennium Development Goals (MDGs), UNDP has concentrated on coordinating global and national efforts to reach them, including the overarching goal of cutting poverty in half by 2015. Its focus is helping countries build and share solutions to the challenges of democratic governance, poverty reduction, crisis prevention and recovery, environment and energy, and HIV/AIDS. UNDP also helps developing countries attract and use aid effectively.

In 1994, in direct response to UNCED, James Gustave Speth, a well-known environmentalist who was then the UNDP administrator, made a strategic decision to strengthen UNDP's environmental and sustainable development capacity by establishing the Energy and Environment Group, which, since its origin, has worked to support

UNDP's overall efforts to help countries successfully design and carry out programs that support the implementation of Agenda 21 and the Rio conventions, in addition to the MDGs. This group works in six areas of high priority:

1. frameworks and strategies for sustainable development;
2. effective water governance;
3. access to sustainable energy services;
4. sustainable land management to combat desertification and land degradation;
5. conservation and sustainable use of biodiversity; and
6. national/sectoral policy and planning to control emissions of ozone-depleting substances and POPs.[46]

UNDP is also one of the three implementing agencies of the Global Environment Facility (GEF) (see Box 2.6) and is the lead UN agency in building the capacity of developing-country governments for sustainable development activities under its Capacity 2015 program, which aims to develop the capacities needed by developing countries and countries in transition to a market economy to meet their sustainable development goals under Agenda 21 and the MDGs at the local level. UNDP also assists in building capacity for good governance, popular participation, private- and public-sector development, and growth with equity, all of which are necessary in promoting sustainable human development.

In spite of UNDP's intentions, a 2008 evaluation of UNDP's work in energy and environment found that beginning in 2000 the UNDP administrator significantly downgraded environment and natural resource management as having relatively little to contribute to the core UNDP mandates to reduce poverty and improve governance, which produced a sharp decline in the number of core staff positions working on environmental issues. At present, most of the staff working on environment and energy are supported by GEF funding. UNDP's reliance on the GEF to support its environmental and energy work has caused high-priority national environment and sustainable development issues—such as environmental health, water supply and sanitation, and energy management—to be replaced by GEF priorities related to climate-change mitigation, biodiversity, and international waters.[47]

IGOs may influence state policy by focusing normative pressures on states regarding the environment and sustainable development, even when no formal international agreement exists on the norm.[48] UNDP has gone the farthest of any UN agency in this regard, calling for the allocation of resources for human development (health, population, and education) by donor countries and developing-country governments, at particular levels, as a norm in the context of what it calls "sustainable human development." Through its annual Human Development Report, which ranks nations accord-

BOX 2.6   WHAT IS THE GEF?

GEF

The Global Environment Facility (GEF) is the largest international funder of projects that address global environmental issues. It provides grants to developing countries and countries with economies in transition for projects in six focal areas: biodiversity, climate change, international waters, land degradation, the ozone layer, and POPs. The GEF is also the designated financial mechanism for four global environmental agreements: CBD, UNCCD, UNFCCC, and the Stockholm Convention on POPs. For each of these conventions, the GEF helps eligible countries meet their regime obligations under rules and guidance provided by the conventions and their COPs. The GEF is also associated with other regimes, including several global and regional agreements that address transboundary water systems.

Since its creation in 1991, the GEF has provided more than $8.6 billion in grants and leveraged more than $36 billion in cofinancing for over 2,400 projects in more than 165 countries. Originally a pilot program of the World Bank, governments agreed to restructure the GEF in 1994 and moved it out of the World Bank system. The decision to make the GEF an independent institution was designed in part to enhance the involvement of developing countries in the decision-making process and in the implementation of the projects. Since 1994, the World Bank has served as the trustee of the GEF trust fund and provided administrative services. Many other international organizations—including UNDP, UNEP, FAO, and several regional development banks—as well as NGOs and other actors, work with national governments to implement GEF-funded projects.

The GEF Secretariat handles the organization's day-to-day operations. Based in Washington, D.C., it reports directly to the GEF Council and GEF Assembly. The GEF Council, the main governing body, functions as an independent board of directors with primary responsibility for developing, adopting, and evaluating GEF programs. Comprising representatives from sixteen developing countries, fourteen developed countries, and two countries with transitional economies, the council meets twice each year. All decisions are reached by consensus. The GEF Assembly includes representatives from all 177 member countries. It meets every three to four years and is responsible for reviewing and evaluating the GEF's general policies, operation, and membership. The assembly also considers and approves proposed amendments to the GEF Instrument, the document that established the GEF and sets the rules by which it operates.

These are official GEF figures as of September 2009; see www.gefweb.org/interior_right.aspx ?id=50. For more information on the GEF, see its official website at www.gefweb.org.

ing to their provision of these social services, UNDP pressures developing countries into devoting more of their budgets to these social sectors.

MULTILATERAL FINANCIAL INSTITUTIONS

In terms of direct impact on the development and environmental policies of developing states, the most powerful IGOs are the multilateral financial institutions, including the World Bank, the International Monetary Fund (IMF), and the regional development banks, because of the amount of financial resources that they transfer to developing countries every year in support of particular development strategies and economic policies. Within these IGOs, donor countries are the dominant players, and voting is weighted according to the size of a country's contributions. The United States has the most power in the World Bank and the Inter-American Development Bank. Japan has the most power in the Asian Development Bank.

Environmental activists have viewed the World Bank's influence on the policies of its borrowers as contributing to unsustainable development (see Box 2.7). Historically, the bank was driven by the need to lend large amounts of money each year, by a bias toward large-scale, capital-intensive, and centralized projects, and by its practice of assessing projects according to a quantifiable rate of return (how the loan contributes to conventional gross national product calculations) while discounting longer-term, unquantifiable social and environmental costs and benefits. In the 1970s and 1980s, the World Bank supported schemes to colonize rain forests in Brazil and Indonesia, cattle-ranching projects in Central and South America, tobacco projects in Africa that contributed to accelerated deforestation, and a cattle-development project in Botswana that contributed to desertification.[49]

In response to persistent, well-orchestrated pressure from NGOs, criticism by some prominent members of the U.S. Congress, and calls for it to become part of the solution to global environmental problems rather than a contributor, the World Bank began a process of evolution in the mid-1980s toward greater sensitivity to the environmental implications of its lending. It refused to provide new support for some of the worst projects in Brazil and Indonesia, created an environment department, began to build an environmental staff, and financed more explicitly environmental programs.

This process accelerated in the 1990s as the bank took concrete steps in the area of the environment. In 1990 and 1991, it became an implementing agency of the nascent GEF and the Multilateral Fund of the Montreal Protocol. It thus enjoyed the largest portfolio of global environmental projects of all multilateral institutions, albeit funded by other donors.

BOX 2.7   WHAT IS THE WORLD BANK?

The World Bank is the largest source of international financial and development assistance to developing countries. It is not a bank in the conventional sense but a group of development institutions owned by 185 member countries. Together they provide low-interest loans, interest-free credits, and grants to developing countries for a wide array of purposes that include investments in education, health, public administration, infrastructure, financial and private-sector development, agriculture, and environmental and natural resource management.

The World Bank comprises a number of different institutions. The United States and its allies created the first, the International Bank for Reconstruction and Development, in 1944 to facilitate post–World War II reconstruction. Over the years it was joined by four other institutions (the International Development Association, the International Finance Corporation, the Multilateral Guarantee Agency, and the International Center for the Settlement of Investment Disputes), and their collective mandate changed to global poverty alleviation and economic development. Today the World Bank focuses on:

- reducing poverty and developing sustainable growth practices in the poorest countries, especially in Africa;
- meeting the special challenges of fragile states, including postconflict countries;
- developing solutions as well as financing for middle-income countries;
- solving global public-goods issues and addressing regional and global issues that cross national borders, such as climate change, infectious diseases, and trade;
- supporting development and opportunity in the Arab world; and
- delivering knowledge and learning services to support development.

For more information, see the World Bank website at www.worldbank.org.

With regard to forests, the bank has combined investments in conservation and capacity building in selected tropical-forest countries with policy dialogues aimed at eliminating the worst distortions in the sector. It adopted a new forest policy in 1991 that precluded support for commercial logging in primary tropical forests. The biggest obstacle to success in the bank's approach was a lack of political will on the part of governments of states that intensively exploit forests.

In Indonesia, the bank implemented two loans in the late 1980s and early 1990s for the development of a forest database and institution building, but a later project proposing ambitious policy and institutional reforms had to be abandoned during preparation because the Suharto government resisted key policy reforms.[50] In 1998, the bank negotiated a major structural adjustment loan with Indonesia as part of the economic rescue package, which included pledges to carry out some far-reaching reforms in the logging-concession system. But when Indonesia failed to deliver on its pledges, the bank was unwilling to suspend payments because its interests in reviving the economy trumped environmental concerns (see the discussion of adjustment lending below).

Perhaps reflecting an implicit recognition of its past failure to leverage changes in clients' forest-management policies, in 1998 the bank tried a different strategy on forests and launched the World Bank–World Wildlife Fund (WWF) Alliance for Forest Conservation and Sustainable Use. The Forest Alliance represents a sharp shift in the bank's past approach to one that (1) openly acknowledges the critical problems of commercial logging, the illegal practices in the forest sector, and the frequently corrupt nexus between officials and economic elites; (2) identifies specific measures and ambitious global forest-policy goals; and (3) employs a combination of financial resources, technical assistance, and public pressures on government to support sustainable forest management. During the first phase of the alliance (1998–2005), 55 million hectares (212,000 square miles) of new protected areas were established, 70 million hectares (270,000 square miles) of protected areas were brought under improved management, and some 31 million hectares (120,000 square miles) of forests outside protected areas were brought under sustainable management. In May 2005, the World Bank and WWF announced an ambitious global program aimed at reducing global deforestation rates by 10 percent by 2010. This is the first step toward achieving zero-net deforestation by 2020 and, going further, to increase forest cover and quality beyond 2000 levels by 2050.[51]

The Forest Alliance has played a pivotal role in facilitating regional initiatives in the developing world and has been working actively with the private sector to promote responsible forest practices, for instance, by supporting the Brazilian government's Amazon Regional Protected Areas program. This ten-year program will protect 12 percent of the Brazilian Amazon and establish a $220 million trust fund to support the ongoing management of this protected-areas network. Its scope is equivalent to building the entire U.S. national parks system in ten years.[52]

On biodiversity, the bank adopted a new policy of not supporting projects that would result in significant conversion or degradation of habitats officially designated as critical—a limitation that severely hinders its application. In 1996, the bank presented its first "biodiversity assistance strategy," which emphasized the importance of integrating biodiversity concerns into country assistance strategies, to the CBD COP.

As an implementing agency of the GEF—the principal financial mechanism for the CBD—and in implementing its biodiversity assistance strategy, the bank has pledged publicly to integrate global biodiversity concerns into relevant portions of its lending portfolio. In 1996, it established a program to identify opportunities for promoting development objectives and global environmental benefits in loan projects when preparing country lending strategies for each client government. But the bank devoted too few budgetary resources and too little staffing to the program, and as a result its country assistance strategies, written in 1996 and 1997, seldom made the linkages between renewable-resource problems and biodiversity loss.[53] However, the biodiversity portfolio of the World Bank has shown steady growth over the past two decades. Between 1988 and 2008, the bank approved 598 projects in 122 countries that fully or partially supported biodiversity conservation and sustainable use. Of these, 277 projects have been completed. This biodiversity portfolio represents over $6 billion in biodiversity investments, including bank contributions and leveraged cofinancing. Although a very small part of the bank's overall lending, this biodiversity funding has made a substantial contribution to helping client countries meet their obligations under the CBD as well as to implementing the convention's work programs and priorities.[54]

World Bank support in the area of biodiversity also involves the establishment and strengthening of protected areas (including activities in buffer zones), the sustainable use of biodiversity outside protected areas, the eradication of alien species, and biodiversity conservation through improved management and sustainable use of natural resources in the production landscape. There is also an increasing focus on improving natural resource management and mainstreaming biodiversity into forestry, coastal zone management, and agriculture.

With regard to climate change, the bank's longtime role as a financier of large conventional fossil fuel power projects has often conflicted with the objective of the UNFCCC and the Kyoto Protocol to reduce GHG emissions. From 1997 to 2007, according to WWF-UK, the World Bank financed twenty-six gigatons of CO_2 emissions—about forty-five times the annual emissions of the United Kingdom.[55] In 1997, the World Bank stated that it would begin to "routinely calculate the potential impact of all its energy projects on climate change and, where there is cause for concern, assist developing country clients to finance more climate-friendly options."[56] According to a 2002 report by the progressive Sustainable Energy and Economy Network, however, five years after that commitment, the World Bank still did not "routinely calculate" its projects' potential climate-change impact and only rarely did "its project reviews consider carbon dioxide emissions, the truest indicator of the climate change impact of its portfolio."[57] The World Bank Group states that it has committed more than $11 billion to renewable energy and energy efficiency in developing countries since 1990.[58]

However, according to studies by WWF-UK,[59] the Sustainable Energy and Economy Network, and other researchers, the World Bank fossil fuel projects still dominate. The Sustainable Energy and Economy Network's study shows World Bank Group coal, oil, and gas lending was up 94 percent between 2007 and 2008, reaching over $3 billion. Coal lending alone increased an astonishing 256 percent in the same period.[60] By comparison, the bank reported that renewable-energy and energy-efficiency lending rose 87 percent from 2007 to 2008, with the vast majority going to support large hydropower projects and supply-side energy efficiency.[61] However, an independent analysis by the bank's Information Center suggests that if you exclude large hydropower projects and efficiency, World Bank Group funding for renewables in 2008 actually dropped by 42 percent from 2007.[62]

The IMF (see Box 2.8) was slower than the World Bank and regional banks to acknowledge the need to take environmental considerations explicitly into account in its lending operations; it defined its role as limited to helping countries achieve a balance of payments and pay off their international debts. Only in 1991 did the IMF executive board consider for the first time the extent to which the IMF should "address environmental issues." It decided that the IMF should avoid policies that might harm the environment but that it should not conduct research or build up its own expertise on the possible environmental consequences of its policies.[63] In 1996, the IMF and the World Bank put in place a joint initiative for heavily indebted poor countries that aimed to reduce the debt-service burden of eligible countries to sustainable levels and to help them exit from the debt-rescheduling process; in turn these countries must adopt and pursue strong and sustained programs of adjustment and reform. This initiative is supposed to help eliminate external debt as an impediment to achieving sustainable development.[64]

Because the World Bank addresses environmental issues and supports an extensive work program on environmental and other sectoral issues, the executive board of the IMF decided early that the IMF should not duplicate the bank's work in this area. The IMF also believes that its mandate and expertise constrain its ability to address environmental issues to specific types of work. The IMF's involvement in environmental policy is thus limited to areas that have a serious and perceptible impact on a country's macroeconomic outlook or on the effectiveness of macroeconomic policy instruments in achieving domestic and external stability. For example, the IMF's climate-change activities focus on providing advice to member countries where climate change can have a significant impact on economic and financial stability, including guidance as to the impact on financial markets, managing climate-related risks, addressing the relationship between food and fuel subsidies, and GHG emissions pricing, among other macroeconomic and fiscal issues.[65] The IMF also assists countries with environmental tax policy for pollution and management of renewable resources, such as forests. Even in these

BOX 2.8   WHAT IS THE IMF?

The International Monetary Fund (IMF) works to foster global growth and economic stability. It provides policy advice and financing to countries in economic difficulties and also works with developing nations to help them achieve macroeconomic stability and reduce poverty. Founded in 1944 and headquartered in Washington, D.C., the IMF is a specialized agency of the United Nations but has its own charter, governing structure, and finances. The highest decision-making body of the IMF, the Board of Governors, consists of one governor and one alternate governor for each of its 185 member countries. However, voting power among the governors is distributed based on the size of each country's share of the global economy. Thus, the United States, Japan, and EU countries wield primary influence. In June 2009, for example, Angola had 0.13 percent of the board's voting power, while the United States had 17.09 percent.

The IMF's work focuses on three main areas: economic surveillance, lending, and technical assistance. Surveillance refers to the monitoring of economic and financial developments and the provision of policy advice aimed especially at crisis prevention. The IMF also lends to countries with balance-of-payments difficulties, providing temporary financing and supporting policies aimed at correcting the underlying problems. It also provides loans to low-income countries aimed especially at poverty reduction. Finally, the IMF provides countries with technical assistance and training in its areas of expertise. In recent years, the IMF has employed elements of its surveillance and technical assistance work to help develop standards and codes of good practice as part of international efforts to strengthen the global financial system. Financing for IMF activities comes mainly from the money that countries pay as their capital subscription when they become members. The size of these payments also varies by the size of their economies.

"IMF Members' Quotas and Voting Power, and IMF Board of Governors," IMF, www.imf.org/external/np/sec/memdir/members.htm. For general information on the IMF, see www.imf.org.

respects, the IMF sometimes runs into obstacles. At times, a member country does not have a national environmental action plan or a stated national strategy to protect the environment. Even where they do exist, such plans or strategies are sometimes not specific enough to allow the IMF staff to consider their macroeconomic implications. Sometimes, the authorities themselves are not fully committed to environmental objectives because of pressure from one or more interest groups or because these objectives conflict with short-run economic growth or with some other objective of the country's policy makers. Thus, the IMF argues, it can integrate environment into its policy dialogue only to the extent that member countries allow it to do so.[66]

When Indonesia's economy collapsed in 1997 and 1998 and had to be rescued by major loans from the IMF and the World Bank, a unique opportunity presented itself to hold the government of Indonesia accountable for reforming its forest system. The policy reforms negotiated by the IMF with the Suharto regime in early 1998 included pledges to reform the logging-concession system and to "reduce land conversion targets to environmentally sustainable levels."[67]

In July 1998, the World Bank followed the IMF agreement with its own $1 billion structural adjustment loan to post-Suharto Indonesia, which went further on forest-policy reform. It required that the Indonesian government prepare an accurate map of the forest areas of key provinces based on recent satellite imagery and identify priority conservation areas. Pending completion of the mapping exercise, the government was required by the loan agreement to "implement and maintain a moratorium on conversion of state forest areas."[68] But the government failed to make good on its pledges. The Ministry of Forestry argued that it could not turn down applications from companies that had already invested in the conversion process. Some applications were still being approved, despite the pledged moratorium. Moreover, no list of applications was ever published; nor was a public review carried out.[69]

Nevertheless, despite this failure to comply with the terms of a critical forest-policy reform, the World Bank went ahead with disbursement of the second tranche of $400 million in February 1999. Then it signed a second adjustment loan in May 1999, which was disbursed immediately upon signing.[70] The World Bank thus let a big opportunity to leverage policy reform in the Indonesian forest sector go by without decisive action. The failure to hold Indonesia accountable for the most elementary forest-policy reforms cannot be explained by pointing at the bank staff involved; instead, it reflected the political preferences held by the finance ministries of the major funders of the World Bank and the IMF. While more than a decade old, the Indonesian case still resonates among experts as a lesson to be learned about lost opportunities for multinational financial institutions to have a positive impact on global environmental politics.

In the 1990s, after twenty years of standard structural adjustment policies and more than forty years of traditional World Bank loans, the international development community recognized that the economic gap between OECD and middle-income countries and some one hundred less-developed countries continued to widen considerably with no sign of abating. As well, the number of poor, particularly the rural poor, had

PHOTO 2.2 **Jubilee and other NGOs protest World Bank and IMF policies.**
Photo by Orin Langelle, Global Justice Ecology Project.

not significantly diminished despite the promise that structural reforms were designed to benefit the world's 2 billion poor.[71] The failure of these policies led to an institutional crisis in the major development institutions in the mid-1990s. In response, the World Bank, the IMF, and bilateral development agencies reoriented their investment priorities and agreed to make poverty alleviation their overarching and unifying goal. From that apparent policy reorientation, a new set of investment guidelines and conditionalities has been established, particularly in the case of the World Bank and IMF, in the form of the poverty-reduction strategy papers (PRSPs). PRSPs, meant to be developed primarily by national governments, establish each country's national development strategy, against which development assistance is to be charted and assessed. Moreover, the UN MDGs embody the commitment to alleviate poverty and to increase country "ownership" of national development strategies.

Critics charge that the MDGs and PRSPs both fail to recognize that the rural poor, constituting more than 70 percent of the world's poor, have an immediate survival dependence on access to use and sound management of natural resources. Deprived of their natural resource assets, the rural poor either suffer major declines in living standards or migrate to urban areas. The MDGs and PRSPs ignore this relationship and view the environment, as in the past, as a separate sectoral issue and priority rather than as the foundation for attaining all other development goals.[72]

REGIONAL AND OTHER
MULTILATERAL ORGANIZATIONS

Regional and other multilateral organizations also play an increasing role in environmental politics. Some, such as the regional fisheries management organizations, are specific functional groups that have taken on environmental responsibilities out of necessity. Others have broad political and economic agendas that include significant environmental issues. Still others have been specifically established to address environmental concerns.

The European Union (EU) is the only regional organization whose decisions obligate its members. In the 1950s, six European countries decided to pool their economic resources and set up a system of joint decision making on economic issues. To do so, they formed several organizations, of which the European Economic Community was the most important (the name was eventually shortened to the "European Community").[73] The group grew in size, and the 1992 Maastricht Treaty introduced new forms of cooperation between the then twelve members on issues such as defense, justice, and home affairs, including the environment. By adding this intergovernmental cooperation to the existing "community" system, the Maastricht Treaty created the European Union. The EU is unique in that its now twenty-seven member states have set up common institutions to which they delegate some of their sovereignty so that decisions on specific matters, including agriculture, fisheries, and trade, can be made at the European level. Both individual EU member states and the EC itself, as a "regional economic integration organization," can ratify and join global environmental agreements.[74] During regime negotiations, EU states negotiate as a single entity, which gives their negotiating positions considerable importance.

Collective environmental action by EU states began in 1972 (then as the EC) with the first in a series of action plans. During the first four action plans, the community adopted more than two hundred pieces of legislation, chiefly concerned with limiting pollution by introducing minimum standards, including for waste management and air and water pollution. Today, the EU strives to achieve sustainable development, and a high degree of environmental protection is among its absolute priorities.

The sixth action program for the environment sets out EU priorities up to 2010. Four areas are highlighted: climate change, nature and biodiversity, environment and health, and the management of natural resources and waste. Measures to achieve these priorities are outlined: improving the application of environmental legislation, working together with the market and citizens, and ensuring that other policies take greater account of environmental considerations. According to the Maastricht Treaty, an objective of EU environment policy is to promote measures at the international level to deal with regional or global environmental problems.[75]

Climate change is currently a particular priority for the EU. In December 2008, after eleven months of legislative work, the European Parliament gave its backing to the EU's climate-change package, which aims to ensure that the EU will achieve its climate targets by 2020: a 20 percent reduction in GHG emissions, a 20 percent improvement in energy efficiency, and a 20 percent share for renewables in the EU energy mix (see Chapter 5).[76]

The Organization of American States (OAS), one of the oldest regional organizations, was also the first to hold a presidential summit specifically focused on the environment when it convened the Summit of the Americas on Sustainable Development in Bolivia in December 1996. The Office for Sustainable Development and Environment is the principal technical arm of the OAS General Secretariat for responding to the needs of member states on issues relating to sustainable development within an economic-development context. With the objective of establishing concrete means to strengthen sustainable development, heads of state and government at the Bolivia summit conferred responsibility to the OAS for formulating a strategy for promoting public participation in decision making for sustainable development.

At the second Summit of the Americas in 1998, governments acknowledged the OAS's effort and instructed it, through the inter-American CSD, to continue to fulfill the previous summit's mandates. Leaders also requested that other entities of the inter-American system and the United Nations work to strengthen cooperation in implementing mandates from the Summit on Sustainable Development. By the third Summit of the Americas, the issues to be addressed concerning sustainable development were well established. The third summit therefore focused on the mechanisms for moving these issues forward in hemispheric and international forums. The enactment and enforcement of multilateral environmental agreements and support for participation in the 2002 WSSD were emphasized. Active use of inter-American institutions such as the OAS and the Pan-American Health Organization to implement the sustainable development agenda was also encouraged. The sustainable development agenda is a major element of the Summits of the Americas and now includes specialized ministerial meetings, experts' groups, and interagency task forces to address these issues. As of 2007, the Department of Sustainable Development executed over fifty multicountry programs and projects with a combined (cofinancing) value of approximately $80 million, or approximately $10 million per annum.[77]

The African Union, which evolved out of the Organization of African Unity in 1999, includes the promotion of sustainable development as one of its official objectives. At its inaugural summit in mid-2001, the African Union adopted the New Partnership for Africa's Development (NEPAD) as a blueprint for the continent's future development. The primary objective of NEPAD is to eradicate poverty in Africa and to place African countries on a path of sustainable growth and development in an effort to halt the continent's marginalization in the globalization process. NEPAD recognizes the need to protect the environment not only for Africa's benefit but also for the many natural resources of global importance the continent holds, including a wide range of flora and fauna, paleoanthropological resources, and immense forests that act as carbon sinks. These resources could be degraded without support from the international community. Implicit in NEPAD's approach is the need for the developed world to support Africa's sustainable development, not only for the sake of Africans but also for the wider global community.

In 2003, the African Union adopted the NEPAD Environmental Action Plan. The plan is organized into clusters of program and project activities to be implemented over a ten-year period dealing with land degradation, drought, and desertification; wetlands; invasive species; marine and coastal resources; cross-border conservation of natural resources; and climate change.[78]

Asia-Pacific Economic Cooperation (APEC), which formed in 1989 in response to the growing interdependence among Asia-Pacific economies, includes in its work the consideration of three categories of environmental issues: air, atmospheric, and water pollution, especially those related to energy production and use; resource degradation; and demographic shifts, including rural out-migration, food security, and urbanization. APEC had a major setback in 1998 as a result of the spread of the Asian financial crisis. However, at their November 1998 meeting in Kuala Lumpur, Malaysia, the APEC economic leaders reiterated their "commitment to advance sustainable development across the entire spectrum of [their] workplan including cleaner production, protection of the marine environment and sustainable cities."[79]

The first APEC ocean-related ministerial meeting was held in South Korea in April, 2002, its theme being "Toward the Sustainability of Marine and Coastal Resources." Sustainable fisheries, ocean science and technology, marine environmental protection, and integrated coastal management were discussed. During the meeting, ministers adopted the Seoul Oceans Declaration. In September 2007, the APEC leaders adopted a Declaration on Climate Change, Energy Security and Clean Development, which expressed commitment to the global objective of stabilizing GHG concentrations in the atmosphere and called for a post-2012 international climate-change arrangement that "strengthens, broadens and deepens the current arrangements and leads to reduced global emissions of greenhouse gases."[80]

The Group of 77 (G-77), which functions as the "negotiating arm of the developing countries" within the UN system, is an important international entity in environmental politics.[81] The G-77 was established in 1964 by seventy-seven developing countries at the end of the first session of the United Nations Conference on Trade and Development in Geneva. Although its membership has grown to 130 countries, the original name was retained because of its historic significance. China, which has the status of

associate member, also plays an influential role in the G-77. As the larges
coalition in the United Nations, the G-77 provides the means for the de
to articulate and promote its collective economic interests, enhance its joint nego-
ating capacity on all major international economic issues in the UN system, and promote economic and technical cooperation among developing countries.[82] Since the
early 1990s, as environmental issues have become increasingly intertwined with economic issues, and as more developing countries have become involved in the negotiation of multilateral environmental agreements, the G-77 has played a key role in
these negotiations.

The OECD is also an actor on the international environmental stage. It has played
a major role in promoting sustainable consumption and production within its member
states and has provided a great deal of background information and support to its
members on such issues as climate change, trade and environment issues, and transport and the environment.

States have also created regional organizations explicitly to address environmental issues. One such organization is the Pacific Regional Environment Programme (SPREP).[83]
Created in 1982, SPREP has developed a framework for environmentally sound planning and management suited to the Pacific island region. In order to improve and protect the environment, SPREP's action program aims to build national capacity in
environmental and resource management. SPREP also provides capacity building,
training, and support for member states to improve their ability to represent their interests in international negotiations and UN global conferences.

The African Ministerial Conference on the Environment is a permanent forum
where African ministers of the environment discuss mainly matters of relevance to
the environment of the continent. It was established in 1985 when African ministers
met in Egypt and adopted the Cairo Programme for African Cooperation. The conference is convened every second year.

The Central American Commission on Environment and Development was established in 1989 to enable improved regional cooperation on environment and development issues. Since then, the commission has adopted different regional agreements
on the conservation of biological diversity, climate change, transboundary movements
of hazardous wastes, the management and conservation of forest ecosystems, sustainable development in oceans and coastal areas, and access to genetic resources.[84]

NONGOVERNMENTAL ORGANIZATIONS

The emergence of the global environment as a major issue in world politics coincided
with the emergence of NGOs as important actors in environmental politics.[85] Although

business organizations are often included in the UN definition of an NGO, we use the term here to denote an independent, nonprofit organization not beholden to a government or a profit-making organization.

NGO influence on global environmental politics stems from three principal factors. First, NGOs often possess expert knowledge and innovative thinking about global environmental issues acquired from years of focused specialization on the issues under negotiation. Second, NGOs are acknowledged to be dedicated to goals that transcend narrow national or sectoral interests. Third, NGOs often represent substantial constituencies within their own countries and thus can command attention from policy makers because of their potential ability to mobilize these people to influence policies and even tight elections.

In the industrialized countries, most NGOs active in global environmental politics fall into one of three categories: organizations affiliated with international NGOs (INGOs), that is, NGOs with branches in more than one country; large national organizations focused primarily on domestic environmental issues; and think tanks, or research institutes, whose influence comes primarily from publishing studies and proposals for action.

Some INGOs are loose federations of national affiliates; others have a more centralized structure. Friends of the Earth International, based in Amsterdam, is a confederation of seventy-seven national independent affiliates, half of which are in developing countries. At an annual meeting, delegates democratically set priorities and select five or more campaigns on which to cooperate. Greenpeace is one of the largest INGOs; it has offices in forty-one counties and more than 2.8 million financial supporters and members.[86] Its international activities are tightly organized by a well-staffed headquarters (also in Amsterdam) and guided by issues and strategies determined at an annual meeting.

The Switzerland-based global conservation organization WWF (formerly known as the World Wildlife Fund and the World Wide Fund for Nature) is the world's largest, and one of its most experienced, independent conservation organizations. It has 5 million members worldwide and works in one hundred countries. WWF's mission is the conservation of nature and the preservation of biodiversity and healthy ecological systems through the protection of natural areas and wild plants and animals, sustainable use of renewable resources, more efficient energy use, and reducing pollution. It also works on cross-cutting sustainability issues, including climate change, toxics, trade and investment (e.g., WTO rules), indigenous and traditional peoples (e.g., intellectual property rights), the impacts of tourism and what WWF sees as the root causes of biodiversity loss: poverty, migration, macroeconomic policies, and poor enforcement of environmental legislation.

The European Environmental Bureau, organized in 1974, is now a confederation of more than 140 environmental citizen organizations based in EU member states. The bureau seeks to help improve EU environmental policies and sustainable development policies by effectively integrating environmental objectives in horizontal and sectoral policies of the EU and ensuring compliance with effective strategies to realize these objectives.

The second category of NGOs includes the big U.S. environmental organizations, almost all of which have international programs.[87] Some, such as the Sierra Club, the National Audubon Society, and the National Wildlife Federation, were formed in the late nineteenth and early twentieth centuries around conservation issues. Others, including Environmental Defense and the Natural Resources Defense Council, arose in the early 1970s in an attempt to use legal, economic, and regulatory processes to affect national policy, with an initial focus on air and water pollution. Along with Friends of the Earth USA, they have come to play effective roles in related international issues, particularly in the negotiations on climate and ozone and efforts to reshape the policies of the multilateral development banks. Other organizations with more specific agendas have also become more internationally active on their issues; among these are Defenders of Wildlife and the Humane Society. Total membership in the United States in national environmental organizations increased rapidly in the 1970s and 1980s to an estimated 13 million people before declining slightly during the 1990s and 2000s.[88]

Environmental think tanks, normally funded by private donations or contracts, rely primarily on their technical expertise and research programs to influence global environmental policy. Prominent examples include the World Resources Institute, which publishes well-respected reports on the global environment and policy studies on specific issues. Publications from the Worldwatch Institute have often identified new problems and suggested alternative approaches to international issues. The International Institute for Environment and Development in London drew early attention to the connection between the environment and poverty in developing countries. In a few countries, government-funded, but nevertheless independent, institutes seek to influence both the policies of their own governments and international negotiations. The International Institute for Sustainable Development (IISD) of Canada and the Stockholm Environment Institute of Sweden have played such roles. These organizations all collaborate with colleagues in other countries.

Unlike the environmental NGOs of the North, environmentalism in developing countries grew out of what some of its founders saw as a "lopsided, iniquitous and environmentally destructive process of development" and is often interlinked with questions of human rights, ethnicity, and distributive justice.[89] Southern NGOs have tended to stress land use, forest management, fishing rights, and the redistribution of power over natural resources rather than ozone depletion and global warming.[90] They also tend to be more critical of consumerism and uncontrolled economic development than their colleagues in the North. But there are many exceptions, such as the Chilean and Argentinean NGOs interested in the ozone layer and the NGOs in low-lying coastal areas or small islands that are concerned about climate change. Developing-country NGOs have often become involved in international policy issues through opposition to multilateral bank projects and government policies that displace villages or threaten rain forests, and they tend to regard transnational corporations as enemies of the environment. Inherently critical of their governments on most domestic policies, NGO members who are committed to environmental protection have often been harassed, subjected to political repression, and jailed. In some countries, however, they have acquired political legitimacy and a measure of influence on national environmental-policy issues.

India, which is symbolic of a number of developing countries, has an environmental movement whose origins date back to the Chipko movement, which started in the Garhwal Himalaya in April 1973. Between 1973 and 1980, more than a dozen instances were recorded in which men, women, and children threatened to hug forest trees rather than allow them to be logged for export. Unlike environmentalists in the North, however, the peasants were not interested in saving the trees but in using the forest for agricultural and household requirements.[91]

The Chipko movement was the forerunner of, and the direct inspiration for, a series of popular movements in defense of community rights to natural resources, some of which continue to this day. Some of these struggles revolved around forests; in other instances, around the control and use of pasture lands, minerals, or fisheries. Most of these conflicts have pitted rich against poor: logging companies against hill villagers, dam builders against forest tribal communities, multinational corporations deploying trawlers against traditional fisherfolk in small boats.[92]

Some of the most important aspects of Brazil's environmental movement can be traced to the 1980s, when rubber tappers organized to resist destruction of the forests that supported them and which they had tended for decades. In 1989, after a cattle rancher murdered Chico Mendes, a key leader of the rubber tappers, popular support grew and the Brazilian government began to take more meaningful action. The country set aside "extractive reserves" to protect forests where tapping and other sustainable extraction could continue.

In Sarawak, Malaysia, loggers cleared 2.8 million hectares, or 30 percent, of the forest between 1963 and 1985. Many of the timber licenses issued by the Sarawak government covered the customary land of the natives who depend on the forests for food and shelter—indeed, for their very survival. Beginning in early 1987, natives started erecting blockades across timber roads in a desperate attempt to stop the logging.[93]

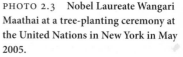

PHOTO 2.3   Nobel Laureate Wangari Maathai at a tree-planting ceremony at the United Nations in New York in May 2005.
Courtesy IISD/*Earth Negotiations Bulletin.*

Logging protests and blockades continue in Malaysia, with aggressive deforestation activities producing serious disputes like those that occurred during July and August 2009.[94]

The Green Belt Movement, based in Kenya, is an influential grassroots NGO that focuses on conservation, community development, and capacity building. Founded in 1977 by Professor Wangari Maathai (under the auspices of the National Council of Women of Kenya), it aims to create a society of people who consciously work for the continued improvement of their environment and for a greener, cleaner Kenya. Programs include tree planting, biodiversity conservation, civic and environmental education, advocacy and networking, food security, and capacity building for women and girls. In 2004, Maathai received the Nobel Peace Prize for her efforts with the Green Belt Movement—the first Nobel Peace Prize given to an environmentalist.[95]

Many environmental and development battles continue to be fought at the community level in developing countries, but some NGOs and coalitions in those countries also tackle a broader range of environmental and development issues. The Third World Network, for example, is an independent nonprofit international network of organizations and individuals involved in issues relating to development, the Third World, and North-South issues. Its mission is to bring about a greater articulation of the needs and rights of peoples in the Third World, a fair distribution of world resources, and forms of development that are ecologically sustainable and fulfill human needs. To this end, the Third World Network conducts research into economic, social, and environmental issues pertaining to the South; publishes books and magazines; organizes and participates in seminars; and represents southern interests and perspectives at international fora such as UN conferences and processes. Headquartered in Penang, Malaysia, the Third World Network also has regional offices in Goa, India, and Geneva, Switzerland. It also has affiliated organizations in several Third World countries, including Bangladesh, Brazil, Ethiopia, Ghana, India, Malaysia, Mexico, Peru, the Philippines, Senegal, South Africa, Thailand, and Uruguay.[96]

The Center for Science and Environment in India seeks to increase public awareness of scientific, technological, environmental, and developmental issues and to search for solutions that people and communities can implement themselves. It works on a wide range of issues in India, including air and water pollution, human health, climate change, and monitoring the environmental performance of Indian industry. Like the Third World Network, it is also involved at the global level and represents southern interests and perspectives at international fora.[97]

Developing-country NGOs often form national-level coalitions, such as the Indonesian Forum for Environment, which unites over four hundred environmental organizations countrywide. Indigenous minorities in the five Amazon basin countries have also organized their own national-level coalitions, which, in turn, have formed a coordinating body (called COICA, for its Spanish name) to lobby for a voice in all Amazon development projects affecting them. Indeed, recognition of indigenous groups at the Rio Earth Summit, including in Chapter 26 of Agenda 21, combined with their highly visible participation in subsequent global conferences and the work of the CBD, have boosted the rights of indigenous peoples and provided them with a way to influence international environmental negotiations.

International coalitions of NGOs working on a specific environmental issue have also become a means of increasing NGO influence. The Antarctic and Southern Oceans Coalition brings together over one hundred environmental organizations working to ensure that the Antarctic continent, its surrounding islands, and the great Southern Ocean survive as the world's last unspoiled wilderness. The Climate Action Network, formed in 1989, has more than 340 member organizations around the world that work to promote government and individual action to limit human-induced climate change.

North-South NGO alliances have sometimes been effective in influencing international events. An alliance between U.S. NGOs and indigenous opponents of rain forest destruction brought worldwide attention to Brazilian policy in 1986. Together, these groups helped stop the World Bank's Polonoreste project, an Amazonian road-building and colonization scheme, persuaded President José Sarney to halt the tax incentives for agriculture and ranching that had stimulated the Amazon land boom, and persuaded members of the U.S. Congress and officials of the Inter-American Development Bank to support extractive reserves.[98]

A coalition of northern and southern NGOs, ranging from the Third World Network to the Council of Canadians, used e-mail and electronic conferencing to organize swift opposition to the Multilateral Agreement on Investment. The prospective treaty to liberalize international investment rules was being negotiated behind the closed doors of the OECD.[99] The OECD canceled negotiations, acknowledging that the NGOs had aroused enough opposition in many countries to derail the process.[100]

But relations between NGOs are not always smooth. There has long been a rift within the Climate Action Network between northern and southern NGOs regarding the balance of climate responsibility and associated commitments under the Kyoto Protocol. There was a similar division in the pre-UNCED discussions of a forest treaty. In this matter, also, the southern NGOs' position tended to parallel that of their governments. A southern resentment of northern NGOs sometimes persists, especially at the big international conferences where the better-prepared, better-financed U.S. and European NGOs are heavily represented.

Despite potential tensions, however, there have been many instances of close North-South NGO cooperation. One example is the Pesticide Action Network, a network of more than six hundred participating NGOs, institutions, and individuals in more than ninety countries working to replace hazardous pesticides with ecologically sound alternatives. Five autonomous regional centers coordinate its projects and campaigns. The Pesticide Action Network and partner groups from around the world have been working together to lobby for the phaseout of POPs during the negotiation and implementation of the Stockholm Convention on Persistent Organic Pollutants, an international treaty that sets mandatory timetables for POP phaseouts and provides technical and financial assistance to help developing countries eliminate POPs.

Another successful coalition of North-South NGOs has been the International POPs Elimination Network (IPEN), which works for the global elimination of POPs on an expedited, yet socially equitable, basis. Founded by a small number of NGOs, IPEN was formally launched with a public forum in Montreal in June 1998 during the first session of formal negotiations on creating a global treaty to control and/or eliminate POPs. Throughout the five negotiating sessions, IPEN grew to become a coalition of more than 350 public health, environmental, consumer, and other NGOs in sixty-five countries. The network worked to mobilize grassroots support for a global treaty to eliminate POPs. It also leveraged the resources and created a forum for NGOs and activists from around the world to participate in the negotiations. IPEN coordinated NGO conferences and workshops at each of the five negotiating sessions.[101]

One of the most important organizations through which NGOs influence environmental politics is the International Union for the Conservation of Nature and Natural Resources (IUCN), which brings together more than 1,000 member organizations in 140 countries, including more than 200 government and 800 NGOs, and some 11,000 scientists and experts in a unique worldwide partnership. Governed by a general assembly of delegates from its member organizations that meets every three years, the IUCN has had a major influence on global agreements on wildlife conservation. Although member government organizations, which often embrace only broad consensus positions, tend to limit the group's actions, IUCN has been successful in drafting environmental treaties and assisting in monitoring their implementation.

Influencing Environmental Regime Formation

NGOs can attempt to influence the development, expansion, and implementation of international regimes in various ways, such as:

- influencing the global environmental agenda by defining a new issue or redefining an old one;
- lobbying governments to accept a more advanced position toward an issue, by advancing new proposals, carrying out consumer boycotts and educational campaigns, or bringing lawsuits;
- proposing draft texts to be included in conventions in advance of conferences;
- lobbying and participating in international negotiations;
- supporting ratification and implementation of the regime by the government in their host country;
- providing reporting services;
- raising public awareness of particular issues;
- assisting implementation of the regime, particularly in developing countries; and
- monitoring the implementation of conventions and reporting to the secretariat and/or the parties.

One example of an NGO influencing the global environmental agenda is the role played by WWF and Conservation International in creating the demand for banning commerce in African elephant ivory. In particular, the groups published a detailed report on the problem, circulating it to the parties to the Convention on International Trade in Endangered Species of Wild Fauna and Flora (CITES), and engaged in public education campaigns.

Pressing for changes in the policy of a major actor is sometimes the best way for NGOs to influence an international regime. In efforts to protect the ozone layer, during the late 1970s the U.S. Clean Air Coalition, a group of national environmental organizations, successfully lobbied for a domestic ban on aerosols and the regulation of CFCs. Because they lobbied for a total phaseout of CFCs before negotiations on the Montreal Protocol began, they contributed to U.S. international leadership on this issue. Similarly, three U.S. NGOs working with pro-treaty **biotechnology** firms were a major influence in the Clinton administration's decision to reverse the Bush administration's position and sign the Biodiversity Convention.[102]

Greenpeace's monitoring of and reporting on the toxic waste trade was a key factor in encouraging a coalition of countries to push for a complete ban on North-South waste trade under the Basel Convention. The Inuit Circumpolar Conference, an NGO representing 150,000 Inuit of Alaska, Canada, Greenland, and Chukotka (Russia), participated in negotiations that produced the Stockholm Convention on Persistent Organic Pollutants, and their stories concerning the dangers that toxic chemicals pose for the future of their people put a human face on the need to eliminate POPs.

Although effective consumer boycotts are rare in international environmental politics (they are more common on local and national issues), an NGO-organized boycott of Icelandic products, including protests of fast-food and supermarket chains that sold fish caught by Iceland's fishing fleet, because of Iceland's pro-whaling stand, contributed to a temporary two-year halt to that country's whaling in 1989.[103] Other notable NGO-led boycotts include Mitisubishi making concessions on forest policy following a campaign spearheaded by Rainforest Action Network and Shell agreeing to dispose of its offshore Brent Spar oil platform on land (rather than dumping it at sea as originally planned).[104]

NGOs can influence international regimes in a more specialized way by writing potential text for inclusion in a convention or amendment and circulating it in advance of the negotiations in the hope that it will be formally supported and submitted by a national delegation. In exceptional cases, this strategy can even include developing an entire draft convention. Few NGOs have the staff resources to devote to such a task, and only IUCN has succeeded in having draft conventions used as the basis for negotiations. The Convention Concerning the Protection of the World Cultural and Natural Heritage, signed in 1972 in Paris, was based on a draft produced by IUCN. CITES, signed in 1973, was the result of an IUCN initiative that went through three drafts over nearly a decade.[105]

NGOs have become especially active and well organized in lobbying at international negotiating conferences. The COPs to most environmental conventions permit NGO observers, enabling NGOs to be actively involved in the proceedings. Certain NGOs specialize in the meetings of particular conventions and over the years have acquired a high level of technical and legal expertise. The Humane Society of the United States has been lobbying at meetings of the International Whaling Commission (IWC) since 1973, and Greenpeace has been active in the COP to the London Convention since the early 1980s. The Climate Action Network was extremely active in the negotiation of the UNFCCC and the Kyoto Protocol, and it has also participated in the negotiations to strengthen the climate regime. The Pesticide Action Network and IPEN have been active in lobbying at negotiations for the Stockholm Convention on POPs.

NGOs also influence international conferences by providing scientific and technical information and new arguments to delegations already sympathetic to their objectives. In the process leading up to the whaling moratorium, NGOs supplied factual information on violations of the whaling convention as well as scientific information not otherwise available to the delegations.[106] In some circumstances, NGOs have a particularly strong influence on a key delegation's positions, an example being the 1991–1992 biodiversity negotiations when WWF-Australia and other NGOs were consulted on major issues in the convention before the Australian delegation adopted positions.[107] The Foundation for International Environmental Law and Development has assisted AOSIS within the context of the climate-change negotiations, providing AOSIS with advice and legal expertise, enabling the alliance to wield greater influence in the climate negotiations.[108] Greenpeace provided a great deal of technical support to African and other developing countries supporting a ban on the dumping of hazardous wastes in developing countries during the negotiation of the Basel Convention.

NGOs can also provide useful reporting services during these conferences. Since 1972, NGOs at selected UN-sponsored environmental conferences have published *ECO*, which provides a combination of news stories and commentary. The *Earth Negotiations Bulletin*, published by IISD, has provided objective reports of many different environment and development negotiations since 1992.[109] Countries cannot easily or effectively report about ongoing negotiations on their own. Were a government to attempt to provide such information, the reports would be derided as biased. If the United Nations or a formal secretariat published daily reports, they would have the status of official documents, and member governments would have difficulty agreeing on their content, style, and tone. However, because the NGO community, including impartial research institutions like IISD, are already providing the information, governments and international organizations have little incentive to step in.[110]

NGOs can sometimes assist governments in implementing the provisions of environmental regimes. This can include offering assistance in drafting national legislation, providing technical and scientific assistance on relevant issues, and brokering the provision of essential financial support.

NGOs can also influence regime formation by monitoring compliance with an agreement once it goes into effect. Investigation and reporting by NGOs can put pressure on parties that are violating provisions of an agreement. They can demonstrate the need for a more effective enforcement mechanism (or for creation of a mechanism where none exists) or help build support for further elaboration or strengthening of the existing regime rules.

This NGO function has been especially important with regard to the CITES and whaling regimes. The international Trade Records Analysis of Flora and Fauna in Commerce (TRAFFIC), a joint wildlife-trade-monitoring program of WWF and IUCN, plays a vital role in supplementing the CITES Secretariat in monitoring the compliance of various countries with CITES bans on trade in endangered species.[111] Climate networks in the United States and the EU have produced detailed reviews of countries' national climate action plans. Greenpeace's aggressive reporting of hazardous wastes dumped in violation of the Basel Convention helped build support for a full ban on international shipping of such wastes to non-OECD countries.

NGOs and International Institutions

Influencing the structure and policies of major international institutions active in global environmental politics poses a different set of challenges to NGOs. The international NGO community has taken on a wide range of global institutions, from the World Bank and the GEF to the International Tropical Timber Organization and the WTO. These institutions have different characteristics that impact the ability of NGO efforts to influence their policies.

The most successful NGO effort was influencing the restructuring of the GEF, on which southern and northern NGOs were in full agreement. NGOs were highly critical of the GEF as administered by the World Bank during its 1991–1993 pilot phase. They supported the developing-country position for the creation of a GEF Secretariat independent of the World Bank and for a transparent and more democratic project-approval process.[112]

U.S. NGOs were also effective in forcing changes in the lending of multilateral development banks—primarily because of the importance of the U.S. Congress in providing funding for the banks.[113] Between 1983 and 1987, U.S. environmental NGOs in alliance with fiscal conservatives persuaded congressional appropriations subcommittees to sponsor legislation directing the banks' U.S. executive directors to press for environmental reforms. As a result, by 1986, the United States began voting against particularly egregious World Bank loans, actions that in 1987 helped prompt a commitment from former World Bank president Barber Conable to pay greater attention to the environment.

In the late 1980s, NGO campaigning for bank reform began to focus on issues of public participation and accountability. About 150 NGOs worldwide participated in some fashion in a campaign to spur greater openness and accountability and to encourage more equitable debt reduction and development strategies that were less destructive to the environment. Today, partly as a result of this high-profile pressure, about half of the bank's lending projects have provisions for NGO involvement in their implementation, up from an average of only 6 percent between 1973 and 1988. The

TABLE 2.1   NGO Participation at WTO Ministerial Conferences, 1996–2005

	ELIGIBLE NGOS	NGOS REPRESENTED
Singapore, 1996	159	108
Geneva, 1998	153	128
Seattle, 1999	776	686
Doha, 2001	651	370
Cancún, 2003	961	795
Hong Kong, 2005	1,065	836

Source: "NGO Participation in Ministerial Conference Was Largest Ever," WTO, October 6, 2003, www.wto.org/english/news_e/news03_e/ngo_minconf_6oct03_e.htm; Accreditation Centre, Hong Kong Ministerial Conference, "NGOs Attendance to the WTO Sixth Ministerial Conference," WTO, December 2005, www.wto.org/english/thewto_e/minist_e/min05_e/list_ngo_hk05_e.pdf.

bank has even included NGOs such as Oxfam International in multilateral debt-relief discussions.

Much more difficult for NGOs is the trade-and-environment issue, to which they turned their attention only in the 1990s. The goal of the General Agreement on Tariffs and Trade (GATT), determined more than sixty years ago, was to reduce tariffs and other trade barriers. The GATT never had provisions for NGO observers. Environmental activists have been campaigning for increased transparency, participation, and accountability in the WTO since its establishment in 1994, portraying it as a secretive organization lacking accountability. They argue that NGOs can play a crucial role in making the world trading system more transparent and accountable.[114] Before the third WTO ministerial talks, which took place in Seattle in December 1999, many believed that although NGO demands for participation were unlikely to be met in the near future, governments were attempting to engage in a more open manner with many development and environmental organizations.[115] In the aftermath of the violent street protests during the Seattle meeting, however, the WTO decided to hold its next ministerial meeting in Doha, Qatar, where, through visa requirements, restrictive security, and the higher cost of travel, they could easily limit NGO access and prevent street protests (see Table 2.1). Although NGO attendance has increased in subsequent years, NGOs still criticize the WTO for lack of transparency in decision making.

CORPORATIONS

Private business firms, especially multinational corporations, are important and interested actors in global environmental politics. Their core activities, although often essential, consume resources and produce pollution, and environmental regulations often directly affect their economic interests. Corporations also have significant assets for influencing global environmental politics. They have good access to decision makers in most governments and international organizations and can deploy impressive technical expertise on the issues in which they are interested. They have national and international industrial associations that represent their interests in policy issues, as well as significant financial and technical resources important to developing solutions.

Corporations often oppose national and international policies that they believe will impose significant new costs on them or otherwise reduce expected profits. Indeed, at times, corporations have worked to weaken several global environmental regimes, including ozone protection, climate change, whaling, hazardous waste, chemicals, and fisheries. Corporations sometimes support an international agreement if it will create weaker regulations on their activities than those that they expect to be imposed domestically.

At the same time, however, corporate interests vary across companies and sectors, and at times some corporations support creating strong national and international environmental policy. When faced with existing strong domestic regulations on an activity with a global environmental dimension, corporations are likely to support international agreements that will impose similar standards on competitors abroad. For example, on fisheries-management issues, U.S. and Japanese fishing industries are more strictly regulated on various issues of high-seas fishing, particularly quotas on bluefin tuna and other highly migratory species, than other Asian fishing states (Republic of Korea, China, Taiwan, and Indonesia); their respective fishing industries therefore pushed the United States and Japan to take strong positions on regulation of high-seas fishing capacity in FAO negotiations in 1998.

A particular industry's interests regarding a proposed global environmental regime are often far from monolithic. On ozone, climate change, biodiversity, and fisheries, industries have been divided either along national lines or among industry sectors or subsectors. On climate, European-based energy firms have traditionally been more willing to see such agreements as business opportunities because they have had experience in using greater energy efficiency to become more profitable, whereas U.S.-based firms, which until recently had far less experience, have been much more resistant to such plans.

But even the energy industry is not united on the issue of climate change. Royal Dutch Shell and BP have decided to seek a seat at the table rather than remain in opposition, joining the Pew Center on Global Climate Change's Business Environmental Leadership Council and reduced their GHG emissions by at least 10 percent from 1990 levels by 2002.[116] A number of utilities across the country are moving aggressively to increase the production of electricity from solar and wind technologies. U.S. automobile manufacturers have also noted opportunities for future markets by investing in hybrid and other technologies that could reduce CO_2 emissions. At the same time, however, the Alliance of Automobile Manufacturers challenged California's right to pass a law requiring automakers to achieve "the maximum feasible and cost-effective reduction" of GHG emissions beginning with model year 2009 vehicles. Although some tout their "green" image and have significantly expanded the market for hybrids and other advanced-technology vehicles, during the Bush administration European and Japanese automakers joined their U.S. counterparts to prevent California and other states from making a commitment to reduce GHG emissions from automobiles.[117] This policy was overturned by the Obama administration in 2009.

When companies see a positive stake in a global environmental agreement, they can dilute the influence of other companies that seek to weaken it. In 1992, the Industrial Biotechnology Association opposed the Biodiversity Convention because it feared the provisions on intellectual property rights would legally condone existing violations of those rights.[118] But the issue was not a high priority for most of the industry, and two of its leading member corporations, Merck and Genentech, believed the convention would benefit them by encouraging developing countries to negotiate agreements with companies for access to genetic resources. After those companies joined environmentalists in calling for the United States to sign the convention in 1993, the Industrial Biotechnology Association came out in favor of signing it.[119]

Similarly, when U.S. industries interested in promoting alternatives to fossil fuels began lobbying at meetings of the INC for the climate convention in August 1994, they reduced the influence of pro-fossil fuel industries, which had previously monopolized industry views on the issue. Similarly, because insurance companies are concerned about the increased hurricane and storm damage that climate change may cause, they are proactive in supporting targets and timetables for GHG emissions reductions. The insurance industry has tried to raise awareness among corporations regarding the dangers of climate change, including by conducting research projects on its negative economic consequences as well as the future impacts of storms and floods.[120] UNEP and several industry leaders established the Insurance Industry Initiative to incorporate environmental considerations into internal and external business activities. In 2003 the UNEP Insurance Industry Initiative merged with UNEP's Financial Institutions Initiative. The resulting UNEP Finance Initiative, through its climate-change working group, provides input into the work of the UNFCCC and communicates the concerns of some leading players in the financial sector regarding the need for climate mitigation and adaptation activities.[121] At the fourteenth COP to the UNFCCC, Munich Re, one of the world's biggest reinsurance companies, addressed the need to incorporate climate-risk insurance as a viable option for reducing the negative effects of global warming. Climate-risk insurance solutions can reduce the financial risks posed by an increasing number of weather-related catastrophes, especially in developing countries.[122]

Corporate Influence on Regime Formation

Corporations impact global environmental regimes by influencing regime formation and by undertaking business activities that either weaken a regime or contribute to its effectiveness. To influence the formation of regimes, corporations attempt to:

- shape the definition of the issue under negotiation in a manner favorable to their interests;
- fund and distribute targeted research and other information supportive of their interests;
- initiate advertising campaigns to influence public opinion;
- persuade an individual government to adopt a particular position on a regime being negotiated by lobbying it in its capital; and
- lobby delegations to the negotiating conference on the regime.

Corporations had great success during the issue-definition phase associated with creation of the International Convention for the Prevention of Pollution of the Sea by Oil (1954). The major oil companies and global shipping interests (most of which the oil companies owned directly or indirectly) were the only actors with the technical expertise to make detailed proposals on maritime oil pollution. The technical papers submitted by the International Chamber of Shipping, comprising thirty national associations of shipowners, and the Oil Companies International Marine Forum, representing the interests of major oil companies, defined the terms of the discussion[123] and ensured that the convention would be compatible with oil and shipping interests—and quite ineffective in preventing oil pollution of the oceans. That degree of success in defining an issue is unlikely to recur in the future because governments and NGOs now have more expertise on issues being negotiated; furthermore, NGOs are better organized and more aggressive.

In most global environmental issues, corporations have relied on their domestic political clout to ensure that governments do not adopt strong policies adversely affecting their interests. The domestic U.S. industry most strongly opposed to a ban on hazardous waste trade, the secondary-metals industry, helped persuade U.S. officials to block such a ban in the negotiation of the Basel Convention. And on ozone depletion, Japan agreed to a phaseout of CFCs only after some of its largest electronic firms agreed they could eliminate their use by 2000.

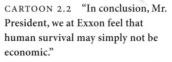

CARTOON 2.2   "In conclusion, Mr. President, we at Exxon feel that human survival may simply not be economic."
© Richard D. Willson, reprinted with permission.

For many years, industry lobbying in the United States succeeded in reducing the executive branch's flexibility in the climate-change negotiations. Some of the most powerful trade associations launched the Global Climate Information Project in 1997. Through a multi-million-dollar print and television advertising campaign, the project cast doubt on the desirability of emissions controls in the Kyoto Protocol, then entering the final stages of negotiation, by arguing that such controls would raise taxes on gasoline, heating oil, and consumer goods and reduce the competitiveness of American businesses. An alliance of business and labor succeeded in persuading the U.S. Senate to vote 95–0 for a resolution stating that the United States should not participate in a climate treaty that would require U.S. GHG reductions without similar commitments from developing countries or would result in serious harm to the U.S. economy.[124]

Industry associations have been actively involved in influencing negotiations in several other global environmental regimes. Sometimes, industries with particular technical expertise or relatively unchallenged influence over the issue have been part of a key country's delegation. For example, the Japanese commissioner to the IWC has generally been the president of the Japanese Whaling Association.[125] U.S. and Canadian food manufacturers have participated on U.S. delegations to the FAO's Codex Alimentarius Commission, which sets international food standards.[126] The Israeli delegation to some ozone-layer negotiations included officials from a methyl bromide manufacturer during key negotiations on expanding controls on the chemical.[127] The Global Climate Coalition, an industry group, worked closely with the delegations from the United States and Saudi Arabia during the negotiation of the UNFCCC.

Like NGOs, representatives of corporate interests lobby negotiations on environmental regimes primarily by providing information and analysis to the delegations most sympathetic to their cause. During the climate-change negotiations, for example, coal and oil interests actively advised the U.S., Russian, and Saudi delegations on how to weaken the regime.[128] Industry groups had a particularly strong presence at the negotiating sessions for the Cartagena Protocol on Biosafety. Their interest in participating in the negotiations grew during the talks: Eight industry groups were represented at the first round of negotiations in 1996, and twenty such groups from many different countries were present at the final meetings in 1999.[129] Individual corporations, among them Monsanto, DuPont, and Syngenta (formerly Novartis and Zeneca), also sent their own representatives to many of the meetings.

Corporations also may facilitate or delay, strengthen or weaken global environmental regimes by direct actions that have an impact on the environment. They may take these actions unilaterally or based on agreements reached with their respective governments. Such actions can be crucial to a government's ability to commit itself to a regime-strengthening policy. The climate and ozone regimes are particularly sensitive to the willingness of corporations in key countries to take actions that will allow the international community to go beyond the existing agreement.

In the ozone-protection issue, the U.S. chemical industry delayed movement toward any regime for regulating ozone-depleting CFCs in the early 1980s, in part by reducing their own research efforts on CFC substitutes.[130] Subsequently, DuPont gave impetus to an accelerated timetable for a CFC phaseout by unilaterally pledging to phase out their production of CFCs ahead of the schedule already agreed to by the Montreal Protocol parties. In 1989, Nissan and Toyota pledged to eliminate CFCs from their cars and manufacturing processes as early as the mid-1990s. In 1992, Ford Motor Company pledged to eliminate 90 percent of CFC use from its manufacturing processes worldwide by the end of that year and to eliminate all CFCs from its air conditioners and manufacturing by the end of 1994.

Early in the climate-change negotiations, the Japanese auto industry, which accounts for 20 percent of Japan's CO_2 emissions, adopted a goal of improving fuel efficiency by 8.5 percent above its 1990 level by 2000, encouraging the Japanese government to make a commitment to stabilize national CO_2 emissions at 1990 levels by 2000.[131] More recently, numerous corporations around the world have pledged to reduce their GHG emissions and to improve their environmental accounting.[132]

Industry and Nonregime Issues

Corporations have their greatest political influence on a global environmental issue when there are no negotiations on a formal, binding international regime governing the issue. Under those circumstances, they are able to use their economic and political clout with individual governments and international organizations to protect particular economic activities that damage the environment.

For example, in the past, the agrochemical industry enjoyed strong influence on the FAO's Plant Protection Service, which was responsible for the organization's pesticide activities. The industry's international trade association even had a joint program with the FAO to promote pesticide use worldwide until the 1970s.[133] This influence was instrumental in carrying out the industry's main strategy for avoiding binding international restrictions on its sales of pesticides in developing countries. Instead of binding rules, the FAO drafted a voluntary "code of conduct" on pesticide distribution and use between 1982 and 1985 in close consultation with the industry.

Although corporations usually resist strong international environmental agreements not in their interest, in recent years certain corporations have been positioning themselves as advocates of global sustainable development, including, BP, DuPont, General Electric, Royal Dutch Shell, and United Technologies. With their environmental behavior under greater public scrutiny and consumers pressuring them for environmentally friendly products, these corporations have discovered that preventing pollution is good for profitability. As a result, a group of corporate leaders has emerged who support some of the main aspects of the new paradigm of sustainable development as well as the development of certain environmental regimes.

In 1991, at the request of UNCED Secretary-General Maurice Strong, Swiss industrialist Stephan Schmidheiny enlisted a group of forty-eight chief executive officers of corporations from all over the world to set up the Business Council on Sustainable Development to support the objectives of the Earth Summit. The business council issued a declaration calling for changes in consumption patterns and for the prices of goods to reflect environmental costs of production, use, recycling, and disposal.[134] In January 1995, the business council and the World Industry Council for the Environment, an initiative of the International Chamber of Commerce, merged into what is today a coalition of two hundred international companies united by a shared commitment to sustainable development via the three pillars of economic growth, ecological balance, and social progress. Drawing members from thirty-five countries and more than twenty major industrial sectors, the resulting World Business Council on Sustainable Development addresses a range of issues, including corporate social responsibility, access to clean water, capacity building, sustainable livelihoods, harmonizing international trade law with multilateral environmental agreements, and developing public-private partnerships in key areas of sustainable development, including energy and climate.[135]

TREATY SECRETARIATS

Treaty secretariats are a specific type of international organization established by an international treaty to manage the day-to-day operation of the treaty regime.[136] Their staffs consist of international civil servants tasked with pursuing the treaty's objectives. Most treaty secretariats are established initially to administer the process of negotiating the treaty and convening follow-up meetings, but their role usually shifts after the adoption and entry into force of the treaty to facilitating regime operations and helping parties implement their commitments. Yet, despite common core functions, secretariats vary considerable in their size, funding, additional responsibilities, degree of activism, and linkages to other secretariats and treaties.

Secretariats are located in disparate parts of the world, have varying levels of autonomy, and focus on separate, but interrelated, environmental problems. The CBD Secretariat is located in Montreal; UNCCD and the UNFCCC are in Bonn; CITES and the Basel, Rotterdam and Stockholm conventions are in Geneva; and the Ozone Secretariat is in Nairobi. Some secretariats, like the Convention on Migratory Species Secretariat (Bonn), serve more than one convention. Some of the larger secretariats, like the UNFCCC Secretariat, have well over one hundred professional members, while the Secretariat of the Ramsar Convention on Wetlands (Gland, Switzerland) has less than fifteen. Several secretariats, such as those for the ozone, biodiversity, and chemicals regimes, are part of UNEP. Some, like the Climate Secretariat, are administered by the UN Secretariat or other UN agencies.

Treaty secretariats have a number of core tasks that include:

- arranging and servicing meetings of the COP and all subsidiary bodies;
- preparing and transmitting reports based on information received from the COP and subsidiary bodies;
- preparing reports on secretariat implementation activities for the COP;
- ensuring coordination with relevant international bodies and NGOs;
- liaising and communicating with relevant authorities, nonparties, and international organizations;
- compiling and analyzing scientific, economic, and social data and information;
- monitoring adherence to treaty obligations;
- giving guidance and advice to parties; and
- providing expert technical advice to parties.[137]

Increasingly, treaty secretariats are also involved in raising funds for treaty implementation and awareness-raising activities and to provide training, capacity building, and technical assistance to developing countries. In some cases, such as the chemicals regimes, UNEP works to help raise the additional funds. Secretariats can also create synergies by means of coordination and cooperation with other secretariats. The need for close cooperation is obvious: integrated ecosystems are approached by fragmented international management. For example, the success of the UNFCCC is directly conditioned by at least ten other international treaties, while the CBD intersects with dozens of international conventions.[138]

Treaty secretariats may influence the treatment of global environmental issues in ways that are quite similar to the international organizations discussed earlier in this chapter. A secretariat's level of influence depends largely on its mandate, its funding, and the professional and personal commitment of the staff. Essentially, however, treaty secretariats have two overarching areas of impact:

1. Treaty secretariats can influence the behavior of actors by changing their knowledge and belief systems.
2. Treaty secretariats can influence political processes through the creation, support, and shaping of norm-building processes for issue-specific international cooperation.[139]

Treaty Secretariats as Knowledge Brokers

Environmental treaty secretariats embody the institutional memory of the regime they serve. A secretariat provides continuity for negotiations that stretch through numerous sessions over a period of years (both during the negotiation and the implementation of the treaty), during which there may be considerable turnover among government negotiators.[140] However, more specifically, they possess expert knowledge of various categories: technical and scientific knowledge on the policy problem at stake, administrative and procedural knowledge (which they will often generate themselves), and the diplomatic knowledge that is paramount to deal with the complex interlinkages characteristic of international regimes, particularly in the environmental field.[141]

As knowledge brokers, secretariats are in a position to manage and even control the horizontal flow of information between national governments and the vertical flow of information between international organizations, national governments, and even local stakeholders. This information can take the form of syntheses of scientific findings, such as the Ozone Secretariat's reports on the impact of HCFCs, chemicals controlled under the Montreal Protocol, on climate change. Reports like these are not trivial in international political processes. Indeed, knowledge brokers can significantly influence the creation, content, and effectiveness of international institutions. Even though many secretariats do not have the means or the mandate for actual scientific research, they have the ability to collect and disseminate scientific knowledge. For example, the CBD Secretariat maintains close links with the scientific community through processes such as the Millennium Ecosystem Assessment, international scientific cooperative programs such as DIVERSITAS, and the participation of staff members in relevant scientific symposia. The secretariat gathers scientific information on the different natural science issues of biodiversity conservation in the various ecosystems such as mountains, wetlands, forests, and so forth, as well as on administrative, social, legal, and economic aspects of the problems, for instance, of access and benefit-sharing. This knowledge is processed and made available through preparatory documents, the secretariat's website, periodic reports, a newsletter, and a comprehensive handbook.[142]

Along these lines, knowledge and information management is another key role for treaty secretariats. The COP, its subsidiary bodies, national policy makers, NGO and corporate stakeholders, and other interested actors, such as media, science, and civil society, draw on and interpret the information and documentation compiled and disseminated by the secretariat in their analytical, political, and scientific assessments and the related discourses.[143] The frequency of visits to and downloads from its website highlights the usefulness of the Climate Secretariat's role in information management. Website usage grew from 309,657 visits in 1999 to nearly 7.4 million in 2008. In 2008 alone, 2.41 terabytes (24,100 gigabytes) of information were downloaded.[144] The website contains information about the regime and ongoing negotiations, progress in implementation of the UNFCCC and the Kyoto Protocol, official documents, and background data and other information on climate change.

Secretariats can also act as a knowledge broker by convening expert panels and academic assessments, which can help to raise concern among external actors to the level needed to have an impact on political activity. For example, the UNFCCC Secretariat holds numerous workshops on scientific and technical topics related to the convention's mandate. It also promotes the use of side events during meetings of the COP or the subsidiary bodies where scientists and other nongovernmental experts share information with policy makers and with each other.

Treaty Secretariats and the Political Process

Treaty secretariats can influence political processes through the creation, support, and shaping of norm-building processes for issue-specific international cooperation, such as the advance informed-agreement provisions in the Biosafety Protocol and the PIC procedure under the Rotterdam Convention. They can initiate conferences to follow up on treaties or to introduce relevant new topics to the parties. They are usually in charge of administering negotiations on the implementation or expansion of the regime. In this case, secretariat staff can exercise considerable influence "even when they are not key players during the negotiation stage."[145] For example, the Biodiversity Secretariat demonstrated a balanced and continuous effort to facilitate dialogues and negotiations on the issue of biosafety, which contributed to the successful adoption of the Cartagena Protocol. The same holds for the facilitation of the preparation and negotiation process on the access and benefit-sharing provisions of the CBD.[146]

Secretariats can also influence the political process through capacity building. While secretariats are not funding agencies or responsible for providing resources for on-the-ground activities, some do play enabling roles for capacity building at the national and local levels. For example, a secretariat provides basic informational materials on its convention and its sociopolitical implications, such as those developed by the UNCCD Secretariat. The Ozone Secretariat produces training materials for customs agents. The CITES Secretariat provides training materials for wildlife enforcement officers. The Rotterdam Convention Secretariat provides a training manual to explain the convention and its obligations to those responsible for the export of chemicals. Some secretariats, including the Montreal Protocol, provide booklets and games that explain the issues to children (i.e., "The Ozone Story" and the Ozzy Ozone game [Photo 2.4] and the UNESCO/UNCCD teachers kit on desertification).

Some secretariats and the chief administrators stick closely to their administrative and facilitative roles, performing only those tasks specifically assigned to them. Others, while also performing the normal administrative and facilitative roles, are more proactive. They seek to push the agenda, looking for new initiatives and trying to get governments to support and implement them.[147] Secretariats in the latter category benefit from skillful and charismatic leadership. UNEP executive director Mostafa Tolba did this in the early years of the ozone regime—inviting, cajoling, and pressuring somewhat reluctant or disinterested governments to come back to the bargaining table to expand the regime. With UNEP designated as the secretariat and administering the process, Tolba played a central and personal role in the negotiations that produced the 1987 Montreal Protocol and a historic expansion of the treaty in 1990, initiating ideas and advancing concerns that might have otherwise been overlooked and pushing negotiators toward compromise solutions on difficult issues.[148] He played a similar role during negotiations that created the Basel Convention on the Control of Transboundary Movements of Hazardous Wastes and Their Disposal.

More often than not, however, the secretariat's role in the negotiations is less overt and more facilitative—the important but often unrecognized, and sometimes pivotal, role of promoting a smooth process, which can be crucial in steering negotiations toward a successful outcome.[149] For example, the Climate Secretariat tends not to generate and broker analytical knowledge on climate change and related economic or regulatory policies; instead it mainly processes and administers factual information. In other words, the secretariat does not exert influence on the parties about whether a particular decision or action is politically desirable and should be taken in order to mitigate or adapt to climate change. Rather, it influences how things are done once parties have agreed that measures have to be taken.[150]

PHOTO 2.4   The Ozzy Ozone Game, the objective of which is to become an ozone-layer protector, was developed by UNEP under the Multilateral Fund. Ozzy Ozone helps educate children about how to protect themselves from the sun's harmful ultraviolet rays and gives practical tips on how to enjoy the sun safely and how to help save the earth's ozone layer.
Courtesy IISD/*Earth Negotiations Bulletin.*

Nevertheless, it is important to note that treaty secretariats sometimes become more active players in global environmental politics than some governments and other actors may prefer. When secretariats move beyond fulfilling their basic functions and begin influencing global discourse through knowledge management, advancing the institutionalization or expansion of a convention, or proactively assisting in capacity building, they become stakeholders in their own right. Government officials occasionally upbraid secretariat officials for moving beyond a purely facilitative role, arguing that secretariats should not impact policy development.[151] At other times they are praised for acting in pursuit of the stated goals of the regime. Thus, in many respects, determining the most effective or legitimate role for a secretariat within a given issue area remains an open question.[152]

CONCLUSION

State and nonstate actors play key roles in the creation and implementation of national and international environmental policy. State actors play the primary roles in determining the outcomes of issues at stake in global environmental politics, but nonstate actors—IGOs, NGOs, corporations, and treaty secretariats—influence the policies of individual state actors toward global environmental issues as well as the international negotiation process itself. Whether a state adopts the role of lead state, supporting state, swing state, or veto state on a particular issue depends primarily on domestic political factors and on the relative costs and benefits of the proposed regime. But international political-diplomatic consequences can also affect the choice of role.

IGOs, especially UNEP, WMO, and FAO, have played important roles in regime formation by helping to set the international agenda and by sponsoring and shaping negotiations on global environmental regimes and soft-law norms. The CSD has called attention to issues that should be on the international agenda as well as areas where there has been a failure to implement recommendations contained in Agenda 21. The **Bretton Woods institutions** (World Bank and IMF) and certain UN agencies, particularly UNDP and FAO, influence state development strategies through financing and technical assistance. IGOs also seek to exert influence on state policy through research and advocacy of specific norms at the global level. Treaty secretariats, a subset of IGOs, can influence the behavior of political actors by acting as knowledge brokers and through the creation, support, and shaping of intergovernmental negotiations and cooperation.

NGOs influence the environmental regimes by defining issues, swaying the policy of a key government, lobbying negotiating conferences, providing information and reporting services, proposing convention text, and monitoring the implementation of agreements. They have also sought to change the policies and structure of major international institutions, such as the World Bank and the WTO, with varying degrees of success. They have been more successful when the target institution depends on funding from a key state that the NGOs can influence and less successful when the institution is relatively independent or has no tradition of permitting NGO participation in its processes.

Corporations have been active in international relations longer than NGOs and can also influence regime creation and expansion. Corporations and industry groups utilize technical expertise, privileged access to certain government ministries, and political clout with legislative bodies in attempts to veto or weaken—or in some situations strengthen—particular aspects of a regime. They can also directly affect the ability of the international community to meet regime goals by their own actions. They are able to maximize their political effectiveness in shaping the outcome of a global environmental issue when they can avert negotiations on a binding regime altogether.

DISCUSSION QUESTIONS

1. In what ways do the domestic politics of various states influence their policies toward global environmental issues?

2. Why might some states feel that there are "winners" and "losers" in a particular proposal for international cooperation on the environment, even though it may be in the interest of all states?

3. Discuss different ways that international organizations can affect global environmental politics. To what extent have they contributed to regime formation?

4. What role do multilateral banks and bilateral development-assistance programs play in global environmental politics?

5. How have NGOs contributed to the development of international environmental policies and regimes?

6. What NGOs would you expect in a coalition on climate change? Biodiversity? Why? What governments would they be likely to befriend or criticize?

7. How do particular U.S. industries affect the position of the U.S. government on international environmental issues?

8. Do you believe it appropriate for environmental NGOs or industry groups to try to impact global environmental politics? Do you believe there are situations, stages in a regime's development, or issues when their involvement is appropriate? Inappropriate?

9. Develop a profile of any of the states frequently mentioned in this chapter—the United States, the European Union, China, India, Indonesia, Mexico, Brazil, and Malaysia—and describe how actively they play lead or blocking roles. Could you do the same for Russia? What other countries are conspicuously absent?

3

The Development of Environmental Regimes: Air Pollution, Hazardous Wastes, and Toxic Chemicals

The development of global environmental regimes often involves four processes or stages: issue definition, fact finding, bargaining on regime creation, and regime strengthening. Within each environmental issue, the sequencing of these stages and the length of time that each takes vary greatly. The stages are also not always distinct; the issue-definition stage may overlap the fact-finding stage, which may, in turn, overlap the bargaining stage. Nevertheless, examining negotiations through these stages or phases provides a framework that reduces some of the complexities of multilateral negotiation to a more manageable level for understanding and analysis.

Issue definition involves bringing the issue to the attention of the international community and identifying the scope and magnitude of the environmental threat, its primary causes, and the type of international action required to address the issue. An issue may be placed on the global environmental agenda by one or more state actors, by an international organization (usually at the suggestion of one or more members), or by a nongovernmental organization (NGO). The actors who introduce and define the issue often publicize new scientific evidence or theories, as they did for ozone depletion, transboundary air pollution, fisheries, toxic chemicals, and climate change. But issue definition may also involve identifying a radically different approach to international action on a problem, as it did for whaling, desertification, the hazardous waste trade, toxic chemicals, and endangered species.

Fact finding involves efforts to build consensus on the nature of the problem and the most appropriate international actions to address it through an international process of studying the science, economics, policy, and ethics surrounding the issue. Fact-finding efforts in different issue areas vary from well developed to nonexistent. A successful example would be a mediating international organization that brings key policy makers together in an attempt to establish a baseline of facts on which they can agree (as the United Nations Environment Programme [UNEP] did in building support for negotiations on persistent organic pollutants [POPs]). When there is no such mediated process of fact finding and consensus building, the facts may be openly challenged by states opposed to international action (this occurred early in international discussions regarding the ozone layer as well as with climate change).

The fact-finding stage often shades into the bargaining stage. Meetings ostensibly devoted to establishing the scope and seriousness of the problem may also try to spell out policy options. During this stage, a lead state may begin to advance a proposal for international action and try to build a consensus behind it. International cleavages and coalitions begin to form.

The nature of global environmental politics means that regime proponents face difficult questions during the bargaining process. To be truly effective, a regime to mitigate a global danger such as ozone depletion or climate change must have the participation of virtually all the states contributing to the problem. However, at some point, negotiators must determine whether to go ahead with a less than optimal number of signatories or to accommodate veto-state demands. Can a regime successfully address the problem without the participation of key nations? Or, can an agreement be considered a success if it has universal support but has been weakened by compromises with veto states?[1] The outcome of the bargaining process depends in part on the bargaining leverage and cohesion of the veto coalition. The veto states can prevent the creation of a strong international regime by refusing to participate in it, or they can weaken it by insisting on concessions that create a toothless regime. However, one or more key members of the veto coalition usually make major concessions that make regime creation or regime strengthening possible. In certain cases, a regime may form without key members of the veto coalition and thus remain relatively ineffective, as in the Kyoto Protocol. In other cases, as happened with forests, a regime cannot be created.

Regime building does not end with the signing and ratification of a global environmental convention. Once established, a regime can be strengthened, its central provisions made clearer or more stringent through further bargaining. Regime strengthening may occur because new scientific evidence becomes available, because political shifts occur in one or more major states, because new technologies make addressing the environmental issue less expensive, or because the existing regime is shown to be ineffective in bringing about meaningful actions to reduce the threat.

The process of regime strengthening is encouraged by the review process that takes place at the periodic meetings of the Conference of the Parties (COP) mandated by most global environmental conventions. Regime strengthening may take one of three forms:

1. The COP can adopt a protocol that establishes concrete commitments or targets, as in the cases of the parties to the Vienna Convention negotiating the Montreal Protocol, the parties to the United Nations Framework Convention on Climate Change (UNFCCC) negotiating the Kyoto Protocol, and the parties to the Convention on Long-Range Transboundary Air Pollution (LRTAP) negotiating protocols on sulfur dioxide (SO_2), nitrogen oxide (NO_x), and volatile organic compounds (VOCs).
2. The COP can formally amend the treaty. Examples include expanding the lists of chemicals controlled in the ozone and POPs regimes, uplisting the African elephant and big-leaf mahogany in the Convention on International Trade in Endangered Species of Wild Fauna and Flora (CITES), and establishing a moratorium on commercial whaling by the International Whaling Commission (IWC).
3. In some treaties, the COP can make decisions requiring important new actions by the parties without amending the convention or creating a new protocol, as in tightening the phaseout schedules in the Montreal Protocol, adding to the list of chemicals covered in the prior-informed-consent regime under the Rotterdam Convention, and adopting conservation measures by regional fisheries management organizations.

The adoption of protocols is often used to strengthen regimes that began with a framework convention. A framework convention does not establish detailed, binding commitments, such as targets or timetables for national actions, usually because the negotiators either could not or were not in a position to reach agreement on such measures. Rather, the framework convention requires sharing of information, study of the problem, and perhaps national plans or strategies aimed at reducing the threat. Creating a conference of the parties allows further negotiations on more concrete, binding actions that take the form of one or more protocols.

This two-stage approach allows the international community to establish the institutional and legal framework for regime strengthening even when no agreement exists on the specific actions to be taken. However, the framework convention-protocol approach has been criticized for taking too much time. For example, it took more than six years to negotiate the Climate Change Convention and the Kyoto Protocol, and it took more than seven years for the protocol to enter into force. Yet the two-stage approach is often a negotiating necessity. The weaker framework convention is chosen because that represents the limit of what veto states would accept. It is usually simply impossible to reach an agreement on targets and timetables because veto states, often due to domestic economic and political forces, dictate the slower pace.

Protocols to a framework convention are treated as an entirely new agreement and must be ratified by a certain number of signatories, as specified in the protocol itself, thus requiring that each party "opt in" via formal ratification if it agrees to be bound by the terms of the protocol.

Regime strengthening by formal amendment normally requires reaching decisions by consensus, with all parties agreeing, or if that is not possible, some treaties allow for approval by "supermajority" vote (usually two-thirds or three-fourths of those present and voting).[2] In many cases, states must then formally ratify the amendment, similar to the treaty itself. A state that chooses not to ratify the amendment is not bound by it. In some regimes, amendments do not require ratification to become binding commitments, but most of these treaties allow parties to opt out of the amendment if they do not support it. For example, CITES and the IWC allow amendment by two-thirds and three-fourths majorities, respectively, but both have opt-out provisions for amendments. The Basel Convention requires specific steps to "opt in" by parties willing to be bound by the amendment. The Stockholm Convention allows each state that ratifies the treaty to choose if it will be immediately bound when additional chemicals are added to the regime or if it wants to opt in each time controls are placed on a new chemical. These and other opt-out and opt-in arrangements allow changes to take effect, at least for some parties, without long ratification delays, but they also risk the blocking of effective action if key states do not support it.

Some environmental regimes allow parties to mandate new or stronger actions without a formal amendment or protocol procedure. These mechanisms exist to allow parties to change regime terms or technical details rapidly in response to new information. For example, the Montreal Protocol allows the Meeting of the Parties to adjust the targets and timetables for chemicals already controlled by the regime. Such decisions should be reached by consensus, but if all efforts at consensus fail, the treaty allows voting approval by a supermajority, although no vote has ever been held in the ozone regime. New ozone-depleting chemicals can be added to the protocol only by formal amendments, which require ratification. However, once a chemical is listed in the treaty, this innovative "adjustment mechanism" allows parties to strengthen the protocol's controls rapidly in response to new scientific information and technological developments. The Basel Convention allows "substantive decisions" to be made by a two-thirds majority of those present and voting, without any opt-out provision for those who oppose it, which is how the ban on the trade in hazardous wastes was adopted. The Stockholm Convention provides for the COP to change certain technical annexes and other aspects of the convention, with no opt-in or opt-out provisions (although changes to other aspects of convention require either formal amendments with ratifications or include opt-in or opt-out provisions). Many other regimes allow the COP to make binding decisions on matters related to regime implementation, operation, or other issues provided that the decisions do not alter the text of the treaty. In most cases these decisions are reached by consensus (albeit sometimes with some states not perfectly happy), but many regimes allow for supermajority votes if consensus cannot be reached.

In this chapter and chapters 4 and 5, we analyze eleven important global environmental issues on which there have been multilateral negotiations during the past forty years. Each issue is analyzed according to the stages of negotiation and the role of veto coalitions in shaping the outcomes of bargaining. This sample of issues represents a wide range of environmental and political circumstances. It shows the similarities and differences in the political processes and provides a basis for addressing the question of why states agree to cooperate on global environmental issues despite divergent interests. The cases are presented chronologically and by issue area. In this chapter we discuss regimes that address toxic pollutants and wastes (transboundary air pollution, the hazardous waste, and toxic chemicals). In Chapter 4 we discuss the stratospheric-ozone and climate regimes, which both address global atmospheric issues. In Chapter 5 we analyze six regimes that address species, natural resources, and habitat protection (whaling, trade in endangered species, biodiversity loss, fisheries depletion, desertification, and forests).

TRANSBOUNDARY AIR POLLUTION

Transboundary air pollution provides an example of an issue in which a veto coalition forced creation of a weak regime. Over time, however, new scientific evidence concerning the problem as well as internal political developments helped to change the position of key states, which then switched from being veto states to advocating a strong regime. This allowed for a significant strengthening of regime rules through a series of increasingly ambitious protocols. But the evidence had limited impact on the policies of other veto states. Although these states did not block the regime strengthening, they did not sign or ratify several key protocols, reducing their impact.

In the 1960s, emissions of SO_2 and NO_x became an international problem after developed countries raised the heights of their industrial chimneys by as much as six times so that pollutants would disperse into the atmosphere. Previously, industries had polluted only their immediate surroundings, but now they exported pollution great distances downwind, including across national borders.

The issue-definition stage for transboundary air pollution regime began in the late 1960s with Sweden as the lead actor. In 1968, Swedish scientist Svante Oden presented scientific evidence showing that the long-range transport of SO_2 emissions was the source of Swedish aquatic acidification. Sweden advanced its efforts to put long-range

PHOTO 3.1   Transboundary air pollution became a problem in the 1960s as the heights of industrial chimneys were increased by as much as six times so that pollutants would disperse into the atmosphere.

transboundary air pollution on the international agenda by offering to host the first UN environmental conference in 1972 in Stockholm.

Despite little or no interest on the part of most European governments, in 1972 Sweden and other Nordic states succeeded in persuading the Organization for Economic Cooperation and Development (OECD) to begin monitoring transboundary air pollution in Europe. The OECD monitoring program from 1972 to 1977 acted as an international fact-finding mission that confirmed the export of air pollution across national boundaries as a problem requiring international cooperation. Interest started to build following the 1975 Helsinki Conference on Security and Cooperation in Europe when the Soviet Union proposed a high-level East-West meeting to discuss the environment, energy, and transport. The Soviet Union's primary motivation was apparently to continue the process of détente in a policy realm other than human rights or arms control. The task of coordinating the discussions fell to the United Nations Economic Commission for Europe (UNECE), which includes eastern and western Europe, the entire area that comprised the former Soviet Union, the United States, and Canada.[3]

States that received imports of acid rain[4]—notably Sweden, Finland, and Norway—took the initiative to negotiate for stringent and binding regulations on emissions of SO_2 and NO_x.[5] The net exporters of acid rain formed a veto coalition, united mostly by their shared reliance on coal-fired power stations, which accounted for two-thirds of SO_2 emissions. This veto coalition included the United States, United Kingdom, Federal Republic of Germany (West Germany),[6] Belgium, and Denmark, with the United Kingdom and West Germany taking the lead role.[7] The veto coalition rejected agreements that included specific commitments to reduce emissions. Only after pressures from Norway and Sweden did West Germany and the United Kingdom accept vague obligations, as part of the framework convention, to reduce transboundary air pollution "as far as possible."

The LRTAP convention was agreed to in Geneva in 1979. Thirty-five countries signed the convention. Its goal is to limit, gradually reduce, and prevent air pollution, including long-range transboundary air pollution. Parties are required to develop policies and strategies to combat the discharge of air pollutants and to cooperate through information exchange, consultation, research, and monitoring.

LRTAP can be fairly described as both a framework convention and a "lowest-common-denominator" compromise. The convention established the principle that transboundary air pollution should be reduced as much as economically feasible and created a mechanism for collecting and disseminating information on air pollution flows, national reduction strategies, and abatement technologies. But LRTAP included no specific binding targets and timetables, and veto states rejected any commitment they thought might be significantly costly. LRTAP did represent two important advances, however. First, it marked acceptance by Eastern Europe and the Soviet Union of Western norms concerning transboundary air pollution as well as their participation in ongoing Western monitoring and reporting programs. Second, it created institutional mechanisms for information and, perhaps most importantly, for facilitating regime strengthening.[8]

LRTAP parties meet annually at sessions of the Executive Body (which is equivalent to a COP) to review issues, decide upon future priorities, and delineate a work plan for the coming year. Three main subsidiary bodies support the regime and report to the Executive Body. The Working Group on Effects focuses on the impacts of pollution. The Cooperative Programme for Monitoring and Evaluation of the Long-Range Transmission of Air Pollutants in Europe Steering Body oversees the program that undertakes atmospheric monitoring, emission inventories and projections, and other information. The Working Group on Strategies and Review is the principal negotiating body for the convention. It assesses scientific, technical, and policy information relevant to reviewing existing protocols and negotiates new protocols and revisions to existing ones (which the Executive Body considers for final adoption).

That process of regime strengthening started early in the 1980s when new and more convincing scientific evidence revealed significant damage to European forests and historic buildings from acid rain.[9] Some major exporters of acid rain, especially West Germany, began to change their stance in the early 1980s because of domestic concerns about forest death, which was especially pronounced in the Black Forest, and the new links to air pollution and acid rain. At the first meeting of the signatory parties in 1983, Norway and Sweden resumed their lead positions and proposed a 30 percent reduction in SO_2 emissions, from 1980 levels, by 1993. They were supported by three defectors from the veto coalition: West Germany, which was seeing forest damage and new public concern, and France and Italy, which had less reason to hold out because they relied heavily on nuclear and hydroelectric power.[10] The United States and the United Kingdom continued to oppose binding emissions reductions as part of LRTAP.

In a departure from diplomatic tradition, during the negotiations some states committed themselves to large unilateral reductions, attempting to set a standard by which other states would be judged and thus create momentum toward an agreement. At a conference in Ottawa in March 1984, ten states pledged to reduce SO_2 emissions by 30 percent and to substantially reduce other pollutants, especially nitrous oxide. The size and commitment of the "Thirty-Percent Club" helped to shift the talks, moving some other states toward agreement. The resulting Protocol on the Reduction of Sulfur Emissions or Their Transboundary Fluxes by at Least 30 Percent (also known as the Helsinki Protocol) was finalized in 1985 and signed by twenty-one states.[11] The protocol came into force in September 1987 but lacked the adherence of three major exporters of acid rain: the United States, the United Kingdom, and Poland, which together represented more than 30 percent of total world SO_2 emissions.[12] Though the remaining veto states could not block the agreement, their nonparticipation weakened it.

Nearly a decade later, increased scientific evidence and greater coherence among European states—as part of European Union (EU) strengthening—produced a second, updated sulfur protocol. The 1994 Protocol on Further Reduction of Sulfur Emissions (often called the Oslo Protocol) was immediately signed by twenty-eight parties to the convention, including the United Kingdom.[13] Unlike its predecessor, the agreement established different requirements for each country, the aim being to attain the greatest possible effect for the environment at the least overall cost. Retaining 1980 levels as a baseline and using an "effects-based" approach setting "target loads" based on calculated critical loads, states agreed to different emissions reductions by 2000, 2005, and 2010. Together, these cuts represented a 60 percent reduction in emissions levels.[14] The agreement also contained some specific, but not very rigorous, requirements for large combustion plants, mandating that parties control and reduce their sulfur emissions and ensure that sulfur depositions from these plants did not, in the long term, exceed critical loads—the level that the natural environment could absorb without sustaining excessive harm. This protocol came into force in August 1998. The United States and Poland remain nonparties, although Poland's 2004 entry into the European Union led it to support LRTAP in principle as well as implement certain pollution controls relevant to the agreement.

Following the first sulfur protocol, lead states initiated negotiations to reduce NO_x emissions. Austria, the Netherlands, Sweden, Switzerland, and West Germany advocated a 30 percent reduction in emissions by 1994. Other countries pressed for lower reductions. The United States argued that it should receive credit for previous abatement measures; otherwise, the new rules would essentially punish countries that had already taken steps to reduce air pollution. The resulting agreement, known as the 1988 Sofia Protocol, signed by twenty-three European countries, the United States, and Canada, reflected a compromise between the lead and veto states.[15] It required a freeze of NO_x emissions or transboundary flows at 1987 levels while allowing most countries to postpone compliance until 1994 through credits for reductions in previous years—a concession to U.S. demands. In this case, the veto states succeeded in weakening regime terms compared to the initial demand of the lead states.

Continuing to address new issues, in November 1991, the parties adopted a protocol on volatile organic compounds (i.e., hydrocarbons), a major air pollutant involved in the formation of ground-level ozone. The VOC negotiations included three broad sets of national positions. The majority of countries supported an across-the-board 30 percent reduction in VOC emissions. Countries with minimal ozone problems (the result of meteorological and geographical conditions), including the Soviet Union, Norway, and Canada, wanted only to reduce VOCs in regions responsible for transborder fluxes. Most Eastern European countries, meanwhile, would commit only to a freeze. Eventually, governments agreed to a VOC protocol that listed three forms of regulation (based on the three sets of national positions), and governments could choose which regulations they preferred.[16] Most signatories committed themselves to reducing their emissions by at least 30 percent by 1999, although with five different base years between 1984 and 1990 because countries were permitted to select their own base year.[17] The protocol currently has twenty-three parties, but not the United States or Russia. Once again, veto states won significant concessions regarding the measures they would need to implement or simply chose not to participate at all (although as in most other LRTAP issues, the United States already had meaningful air-pollution measures in place as part of the Clean Air Act and associated domestic legislation).

Following completion of the second sulfur protocol, outlined above, some lead states began pushing for negotiations on two new issues, emissions of heavy metals and POPs, which appeared at first to be outside LRTAP's focus. To create a sufficiently large coalition to ensure that negotiations would begin, the governments primarily interested in POPs negotiations and those more interested in talks on heavy metals agreed to support both initiatives—and that the negotiations should proceed simultaneously.

The Protocol on Heavy Metals was adopted on June 24, 1998, in Aarhus, Denmark.[18] It targets airborne emissions of three particularly harmful metals: cadmium, lead, and mercury. The protocol aims to cut emissions from industrial sources, combustion processes, and waste incineration. The protocol also requires that parties phase out leaded gasoline. It introduces measures to lower heavy-metal emissions from other products, such as mercury in batteries, and proposes the introduction of management measures for other mercury-containing products, such as thermometers, fluorescent lamps, dental amalgam, pesticides, and paint.

The Protocol on Persistent Organic Pollutants was also adopted on June 24, 1998, in Aarhus.[19] Canada and Sweden were the lead states on POPs, because POPs tend to bioaccumulate in the Arctic and have had an impact on Arctic populations in both countries.[20] Canada was so concerned about POPs that it agreed to support holding negotiations on metals, an issue on which it might otherwise have joined a veto coalition, in exchange for greater European support for talks on POPs. The protocol establishes binding controls on fifteen POPs: eleven pesticides, two industrial chemicals, and three by-products/contaminants. It bans the production and use of some products outright and schedules others for elimination at a later stage. The protocol also includes provisions for dealing with the wastes of products that will be banned. The negotiation and content of the Aarhus Protocol helped build support for creating a global POPs treaty, a process that resulted in the 2001 Stockholm Convention.

The formal fact-finding process began with a special task force established to investigate POPs, which met from 1991 to 1994. Assessments continued in 1995 and 1996 in the preparatory working group, and formal negotiations began in 1997. A significant issue in the negotiations was deciding which substances the protocol would cover. Most European countries, led by Sweden, advocated a large list of POPs. The United States, a veto state, favored a more limited list. Negotiators addressed the disagreement by establishing a set of criteria that they then used to screen the POPs. They ranked them according to toxicity and bioaccumulation potential and then assessed their long-range transport risk. While this resolved several issues, the United States blocked inclusion of several chemicals that remained in dispute, including pentachlorophenol. The United States argued that this wood preservative, which is widely regulated in Europe, should not be considered a POP and threatened not to sign the protocol if it included pentachlorophenol. The United States won primarily because Sweden and other countries thought it crucial for the United States to become a party to the protocol, if not immediately then in the future, and because the agreement included provisions for placing controls on additional POPs in the future.[21] The Aarhus POPs protocol currently has twenty-nine parties. The United States is not a party.[22]

By the mid-1990s evidence began to accumulate that the existing sulfur, NO_x, and VOC protocols were insufficient to achieve the goals of the original convention. Studies showed that the acidification problems remained severe, and about 70 percent of the population living in European cities equipped with monitoring stations were being exposed to pollution levels above EU air-quality standards.[23] As a result, in 1995, Sweden, which had recently joined the EU, began to press for the development of a more comprehensive EU acidification strategy. New scientific initiatives emerged within both LRTAP and EU frameworks aimed at producing the scientific groundwork for a new "multipollutant approach." These served as issue-definition and fact-finding mechanisms for a new idea to address multiple effects (acidification, tropospheric ozone formation, and eutrophication) and multiple pollutants (NO_x, VOCs, SO_2, and ammonia) within a single agreement.[24]

Negotiations on a possible eighth LRTAP protocol began in early 1999. Austria, Denmark, Finland, Netherlands, and Sweden supported fairly substantial reductions in emissions of the four pollutants (NO_x, VOCs, SO_2, and ammonia). Partly as a result of increasing domestic concern about air pollution, an early veto state and big emitter, the United Kingdom, joined the lead states and showed constructive negotiating flexibility.[25] The Eastern European countries, including Russia, however, were not much more constructive than in previous negotiations. The overall improvements in East-West relations in the post–Cold War 1990s had not produced greater flexibility. Similarly, the high emitters—Germany, France, and Italy—remained a potential veto coalition due to their concerns about the cost of large emissions reductions.[26]

Despite these initial positions, however, negotiations concluded successfully, and governments adopted the Protocol to Abate Acidification, Eutrophication and Ground-Level Ozone, in Gothenburg, Sweden, in December 1999.[27] The Gothenburg Protocol set 2010 emission limits for SO_2 and other sulfur compounds, NO_x, VOCs, and ammonia. Each country's individual ceilings depend on the impact that its emissions have on public health and on the vulnerability of the environment they pollute. Countries producing emissions with the most severe health or environmental impact and whose emissions are the cheapest to reduce will make the biggest cuts. Collectively, by 2010, Europe's sulfur emissions should be cut by 63 percent, NO_x emissions by 41 percent, VOC emissions by 40 percent, and ammonia emissions by 17 percent, compared to their 1990 levels. The protocol also set limits for specific emission sources (e.g., electricity production, dry cleaning, cars and trucks) and required that countries use the best available techniques to keep emissions down.

Most of the twenty-five countries that have ratified the 1999 Gothenburg Protocol (which include all the major EU countries and the United States) will meet their obligations.[28] Sulfur emissions have probably been reduced further than agreed (because of a reduction in the use of coal), and as a result, the acidification of forests and lakes has declined in many parts of Europe. However, the reduction of NO_x emissions from cars and trucks has proceeded more slowly than expected, and in large parts of Europe, exposure to particulate matter and ozone in the air remains higher than recommended by the World Health Organization.[29]

In December 2007, the LRTAP Executive Body instructed the Working Group on Strategies and Review to begin negotiations on revising the Gothenburg Protocol. Governments hope to complete negotiations in December 2010. The revised agreement will likely include more stringent 2020 limits for sulfur, NO_x, VOC, and ammonia emissions, emissions ceilings for particulate matter, updated technical annexes and guidance documents (which assist countries in implementing best technologies and practices), and nonbinding emission targets for 2050 to allow countries and corporations to make long-term plans.

Other current action within LRTAP includes reviewing (with the possibility of revising) the protocols on POPs and heavy metals, working toward ratification and implementation of the convention and its protocols across the entire UNECE region

TABLE 3.1   Total EU-27 LRTAP Convention Emissions

EU-27*	1990	1995	2000	2005	2006	Change 1990–2006
NO_x	17,101	14,576	12,581	11,406	11,199	–35%
CO	64,660	50,791	39,434	32,240	30,200	–53%
NMVOC	16,868	13,501	NA	9,596	9,391	–44%
SO_x	26,217	16,719	9,928	8,227	7,946	–70%
NH_3	5,118	4,395	N/A	4,068	4,001	–22%

			2000	2005	2006	Change 2000–2006
PM_{10}[†]			1,936	1,760	1,726	–11%
$PM_{2.5}$[†]			1,324	1,212	1,181	–10.8%

Chemicals measured:

NO_x: Nitrogen oxides

CO: Carbon monoxide

NMVOC: Nonmethane VOCs

SO_x: Sulfur oxides

NH_3: Ammonia

PM_{10}: Particles measuring ten micrometers or less (micrometer is a millionth of a meter)

$PM_{2.5}$: Particles measuring 2.5 micrometers or less

* EU-27: All twenty-seven EU member states
† Reporting of particulate matter emissions was requested only for years since 2000.

Data source: European Environment Agency, *Annual European Community LRTAP Convention Emission Inventory Report, 1990–2006,* EEA Technical Report No 7/2008 (Copenhagen: EEA, 2008), 7. Available at www.eea.europa.eu/publications/technical_report_2008_7.

(with special focus on Eastern Europe, the Caucasus, and Central Asia, including states that were once part of the Soviet Union and thus remain in the UNECE), and sharing its knowledge and information with other regions and global environmental regimes.

Like several other regimes negotiated in the 1970s and 1980s, the international regime for transboundary air pollution has lent itself to regular strengthening. LRTAP includes a regular review process that relies on increasing scientific evidence, an understanding of the environmental and health impacts of transboundary air pollution, and the negotiation of protocols. In the initial negotiations, a group of veto states, usually led by the United Kingdom, Germany, and/or the United States, either refused to join particular protocols or demanded that they be watered down. However, while the United States and Russia remain outside several of the regime's agreements, the increasing importance of sustainability and the precaution in EU policy, the EU's expanding size and influence, and greater scientific knowledge and public awareness of the dangers posed by air pollution have produced stronger agreements, such as the Gothenburg Protocol and its successor, and have begun to increase the number of states party to LRTAP and its most important protocols.

HAZARDOUS WASTE

Hazardous waste can be defined as any discarded material that can damage human health or the environment. It includes materials that consist of or contain heavy metals, toxic chemicals, infectious medical wastes, and corrosive, flammable, explosive, or radioactive substances. Estimates vary, but several billion tons of hazardous waste are generated each year. Industrialized countries generate the vast majority of this waste. It is generally accepted that about 10 percent of generated hazardous wastes are shipped across international boundaries. Most of this movement is between OECD countries, but an increasing amount of waste is being exported to developing countries.

As laws regulating hazardous waste disposal grew in OECD countries, individual firms sought cheaper sites for their disposal. As a consequence, North-South hazardous waste shipments increased significantly in the 1970s and 1980s. Developing countries, particularly the poorer states in Africa, Central America, South Asia, and the Caribbean, were tempted by offers of substantial revenues for accepting wastes but lacked the technology or administrative capacity to dispose of them safely. Some of this trade was legal, but much was not, with the wastes entering the countries covertly as a result of bribes to corrupt officials or labeled as something else (such as old, decaying batteries mixed with new ones or obsolete pesticides sold as new, safer alternatives). In some cases, businesses interested in recycling products that contain hazardous materials (such as the ship-breaking industry in South Asia or parts of the electronic waste, or **e-waste**, industry) ignored or prevented effective environmental and human-health protections.

During this period several notorious cases of illegal dumping also occurred. In one example, the cargo ship *Khian Sea* went to sea in 1986 in search of a disposal site for 14,000 tons of incinerator ash containing high levels of lead, cadmium, and other heavy metals. The ash came from incinerators in Philadelphia. It had previously gone to New Jersey, but New Jersey refused to accept any more after 1984. The ship spent almost two years at sea, looking for a place that would accept its cargo, during which it changed its name twice. In January 1988, it dumped 4,000 tons of ash in Haiti; it dumped the remaining 10,000 tons in November at different spots in the Atlantic and Indian oceans.

CARTOON 3.1   "Looks like they've heard of us."
© Los Angeles Times News Syndicate, reprinted with permission.

The issue-definition stage began in 1984 and 1985 when a UNEP working group of legal and technical experts developed a set of voluntary guidelines (the Cairo Guidelines) on the management and disposal of hazardous wastes. The guidelines specified prior notification of the receiving state of an export, consent by the receiving state prior to export, and verification by the exporting state that the receiving state has requirements for disposal at least as stringent as those of the exporting state.

These soft law guidelines did not satisfy some key actors, however, most notably African states that received the bulk of illegal hazardous waste exports. They characterized the international hazardous waste trade as a form of exploitation of poor and weak states by advanced countries and businesses and sought to define the issue as a problem that required an outright ban rather than regulation. This characterization drew support from NGOs and some officials in the industrialized states, particularly in Europe.

In 1988, parliamentarians from the European Community joined with representatives of sixty-eight developing states from Africa, the Caribbean, and the Pacific in demanding arrangements banning international trade in wastes. Developing countries, speaking together initially through the international coalition known as the **Non-**

Aligned Movement, also called for industrialized countries to prohibit waste exports to developing countries.[30]

The bargaining stage began in 1987 when UNEP, at the request of governments, organized formal negotiations on a global convention to control international trade in hazardous wastes. During the next eighteen months, major differences emerged between African and industrialized countries. African states wanted a total ban on such waste exports and export-state liability in the event of illegal traffic in wastes, in part because many developing countries did not possess the administrative, technical, or financial ability to enforce a ban on their own. Waste-exporting states wanted a convention that would permit the trade, providing that importing countries were notified and agreed to accept it—something known as an informed-consent regime.

The final bargaining stage took place in Basel, Switzerland, in March 1989, where the veto coalition, led by the United States, took advantage of the fact that exporting states could continue to find poor countries willing to accept wastes. At the time, the United States exported only about 1 percent of its hazardous wastes (although this was a large amount by weight), mostly to Canada and Mexico, but it led the veto coalition largely because of an ideological position that rejected limitations on its right to export. The veto coalition gave the ban supporters a choice: Accept an informed-consent regime or get none at all. The Organization of African Unity proposed amendments to ban the export of wastes to countries that lack the same level of facilities and technology as the exporting nations and to require inspection of disposal sites by UN inspectors, but many industrialized countries rejected the amendments.[31]

The 1989 Basel Convention on Control of Transboundary Movements of Hazardous Wastes and Their Disposal prohibited the export of hazardous wastes to countries with less advanced storage and disposal facilities unless the importing state had detailed information on the waste shipment and gave prior written consent.[32] Agreements between signatory and nonsignatory states were permitted, although they needed to conform to the terms of the convention. Critics charged that the convention did not go further than the existing regulations in most industrialized countries—regulations that had already failed to curb legal or illegal waste traffic. Moreover, the convention suffered from a lack of precision on key definitions, such as "environmentally sound" and even "hazardous wastes," and contained no liability provisions.[33]

As with other global environmental issues, the signing of the Basel Convention began a new phase of maneuvering and bargaining for a stronger regime. Surprisingly, however, this process did not take place entirely within the Basel Convention. In April 1989, soon after the formal adoption of the Basel Convention and three years before it entered into force, thirty states (not including the United States) and the European Community (EC) pledged to dispose of most of their wastes at home and to ban the export of hazardous wastes to countries that lacked the legal and technological capacity to handle them.[34] Later in 1989, the EC reached agreement, after extended negotiations, to ban waste shipments to sixty-eight former European colonies in Africa, the Caribbean, and the Pacific. The EC had sought an exception for exports to countries with "adequate technical capacity," but developing countries insisted on a total ban.[35] This concession by the EC likely reflected particular concerns of several key states. This included a French foreign policy decision to prioritize cultural and economic ties with France's former colonies, all of which opposed waste exports to Africa; heavy pressure on the United Kingdom from its former African colonies, which also opposed waste exports to Africa; and West Germany's lack of interest in exporting to developing countries.

In perhaps the most important development outside the Basel regime, in January 1991, twelve African states signed the Bamako Convention, which would ban all imports of hazardous wastes into their countries. To date, twenty-three African countries are party to the convention, which underlined African determination to end the international hazardous waste trade.[36] The Bamako Convention, combined with the other unilateral and multilateral policies to ban hazardous waste exports to Africa, initially created a stronger hazardous waste regime outside the Basel Convention than within it, at least until the Basel Convention was strengthened.[37]

The Basel Convention came into effect in May 1992 as a weak regime, without ratification by any of the major exporting states that composed the victorious veto coalition during the negotiations.[38] In less than two years, however, growing demands for a complete ban on hazardous waste trade would transform the Basel Convention into a stronger regime. By early 1994, more than one hundred countries had passed domestic legislation banning the import of hazardous wastes, although not all of them had the administrative capacity to do so unilaterally.[39] Some of the credit must go to Greenpeace, which published a report documenting 1,000 cases of illegal toxic waste exports.[40] Even the United States, although not a party to the regime, signaled it would support a ban on hazardous waste exports if it exempted scrap metal, glass, textiles, and paper, which are widely traded for recycling.[41]

At the second COP (COP-2), a broad coalition pressed for a complete ban on hazardous waste exports from OECD countries to non-OECD countries, including those exported for recycling.[42] They argued that shipments of recyclables often were not recycled but just dumped in a developing country and that the OECD countries would never reduce their waste as long as they could ship it to developing countries.

The Group of 77 (G-77), the lead coalition, called for a ban to go into effect immediately. Denmark was only a step behind, calling for a ban to begin in 1995. The United Kingdom, Australia, Germany, the Netherlands, Japan, Canada, and the United States wanted to exempt recyclables. China and the former socialist states of Central and Eastern Europe came out in favor of the G-77 proposal. Greenpeace also made an important contribution to the G-77 position. Reporting on a seven-year study that closely examined more than fifty recycling operations in non-OECD countries, Greenpeace produced concrete evidence of widespread dumping of hazardous wastes that had been falsely labeled and shipped as "recyclables"[43] as well as many shipments of recyclables that had not been recycled at all but just dumped in developing countries.[44]

Despite intensive lobbying by exporting countries, particularly in support of allowing bilateral agreements on hazardous waste exports for recycling, the G-77 remained firm, agreeing to negotiate only on the timetable for implementing a ban. Confronted with non-OECD unity, the veto coalition began to divide, with some withdrawing their opposition. The veto coalition was also weakened because several veto states, including the United States, had not ratified the Basel Convention itself and, as nonparties, were technically outside the decision-making process. They could speak in opposition to the ban, but they could not vote, and their views did not officially count as opposing the emerging consensus. When debate ended, COP-2 approved the ban. The remaining veto states obtained nothing more than a delay in the full implementation of a total export ban.

FIGURE 3.1   Evolution of transboundary movements of waste among parties to the Basel Convention

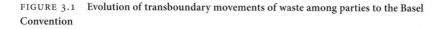

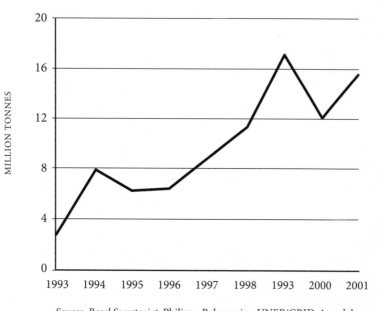

Source: Basel Secretariat; Philippe Rekacewicz, UNEP/GRID-Arendal, reproduced from http://maps.grida.no/go/graphic/trends-in-transboundary-movement-of-waste-among-parties-to-the-basel-convention.

COP-3 significantly strengthened the ban by adopting it as a formal amendment to the convention (it had been approved in a far less legally binding form at COP-2). The Ban Amendment prohibits export of hazardous wastes for final disposal or recycling from countries listed in Annex VII of the convention (currently the EU, the OECD, and Liechtenstein) to non–Annex VII countries. The Ban Amendment does not use an OECD/non-OECD distinction and thus is not in itself a barrier for developing countries to retain the option of receiving OECD hazardous wastes because they can do so by joining Annex VII. The amendment needs to be ratified by three-fourths of the parties present at COP-3 in 1995 to enter into force. By late 2009, this still had not occurred.

The most controversial aspect of the Ban Amendment is the prohibition on exports of wastes intended for recovery and recycling, such as scrap metal. Many industrialized countries, as well as an increasing number of developing ones (including China and India), have significant economic interests in the maintenance of a lucrative trade in wastes for recycling—including ships, electronics, metals, glass, papers, and some chemicals. As a result, not only has the Ban Amendment not entered into force, but the total amount of waste shipments rose sharply during the first decade of the convention's existence (see Figure 3.1).

Another debate regarding the Ban Amendment centered on the question of which wastes were defined as "hazardous" for the purposes of recycling and recovery and thus covered within the scope of the convention. To remedy this situation, a COP-authorized technical working group drew up lists of banned and exempted wastes. COP-4 approved these lists; in doing so, it diffused the industry argument that nobody knew what the ban was banning. Supporters of the Ban Amendment hoped that the new lists would speed its ratification and implementation. Countries that had not ratified the amendment still supported the lists, as they provided greater clarity to other elements of the convention as well as the ban.

Parties have also worked to strengthen the convention by addressing the issue of liability. In December 1999, COP-5 adopted the Basel Protocol on Liability and Compensation, which addresses developing countries' concerns that they lack sufficient funds and technologies to prevent or cope with the consequences of illegal dumping or accidental spills. The protocol seeks to deter these by establishing provisions for determining liability and compensation for damage resulting from the legal or illegal transnational movement of hazardous wastes. By late 2009, the liability protocol had received only nine out of the twenty instruments of ratification necessary for entry into force.[45]

COP-6, held in Geneva in December 2002, agreed upon a prioritized plan for implementing the Basel Convention over the next decade. The plan emphasized the need to tackle priority waste streams such lead-acid batteries, **polychlorinated biphenyls**

(PCBs), used oil, electronics, and obsolete pesticides. Parties also streamlined the institutional architecture of the convention, created a compliance mechanism to review and assist implementation, and confirmed the role of the Basel Convention regional centers to facilitate implementation in developing countries through building capacity, educating the public, collecting data, reporting, promoting environmentally sound waste management, easing the transfer of cleaner production technologies, and helping to train customs officials. There are now fourteen such centers located in different parts of Africa, Asia, eastern Europe, and Latin America. Additional centers may be created in the future.[46]

At COP-7 in 2004, parties adopted a variety of decisions on expanding or implementing the regime, including new technical guidelines to assist industry and government officials in managing hazardous waste in an environmentally sound manner. Guidelines are now in place for nearly twenty different types of hazardous wastes, including organic solvents, waste oil, biomedical and health-care wastes, POPs, PCBs, a variety of chemicals, obsolete ships, and mobile phones. Financial issues remained a serious concern, however. Delegates from some developing countries told observers that efforts spent developing and revising the technical guidelines mattered little to most developing countries since they did not have the financial resources or cadres of technically trained personnel to administer and enforce them.[47]

Only a few months before COP-8 convened in Nairobi, Kenya, in November 2006, an egregious incident of hazardous waste dumping in Côte d'Ivoire served to highlight the original purpose of the convention and the dangers associated with hazardous waste. An old chemical tanker carrying more than four hundred metric tons of heavily contaminated wash water (water used to clean its holds) sailed to Nigeria to deliver a different cargo and then docked in Abidjan, a port city of 5 million people and the economic (and former official) capital of Côte d'Ivoire. Under the cover of night, the contaminated wastewater was transferred to tanker trucks belonging to a local company, which then dumped it at sixteen different open-air sites around the city, many near water supplies or fields growing food. At least fifteen people died, thousands were hospitalized, and over 100,000 sought medical treatment, overwhelming local hospitals. Many fishing, vegetable, and small livestock activities were halted, associated businesses closed, and workers laid off. Protests erupted over suspicions of (unproven) government corruption in the scandal.[48]

The Côte d'Ivoire incident highlighted the absence of effective tracking systems for the transboundary movement of hazardous waste and concern that these shipments, both legal and illegal, might be producing more environmental damage than recognized. COP-8 strongly condemned the incident and called for immediate technical and financial assistance from able member states to support implementation of an emergency plan developed by Côte d'Ivoire.[49]

In addition to addressing the Abidjan incident, COP-8 took more than thirty decisions concerning issues on the normally crowded COP agenda. Among the issues discussed were many that build on work from previous COPs, including continued implementation of the strategic plan, operations of the Basel Convention regional centers, updates to technical guidelines, adoption of new guidelines on certain chemicals wastes, achieving greater synergies and cooperation with other, related conventions, the membership and work of the Compliance Committee, the secretariat's budget, and the 2007–2008 work plan for the convention up to the next COP.

COP-8 also included serious discussions of electronic waste, or e-waste. E-waste includes discarded, broken, or obsolete electronic devices, including computers, printers, and monitors; televisions and phones; CD, DVD, and MP3 players; and their parts and components. Much of this equipment contains hazardous materials, including heavy metals such as lead, cadmium, beryllium, and a variety of toxic chemicals, including certain flame retardants. Processing e-waste, particularly in developing countries, can cause serious pollution and health problems if proper care is not taken to protect workers and prevent release of the pollutants into the environment via direct dumping, poorly designed and operated landfills, or incinerator exhaust or ashes.

At COP-8, delegates agreed on the importance of effectively managing this waste, large quantities of which get dismantled or disposed of in developing countries. However, some expressed concern for the convention's ability to mandate particular controls on e-waste effectively or to provide the financial resources necessary to improve e-waste management in many developing countries. Some parties supported using the convention to seek reductions in the amount of e-waste produced by requiring effective recovering and recycling programs that would prevent the items from entering the waste stream or being shipped to developing countries where they are broken apart and harvested for materials. While the meeting could not reach consensus on particular commitments to minimize e-waste production or mandate how it is handled, it did agree on a general declaration to symbolize the importance of the issue and announce that the regime would begin addressing it.[50]

The ninth meeting of the COP to the Basel Convention convened in June 2008 in Bali, Indonesia.[51] Among other decisions, the parties adopted five technical guidelines and an overall guidance document for the environmentally sound management of used and end-of-life mobile phones. The guidelines address awareness raising on design considerations relevant to reducing hazardous waste and improving recycling, collecting used and end-of-life mobile phones, transboundary movement of collected phones, refurbishment, and recovering and recycling material from end-of-life mobile phones. The guidelines built on, and resulted from, the Mobile Phone Partnership Initiative, launched in 2002, in which mobile phone manufacturers and service providers

PHOTO 3.2   A Chinese child sits among a pile of wires and e-waste. Children can often be found dismantling e-waste containing many hazardous chemicals known to be potentially very damaging to children's health.
© Greenpeace/Natalie Behring.

in partnership with the Basel Convention worked to develop and promote the environmentally sound management of end-of-life mobile phones.

COP-9 also moved to bring this process to e-wastes. While some have expressed concern that involving companies would weaken e-waste efforts, others believed that the market image, financial interests, and technical expertise of many computer and electronic companies could form the basis for productive partnerships similar to the mobile phone experience (which some had viewed as a kind of experiment). To this end, COP-9 agreed to establish the Partnership for Action on Computer Equipment patterned after the mobile phone process, which will promote dialogue among governments, industry, NGOs, and academic experts; develop technical guidelines and a certification program for environmentally sound repair, refurbishment, and recycling of computer equipment and components; offer expert advice and participation in relevant initiatives; and work with the Basel Convention and its parties to develop and promote solutions.[52]

With regard to long-term planning, COP-9 established a process to review the effectiveness of the convention, its extant implementation, and the current long-term strategic plan, which runs through 2010, and to initiate drafting of a new strategic plan. During the COP, many parties called the current "Strategic Plan to 2010" a success in providing guidance to parties, the secretariat, regional centers, other conventions,

NGOs, and corporations regarding the regime's priorities, where to focus efforts, and how to allocate limited resources.[53] However, some delegates noted that many activities of the current plan had not been carried out due to inadequate financial resources; thus, the success of a new plan would depend on the provision of adequate financial and technical assistance both to the Basel Convention regional centers and to developing countries to assist them in implementing the convention. COP-9 made some progress on issues related to long-term financing, but resolution of several key issues, in particular the financing of Basel Convention regional centers, was deferred to future meetings.

COP-9 also included a renewed effort to move forward on the Ban Amendment, which had yet to enter into force, but no final agreement could be reached. At the end of the meeting, in the absence of a substantive agreement, the president of the COP issued a "president's statement" urging parties to cooperate on a series of steps that would achieve the ban's core objective—to protect vulnerable populations from the environmental and health threats posed by hazardous wastes—which all parties supported. These initiatives seek to improve national capacities to monitor and trace shipments of hazardous wastes as well as to monitor, detect, and control illegal traffic; to establish criteria for classifying materials as hazardous in relation to the ban; and to require a prior informed consent (PIC) procedure and use of the precise custom codes.[54]

Some of the strongest supporters of the Ban Amendment had hoped COP-9 would resolve several key legal and technical debates obstructing the amendment, issue a strong statement calling for ratification, or even declare the amendment in force. Such outcomes were unrealistic.[55] The president's statement received support from many parties (including some that had already ratified the amendment and some that have stated they will not ratify it) as the first opportunity for open discussion on the underlying intent of the Ban Amendment in many years. Switzerland and Indonesia offered to jointly initiate a follow-up process that could contribute to the more substantive and productive discussion at COP-10.

Finally, perhaps, COP-9's most lasting achievement was the formal decision to build synergies with the Rotterdam and Stockholm conventions. Basel COP-8 and the COPs of the Rotterdam and Stockholm conventions created an ad hoc joint working group to prepare joint recommendations on enhanced cooperation and coordination among the three conventions at the administrative and programmatic levels for consideration by their respective COPs for possible adoption and implementation. The central idea is to create and implement more effective global policy on hazardous chemicals and to reduce expenses by getting the three conventions, their secretariats, and their subsidiary bodies to coordinate implementation activities, eliminate duplicated efforts and staff positions, and produce reinforcing synergies that enhance the three interrelated regimes.

Basel COP-9 was the first to address these recommendations, and after some debate the parties agreed to adopt the recommendations in their entirety. The extensive recommendations focused largely on organizational issues, including establishment of joint secretariat services with regard to information management, public awareness, budget cycles, and common administrative functions. Many considered this a significant step toward streamlining international processes and saving resources for implementation. The recommendations also advocated better national and international coordination on issues common to the three conventions, cooperative use of regional centers, **joint implementation** efforts in developing countries, synchronized and simplified reporting under the regimes, coordinated COPs, and convening a joint COP to decide how to implement the recommendations. At the same time, the working group emphasized the autonomy of each convention, "alleviating the concerns expressed in the past by some developing countries that by creating strong links with the other conventions the Basel Convention might lose its thrust and uniqueness."[56]

Following its approval by the Basel COP-9 in 2008, the proposal went to the fourth meeting of the COP to the Rotterdam Convention in October 2008 and then to the fourth meeting of the COP to the Stockholm Convention in May 2009. Both COPs approved the recommendations unanimously and without amendment, and a historic joint COP of all three conventions will convene in February 2010 to outline their implementation. Implementing these proposals will likely enhance the effectiveness of the conventions, promote cost-savings at the national and secretariat level, and allow more resources and attention to shift toward implementation. Indeed, in general these types of steps help address several obstacles to effective environmental policy, which will be discussed further in Chapter 6, including poorly designed, uncoordinated, or contradictory regimes, overburdened national bureaucracies, and inadequate resources. This process could also serve as a model that stimulates similar efforts in other areas or even broader discussions on other issues (e.g., species or habitat protection) or on overlapping issue areas (e.g., deforestation and climate change).

In conclusion, the relatively strong global regime for managing hazardous waste and its international movement is far different from the original weak regime created in 1989. The expanded Basel Convention has been central to the elimination of some of the worst forms of toxic-waste dumping by industrialized countries in developing ones, contributed to improved management of certain hazardous wastes, and put into place frameworks, guidelines, and partnerships that, if implemented, could portend dramatic improvements in the future. The evolution of the Basel Convention shows how veto power can dissipate under pressure from a strong coalition that includes all the developing countries, along with the added support of various key OECD countries. The pressure and publicity generated by the activities of several key NGOs, especially Greenpeace and the Basel Action Network, has also had an impact on overriding the veto coalition against restricting the waste trade. Once the hazardous waste-trade issue became a political symbol uniting developing countries behind the demand for a complete ban, it overcame the leverage of waste exporters that had weakened the regime in 1989. And once the regime branched out toward selected efforts to help reduce the creation of certain wastes and improve the management of all wastes, it expanded its network of supports and increased its relevance.

Yet the hazardous waste regime faces many challenges. Both the production and transboundary movement of hazardous waste continue to grow. While many promising policy initiatives and economic incentives have emerged to promote more effective recycling of some aspects of this waste, some central goals of the current regime—to reduce the amount of waste produced, limit its movement, and induce its environmentally sound management—have become more difficult to achieve. In addition, the increasing industrialization of many developing countries could create significant waste movements between them. Moreover, as these changes occur, the Ban Amendment and Liability Protocol still have not received enough ratifications to enter into force, and the United States still has not ratified the Basel Convention. Long-standing issues, such as the export of hazardous wastes for recycling, and issues that have gained increasing recognition in the last decade, including e-waste and the dismantling of toxic ships, will require increasing attention, as will the newest challenge of dramatically and effectively increasing cooperation and coordination between the Basel, Rotterdam, and Stockholm conventions. Finally, parties must continue to grapple with the challenge of securing sufficient funding to support key regime priorities, to expand the Basel Convention regional centers so they can become nodes for technical assistance and implementation activities for all the chemicals conventions, and to assist developing countries in implementing key aspects of the regime.

TOXIC CHEMICALS

The systematic development and use of chemicals for commercial purposes began after World War II. Of the 6 to 7 million chemical substances known in industry and scientific research, close to 70,000 have been produced for regular use in the industrial, agriculture, and service sectors.[57] Not all chemicals are hazardous, of course, but toxic chemicals are produced or used in virtually every country in the world. In the United States, more than 2,000 are usually listed under the Toxic Substances Control Act.[58] About 80 percent of chemicals are used in developed countries, but consumption in developing countries is increasing rapidly. Toxic chemicals include poisons, carcinogens, teratogens (affecting offspring), mutagens (affecting genes), irritants, narcotics, and chemicals with dermatological effects. Toxics are released into the environment through the normal use of certain products (e.g., pesticides and fertilizers), industrial and manufacturing practices that involve or produce hazardous chemicals, leakage from wastes, mismanagement, accidents, and intentional dumping. Once they have been dispersed into the environment, the complete cleanup of many toxic chemicals is difficult, sometimes impossible, and their harmful effects can continue for many years.

A number of international treaties, international organizations, and soft-law mechanisms address the threats that toxic chemicals pose to human health and the environment. These include the 1998 Rotterdam Convention on the Prior Informed Consent Procedure for Certain Hazardous Chemicals and Pesticides in International Trade, the 1998 Aarhus Protocol on Persistent Organic Pollutants (a protocol to LRTAP, discussed earlier in this chapter), the Inter-Organization Programme on the Sound Management of Chemicals (IOMC), the Intergovernmental Forum on Chemical Safety (IFCS), the Strategic Approach to International Chemicals Management (SAICM) initiative, UNEP Chemicals, the Food and Agriculture Organization's (FAO) work on hazardous pesticides, and elements of the Basel Convention. But perhaps the most important part of the global chemicals regime, and the focus of this section, is the 2001 Stockholm Convention on Persistent Organic Pollutants, the only chemicals treaty that includes binding global controls on the production, use, and emissions of specific toxic chemicals.

The issue-definition phase for toxic chemicals began in the 1960s when concern started to grow about potentially negative impacts from pesticides and other chemicals. Instrumental in this process were groundbreaking publications, especially Rachel Carson's *Silent Spring*, and high-profile accidents, such as the 1968 tragedy in Yosho, Japan, where many people were poisoned after eating rice contaminated with high levels of PCBs. In the late 1960s and early 1970s, new risk assessments led many industrialized countries to adopt domestic regulations on a relatively small set of hazardous chemicals. The United States, for example, banned DDT in 1972 and initiated controls on PCBs in 1976.[59] During this period, the OECD became one of the first international organizations to address toxic chemicals. Its initial efforts focused on information exchange and improving scientific and policy measures in the industrialized countries.

Stimulated in part by work done on hazardous chemicals at the 1972 United Nations Conference on the Human Environment,[60] governments adopted several multilateral agreements in the 1970s and early 1980s to help protect oceans, regional seas, and rivers from dumping and pollution.[61] In 1976, UNEP created the International Register of Potentially Toxic Chemicals to gather, process, and distribute information on hazardous chemicals. The FAO and UNEP led the development of the 1985 International Code of Conduct for the Distribution and Use of Pesticides and the 1987 London Guidelines for the Exchange of Information on Chemicals in International Trade. Unfortunately, many developing countries lacked the regulatory infrastructure that would enable them to use the information made available through these initiatives.[62]

In 1989, amendments to the FAO Code of Conduct and the UNEP London Guidelines created a voluntary prior informed consent (PIC) procedure to help countries, especially developing countries, learn about chemicals that had been banned or severely restricted in other countries so that they could make informed decisions before they allowed them as imports. Although the voluntary PIC system was seen as a victory for NGOs, which had long called for its adoption, and for developing countries, because they hoped it would allow them to regulate such imports, many believed that a voluntary system would prove insufficient.[63]

The fact-finding process coincided with the Earth Summit in Rio when delegates agreed to devote an entire chapter in Agenda 21 to chemicals. Among other actions, Agenda 21 called on states to create a mandatory PIC procedure and to improve coordination among the many national agencies and international organizations working on chemicals or related issues. To this end, governments created the IFCS in 1994 to address coordination among governments and the IOMC in 1995 to address coordination among international organizations.[64] The fact-finding process continued in these two bodies.

In response to Agenda 21, UNEP and FAO jointly convened formal global negotiations in 1995 with the goal of adopting a binding PIC procedure. The result was the 1998 Rotterdam Convention on the Prior Informed Consent Procedure for Certain Hazardous Chemicals and Pesticides in International Trade, which mandates that parties export certain toxic chemicals only with the informed consent of the importing party.[65]

During this period, concern had also grown regarding a particular set of toxic chemicals known as persistent organic pollutants, or POPs. Scientists and policy makers usually define POPs as possessing four key characteristics: toxicity, persistence, bioaccumulation, and long-range environmental transport. Some believed that international action might be warranted to limit their production and use.

POPs are among the most toxic pollutants released into the environment. Observed or suspected impacts of POPs on wildlife and humans include reproductive disorders, birth defects, cancers, developmental impairment, damage to central and peripheral nervous systems, immune system impairment, and endocrine disruption.[66] POPs are also stable and persistent compounds that resist photolytic, chemical, and biological degradation. This means that once released into the environment, most POPs remain toxic for years before breaking down.

POPs also bioaccumulate. Once ingested, they are readily absorbed by, and remain in, the fatty tissue of living organisms. Over time, POPs concentrations can build up in animals and people, potentially reaching 10,000 times the background levels found

FIGURE 3.2　Migration of POPs

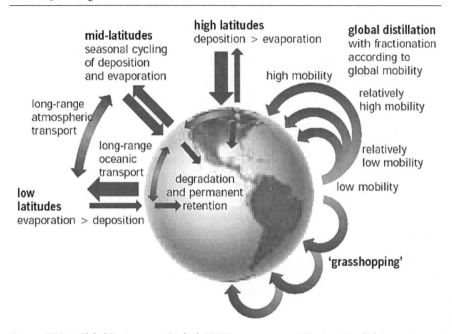

Source: GEO-3: Global Environment Outlook, UNEP, www.unep.org/Geo/geo3/english/ fig212.htm.

in the surrounding environment. Fish, birds, mammals, and humans can absorb high concentrations of POPs quickly if they eat multiple organisms in which POPs have already accumulated. Mammals and people can then pass these chemicals to their offspring through breast milk.

Finally, POPs engage in long-range transport across national borders and can be found in ecosystems, waterways, animals, and people thousands of kilometers from the nearest location of their production, use, or release. POPs travel through air currents, waterways, migrating animals, food chains, and a process known as the "grasshopper effect," in which POPs released in one part of the world can, through a repeated process of evaporation and deposit, be transported through the atmosphere to regions far away from the original source (see Figure 3.2).

In the 1980s and 1990s, Canada and Sweden played lead roles in the issue-definition and fact-finding phases by both supporting POPs research and putting POPs on the agenda of several international forums. Much of this work had been initiated after a study found very high levels of certain POPs in wildlife and even the breast milk of Inuit women in northern Canada, thousands of miles from the nearest source of emissions. These findings and subsequent studies added a normative component to the

CARTOON 3.2   "I ordered
mussels, not PCB, DDT, dieldrin, aldrin and lindane."
Source: "'The Dirty Dozen'
and Others," UN Atlas of the
Oceans, www.oceans
atlas.org/servlet/CDSServlet
?status=ND0yNjAxJjY9ZW
4mMzM9KiYzNz1rb3M~.

issue-definition phase because POPs were now seen as a threat to the food chain, and
thus the cultural survival, of the Inuit.[67]

The issue-definition phase reached a turning point in May 1995 when UNEP's Governing Council called for an international assessment of twelve POPs known as the
"dirty dozen": nine pesticides (aldrin, chlordane, dieldrin, DDT, endrin, furans, heptachlor, mirex, and toxaphene); two industrial chemicals (PCBs and hexachlorobenzene, which is also a pesticide); and dioxins and furans, two unintentionally produced
by-products created by burning certain substances or by other industrial activities.
UNEP acted in response to growing scientific data regarding the transnational movement and toxicity of POPs, increasing evidence of POPs in various food chains, and
the cumulative political efforts of the lead states, NGOs, and representatives of the
Inuit and other indigenous peoples whose traditional food sources were becoming
contaminated by POPs.[68]

In response to UNEP's call, the IOMC established a UNEP/IFCS ad hoc working
group on POPs to proceed with fact finding. In June 1996, the working group concluded that scientific evidence supported international action to reduce the risks posed
by POPs. In February 1997, the UNEP Governing Council endorsed this conclusion
and authorized formal negotiations aimed at creating a global POPs treaty.

The fact-finding process continued in eight regional workshops on POPs that UNEP and the IFCS convened in preparation for the negotiations. More than 138 countries participated in the workshops, which greatly increased awareness of POPs issues, particularly in developing countries and countries with economies in transition.[69] Preparations also included studying previous negotiating processes on chemicals and specific aspects of the Rotterdam PIC Convention, the Aarhus POPs Protocol to LRTAP, the Montreal Protocol, and other international treaties to see what lessons could be learned to help governments create an effective regime.[70]

The bargaining process began in June 1998 and lasted three years. Individual sessions included five official weeklong meetings of the Intergovernmental Negotiating Committee (INC), the main negotiating body; two meetings of the Criteria Expert Group, which focused on developing procedures for identifying and adding new chemicals to the treaty; a formal intersessional consultation on issues related to financial and technical assistance (FTA); numerous formal contact groups; and countless informal consultations.[71]

During the negotiations, the EU, Canada, NGOs, and representatives of northern indigenous peoples played the lead role in support of a strong regime. Indeed, the POPs negotiations were notable for the prominent role given to the Inuit and other northern indigenous peoples to speak to delegates and the press concerning the threats that POPs posed not only to their health but also to their cultural heritage of subsistence hunting and fishing.

Countries playing veto roles shifted according to the issue in question. Interestingly, no governments opposed the creation of strong controls on the dirty dozen. The issue-definition and fact-finding phases, combined with efforts that took place before the negotiations, produced a ringing endorsement at INC-1 of the need for global regulations. This reflected a general acceptance of the science regarding POPs and the relatively modest adjustment costs given that industrialized countries had already established significant controls on the dirty dozen.

With regard to specific issues, the EU and NGOs supported creating controls on chemicals beyond the dirty dozen (as was done in the Aarhus POPs Protocol to LRTAP), but these efforts were opposed by a broad veto coalition that included many developing countries, the United States, Japan, and companies that made the chemicals in question. African countries and health-related NGOs strongly opposed the elimination of DDT because its use was essential for battling mosquitoes that spread malaria (malaria kills nearly 1 million people a year).[72] This position quickly gained near-universal support. Although there was general agreement on the need to phase out the rest of the dirty dozen, Australia, Brazil, China, India, Indonesia, the United States, and other countries stated they needed individual exemptions for very specific uses of certain chemicals, at least for a short period. Negotiators quickly agreed on the concept of exemptions, although a variety of views existed on which chemicals or uses deserved such exemptions and how they should be administered. As they had in previous negotiations on biodiversity, climate, and desertification (see chapters 4 and 5), industrialized and developing countries disagreed strongly on the mechanism for providing financial assistance. Resolving these and other issues required difficult and detailed negotiations.

The resulting 2001 Stockholm Convention on Persistent Organic Pollutants seeks to protect human health and the environment by eliminating or reducing the production, use, trade, and emission into the environment of twelve POPs.[73] In particular, all parties must eliminate the production and use of aldrin, chlordane, dieldrin, endrin, heptachlor, hexachlorobenzene, mirex, PCBs, and toxaphene. Parties must restrict the production and use of DDT except for that needed for disease-vector control, especially against malaria mosquitoes, when there are no suitable and affordable alternatives.[74] Parties must minimize the creation and release of dioxins and furans into the environment. To ensure an effective phaseout process, parties must also ban the import or export of POPs controlled under the convention (except for narrowly defined purposes or environmentally sound disposal); promote the use of the best available technologies and practices for reducing emissions, replacing existing POPs, and managing POP wastes; and take steps to prevent the development and commercial introduction of new POPs.

Although there was no debate on the need to control the dirty dozen, as noted above several prominent countries supported the continued but limited use of certain POPs for selected purposes if economic, safety, or other conditions made an immediate phaseout too difficult. For example, Russia, the United States, and many other countries noted that PCBs were once widely used in electrical transformers and other equipment, and although equipment using new PCBs was no longer produced, hundreds of thousands of tons of PCBs were still in use in existing equipment. Australia and China supported using mirex to control termites in remote areas. Botswana and China supported continued use of chlordane to protect wooden dams and certain other structures from termites. Other parties argued they would need small amounts of aldrin for use as an insecticide during the transition to alternatives.

Therefore, in addition to the broad health-related exemption granted for DDT, a specific exemption for PCBs allows countries to maintain existing equipment containing PCBs until 2025. Parties are also allowed to exercise "country-specific exemptions" that permit the continued use of small amounts of specific POPs for essential applications for five years (for such things as termite control), after which an extension must be granted by the COP.

One of the most important factors in the long-term effectiveness of a global environmental regime is the process it contains for increasing the scope and strength of its environmental protections. For a treaty to be effective over time, it must be able to adapt and grow in response to new information. However, it can be difficult for negotiators to balance the competing legitimate concerns and preferences relevant to this issue (e.g., a preference for rapid regime flexibility versus a preference for sovereign control of the amendment procedure, a preference for a strong precautionary approach versus preference for a strong risk-analysis or cost-benefit approach, and preference for a system that allows for vigilant expansion of environmental protection versus a system that provides stable expectations for governments and corporations).

To this end, the Stockholm Convention establishes scientifically based criteria and a specific step-by-step procedure for identifying, evaluating, and adding chemicals to the convention. This critical feature of the regime, which ensures its continued relevance beyond the dirty dozen, took a long time to develop. EU states had advocated a process that would emphasize the precautionary principle and allow the addition of chemicals relatively easily and quickly. The United States, Japan, and Australia, among others, wanted a more regimented mechanism that required explicit risk analyses and clear evidence of existing harm before the COP could add a chemical.[75]

The resulting process represents a working compromise between these views that incorporates precaution, risk analysis according to set criteria, use of experts, flexibility, and sovereign control by the parties[76] (see Figure 3.3). Under the treaty, any party may nominate a chemical for evaluation. A POPs Review Committee (POPRC), made up of thirty-one experts nominated by parties, then works on behalf (and under the oversight) of the COP to examine the nominated chemical in detail. The POPRC first determines whether the substance meets the criteria for status as a POP under the convention (as set out in Annex D) by examining its toxicity, persistence, bioaccumulation, and potential for long-range environmental transport. If a substance meets the POPs criteria, the committee then drafts a risk profile to evaluate if emissions of the substance would produce significant adverse environmental or human-health impacts. If the POPRC determines it would, the committee develops a risk-management evaluation that assesses the costs and benefits of international controls. Finally, based on these analyses, the POPRC then decides to recommend, or not to recommend, that the COP consider controlling the substance under the convention. In carrying out these tasks, the POPRC is instructed to use specific scientific criteria for identifying and evaluating candidate POPs (as set out in Annex D of the convention), to use specific information requirements for developing a risk profile for candidate POPs (Annex E), to consider socioeconomic impacts of controlling a POP in developing the risk-management evaluation (Annex F), and to take a strong perspective of precaution. Indeed, as demanded by the EU, precaution informs the process in such a way that the absence of strict scientific certainty does not prevent the COP from controlling a potentially hazardous substance.[77]

148

FIGURE 3.3 **Process for adding new chemicals to the Stockholm Convention**

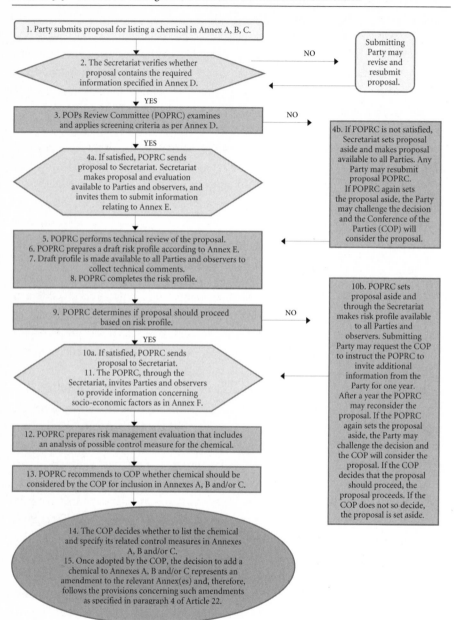

At the same time, sovereign control is preserved, as demanded by the United States and other countries. All parties have opportunities for a full hearing on any candidate POP. Parties can submit comments and suggest changes to POPRC outputs before they become final. The COP, not the POPRC, holds final decision-making authority. And each party, if it chooses, can decide if it wishes to be bound by a particular decision to add a chemical.

To organize the control measures and make the addition of chemicals more orderly, the convention establishes three annexes that group substances by the type of restrictions placed on them. Annex A lists substances slated for elimination, such as aldrin, chlordane, dieldrin, endrin, heptachlor, hexachlorobenzene, mirex, PCBs, and toxaphene. Any new chemical slated for elimination will also be listed in this annex. Annex B lists substances like DDT, whose production and use will be severely limited. Annex C lists unintentionally produced substances, like dioxins and furans. Parties agree to take specific steps to minimize emissions of these substances. Listing chemicals in the annexes means that adding new chemicals only requires amending the annex, not the main body of the convention. This allowed negotiators to create opt-in or opt-out provisions governing how parties can choose to be bound by the amended annexes. While potentially confusing, the entire package makes it easier to add chemicals and speeds the implementation of the new controls. At the same time, the opt-in or opt-out provisions also allow parties not to participate in a given amendment to add new chemicals to the convention if they so choose.

Another critical feature of the convention is the financial mechanism that assists developing countries and countries with economies in transition in meeting their treaty obligations. Under the convention, industrialized countries must provide new financial resources, albeit at unspecified levels, and promote the transfer of technical assistance. Although nearly all negotiators acknowledged the importance of providing FTA, there were diverse views regarding the proper level and delivery mechanisms. Developing countries strongly supported creating a new stand-alone financial institution patterned after that developed under the Montreal Protocol. They opposed designating the Global Environment Facility (GEF) as the financial mechanism because of concerns about the GEF's willingness both to address POPs as a priority area and to follow direction on POPs-related issues from the Stockholm Convention COP. The G-77 also insisted that all FTA be new and additional to current programs so that POPs-related activities did not mean less FTA in other areas. Donor countries countered that the GEF could provide important efficiencies and expertise and that new FTA programs could be bundled and augmented with existing programs in other forums, such as the Rotterdam and Basel conventions.

In the final compromise, the GEF was designated as the main financing mechanism but only on an interim basis.[78] Industrialized countries agreed to provide new

PHOTO 3.3   WWF protesters outside POPs INC-4 negotiations in Bonn, Germany, in March
2002.
Courtesy IISD/*Earth Negotiations Bulletin.*

and additional financial resources for POPs, and the COP gives instructions to, and
regularly reviews the performance of, the GEF with regard to its role as the convention's
financial mechanism. In response to the concerns expressed during the negotiations,
the GEF created a dedicated POPs program, and the industrialized countries have dedicated increasing levels of funds to POPs during the GEF's replenishment. Since 2001,
the GEF has allocated nearly $400 million to POPs projects, first in the areas of capacity
building and preparation of national implementation plans and now increasingly for
implementation projects. The GEF has also leveraged more than $450 million of fund-
ing from other sources—primarily from governments but also from the private sector,
international organizations, foundations, and NGOs—to support these and other POPs
projects. GEF support activities have taken place in more than 135 countries.[79]

The Stockholm Convention entered into force in 2004. It currently has more than
160 parties.[80] Most countries in the world and all the major producers and users of
toxic chemicals have ratified the convention except for Malaysia, Russia, and the United
States. Although the Bush administration supported the treaty and intended to push
for its ratification by the Senate, the terrorist attacks on September 11, 2001, put the

White House on a war footing, allowing a few opponents in the Senate to block consideration of the treaty out of concern for how the regime might expand.[81] Yet, this may have been a tactical error because, as a nonparty, the United States may speak at the COPs, but its voice does not count in actual decision making; nor does it have vote on the POPRC. As a major donor to the GEF, a major trade partner, and a large producer and consumer of chemicals, the U.S. voice at the negotiations is respected. While the United States can effectively support lead coalitions, however, it cannot act as a veto state on issues relating to regime expansion.

The regime-strengthening process began almost as soon as the convention was adopted. In particular, a series of negotiating sessions convened before COP-1 in May 2005 in Punta del Este, Uruguay. Because of this preparatory work, COP-1 succeeded in adopting decisions on the budget, the financial mechanism, and the POPRC, among other issues.[82]

Work by the POPRC

Sixth months later, the POPRC held its first meeting.[83] The committee addressed several operational issues, such as developing procedures for handling confidential information, delineating procedures for the participation of additional experts, and outlining work to be done between formal sections. POPRC-1 then began consideration of the first five chemicals proposed by parties for possible inclusion in the convention: chlordecone and hexabromobiphenyl, nominated by the European Union; lindane, nominated by Mexico; pentabromodiphenyl ethers, nominated by Norway; and perfluorooctane sulfonate (PFOS), nominated by Sweden. Nominating states act as lead states on that substance, although in many instances parties work together as a coalition of lead states, and one particular party puts forth the formal nomination for political reasons (either within a country or within the regime).[84]

This pattern has continued. At each meeting the POPRC addresses key procedural issues; considers chemicals nominated by parties; develops, revises, and finalizes risk profiles and risk-management evaluations, taking into account comments from parties and observers; and outlines work that will be done by members before the next POPRC meeting or COP. The POPRC meets each year, usually in October, so that its work and progress can be considered in a timely fashion by the COP during its biannual meetings.

In 2006, POPRC-2 adopted risk profiles for the five substances considered at its first meeting. Following a positive review by COP-3 on the progress of its work, in 2007, POPRC-3 approved risk-management evaluations for five chemicals and formally recommended that COP-4 consider adding these substances to the convention when it met in 2009. POPRC-3 adopted risk profiles for four additional chemicals: commercial octabromodiphenyl, pentachlorobenzene, and alpha and beta hexachlorocyclohexane.

They decided that these chemicals are likely, as a result of their long-range environmental transport, to lead to significant adverse human-health or environmental effects such that global action is warranted. In October 2008, POPRC-4 approved these risk-management evaluations and recommended that COP-4 consider listing these chemicals in the control annexes. All nine of the proposed chemicals were listed in the convention by COP-4. POPRC-4 also discussed a draft risk profile for a newly nominated chemical (short-chained chlorinated paraffins) and began criteria evaluations of several others. This work continued at POPRC-5 in 2009.

The nominations of new chemicals by parties and subsequent action by the POPRC and the COP, in just the first five years of the regime's operation, proved that the procedure for adding new substances to the convention did indeed work and that consideration of new chemicals could be done according to an orderly schedule that allowed sufficient time to examine the scientific issues and prepare materials for the COP. It also confirmed that lead states, particularly countries within the EU, intended to nominate and support consideration of additional chemicals in accordance with the precautionary principle.

At the same time, events during POPRC-4 and POPRC-5 also revealed potential obstacles to adding controls on a large number of chemicals beyond those under current consideration. As noted by POPRC participants and reported in the *Earth Negotiation Bulletin*, POPRC-4 "marked a shift in the work of the Committee from considering what are commonly referred to as 'dead' chemicals to those 'live' chemicals that are still in use in many parts of the world."[85] By creating the POPRC, the Stockholm Convention attempted to separate the scientific and technical consideration of nominated POPs, which are the purview of the POPRC, from the economic and political concerns of parties, which are discussed by the COP. The POPRC's job is to review a substance and make recommendations, based on criteria laid out in the convention, as to whether the substance is a POP and whether its capacity for harm warrants consideration for inclusion in the convention. It is then up to the COP to make that consideration—to weigh the environmental, economic, political, and precautionary costs and benefits and make a decision. In essence, the POPRC addresses whether the convention can control a substance. Then the COP decides if it should.

The lines can blur, however, because the convention asks the POPRC to include certain socioeconomic considerations in the risk-management evaluation phase. This was not an important issue on most of the substances that the POPRC considered at its first meetings, but the shift to evaluating toxic chemicals still in production presents a new challenge. At POPRC-4, some participants took positions that appeared to reflect their home country's economic and political views as much as a technical evaluation of the POP's toxicity, persistence, bioaccumulation, long-range environmental transport, and consequential risks to human health and the environment. This produced some strong exchanges during POPRC-4 and POPRC-5 and some contentious votes (almost all regime decisions are made by consensus). How the regime navigates the transition from dead to live chemicals could represent the "true test" of both the POPRC process[86] and the long-term success of the regime.

Work by the COP

While the process of adding chemicals was unfolding in the POPRC, COP-2, COP-3, and COP-4 pushed the regime forward on other issues. COP-1 in 2005 had taken a number of decisions needed to start key regime operations. COP-2 in 2006 faced the more difficult challenge of beginning several long-term substantive processes necessary to ensure the effective implementation of the convention. These included, among other things, processes to evaluate the financial mechanism, including the role of the GEF; to monitor and evaluate the effectiveness of the regime in reducing the presence of POPs in the environment; to examine whether the convention should seek synergies via close collaboration with the other chemicals conventions (discussed above in the section above on the Basel Convention); and to enhance provision of technical assistance and capacity building, including the potential use of new regional centers (as favored by some developing countries) or collaboration with other regimes (favored by some donor countries). Debates on many of these issues took more difficult turns than the comparatively celebratory discussion held at COP-1, but in the end COP-2 took the decisions required to keep the regime on course.

In 2007, COP-3 convened in Dakar, Senegal. Faced with the knowledge that future COPs would meet biannually, parties grappled with the challenge of reaching decisions that would support and enhance normal regime operations and implementation for two years rather than just one. They also needed to complete procedures for several major reports, reviews, and decisions scheduled for consideration at COP-4 in 2009. To this end, COP-3 took decisions on issues related to budgets and work plans for 2008 and 2009; the work of the POPRC to date and clarifying procedural issues to assist its work; measures to reduce or eliminate releases from wastes; guidelines for identifying and measuring dioxin and furan emissions; guidelines for using the best available techniques and best environmental practices to reduce POPs emissions; clarifying and expanding details concerning the DDT controls; improving the reporting requirements; promoting information exchange; and several issues surrounding national implementation plans (the documents that states must develop that outline how they intend to implement the convention). Yet, even with action in all these areas, four other issues with significant long-term importance dominated discussions at COP-3: synergies, technical and financial assistance, creation of noncompliance procedures, and methods to evaluate regime effectiveness.

For several years the EU, Switzerland, and others have played lead roles in various regimes pushing the concept of creating formal coordination among the three main chemical and waste conventions to achieve synergies and reduce costs. In 2005 and 2006, as noted above, the Basel, Rotterdam, and Stockholm COPs had established an ad hoc joint working group on synergies to examine the issue, develop background materials, and draft recommendations. Although this process was far from complete, by the time of POPs COP-3 in 2007, work by the ad hoc joint working group had helped to clarify key concepts, purposes, and potential outcomes of the process. The "concept of synergies [had been transformed] from a nebulous norm into a series of practical actions, such as adopting a streamlined reporting system, that parties see as being beneficial."[87] In Dakar, parties strongly supported the initiative—unlike in previous COPs where developing countries expressed significant concern that the process would divert attention and resources away from technical assistance. The final proposal of the ad hoc working group, submitted in 2008, was considered first, by virtue of the calendar, by the Basel and Rotterdam COPs prior to POPs COP-4 in May 2009.

On FTA, COP-3 took several decisions to advance its working relationship with the GEF; discussions were made easier by the replenishment of the GEF that included increased funding for POPs. Parties provided additional guidance to the GEF regarding priority funding areas and established final procedures for reviewing the financial mechanism at COP-4. Developing countries continued to express concern regarding the long-term availability of sufficient resources, and they stated where they believed the GEF could improve, but the tone of the discussions had become more positive in comparison to the far more difficult debates during the creation of the regime and even at COP-2. COP-3 also confirmed that regional centers would be the principle nodes for capacity-building and technical-assistance activities under the convention and developed a procedure for officially designating these centers at COP-4.

Creating a noncompliance procedure has proven a difficult or impossible task for most environmental regimes, despite the priority given the issue by some influential parties. COP-3 and COP-4 followed this pattern. Article 17 of the Stockholm Convention states that the COP will develop "as soon as practicable . . . mechanisms for determining noncompliance with the provisions of this Convention and for the treatment of Parties found to be in noncompliance." The EU places great emphasis on developing a robust noncompliance procedure and plays a strong leadership role on the issue. Several industrialized countries, such as Switzerland, support this position. Several other industrialized countries and some developing countries attach less importance to the issue, acting as potential swing states. A large group of developing countries, often led by China and India, constitute a powerful veto coalition. They link implementation and effectiveness to the provision of financial resources and argue that a noncompliance procedure can only be developed after such assistance has been provided. They emphasize that any procedure related to compliance, with regard to developing countries, should be not punitive but assistance oriented. It should focus on identifying obstacles to effective compliance in a given party so that additional assistance can be targeted effectively.

Attempts to resolve these differences during negotiation of the convention failed, leading to the compromise language in Article 17, which, unlike nearly all the other parts of the convention requiring action by the COP, carries no deadline. COP-1 created an open-ended working group on noncompliance to allow delegates extended periods to consider the issue in the hope of reaching agreement on a procedure. However, discussions yielded little substantive progress (and sometimes generated heated debates) beyond a preliminary draft text covered with "square brackets" and alternative formulations supported by different groups. (Square brackets are used to indicate portions of a draft document on which parties do not agree.) Working group discussions during COP-3 made some progress, but significant differences remained on fundamental issues, including the ultimate objective and underlying principles of the noncompliance procedure, how to initiate action on potential cases of noncompliance (developing countries reject giving either the secretariat or other parties the authority to initiate the procedure), and the composition and decision-making processes for the compliance committee. These disagreements continued during discussions prior to and during COP-4, and further discussion was deferred to COP-5 in 2011.

Far more progress was made on the effectiveness evaluation. COP-2 had agreed to implement a global monitoring plan to gather data on POPs levels in humans and the environment, largely by utilizing and adding existing national and international programs. An ad hoc technical working group oversaw the initial stages of this process and was tasked to prepare recommendations to the COP on possible procedures for the effectiveness evaluation, which the convention required parties to adopt at COP-4. At COP-3, parties reviewed this work and agreed to create a permanent expert group to oversee the monitoring plan, examine the data, and undertake the effectiveness evaluation of the convention on behalf of the COP. Parties agreed that the expert group would consist of three representatives from each of the five UN regions. This was a compromise between industrialized countries that wanted a small group to enhance effectiveness and cost-efficiency and developing countries that feared they would lack sufficient representation in a very small group.

Following two years of extensive intersessional work, COP-4 convened in Geneva in May 2009. Although delegates addressed the normal agenda of issues related to regime operations and implementation, two issues dominated discussions at COP-4: adding new chemicals to the convention and financial resources and technical assistance.[88]

The lead states on listing chemicals included the nominating party supported by different parties, depending on the substance. The one constant was the strong support of the EU and its member states for listing each of the nine substances under discussion. Veto states varied depending on which countries opposed listing the chemical (a significant issue only in the case of PFOS) or insisted on significant exemptions that would allow continued use of the chemical for certain applications. Veto states were empowered to the extent that they were willing to prevent consensus on listing a chemical unless certain exemptions were allowed; could credibly claim they would opt out of an amendment (this only worked for countries such as China, India, Iran, Pakistan, and some others that produced or used sufficient quantities of a substance to threaten the effectiveness of the controls); or were willing to withhold support on an unrelated issue if their position was not adopted.

An important issue for some chemicals was the annex in which they would be placed. Lead states pushed for inclusion of chemicals in Annex A, which mandates elimination. Veto states pushed for one or two chemicals to be placed in Annex B, which establishes severe restrictions but no near-term elimination. Parties also disagreed on the category of potential exemptions that should be applied to a chemical. Lead states argued that only special exemptions for specific, time-limited uses be allowed. Other states supported the more lenient "acceptable purpose" category, which allowed larger and less controlled levels of exempted use. Finally, many of the most contentious listing issues were interrelated from a bargaining standpoint. For example, a veto state could offer to relent on listing or acceptable purposes for one chemical in exchange for the creation of more special exemptions for another substance.

The suite of intersecting issues on financial resources and technical assistance was equally complex. Among other issues, the parties needed to select regional centers through which capacity building and technical assistance would flow; review reports on the operations and extant effectiveness of the financial mechanism, particularly the GEF; review needs-assessment reports on the potential overall costs for developing countries to implement the regime and take decisions in response to this information regarding the mobilization of resources, including desires for POPs-related funding levels in the upcoming negotiations on replenishing the GEF; and provide updated guidance to the GEF regarding how the COP wants it to operate in supporting the convention.

Further complicating matters, the bargaining strategies of many participants, as expected, caused these and other issues to become interlinked. This forced the meeting to search for a complex package deal that almost prevented decisions on issues where there was no disagreement. For example, many developing countries would not allow a decision on the listing of chemicals until a satisfactory resolution was reached on the package of FTA issues. The EU also attempted to include noncompliance as part of the overall compromise package. China, India, and others essentially refused to consider a package that included a noncompliance procedure. Some countries dug in their heels on issues relating to certain chemicals in an attempt to get movement on other chemicals or on an unrelated issue.

In the end, these linkages produced a stalemate that almost derailed the meeting. Late Friday night, six hours after the meeting was scheduled to end, delegates were openly speaking of the possibility that negotiations would have to be suspended, without decisions being taken, and reconvened later in the year. Finally, after 4:00 a.m. on Saturday morning, long after the interpreters had left the building, a final compromise allowed the COP to adopt a package of decisions on new chemicals and issues relating to financial resources and technical assistance. Although some delegates worried that the exhausting and sometimes heated negotiations might set a negative precedent, others emphasized that COP-4 had taken many very important decisions that would define the global regime on toxic chemicals for years to come. In particular, COP-4:

- *added nine new chemicals to the Stockholm Convention.*[89] Of the twenty-one POPs listed in the convention as of 2010, seventeen are slated for total elimination (Annex A), two are severely restricted (Annex B), and two are unintentional by-products requiring specific efforts to minimize their emissions (Annex C). As with the dirty dozen, in cases where complete elimination of one of the newly listed substances would produce significant health, economic, social, or logistical impacts, parties are also allowed to utilize "country-specific exemptions" that permit the continued use of a specific POP for a narrowly defined application for a certain number of years.

- *issued the final approved needed to begin the groundbreaking synergies initiative that will create close collaboration between the Basel, Rotterdam, and Stockholm conventions.* Over time, certain operational elements within their secretariats and regional centers will likely combine. Some regime functions, such as national reporting, technical guidelines, public awareness campaigns, technical- and financial-assistance activities, and information exchange, will also likely merge while others will become far more coordinated. An extraordinary COP will convene in 2010 to begin setting priorities, developing work plans, and initiating action.

- *finalized the process for evaluating the convention's effectiveness in reducing POPs over time.* A global monitoring program building on various national and regional monitoring systems will seek to produce a worldwide picture of trends in the quantity and types of POPs present in humans and the environment. An expert body will oversee this effort, draft reports, offer preliminary effectiveness evaluations, and report to the COP.

- *endorsed Stockholm Convention centers in Brazil, China, Czech Republic, Kuwait, Mexico, Panama, Spain, and Uruguay as official nodes for capacity building, transfer of technology, and technical assistance.* These will be reviewed at COP-6. Four additional centers, most likely in Algeria, Iran, Russia, and Senegal, will be selected at COP-5.

- *reaffirmed the GEF as the principle entity for the financial mechanism.* COP-4 called on donors to take the funding-needs assessment of developing countries, as revealed in their national implementation plans, and the listing of new chemicals in the convention into full consideration during the fifth replenishment of the GEF. It also requested that the GEF continue its efforts, called for by previous COPs, to streamline the processes for applying for and receiving financial assistance.

- *endorsed establishment of a global DDT partnership.* This network of global stakeholders—including doctors, health agencies, NGOs, international organizations, national governments, corporations, and scientists—will work to hasten development and deployment of more effective and cost-efficient alternative products, methods, and strategies to control malaria than the use of DDT. The partnership operates on the understanding that the first priority is controlling malaria and that the convention allows countries to use DDT to combat malaria and other diseases until proven alternatives exist.

- *created the PCB Elimination Network to strengthen efforts to manage, phase out, and dispose of equipment containing PCBs in an environmentally sound manner.* The network is expected to include experts from multiple treaty secretariats, international organizations, governments, NGOs, research institutions, industry, and business, who will exchange information, establish data sets, evaluate whether PCB use is declining, initiate and support pilot programs, and develop recommendations for further action.

The global regime for toxic chemicals has expanded significantly since governments adopted the Stockholm Convention in 2001. Nine new chemicals have been added to the control regime. The POPRC continues to evaluate candidate POPs nominated by parties. The GEF has created a dedicated funding stream and has contributed more than $400 million directly to POPs projects. POPs activities and regional centers have been selected to serve as nodes for capacity building and technical assistance. Technical guidelines have been developed to help measure and reduce dioxin and furan emissions as well as emissions of POPs waste. Efforts are under way to create significantly greater levels of coordination between the chemicals regimes. Global networks have been created in an attempt to speed development of alternatives to DDT and the phaseout of PCBs. Awareness of toxic chemicals has increased in many national governments.

Like the other regimes discussed in this book, however, the Stockholm Convention faces several challenges. One of the most basic is attracting ratifications from the few large producers and consumers of toxic chemicals that are not yet parties: Ireland, Italy, Malaysia, Russia, and the United States.[90]

The Stockholm Convention must also overcome the challenges inherent in addressing "live" chemicals still in production and use. POPRC-4 and COP-4 took the first difficult steps in this direction, particularly in debates on listing PFOS. Significantly reducing emissions of the twenty-one substances currently in the control regime will be considered a success. However, many more chemicals known to be hazardous exist, and concern is rising over a new class of endocrine disruptors that may impact humans at very low doses and might be found in some brands of everyday products, including plastics, pesticides, and detergents.

Exemptions represent another challenge. Accepted-use and country-specific exemptions are political necessities that overcome the lowest-common-denominator problem by establishing asymmetrical controls. By reducing the adjustment costs of potential veto states, they allow a higher common policy for most of the world. At the same time, if these exemptions last forever, they can severely weaken the impact of listing a particular chemical, especially if the country in question both produces and consumes the substance. Although countries have retired their special exemptions for most of the dirty dozen Annex A substances, the chemicals listed in Annexes A and B at COP-4 contain a far larger list of potential exemptions. Lead states see this as a necessary compromise. However, for the regime to be effective over the long term, the COP must prevent parties from renewing these exemptions if there is evidence of nontoxic alternative substances or practices.

Another lingering challenge, common to all environmental regimes, is the need for more financial and technical resources to assist developing countries' transition away from the use of as many toxic chemicals as possible and to better manage those that remain. While donor countries and the GEF have significantly increased assistance, further regime strengthening will require the availability and proper application of sufficient FTA.

Opinions vary widely among parties and outside experts regarding the proper purpose, the most efficacious design, and even the necessity of a noncompliance procedure. However, while one might argue that the regime may not require one to remain effective, the continuing deadlock on the issue has the potential to impact discussion on other matters negatively. Resolving this deadlock in a manner that addresses the common goal of regime effectiveness would remove a potential political problem.

Finally, the synergies initiative presents a huge challenge and opportunity. Establishing effective, institutionalized coordination, collaboration, and selective consolidation among the Stockholm, Rotterdam, and Basel conventions will not be easy, but it is a necessary first step toward a coherent international approach to highly toxic substances that establishes environmentally sound, implementable controls on all aspects of their life cycle. Many parties recognize the need for a comprehensive approach, and this has been called for as well by several international forums, including the 2002 World Summit on Sustainable Development, the UNEP Governing Council, the Intergovernmental Forum on Chemical Safety, and UNEP's Strategic Approach to International Chemicals Management initiative. The greater efficiencies and productive synergies of closer collaboration and even merging appropriate aspects of the conventions can raise their collective profiles, augment more successful and less costly implementation, and provide more opportunities for regime expansion in the future.

CONCLUSION

These three cases of pollution-control regimes demonstrate how both state and non-state actors have come together to address problems of transboundary air pollution, hazardous waste, and the toxic chemicals known as persistent organic pollutants. The negotiation of a strong global environmental regime almost always depends on inducing one or more key states in a veto coalition to go along with one or more of the core proposed provisions of the regime. By strong, we mean an agreement that includes obligations or norms that make it sufficiently clear that parties can be held accountable for implementing them and that calls for reasonable actions expected to have an impact on the problem if they are implemented. Whether a regime succeeds in addressing an environmental threat depends, of course, on how strong the regime is in the above sense and on the degree to which parties comply with its core provisions.

In these cases, numerous issues had an impact on the negotiations and the politics. New scientific evidence helped move veto states on some issues (acid rain and POPs). International political considerations played a role in the Basel Convention, where French and British desires to maintain close relations with former colonies factored into their views on the hazardous waste trade. Domestic political and ethical concerns played a key role in making Canada a lead state in the Stockholm Convention negotiations. Regime formation also requires leadership by one or more states committed to defining the issue and proposing a detailed policy approach as the basis for the regime. In these cases states motivated by particular vulnerabilities played lead roles: Sweden, Finland, and Norway on acid rain; African countries on hazardous waste; and Canada and some European countries on POPs. However, in none of the three cases has the United States played a lead role. When the United States plays a veto role or does not become a party to a treaty, as in the case of the Basel and Stockholm conventions and some LRTAP protocols, the result is a weaker regime.

The next chapter will look at two other pollution-control regimes that involve a different type of problem: global atmospheric pollution. Chapter 5 will then examine the differences between these types of global pollution-control regimes and global regimes that address the conservation and sound management of natural resources. The conclusion to Chapter 5 will then review and compare all eleven case studies.

DISCUSSION QUESTIONS

1. How has scientific evidence altered the positions of government negotiators in these cases? What role does scientific uncertainty play? What role does the precautionary principle play? What are the challenges of utilizing the precautionary principle in these cases?

2. What were the primary motives of the veto coalitions in each of these cases? Why did the coalitions weaken in some cases?

3. Trace the role of a particular state in each of these three negotiations and try to assess the extent of its involvement in leadership or blocking roles.

4. What are some of the underlying economic factors that impact pollution-control regimes such as these?

5. How do the challenges of finance, technology transfer, and capacity building differ between LRTAP, the Basel Convention, and the Stockholm Convention? How are they similar?

6. What are the strengths and weaknesses of the process of strengthening the Stockholm Convention by adding new chemicals? What aspects of that framework might work for other regimes?

4

The Development of Environmental Regimes: Stratospheric Ozone and Climate Change

The global regimes to protect stratospheric ozone and mitigate the severity and impacts of climate change share important similarities. Both address critical atmospheric issues. The two regimes started with framework conventions before adding regulatory protocols. Like the regimes on air and toxic pollutants, both include very specific rules to limit particular substances from entering the environment. They have been significantly influenced by scientific bodies and economic interests. Both allow developing countries greater time to implement the controls and have provisions for them to receive financial and technical assistance (FTA).

Yet, important differences exist as well. The ozone regime quickly expanded its scope, has strong and effective control mechanisms, covers all major emitters of ozone-depleting substances (ODS), and is widely considered to be a success. The climate regime has developed at a slower pace. It does not yet include the rules necessary to mitigate climate change in the long term, does not yet place binding controls on all major greenhouse gas (GHG) emitters, and few would call it a success. While both regimes have scientific bodies to advise them, they interact with them very differently and as a result the scientific bodies have different impacts. The ozone regime has nearly eliminated many ozone-depleting chemicals, especially in the industrialized nations, and now focuses on implementing the remainder of its controls. While only five years younger, the climate regime must still go through many more difficult negotiations on creating the controls necessary to prevent significant and damaging change to the earth's climate.

Like the regimes on air and toxic pollutants discussed in Chapter 3, the ozone and climate regimes seek to prevent specific chemicals or substances from endangering humans and the environment. However, they differ from those regimes in that the impacts of ODS and GHG emissions affect human, plant, and animal life across the planet. The scale of the emissions and the impacts, as well as the challenges in creating effective regimes, sets these two apart from other pollution-control regimes.

This chapter examines these two regimes. As in the previous chapter, each issue is analyzed according to the stages of negotiation and the role of lead states and veto coalitions in shaping the outcomes of bargaining. We also highlight other important causal factors, outline key aspects of their design and expansion, delineate current global policy for each issue, and examine their similarities and differences in more detail.

OZONE DEPLETION

Ozone is a pungent, slightly bluish gas composed of three oxygen atoms (O_3). Of naturally occurring ozone, 90 percent resides in the **stratosphere**.[1] This "ozone layer" helps to shield the earth from ultraviolet radiation produced by the sun and plays a critical role in absorbing ultraviolet B radiation. Because large increases in ultraviolet B radiation would seriously harm nearly all plants and animals, the ozone layer is considered an essential component of the natural systems that make life on earth possible.

In the 1970s, scientists discovered that certain man-made chemicals, called chlorofluorocarbons (CFCs), posed a serious threat to stratospheric ozone.[2] CFCs release chlorine atoms into the stratosphere that act as a catalyst in the destruction of ozone molecules. Created in the 1920s to replace flammable and noxious refrigerants, CFCs are inert, nonflammable, nontoxic, colorless, odorless, and wonderfully adaptable to a wide variety of profitable uses. By the mid-1970s, CFCs had become the chemical of choice for coolants in air conditioning and refrigerating systems, propellants in aerosol sprays, solvents in the cleaning of electronic components, and the blowing agent for the manufacture of flexible and rigid foam. Scientists later discovered other ODS, including halons (a very effective and otherwise safe fire suppressant), carbon tetrachloride, methyl chloroform, and methyl bromide. Each can release ozone-destroying chlorine or bromine atoms into the stratosphere.

The economic importance of these chemicals, especially CFCs, made international controls very difficult to establish.[3] The absence of firm scientific consensus on the nature and seriousness of the problem, a strenuous antiregulatory campaign by corporations producing or using CFCs, concerns for the cost of unilateral regulation, worries on the part of developing countries that restricting access to CFCs would slow economic development, and opposition by the then European Community (EC) prevented effective action for many years.

The political definition of the ozone-depletion issue began in 1977. The fact-finding process lasted many years, however, because scientific estimates of potential depletion fluctuated widely during the late 1970s and early 1980s, and no evidence emerged in nature to confirm the theory. Indeed, when the bargaining process formally began in 1982, the exact nature of the threat was unclear even to proponents of international action.[4]

The United States, which at that time accounted for more than 40 percent of worldwide CFC production, took a lead role in the negotiations in part because it had already banned CFC use in aerosol spray cans, which accounted for a large percentage of total use at that time, and wanted other states to follow suit. However, for an ozone-protection policy to succeed, it was essential that all states producing and consuming CFCs be part of the regime. Thus, the EC, which opposed controls, constituted a potential veto coalition because its member states also accounted for more than 40 percent of global CFC production (exporting a third of that to developing countries). West Germany supported CFC controls, but the EC position was effectively controlled by the other large producing countries—France, Italy, and the United Kingdom—which doubted the science, wanted to preserve their industries' overseas markets, and wished to avoid the costs of adopting substitutes. Japan, also a major producer and user of CFCs, supported this position.

Large developing countries, including Brazil, China, India, and Indonesia, formed another potential veto coalition. Their bargaining leverage stemmed from their potential to produce very large quantities of CFCs in the future—a situation that would eventually eviscerate the effectiveness of any regime.[5] Although most developing countries did not play an active role early in the regime's development, they eventually used this leverage to secure a delayed control schedule and precedent-setting FTA.

Although negotiations began with an explicit understanding that only a possible framework convention would be discussed, in 1983, the lead states (the United States, Canada, and the Nordic states) proposed adding binding restrictions on CFC production to the treaty. The veto coalition, led by the EC, steadfastly rejected negotiations for regulatory protocols. Thus, the regime's first agreement, the 1985 Vienna Convention for the Protection of the Ozone Layer, affirmed the importance of protecting the ozone layer and included provisions on monitoring, research, and data exchanges but imposed no specific obligations to reduce the production or use of CFCs. Indeed, it did not even mention CFCs. However, because of a last-minute U.S. initiative, states did agree to resume negotiations if further evidence emerged supporting the potential threat.

Only weeks after nations signed the Vienna Convention, British scientists published the first reports about the Antarctic ozone hole.[6] Although the hole had been forming annually for several years, the possibility of its existence fell so far outside the bounds of existing theory that computers monitoring satellite data on stratospheric ozone had ignored its presence as a data error. Publication of its existence galvanized proponents of CFC controls, who argued that the hole justified negotiations to strengthen the nascent regime (despite the lack of firm evidence linking the hole to CFCs until 1989).[7] Thus, faced with domestic and international pressure, the veto states returned to the bargaining table in 1986. This round of negotiations concluded with the 1987 Montreal Protocol.

The lead states in the Protocol negotiations—a coalition that now included Canada, Finland, Norway, Sweden, Switzerland, and the United States—initially advocated a freeze, followed by a 95 percent reduction, in production of CFCs over a period of ten to fourteen years. The industrialized-country veto coalition—the EC, Japan, and the Soviet Union—eventually proposed placing a cap on production capacity at current levels. Lead states argued that a capacity cap would actually allow for an increase in real CFC production because many manufacturers outside the United States already possessed significant excess production capacity. Thus, even if a cap was imposed, European producers could increase their actual output of CFC production while maintaining their current capacity, gaining economic benefits from the regime. Consistently rejecting this proposal, lead states issued a series of counterproposals before eventually offering a 50 percent cut as a final compromise during the final stages of the negotiations. As late as April 1987, the EC stated it could not accept more than a 20 percent reduction but relented in the final days of negotiations in Montreal in September.

The 1987 Montreal Protocol on Substances That Deplete the Ozone Layer mandated that industrialized countries reduce their production and use of the five most widely used CFCs by 50 percent. Halon production would be frozen. The expanded regime also included scientific and technological assessment panels, reporting requirements, potential trade sanctions for countries that did not ratify the agreement, and a robust procedure for reviewing the effectiveness of the regime and strengthening controls through amendments and adjustments.[8] To gain the acceptance of the developing-country veto coalition, delegates agreed to give developing countries a ten-year grace period, allowing them to increase their use of CFCs before taking on commitments.

The 1987 Montreal Protocol is widely considered a historic achievement in global environmental politics because it was the first treaty to address a truly global environmental threat, required significant cuts in the production and use of several very important chemicals, was taken in the absence of scientific proof concerning the problem, and contained clear mechanisms for possibly expanding the treaty in response to new information. However, it is important to note that the original protocol (before its significant amendment and expansion in the 1990s) addressed only the eight most widely produced CFCs and halons (ignoring, at least for the time being, other known ODS), neglected to require that alternatives to the controlled chemicals must not damage the ozone layer, included no provisions for independent monitoring of ODS production and use, and contained no real provisions for providing FTA to developing countries that joined the regime. While hailing the protocol as a great success, some of those most worried about the problem doubted at the time that the 1987 agreement would be sufficient to truly safeguard the ozone layer.[9]

The ten-year evolution of the EC position from rejecting all discussion of control measures to proposing a production cap to accepting a compromise 50 percent reduction target reflected several factors: disunity within the EC (Belgium, Denmark, the Netherlands, and West Germany supported strong CFC regulations), the personal role played by United Nations Environment Programme (UNEP) executive director Mostafa Tolba, diplomatic pressures by the United States, pressure from European nongovernmental organizations (NGOs), and reluctance by the EC to be seen as the culprit should negotiations fail to produce an agreement. The evolution of the lead-state position from seeking a near 95 percent cut to accepting a 50 percent cut reflected the need to include the Europeans in the protocol. A regime that did not include countries responsible for 40 percent of global production could not succeed. Thus, the lead states believed it was better to compromise at 50 percent cuts (even though these carried far higher adjustment cost for the lead states, as they had already taken all the lost-cost reduction measures while the Europeans had done almost nothing), in the hope that these could be increased in light of future scientific information, rather than to create a regime without the EC.

Within months of the Montreal accord, new scientific evidence emerged that supported strengthening the regime. In late 1987, scientists announced that initial studies suggested that CFCs probably were responsible for the ozone hole, which continued to grow larger every year, although natural processes peculiar to Antarctica contributed to its severity. Studies during the next two years confirmed these findings. In March 1988, satellite data revealed that stratospheric ozone above the heavily populated Northern Hemisphere had begun to thin.[10] Finally, the 1989 report of the regime's own Scientific Assessment Panel signaled conclusively that the world's scientific community had reached broad agreement that CFCs had indeed begun to deplete stratospheric ozone.[11]

This period also saw changes in the pattern of economic interests. In 1988, DuPont announced that they would soon be able to produce CFC substitutes. They were followed the next year by other large chemical companies, including several in Europe. Now that they could make substitutes, the major CFC manufacturers no longer opposed a CFC phaseout but lobbied instead for extended transition periods and against controls on their new alternatives, particularly hydrochlorofluorocarbons (HCFCs)—a class of CFC substitutes that deplete ozone but at a significantly reduced rate. In response to these scientific and economic changes and to increased pressure from domestic environmental lobbies, the EC abruptly shifted roles.[12]

At the second Meeting of the Parties to the Montreal Protocol (MOP-2) in London in June 1990, EC states assumed a lead role during the difficult negotiations that eventually produced the first set of amendments and adjustments that significantly strengthened the regime.[13] The London Amendment required that the production and use of the eight CFCs and halons controlled in 1987, plus many other ODS, including carbon tetrachloride and all other CFCs and halons, would now be phased out by 2000. Methyl chloroform would be phased out by 2005. The accelerated control schedules represented a huge achievement. In 1985, the industrialized countries could not even agree to name CFCs as an ODS as part of the Vienna Convention. Now, only five years later, they had agreed to eliminate CFCs and several other chemicals by 2000. This represented the first binding global agreement to eliminate specific chemicals that harm the environment.

Because the long-term success of the ozone regime also depended on getting large developing countries to participate, a second historic achievement during MOP-2 in London was creation of the Multilateral Fund for the Implementation of the Montreal Protocol. The first such fund established under an environmental agreement (it predates, and influenced the creation of, the Global Environment Facility), the Multilateral Fund was established to help developing countries and "countries with economies in transition" implement the protocol, including by using alternatives to CFCs and other ODS.[14] The fund addressed demands by Argentina, China, India, Indonesia, and other large developing countries that had refused to join the regime without FTA, especially with regard to the replacement chemicals. The fund meets the incremental costs to developing countries of implementing the control measures of the protocol and finances clearinghouse functions, country studies, technical assistance, information, training, and costs of the fund secretariat. The incremental costs in this case are the extra expense of producing or using the alternatives to, for example, CFCs rather than the CFCs themselves.

The Multilateral Fund is replenished every three years and administered by an Executive Committee made up of seven donor and seven recipient countries. Replenishment levels are negotiated by the MOP. The total budget for the 2009–2011 triennium is $490 million.[15] Since its establishment, the fund has disbursed over $2.3 billion to support more than 4,600 projects in 148 countries[16] and is widely considered a key ingredient in the success of the ozone regime. As noted, China, India, and several other large developing countries would likely not have joined the regime without it. Perhaps as importantly, later in the regime's development, developing countries accepted accelerated phaseout schedules in part because the existence and generally effective operation of the fund gave them confidence that financial assistance would be available to assist them in implementing the new controls.

Parties strengthened the regime again in 1992 at MOP-4 in Copenhagen. They acted in response to increasing evidence of serious and accelerating ozone-layer depletion as well as significant progress in the deployment of CFC substitutes. Delegates accelerated the existing phaseouts and added controls on additional chemicals, including methyl bromide, a toxic fumigant used in agriculture and once the second most widely used insecticide in the world by volume, and HCFCs, which parties agreed to phase out by 2030 (with all but 0.5 percent being eliminated by 2020).[17] MOP-4 also established the Implementation Committee, which examines cases of possible noncompliance and makes recommendations to the MOP aimed at securing compliance.[18]

By the conclusion of the 1992 negotiations, the EU and United States had completed a near reversal of their respective roles during the 1970s and 1980s. In 1993, the EU argued for the importance of eliminating all threats to the ozone layer as soon as possible—the first in a series of attempts to accelerate HCFC controls.[19] Meanwhile, a veto coalition that included the United States (the key lead state in the 1970s and 1980s), Australia, China, and India argued that further restrictions on HCFCs would not reduce enough total damage to the ozone layer to justify the extra costs; would prevent firms that had made significant and good-faith investments in HCFC technologies from recouping their investment; would mean greater use of hydrofluorocarbons (HFCs), which, while not ozone depleting, are very potent GHGs (and manufactured at the time almost exclusively by European companies); and would detract attention from other available measures that could have a greater impact on the ozone layer.

A similar division developed with respect to methyl bromide. Since the early 1990s, NGOs had called for a rapid phaseout of methyl bromide because of its threat to both human health (as a toxic pesticide) and the ozone layer (as an ODS). Many industrialized countries, including the United States and the EU, had taken steps domestically to limit, and in some cases phase out, methyl bromide and supported regulating it under the protocol and providing corresponding FTA to developing countries. However, the United States had also successfully championed a significant loophole in the ozone regime that allows parties to continue using methyl bromide for "critical agricultural uses" even after the phaseout date. The exemption procedure does require a party application and a review by the MOP but gives the requesting country significant latitude in defining what constitutes a critical use. The United States pushed this exception in response to intense domestic lobbying from influential agricultural interests, particularly in California.

In 1997 (at MOP-9 in Montreal), parties accelerated the phaseout of methyl bromide for industrialized countries to 2005. Developing countries, previously committed only to a freeze by 2002, would now eliminate methyl bromide by 2015 but would also be eligible to receive assistance specifically earmarked for methyl bromide projects from the Multilateral Fund. These were very important developments, especially the new controls for developing countries. However, they were made easier because potential veto states, including the United States, understood that their concerns had already been addressed via the exemption for "critical agricultural uses." MOP-9 also addressed the issue of illegal trade in CFCs, creating a new licensing system for CFC imports and exports of CFCs and a system of regular information exchanges between parties.

At MOP-11, held in Beijing in 1999, the EU lead states finally secured U.S. agreement to strengthen controls on HCFCs, albeit modestly. MOP-11 also agreed to phase out the production of bromochloromethane (a recently developed ozone-depleting chemical) and to require that parties report on their use of methyl bromide for quarantine and preshipment applications. The use of methyl bromide to clean shipping containers as part of quarantine and preshipment procedures is a relatively noncontroversial exempted use of the pesticide, but parties (after a push by lead states) agreed that requiring reports on the amounts used would provide information useful to discouraging unnecessary or excessive applications or the diversion of methyl bromide to other uses. The Beijing amendment also bans trade in HCFCs with countries that have not ratified the 1992 Copenhagen amendment, which introduced the HCFC phaseout.

The next major development in the ozone regime occurred in 2003. Like its predecessors, MOP-15 in 2003 produced decisions on a range of issues relating to regime implementation. However, parties could not resolve significant disagreements concerning requests for the exemptions, known officially as critical-use exemptions (CUEs), which allow for continued use of methyl bromide beyond the phaseout date. Some delegates argued that the exemptions sought by Italy, Spain, the United States, and several other countries were unjustifiably large. The EU also argued that clear, new rules should be established that limit the exemptions to one year, requiring countries to reapply annually. The United States favored multiyear exemptions. With no compromise in sight, delegates took the unprecedented step of suspending the negotiations related to methyl bromide and agreeing to convene an "extraordinary" MOP to try to resolve these and other issues.

The first Extraordinary Meeting of the Parties to the Montreal Protocol convened the following March. After many preliminary discussions, parties reached compromises on several important methyl bromide–related issues, including specific CUEs for 2005, certain conditions for granting and reporting on CUEs, and working procedures for the Methyl Bromide Technical Options Committee. However, delegates could not conclude a long-term agreement regarding the allowable size or duration of exemptions beyond 2005.

BOX 4.1   CHEMICALS CONTROLLED
BY THE MONTREAL PROTOCOL

- *Chlorofluorocarbons* (CFCs) were discovered in 1928 and were considered wonder gases because they are long-lived, nontoxic, noncorrosive, and non-flammable. They are also versatile and from the 1960s were increasingly used in refrigerators, air conditioners, spray cans, solvents, foams, and other applications. CFC-11 has a lifetime in the atmosphere of 50 years, CFC-12 of 102 years, and CFC-115 of 1,700 years.
- *Halons*, which have high ozone-destroying properties, were used primarily in fire extinguishers.
- *Carbon tetrachloride* was used as a solvent, and its lifetime is about forty-two years in the atmosphere.
- *Methyl chloroform*, also used as a solvent, has an atmospheric lifetime of about 5.4 years.
- *Hydrobromofluorocarbons* are not widely used, but they have been included in the Montreal Protocol to prevent any new uses.
- *Hydrochlorofluorocarbons* (HCFCs) were originally developed in the 1950s as refrigerants for air conditioning, and a number of them became the first major replacements for CFCs in several application areas in the 1990s. While much less destructive than CFCs, HCFCs also contribute to ozone depletion. They have an atmospheric lifetime of about 1.4 to 19.5 years.
- *Methyl bromide* is used as a fumigant for high-value crops, pest control, and quarantine treatment of agricultural commodities awaiting export. Total world annual consumption for controlled uses (not including uses for quarantine and preshipment) was about 10,000 tons in 2006. The lifetime is about 0.7 years.
- *Bromochloromethane*, an ODS that some companies sought to introduce into the market in 1998, was targeted by the 1999 amendment for immediate phaseout to prevent its use.

Ozone Secretariat, "Basic Facts and Data on the Science and Politics of Ozone Protection," UNEP, September 18, 2008, http://ozone.unep.org/Events/ozone_day_2008/press_backgrounder.pdf.

As a result, the annual review of methyl bromide CUEs dominated MOP-16 in 2004 as well. Delegates continued the normal MOP process of managing the regime, this time taking decisions that addressed data reporting, improving compliance, and illegal trade in ODS, and many other issues. However, in spite of lengthy discussions, talks did nothing to mend the deep divisions between the lead states and the U.S.-led veto states regarding methyl bromide CUEs. Moreover, the meeting appeared to confirm that certain powerful agricultural and pesticide lobbies had been able to push their

PHOTO 4.1   Anti–methyl bromide picket signs outside of the first Extraordinary Meeting of the Parties to the Montreal Protocol in Montreal in March 2004.
Courtesy IISD/*Earth Negotiations Bulletin.*

governments (e.g., Israel, Italy, Spain, and the United States) to pursue large, ongoing production and use of methyl bromide in certain sectors via the CUE process.[20] The majority of methyl bromide is produced in the United States and Israel.

The deadlock forced governments to convene a second Extraordinary MOP in July 2005. Delegates again reached agreement on specific CUEs for 2006 but not on the larger issues. The continuing deadlock caused some to worry that the commitment of developing countries to phase out methyl bromide might erode if some industrialized countries continued to request and receive large CUEs. Others feared that the producers and users of alternative pesticides might find their incentives to continue reduced because their promised markets had not materialized. Some noted that there would be negative impacts on the ozone layer if large CUEs receive systematic and long-term approval. In a compromise to begin addressing elements of such concerns, the MOP decided that parties must report on existing stockpiles of methyl bromide (which are created when a country does not use all of the allowance granted in CUEs) and work to limit them to specific uses delineated in previous or current MOP decisions.

As they do every three years, negotiations on replenishing the Multilateral Fund occupied a great deal of attention during MOP-17, held in Dakar, Senegal, in December 2005. Parties agreed to allocate $470.4 million for 2006 to 2008. Although the divisions on methyl bromide CUEs remained, parties decided simply to address the nominations themselves and defer consideration of more controversial elements (which had deadlocked the previous two MOPs), such as the United States' proposal for multiyear CUEs and the EU's proposals to tighten CUEs as well as to speed the methyl bromide phaseout schedule for developing countries. This agreement to disagree was made easier in that the total amount of methyl bromide CUEs requested declined somewhat from the previous year. This pattern continued at MOP-18 in New Delhi in 2006.

MOP-19 convened in Montreal in September 2007. Parties marked the twentieth anniversary of the protocol and adopted the Montreal Declaration, which highlighted the historic and unprecedented global environmental cooperation and success achieved under the regime and reaffirmed their commitment to continue to phase out all ODS.

In a surprising and important development, MOP-19 agreed to move the phaseout of HCFC production and consumption forward by a full decade (to 2020 from 2030 for industrialized countries and to 2030 from 2040 for developing countries) and to increase or add significant interim cuts (75 percent reductions in 2010 and 90 percent by 2015 for industrialized countries and 10 percent in 2015, 35 percent in 2020, and 67.5 percent in 2025 for developing countries).[21] This agreement, heralded worldwide in environmental-policy circles, represented an important accomplishment for addressing both ozone depletion and climate change (as noted above, HCFCs are also powerful GHGs). It was one of the most significant developments in the ozone regime in nearly a decade and revealed new attitudes on the part of former veto and swing states. The United States, one of the key veto states on HCFCs in the past, suddenly switched to a lead position on accelerating their phaseout, emphasizing the positive climate aspects of the move. Indeed, in an example of the political interlinkages that sometimes arise in environmental politics, in addition to protecting the ozone layer, the United States apparently wanted a climate victory in the ozone negotiations to buttress its image and negotiating position in the parallel climate-change talks. China, the biggest producer of HCFCs, a long-time opponent of an accelerated phaseout and the key developing-country veto state along with India, shifted from a veto to a swing role. China is the world's leading manufacturer of air conditioners that use HCFC-22 as a refrigerant. However, after initially blocking the agreement, China eventually agreed to the new requirements in exchange for political commitments that the next replenishment of the Multilateral Fund would include substantially more funding for HCFC alternatives. Australia, India, Russia, and other former veto or swing states also did not block agreement. Despite their positions at previous MOPs and concern for the feasibility and cost of speeding HCFC elimination, they eventually accepted lead state arguments in support of the new controls and also evidently did not want the blame for scuttling a deal on the protocol's anniversary. "An agreement on HCFCs was therefore timely and served several interests. Many developing country delegates saw new policy commitments on HCFCs as a way to ensure continued availability of funding to Article 5 parties. Industrialized countries saw an agreement on accelerated phase-out of HCFC as an easy win for climate, through action by both developed and developing countries."[22]

PHOTO 4.2   The Montreal Protocol Meeting of the Parties in 2008 in Doha, Qatar.
Courtesy IISD/*Earth Negotiations Bulletin.*

On methyl bromide, while delegates to MOP-19 neither resolved nor really addressed the core underlying disputes, they did reach agreement on a much smaller level of CUE requests. The surprising 40 percent drop in approved CUEs from MOP-18 confirmed the declining CUE trend and might be seen in the future as an important moment in efforts to eliminate methyl bromide. Parties also took other decisions, including enhanced voluntary efforts to monitor and combat illegal trade in ODS (a subject of discussions for many years) and, most importantly, to accelerate the phaseout of HCFCs.

In 2008, the MOP met in Doha, Qatar, and included two impressive milestones. Parties marked the closure of the last production facilities for CFCs in India and China. The meeting also went paperless, becoming the first MOP to replace the avalanche of official documents produced during a global environmental meeting with electronic versions.[23]

The substantive debate was dominated by negotiations on the triennial replenishment of the Multilateral Fund, which for the first time now needed to include funding for HCFC phaseout activities. Many developing countries had joined the consensus to accelerate HCFC controls during the previous MOP only because the decision also stated "that the funding available through the Multilateral Fund for the Implementation of the Montreal Protocol in the upcoming replenishments shall be stable and sufficient to meet all agreed incremental costs to enable [developing country] Parties to comply with the accelerated phase-out schedule."[24] Thus, this was an important negotiation for continuing the constructive atmosphere of the ozone regime. Having spent so many years working on these issues, however, perhaps it was no surprise that after the detailed, but fundamentally constructive, negotiations, parties agreed on $490 million for the 2009–2011 replenishment, which was nearly in the middle between the initial bargaining positions of the donor and developing countries (positions set in part by studies done by one of the regime's technical advisory expert panels, the Technology and Economic Assessment Panel).[25] Yet, future negotiations may be more contentious if HCFC funding requirements increase. The fund's Executive Committee and the MOP must also address key and potentially divisive operational issues, such as the date for determining a country's level of HCFC consumption and production eligible for funding and the rules regarding "second conversions," or situations in which a plant that already converted from CFC to HCFC production using Multilateral Fund resources now sought funding for conversion away from HCFCs.

Both the Doha MOP and the 2009 MOP in Egypt also addressed ODS destruction. Thousands of tons of CFCs and halons and other controlled substances exist both in stockpiles of unused ODS and in so-called ODS banks, the name given to ODS contained in existing equipment and products that are either still in use, are in storage, or have been discarded as waste. Parties understand the need to manage stockpiles and banks carefully to avoid their release into the air, something that could threaten the impact of the regime. This is not always done. Destruction represents the only permanent solution as it means breaking the ODS down into inert components. Reports discussed at the meeting indicate that more than 5 million tons of ODS banks already exist (with about 1 million tons easily available for recovery and destruction). This number will increase dramatically as most developing countries cease production and use of new CFCs, halons, and carbon tetrachloride in 2010 and all countries begin to implement the accelerated HCFC phaseout.

Many industrialized countries have programs in place to deal with ODS banks, but crucial challenges remain, especially in developing countries. In Doha, delegates agreed that the regime's technical panels should continue studying the issue and, more importantly, instructed the Multilateral Fund to pay for pilot projects in developing countries on the collection, storage, and destruction of ODS banks. At future MOPs the parties must decide how, and to what extent, to fund destruction activities in developing countries. The mandate of the Multilateral Fund allows for funding pilot projects on almost any issue, but it does not explicitly include covering the costs of ODS destruction or managing stockpiles and banks. This would require adjusting elements of the fund and larger replenishments in the future. While such steps are logical, it is not clear that current economic and political conditions will allow for significant expansion of the fund. Other environment regimes also face the challenge of how to fund regime expansion into environmentally important but potentially expensive areas.

These and other issues were on the agenda at MOP-21 in 2009 and will also be discussed at future ozone meetings. Indeed, the regime still faces significant challenges. Despite its many successes, stratospheric ozone levels remain lower than before CFCs starting attacking them, the Antarctic ozone hole remains near its worst levels, and skin cancer cases continue to rise and could multiply in the next decade. The regime is on pace to reverse all these impacts, a historic accomplishment, but doing so requires completing the phaseout of CFCs in all developing countries, implementing and funding the transition away from HCFCs, and ensuring that HCFCs are not replaced by substances with high global-warming potential or other harmful environmental impacts. Methyl bromide remains a contentious issue despite the reduction in CUE totals. The need to increase, manage, and fund ODS destruction will increase in importance over the next several years. Parties must also eliminate the illegal trade of ODS, find alternatives for the few remaining exempted uses of halons, and address any new chemicals found to threaten the ozone layer. Finally, maintaining stable and appropriate funding to assist developing countries in implementing the regime will remain central to its effectiveness, its sense of constructive cooperation, and its positive impact on global environmental politics in general. How parties address these challenges will determine the continued growth and ultimate success of the ozone regime.

The history of global ozone policy illustrates the role that veto coalitions can play in weakening regime rules, as well as how states sometimes shift roles as a result of increasing scientific evidence, domestic political pressures, and changing economic interests. It is also the best example of a global environmental regime that has been continually strengthened in response to new scientific evidence and technological innovations.

Indeed, when one combines all the amendments and adjustments to the Montreal Protocol, the current set of binding controls is truly impressive. The protocol currently controls ninety-six chemicals. Industrialized countries phased out halons in 1994; CFCs, carbon tetrachloride, methyl chloroform, and hydrobromofluorocarbons in 1996; bromochloromethane in 2002; and methyl bromide in 2005—although various exceptions exist that allow continued use of small amounts of certain substances. They must phase out almost all HCFCs by 2020. Developing-country parties phased out hydrobromofluorocarbons in 1996 and bromochloromethane in 2002. They must phase out CFCs, halons, and carbon tetrachloride in 2010, methyl chloroform and methyl bromide by 2015, and HCFCs by 2030 (see Table 4.1).

The ozone regime stands as perhaps the strongest and most effective global environmental regime and now boasts universal ratification (196 parties). The worldwide production of CFCs fell from about 1.1 million tons in 1986 to 35,000 tons in 2006.[26]

TABLE 4.1   Montreal Protocol Chemical Controls

CHEMICALS	DEVELOPED COUNTRIES PHASEOUT SCHEDULE	DEVELOPING COUNTRIES PHASEOUT SCHEDULE
Chlorofluorocarbons (CFCs)	Phase out by 1996	Phase out by 2010
Halons	Phase out by 1994	Phase out by 2010
Carbon tetrachloride	Phase out by 1996	Phase out by 2010
Methyl chloroform	Phase out by 1996	Freeze by 2003 at average 1998–2000 levels, reduce by 30 percent by 2005 and 70 percent by 2010, and phase out by 2015
Hydrobromofluorocarbons (HBFCs)	Phase out by 1996	Phase out by 1996
Hydrochlorofluorocarbons (HCFCs)	Reduce by 35 percent by 2004, 75 percent by 2010, 90 percent by 2015, and phase out by 2020, allowing 0.5 percent for servicing purposes during the period 2020 to 2030	Freeze by 2013 at the average 2009–2010 levels; reduce by 10 percent by 2015, 35 percent by 2020, 67.5 percent by 2025; phase out by 2030, allowing for an annual average of 2.5 percent for servicing purposes during the period 2030 to 2040.
Methyl bromide (CH$_3$Br)	Phase out by 2005	Freeze by 2002 at average 1995–1998 levels, reduce by 20 percent by 2005, and phase out by 2015
Bromochloromethane (BCM)	Phase out by 2002	Phase out by 2002

Source: Ozone Secretariat, "Basic Facts and Data on the Science and Politics of Ozone Protection," UNEP, September 18, 2008, http://ozone.unep.org/Events/ozone_day_2008/press_backgrounder.pdf.

FIGURE 4.1   **Worldwide production of CFCs, HCFCs, and HFCs**

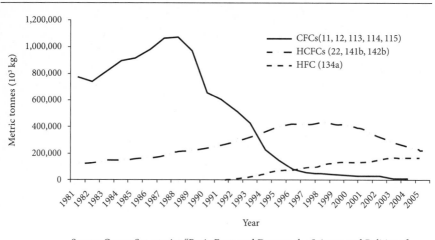

Source: Ozone Secretariat, "Basic Facts and Data on the Science and Politics of Ozone Protection," UNEP, September 18, 2008, http://ozone.unep.org/ Events/ozone_day_2008/press_backgrounder.pdf.

Worldwide production of CFCs, also near 1.1 million tons in 1986, will be nearly eliminated during 2010. HCFC production has peaked. The Ozone Secretariat calculates that without the Montreal Protocol, global CFC consumption would have reached about 3 million tons in 2010 and 8 million tons in 2060, resulting in a 50 percent depletion of the ozone layer by 2035[27] (see Figure 4.1). Studies estimate this would have caused 130 million more cases of cataracts, 19 million additional cases of non-melanoma skin cancer, and 1.5 million more cases of melanoma cancer.[28] Many animal and plant species would also have seen very significant and negative impacts.

The ozone regime has also delivered substantial climate benefits. Because most ODS are also potent GHGs, just those eliminated prior to 2000 prevented the equivalent of approximately 25 billion tons of carbon dioxide (CO_2) emissions[29]—or several times as much as the initial targets of the Kyoto Protocol.[30] Looking forward, the 2007 agreement to speed the phaseout of HCFCs will eliminate about 7 to 9 metric tons of HCFCs, equal to the CO_2 produced by 100 million cars.[31]

Most parties continue to meet their commitments to reduce or eliminate the production and consumption of ozone-depleting chemicals, and as a result the atmospheric concentrations of these chemicals are declining. While the future is far from certain, if countries fully implement all the requirements in the ozone regime (still a big "if"), then the ozone layer over most of the earth could fully recover around 2050, with the more extensive depletion above Antarctica following late in the century. This would represent one of the greatest successes in global environmental policy.

CLIMATE CHANGE

The release of heat-trapping greenhouse gases from human activities, including the burning of fossil fuels and deforestation, is intensifying the natural greenhouse effect and warming the planet. Relatively small amounts of warming can cause surprisingly large changes in climate. Anthropogenic warming is already being observed and will increase as GHGs increase.

The resulting climate change will produce a host of mostly negative and potentially very harmful impacts. These include increased incidence of drought and floods, expanded ranges for certain crop-eating pests and tropical diseases (such as malaria), sea level rise, significantly higher extinction rates, disruption of global and regional weather patterns, ocean acidification, and potentially very serious damage to regional freshwater resources and food production, coral reefs, mountain ecosystems and even the Amazon basin. Many of these impacts are already beginning to occur, some much more quickly than expected.[32] Significantly reducing the amount of greenhouse gases released from human activity will reduce, or mitigate, the extent of future impacts.

Climate change is the prototype of the global commons issue. The earth's climate system affects all nations, and broad international cooperation is required to mitigate the threat of global warming. The negotiation of a regime to mitigate global climate change has been complicated by the multiple sources of emissions that contribute to global warming; by scientific uncertainties, especially the chemistry of the atmosphere; and by dependence on global climate modeling, which is not yet an exact science.[33] Even more importantly, however, energy is central to every nation's economy, and the policy changes required to reduce GHG emissions raise difficult political questions about who should bear the immediate economic costs and how to allocate the potential long-term benefits. Even to stabilize the amount of CO_2 in the atmosphere (which would not reduce the warming caused by emissions already in the atmosphere) would require cutting current emissions by roughly one-half or more. That would necessitate major gains in conservation and a switch from coal and oil to natural gas and renewable sources, all of which would affect powerful economic and political interests in some of the most important emitters of GHGs.

GHG emissions from the burning of fossil fuels account for roughly 80 percent of total world emissions, and deforestation and methane emissions contribute most of the rest. Fossil fuel burning has increased atmospheric concentrations of CO_2 by 30 percent since preindustrial times (see Figure 4.2). The top twenty emitters of CO_2, led by China (20 percent) and the United States (19 percent), account for about 76 percent of the world's emissions (see Table 4.2 and Figure 4.3).

FIGURE 4.2   Atmospheric concentration of CO_2, 1744–2008

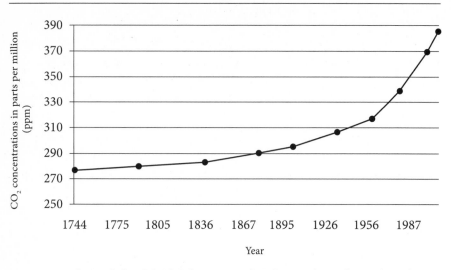

Source: Carbon Dioxide Information Analysis Center website at http://cdia.ornl.gov.

FIGURE 4.3   Global CO_2 emissions from fossil fuel burning, 2006

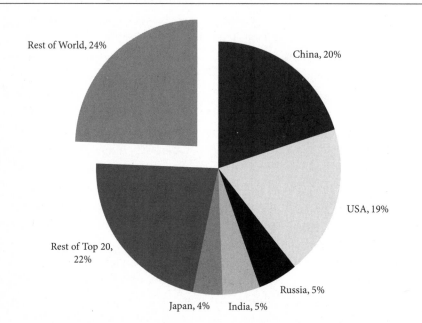

Data source: Tom Boden, Gregg Marland, and Robert J. Andres, *National CO_2 Emissions from Fossil Fuel Burning, Cement Manufacture, and Gas Flaring: 1758–2006* (Oak Ridge, TN: Carbon Dioxide Information Analysis Center, Oak Ridge National Laboratory, 2009), http://cdiac.ornl.gov/trends/emis/tre_tp20.html.

TABLE 4.2   2006 Top Twenty Emitting Countries by Total Fossil Fuel CO_2 (1,000 Metric Tons of Carbon)

COUNTRY	1990 EMISSIONS	2006 EMISSIONS	PERCENTAGE CHANGE	2006 PER CAPITA EMISSIONS
China	658,554	1,664,589	+153	1.27
United States	1,326,725	1,568,806	+18	5.18
Russia	565,901*	426,728	−25	2.99
India	188,344	411,914	+119	0.37
Japan	319,704	352,748	+10	2.80
Germany	276,425	219,570	−21	2.67
United Kingdom	156,481	155,051	−1	2.56
Canada	122,739	148,549	+21	4.55
South Korea	65,901	129,613	+97	2.68
Italy	115,925	129,313	+12	2.19
Iran	61,954	127,357	+106	1.81
Mexico	104,907	118,950	+13	1.13
South Africa	90,963	113,086	+24	2.39
France	108,576	104,495	−4	1.71
Saudi Arabia	58,646	104,063	+77	4.38
Australia	79,943	101,458	+27	4.90
Brazil	56,966	96,143	+69	0.51
Spain	62,497	96,064	+54	2.18
Indonesia	41,032	90,950	+122	0.41
Ukraine	166,770*	87,043	−48	1.86
TOTAL TOP 20	3,896,282	6,246,490	+60	2.43
GLOBAL TOTAL	6,144,000	8,230,000	+34	1.25

* 1992 figures.

Data source: Tom Boden, Gregg Marland, and Robert J. Andres, National CO_2 Emissions from Fossil-Fuel Burning, Cement Manufacture and Gas Flaring: 1758–2006 (Oak Ridge, TN: Carbon Dioxide Information Analysis Center, Oak Ridge National Laboratory, 2009), http://cdiac.ornl.gov/trends/emis/tre_tp20.html.

Key participants in the negotiations on climate change have defined their interests in a manner more closely correlated with their perceptions of the costs of the regime than with their perceptions of vulnerability to the threat. The perceived costs of addressing climate change, moreover, relate primarily to the country's "energy culture," that is, its historical experience with fossil fuels in relation to its economic growth. Because governments argue that they cannot estimate the eventual costs of mitigation measures in overall economic growth without far more information, perceptions of costs are usually shaped by their overall biases regarding energy policy.[34] Thus, three groups of states were initially distinguished:[35]

- *States with few indigenous fossil fuel resources and relatively dependent on imported energy and thus have learned to maintain high living standards while reducing their use of fossil fuels:* This group includes Japan and most European Union (EU) states, including Denmark, Finland, France, Italy, the Netherlands, and Sweden.
- *States with large supplies of cheap energy resources and a culture of highly inefficient energy use:* This group includes Brazil, China, India, Mexico, Russia, and the United States.
- *States highly dependent on fossil fuel exports for income:* This group includes the Arab oil states, Australia, Norway, and, initially, the United Kingdom.

The "energy culture" of states generally determined whether a state would join a lead- or veto-state coalition with regard to commitments to GHG emissions targets and timetables. The EU was the leader in pushing for targets and timetables during the 1990s, and the United States was the main veto state. Brazil, China, India, Russia, and Saudi Arabia have consistently played veto roles. Small island developing states are the other prominent set of lead states. Their extreme exposure to rising sea levels and stronger storms make them perhaps the most vulnerable countries to the impacts of climate change and strong advocates for international action.

There have also been some exceptions: Norway and Australia were early lead states, mainly because domestic political pressures and an initial focus on vulnerability drove their positions, but they later retreated to veto roles in negotiations over targets and timetables. The United Kingdom now supports a strong climate regime, despite being a fossil fuel exporter, because its overall energy and industry policies have transitioned to a greater emphasis on energy efficiency and natural gas and a lesser one on coal. Japan was initially part of a veto coalition but has shifted its position over time and now gives more support to the regime to fight climate change, although it still appears to be questioning the practicality of future emissions commitments.

Scientists have long known that the buildup of CO_2 in the atmosphere can cause climate change. But the process of issue definition began to accelerate in 1985 and 1986. The World Meteorological Organization (WMO) and UNEP took the first major

BOX 4.2   CHINESE FOSSIL FUEL EMISSIONS

The People's Republic of China has surpassed the United States as the world's largest emitter of CO_2. According to reported energy statistics, coal production and use in China have increased tenfold since the early 1960s. Similarly marked increases have occurred in the use of oil and natural gas. As a result, Chinese fossil fuel CO_2 emissions have grown a remarkable 79.2 percent since 2000 alone. This is quite a change since 1950, when China stood tenth among nations based on annual fossil fuel CO_2 emissions. From 1970 to 1996, China's fossil fuel CO_2 emissions grew at an annual rate of 5.3 percent. Growth has occurred largely in the use of coal—which is not surprising, given China is the world's largest coal producer—accounting for 98.7 percent of the emissions total in 1950 and 72.9 percent in 2006. China is also the world's largest hydraulic cement producer, a major source of CO_2 emissions. In 2006 China produced over 1.2 billion metric tons of hydraulic cement, or roughly 47 percent of the world's production. Emissions from cement production account for 9.8 percent of China's 2006 total industrial CO_2 emissions. China's population has doubled over the past four decades and now exceeds 1.3 billion people. Per capita emissions increased considerably over this period, and 2006 marked the first year China's per capita emission rate (1.27 metric tons of carbon) exceeded the global average (1.25 metric tons of carbon). Nevertheless, as the Chinese have argued within the context of global climate-change negotiations, its per capita emissions are less than one-quarter of the United States'.

T. A. Boden, G. Marland, and R. J. Andres, *Global, Regional, and National Fossil-Fuel CO_2 Emissions* (Oak Ridge, TN: Carbon Dioxide Information Analysis Center, Oak Ridge National Laboratory, U.S. Department of Energy, 2009), http://cdiac.ornl.gov/trends/emis/tre_prc.html.

step with a 1985 conference in Villach, Austria, that produced a new scientific consensus that global warming was a serious possibility.[36] And in 1986, WMO, the National Aeronautics and Space Administration, and several other agencies issued a three-volume report concluding that climate change was already taking place at a relatively rapid rate. The unusually hot summer of 1988 accelerated media and congressional attention in the United States, and even thrust the climate issue into the presidential campaign. Congressional testimony by prominent U.S. scientists suggesting that the climate was already changing, primarily because of CO_2 emissions, further contributed to the definition of the climate-change issue.[37]

The fact-finding process coincided with the issue-definition stage. In 1988, the WMO and UNEP organized the Intergovernmental Panel on Climate Change (IPCC) in an attempt to establish a common factual basis for negotiations that would focus on policy options.[38] The First Assessment Report of the IPCC—approved by the participating states after long, grueling negotiations in August 1990—reaffirmed that global warming is a serious threat. The report predicted that if states continue to pursue "business as usual," the global average surface temperature would rise at a rate of change unprecedented in human history. However, despite the success of the first IPCC report in establishing a stronger scientific consensus on climate change, it failed to establish a consensus on the economics of the problem, which was one of the key points of contention during subsequent negotiations.

The initial coalition of lead states (Finland, the Netherlands, Norway, and Sweden) squared off with the United States, as leader of the veto coalition, first on whether to hold global negotiations on climate change and then on whether the negotiations should seek to produce a protocol containing specific obligations on emissions. The lead states wanted to negotiate a framework convention in parallel with negotiations for a protocol limiting emissions, to be completed no later than a year after the convention. The United States insisted on holding talks only on a framework convention, with no parallel negotiations on protocols, arguing that regulating carbon releases would require major changes in fossil fuel consumption and, consequently, lifestyles and the industrial structure. In October 1990, however, Japan broke ranks with the United States on the issue by committing itself to stabilizing its GHG emissions at 1990 levels by 2000. That left the United States and the Soviet Union alone among industrialized countries rejecting a target and timetable for controlling emissions in a future climate regime.[39]

Formal negotiations for a climate convention began officially in February 1991 under the auspices of the Intergovernmental Negotiating Committee for a Framework Convention on Climate Change, which was created by the United Nations General Assembly. The EC led the negotiations by virtue of its previous announced commitment to lower its joint CO_2 emissions to 1990 levels by 2000. Australia, Austria, Denmark, Germany, Japan, the Netherlands, and New Zealand also committed themselves to reducing their emissions by 2000 or 2005.

Had binding commitments for controlling GHG emissions been included in the text, developing countries' agreement would have been crucial to the regime. The biggest rapidly industrializing countries (Brazil, China, and India) already accounted for 21 percent of global emissions in 1989 (about the same as the United States), and as their economies grew, their emissions levels would certainly rise. Because they viewed fossil fuels as a vital component of their success as potential industrial powers, they formed a potential veto coalition.[40]

The negotiating session in February 1992 ended without resolution of the issue of a stabilization target and timetable. British, Dutch, German, and other EC member governments sent officials to Washington before the next meeting in April in an unsuccessful effort to persuade the United States to go along with a commitment to stabilize emissions at 1990 levels by 2000. Then, during the April session, President George H. W. Bush personally called Prime Minister Helmut Kohl of Germany and asked him to drop his government's demand for the stabilization commitment in return for Bush's participation in the upcoming Earth Summit. Bush announced his decision to attend the Rio conference only after the final draft text of the convention was completed without reference to binding commitments to controlling GHGs.[41]

In June 1992, countries gathered in Rio for the United Nations Conference on Environment and Development (UNCED), and during the proceedings 154 countries signed the United Nations Framework Convention on Climate Change (UNFCCC). At this point, forty industrialized countries, including Australia, Japan, Russia, Ukraine, and the United States, as well as countries in the EC, agreed to take the leading role in reducing GHG emissions, as they were now identified in the text of the UNFCCC as Annex I parties.[42] The UNFCCC states that Annex I parties should take steps to reduce their GHG emissions in 2000 to "earlier levels"—a phrase interpreted by the EC to mean 1990 levels—but does not commit governments to hold emissions to a specific level by a certain date. Nor does it address emissions-reduction targets after 2000. But the text does provide for regular review of the "adequacy" of the commitments.

The UNFCCC entered into force in March 1994 after ratification by the minimum-necessary fifty states.[43] Today, more than 190 countries are parties. While the veto power exercised by the United States and, to a lesser extent, Russia, prevented the inclusion of binding targets and timetables in the UNFCCC, it could not prevent efforts to begin negotiations on a binding protocol. The EC issued a statement upon signing the convention calling for an early start on negotiation of a protocol with binding targets and timetables. Germany joined with an international network of NGOs and small island developing states to press for a significant strengthening of the regime. Then, in 1993 and 1994, the Bill Clinton administration effectively reversed the Bush policy of opposition to such negotiations, moving the United States from a clear veto state to more of a swing state, ensuring that such talks would occur.

Kyoto Protocol

The first Conference of the Parties (COP) to the UNFCCC convened in March 1995. In addition to its work on initiating implementation of the climate regime under the UNFCCC, the COP agreed to negotiate, by the end of 1997, quantitative limits on GHG emissions beyond 2000. The COP created a new subsidiary body, the Ad Hoc Group on the Berlin Mandate, to conduct the negotiations (COPs often place large and potentially divisive issues into separate subsidiary bodies that can meet more frequently). However, the COP could not agree if the new limits on GHG emissions should represent real reductions from current levels, as opposed to simply reduced levels of future emissions, or which countries would be subject to the new commitments. The EU supported a commitment of substantial reductions, but the JUSCANZ group (Japan, the United States, Canada, Australia, and New Zealand), which constituted a new veto coalition, opposed negotiations for reduced emissions. The ad hoc group met eight times between August 1995 and December 1997. Halfway through the process, the second COP met in July 1996 and adopted the IPCC's Second Assessment Report of December 1995. The IPCC report concluded that the earth's temperature had increased by 0.3 to 0.6 percent—nearly 1 degree Fahrenheit over the previous one hundred years—and that there was a "discernible human influence" on climate. The report predicted an increase of another 2 to 6 degrees Celsius over the next century if the trend in atmospheric CO_2 concentrations was not reversed.

The EU maintained its lead-state role by tabling a proposal to reduce emissions of the three main GHGs (carbon dioxide, methane, and nitrous oxide) from 1990 levels by at least 7.5 percent by 2005 and by 15 percent by 2010. The EU proposal would allow some EU member countries, such as Germany, to undertake deeper emissions reductions and poorer EU states to accept lower targets provided the overall EU reduction reached the 7.5 percent required of other countries. In sharp contrast, the United States proposed stabilizing emissions of six GHGs (including three whose impacts were less quantifiable) at 1990 levels by 2008 to 2010 for all Annex I parties.

The United States also proposed allowing countries to meet their targets through emissions trading with other parties. Countries able to exceed their emissions-reduction requirements would be able sell those excess reductions, or credits, to a country that was having trouble meeting its targets. In theory, this would allow countries with more inexpensive options to make more reductions while allowing countries that only had very expensive options to do less. If the system worked, it would encourage greater technological innovation (as some countries sought to sell credits for profit) while allowing the world as a whole to achieve the same GHG reductions at a lower cost.

The EU did not oppose the concept of emissions trading but objected to the specific U.S. proposal because it established few specified conditions for how the trading would occur. The EU and many developing countries were particularly concerned that the U.S. proposal would assign emissions reductions to Russia and former Soviet bloc states in Central and Eastern Europe. These emissions were referred to as "hot air" because these countries' emission levels were already down more than 30 percent from 1990 because so many obsolescent plants had been shut down following the collapse of communism and the ongoing restructuring of their economies. Because emissions-reduction and -trading levels would be pegged to 1990 levels, these countries would be able to sell emissions-reduction credits for emissions that did not really exist (hot air). This would allow parties buying the hot air to meet their reduction targets on paper but without actually reducing GHG emissions. Some developing countries objected to trading on more general grounds, arguing that it would allow countries that purchase credits to delay the start of serious efforts to transition away from fossil fuels. Since such steps would be necessary eventually, it would be less expensive and more effective in the long run, and perhaps fairer as well, if all countries began the process immediately. For the same reasons, some other parties argued the proposed protocol should allow parties to fulfill only a certain percentage of their required reductions through trading.

Meanwhile, Australia opened up another important issue in the diplomatic struggle, arguing that because its economy depended far more heavily on exports of fossil fuels than the average Annex I party, it should not have to reduce its emissions as other countries. This demand for differentiation became another way for the veto coalition to seek to reduce its costs for complying with a possible targets-and-timetables agreement by allowing some states to justify lower targets.

As parties gathered for the third meeting of the COP in 1997 in Kyoto, the planned deadline for adopting a protocol, the differences between lead and veto states continued to widen rather than narrow. The United States, which had previously supported equal reductions for all industrialized-country parties, endorsed the concept of differentiation to take into account the greater economic burdens that equal reductions would impose on certain states. The U.S. delegation also took the position that it could not accept any emissions reductions unless developing countries also agreed formally to control their emissions—a condition mandated by a unanimous vote in the U.S. Senate that was clearly unacceptable to developing countries. New Zealand similarly demanded that developing countries specify by 2002 how much they would slow their emissions over the subsequent twelve years.

Following a week and a half of intense negotiations, the parties finally adopted the Kyoto Protocol.[44] The protocol requires industrialized-country parties to reduce their collective emissions of six GHGs by at least 5.2 percent below their 1990 levels between 2008 and 2012 (see Table 4.3). Although it adopted no formula for differentiation based on objective characteristics of the party, the protocol does differentiate national targets based on bargaining between and among veto states and the EU. The national targets vary from a 10 percent increase for Iceland (which already had very low emissions due to its reliance on geothermal and hydroelectric power) and an 8 percent increase for Australia to 8 percent reductions for the EU and most of the countries in eastern Europe. The United States agreed to accept the target of a 7 percent reduction but won a concession that the three newer GHGs would be calculated from a 1995, rather than a 1990, baseline. This not only made the target much less demanding but also revealed the first of a number of limitations of the protocol's potential success.

TABLE 4.3   Kyoto Protocol Annex B:
Party Quantified Emission Limitation or
Reduction Commitment (Percentage
Change from 1990 Base Year)

COUNTRY	KYOTO TARGET
Australia	+8
Austria	−8
Belgium	−8
Bulgaria*	−8
Canada	−6
Croatia	−5
Czech Republic*	−8
Denmark	−8
Estonia*	−8
European Community	−8
Finland	−8
France	−8
Germany	−8
Greece	−8
Hungary*	−6
Iceland	+10
Ireland	−8
Italy	−8
Japan	−6
Latvia*	−8
Liechtenstein	−8
Lithuania*	−8
Luxembourg	−8
Monaco	−8
Netherlands	−8
New Zealand	0
Norway	+1
Poland*	−6
Portugal	−8
Romania	−8
Russian Federation*	0
Slovakia*	−8
Slovenia*	−8
Spain	−8
Sweden	−8
Switzerland	−8
Ukraine*	0
United Kingdom	−8
United States	−7

* Countries undergoing
the process of transition
to a market economy.

The U.S. proposal for a formal commitment by developing countries to control and eventually reduce their emissions was dropped after China, India, and other developing-country parties attacked it, making clear that they constituted a broad and firm veto coalition on the issue and would not compromise. Even an opt-in position that would have provided for voluntary adoption of an emissions target by non–Annex I states was vetoed by their delegations.

To alleviate the costs of achieving its emissions targets, the Kyoto Protocol recommends that countries use three "flexibility mechanisms": the **Clean Development Mechanism** (CDM), **joint implementation**, and **emissions trading**.[45] Although many argued that the environmental integrity of the protocol and inequity among member states represent potential weaknesses in the flexibility mechanisms, proponents successfully argued that they were necessary to achieve widespread consensus to lower emissions below 1990 levels.

The CDM is a procedure under the Kyoto Protocol by which developed countries may finance or invest in projects that avoid GHG emissions in developing countries; for doing so, they receive credits that they may apply toward meeting mandatory limits on their own emissions.

Joint implementation is similar to the CDM, but instead of involving cooperation between developed and developing countries, it promotes collaboration between industrialized countries and countries with economies in transition (the former Soviet bloc). For example, a joint implementation project could involve German support for replacing a coal-fired plant in Romania with a more efficient energy source. All parties involved must approve joint implementation projects, which must result in emissions reductions or removals greater than any that would have otherwise occurred.

The third Kyoto mechanism is emissions trading, whereby an Annex I party with excess emissions credits sells its credits to another Annex I party unable to meet its commitments. However, as noted above, some expressed concern that this could allow the United States and others to accomplish many of their reductions by acquiring emissions credits from Russia, which, along with Ukraine, was not required to reduce emissions below 1990 levels.[46] The developing countries had initially opposed that provision but finally agreed in order to avoid a complete collapse of the negotiations.

Despite the Kyoto Protocol's adoption, many challenges remained on the horizon. The Kyoto Protocol could enter into force only after ratification by fifty-five parties to the convention, accounting for at least 55 percent of the CO_2 emissions in 1990. Designed to ensure that the protocol would have a meaningful impact if it entered into force, the requirement also provided bargaining leverage for industrialized countries, which could withhold ratification in exchange for compromises on particular uses. Thus, while most developing countries and small island states ratified immediately, many

Annex I parties signaled their intention to use subsequent COP meetings as forums to address remaining concerns and negotiate more favorable terms before they ratified.

UNFCCC COP-4 in 1998 adopted the Buenos Aires Plan of Action, which set a two-year deadline to strengthen UNFCCC implementation and prepare for the entry into force of the Kyoto Protocol. Among other things, the meeting also set the stage for future discussions on important details concerning the operation of the three flexibility mechanisms, including the concept of supplementarity, the requirement that the mechanisms can be used only in addition to significant domestic action to meet a country's targets. When that deadline approached two years later in The Hague, the issue of if and how to include carbon sinks (forests and other ecosystems that absorb CO_2 from the atmosphere) within the CDM proved to be the most difficult to resolve. The EU favored limited use of the mechanisms in meeting emissions targets and also proposed a "concrete ceiling" on the use of carbon sinks, seeking to limit how much a country could attempt to offset actual emissions reductions by creating or protecting natural sinks.[47] The United States, which on this issue was aligned with a new veto coalition known as the Umbrella Group (Australia, Canada, Iceland, Japan, New Zealand, Norway, Russia, and Ukraine), pushed for liberal use of the mechanisms, especially the CDM, and would not agree to ceilings on carbon sinks.

Not until the seventh COP, held in Morocco in November 2001, did delegates finally reach agreement on ways to operationalize the Kyoto Protocol and complete the mandate set forth in Buenos Aires three years before. The EU and the developing countries (who negotiated on these issues as a bloc through the coalition known as the Group of 77) remained steadfast in their goal to achieve full ratification of the Kyoto Protocol, even though it required concessions on some of the demands of Umbrella Group countries. Australia, Canada, Japan, and Russia were able to use the ratification card (their ratification was necessary for the protocol to enter into force) to push for a weaker compliance system, lower eligibility requirements for mechanisms, greater state sovereignty, and minimized requirements for providing information on carbon sinks. Resolving these issues made it more likely they would ratify the protocol because it would be easier and less expensive for them to meet their Kyoto obligations since they could utilize the flexibility mechanism more and control domestic emissions less.[48]

Despite the progress made on elaborating the implementation details of the Kyoto Protocol, however, one major question remained: Would the protocol ever enter into force? Many thought that the Kyoto Protocol had received a death sentence when President George W. Bush announced he would not seek U.S. ratification of the agreement in March 2001: "I oppose the Kyoto Protocol because it exempts 80 percent of the world, including major population centers such as China and India, from compliance, and would cause serious harm to the U.S. economy," he wrote. Bush further referred to "the incomplete state of scientific knowledge of the causes of, and solutions to, global

THE CHRISTIAN SCIENCE MONITOR *Bennett*

CARTOON 4.1   "Kyoto Protocol."
By Clay Bennett. Reproduced with permission from the July 25, 2001 issue of *The Christian Science Monitor* (www.CSMonitor.com). © 2001 *The Christian Science Monitor.*

warming."[49] Although Kyoto could enter into force without the United States, the U.S. decision not to ratify played a large role in delaying the decisions of other economically powerful countries. Furthermore, under most scenarios, the protocol would need the ratification of at least all members of the European Union, as well as Canada, Japan, and the Russian Federation, to enter into force without the United States.

By mid-2004, Russia had become the focus of attention. With more than 120 countries having ratified already—including more than thirty Annex I parties—representing 44 percent of that group's 1990 emissions, the 55 percent threshold required for Kyoto's entry into force as a legally binding international treaty was now tantalizingly close, even without U.S. involvement. If Russia, which represented 17.4 percent of 1990 emissions, signed up, the treaty would have more than enough support to push it over the top.[50]

Interestingly, most observers believed that Russia would likely gain economically from ratifying the protocol because emissions trading would enable it to sell credits for emissions that had already been eliminated as a result of the fall of communism that left its heavy industry in ruins. Also, as an economy in transition, such opportunities to attract foreign investment made the emissions-trading mechanism particularly appealing. Russia would also likely receive substantial financial aid for preserving and expanding its Siberian forests via the CDM's use of carbon sinks. While these factors played a significant role, in the end it was Russia's desire for admission into the World Trade Organization (WTO) that provided the final incentive. The EU had told Moscow that it would support Russia's admission only after it ratified the Kyoto Protocol. On November 18, 2004, Russia ratified the protocol, which then entered into force on February 16, 2005 (the protocol, like most treaties, specifies a ninety-day delay between the final ratification required for entry into force and the actual entry into force). As of late 2009, 188 countries and the European Community had ratified the Kyoto Protocol. The United States is the only industrialized country that has not ratified.[51]

Post-Kyoto Commitments

Yet, even before the Kyoto Protocol entered into force, significant attention had already turned to the question of what would happen when the first commitment period ended in 2012. Article 3.9 of the protocol provides for commitments for subsequent periods for Annex I parties. Neither the precise nature nor the duration of such commitments is specified. In theory, a second commitment period (together with the issue of which parties it applies to and in what ways) could be negotiated under the framework provided by the protocol or as part of a new protocol under the UNFCCC.[52]

Many believed that due to a range of economic, political, and diplomatic considerations, negotiations on a successor regime to the Kyoto Protocol's first commitment period would have to begin in 2008 to avoid a gap between the first commitment period and subsequent commitment periods (many believe a gap between commitment periods would create counterproductive uncertainty and complications for countries and industry). Negotiations on a successor agreement, which could be a new protocol, were expected to take at least two years, and the new agreement's entry into force could take at least another two years after its adoption. Yet achieving consensus on the nature of such an agreement—including its goals and requirements, burden sharing, inclusion of requirements for developing countries, and means to ensure participation by both the United States, the world's largest per capita emitter of GHGs, and China, the world's largest total GHG emitter—would not be easy. The first challenge, however, was to reach an agreement to begin formal negotiations and achieve consensus on the terms of reference for the negotiating process. To provide incentive for achieving this preliminary step, parties set a deadline—the December 2007 Climate Change Conference in Bali, Indonesia.

To facilitate these initial deliberations, two parallel processes were established at the eleventh COP to the UNFCCC and the first MOP to the Kyoto Protocol in Montreal, Canada, in December 2005 (as related agreements within the same regime, the

UNFCCC COP also serves as the protocol's MOP).[53] The first process, titled "Dialogue on Long-term Cooperative Action to Address Climate Change by Enhancing Implementation of the Convention," was established under the UNFCCC. In this process, parties were expected to exchange experiences and analyze strategic approaches for long-term cooperative action to address climate change, including advancing development goals in a sustainable way, addressing action on adaptation, realizing the full potential of technologies, and realizing the full potential of market-based options.[54] The dialogue included all parties to the convention and scheduled four sessions in 2006 and 2007, leading up to Bali. The second process, the "Ad Hoc Working Group on Further Commitments from Annex I Parties under the Kyoto Protocol," was established under the Kyoto Protocol to examine further commitments from Annex I parties.[55] As a working group established under the Kyoto Protocol, it would not consider commitments from developing countries (non–Annex I parties) and those Annex I countries that had not yet ratified the Kyoto Protocol, namely the United States and, until December 2007, Australia. These issues could only be discussed under the UNFCCC process. This reveals why two processes were necessary—so that all types of potential future regime policies could be discussed by all the relevant countries.

The two new groups had the advantage that, while official meetings, they were not established as formal negotiating sessions and thus allowed participants to explore different ideas for post-2012 commitments through the use of panel and expert presentations, guided discussions, and workshops. Yet, as became apparent after COP-12 in Nairobi, Kenya, in December 2006, uncertainty still surrounded the post-2012 agenda, especially the roles to be played by some of the key players, primarily the United States and China and, to a lesser degree, Saudi Arabia, India, and other members of the Group of 77, who were all poised to act as veto states on some issues during the next phase of negotiations.

After two years of these informal meetings, delegates arrived in Bali in December 2007.[56] UN negotiators have an uncanny ability to use all available time and space to exercise options and create package deals. Therefore, no one really expected the conference to end before the final day, likely after several late- or all-night negotiating sessions. Negotiators at these meetings do not like to admit failure and are often willing to agree to a "lowest-common-denominator" agreement so as not to be accused of failing to reach any agreement at all. This process appeared to be unfolding in Bali despite the fact that only an agreement to begin formal negotiations and the terms of reference for this negotiating process were the subject of the negotiations. Delegates did not need to agree on emissions-reduction targets, technology transfer, deforestation, adaptation, or commitments for developing countries . . . yet.

Heading into Bali, there were several possible outcomes:

A new negotiating forum: Delegates could decide, following the 1995 Berlin Mandate model, to create a new ad hoc working group tasked with negotiating a post-2012 "arrangement." The new arrangement could be a totally new protocol (that is, not Kyoto Protocol II), an extension of the Kyoto Protocol's limited quotas past 2012, or a new, non–legally binding agreement concentrating on voluntary commitments. The relative strength or weakness of this outcome would depend on the working group's terms of reference and the political will of the negotiators.

The status quo: Delegates could renew the mandates of the two processes (the Dialogue on Long-term Cooperative Action and the Ad Hoc Working Group on Further Commitments) so they could continue less formal discussions for another year or two. This would signify that the delegates could not reach any other agreement at that time but were willing to continue discussions until an agreement became possible.

A variation on the status quo: Delegates could agree to renew the mandate of only one of the two bodies discussed in the point above. If the ad hoc working group continued, this would exclude countries who were not parties to the Kyoto Protocol. If the dialogue continued, the focus could be forward-looking (a new protocol) or limited to the existing UNFCCC, depending on what direction parties were willing to take.

Stalemate: Delegates could decide that they were unable to reach an agreement to renew the mandates of the dialogue or the ad hoc working group or to establish a new body to negotiate a post–Kyoto Protocol arrangement. If this were the case, delegates would probably agree to revisit the issue at the fourteenth COP in December 2008 in Poznań, Poland—notably, after the U.S. presidential elections.

Although all these (and other) options existed, many believed it crucial to achieve some type of negotiating mandate in Bali. If no mandate emerged to negotiate binding post–Kyoto Protocol targets, a post-2012 gap would become more likely, which in turn could have a negative effect on the emerging European-centered carbon-trading market and undermine the increasing expectations in many industries that a new global agreement is inevitable and that they need to prepare for a more "carbon-constrained" future. The absence of a global framework would make it more likely that domestic policy makers worried about climate change would develop new and very different measures to fight climate change, which, if there was no concern for how these might impact the global negotiations, could create an increasingly fragmented system that

PHOTO 4.3   **Climate-change negotiations in Bali were often so crowded that delegates sat on the floor.**
Courtesy IISD/*Earth Negotiations Bulletin.*

might make a strong global agreement even more difficult. Finally, a failure in Bali to create a negotiating framework that included the issues of prime importance to developing countries—technology transfer, capacity building, and adaptation—would likely make many developing countries less inclined to begin or continue substantive efforts to cut carbon emissions.

In addition to the perception that an agreement was badly needed to keep global climate policy on track, the strong international reaction to the IPCC's Fourth Assessment Report and consequential sense of urgency about climate change had a significant impact on the negotiating atmosphere in Bali. The report, released in stages during 2007, included the strongest consensus statements to date regarding how humankind was impacting the climate, the range of impacts that were already being observed, and the significant threats that existed if efforts were not taken to reduce GHG emissions and protect sinks (climate mitigation), as well as to prepare for the impacts that can no longer be avoided (climate adaptation).

Delegates took more than the scheduled two weeks to reach consensus in Bali on a process to negotiate a post-2012 agreement, but they did succeed. On Saturday afternoon, December 15, 2007, twenty-four hours after the conference's scheduled conclusion, ministers and other high-level officials agreed to a series of outcomes that together comprise the Bali Action Plan. These decisions provided guidance and direction for a series of meetings over the subsequent two years under both the convention and protocol, with the aim of concluding a comprehensive framework for the post-2012 period at COP-15 and COP/MOP-5 in Copenhagen, Denmark, in December 2009. At the heart of the Bali road map were the negotiating tracks to be pursued under the newly launched Ad Hoc Working Group on Long-term Cooperative Action (convention track) and the existing Ad Hoc Working Group on Further Commitments for Annex I Parties under the Protocol (protocol track).

Under the convention track, for the first time parties had a negotiating agenda that encompassed discussions on enhanced national and international action on mitigation (including both developed and developing countries), enhanced action on adaptation,

---

BOX 4.3 IPCC FOURTH ASSESSMENT REPORT

The IPCC's Fourth Assessment Report (AR4) was released in four installments during 2007. AR4 made a major scientific contribution to the understanding of climate change and had an impact on the negotiations of the Bali Action Plan in December 2007.

Working Group I's contribution on climate-change science was released in February 2007. The document summarizes progress in understanding the drivers of climate change, observed climate change, climate processes, and estimates of projected future climate change. The report contains the strongest global scientific consensus statement to date regarding the extent and causes of climate change, expressing greater than 90 percent certainty that human activities have caused most of the observed warming over the past half century. The report notes that the rate of warming and sea-level rise accelerated during the twentieth century and details how other important consequences of climate change, such as more intense precipitation, droughts, and heat waves, have likely already begun to occur.

Working Group II's report, released in April 2007, focuses on impacts, adaptation, and vulnerability and summarizes the current understanding of the impacts that climate change has already had, and will continue to have, on natural, managed, and human systems, their vulnerabilities, and their capacity to adapt. Particularly obvious impacts that have already occurred include widespread changes in ice and snow cover, earlier spring biological events in natural and managed ecosystems, and changes in water temperature and flows in rivers, lakes, and oceans. The report presents projections of impacts on policy-relevant sectors, including water, ecosystems, food, coastal systems, industry, settlement and society, and health, as well as on major regions, including Africa, Asia, Australia and New Zealand, Europe, Latin America, North America, polar regions, and small islands.

The third installment to the IPCC AR4 was released in May 2007. The Working Group III report analyzes options to reduce GHG emissions in main economic sectors as

technology transfer, and provision of financial resources and investment. Since the negotiations took place under the framework of the convention, they included all parties with major GHG emissions—including the largest developing countries and the United States. On the protocol track, the working group continued to analyze mitigation potentials and ranges of emissions-reduction objectives for Annex I parties, examine possible means to achieve mitigation objectives under the Kyoto Protocol, and consider potential further commitments by Annex I parties.

In December 2008, the political contexts for the COP and MOP meetings during the Poznań Climate Conference were quite different than they had been in Bali only a year

---

IPCC Fourth Assessment Report (continued)

well as other mitigation strategies. Short- and long-term strategies are examined under a variety of different global socioeconomic assumptions. The report addresses the implications of different short-term strategies for achieving long-term goals and the relationship between mitigation and sustainable development. Among its central findings are that the economic costs of the most serious impacts of climate change, in the absence of mitigation efforts, will very likely exceed the costs of mitigation efforts that would likely prevent those impacts; delaying the start of mitigation efforts usually increases their long-term cost; and both mitigation and adaptation efforts are necessary to address climate change.

The final installment, the AR4 Synthesis Report released in November 2007, includes the following key findings:

- There is strong certainty that most of the observed warming of the past half century is due to human influences, and there is a clear relationship between the growth in manmade GHG emissions and the observed impacts of climate change.
- The climate system is more vulnerable to abrupt or irreversible changes than previously thought.
- Avoiding the most serious impacts of climate change, including irreversible changes, will require significant reductions in GHG emissions.
- Mitigation efforts must also be combined with adaptation measures to minimize the risks of climate change.

IPCC, *Fourth Assessment Report: Climate Change 2007* (Geneva: IPCC, 2007), www.ipcc.ch/ipccreports/assessments-reports.htm, and "Highlights from Climate Change 2007: Synthesis Report of the IPCC Fourth Assessment Report Summary for Policy Makers," Pew Center for Global Climate Change, www.pewclimate.org/docUploads/PewSummary_AR4.pdf.

earlier. As noted above, in Bali, the negotiating atmosphere reflected the need to come to some agreement to keep the regime on track, as well as an increased sense of urgency concerning the climate change problem in response to the IPCC's Fourth Assessment Report. In Poznań, by contrast, the negotiations took place against the backdrop of the rapidly worsening global financial situation. Many were concerned that aspirations for climate policy would fall victim to the economic crisis—and even the most optimistic observers expected the financial crisis to have an impact on the process.[57]

The EU and other lead states at the Poznań Climate Conference tried to stress their ongoing commitment to combating climate change, arguing that transitioning to a low-carbon society entails not only costs but also important economic opportunities and important long-term benefits. However, during the early stages of the conference, protracted negotiations were also taking place within the EU itself regarding important details of its climate and energy policy package, which centers on a pledged 20 percent GHG-emissions-reduction target by 2020. A number of EU governments were expressing concern about the short-term costs of the package given the economic crises, which caused some delegates in Poznań to question whether the EU's leadership on climate policy was faltering.

On the last day of the Poznań conference, delegates were pleased to hear news that agreement had been reached in Brussels (even though some NGOs criticized the concessions made to secure the compromise). The announcement provided additional details regarding implementation of the EU pledge to reduce its GHG emissions by 20 percent by 2020, as well as to increase its use of renewable energy to 20 percent of total energy use and to increase energy efficiency by 20 percent. The announced package, covering the period from 2013 to 2020, included information on how EU states would divide up the required reduction rules for the third phase of the EU Greenhouse Gas Emissions Trading Scheme and detailed individual emission targets for EU member states in sectors not covered by the trading scheme.[58]

In contrast to worries concerning potential EU backtracking, Barack Obama's victory in the 2008 U.S. presidential election was a source of optimism in the days leading up to the Poznań meetings. Obama promised to make climate change a high priority and highlighted a green-energy economy as a remedy for the ongoing economic crisis. In Poznań, however, the United States was still represented by the Bush administration and remained relatively subdued during the official negotiations. Some delegates and observers also believed that the financial crisis would certainly impact congressional willingness to support a severe change in U.S. climate policy. Some felt that the consequential uncertainty about the U.S. position in 2009 caused other countries to refrain from making significant political advances in Poznań. In addition, developing countries, as expected, declined to make significant moves, choosing to wait for the industrialized countries to clarify their positions on emissions reductions and financing before entering into serious discussions on what actions they would be willing to take. Given this background, many participants agreed that the political circumstances surrounding the Poznań conference were not ideal for major political breakthroughs.[59]

Many issues must be resolved before a new agreement can be reached. Officially negotiations were scheduled to conclude in December 2009 in Copenhagen. While it was increasingly likely that countries would seek only to reach agreement on a general architecture in Copenhagen and fill in the details later, or even agree to postpone the conclusion date, they had to overcome a host of obstacles standing in the way of an effective post-2012 climate regime. Many of the major issues on the table revolved around the nature of emissions-reduction commitments beyond 2012: Should these commitments be legally binding or voluntary? Which countries would have to reduce their GHG emissions? What targets and timetables should be established? Should these be short- or long-term targets, or both? Should the controls address GHG emissions in general, like Kyoto, or should they include action on specific sources of emissions, like cement production or deforestation? What types and levels of new technology transfer and financial assistance, if any, should be provided to developing countries? Should developing countries be required to adopt particular commitments in exchange for such assistance? Should the new agreement take the form of a new protocol, an extension of the Kyoto Protocol, an amendment to the convention, or some other agreement? How should the regime balance actions to mitigate climate change and those to help countries adapt to it?

At the **Group of Eight** (G-8) summit in July 2009, leaders from Canada, France, Germany, Italy, Japan, Russia, the United Kingdom, and the United States agreed to a statement setting the goal of holding global warming to an increase of 2 degrees Celsius (3.6 degrees Fahrenheit) above preindustrial levels by 2020. The EU has also promoted 2 degrees as a goal that the global climate regime itself should adopt. The G-8 also set a long-range target of cutting GHG emissions by 50 percent worldwide and by 80 percent among industrialized countries by 2050. However, they were unable to reach agreement on any short-term targets and did not include any targets for emissions cuts for developing countries. Instead, they "called upon major emerging economies to undertake quantifiable actions to collectively reduce emissions significantly below business-as-usual by a specified year."[60] The endorsement of the long-range goals by Japan, Russia, and the United States represented a significant development, but the statement did not indicate what cuts their leaders were willing to accept for their own countries.

The future of the climate regime still hangs in the balance. Whether the G-8, the bilateral talks between the United States and China, bilateral talks between the EU and several large developing countries, or the two working groups under the UNFCCC and the Kyoto Protocol will contribute to an agreement in Copenhagen is unknown as this book goes to press. However, securing agreement from traditional veto states,

BOX 4.4   UP-TO-DATE RESOURCES ON THE
CLIMATE-CHANGE NEGOTIATIONS

The following websites provide up-to-date information about and analysis from several different perspectives of the outcome of the Copenhagen Climate Change Conference and the negotiations that will follow:

United Nations Framework Convention on Climate Change: http://unfccc.int

United Nations Framework Convention on Climate Change E-newsletter: http://unfccc.int/press/news_room/newsletter/items/3642.php

Earth Negotiations Bulletin/International Institute for Sustainable Development: www.iisd.ca

Climate Action Network: www.climatenetwork.org

Pew Center on Global Climate Change: www.pewclimate.org

Third World Network: www.twnside.org.sg

Tiempo Climate Newswatch: www.tiempocyberclimate.org/newswatch

World Resources Institute: www.wri.org/climate/cop-15

Wuppertal Institute for Climate, Environment and Energy: www.wupperinst.org/en/home

like China, India, the United States, and others who do not support emissions caps for developing countries will require creativity and compromise. The continued injection of science into the policy-making process, along with the focus on the key elements of long-term cooperation in the Bali road map—mitigation (reducing emissions of GHG and protecting sinks), adaptation to climate change, and the necessary FTA to developing countries—may help the various veto coalitions to make the necessary compromises for a stronger climate regime in the future.

CONCLUSION

The ozone and climate regimes share important similarities. Both address the earth's atmosphere. Both attempt to prevent changes to a critical natural system; significant change to either would affect nearly all life on earth.[61] Each addresses a system that exists within a dynamic equilibrium but has certain so-called tipping points. This means that human action can impact the ozone layer and global climate system to a certain degree without changing either significantly, but once these impacts reach a certain level, then it becomes essentially impossible to prevent significant negative changes to these systems or to reverse the changes (or "fix" the problem) for a very long time.

Like the regimes for transboundary air pollution and toxic chemicals discussed in Chapter 3, both the ozone and climate regimes establish binding controls, including targets and timetables, to limit emissions of specific substances. Both regimes started with framework conventions that established important goals, norms, institutions, and procedures. Governments then negotiated protocols that established specific binding emissions reductions. Both regimes impact important economic sectors, and their control measures faced significant opposition from powerful national and international interests. Both include references to the importance of addressing their issues in a precautionary manner. Both follow the principle of common but differentiated responsibilities by mandating that industrialized countries address the issue first, since they are responsible for creating the problem and have the necessary resources to address it. Each includes provisions for developing countries to receive technical and financial assistance to help them meet their regime obligations.

The two regimes are also interrelated. Many of the chemicals that deplete the ozone layer and many of the substances developed to replace them are also powerful GHGs. Thus, by reducing CFC emissions, the ozone regime helped to address climate change, but by promoting certain CFC substitutes, such as HCFCs, the ozone regime complicated matters and actually contributed to GHG emissions. At the same time, accelerating climate change is actually slowing recovery of the ozone layer. While climate change is warming the atmosphere nearest the earth's surface, the troposphere, it is also cooling the stratosphere. A cooler stratosphere produces conditions that accelerate the chemical reactions that deplete ozone.

Yet, in other ways, the ozone and climate regimes are quite different. The ozone regime is widely considered to be among the most effective examples of international environmental policy. The climate regime has likely slowed the growth of GHG emissions, but global emissions have still increased significantly since the regime formed in 1992, serious impacts of climate change are already being observed, and the odds have increased that very serious, even catastrophic, changes will occur in the future. The regimes have also developed at very different speeds. Governments concluded negotiations on the framework treaty for the ozone regime in 1985, eleven years after the discovery that CFCs might threaten stratospheric ozone. Scientists first discovered that increasing GHGs would warm the atmosphere more than one hundred years before the UNFCCC was adopted.

While both regimes establish targets and timetables, in the ozone regime, all industrialized countries must meet essentially the same standards, while in the climate regime, different industrialized countries have very different targets for reducing emissions of GHGs. Developing countries accepted binding controls to reduce the use of ODS under the Montreal Protocol, but there were no binding commitments to reduce GHG emissions under the Kyoto Protocol. Finally, governments expanded and strengthened the ozone regime much more quickly than the climate regime, primarily because of scientific consensus and the availability of substitutes for ozone-depleting chemicals. With regard to the climate regime, while the IPCC has provided the scientific consensus that climate change is occurring, the economic impacts of climate-change mitigation and the fact that much of the world's economy is fueled by coal, oil, and natural gas—fossil fuels that contribute most to CO_2 emissions—have made it difficult for governments to reach agreement on necessary emissions reductions.

These differences, like the those between the regimes examined in Chapter 3, reflect a variety of factors, including characteristics of the issue area; the evolution of scientific consensus on the issues; the identity and interests of the major actors, especially the lead and veto states; how the regime moved through the stages of regime development; the evolution of economic and political interests underlying the issue area; and the presence or absence of well-known obstacles to effective cooperation (discussed in Chapter 6). This contrasts somewhat with global regimes that address the conservation of endangered species and natural resources. Chapter 5 examines six regimes for natural resource conservation and management and how they differ from pollution-control regimes. The conclusion to Chapter 5 will also review and compare all eleven case studies presented in chapters 3 to 5.

DISCUSSION QUESTIONS

1. Why has scientific evidence had a greater impact on the ozone regime than the climate regime? Why is it harder to alter the positions of government negotiators in the climate regime?
2. Consider the veto coalitions opposing strong action on the issues in this chapter. What are the primary motives of each individual member? What weakened those coalitions?
3. Trace the stance of a particular state on climate change and ozone depletion and try to assess the extent of its involvement in leadership or blocking roles.
4. What might be the effect on climate change of growing economic prosperity or recession in the United States or other countries?
5. Compare and contrast the political, economic, and environmental factors that influenced the evolution of the climate and ozone regimes.

5

The Development of Environmental Regimes: Natural Resources, Species, and Habitats

Like the international environmental-protection and pollution-control regimes described in chapters 3 and 4, regimes designed to conserve natural resources also have to overcome conflicts between states' economic and political interests, concerns for protecting state sovereignty, and different opinions regarding the importance of, and how to implement, the principles of common but differentiated responsibilities, precaution, and additionality. The actors are the same: states, international organizations, NGOs, corporations, treaty secretariats, and scientific bodies. The lead states push for greater international cooperation to address a common issue, and the veto states attempt to block agreement or demand certain concessions before they will consent to participate. However, natural resource regimes face the additional challenge of trying to protect and manage physical and living resources—such as forests, rivers, whales, fish stocks, and endangered species—that are of international importance but exist within the boundaries of one or more sovereign states or beyond the boundaries of any state.

The regimes described in this chapter focus on shared natural resources—physical or biological systems that extend into or across the jurisdictions of two or more states. Shared natural resources include nonrenewable resources (for example, pools of oil that are under land or water subject to the jurisdiction of two or more states), renewable and biological resources (fish stocks, birds, mammals), and complex ecosystems (forests, regional seas, river basins, coral reefs, and deserts).[1] However, shared resources are not only of interest to adjacent or neighboring states; they may also link states far removed from each other geographically, as in the case of migratory birds. Similarly, shared natural resources may impinge on the commons, as well as on the jurisdictional zones, of two or more states. Many marine mammals, including whales, move through the waters of several coastal states as well as the waters that are part of the high seas, beyond a country's **exclusive economic zone**.[2]

The international management of natural resources must also address transboundary externalities, which arise when activities that occur within the jurisdiction of an individual state produce results that affect the welfare of those residing in other states.[3] Such situations involve a very difficult question, one central not only to environmental but also to human rights and humanitarian issues: When does the international community have a legitimate interest, right, or obligation to seek significant changes in the domestic affairs of individual states because the activities occurring within their jurisdictions pose severe threats to the well-being of others or to international society as a whole? For example, should states still have unfettered rights to cut huge tracts of their forested land for timber or agriculture since these forests benefit the entire world as biodiversity reserves and as carbon sinks that mitigate climate change? Do countries have a right to try to change how other states manage ecosystems with rich biological diversity because the loss of particular plants and animals could prevent the discovery of new drugs that might cure cancer or other diseases around the world? Do states have the right to tell other states to stop killing, buying, and selling endangered species because extinction is now a global concern? Should the ethical perspectives of a large group of countries regarding whales, elephants, or turtles impact the activities of a smaller set of countries that do not share these views?

In addition to national sovereignty issues, efforts to negotiate regimes to deal with biodiversity, endangered species, forests, fish stocks, and land-management issues may also have consequences for particular economic-development strategies or efforts to promote free trade. Are states free to impose restrictions on imports from other countries if their production involves practices that are unacceptable on environmental grounds, such as catching shrimp in a way that endangers sea turtles? Should a country be prevented from developing a tropical timber industry, which could have major short-term economic benefits, because of the consequences of biodiversity loss?

Finally, pollution-control regimes, such as those for ozone, climate change, POPs, and air pollution, are often based on clear and measurable targets and timetables. Many natural resources regimes, especially those for biodiversity and desertification, do not lend themselves to those types of rules. Effective protection and management of natural resources often requires a complex set of new policies that seek to address a host of factors that threaten the resource. It is also often more difficult to develop effective indicators to measure implementation or to determine the impact of the regime on the resources it is supposed to manage or conserve.

This chapter examines six cases that look at different aspects of international natural resource management. The International Convention for the Regulation of Whaling and the Convention on International Trade in Endangered Species of Wild Fauna and Flora (CITES) present two very different examples of regimes that manage endangered species and illustrate the politics and economics involved in the sustainable management of whales, elephants, and big-leaf mahogany. The Convention on Biological Diversity (CBD) highlights North-South contrasts in the distribution of biodiversity resources and the many ways that natural resource management can conflict with important economic, social, and political interests. The fisheries regime illustrates the importance and difficulty of managing resources that move between areas of national jurisdiction and the global commons. The desertification regime is closely involved with sustainable development issues as it tries to improve land management that has an impact on environmental sustainability and economic and social development. Finally, the case of forests demonstrates what happens when the international community cannot reach agreement on the establishment of a global regime and raises the question of whether legally binding treaties are always the appropriate answer for addressing global environmental problems.

As in the previous two chapters, we analyze each issue according to the stages of negotiation and the role of veto coalitions in shaping the outcomes of bargaining. We also highlight other important causal factors, outline key aspects of their design and expansion, delineate current global policy for each issue, and examine their similarities and differences in more detail.

WHALING

The development and expansion of global policy to safeguard whales illustrates the transformation of an international regime from one that allowed virtually unregulated exploitation of an endangered species into a framework for global conservation, despite the continued resistance of a strong veto coalition. Despite this transformation, however, the international whaling regime sits at a crossroads. The balance of power in the regime's decision-making body, the International Whaling Commission (IWC), rests narrowly with the states favoring a whaling ban. The veto coalition, growing in support and empowered by its ability to exit the relevant international agreement at any time, is gaining ground. Although recent advances in population monitoring and technology offer the prospect of developing a biologically sound system of management, desires to uphold national sovereignty and strong emotions on both sides of the issue threaten to create an impasse that, if left unresolved, could endanger the regime.

Indeed, to a significant degree, emotions and concerns for national sovereignty influence the global debate on whaling more than detailed scientific analysis or national economic interests (whaling no longer represents a significant economic enterprise on a global or even national basis). For some governments and many environmental nongovernmental organizations (NGOs) in the United States and Europe, whaling is seen as both an act of unnecessary human cruelty to an intelligent species and a powerful symbol of environmental overexploitation. To whaling states, harvesting whales represents the right to preserve cultural traditions, maintain coastal livelihoods, and exercise national sovereignty.

In 1946, the long history of the overexploitation of whales, which threatened many species with extinction, led to the establishment of the International Convention for the Regulation of Whaling. The convention prohibited killing certain endangered whale species, set quotas and minimum sizes for whales caught commercially, and regulated whaling seasons. The convention was not, however, a prohibition regime but a club of whaling nations designed to manage the catch. The regime's designated decision-making body, the IWC, met in secret each year to haggle over quotas set so high that far more whales were being killed annually under the new regime than before the regulations had gone into effect. Indeed, the total number of whales killed more than doubled between 1951 and 1962. The IWC also had no power to enforce its regulations on the size of catch or even its ban on killing endangered species. Although the major whaling nations were members of the IWC, many developing countries, including Brazil, Chile, China, Ecuador, Peru, and South Korea, had refused to join or abide by its restrictions. They allowed "pirate" whalers, often financed by sales to the Japanese, to operate freely.

The process of fact finding and consensus building played virtually no role in relations among IWC members. Scientific knowledge was usually subordinated to political and economic interests. The IWC's scientific committee routinely produced data and analyses supporting continued commercial exploitation, and no outside international organization existed that could facilitate a different framework for decisions based on the scientific facts on whaling. Given this situation, it is not surprising that by the 1960s, the survival of the largest species, the blue whale, was in doubt, finback stocks were dwindling, and many other species were experiencing population declines as whalers filled their quotas with younger and smaller whales.

Increasing public awareness of the diminishing stocks, including the potential extinction of blue whales, combined with the emerging environmental movement, began to turn the tide against commercial whaling. The plight of the whales seized the imagination of many Americans, who were beginning to learn more about the intelligence of cetaceans, and the new awareness led to broad popular support for meaningful protections. Responding to the 1969 Endangered Species Act, the United States declared eight whale species endangered in 1970 and began to take the lead in defining the whaling issue internationally.[4]

Placing the issue of whaling in the context of the broader international environmental agenda, the United States first proposed an immediate moratorium on commercial whaling at the 1972 United Nations Conference on the Human Environment. Adopted unanimously by fifty-two of the counties attending the conference, the proposal signaled strong international support for a moratorium. However, because it had not been generated through the IWC, it carried no force of law within the whaling regime itself. In the IWC, the whaling states (Chile, Iceland, Japan, Norway, Peru, and the Soviet Union) not only constituted a powerful veto coalition (that could even choose to leave the regime if they wished) but also held a near majority. A proposal for a whaling moratorium was defeated in the IWC by a vote of six to four, with four abstentions.

Seeing the need to seek change within the whaling regime itself and taking advantage of the fact that the IWC does not limit membership to whaling nations, the United States, Sweden, and other conservationist states sought to overcome the veto coalition by recruiting nonwhaling states into the commission. Thus, rather than pursuing regime transformation through a process of fact finding and consensus building within the IWC, this group sought to assemble the three-fourths majority required to institute a whaling ban. Between 1979 and 1982, the antiwhaling coalition recruited the Seychelles and a number of other developing states, most of which viewed the whaling issue from the perspective that the oceans and their natural resources are the "common heritage of humankind."[5]

The United States, as the lead state, also sought to weaken the veto coalition through the threat of economic sanctions. It used domestic legislation to ban imports of fish products and to deny fishing permits within the United States' two-hundred-mile exclusive economic zone to countries violating international whale-conservation programs. This action put pressure on Chile and Peru, both heavily dependent on U.S. fishing permits and markets, to comply with the conservation programs.

By 1982, enough developing-country nonwhaling nations had joined the IWC to tilt the balance decisively. A five-year moratorium on all commercial whaling, to take effect in 1985, was passed twenty-five to seven, with five abstentions. Four of the veto-coalition states (Japan, Norway, Peru, and the Soviet Union), which accounted for 75 percent of whaling and almost all consumption of whale meat and other whale products, filed formal reservations to the moratorium but chose not to defy it openly when it went into effect.

Japan, Norway, and the Soviet Union had all formally ended commercial whaling activity by the 1987–1988 whaling season. Soon after, however, Japan, Iceland, and Norway unilaterally began the practice of what they called "scientific" whaling, which is permitted under the whaling convention. Most IWC members found no scientific merit in this whaling, which was conducted by commercial ships, because it killed hundreds of minke whales annually. However, other economic and political interests weakened the ability of the United States and other countries to pressure whaling states to end this practice. For example, to avoid a probable Japanese retaliation targeting U.S. fish exports, the United States decided not to ban imports of $1 billion in Japanese seafood annually as retaliation for Japan's whaling, instead choosing the lesser sanction of denying the Japanese permission to fish in U.S. waters. The United States also reached successive bilateral agreements in 1987 and 1988 with Iceland, condoning its "scientific" whaling in part because Washington feared it might be denied use of its air force base in Reykjavik. Only a boycott of Icelandic fish products and other protests organized by conservationists, who were unburdened with such broader concerns, persuaded Iceland to pledge a halt in whaling, at least until 1991.[6] The Soviet Union, meanwhile, continued whaling in spite of the moratorium, bringing in the world's second-largest catch in the 1980s.[7] In addition, underreporting of the Soviet catch during that decade may very well have distorted the estimates of surviving stocks.

Although the adoption of "scientific" whaling programs and a request for a change in the status of the Northeast Atlantic minke whales from "protection stock" to "sustainable stock" represented interim attempts to allow whaling to continue, the whaling states had their sights set on the larger target of repealing the whaling moratorium. At the 1990 IWC meeting, however, with the five-year moratorium ending, the United States led a majority of IWC members in blocking a proposal that would have allowed limited commercial whaling in the Atlantic and instead extended the moratorium for another year. In response, Iceland, Japan, and Norway threatened to use the ultimate weapon of leaving the IWC if the moratorium was not overturned at the next meeting. Only Iceland followed through with the threat, however, leaving the commission in 1992.

Before the 1993 IWC meeting in Kyoto, Japan and Norway prepared for another attempt to end the whaling ban. Norway announced its intention to resume modest commercial whaling (160 minke whales from the North Atlantic) in the 1993 season, reportedly because Prime Minister Gro Harlem Brundtland needed the Arctic whaling communities' votes in a tight upcoming election. Japan planned to request authority to resume the commercial whaling of a limited number of Antarctic minkes and for the harvest of fifty more by village fishermen off the Japanese coast. Meanwhile, both governments spent large amounts of money and effort on public relations in nonwhaling countries to promote the position that minke whales were no longer endangered and that whaling villages, severely impoverished by the moratorium, were being denied the right to pursue a cultural tradition.[8] In addition, Japan induced six Caribbean IWC members to support its position by providing funds for new fishing vessels and paying their annual IWC membership fees.[9] Despite these efforts, the IWC again voted to extend the whaling moratorium for another year, rejecting Japan's requests. Norway resumed limited whaling in 1993 in spite of the moratorium but came under increased international pressure when President Bill Clinton's administration certified Norway as eligible for U.S. trade sanctions and the U.S. House of Representatives called unanimously for their application. President Clinton delayed the application of sanctions pending efforts to convince Norway to end its defiance of the moratorium.

The regime was further strengthened at the 1994 IWC meeting in Mexico by the adoption of a long-term no-catch area for all whales inhabiting waters below 40 degrees south latitude. The action created the Southern Ocean Whale Sanctuary, an Antarctic whale sanctuary that could protect up to 90 percent of the estimated 3.5 million remaining great whales. The whaling nation most affected by the vote was Japan, which was taking three hundred minkes from the Antarctic annually, ostensibly for scientific purposes. Nevertheless, Japan and Norway continued to defy both the whaling moratorium and the provisions for a no-catch area. In 1997, Norway hunted five times as many whales as it did in 1992, and Japan continued to hunt whales in the Antarctic whale sanctuary.[10]

Responding to the standoff on the whaling moratorium and broad consensus among antiwhaling nations that "scientific whaling" simply provided a front for commercial harvesting, Ireland made a compromise proposal at the 1997 IWC meeting in Monaco that would end the moratorium on commercial whaling, terminate the practice of scientific whaling, bring commercial whaling back under the control of the commission, and establish strong rules to govern it. Central to the Irish initiative was the proposal that the IWC formally adopt, as a package, a new Revised Management Scheme, a regulatory mechanism that includes scientific guidelines for setting catch limits and incorporating population uncertainty levels (the Revised Management Procedure), guidelines and methods for monitoring and inspection, area restrictions (such as permitting coastal whaling within two hundred miles of countries having a long whaling tradition as well as designating a global whale sanctuary), prohibiting international trade in whale products, and ending the practice of scientific whaling.

The IWC did not take a vote on the Irish proposal at either its 1997 or 1999 meetings, voting instead to defer a decision. This occurred even though a majority of governments appeared to support the proposal, at least privately,[11] in part because many nations supportive of whale protection did not openly support the Irish proposal. Nervous about being criticized by environmental and animal-welfare organizations, they were reluctant to endorse a plan that would officially allow commercial whaling, even though the present strategy of a simple moratorium on whaling allowed more and more whales to be killed each year[12] (see Figure 5.1).

FIGURE 5.1   Scientific whaling catches since 1985

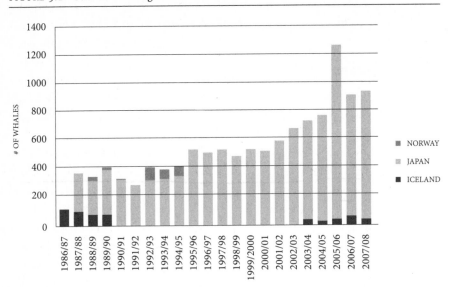

Note: In 1987 and 1988, Iceland had a scientific permit, and Japan and
Norway caught whales in defiance of the moratorium. Beginning in
1993 and 1994, Japan did all of the scientific whaling, and Norway
continued to catch whales in objection to the moratorium (only its
"scientific" whaling figures are included here). Iceland did not kill any
whales from 1989 to 2003 but resumed whaling after rejoining the
IWC in 2002.

Source: "Catches Taken: Under Scientific Permit," IWC, August 10, 2008,
www.iwcoffice.org/conservation/table_permit.htm.

The bitter stalemate over the moratorium on commercial whaling and the loophole
for scientific whaling continues. Japan conducts scientific whaling on a large scale.
Norway continues to set its own commercial quotas for minke whales in defiance of
the IWC ban and kills approximately two to seven hundred whales each year.[13] Iceland
significantly increased its self-targeted quotas in 2009. The fact that whaling essentially
continues to increase, with certain actors effectively ignoring the regime, has raised
concern about the IWC's future role. Observers note the regime's ability to control
whaling activities faces several major challenges: the buildup of a pro-whaling coalition
within the IWC, outright defiance of international whaling rules, misuse of scientific
whaling, the potential for weakened support for the moratorium, and the use of other
processes, including CITES, to attempt "end runs" around IWC prohibitions.

In a development reminiscent of the building of the antiwhaling coalition in the
late 1970s and early 1980s, an alliance to reverse the whaling ban has been steadily

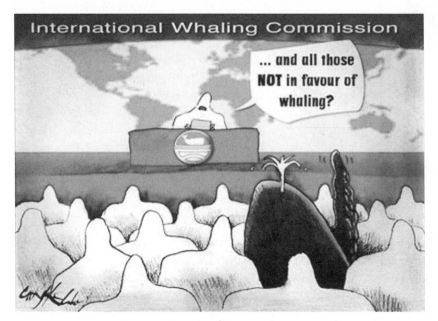

CARTOON 5.1 "International Whaling Commission."
© Chris Kelly, reprinted with permission; www.chriskelly.net.au.

growing since the early 1990s. This coalition has been built largely by Japan, which has engaged in what opponents label "vote buying," that is, building support for its position on whaling through foreign aid and paying IWC membership fees for small-nation coalition members. The head of Japan's Fisheries Agency confirmed this practice, but government officials subsequently denied it.[14] By 2005, the IWC had grown to sixty members, with the antiwhaling bloc holding only a slight simple majority. Although gaining a simple majority would be insufficient to overturn the moratorium, it would allow the veto coalition to affect other aspects of the regime, for instance, by abolishing the conservation committee.[15] Japan proposed overturning the moratorium once again at the 2005 IWC meetings in Ulsan, South Korea, but the proposal was defeated by a vote of twenty-nine countries in favor of retaining the moratorium, twenty-three countries supporting Japan, and five abstentions. Another Japanese proposal would have allowed the use of secret ballots for IWC proposals, lessening the transparency of decision making within the commission and attempting to further strengthen the veto coalition. This proposal was also defeated.

Although the whaling moratorium suggests a strong degree of protection for whales, it is severely weakened by outright defiance of the whaling moratorium, incursions into the whale sanctuaries (in both the Southern and Indian oceans), and the use of loopholes in the regime such as scientific whaling. Norway registered a formal reservation to the moratorium at the time of its passage and, despite significant international pressure for it not to do so, has since conducted commercial whaling outside the control of the IWC. Japan, on the other hand, has conducted its whaling operations mostly under the banner of scientific whaling while also seeking to weaken the controls over sanctuary areas and the moratorium itself. Nations engaged in scientific whaling defend the practice by pointing to the large amount of scientific data it has generated. Some of these data, including stomach contents and reliable estimates of age, cannot be collected without taking whales. However, many scientists contend that although the data are collected using a high degree of scientific rigor, the resulting information does not provide new and important information relevant to the management of stocks but instead largely supports previous knowledge.[16]

Pro-whaling nations have also attempted an "end run" around the IWC by seeking to reduce species protections for whales in CITES. During the thirteenth CITES Conference of the Parties (COP) in 2004, Japan entered a proposal to downlist three populations of minke whales from Appendix I (endangered) to Appendix II (may become endangered); this proposal was rejected, however, as were similar proposals in 1997, 2000, and 2002.[17] Beginning in 1979, and affirmed by Resolution 11.4 at the twelfth CITES COP in 2000, the position of CITES has been to ensure that no conflict exists between treaties and to support the IWC moratorium by maintaining Appendix I listings for all whale species.[18] Downlisting in CITES may not affect the measures imposed by the IWC on its member states, but it would remove barriers to international trade in whale species, thus opening international markets if commercial whaling resumes; it would also provide an important negotiating argument for the veto coalition.

In 2006, the IWC at its annual meeting in St. Kitts and Nevis adopted a declaration by a closely divided vote of thirty-three in favor, thirty-two against, with one abstention, that aimed to break the deadlock. Delegates noted that after fourteen years of discussion and negotiation, "the IWC had failed to complete and implement a management regime to regulate commercial whaling" and declared their "commitment to normalizing the functions of the IWC."[19] In addition, at this meeting American William Hogarth took over as IWC chairman for a three-year term.

Hogarth, a biologist who has managed fisheries throughout his career, decided to focus his efforts on the future of the IWC and, to this end, bring in outside conflict-resolution experts and work toward a compromise. At Hogarth's initiative the IWC agreed to convene an intersessional meeting in London in March 2008 to discuss the future of the IWC and to explore an approach to conflict resolution. The meeting focused on matters of process and not on matters of substance. Contracting governments were encouraged to share their concerns and methods to improve the functioning of the commission. Three internationally recognized experts in the handling of challenging international issues, Special Adviser Calestous Juma, Ambassador Alvaro de Soto, and Ambassador Raul Estrada-Oyuela, were selected to offer guidance in the use of the consensus approach to conflict resolution.[20]

The results of the March 2008 meeting were presented to the IWC in June 2008 at its sixtieth meeting in Chile. Delegates agreed to a procedure aimed at reform of the IWC and agreed to set up a small working group on the future of the IWC to meet intersessionally. The task of the small working group, which is chaired by Ambassador de Soto, is to "assist the Commission to arrive at a consensus solution to the main issues it faces, to enable it to best fulfill its role with respect to the conservation of whale stocks and the management of whaling."[21] The group met in Florida in December 2008, then held another intersessional meeting in March 2009.

The small working group recommended that the IWC address a set of issues requiring immediate action, including Japanese scientific whaling, Japanese coastal whaling, sanctuaries, and whale watching/nonlethal use. A set of compromise packages was put forward that either would phase out Japan's scientific whaling program in the Southern Ocean in exchange for Japan's being allowed to take an unspecified number of minke whales off its coast in the North Pacific or would allow Japan's scientific whaling program to continue in the Southern Ocean if it adhered to annual limits set by the IWC's Scientific Committee.[22] The IWC took no decision on these recommendations but noted that the small-group process was making progress and should continue with a goal to achieving consensus by 2010.

When the IWC held its sixty-first annual meeting in 2009 in Madeira, Portugal, its membership had grown to eighty-five countries.[23] The Scientific Committee's report attested to the regime's success by noting that East African humpback whales had recovered to over 65 percent of their pre-exploitation size. The committee also reported positive evidence of increases for several other stocks of humpback, blue, and right whales in the Southern Hemisphere, although several remain at reduced levels compared to their prewhaling numbers.[24] Despite this progress, however, the IWC was unable to address the issues of scientific whaling, special-permit whaling, a Danish request to allow more aboriginal subsistence whaling in Greenland, or the establishment of a Southern Atlantic Whale Sanctuary. Most of these issues were put on hold pending the outcome of the discussions on the IWC's future. The IWC agreed that the small working group should continue its work and report back at the sixty-second IWC meeting in Morocco in May 2010. In the meantime, the IWC established a "support group" to assist newly elected IWC chair Cristian Maquieira, a seasoned environmental diplomat from Chile, in preparing documentation for the next meeting of the small working group. The members of this support group represented both whaling and antiwhaling nations, including Antigua and Barbuda, Australia, Brazil, Cameroon, Germany, Iceland, Japan, Mexico, New Zealand, Saint Kitts and Nevis, Sweden, and the United States.[25]

Critics of the package under discussion by the small working group, including NGOs like WWF, pointed out that the package makes no mention of other whaling nations, such as Iceland and Norway, which whale in defiance of the IWC's commercial whaling moratorium. Iceland recently announced a quota of one hundred fin whales—an endangered species—which is a dramatic increase over its original self-assigned quota of nine. Iceland also almost doubled its quota of minke whales. WWF argued that no package will heal the IWC if it "deals exclusively with one whaling nation and ignores the rest. The world's whales will not be saved until all governments commit to their conservation together. It is time to bring the IWC into the 21st century—as a whale conservation organization."[26]

Over the years, the IWC has evolved from a "whalers' club," where regulatory limits were established based on the power of the competing economic interests of whaling nations, into an international body in which "exclusive reliance on arguments grounded in moral beliefs have decreased the whaling states' commitment to the process of collective decision making, with scientific and commercial whaling aimed at circumventing IWC regulations becoming increasingly common."[27] This shift in discourse has been driven by strong emotions, and at times it almost seems that whales have become a casualty of the process rather than the focus of scientifically informed international cooperation to protect a threatened species.

The pro-whaling countries in the veto coalition fear losing their sovereign right to take ocean resources in international areas outside territorial limits. There is concern that the moratorium on whaling is the first step down a slippery slope whereby other depleted fish stocks will become off-limits. On the other hand, antiwhalers fear that agreement with any exception to the moratorium will degenerate into an open season on whales. As a result, both groups feel entirely justified in refusing to work together to reach points of agreement for fear of an outcome undesirable to "their" side.[28]

For antiwhaling nations and NGOs (including WWF, Greenpeace, the International Fund for Animal Welfare, and Cetacean Society International), whaling is emblematic of the short-sighted degradation of this planet. They argue that whaling is inexcusably cruel and endangers an already scarce species, compounding the threats whales face from global warming, noise and chemical pollution, physical strikes by ships, and net entanglements.[29]

The building of coalitions on both sides of the commercial whaling moratorium has been characterized more by political maneuvering than by a process of fact finding and consensus building. Science appears to have played a marginal role in decision making, with its credibility diminished by the practice of commercial whaling being carried out under the banner of scientific whaling. However, recent advances in the ability to monitor whale populations and the intersessional work of the small working group may break this deadlock and lead to more emphasis on scientifically based management above economics and morality.

INTERNATIONAL TRADE IN ENDANGERED SPECIES

The regime governing trade in endangered species centers on the Convention on International Trade in Endangered Species of Wild Flora and Fauna, commonly known as CITES. The treaty combats overexploitation of wild animals and plants by delineating threatened species, establishing rules regarding their trade, and imposing trade sanctions against violators.[30]

CITES is really an umbrella regime containing a multitude of smaller "regimes within regimes" that address specific species. Under this umbrella, proponent and veto coalitions vary across the specific agreements on individual species (or groups of species) and often cross traditional North-South divisions.[31] In contrast to the broader biodiversity regime discussed later in this chapter, CITES focuses on a single cause of species loss, contains generally clearer, stronger, and more straightforward protection targets and corresponding regulations, and lacks the North-South struggle over intellectual property rights (IPR) issues.

International trade in exotic wildlife is an enormous and lucrative business. Approximately 350 million individual plants and animals,[32] as well as their parts and derivatives, are bought and sold each year with an estimated value of $240 billion a year.[33] Much of this multi-billion-dollar trade is illegal. Indeed, illegal trade in wildlife is the third largest international market in illicit goods, behind only drugs and weapons.[34] The worldwide market for animals and their parts and derivatives plays an important role in species loss by producing significant incentives to overexploit particular natural resources both legally and illegally.[35] Moreover, many "range" countries, the nations in which traded species naturally reside, lack the monitoring or enforcement capacity needed to regulate legal and prevent illegal harvests.

Created by governments in 1973, CITES currently protects over 33,000 species against illegal trade. There are currently 175 parties to the convention. A COP meets every two to three years to decide how to regulate trade in species in different degrees of danger. The United Nations Environment Programme (UNEP) provides the secretariat, which administers the regime on behalf of the parties.

CITES creates three categories of species according to the threat to their existence, with various levels of controls for each category. Species listed in Appendix I are threatened with extinction and are not to be traded except for scientific or cultural endeavors. Species listed in Appendix II, while not yet endangered, are considered to be affected by international trade, which, if left unregulated, would endanger them. Before a country can allow exports of an Appendix II species, a scientific authority must determine that the proposed export will not be detrimental to the survival of the species. The decision to list a particular species in Appendix I or II requires a vote by the parties. Species listed in Appendix III are listed voluntarily by range states seeking cooperation in the control of international trade and do not require a vote. As of 2009, Appendix I lists more than 900 species; Appendix II, over 33,000; and Appendix III, more than 170.[36]

In the negotiations that created CITES, countries expressed strong support for the overall goal of protecting endangered species. Nations where the traded species lived also supported (and continue to support) CITES because it helped protect their valuable wildlife resources from poachers and illegal traders. Importing countries supported (and continue to support) the regime because it protected the interests of their legitimate dealers. Differences arose, however, concerning how to list specific species that would be restricted from trade. Many countries wanted a system that would require all parties to protect a species if a majority voted to list it. Others insisted on a system that would protect both economic interests and the principle of sovereign control. In the end, a potential veto coalition forced the convention's strongest proponents to allow a party to enter a reservation to (i.e., "opt out" of) the listing of a species as controlled or banned if the party claimed an overriding economic interest in continuing to exploit it. Such a reservation makes that party, in effect, a nonparty with regard to that particular species. Listing decisions are made on a two-thirds supermajority voting system, so member states' option to enter a reservation to a specific Appendix I or II listing constrains negotiations. In certain circumstances, this can give some states de facto veto power over a listing. If one or a few states control the great majority of trade in a species, they can essentially veto the effectiveness of a listing by entering a reservation to it. However, it takes two countries (an exporter and an importer) to overcome a CITES listing, and in cases where reservations exist by range states, it is not unusual for importing countries to pass national laws that are stricter than CITES in an effort to prevent loopholes. The effects of the so-called veto power are, however, more evident when dealing with marine species, where species are introduced directly from the sea and the two-party relationship does not take place.

Each member party is required to adopt national legislation that corresponds to the species listings of CITES. They have to designate two authorities on a domestic level, a management authority and a scientific authority. The scientific authority advises the management authority, which is in charge of issuing permits and certificates, in keeping with the CITES appendices. These authorities work in correlation with customs offices, police departments, and other appropriate agencies to record species trading and report to CITES. Thus, the operation and enforcement of CITES can be compromised when national and local officials do not, or cannot, enforce it.

CITES has three main operational bodies: the Standing Committee, the Animals Committee, and the Plants Committee. The Standing Committee oversees and helps to coordinate the workings of other bodies with policy guidance and budget management. The committees for animals and plants work between COPs and report to the COP about their respective mandates. The main implementation tool used by these bodies to monitor CITES's effectiveness is a review of significant trade (RST), a process whereby the bodies evaluate trade data pertaining to specific species, delving deeper if anything out of place is noticed. However, CITES's capacity to actually reduce illegal trade using this process is minimal. The RST relies on data reported by countries through government agencies; these statistics include information only on legal trading. As one of the major causes of species loss is illegal trading, this process may serve merely to pressure governments to comply with CITES listings without having much of an effect on the illegal movement of species and their derivatives.

In fact, the illegal wildlife trade is a growing illicit economy, estimated to be worth at least $5 billion and potentially in excess of $20 billion annually. Some of the most lucrative illicit wildlife commodities include tiger parts, caviar, elephant ivory, rhino horn, and exotic birds and reptiles. Demand for illegally obtained wildlife is ubiquitous, and some suspect that illicit demand is growing[37] (see Table 5.1). Illicit wildlife trade

TABLE 5.1   Selected Illicit Wildlife Trade and Estimated Retail Value

ILLEGALLY TRADED WILDLIFE	ESTIMATED RETAIL VALUE
Elephants	$121–$900 per kilogram of ivory
Rhinos	$945–$50,000 per kilogram of rhino horn
Tibetan antelopes	$1,200–$20,000 per shatoosh shawl
Big cats	$1,300–$20,000 per tiger, snow leopard, or jaguar skin; $3,300–$7,000 per set of tiger bones
Bears	$250–$8,500 per gallbladder
Sturgeon	$4,450–$6,000 per kilogram of caviar
Reptiles and insects (often live)	$30,000 per oenpelli python; $30,000 per komodo dragon; $5,000–$30,000 per plowshare tortoise; $15,000 per Chinese alligator; $20,000 per monitor lizard; $20,000 per shingleback skink; $8,500 per pair of birdwing butterflies
Exotic birds (often live)	$10,000 per black palm cockatoo egg ($25,000–$80,000 per mature breeding pair); $5,000–$12,000 per hyacinth macaw; $60,000–$90,000 per lear macaw; $20,000 per Mongolian falcon
Great apes (often live)	$50,000 per orangutan

Source: Liana Sun Wyler and Pervaze A. Sheikh, *International Illegal Trade in Wildlife: Threats and U.S. Policy* (Washington, DC: Congressional Research Service, March 3, 2008), 1. Available at http://fpc.state.gov/documents/organization/102621.pdf.

uses complex distribution networks connecting raw material from source states and producers of wildlife products to customers.[38] Illicit wildlife trade networks can involve a combination of any of the following: (1) village hunters, who trade small wildlife as a source of subsistence cash income or kill some wildlife to protect their people and crops from attacks; (2) wildlife experts; (3) criminal entities, sometimes including terrorists, rebels, drug traffickers, and others, able to evade detection and transport and secure the products as well as launder the proceeds; (4) legitimate businesses serving as a front for the trade; (5) corrupt government officials to facilitate import and export; and (6) consumers willing to pay for the contraband.[39] Traffickers are reportedly connected globally to suppliers of exotic animals in developing countries, consumers at upscale art galleries, safari operators guiding hunters to illegal animal trophies, and international and interstate networks of wildlife exporters, taxidermists, and wildlife retailers.[40]

The Internet has contributed to the growth of the illegal wildlife trade, providing an unprecedented technological platform for a burgeoning, undocumented trade in endangered animals, alive and dead[41] (see Box 5.1). The ability to scan the globe for buyers or sellers without leaving one's office, to mask one's identity with increasingly sophisticated technology and software, and to buy and sell online, without ever having to meet even a middle man, are just three aspects of Internet-based endangered-species crime that challenge the abilities of national and international law enforcement officials. In addition, many national laws aimed at regulating wildlife trade to ecologically sustainable levels do not yet address aspects of illicit Internet sales, and some states have few laws governing Internet commerce at all. Even where laws exist, enforcement is often inadequate because officials do not have the capacity to address Internet crime or because they are not focused on online trafficking in wildlife.

The state of two species, African elephants and big-leaf mahogany, illustrates CITES's efforts to curb species loss and exemplifies the difficulties inherent in negotiations between numerous parties. Because of the number and different geographical distributions of species endangered by international trade, as well as variation in the countries where market demand for a given species exists, the proponent and veto coalitions and the comparative difficulty of obtaining a listing differ between species.

African Elephants

The African elephant was first listed under CITES Appendix II in 1977. Beginning in the early 1980s, African elephant populations began to decline precipitously, falling from 1.3 million in 1979 to 625,000 in 1989.[42] Most of this decline was due to illegal poaching to provide ivory for international markets, triggering calls for more serious action. In 1985, to control the international traffic, CITES established a system of ivory export quotas in the countries with elephant herds. Declines continued, however, and

BOX 5.1   ENDANGERED SPECIES ONLINE

The International Fund for Animal Welfare has conducted four investigations since 2004 into potentially illegal trade in endangered species on the Internet. The most recent investigation in 2007 spanned three months, involved six one-week snapshot investigations on 183 publicly accessible websites in eleven countries, and looked at both the wildlife products and live-animal trade in primates, birds, reptiles, big cats, bears, elephants, rhinoceroses, sharks, Tibetan antelopes, and sturgeon.

In a six-week period, International Fund for Animal Welfare investigators tracked 7,122 online auctions, advertisements, and communiqués offering trade in CITES Appendix I–listed wildlife, as well as a notable number of Appendix II–listed species, for sale both domestically and internationally. The final tally of verifiable commerce was approximately $3.8 million in advertisements and nearly $450,000 in final sales. While these figures are already high, they become even more sobering when we consider that many sites do not offer an advertised sale price, and only eBay provides the means for tracking final sales; a comprehensive tally would likely be much higher.

In 2007, eBay announced a ban on cross-border trade in elephant ivory, meaning that sales across country lines would be prohibited. Yet, a year after the announcement of the ban, eBay-based sales were found responsible for 83 percent of all ivory identified by investigators and a full 63 percent of all trade in this investigation, a significant amount of which shipped internationally. This demonstrates one of the key issues in global Internet trade: A strong policy without adequate enforcement is ineffective.

eBay Numbers (U.S.)
Results of the International Fund for
Animal Welfare's 2007 three-month investigation:

Total ivory items tracked	3,667
Total ivory final sales recorded	1,847 (50.37 percent)
Dollar value of recorded ivory	$369,885.39
Estimated annual ivory commerce	$3.2 million
Estimated ivory listing fees	$3,278
Estimated commissions paid on ivory sales	$11,445.87
Estimated eBay ivory profits per year	$127,606.87

International Fund for Animal Welfare, *Killing with Keystrokes* (Yarmouth Port, MA: IFAW, 2008), www.ifaw.org/Publications/Program_Publications/Wildlife_Trade/Campaign_Scientific_Publications/asset_upload_file848_49629.pdf.

PHOTO 5.1   **Examining poached elephant tusks.**
Photo by Rob Barnett/TRAFFIC.

a study sponsored by WWF and Conservation International concluded that African elephants were being harvested at a rate far exceeding that considered sustainable. This rate of loss, driven primarily by the international trade in ivory, led to increasing calls to place African elephants in Appendix I of CITES and establish a worldwide ban on trade in African elephant ivory.

The bargaining stage began at the seventh CITES COP in October 1989 when an odd international coalition consisting of Austria, the Gambia, Hungary, Kenya, Somalia, Tanzania, and the United States initiated an effort to list the African elephant in Appendix I and ban trade in ivory products entirely. Another unlikely coalition, uniting foes in southern Africa's struggle over apartheid (Botswana, Malawi, Mozambique, South Africa, Zambia, and Zimbabwe), opposed the listing. Underlying their resistance was the fact that several southern African herds had grown in the 1980s due to conservation efforts financed through limited hunting of elephants and commercial trade of elephant parts. Despite this resistance, a two-thirds majority of all CITES parties voted to place all African elephant herds in Appendix I.[43] The southern African states lodged reservations against the ban and announced plans to sell their ivory through a cartel, with the proceeds to be used to finance conservation.[44]

It was Japan, however, not the African states, that determined the viability of the regime. In 1989, the worldwide ivory market was worth an estimated $50 to $60 million annually. Japan dominated this market, importing more than 80 percent of all

African ivory products, making it the potential leader of a veto coalition.[45] As the major consumer nation, Japan had been expected to enter a reservation, allowing a significant portion of the market to remain viable and effectively vetoing the ban. Facing heavy pressure from NGOs, the United States, and the European Community (EC), Japan eventually decided not to oppose the ban, and world prices for raw ivory soon plunged by 90 percent.[46]

In the 1990s, three southern African countries (Botswana, Namibia, and Zimbabwe) called for an end to the ivory trade ban, proposing that the African elephant be "downlisted" from CITES Appendix I to Appendix II. Efforts to this effect were initiated unsuccessfully at CITES meetings in 1992 and 1994.[47]

At the tenth COP in June 1997 in Harare, Zimbabwe, the debate over the proposal by the three southern African range states and Japan for a "split" downlisting of the elephant populations in their countries was long and acrimonious. The three range states argued that their herds had grown to a combined total of about 150,000 and that continued inability to exploit the herds commercially was costing them revenues that could be used to increase their conservation budgets. The United States and other parties feared that even partial easing of the trade ban would result in a new flood of illegal trade in ivory and cited deficiencies in enforcement and control measures in the three African countries and Japan identified by the CITES panel of experts. They pointed out that, without adequate controls in place, it would be extremely difficult to track where elephant tusks originated.

In the end, a committee of nineteen CITES members worked out a compromise under which each of the three states could get permission to sell a strictly limited "experimental quota" of ivory under a stringent set of conditions.[48] A heavily regulated one-time sale of ivory from these countries was also approved after monitoring deficiencies were adequately addressed. All experimental sales went to Japan, with all funds obtained by the sale to be invested in elephant-conservation efforts.[49] The split downlisting was maintained at the eleventh COP in 2000, but no further ivory sales were authorized.

At the twelfth COP in 2002, Botswana, Namibia, and South Africa once again advanced a proposal for the limited sale of ivory. This proposal was accepted after the removal of an annual quota and the establishment of strict monitoring and verification conditions. It was agreed that 20,000, 10,000, and 30,000 kilograms from Botswana, Namibia, and South Africa, respectively, would be traded in a single shipment.

Again in 2004, at the thirteenth COP, Namibia proposed a 2,000 kilogram annual quota of raw ivory, in addition to the trade of worked ivory, leather, and hair products. The proposal involving raw ivory was rejected, but Namibia was allowed to participate in trade in leather and hair products and noncommercial trade in worked ivory amulets known as *ekipas*.[50]

At the fourteenth COP in 2007, the Trade Records Analysis of Flora and Fauna in Commerce (TRAFFIC) reported that illegal trade in ivory had increased since 2005 and implicated the countries of Cameroon, China, the Democratic Republic of Congo, Nigeria, and Thailand as the major players. Four proposals to amend the appendices and annotations governing trade for African elephants were presented. After negotiations, an all-African consensus was reached and subsequently adopted. The agreement keeps the allowance of the one-off sale approved at COP-12, along with the trade in leather and hair products and *ekipas* approved at COP-13. In addition to the quantities of raw ivory agreed to at COP-12, Botswana, Namibia, South Africa, and Zimbabwe received permission to have a one-off sale of raw ivory that had been registered in government stocks prior to January 31, 2007.[51]

The decision bars additional proposals for ivory trade for nine years following the one-off sale and also allows for the Standing Committee to stop the agreed-upon trade if noncompliance arises. The proposal also commissions the Standing Committee to propose a decision-making mechanism for ivory trade in time for COP-16 and states that the secretariat should establish a specific fund for African elephants. Range states must develop an action plan regarding the elephants as well. COP-14 also saw the adoption of the new Action Plan for the Control of Trade in African Elephant Ivory, which emphasizes the need to enforce national legislation and promote public awareness among range states, for parties to report to the convention on seizures and legislation, and for the secretariat to provide assistance to range states.[52]

In July 2008, at the fifty-seventh meeting of the CITES Standing Committee, delegates gave the go-ahead for the one-off sale of ivory and agreed that China could join Japan as an approved bidder on the ivory. The total amount of ivory to be sold was 108 tons, with Botswana allowed 43,682.91 kilograms; Namibia, 9,209.68 kilograms; South Africa, 51,121.8 kilograms; and Zimbabwe, 3,755.55 kilograms.[53] The secretariat visited all four African countries to verify the quantity and legality of ivory stocks before allowing the sale to proceed. The sale took place in October and November 2008 with a total profit of nearly $15.5 million to the four southern African states.[54]

Most environmental groups met the Standing Committee's decision with anxiety. Many conservationists fear that the approval of China as a trading partner will fuel poaching, increasing the threat to the endangered elephants. China is known to be the number one consumer of ivory products, and the country has a history of failing to regulate the trade. Increased poaching for China's markets could undo all of the strides CITES has made in protecting African elephants.

Big-Leaf Mahogany

Trade in mahogany is a very lucrative business. With an average price of $1,700 per cubic meter of wood, global sales approached $200 million in 2004.[55] High international demand has put incredible pressure on mahogany populations. Honduran and Caribbean mahogany were once staples of the timber market but are now commercially extinct due to overexploitation. With these species unavailable for large-scale, profitable harvest, the market shifted its focus to big-leaf mahogany, with predictable results. In Central America alone, big-leaf mahogany coverage fell from 45 million hectares in the 1940s to 13 million hectares in the 1990s.[56] While not as dramatic as that of the African elephants, this decline still signaled an alarming trend.

Despite the notable population decline in the 1980s, mahogany did not immediately emerge as a candidate for a CITES appendix listing. In 1992, at the eighth COP, the United States and Costa Rica put forth a proposal for an Appendix II listing for big-leaf mahogany. In response, a subset of Latin American range states argued that insufficient information regarding the population declines and inadequate national infrastructures could not effectively support trade restrictions. As a result, the proposal failed to garner the required votes.

Negotiations continued over the next several years. At the ninth COP in 1994, the Netherlands and El Salvador proposed an Appendix II listing. This proposal failed by only six votes. Taking what unilateral action it could, in 1995 Costa Rica voluntarily listed big-leaf mahogany as a CITES Appendix III species. In 1997, at the tenth COP, the United States and Bolivia made a third attempt to list mahogany in Appendix II, a proposal that was once again narrowly rejected. However, that same year, Bolivia, Brazil, Colombia, Mexico, and Peru voluntarily listed big-leaf mahogany under Appendix III.

Some range states that opposed further action hoped that placing big-leaf mahogany in Appendix III would retard the progression of an Appendix II listing. Proponents of an Appendix II listing maintained that the voluntary Appendix III listings did not offer sufficient guarantees that trade would consist only of legally obtained timber or that the harvest did not threaten the survival of the species. For example, Brazilian border authorities often do not require CITES certificates of origin from timber imports from Bolivia and Peru, allowing illegal trade to continue.[57]

While the proposal for an Appendix II listing did not succeed, the COP did create a working group, supported by both import and export countries, to examine the population status, management, and trade of big-leaf mahogany throughout its entire range. In 2000, at the eleventh COP, delegates established additional working groups to continue the collection of scientific information to help frame the negotiations.

As information began to accumulate, Nicaragua and Guatemala tried again to list big-leaf mahogany in CITES Appendix II in 2002. Their proposal pointed to evidence that the status of the species had not changed in the five years since it was listed in Appendix III due to weak implementation and lack of political will.[58] Brazil continued to oppose the proposal, emphasizing that an Appendix II listing would produce trade barriers and prevent access to markets, as well as restrict national sovereignty over natural resources. Despite this opposition, the fourth attempt to list big-leaf mahogany in Appendix II was successful, and the listing entered into force in November 2003.

At the fifteenth meeting of the Plants Committee in May 2005, the Big-Leaf Mahogany Working Group was reestablished due to increasing concern over the implementation and enforcement of the Appendix II listing. Range states were having difficulty identifying means to reduce trade in, and to allocate resources toward the fight for, big-leaf mahogany, and they needed capacity-building help from the convention. The working group's mandate called for it to prepare and adopt regional action plans, undertake inventories in range states, and report on progress at the sixteenth meeting of the Plants Committee in 2006. While some progress was made among range states between the fifteenth and sixteenth meetings, widespread illegal logging of big-leaf mahogany continued, and efforts made by range states were unclear and insufficient.

COP-14 in 2007 made little progress on the issue of the big-leaf mahogany trade, but it did task the Plants Committee with developing principles and criteria for nondetriment findings (assuring that export of the species will not adversely affect the wild population) for timber species. Range states were encouraged to deny imports or exports of big-leaf mahogany that failed to provide proof of legal origin and to continue working on forest-management plans. COP-14 did not reach conclusions on all big-leaf mahogany issues, referring several back to the Plants Committee.

During the seventeenth meeting of the Plants Committee in April 2008, only ten range states reported on their creation of nondetriment findings. In light of such little progress, the Plants Committee decided to include big-leaf mahogany in an RST for the following range states: Belize, Bolivia, Colombia, Costa Rica, Dominican Republic, Ecuador, El Salvador, Guyana, Honduras, Nicaragua, Panama, Peru, St. Lucia, St. Vincent and the Grenadines, and Venezuela. The RST may prove an opportunity for range states to receive aid in improving their national action plans and securing funding and technical assistance to do so. Whether this will be a large-enough step to reduce trade in big-leaf mahogany remains to be seen.

The cases of African elephant ivory and big-leaf mahogany help to illustrate several distinctive features of the CITES regime. First, and as noted above, CITES is actually an umbrella regime enveloping a multitude of "mini regimes" across which states' political and economic interests vary from species to species. These mini regimes, while sharing a common organizational structure, are all characterized by an individual set of developmental stages, proponents, and coalitions that often consist of unusual alliances that cross traditional North-South lines. Veto coalitions can be led by producer nations, as was the case with big-leaf mahogany, or by both producer and consumer nations, as was the case with elephant ivory. In both cases, range states split over listing. With ivory, the split largely reflected differences in the viability of central versus southern African elephant populations. Central African states with rapid elephant population declines and high levels of poaching supported an Appendix I listing. Southern African states with growing elephant populations opposed the ban. The consensus reached by all African range states at COP-14 was a major achievement considering the difficulties associated with negotiating among several states. Political climates and economics create a very fragile landscape in negotiating the rules governing trade in potentially lucrative animal species.

With big-leaf mahogany, range states with commercially extinct populations tended to favor an Appendix II listing. States with active legal trade (despite their also having a high level of illegal trade) tended to oppose listing out of concern that it would promote a perception that mahogany was an "endangered species" and harm the image of legally traded products.[59] The United States, the largest consumer of big-leaf mahogany, supported listing as a means to assure that any imports were legally obtained. The largest consumer of elephant ivory, Japan, opposed that listing due to commercial concerns but did not register a reservation to the listing due to broader political concerns.[60]

Second, the role of science in the listing of species can also vary by species. While logically associated with the stages of issue definition and fact finding, scientific knowledge can also play an important role in bargaining and regime strengthening. The case of African elephants demonstrates an important scientific role in issue definition and fact finding, via the documentation of the initial population crashes, as well as in the bargaining and regime-strengthening stages, via the documentation of different population trajectories for southern and eastern African elephant populations. Documentation of population declines was also important in raising the profile of big-leaf mahogany.

Third, the development of modern techniques for genetic analysis of living plants or animals, as well as plant and animal parts or extracts, has transformed the monitoring of trade in endangered species and can lead to the ability to produce appendix listings that work at a finer population scale. Fourth, both the elephant and mahogany cases show that although scientific knowledge can inform debates, economic and political factors that science cannot inform often determine specific courses of action, which is similar to the whaling case study. Strong commercial interests on the part of consumer nations or issues such as national sovereignty may lead nations to oppose listings despite strong evidence of declining populations.

Finally, the success of CITES listing in controlling population declines also varies by species. CITES listing can be ineffective in stopping overexploitation, particularly if important trading countries file a reservation to the listing, trade is predominantly domestic rather than international (e.g., trade in Chinese tigers and tiger parts), factors other than trade are more important in driving loss (e.g., habitat loss), or monitoring is difficult due to the type of product traded (e.g., sawn wood or plant extracts). CITES listings may also be ineffective when improperly obtained export permits place a veneer of legality over trade in an endangered species, as has been suggested is the case with mahogany.[61] An argument exists that CITES listing could even be detrimental to a species by driving black market trade, although little empirical evidence exists to support this view.[62] Indeed, no species listed in a CITES appendix has become extinct.

CITES is widely considered to be among the most effective global environmental regimes, despite the powerful commercial interests involved and the ability of parties to "opt out" of regulation by entering reservations on particular species. This case, like those of whaling and ozone depletion, illustrates the importance of bans or prohibitions as an effective mechanism for regulating activities that threaten the environment, natural resources, or wildlife. However, as threats to endangered species continue to multiply and avenues for trade in endangered species proliferate over the Internet, the coming years will present future challenges to the CITES regime.

BIODIVERSITY LOSS

Over the past fifty years, humans have changed ecosystems more rapidly and extensively than during any comparable period in human history, largely to meet rapidly growing demands for food, fresh water, timber, fiber, and fuel. This has resulted in a substantial and largely irreversible loss in the diversity of life on earth.

This was one of the key findings of the second Millennium Ecosystem Assessment report, "Biodiversity and Human Well-being," released in 2005.[63] Biological diversity, or biodiversity, is most often associated with the earth's vast variety of plants, animals, and microorganisms, but the term encompasses diversity at all levels, from genes to species to ecosystems to landscapes. Approximately 1.75 million species have been identified, mostly small creatures, such as insects. Many scientists believe that there could be as many as 13 million species, although individual estimates range from 3 to 100 million. Ecosystems are another aspect of biodiversity. In each ecosystem, including those that occur within or between forests, wetlands, mountains, deserts, and rivers, living creatures interact with each other as well as with the air, water, and soil around them; in this way, they form an interconnected community. Biodiversity also includes genetic differences within species, such as different breeds and varieties, as well as chromosomes, genes, and genetic sequences (DNA).

According to the Millennium Ecosystem Assessment, humans have increased species extinction rates by as much as 1,000 times over background, or natural, rates of extinction. Some 12 percent of birds, 23 percent of mammals, 25 percent of conifers, and 32 percent of amphibians are threatened with extinction. The world's fish stocks have been reduced by an astonishing 90 percent since the start of industrial fishing. Although the loss of species is seen as a threat to the well-being of future generations of humans, the formation of a regime for conserving biodiversity has suffered from differences concerning the definition of the problem, the application of the principle of national sovereignty versus that of the common heritage of mankind,[64] and resistance to strong legal obligations by a veto coalition of developing states holding most of the world's biodiversity, as well as inconsistent commitment from the United States and several other key industrialized states.

By the early 1980s, scientific consensus emerged that the rate of species extinction had increased alarmingly. In response, the General Assembly of the International Union for the Conservation of Nature and Natural Resources (IUCN) initiated a process aimed at producing a preliminary draft of a global agreement on conserving the world's genetic resources.[65] The United States also helped put the issue of biodiversity loss on the international agenda, encouraging the UNEP Governing Council in 1987 to create an ad hoc working group of experts to study an "umbrella convention" to rationalize activities in biodiversity conservation.[66] But it quickly became apparent to the experts that an umbrella convention would be an unworkable approach to the problem.

As the UNEP ad hoc working group continued its work and began the process of issue definition in 1990, the idea of a biodiversity convention became entangled in North-South struggles over plant genetic resources and IPR. The debate took shape around the "ownership" of genetic resources, with southern states arguing for explicit state sovereignty over the genetic resources within their borders and northern states arguing the view, previously accepted under international law, that these resources form part of the "common heritage of mankind." However, in 1983, when the non-binding International Undertaking on Plant Genetic Resources for Food and Agriculture was adopted by the Food and Agriculture Organization (FAO) Conference, eight developed countries in which major seed companies were located (Canada, France, Japan, New Zealand, Switzerland, the United Kingdom, the United States, and West Germany) were reluctant to apply the principle of common heritage to their modern varieties because of possible IPR implications. The FAO International Undertaking, the first comprehensive international agreement dealing with plant genetic resources for food and agriculture, was based on the principle that plant genetic resources are a heritage of mankind and consequently should be available without restriction. As a result of the novelty requirement of IPR protection, traditional and farmers' varieties have been regarded as "prior art" within the public domain and have been effectively part of the common heritage of humanity, but modern varieties have been considered private property. This asymmetry between improved and traditional **germplasm** has led to a sense of unfairness among developing countries: Their germplasm could be acquired, shared freely, and used in the development of modern varieties, which would then be protected by exclusive property rights. They consequently used the principle of national sovereignty over genetic resources to correct this asymmetry.

Some developing countries began to insist that genetic resources belong to the states in which they are located and that access should be based on a "mutual agreement between countries." They also argued for the inclusion of provisions for noncommercial access to biotechnologies based on plant genetic resources found in the South as a central element in any biodiversity convention. Most industrialized countries initially opposed the inclusion of biotechnology in the convention and attempted to define the scope of the regime to include only the conservation of biodiversity in the wild and mechanisms to finance such efforts.[67]

Formal negotiations on what would become the Convention on Biological Diversity (CBD) were completed in five sessions over nine months from July 1991 to May 1992. Four factors shaped the bargaining stage, polarized largely along North-South lines: the veto power of developing countries over biodiversity-conservation provisions, the veto power of industrialized countries over technology-transfer and financing provisions, the aggressive role played by UNEP executive director Mostafa Tolba, and the implicit deadline imposed by the Earth Summit in Rio in June 1992.

Under the objectives of biodiversity conservation, sustainable use of its components, and the fair and equitable sharing of the benefits arising out of the use of genetic resources, the resulting regime obligates parties to inventory and monitor biodiversity, incorporate the concepts of conservation and sustainable development into national strategies and economic development, and preserve indigenous conservation practices. The unwillingness of key actors to consider quantitative targets for the percentage of land that should be set aside for biodiversity conservation narrowed the scope of the CBD's conservation provisions. Germany informally raised the idea early in the negotiations, but a veto coalition led by developing countries holding a large proportion of the world's biodiversity (Brazil, Indonesia, and Mexico) vociferously opposed such stringent provisions. Interestingly, most European countries also opposed such targets because they thought they could embarrass developed countries that had already cut down most of their forests in past centuries.[68]

The regime relies more on economic incentives than on legal obligations for biodiversity conservation, putting access to genetic resources under the authority of the state in which they are found and calling for access to be granted on "mutually agreed terms." Thus, companies interested in prospecting for genetic resources in a particular country have to negotiate with government entities over the terms of that access, including royalties from any biotechnologies transferred from the genetic resources included within the agreement. Such deals are intended to provide a new economic incentive for developing countries to conserve biological resources.

The most contentious issues—the transfer of technology and financing—resulted in compromises that left most of the major actors unsatisfied. On technology transfer, a struggle developed between India, on behalf of the Group of 77 (G-77), and the United States concerning language governing the obligation of biotechnology companies in industrialized countries to disseminate knowledge and access to patented technologies. The United States succeeded in guaranteeing that technology transfers would protect IPR. India insisted that this guarantee be linked to an ambiguous compromise paragraph ensuring that IPR will be "supportive of and . . . not run counter to" the convention's objectives, a paragraph opposed by the United States as hostile to IPR.[69]

Debate concerning the convention's financial mechanism proved equally divisive. Donor countries and most Latin American states supported mandating the Global Environment Facility (GEF) to serve as the funding mechanism for the convention. Asian and African states, led by India and Malaysia, argued for creating a freestanding biodiversity fund independent of the GEF, which they believed donor countries controlled.

During the final negotiating session in May 1992, UNEP executive director Mostafa Tolba, confronted with the possibility that countries might fail to reach an agreement in time for the Rio conference, took over the negotiations personally. This included replacing the designated chair and drafting and submitting compromise texts to the delegations. He proposed that the convention designate the GEF as the interim funding mechanism but call for greater GEF transparency and democracy with respect to this role. The CBD COP would exercise authority over the GEF in its capacity as the financial mechanism, a proposition that appeared to leave open the possibility that the COP could determine levels of financial resources to be contributed by donor countries. Tolba submitted the text to the delegations as a fait accompli to be accepted or rejected shortly before the diplomatic conference that would formally adopt the convention.[70] Although the industrialized countries had concerns, particularly regarding the financial mechanism, they believed the proposed text offered the best agreement that could be reached in time for the treaty to be opened for signature at the Earth Summit only ten days later. They chose to issue their own interpretations of the text on financing and to sign the convention in Rio.

At the June 1992 Earth Summit, 153 countries signed the convention. The United States refused to do so, citing the provisions on financing and IPR. The United States reversed its position after the Clinton administration came into office and signed the convention in June 1993.[71] The United States has not ratified the convention, however, and is not yet a party.[72] The convention entered into force on December 29, 1993, and has been ratified by 191 countries.[73]

The process of regime strengthening for the CBD has been less focused than in some of the other major global environmental regimes. This reflects the more diffuse nature of the regime's rules and norms, the absence of a strong lead-state coalition, the absence of an enforcement mechanism, and a general lack of political will to strengthen the regime. The key challenges for strengthening the regime include identifying global conservation priority areas and developing protocols or work programs on conservation and/or sustainable use in particular sectors, avoiding distractions that divert attention away from key issue areas, and addressing several controversial issues, such as access to genetic resources and benefit-sharing.

Over the past fifteen years, the COP has made some progress in the first two areas by developing seven work programs that address the conservation of several areas of special concern in sustaining biodiversity and providing critical ecosystem services: mountain regions, dry and subhumid lands, marine and coastal areas, islands, inland waters, agricultural systems, and forests.[74] Drafting these work programs proved a long and arduous process. Discussions began at the first COP in 1994, but parties did not adopt the first program until 1998. However, the programs' current conservation measures are largely ineffective because they lack precise, binding language. The formation of various veto coalitions based on common economic or political interests regarding a particular issue has further inhibited effective policy. For example, major forest-product-exporting countries, including Brazil, Canada, and Malaysia, ensured that the convention would not take the lead on forests by blocking the development of a strong work program in this issue area.

Cartagena Protocol on Biosafety

The COP's decision to negotiate a protocol on biosafety (on the basis of Article 19.3 of the convention) further hindered progress in drafting and implementing ecosystem-focused work programs. These negotiations took up much of the parties' time and energy between 1996 and 2000. Biosafety refers to a set of precautionary practices to ensure the safe transfer, handling, use, and disposal of **living modified organisms (LMOs)** derived from modern biotechnology. Many countries with biotechnology industries had domestic biosafety legislation in place, but there were no binding international agreements on the problem of genetically modified organisms that cross national borders. Biotechnology, particularly its agricultural applications, remains a highly controversial issue. Policy responses vary widely in different legal orders, the most well-known example being the contrasting approaches of the United States and the European Union (EU), with the latter calling for a precautionary approach toward modern biotechnology. In 1999, several European governments joined European environmental NGOs in calling for a moratorium on the import of genetically modified foods. Although the moratorium ended in 2004, it did provoke a World Trade Organization (WTO) dispute between the United States and the EU, which was decided in favor of the United States in 2006 (see Chapter 7).[75]

The biosafety protocol was negotiated during a series of six meetings from 1996 to 1999. In February 1999, delegates convened in Cartagena, Colombia, intending to complete negotiations on the protocol. But a veto coalition, called the Miami Group, consisting of the world's major grain exporters outside of the EU (Argentina, Australia, Canada, Chile, the United States, and Uruguay), successfully thwarted efforts to complete the protocol on schedule. The veto coalition argued that the trade restrictions would harm the multi-billion-dollar agricultural export industry, that uncertainty regarding the precise meaning of key provisions created important weaknesses in the protocol, that countries would be able to block importation for reasons based on their own criteria rather than on sound scientific knowledge, and that the increased documentation required under the protocol would create unnecessary and excessive procedures and financial costs.[76] Informal consultations continued over the next year to address outstanding issues and to facilitate discussions between the major coalitions, which included the Central and Eastern European Group, the Compromise Group (Japan, Mexico, Norway, Republic of Korea, and Switzerland, joined later by New Zealand and Singapore), the EU, the Like-minded Group (an informal coalition that included the majority of developing countries but not the major grain exporters), and the Miami Group. Finally, after a week of formal negotiations in Montreal in January 2000, the major coalitions reached an agreement and adopted the Cartagena Protocol on Biosafety.[77] The protocol entered into force in September 2003.

The viability of the Cartagena Protocol hinges on the interplay of economic interests. This has played out in various ways, including the difficulties the parties have had in reaching agreement on documentation requirements for bulk shipments of living modified organisms intended for food, feed, and processing (LMO-FFPs). According to Article 18.2(a) of the protocol, parties were required to make a decision on the detailed requirements for such documentation within two years of the entry into force of the protocol. At the second Meeting of the Parties (MOP) in May 2005, delegates attempted to resolve this issue. Exporting countries expressed concern that labeling shipments that might include LMOs as including them could interfere with trade. Apart from fears that many commodity producers do not have the capability to account for small amounts of LMOs that a shipment might contain, there was widespread concern that stricter documentation requirements could prove costly, restrict market access, and have a negative impact on countries that rely heavily on agricultural exports. Meanwhile, importing countries wanted to set up documentation requirements that would state which LMOs actually were included in a shipment rather than a longer list of LMOs that might be included. Developing-country importers, particularly African parties, stressed that shipments listing all LMOs grown in the exporting countries for direct use as food or feed or for processing, without guidance as to which LMOs were most likely to be contained, posed decision-making challenges, such as the need for additional risk assessments, and capacity challenges to adequately detect and monitor the content of incoming shipments.[78] By the end of the meeting, New Zealand and Brazil played the role of veto states and, expressing serious objections to establishing any rule that would affect commodity trade in general, broke consensus.

Ten months later, at the third MOP in March 2006 in Curitiba, Brazil, parties tried again to reach agreement on documentation requirements. At the beginning of the week, many parties wanted to find a way to bring New Zealand and Brazil "into the fold" and were therefore surprised when other parties took on the role of veto states, notably Mexico, Paraguay, and Peru. Some saw this as evidence of the rapid evolution of biosafety regimes, with an increasing number of countries approving LMOs for production and acknowledging the trade implications of any constraints on LMO-FFP exports. The increased participation in many delegations of representatives of trade and finance ministries, who sometimes replaced more familiar faces from environment and agriculture ministries, further evidenced this shift. This represented a clear recognition of the importance of the trade implications of the protocol and, more specifically, the relationship between the protocol and the WTO. Similarly, exporting parties' preexisting bilateral trade agreements with large nonparties, such as the United States, were widely acknowledged as one of the reasons why some Latin American parties emerged as the ones most likely to resist consensus.[79]

In the end, Brazil shifted positions and, because of its role as host country, played the role of lead state by preparing drafts and promoting compromise to demonstrate its commitment to a successful outcome of the meeting. Thus, under Brazil's leadership, parties agreed on a compromise package that balanced the interests of importing and exporting, as well as of developed and developing, parties. The Curitiba Rules request parties to take measures to ensure that documentation accompanying LMO-FFPs in commercial production clearly states that the shipment contains LMO-FFPs in cases where the identity of the LMO is known through means such as identity preservation systems. In cases where the identity of the LMO is not known through such measures, the Curitiba Rules still allow documentation to state that the shipment may contain one or more LMO-FFPs, and they acknowledge that the expression "may contain" does not require a listing of LMOs of species other than those that constitute the shipment. The rules also provide for reviewing experience gained with these documentation requirements at COP/MOP-5 in 2010.[80]

Access and Benefit-Sharing

Another challenge to regime strengthening is the continuing divisive debate over issues such as access to genetic resources and benefit-sharing. Throughout the process of regime strengthening, developing countries have advocated an increased focus on the convention's third official objective: fair and equitable sharing of benefits arising from the use of genetic resources.[81] This issue relates to the way foreign companies, collectors, researchers, and other users gain access to valuable genetic resources in return for sharing the benefits with the countries of origin and with local and indigenous communities. The discussion addresses three main arguments: state sovereignty and the mandatory disclosure of country of origin in patent applications, the relationship of the original genetic resources and their derivatives, and the protection of traditional knowledge.

Genetic resources, whether from plants, animals, or microorganisms, are used for a variety of purposes ranging from basic research to the development of products. Users of genetic resources may include research institutes, universities, and private companies operating in various sectors such as pharmaceuticals, agriculture, horticulture, cosmetics, and biotechnology. For example, Calanolide A, a compound isolated from the latex of the tree *Calophyllum lanigerum var. auslrocoriaceum* found in the Malaysian rain forest, is used as a treatment for the human immunodeficiency virus type 1 (HIV-1).[82] Another example is the development of an appetite suppressant derived from species of Hoodia, succulent plants indigenous to southern Africa and long used by the San people to stave off hunger and thirst.[83]

In 2002, the World Summit on Sustainable Development called for action to negotiate an international regime to promote and safeguard the fair and equitable sharing of benefits arising out of the utilization of genetic resources within the framework of the CBD, In response, in 2004 the COP mandated the Working Group on Access and Benefit Sharing to elaborate and negotiate the "international regime on access to genetic resources and benefit-sharing" and, at its ninth meeting, in May 2008, in Bonn, Germany, the COP agreed on a schedule of meetings to complete negotiations before its tenth meeting in 2010 in Nagoya, Japan.[84]

Sharp divides between the lead countries (the providers of genetic resources) and the veto coalition (user countries) plagued the access-and-benefit-sharing negotiations. Those arguing the position of provider countries, primarily the Like-minded Group of Megadiverse Countries (see Box 5.2) and the African Group, claimed that the current state of affairs led to unfair distribution of benefits and sought to change it. Those regarded as user countries (i.e., those with industries that commercialize genetic resources)—mostly industrialized countries—were quite content with the status quo, where access to genetic resources was arguably free.

Points of divergence between the major negotiating groups were most visible in the treatment of access to genetic resources. Provider countries pushed for a regime that mostly addresses benefit-sharing by preventing the misappropriation and misuse of genetic resources and their derivatives in order to ensure that benefits flow to the

BOX 5.2   MEGADIVERSE COUNTRIES

The Group of Like-minded Megadiverse Countries was conceived in 2002 as a consultation and cooperation mechanism in order to promote common interests and priorities related to the conservation and sustainable use of biological diversity. The megadiverse countries consist primarily of tropical countries with rich variety in their animal and vegetable species, habitats, and ecosystems. Up to 70 percent of the biological diversity of the planet is located under the jurisdiction of these seventeen megadiverse countries: Bolivia, Brazil, China, Colombia, Costa Rica, Democratic Republic of Congo, Ecuador, India, Indonesia, Kenya, Madagascar, Malaysia, Mexico, Peru, the Philippines, South Africa, and Venezuela.

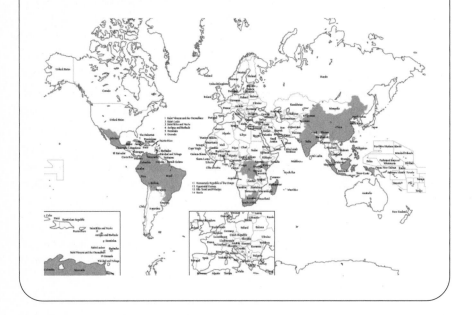

countries of origin. Users argued that both sides need to have incentives for negotiations to progress; therefore, facilitated access[85] should be part of the regime.[86] The one thread of consensus on this issue among developing and industrialized parties appears to be the protection of indigenous and local communities and their traditional knowledge. Article 8(j) of the convention calls on parties to "respect, preserve and maintain knowledge, innovations and practices of indigenous and local communities embodying traditional lifestyles relevant for the conservation and sustainable use of biological diversity; and promote their wider application." Negotiations have progressed in fits and starts since 2004, and with the 2010 deadline fast approaching, it remains unclear what the nature of the resulting agreement, if there is one, will be.[87]

Although parties have made progress on important issues, the biodiversity regime remains surprisingly weak. The complexity of the biodiversity crisis, the multiple levels at which it can be addressed (e.g., ecosystem, species, genes), the North-South contrasts in the distribution of biodiversity resources, and the many ways that biodiversity protection can conflict with important economic, social, and political interests together make drafting action-forcing language a contentious and intractable process. Numerous work programs, working groups, and subsidiary bodies have served to increase the number of meetings each year and decrease parties' focus on any one aspect of the convention, its strengthening, and its implementation. With the current focus on adopting an instrument on access and benefit-sharing, examining the relationship between climate change and biodiversity loss[88] and the challenges they pose to human development, assessing the impact of global trade on the problems associated with invasive alien species (see Box 5.3), and addressing and achieving the 2010 target to achieve a significant reduction of the current rate of biodiversity loss at the global, regional, and national levels,[89] there are no indications that the convention's focus will be narrowed. Action to strengthen the biodiversity regime will depend, in part, on greater commitment by lead states with significant economic, political, or biodiversity resources. Some European states have been active in trying to strengthen the regime, but without greater clout—and the support of developing countries as well as the United States, which remains a nonparty to the regime—the convention will remain unfocused and largely ineffective.

FISHERIES DEPLETION

For many centuries, the ocean's bounties have been viewed as limitless. But for the past three decades, the world's marine fisheries have been in crisis: overexploited to the point that the most valuable fish stocks have been depleted and sometimes virtually eliminated. About 80 percent of the world's marine fish stocks are considered depleted, slowly recovering from depletion, overexploited, or fully exploited[90] (see Figure 5.2). Because fishing fleets can overexploit one fishery and then move on to another, and because fleets continued to catch high levels of lower-value fish even after depleting the most desirable stocks, the fisheries crisis was disguised for many years by the continuing increase in the total global catch figures, which grew from 16.7 million tons in 1950 to 80 million tons in the late 1980s. Since then, the global catch has leveled off and fluctuated between 77 and 86 million tons.[91] Global marine capture production was 81.9 million tons in 2006 (the most recent year for which authoritative figures are available), the third lowest since 1994.[92]

BOX 5.3   INVASIVE ALIEN SPECIES

Invasive alien species are those that, when introduced to new ecosystems outside their natural habitats, threaten biological diversity because of their ability to multiply and cause the destruction of native species. Although only a small percentage of organisms transported to new environments become invasive, they can have extensive and substantial negative impacts on food security, economic development, and plant, animal, and human health.

Most nations already grapple with complex and costly invasive-species problems. Examples include zebra mussels affecting fisheries and electric-power generation; the water hyacinth blocking waterways and decimating aquatic wildlife and the livelihoods of local people; rats exterminating native birds on Pacific islands; and deadly new disease organisms, such as avian influenza A, attacking humans and animals in both temperate and tropical countries. Addressing the problem of invasive alien species is urgent because the threat is growing daily, and the economic and environmental impacts are severe.

The problem of invasive alien species continues to grow, essentially due to global trade, transport, and travel, including tourism, at an enormous cost to human and animal health and the socioeconomic and ecological well-being of the world. Since the seventeenth century, invasive alien species have contributed to nearly 40 percent of all animal extinctions for which the cause is known. They pose the greatest threat to biodiversity in isolated ecosystems, such as islands, as these lack natural competitors and predators that usually control populations of invasives. The annual environmental losses caused by introduced pests in Australia, Brazil, India, South Africa, the United Kingdom, and the United States have been calculated at over US$100 billion.

ECONOMIC IMPACT OF SOME INVASIVE ALIEN SPECIES

SPECIES	ECONOMIC VARIABLE (US DOLLARS/YEAR)	ECONOMIC IMPACT (ONE COIN=APPROX. US$20 MILLION)
Rats (Rattus ruttus and R. norvegicus)	US$19 million per year in losses and damages in the US (Pimentel et al. 2005)	$
Feral pigs (Sus scrofa)	US$800 million per year in losses and damages in the US (Pimentel et al. 2005)	$))))))))))))) $)))))))))))))
Water hyacinth (Eichhornia crassipes) and other alien water weeds	US$100 million per year in costs related to water use to developing countries (GISP 2004b)	$))))
Vegetable leaf miner (Liriomyza sativae)	US$80 million per year for economic losses in China (Li and Xie 2002)	$)))
Small Indian mongoose (Herpestes javanicus)	US$50 million in damages per year in Puerto Rico and the Hawaiian Islands alone (GISP 2004b)	$))
Coffee berry borer (Hypothenemus hampei)	US$300 million per annum in India (GISP 2004b)	$)))))))))

Secretariat for the CBD, *Invasive Alien Species: A Threat to Biodiversity* (Montreal: Secretariat for the CBD, 2009), 6. Available at www.cbd.int/doc/bioday/2009/idb-2009-booklet-en.pdf. Reprinted with permission of the CBD Secretariat.

FIGURE 5.2   **State of the world's fish stocks, 2007**

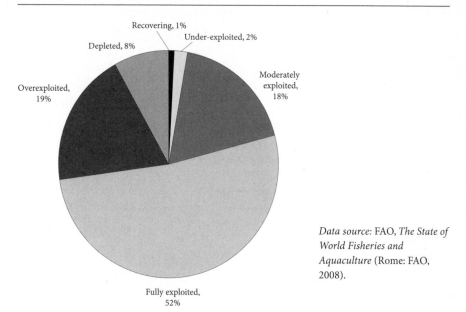

Recovering, 1%

Under-exploited, 2%

Depleted, 8%

Overexploited,
19%

Moderately
exploited,
18%

Fully exploited,
52%

Data source: FAO, *The State of World Fisheries and Aquaculture* (Rome: FAO, 2008).

The primary reason for the worsening condition of fishery resources is the significant increase in the number of fishing vessels and increasingly effective fishing technologies, such as electronic fish-finding equipment, bigger nets, larger storage capacity, more powerful engines, and mechanized hauling gear, all of which give fleets far more catching power than fisheries can support. By the early 1990s, the global fishing fleet had as much as two and a half times more capacity than could be used sustainably.[93] Inadequate regulations on catch and enforcement and illegal, unreported, and unregulated fishing also contributed to the crisis.

Fishery resources are found either under national jurisdiction or in international waters, and often in some combination of the two, a situation that complicates the politics of forming a regime governing the global overfishing problem. The ten biggest fishing states (Chile, China, India, Indonesia, Japan, Peru, the Philippines, the Russian Federation, Thailand, and the United States) account for 67 percent of the global catch.[94] The countries with "distant-water" fishing fleets (Japan, Poland, the Republic of Korea, Russia, Spain, and Taiwan) are responsible for the majority of the catch in international waters. These countries had the greatest potential for vetoing an international agreement to address the overfishing problem.

Of the global fish catch, 95 percent is taken within the two-hundred-mile exclusive economic zones (EEZs) that are under the national jurisdiction of individual coastal states. But some important fish stocks, such as cod and pollack, straddle EEZs and adjacent areas of the high seas. And some highly migratory stocks, especially tuna and swordfish, move long distances, passing through both the high seas and the EEZs of multiple coastal states each year. Straddling and highly migratory fish stocks are particularly important on the Challenger Plateau off the coast of New Zealand, off Argentina's Patagonian Shelf, off the coasts of Chile and Peru, in the Barents Sea, off the coast of Norway, in the Bering Sea, in the Sea of Okhotsk, in the South Pacific Ocean, and on the Grand Banks of Newfoundland outside Canada's two-hundred-mile nautical zone. As many straddling stocks and highly migratory fish stocks have dwindled, coastal and distant-water states each blame overfishing by the other group as the cause.

The first binding global agreement to address overfishing was the United Nations Agreement for the Implementation of the Provisions of the United Nations Convention on the Law of the Sea of 10 December 1982 Relating to the Conservation and Management of Straddling Fish Stocks and Highly Migratory Fish Stocks (United Nations Fish Stocks Agreement). Not surprisingly, the agreement arose from conflicts over straddling and highly migratory fish stocks. Canada was the lead actor in putting the issue of a new global management regime for these stocks on the political agenda. It was unable, however, to put forward a definition that could serve as the foundation for a successful conservation regime.

Canada was motivated to push for formal agreement limiting the freedom of distant-water fishing fleets to exploit these stocks because of a dispute with the EU, especially Spain, about the Spanish fleet's overfishing of the stocks on the Grand Banks outside Canada's EEZ. The regional fisheries management organization responsible for regulating fishing in the Grand Banks area, both within Canada's EEZ and on the high seas, is the Northwest Atlantic Fisheries Organization (NAFO), founded in 1979. From 1986 to 1990, the NAFO failed to enforce high-seas catch limits agreed to by the organization on most of the straddling stocks because the EC had exercised its right to opt out of the regional quotas; Canada, therefore, appealed to the broader international community to adopt a global policy governing the problem.

During preliminary negotiations for the United Nations Conference on Environment and Development (UNCED), a paper from coastal states proposed that new conservation rules should be established for high-seas fisheries but not for fisheries under national jurisdiction. Canada proposed language calling for recognition of the special interests of coastal states in highly migratory stocks and stocks that straddle national EEZs and international waters. The EC disagreed, producing a diplomatic deadlock on the issue. The issue remained unresolved until the Rio conference, when UNCED Main Committee chairman Tommy Koh asked the United States to broker a compromise between Canada and the EC. The result was an agreement to hold an intergovernmental conference under UN auspices "with a view to promoting effective implementation of the provisions of the Law of the Sea on straddling and highly mi-

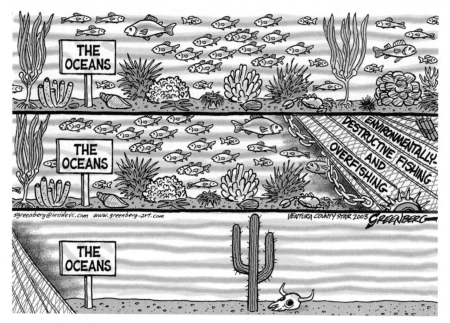

CARTOON 5.2 "Ocean into Desert."
Steve Greenberg, *Ventura County Star* (California), 2003.

gratory fish stocks." The EC agreed to that formula because its diplomats believed the Convention on the Law of the Sea guaranteed the sovereign right of states to fish on the high seas. Canada, however, hoped that the need for conservation would trump that traditional sovereign right.

The United Nations Conference on Straddling Fish Stocks and Highly Migratory Fish Stocks opened in July 1993 under the authority of the United Nations General Assembly (UNGA). The main conflict of interest in the negotiations was between the seventy coastal fishing states and the ten distant-water fishing states. The coastal states, led by the "like-minded" caucus (Argentina, Canada, Chile, Iceland, New Zealand, Norway, and Peru), accused the distant-water fishing states of abusing their right to fish to the detriment of straddling stocks. The distant-water fishing states, led by the EC (on behalf of its distant-water fishing states),[95] Japan, and the Republic of Korea, pointed out that mismanagement of national fisheries by coastal fishing states was just as much to blame for the most serious problems of stock depletion.[96] Both sides were only half right, a conclusion based on the Canadian-EC case: The evidence is clear that there was gross mismanagement and overfishing within the Canadian EEZ and that from 1986 to 1989 the Spanish and Portuguese fleets were consistently catching several times the EC's NAFO allocation of groundfish catch.[97]

As they had during the UNCED negotiations, the like-minded caucus proposed a legally binding agreement that would prescribe conservation rules for high-seas fishing that affected straddling stocks and highly migratory stocks. But the coastal states resisted international rules that would limit their freedom to manage their EEZs. Distant-water states called for nonbinding conservation guidelines that would apply equally to coastal state fisheries and the high seas. They had long argued that the regulation of fishing practices on the high seas should be left to regional or subregional organizations. While the UN conference was going on, consultations were also being held on a nonbinding FAO Code of Conduct for Responsible Fisheries, and the two groups of fishing states took opposite positions about that process: Coastal states insisted that the entire text be bracketed until the UN agreement on straddling stocks and highly migratory stocks was adopted, whereas the distant-water fishing states favored the FAO process because it was voluntary.

Both groups of states were thus separate veto coalitions who were prepared, at least initially, to block agreement on needed measures to conserve stocks effectively. The United States, which is a coastal fishing state and a distant-water fishing state, was in a pivotal position to play the role of lead state in negotiating the regime. Initially, however, the United States was ready to join with the distant-water states to oppose a binding convention because of its close historic ties with the EU and Japan on Law of the Sea issues. The United States had clashed with Canada and other coastal states during the negotiations on the Law of the Sea treaty. But in 1994, officials in the White House and the National Oceanic and Atmospheric Administration who had a strong commitment to conservation intervened in the issue after being lobbied by NGOs. As a result, the United States decided to come out for a binding agreement and began playing the role of lead state.

One of the U.S. contributions to the text was a proposal that the "precautionary approach" to fishing be applied by requiring the adoption of "reference points" (target levels of fishing effort aimed at conserving fish stocks) and measures for rebuilding the stocks, including reduced fishing efforts, if the reference points are exceeded. Canada resisted the application of precautionary reference points within fisheries under national jurisdiction, along with other conservation requirements, as a violation of national sovereignty. The United States pushed Canada and the like-minded caucus to accept certain basic conservation principles and guidelines for their application to straddling stocks on the high seas and within areas under national jurisdiction, but the issue remained unresolved even after the fourth session in April 1995.

The like-minded caucus also pressed the issue of coastal states' right to board and inspect fishing vessels in international waters. It argued that such a right was necessary to ensure compliance with international conservation measures. Traditionally, the enforcement of legal obligations on the high seas had been in the hands of the "flag state" (the state in which the vessel was registered), and distant-water fishing states wanted to maintain the status quo. The United States again sided with the like-minded caucus in supporting wider latitude for high-seas inspection by states other than the flag state under certain circumstances, but the distant-water states continued to resist until the last session.

Before the negotiations could be completed, tensions between Canada and the EU escalated to the use of force over Spanish fishing for turbot, allegedly in violation of NAFO quotas. In September 1994, the thirteen members of NAFO voted to reduce the annual total allowable catch of rapidly declining stocks of turbot by 38 percent and reallocated much of the EU share of the quota to Canada. The EU again used its right to opt out of the quota and set its own, much higher, unilateral quota. In response, in February 1995, the Canadian fisheries minister warned that Canada would not let EU vessels "devastate turbot the way it devastated other ground fish stocks."[98] In March 1995, Canadian ships aggressively pursued and seized or cut the nets of Spanish trawlers outside the Canadian EEZ.

The Canadian actions angered the EU and temporarily polarized the conference. The March–April 1995 round of negotiations was still deadlocked on the issue of the right of coastal states to board ships on the high seas that they suspect of having violated a regional fisheries-conservation measure. The chair's draft allowed wider latitude for such high-seas boarding and inspection than the distant-water states were prepared to accept.

But a new Canadian-EU agreement reached immediately after that round may have contributed to a successful conclusion to the negotiations. Canada compromised on the 1995 quota and agreed to give the EU the same amount as Canada instead of the one-fifth of the Canadian quota that had been authorized by NAFO. Canada also dropped charges against the Spanish trawler it had seized and repealed legislation authorizing such actions in international waters. In return, the EU agreed to a new regime of independent inspectors onboard every EU ship in the NAFO area to ensure that conservation rules were being followed.[99]

In the fifth and final negotiating session in August 1995, distant-water fishing states were still resisting high-seas boarding and the "precautionary approach" to fisheries management. The distant-water fishing states had agreed to boarding and inspecting in principle, but there were still differences about whether the regional fisheries organizations had to reach agreement on procedures governing such boarding and inspecting: Canada insisted that it would not require prior agreement on procedures by the organizations, whereas Japan and South Korea both insisted on regional agreement as a precondition for such boarding and inspection. A compromise was ultimately adopted: States that were parties to regional fisheries organizations could board and inspect vessels on the high seas of parties to the Fish Stocks Agreement

suspected of violating regional conservation measures without prior regional agreement, but only if the regional organization had failed to adopt procedures for such
boarding and inspection for two years prior to the boarding.

As discussed in Chapter 1, the precautionary approach requires that scientific uncertainty not be used as a reason for postponing or failing to take effective conservation
and management measures. Japan was concerned that the coastal states would use the
precautionary approach as an open license to adopt moratoria on fishing as a new
management norm and was reluctant to see it enter into a binding international agreement. But Japan finally accepted the precautionary approach, perhaps because it did
not want to be blamed for the collapse of the negotiations.[100]

Once it was ratified by thirty signatories, the United Nations Fish Stocks Agreement entered into force in December 2001. By September 2009, seventy-five countries had ratified the treaty, but only four of the top ten fishing states (India, Japan,
Russia, and the United States) and the EU are parties to the agreement. China and
the Philippines signed but still have not ratified and remain nonparties. Many of the
other most important fishing states, including Peru, Chile, Malaysia, Mexico, Thailand,
and Vietnam, also remain nonparties, declining even to sign the agreement and consider ratification. Although these countries' support was not needed for the Fish
Stocks Agreement to enter into force, their compliance is essential if the treaty is to
be effective.

Although the agreement represents a major step forward in global cooperation for
conservation of fish stocks, it does not effectively address three key global management
issues. First, regional fisheries organizations that make decisions on management measures such as catch quotas normally allow member states simply to opt out of the decision if they don't like it—this was the weakness that prompted Canada's original push
for a new regime. The second problem is overcapacity in the global fishing fleet. Although the agreement calls for states to take measures to "prevent or eliminate excess
fishing capacity," it does not spell out this obligation or set up a mechanism for implementation. Finally, the agreement does not apply to all fish stocks under national jurisdiction but only to those referred to in the title, or approximately 20 percent of the
global fish catch.

States have created several nonbinding agreements to supplement the regime. In
October 1995, governments adopted an international Code of Conduct for Responsible Fisheries, which provides principles and standards applicable to the conservation,
management, and development of all aspects of fisheries, such as the capture, processing, and trade of fishery products, as well as fishing operations, aquaculture, fisheries
research, and the integration of fisheries into coastal-area management. To support
implementation of the code of conduct, the FAO Technical Guidelines for Responsible
Fisheries were elaborated.[101]

The FAO also developed international plans of action addressing specific issues in implementing the code of conduct. The 1999 International Plan of Action for the Management of Fishing Capacity aims to reduce excess fishing capacity in world fisheries. This is to be achieved through assessment plans to reduce capacity and the strengthening of national and regional organizations to better manage capacity issues. Priority is to be given to those fisheries and fleets that show the effects of overcapacity and overfishing. The 2001 International Plan of Action to Prevent, Deter and Eliminate Illegal, Unreported and Unregulated (IUU) Fishing recommends good practice and calls upon states to adopt national plans of action to combat IUU fishing (see Box 5.4). It describes highly detailed measures to halt IUU fishing, including tougher requirements for vessel authorizations and registers, port-state controls to restrict IUU landings, and market-related measures to prevent IUU catch from being traded or imported.[102]

Although voluntary instruments such as these can be useful, a key problem is their nonbinding nature, which significantly impedes their effectiveness. Thus far, efforts to achieve the fine balance between encouraging widespread and international participation and the effective implementation of the guidelines and measures outlined in these voluntary instruments have not been that successful. Key factors, in addition to their voluntary status, are the lack of both financial and human resources in national fisheries sectors to implement the instruments properly and the fact that about one-third of FAO members still lack fisheries management plans.[103]

In May 2006, the United Nations held a review conference to assess implementation of the Fish Stocks Agreement, as called for in Article 36(2) of the agreement. The review conference recognized that although there had been some progress, much more needs to be done to prevent the further depletion of key fish stocks. The conference recommended a commitment to integrate ecosystem considerations in fisheries management, the urgent reduction of the world's fishing capacity to levels commensurate with the sustainability of fish stocks, urgent strengthening of the mandates of regional fisheries management organizations to implement modern approaches to fisheries, a commitment to develop a legally binding instrument on minimum standards for port-state measures and a comprehensive global register of fishing vessels, expanded assistance to developing countries, and a continuing dialogue to address concerns raised by nonparties, including issues related to boarding fishing vessels and inspections.[104]

The review conference also demonstrated that much has changed since the treaty's 1995 adoption. Parties and nonparties alike now accept certain principles of the treaty that were won only after long hours of negotiations in 1995, such as the ecosystem and precautionary approaches to management. Other provisions, however, remain perennially contentious, such as inspection and boarding. Overall, discussion revealed a shift in dynamics from the original negotiations, which had been divided between two coalitions: the distant-water fishing states and the coastal states. By contrast, in

BOX 5.4   IUU FISHING

Illegal, unreported, and unregulated (IUU) fishing is a global threat to sustainable fisheries and to the management and conservation of fisheries resources and marine biodiversity. IUU fishing includes fishing that violates the laws and regulations of a country or an international agreement, misreporting catches to the relevant national or regional authority, or fishing in a way that undermines management efforts to conserve marine species and ecosystems. IUU fishing occurs around the world and is thought to account for up to 30 percent of catches in some areas. However, since these catches are not recorded, exact amounts are hard to quantify. Failure to report catch and effort data to the regional fisheries management organizations, such as the International Commission for the Conservation of Atlantic Tunas, hampers their ability to conduct vital stock assessments used to manage and rebuild stocks, such as the severely depleted eastern Atlantic and Mediterranean bluefin tuna.

IUU fishing is often an organized criminal activity. For example, a pirate vessel may be owned by a company in the Caribbean that is itself owned by someone in Spain, it may have a Russian skipper and a crew from the Philippines or China, and it may be flagged to Togo. They use various strategies to evade apprehension and avoid laws and agreements to protect fish populations and other marine resources. The pirates often disguise the origin of their illegal catch so well that the fish is often sold legitimately into consumer markets—mainly in Japan, the European Union, the United States, and other developed countries. IUU fishing has enormous consequences. These poachers not only decimate valuable fish populations but also kill tens of thousands of marine animals as bycatch and destroy habitats through their unregulated use of damaging and illegal fishing practices. Annual global economic losses due to IUU fishing are estimated to be about $9 billion, according to an international task force on IUU fishing.

Enhanced port-state control has gained ground in the last decade as a tool to combat IUU fishing. The growing reliance on port states to combat nonsustainable fishing practices stems to a great extent from the failure of flag states to effectively control fishing operations carried out by vessels flying their flag (but which often operate out of different ports). In 2007 the FAO started a process to draft a legally binding instrument on port-state measures to prevent, deter, and eliminate IUU fishing. According to the draft elements of the treaty, fishing vessels that wish to land will be required to request permission from specially designated ports ahead of time, transmitting information on their activities and the fish they have on board, thereby providing authorities an opportunity to assess and detect possible illegalities prior to the vessel's docking. In addition, information-sharing networks will enable countries to deny port access to any vessel previously reported as involved in IUU fishing by other agreement participants or by regional fisheries management organizations.

"IUU Fishing: Background," Environmental Justice Foundation, www.ejfoundation.org/page162.html; "Planned Treaty Will Close Ports to Fish Pirates," FAO, February 3, 2009, www.fao.org/news/story/en/item/9998/icode; and "Fishing Problems: Illegal Fishing," WWF, www.panda.org/about_our_earth/blue_planet/problems/problems_fishing/illegal_fishing.

2006, the divide was between the lead coalition, now the parties, and a potential veto coalition, nonparties, whose continued refusal to ratify the agreement threatens the status of remaining fish stocks.[105] The review conference is scheduled to resume in 2010.[106]

In the regime-formation stage of the Fish Stocks Agreement, not one veto coalition but two—the like-minded caucus of coastal states and the major distant-water states—initially opposed key provisions of the regime. The original impetus for the agreement does not appear to have been a broad demand for conservation of straddling and highly migratory fish stocks as much as Canada's desire to overcome the EU's ability to determine its own catch levels in the Grand Banks fishery.

The U.S. shift from veto state to lead state was undoubtedly a major factor in overcoming the resistance of the two veto coalitions and gave greater impetus to the adoption of innovative conservation measures in the convention. And the willingness of Canada to use physical force on the high seas in its dispute with the EU, with the result that the EU agreed to onboard inspectors on the high seas, probably helped put the issue of boarding and inspecting in a different light for key veto states. Actions by veto states, however, especially some of the main fishing states (such as Chile, China, and Peru, to name a few), and their refusal to ratify the agreement continue to impede the regime's effectiveness. As long as the veto states remain such, the depletion and overexploitation of the world's fish stocks will continue.

DESERTIFICATION

The United Nations Convention to Combat Desertification (UNCCD) is one of only two global regimes established on the initiative of developing countries despite resistance by industrialized countries. Desertification, which affects the lives of 1 billion people in more than 110 countries around the world, had been the subject of international cooperation for nearly three decades, since the first major drought in sub-Saharan Africa, but was put on the UNCED agenda in 1992 only because African countries persisted. As it was the first treaty to be negotiated after UNCED, some looked upon it as a test of whether governments had the political will to follow up on Agenda 21 commitments.

Complexity, vagueness, and disagreement on whether desertification was indeed a "global" problem plagued the issue-definition stage. UNEP and most specialists defined desertification as sustained land degradation in arid, semiarid, and dry subhumid areas resulting mainly from adverse human impact.[107] But the term *desertification* evokes images of deserts advancing and destroying productive land, whereas scientists have found no evidence to support claims that the Sahara is expanding at an alarming

PHOTO 5.2   "Despair": Severe land degradation and desertification has a huge impact on the livelihoods of some of the poorest people on the planet.
2005 UNCCD photo contest, photo by Kushal Gangopadhyay, reprinted with permission.

rate.[108] Foes of a convention exploited that fact: At one point in the UNCED negotiations, the United States proposed that negotiators discard the term *desertification* and suggested substituting land degradation. Some donor countries objected that the designation "global" might imply that treaty-implementation efforts would be eligible for GEF funding.[109]

African countries encountered other problems in defining desertification. First, desertification does not involve resources or life-support systems of global interest, as do other environmental issues on which treaties have been negotiated. It affects countries not suffering from desertification only because it threatens the economies and societies of many other countries. Second, a bewildering array of natural and social factors appears to affect land degradation in drylands, including overpopulation, climatic cycles, social and economic structures, poor pastoral or agricultural practices, bad policies on the part of governments and donors, and North-South economic relations. It was difficult, therefore, to articulate simply and clearly either the nature of the problem or the international actions needed to address it.

Indeed, for many African countries, there is a strong link between poverty alleviation and desertification control. The African countries' definition of the problem emphasized the need for additional funding for as-yet-unidentified activities. These countries hoped that a desertification convention would help them gain access to additional funding through the GEF, which had rejected desertification as one of the global environmental problems it could finance.[110]

Finally, the African countries' attempt to define the desertification issue was hampered because the earlier Plan of Action to Combat Desertification, launched in 1977, was generally acknowledged as a failure. A UNEP evaluation of the plan had blamed the failure on African governments and the donor community for not giving the issue priority. UNEP had also found that only $1 billion of the $9 billion provided by donor agencies from 1978 to 1983 had been spent on direct field projects.[111]

So, when the issue of a desertification convention was first raised during the UNCED process, only France, with its historic ties with Africa, expressed support for the idea. Most industrialized countries and the World Bank argued that the primary problems were the macroeconomic policies of African governments (such as levying excessive taxes on agriculture and failing to grant enforceable property rights) and that policy reforms, better planning, and more popular participation would achieve better results than a new international program or formal agreement.[112] Moreover, the G-77 failed to endorse the African call for a desertification convention in the final communiqué of a key pre-UNCED meeting of developing countries, the 1992 Kuala Lumpur ministerial meeting, which was dominated by host government Malaysia.

Despite these problems in the definition of the issue of desertification, UNCED put it on the global agenda because of African persistence and because the United States unexpectedly supported the African position. At the Earth Summit in Rio, the United States, after opposing a desertification convention throughout the negotiations, shifted to backing such a convention in the hope of winning African support on forests and on the remaining issues in the Rio Declaration.[113] Other industrialized countries then followed suit, but the EC initially resisted the U.S. proposal. Finally, the EC relented, and the call for a desertification convention became part of Agenda 21.[114]

Negotiations by the Intergovernmental Negotiating Committee for the elaboration of an international convention to combat desertification in those countries experiencing serious drought and/or desertification, particularly in Africa (INCD), began in May 1993 and were completed in fifteen months. The formal fact-finding process, carried out in an "information-sharing segment" at the first session of the INCD, focused primarily on socioeconomic strategies for slowing and reversing desertification and on reports from individual countries rather than on scientific understanding of the problem. That process produced general agreement on the importance of such strategies as the integration of arid and semiarid areas into national economies, popular participation in antidesertification efforts, and land-tenure reform.[115] As a result, the convention would be the first to call for affected countries to provide for effective participation by grassroots organizations, NGOs, and local populations—men and women—in the preparation of national action programs.[116]

The bargaining stage revolved not around commitments to environmental conservation actions but around financial, trade, institutional, and symbolic issues. The African countries were the lead states and presented detailed draft sections for every section of the convention, some of which were accepted as the basis for negotiation.

Whether debt and trade issues should be included within the scope of the convention was a central issue that affected the obligations, action programs, and regional annexes, as well as sections on scope, objectives, and principles. The Africans and other developing countries asserted that external debt burdens and commodity prices, among other international economic policy issues, affected their ability to combat desertification. The industrialized countries argued that those North-South economic issues could be negotiated only in other international forums. They did agree to general obligations to "give due attention" to the trade and debt problems of affected countries and so create an "enabling international economic environment" for those countries.

Differences over financial resources and the financial mechanism nearly caused the negotiations to collapse. As in other global negotiations, some members of the G-77 and China demanded commitments to "new and additional" financial resources and creation of a special fund for desertification as the centerpiece of the convention. Industrialized countries acted as a united veto coalition in rejecting provisions for new and additional financing, agreeing only to ensure "adequate" financial resources for antidesertification programs. The developed countries felt they bore no responsibility for the problem of desertification worldwide, a position unlike that for the issues of ozone depletion and climate change, and were therefore unwilling to incur obligations to increase their financial assistance to affected countries.[117] They insisted that the overhead associated with a special fund would reduce the resources needed in the field and that existing resources could be used more effectively. They also vetoed the use of GEF funds unless the project contributed either to the prevention of climate change or to the conservation of biodiversity.

The deadlock on a funding mechanism was broken only after the United States proposed the "Global Mechanism" (GM) under the authority of the conference of the parties, to be housed within an existing organization, which would improve monitoring and assessment of existing aid flows and increase coordination among donors. Developing countries remained dissatisfied because such a mechanism would not increase development assistance to African and other countries suffering from desertification. But they ultimately accepted it as the only compromise acceptable to the donor countries.[118]

The problem of how to reflect the priority to be given to Africa as called for in the UNGA resolution on the convention, while meeting demands from other regions for equitable treatment, arose in negotiating regional annexes to the convention. The African and industrialized countries' delegations originally intended to negotiate a regional implementation annex only for Africa by the deadline of July 1994, but other developing-country delegations demanded that implementation annexes for their own regions be negotiated simultaneously with the one for Africa. In the end, each regional grouping received its own annex, but the priority for Africa was ensured by a special resolution that encouraged donor countries to provide financial support for national action programs in Africa without waiting for the convention to come into force.

The UNCCD was opened for signature in October 1994 and entered into force on December 26, 1996. Today, 193 countries are parties. The convention recognizes the physical, biological, and socioeconomic aspects of desertification, the importance of redirecting technology transfer so that it is demand driven, and the importance of local populations in efforts to combat desertification. The core of the convention is the development of national and subregional/regional action programs by national governments in cooperation with donors, local populations, and NGOs.

The regime-strengthening stage began at the first meeting of the COP in Rome in October 1997 and has been shaky at best. Challenges during the UNCCD's first six years included the definition, establishment, and operationalization of the GM, the financial mechanism created by, and loosely defined in, the convention. Another challenge was reconciling the convention's emphasis on "bottom-up" approaches and involvement at all levels by all relevant actors while remaining an international coordinating body. At the national level, the challenge was to enable affected countries to develop effective action programs in conjunction with donor countries and organizations as well as local communities and NGOs.[119]

Between 1997 and 2003, the COP set up institutional mechanisms to enable effective implementation of the convention. This work and the lack of a dedicated financing mechanism in the convention meant that the first five COPs spent time on procedures and institutions rather than on substance. During this period, they established two subsidiary bodies—a Committee on Science and Technology and a Committee for the Review of the Implementation of the Convention. After a long-fought battle, the convention designated the GEF as the financial mechanism for the convention once the GEF agreed to establish a program to fund projects to combat desertification. A fifth regional implementation annex for Central and Eastern Europe was adopted, and numerous education and awareness-raising programs were conducted. The sixth COP, in Havana in 2003, officially marked the transition from issues of process, institutions, and budgets to concrete action, such as support for stronger efforts and implementation on the ground. This transition has not been easy.

Overall, it took ten years for the convention to make the transition from awareness raising to implementation, but by 2005 it appeared as though the building blocks crucial for success were in place. Eighty-one affected countries had submitted national action programs, synergies had been developed with the climate change and biodiversity

conventions, new initiatives were underway, and there seemed to be a growing understanding in the international community that the Millennium Development Goals
cannot be achieved without an all-out attack on the root causes of rural poverty, to a
large extent brought on by desertification and drought.[120]

However, when the seventh meeting of the COP convened in Nairobi in October
2005, the convention faced an existential crisis as delegates fought acrimoniously over
many of the same issues that had plagued the convention since its negotiation. Unlike
in other natural resource–based treaties discussed in this chapter, the problems facing
the UNCCD do not involve national sovereignty over resources. In this regime, the
only multilateral environmental agreement driven by developing countries, many problems stem from the fact that land degradation is not a priority issue for donor governments. As one developing country official put it, the "scorching breath of the desert is
not readily felt by the prosperous public of the rich North."[121] This relatively low level
of concern is compounded by the donors' persistent distrust of the secretariat.

The tone in Nairobi was also shaped by the critical report of the United Nations
Joint Inspection Unit (an external oversight body). At COP-6 in Havana, parties had
requested the Joint Inspection Unit to review the activities of the secretariat. The report
confirmed, among other things, that the convention had a major identity crisis. "In the
course of the review, it appeared to the Inspectors that from the outset there has been
a lack of common understanding and recognition of the Convention in its true and
proper perspective."[122] The report continued that it seemed unclear whether the convention is environmental, developmental, or both and whether it concerns problems
of a purely local or a global nature. The inspectors also noted, "The very name of the
Convention may perhaps be misleading since the fundamental problem is one of land
degradation, of which desertification is a key element. The failure and/or unwillingness to recognize the Convention in its proper perspective has inevitably led to undesirable consequences."[123] Some of these consequences include the lack of access to
financial support, the lack of a stable financial commitment by the developed-country
parties, the failure to mainstream UNCCD programs and activities into their respective development-support initiatives, and the lack of UNCCD prioritization in affected
country parties, which have had little success in integrating UNCCD objectives into
overall national development plans. The inspectors also noted that in many developed
countries, the ministry of cooperation or foreign affairs has responsibility for the
UNCCD, but these ministries rarely see desertification as a priority issue. Furthermore,
in the developing countries, desertification is generally the responsibility of relatively
weaker environment ministries. Officials designated as UNCCD focal points in both
developed and developing countries are usually not sufficiently senior in the ministries
concerned to effectively promote the convention. As a result, the convention has difficulty in getting the necessary recognition and support.[124]

The Nairobi meeting ended with agreement that in response to the Joint Inspection Unit's report, parties should adopt a long-term strategic plan for implementation of the convention at the next COP. While many admitted that this was not a panacea to the UNCCD's problems, they also hoped that it would help to strengthen the regime.

The strategic plan was developed at a series of intersessional meetings in 2006 and 2007 and brought forward for adoption at COP-8 in Madrid in September 2007. The strategic plan strives to link the work programs of the convention's institutions to a common vision, clarifies their mandates and methods of work, and institutionalizes a results-based management approach. It also sets out operational objectives on issues including awareness raising, policies, improving the flow of science and technology, and capacity building. It also further defines the coordination and respective mandates of the secretariat and the GM so as to enhance coordination and integration.[125]

At the same time that the strategic plan was under development, long-time executive secretary (director) Hama Arba Diallo announced that he would be stepping down. The secretariat in general, and Diallo in particular, had repeatedly come under fire for questionable management practices and lack of transparency.[126] During the COP in Madrid, the UN Secretary-General appointed Luc Gnacadja as the new executive secretary of the UNCCD. Many hoped that the new strategic plan and a new executive secretary would usher in a new phase of successful implementation for the convention.[127] Yet, this has been easier said than done. The parties could not reach agreement on a budget in Madrid, forcing them to convene an extraordinary session of the COP in New York in late November 2007. While many developing countries wanted a budget increase as a display of confidence for the strategic plan and Gnacadja's leadership, developed countries, particularly Japan, were not so willing to open their checkbooks until there was some evidence of more effective management practices.

The UNCCD still faces a number of challenges. The relationship between the GM and the secretariat remains contentious. Many developing countries believe that the GM is not doing enough to increase the flow of financial resources for UNCCD implementation, feel frustrated by its current operation, and believe it should be controlled by the secretariat in Bonn rather than the International Fund for Agricultural Development in Rome. Developed countries, on the other hand, believe that the GM should be an independent broker to mobilize resources. Despite their preferences for either the GM or the secretariat, delegations across the board have highlighted concerns about overlapping activities and lack of coordination and mutual support.[128]

The UNCCD also faces the challenge of bringing more scientific and technological input into its operations. Since the convention's inception, the role of scientists has been marginalized. In its existing institutional architecture, scientific and technological input has been predominantly channeled to the COP through its subsidiary Committee on

Science and Technology and a roster of independent experts, as nominated by the parties. However, the science and technology committee's large and diverse membership renders it rather unwieldy: Different people attend each meeting, and rarely have there been focused and meaningful exchanges on specific issues. Government representatives, many of whom lack the training or expertise to engage in substantive scientific debates, typically dominate discussions. Committee sessions are often marred by procedural quarrels resulting in low-profile, nonauthoritative outputs with little relevance for either the COP or the scientific community.[129]

In short, the UNCCD process lacks an efficient operational mechanism to process and channel practical and scientific expertise for political decision makers. The COP fails to tap the information potentially available from the scientific community, which in turn is unable to draw the attention of the parties to the scientific aspects of the issues on their agenda.[130] To address this problem, at COP-8 parties called for a "scientific-style" conference which took place during the meeting of the Committee on Science and Technology in Buenos Aires, Argentina, in September 2009. There have also been calls for the provision of independent scientific policy advisory services from outside the immediate UNCCD process, referring to the role of the Intergovernmental Panel on Climate Change vis-à-vis the United Nations Framework Convention on Climate Change as a promising model.

While the UNCCD has carved a niche for itself at the interface of environment and development—it is often referred to as "the sustainable development convention"—it still suffers from an identity crisis. Unlike the other treaties described in this volume, the UNCCD is seeking to address poverty, both a cause and consequence of dryland degradation, as well as problems pertaining to sustainable land management, combating desertification, and mitigating the effects of drought. Many parties, in fact, consider the UNCCD a developmental rather than an environmental treaty, stressing that its primary objective is to fight poverty. This dual emphasis reflects serious differences of opinion between developing and developed countries, hindering the effective implementation of the convention. For the same reason, however, developed countries have been reluctant to acknowledge desertification as a global commons problem and to commit substantive financial resources. While this caveat is hardly exclusive to the desertification issue—many other treaties face shortfalls in financial resources—the UNCCD's future success will arguably depend on the effective mediation of divergent perspectives on the environment-poverty nexus and improved understanding of the interlinkages between development and the environment.[131]

Unlike other regimes, the UNCCD's implementation has not been hindered by issues of national sovereignty or scientific uncertainty. In fact, the knowledge and technical skills exist to halt several causes of desertification, but political and economic factors determine whether the expertise is ever put into practice. Implementation has proven difficult because of the nature of the problem, lack of political commitment, and bureaucratic mistrust, often demonstrated by the developed countries, who serve as a veto coalition utilizing the power of the purse. Desertification is a worldwide problem, but solutions are essentially local or regional, not global. The idea of addressing a global "public good" through a global convention, which works with the other Rio conventions (climate change and biodiversity), is not as effective in the UNCCD case.[132] The UNCCD will have to consider which issues in the desertification battle should be addressed in the far-removed and bureaucratic "virtual world" of the international level and which are best decided in the "real world," nationally or locally. Unless the secretariat and the parties can effectively address these issues and the UNCCD can refocus on implementation, within the context of reduced financial contributions and wavering political commitment from some donor parties, the future of the first "sustainable development" convention may be bleak indeed.

FORESTS

The issue of forests is unique among these case studies in that it continues to defy the creation of a comprehensive global regime. The main reasons for this are linked to the complexity of the issue and the successful efforts of a veto coalition. As demonstrated in several other cases, the makeup of a veto coalition can change over time, but only in this issue has the veto coalition changed so much in membership and rationale, yet still blocked the negotiation of a treaty.

Forests cover 3.95 billion hectares, or about 30 percent of the total land area of the world (not including Greenland and Antarctica). Between 1990 and 2005, the global forest area shrank at an annual rate of about 0.2 percent. Losses were greatest in Africa, Latin America, and the Caribbean. However, forest area expanded in Europe and North America. In Asia and the Pacific, forest area expanded after 2000 (see Figure 5.3). In addition to the changes in global forest area, significant changes have also occurred in forest composition, particularly in the conversion of **primary forest** to other types of forests, especially in Asia and the Pacific. It is estimated that since 1990 there has been an annual loss of 50,000 square kilometers (about 19,305 square miles, or twice the size of the state of Vermont) of primary forest, while there has been an average annual increase of 30,000 square kilometers of **plantation forests** and seminatural forests. Primary forests, or forests largely undisturbed by human activity, now comprise only about one-third of global forest area.[133]

According to World Bank estimates, more than 1.6 billion people depend on forests for their livelihoods. The forest-product industry is a source of economic growth and employment, with global forest products traded internationally on the order of $270

FIGURE 5.3   Annual forest cover change, 1990–2005

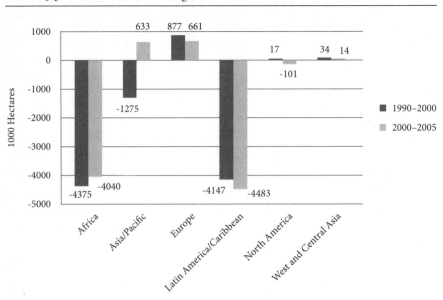

Data source: FAO, *State of the World's Forests, 2009* (Rome: FAO, 2009).

billion. The 13 million hectares of the world's forests lost due to deforestation every year account for up to 20 percent of the global greenhouse gas (GHG) emissions that contribute to global warming. The world's forests and forest soils store more than one trillion tons of carbon—twice the amount found in the atmosphere.[134]

Even as public awareness of the impact of deforestation increased over the last thirty years, the problem continued on a tremendous scale. Although the global rate of deforestation has slowed since the 1990s, deforestation and forest-degradation rates remain high in many African and Latin American countries.[135]

The many causes of forest degradation include overharvesting of industrial wood and fuelwood, overgrazing, fire, insect pests, diseases, storms, and air pollution. Most forests are being cleared to provide land for food and cash crops. Fuelwood is also the main cooking fuel for nearly half the world's people, the poorest of them. Wood is essential for building construction and a host of other uses. Timber exports are a source of foreign exchange for many countries. Although cutting trees and clearing forests make perfect sense to those engaged in these practices, as the trees disappear there are also losers: Forest dwellers, often the poorest and most vulnerable members of society, are deprived of their homes and livelihoods. Fuelwood and other forest products become harder to obtain. Flooding results, land is eroded, and lakes and dams are filled with silt. With fewer trees to soak up carbon dioxide from the atmosphere, the risk of climate change increases. As plant and wildlife species become extinct, biological diversity is reduced.[136]

Countries have been discussing international forest-policy issues within the UN system since the end of World War II.[137] The FAO Conference, which first met in 1945, was the principal global forum for the discussion of international forestry issues from the mid-1940s until 1971, when the FAO established the Committee on Forestry. Since its first session in 1972, this committee has met regularly at two-year intervals to review forestry problems of "an international character."[138] Forest industries and the restoration of timber supplies were prominent topics of early conferences, and they, together with logging and the marketing and utilization of forest products, have remained on the committee's agenda.

Other milestones in the global forest-policy dialogue include the adoption of the International Tropical Timber Agreement in 1983 and the establishment of the International Tropical Timber Organization in 1986 to promote international trade in tropical timber, the sustainable management of tropical forests, and the development of forest industries. The organization's membership represents 90 percent of world trade in tropical timber and 80 percent of the world's tropical forests. Regional initiatives to protect forests and promote their sustainable management have also been developed, including the 1978 Amazon Cooperation Treaty and the 1990 Ministerial Conference on the Protection of Forests in Europe.

The 1992 UNCED marked a turning point in the international forest-policy dialogue and started a new process of issue definition when forests were examined within the context of sustainable development. Negotiations on forests during the UNCED Preparatory Committee quickly became polarized. Three competing public claims to the world's forests were made during the negotiations. The developed countries, which had called for a forest convention in 1990 in the European Parliament and at the Group of Seven Houston summit meeting, ventured that forests could be seen as a global common because all humanity has a stake in forest conservation. On the other side, the G-77, led by Malaysia and India, claimed that forests are sovereign national resources to be used in line with national development objectives. NGOs and indigenous peoples' groups made a third claim: Forests should be seen as local commons, and the best way to achieve forest conservation was to grant secure land-tenure rights to local communities whose livelihoods depend directly on the conservation of forest resources.[139] With rejection of a treaty by the G-77 dooming negotiations on a formal convention, delegates instead negotiated two non–legally binding agreements on forests: the Forest Principles[140] and Chapter 11 of Agenda 21, titled "Combating Deforestation."[141]

During the UNCED negotiations, the United States and Canada tried to link the principle of the sovereignty of countries over their own forest resources with the principles of national responsibility and global concern for forests. Canada, with huge forest re-sources under rapid development, proposed to establish the principle that forests are of interest to the international community, that international standards should be im-plemented in forest management, and that targets and time frames should be included in national forestry plans. But Malaysia and India saw these formulations as an effort to establish the legal principle that forests are "global commons," or part of the "com-mon heritage of mankind," a status that might eventually give industrialized countries the right to interfere in the management of the tropical-forest countries' resources.[142] Malaysia, as the world's largest exporter of tropical timber, had a particularly intense interest in the issue. It was determined to become a "fully developed country" by 2020, using export earnings from timber and other export crops grown on land converted from forests.[143]

The final version of the Forest Principles only hints that forests are a global envi-ronmental issue and drops not only the idea of international guidelines for forest man-agement but also all references to trade in "sustainably managed" forest products. It also gives blanket approval to the conversion of natural forests to other uses. Developed countries widely regarded the agreement as worse than no declaration at all because it appeared to legitimize unsustainable forest-management policies.[144] The Forest Prin-ciples and Chapter 11 of Agenda 21 both reaffirmed the rights of sovereign nations to use their forests in accordance with their national priorities and policy objectives. The Rio agreements also stress the cross-sectoral nature of forests and point out that forests simultaneously provide a wide range of socioeconomic benefits as well as environ-mental values and services.

The Forest Principles agreement and the North-South confrontation over the issue seemed to shut the door on global negotiations on forests. Between 1992 and 1995, however, a series of international meetings and ongoing initiatives, including several joint North-South collaborations, began a new process of maneuvering over sustain-able forest management.[145] These initiatives, which contributed to the review of the Forest Principles and Chapter 11 of Agenda 21 by the Commission on Sustainable De-velopment (CSD) in 1995, helped some key forest countries identify areas of common interest and develop a common international agenda on forests.[146] The result was agreement to begin the next phase of fact finding and bargaining within a new forum, the Intergovernmental Panel on Forests (IPF).

Intergovernmental Panel on Forests

The IPF was possible, in part, because of a Malaysian shift of position. After UNCED, responsibility for international forest negotiations in Malaysia was moved from the Ministry of Foreign Affairs to the Ministry of Primary Industries.[147] Malaysia subse-quently shifted to supporting a convention. A factor here appears to have been the position of the Malaysian Timber Council. Malaysia is one of the few developing countries in which timber corporations conduct substantial logging operations in other countries. Malaysian forest-industry businesses are active in Africa and South America, and the Malaysian Timber Council has openly acknowledged that it supports a convention to enable "access to markets."[148]

With Canada and Malaysia in the lead, the CSD established the IPF with a two-year mandate to build consensus on priority issues in five interrelated categories: implementation of UNCED decisions related to forests at the national and international level; international cooperation in financial assistance and technology transfer; scientific research, forest assessment, and development of criteria and indicators for sustainable forest management; trade-and-environment issues relating to forest products and services; and international organizations and instruments, including the possibility of a forests convention.[149]

By the time the IPF had completed its work in February 1997, it had developed more than one hundred proposals for action on issues related to sustainable forest management, including national forest programs, forest assessment, criteria and indicators, traditional forest-related knowledge, and underlying causes of deforestation.[150] These recommendations, however, did not effectively leverage changes in forest-management policies and practices. Many involved lengthy texts that did not identify key issues and actions to be taken; others did not clearly indicate whether action should be taken at the national or international level. Relatively few suggested regulatory measures, and implementation was left to the country's discretion. The IPF created no mechanism for reporting or follow-up on the recommendations, further limiting their impact on policy. An intergovernmental paper on the implementation of the IPF proposals in 1999 concluded that it was "difficult to single out the impacts of IPF from those induced by macroeconomic changes and other policy processes."[151]

The debate about the need for a global forest convention remained as polarized as it was in 1992; by 1997, however, there was a new alignment of countries. Malaysia and Canada, the lead states, apparently believed that a global agreement on sustainable forestry could be the basis for an officially sponsored, international ecolabel for wood products and that their timber industries could use the label to fend off pressures for certification by the Forest Stewardship Council. The former Canadian natural resources minister, Anne McLellan, said in a 1997 speech to the Canadian pulp and paper industry that Canada was leading a push for a forest convention to secure an internationally recognized ecolabel for wood-based products (see Chapter 7). She linked the project to the threat posed to Canada's forestry industry, the country's largest export sector, by environmental protests and boycotts over clear-cutting of old-growth forests.[152]

The European Union still officially supported the negotiation of a binding treaty. Some of its key member states (France, Germany, and Italy) had long been the staunchest supporters of a global forest treaty. But by 1996, some environmental groups and aid agencies in EU member states had begun to oppose a binding agreement, in part because they saw that no new money would be forthcoming to support it. Germany had started to view it as a potentially dangerous agreement, pushed by some of the very states that had opposed meaningful norms of forest management at UNCED.[153]

Some developing countries, including Costa Rica, Indonesia, Papua New Guinea, and the Philippines, also changed their position to support a convention in the hope that it would generate new sources of development assistance for forests. There was also some movement from the African countries in favor of a convention. At UNCED, African countries had supported the G-77 position against a convention despite an attempt by the Europeans to split the G-77 by promising the sub-Saharan African countries a convention on desertification if they would support a forest convention. By 1997, many African countries were prepared to do so. However, with the major South American countries remaining firmly opposed, the G-77, which seeks to speak with one voice, maintained that it was too early to start negotiations for a convention, but the desirability of a convention would be reassessed at a later stage.[154]

The United States, which had supported a convention in Rio, now opposed it and so became one of the leaders of the veto coalition. The influence of the corporate sector, which opposed a convention on the grounds that it would be interventionist and regulatory, was largely responsible for this shift.[155] Japan, which had also formally endorsed a convention at UNCED without actively supporting it, now opposed the idea, as did Australia and New Zealand, along with the major South American countries, led by Brazil. As another leader of the veto coalition, Brazil's strong resistance to a binding treaty on forests reflected similar fears about environmental requirements finding their way into the agreement. The forest convention issue thus shows how different states—and the timber industry in different countries—can share the same political and economic interests (in this instance freedom from third-party certification by a system that the industry didn't trust) but come out on opposite sides of the issue because of differing assessments of the situation.

There was also a major shift in the NGO community. In Rio, many international NGOs tended to favor a convention if it contained strong conservation commitments and firm provisions respecting the rights and traditions of indigenous forest peoples. But at the IPF, NGOs issued a declaration against a convention. They had noticed the shift by major tropical timber producers such as Malaysia and Indonesia in favor of a convention. Coupled with the long-term support from the Canadian government and the Canadian forest industry, along with support from Finland and Russia, this led NGO campaigners to question which interests and values the convention would actually promote.[156]

THE FAR SIDE®   By GARY LARSON

"And see this ring right here, Jimmy? ... That's another time when the old fellow miraculously survived some big forest fire."

In the end, the IPF was unable to agree on recommendations for a global forest convention. The panel proposed the following three options to the CSD: continue the policy dialogue within existing forums, continue the dialogue through another intergovernmental forum under the CSD, or establish under the authority of the UNGA an intergovernmental negotiating committee on a legally binding instrument. The commission declined to take a decision and passed it to an UNGA special session to review implementation of Agenda 21; in June 1997, the UNGA agreed to establish an Intergovernmental Forum on Forests (IFF) under the auspices of the CSD.[157] In other words, governments supported the need for dialogue but could advance matters no further than the status quo.

Intergovernmental Forum on Forests

The IFF, which held its first meeting in October 1997 and concluded its work in February 2000, was charged with promoting and facilitating implementation of the IPF's proposals for action; reviewing, monitoring, and reporting on progress in the management, conservation, and sustainable development of all types of forests; and considering matters left pending by the panel, particularly trade, finance, and technology transfer, and a possible forest convention.

The same issues that stymied the IPF continued to prove difficult for the IFF. Trade and sustainable-forest-management issues continued to yield some of the most intense debates. Long-held differences between developed and developing countries on the financial resources and provision of new technology also remained unresolved. Canada did not give up its aim of securing agreement on a global forest convention, but the veto coalition of industrialized and developing states opposed to negotiating a forest treaty doomed the Canadian effort. Delegates finally agreed to recommend to the CSD that the UN establish an intergovernmental body called the United Nations Forum on Forests (UNFF) and, within five years, "consider with a view to recommending the parameters of a mandate for developing a legal framework on all types of forests." The language is sufficiently obscure that the lead and veto coalitions both felt they had achieved a successful outcome to the negotiations.

United Nations Forum on Forests

The United Nations Economic and Social Council established the UNFF in 2000 with the goal of promoting "the management, conservation and sustainable development of the world's forests, and to strengthen long-term political commitment to this end."[158] The Collaborative Partnership on Forests was also established to support the work of the UNFF and its member countries and to foster increased cooperation and coordination on forests.[159] The UNFF held eight sessions between 2001 and 2009, attempting to build upon the work initiated by the IPF and IFF. However, according to some observers, a lack of both engagement and consensus hampered progress, and at times the process appeared at risk of complete derailment.[160]

When discussion on a forests convention or other "international arrangement on forests" convened at UNFF-5 in May 2005, the session was supposed to review the effectiveness of the current international arrangement on forests, including the UNFF itself, and also to consider whether negotiations on a global forest convention could be initiated. However, many of the most ardent proponents of a global forest convention were already conceding that a consensus was unlikely to emerge for any type of legally binding agreement.[161] The coalitions that emerged in 1997 were largely unchanged by 2005, and the debate appeared to be as polarized as ever. There was wide agreement that the global forest agenda had made some progress under the UNFF but that deforestation and forest degradation continued at an unsustainably high rate; however, there was no consensus on how to proceed.

Developing countries, although divided on the need for a treaty, were united in their call to implement commitments related to financial resources, capacity building, and technology transfer, which they saw as critical to advancing the management, conservation, and sustainable development of all types of forests.[162] Canada, the EU, Malaysia, and Switzerland continued to act as lead states, although they recognized that a treaty might not be possible and started to look for alternative proposals. The veto coalition, led by Brazil, continued to oppose a treaty, calling instead for the continuation and strengthening of the UNFF and the Collaborative Partnership on Forests. Several compromise proposals began to emerge. Some countries called for a non–legally binding voluntary code of conduct with clear overarching goals and a limited number of targets. Canada, Switzerland, and the United States, among others, supported this proposal, but Brazil and others rejected quantifiable goals and argued that the UNCED Statement of Forest Principles was a code of conduct. Negotiation for targets and timetables began, but although there was tentative agreement about goals and the possibility of negotiating a voluntary code, there was no consensus on the details. NGOs argued that members had engaged in policy talks for too long while deforestation continued unabated and unchallenged. They argued that governments must adopt clear, measurable targets, provide the necessary resources to implement actions to achieve them, and ensure broad participation of NGOs and indigenous peoples.

In the end, countries recognized that without the support of two key players in the veto coalition—the country with the largest timber industry (the United States) and the country with the world's largest tropical forest (Brazil)—no treaty would be possible. Other options were put on the table, but there was still no consensus on the adoption of targets, a voluntary code of conduct, or the consideration of a treaty in the future. With no agreement possible, delegates agreed to reconvene at UNFF-6 in 2006 to try, yet again, to reach consensus on an international arrangement on forests—an agreement that has eluded international makers of forest policy since 1992.

UNFF-6 finally secured the next step in strengthening the international arrangement on forests by deciding to develop a voluntary instrument. To this end, delegates agreed on four "global objectives" on forests: reversing the loss of forest cover and increasing efforts to prevent forest degradation, enhancing forest benefits and their contribution to international development goals, increasing the area of protected forests and areas of sustainably managed forests, and reversing the decline in **official development assistance** for sustainable forest management. They also agreed to continue the work of the UNFF at least through 2015 and to conclude and adopt at its seventh session "a non–legally binding instrument on all types of forests."[163] So, fourteen years after Rio, the idea of a forest treaty seemed to have disappeared off the agenda, despite the efforts of a few staunch supporters, including the Canadians. But most countries expressing interest in a legally binding treaty had no intention of abandoning the UNFF, with many stating that a voluntary instrument was a good first step toward securing a more binding agreement.

Nine months later, UNFF-7 completed negotiation of a non–legally binding instrument on all types of forests, which the UNGA adopted in December 2007.[164] The instrument sets a framework for accomplishing the global objectives on forests and defines its overall purpose as:

- to strengthen political commitment and action at all levels to implement effectively sustainable management of all types of forests and to achieve the shared global objectives on forests;
- to enhance the contribution of forests to the achievement of the internationally agreed development goals, including the Millennium Development Goals, in particular with respect to poverty eradication and environmental sustainability; and
- to provide a framework for national action and international cooperation.

The forum also agreed to consider a financial mechanism to support implementation at its 2009 session. The effectiveness of the international arrangement on forests will be reviewed in 2015, at which time a full range of options will be considered, including a legally binding instrument on all types of forests. UNFF-7 also adopted a focused multiyear program of work from 2007 to 2015, during which period the forum would meet biannually to review implementation of the non–legally binding instrument, sustainable forest management, the global objectives on forests, and the IPF/IFF proposals for action.[165]

When UNFF-8 convened two years later in April 2009, the main agenda item was to reach agreement on how to finance implementation of the non–legally binding instrument. Unlike at previous meetings, this discussion took place against a different backdrop, with increased attention to the role that forests play in climate change. The UK-commissioned Eliasch Review found that close to US$30 billion per year would be required to halve the rate of forest loss and its associated impacts on climate change, an amount far greater than the level of financing produced by the international community to date. The review also estimated the global costs of climate change caused by deforestation at an even more astounding US$1 trillion a year.[166] Documents prepared for UNFF-8 echoed these findings, including a report prepared for the Advisory Group on Finance of the Collaborative Partnership on Forests that concluded there is a need for substantial new and additional funding from all sources to support sustainable forest management and enable effective implementation of the forest instrument. These reports may have increased developing countries' expectations that donors would be more amenable to creating a global forest fund. However, as became clear by the middle of the second week, none of the donors had a mandate to negotiate such a fund.[167]

At this point, the negotiations reflected the North-South division characteristic of many other environmental negotiations because the focus was now on financing and not on the definition of sustainable forest management or the need for a forest treaty. The first co-chairs' draft failed to capture the true magnitude of the chasm between these positions, downplaying the G-77 and China's proposal for a global forest fund, resulting in a time-consuming false start. An entrenched debate over "fund or no fund" dominated the remainder of the session's negotiations, which never progressed past this to discuss more nuanced details, such as how such a fund would be governed. In the end, even a decision to establish an expert group to consider the need for a fund was quashed by lack of agreement over the group's mandate or a timeline for its work, with developing countries, as lead states, pushing for a decision on a fund's establishment sooner rather than later and donor countries, as veto states, aligning to consider the establishment of a fund only at UNFF-10.[168]

One of the donors' main arguments against the creation of a global forest fund was that the forum would run a great reputational risk in creating a fund that might never receive any voluntary contributions, an argument similar to the one made during the negotiations on the UNCCD. This led the donors to take the strong position that a facilitative process was preferable, calling for developing countries to make better use of existing funds. Developing countries turned this argument around, saying that the reputational risk lay in failing to create the fund and consequently failing to produce the needed resources to implement the forest instrument.[169]

This argument did not appear to convince donors, and some delegates went so far as to say that the UNFF was not even the venue in which donors were most likely to produce big results for forest funding. Many reserved such expectations for the Copenhagen climate talks in December 2009 and the anticipated financing mechanism for reducing emissions from deforestation and forest degradation, which some see as the only major hope for generating anywhere near the amount of funding indicated by Eliasch and others. While the source of funds would seem irrelevant at first, many within the forest community worry that a purely climate-oriented source of forest funding risks marginalizing the many other values delivered by forests.[170]

Although it may appear that the international forest-policy debate within the UNFF is dysfunctional at best, the dialogue is in full swing in other fora. The emergence of illegal logging as an issue of concern for the international forest-policy community, coupled with the ineffective UNFF process, have caused some parts of the international community to move away from the issue of sustainable forest management and toward illegal logging as their main area of concern.[171] That the issue of illegal logging is being addressed for the most part through the various Forest Law Enforcement and

Governance ministerial processes (Africa, East Asia, Europe, and North Asia) also suggests a regionalization of the global forest discourse.[172] Illegal forest activities may contribute to increased poverty and conflict, foster a vicious cycle of bad governance, and pose a significant threat to the sustainability of forest ecosystems. According to the World Bank, the (global) annual market value of losses from illegal cutting of forests is estimated at over US$10 billion—more than eight times the total official development assistance flows to the sustainable management of forests.[173]

Another issue that has come to dominate the forest debate is the role of forests in climate change. Deforestation and forest degradation in developing countries are the primary sources of carbon emissions from these countries. Deforestation accounts for 35 percent of carbon emissions in developing countries and 65 percent in the least-developed countries.[174] In 2007, at the Climate Change Conference in Bali, Indonesia, forests received significant attention. The Bali Action Plan addressed mitigation action, including through policy approaches and positive incentives on issues relating to reducing emissions from deforestation and forest degradation in developing countries, as well as the role of conservation, sustainable management of forests, and enhancement of forest carbon stocks in developing countries. As noted above, some in the forest community are concerned that forest-related climate-change options must recognize the comprehensiveness of sustainable forest management, which goes beyond forests' emission and carbon potentials. When only one single good or service under sustainable forest management—such as climate-change adaptation and mitigation—attracts significant financing, there is a risk that this can distort sustainable forest management to the detriment of other goods and services. This issue will likely grow in importance and become more controversial as the climate-change and forests negotiations continue.

CONCLUSION

The cases of environmental regime formation presented in chapters 3 to 5 show that the negotiation of a strong global environmental regime almost always depends on inducing one or more key states in a veto coalition to go along with one or more of the core proposed provisions of the regime. By a strong or effective regime, we mean an agreement that includes obligations or norms that make it sufficiently clear that parties can be held accountable for implementing them and that calls for actions reasonably can be expected to have an impact on the problem if they are implemented. Whether a regime succeeds in addressing an environmental threat depends, of course, on how strong the regime is in the above sense and on the degree to which parties comply with its core provisions. When veto power has been successfully over-

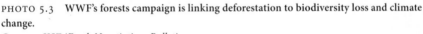

PHOTO 5.3   WWF's forests campaign is linking deforestation to biodiversity loss and climate change.
Courtesy IISD/*Earth Negotiations Bulletin.*

come, and when vital norms or actions have been agreed to, it has been for one of five possible reasons:

1. A veto state changed its own understanding of the problem because of new scientific evidence.
2. A veto state changed its position because its economic interests changed.
3. A veto state had a change of government, and the new government had a different policy toward the issue.
4. A veto state came under effective domestic political pressure to change its policy.
5. A veto state feared negative reactions from other governments or adverse international opinion, which it regarded as more important than its interest in vetoing a specific provision of the regime.

As Table 5.2 shows, in some of these cases one or more veto states either agreed to the central obligation proposed by the lead-state coalition or accepted the regime in general, despite earlier rejection.

New scientific evidence has helped move veto states on some issues (acid rain, ozone depletion, climate change, and persistent organic pollutants) but has been secondary or irrelevant in other issues (whaling, hazardous waste trade, desertification,

TABLE 5.2 Veto States and Regime Creation or Strengthening

ISSUE*	KEY VETO STATES	BASIS OF VETO POWER	VETO-STATE CONCESSION
Acid rain (sulfur dioxide)	Belgium, Denmark, and Germany	Export of sulfur dioxide	Joining the "30 Percent Club"
Ozone depletion	EC	Percent of CFC production	Agreeing to a 50 percent cut
Climate change	United States	Percent of CO_2 emissions	Agreeing to stabilization goals**
Toxic waste trade	EU, Japan, United States	Percent of exports	Agreeing to ban exports
Toxic chemicals	Developing countries who use DDT for malaria control	Percent of use of DDT; global support for increased malaria control	Accepting elimination of DDT but with blanket exception for disease control; accepting regular reviews on continued need for DDT
Whaling	Japan and Norway	Percent of catch	Accepting outcome of the vote on the ban on whaling against depleted populations
African elephant ivory	Japan, southern African states	Percent of imports (Japan); elephant herds (southern African states)	Having no reservation to CITES uplist
Big-leaf mahogany	Bolivia, Brazil, and other exporters	Source of big-leaf mahogany	Having no reservation to CITES uplist
Biodiversity loss	United States	Percentage of financing of GEF; biotechnology	Signing the agreement**
Fisheries depletion	EC, Japan, and the like-minded caucus	Percentage of global catch of straddling and highly migratory stocks	Agreeing to precautionary reference points and new enforcement measures
Desertification	EC, United States	Percentage of ODA	Agreeing to negotiate regime
Forests	Brazil and Latin American countries, United States	Percentage of the world's forests; largest timber industry	No agreement

* This table outlines one aspect of the veto-coalition situation for each case as a point of comparison.

** In both of these cases, veto-state power has not totally been overcome because although the United States in each case made certain concessions in the negotiations, the result was a much weaker treaty.

and African elephants). International considerations were primary in several cases: Japan's concern with economic and diplomatic ties with other major trading nations and its international image helped tilt its stance on the ivory ban. French and British desires to maintain close relations with former colonies factored into their view on the hazardous waste trade. The leading distant-water fishing states dropped their resistance to key provisions in the Fish Stocks Agreement at least in part because they did not want to appear to be blocking the first major global agreement on sustainable fishing. Changing economic interests or new political strategies concerning how to best pursue those interests can also lead veto states to change position. The United Kingdom and France dropped their opposition to phasing out CFCs in part because their chemical industries invented substitutes. Several veto states early in the forest negotiations changed positions when they believed they might secure a treaty that would preserve market access or secure new sources of multilateral funding.

In most of these cases, domestic political developments played a key role in facilitating agreement. Business and industrial concerns have affected the U.S. response to climate change as well as the dispute over methyl bromide in the Montreal Protocol. Concern about persistent organic pollutants in the Inuit communities of northern Canada pushed Canada to the forefront of the negotiations to ban certain types of these substances.

Regime formation also requires leadership by one or more states committed to defining the issue and proposing a detailed policy approach as the basis for the regime. Sometimes, that lead role is played by states motivated by particular vulnerability (Finland, Norway, and Sweden on acid rain; the African countries on the hazardous waste trade and desertification; the small island states on climate change) and sometimes by a state that has an advantageous legal or economic status (the original U.S. call for a phaseout of chlorofluorocarbons).

But as these cases show, the United States has greater diplomatic influence on other state actors and intergovernmental organizations than any other state. When the United States has taken the lead, as it did on ozone depletion, whaling, or the African elephant, the result has been a much stronger regime than would otherwise have been established. In the case of the Fish Stocks Agreement, the lead role played by the United States was crucial to agreement on conservation norms applying on the high seas and within EEZs. But when the United States has been a veto state, as in the LRTAP sulfur dioxide protocol, the Basel Convention, the Biodiversity Convention, and the Kyoto Protocol, the result is a significantly weaker regime.

In the cases of the climate and biodiversity regimes, veto power wielded by key states has not yet been overcome either in the initial negotiations on regime formation or in subsequent negotiations on regime strengthening. The result is two relatively weak regimes, given what is known regarding the magnitude of the problems they seek to address. In negotiations on strengthening the climate regime, the key veto states have been Brazil, China, India, and the United States, which together account for much more than half of global GHG emissions. The United States, hobbled by strong domestic political opposition to a meaningful commitment to emissions reduction, has consistently opposed ambitious targets for reducing GHG emissions and has the greatest impact on the effectiveness of any resulting targets (although the resistance of other countries has also contributed to the result). But the insistence of major developing countries, whose emissions already account for a large proportion of global emissions, that no obligations for controlling emissions be placed on them threatens the effectiveness of the existing regime. While many had hoped that the election of President Barack Obama in 2008 would enable the United States to play more of a lead role in the negotiations, the reality is that domestic economic and political concerns in the United States still do not support any agreement that does not include developing countries. Even though the election of Prime Minister Kevin Rudd in 2007 enabled Australia to ratify the Kyoto Protocol—and the Australian public is much more supportive of reducing GHG emissions than the American public—Australia has not become a lead state, acting instead as more of a swing state.

The absence of an effective lead-state coalition, however, can also contribute to a regime's ineffectiveness, as is true of the biodiversity regime. The fact that the language of the main conservation provisions of the biodiversity treaty remains for the most part more advisory than binding results not only from the presence of veto states but also from the absence of lead states seeking to strengthen the regime. For several reasons (greater complexity, lack of high levels of media interest, less domestic lobbying by environmental NGOs, and the proliferation of working groups), the Biodiversity Convention has not received as much high-level political attention in major states as the climate or ozone treaties. In the case of desertification, although the African countries have formed an active lead-state coalition, their weak political and economic influence has contributed to the ineffectiveness of the regime.

As indicated in the regimes examined in chapters 3 to 5, the international community has been able to negotiate an impressively large number of agreements to reduce environmental threats. This could be interpreted as an indicator of the paradigm shift toward sustainable development. Many of these agreements were believed impossible to achieve only a few years, and sometimes even a few months, before their successful completion. Moreover, many of the more recent agreements were negotiated more rapidly than previous environmental treaties, indicating a process of international learning about how to reach agreement on complex and contentious environmental issues.

Many of these regimes have also grown significantly since the creation of their first agreement. Governments continue to meet and negotiate to add new pollution controls (as in the air-pollution, ozone, and chemicals treaties), list new species (CITES), and even negotiate entirely new protocols within the regime (the Liability Protocol under the Basel Convention, the Kyoto Protocol, the Cartagena Protocol on Biosafety, the LRTAP protocols).

Global environmental regimes now include conventions that enjoy nearly universal participation. Almost every country in the world is a party to the climate change, biodiversity, ozone, and desertification conventions. Finally, some of these regimes (climate, biodiversity, hazardous waste trade, toxic chemicals, and desertification) have the potential to affect fundamental economic development strategies, production technologies, and even domestic political processes in ways supportive of long-term sustainable development.

However, as these cases also demonstrate, not all of these agreements have been successful. Serious obstacles exist to negotiating strong, global environmental treaties. Moreover, negotiating a strong treaty on paper does not mean it will be effective in practice. All of the regimes discussed in these chapters face serious implementation challenges, including compliance, financing, technology transfer, and effective translation of regime rules into national policy. The next chapter focuses on these challenges.

DISCUSSION QUESTIONS

1. In which cases did countries change roles from veto states to lead state or vice versa? Why did these changes occur?

2. What role does the sovereignty debate play in international natural resource management? Why is the debate greater in this area than in the management of air pollution and chemicals?

3. Consider the veto coalitions opposing strong action on the issues in this chapter. What are the primary motives of each individual member? Why did those coalitions weaken?

4. Trace the role of a particular state on a variety of issues and try to assess the extent of its involvement in leadership or blocking roles.

5. Compare and contrast two conventions or protocols and the political, economic, and environmental factors that influenced their evolution.

6. Why is the United Nations Convention to Combat Desertification so challenging to implement? What other issues discussed in this chapter face similar implementation challenges? How might these challenges be overcome in the future?

6

Effective Environmental Regimes: Obstacles and Opportunities

The last forty years have seen an unprecedented explosion of international negotiations and cooperation on global environmental issues. Today, over 150 prominent international environmental agreements have been negotiated, and over 950 multilateral agreements contain at least some provisions addressing the environment.[1] However, simply negotiating an agreement, or even creating an entire regime, does not guarantee environmental protection.

The effectiveness of an environmental regime—the extent to which it produces measurable improvements in the environment—is a function of three factors. First is regime design, particularly the strength of the key control provisions aimed at addressing the environmental threat, but also the provisions on reporting, monitoring, regime strengthening, noncompliance, and financial and technical assistance (FTA). Second is the level of implementation, the extent to which countries (and to a lesser extent international organizations) adopt formal legislation and other regulations to enact the agreement. Third is compliance, the degree to which countries and other actors actually observe these regulations and the extent to which their actions conform to the explicit rules, norms, and procedures contained in the regime.[2]

This chapter examines some of the factors that inhibit or promote effective international environmental regimes. The first section outlines obstacles that can make it difficult to create and implement effective regimes with strong, binding control measures. These obstacles primarily relate to factors at the international level. The second section looks at variables that inhibit effective implementation and compliance. These primarily concern national-level issues. The third section outlines potential avenues to improve compliance. The final section discusses options for increasing the financing available to implement global environmental regimes.

OBSTACLES TO CREATING
STRONG ENVIRONMENTAL REGIMES

This section examines six types of obstacles that can inhibit creation of strong and effective global environmental regimes: (1) systemic or structural obstacles that stem from the structure of the international system, the structure of international law, and the structure of the global economic system; (2) a lack of necessary and sufficient conditions, in particular, public or official concern, a hospitable contractual environment, and capacity; (3) procedural obstacles inherent in international environmental negotiations; (4) obstacles that stem from common characteristics of global environmental issues; (5) obstacles that result from the interconnections of environmental issues, including potential conflicts between solutions; and (6) obstacles to designing effective regimes.[3] Of course, when thinking about these categories of obstacles, it is important to see them as indicative and heuristic rather than exhaustive and exclusive. In the real world, these factors are interrelated, both with each other and with other issues, and their individual and relative impacts vary significantly across countries and issue areas. They also do not prevent effective policy; they simply make it more difficult to achieve.

Systemic Obstacles

Some impediments to creating strong global environmental regimes result from inherent elements of the global political, ecological, legal, and economic systems. One of the broadest is the anarchical structure of international politics. Anarchy, as used here, means the absence of hierarchy, specifically the absence of a world government with recognized authority to maintain order and make rules. For thousands of years, notable statesmen, philosophers, historians, and political scientists have argued that aspects of this structure have broad consequences for international relations.[4] In particular, states tend to believe they can rely only on self-help to ensure their safety, states usually attempt to balance the power of other states through alliances and armaments, states prefer independence over interdependence, and states find that it is often difficult to achieve effective international cooperation.

The last consequence is perhaps the most relevant to environmental regimes. Just as in security or economic issues, the pressures that the system structure places on state actors can make it difficult to create strong, effective environmental regimes (although to a lesser extent than in security issues). Strong states sometimes attempt to dictate terms to weaker states. States worry that other countries might face fewer costs from an agreement (even as both sides benefit environmentally) or that others might gain more economically or politically.[5] For example, the administration of George W. Bush often expressed concern for relative impacts with regard to climate change, arguing that the United States would suffer competitively if it reduced greenhouse gases (GHGs) but China did not.

States can fail to agree when some fear others might "double cross" them by not fulfilling regime obligations or paying their share of the costs.[6] States sometimes try to avoid paying a fair share of the costs, or to free ride, for example, by continuing to emit a certain pollutant when others have agreed to stop, the fear of which can scuttle an agreement or render it ineffective.[7] States sometimes have incentives to pursue policies that appear rational but help destroy a common-pool resource, resulting in a "tragedy of the commons."[8] A current example is the depletion of ocean fisheries, where some countries and fishing fleets catch as much fish as they can, which is good for them individually in the short run, even as the resource is depleted for all of them in the long run. States sometimes fail to locate mutually advantageous policies due to suspicions, a lack of information, market failure,[9] or misperception of the motives, intentions, or actions of other governments.[10] Governments can also compromise environmental negotiations by linking them to unrelated international or domestic political, security, and economic issues.

Another systemic or structural obstacle is the lack of congruence between the global political and ecological systems. The geographic boundaries, operations, and underlying logic of the two systems simply do not match up. The causes, consequences, and geographic scope of environmental problems do not respect national boundaries. Pollution released into the air or water spreads easily to other countries. Chlorofluorocarbons (CFCs) deplete the ozone layer without respect to which country released them. Persistent organic pollutants (POPs) released in the United States or Mexico impact people, animals, and ecosystems in northern Canada. High-seas fisheries and atmospheric chemistry are outside the political control of any one state. The structure of the global political system, which comprises independent sovereign states, is not well suited to address complex, interdependent, international environmental problems whose causes, impacts, and solutions transcend unrelated political boundaries.

This structural conflict has impacted negotiations on global and regional commons issues—such as the atmosphere (ozone depletion and climate change) and the high seas (fisheries and whales)—as well as negotiations on problems where air and water pollution cross national borders. For example, upwind and downwind states can hold different views on the need for strong regimes to control air pollution, as was apparent in the negotiation of the Convention on Long-Range Transboundary Air Pollution (LRTAP) protocols and in the U.S.-Canada acid rain negotiations. Similar problems exist in the management of transboundary waterways. Of the more than 260 river basins around the world, one-third are shared by more than two countries. Nineteen major river basins are shared by five or more states.[11] This significantly complicates efforts to manage pollution, overfishing, and nonsustainable use. For example, ten

African states rely on the Nile River and its tributaries. Cooperative management efforts date back to a 1902 agreement between Ethiopia and Great Britain, but significant disputes continue to threaten the river's health. Egypt has even threatened military action against Sudan, Ethiopia, and Uganda for what it perceives as illegal diversions of water from the Nile, which decrease the river's volume when it reaches Egypt.[12]

A similar conflict exists between the foundations of international law and the requirements for effective international environmental policy. Perhaps the most fundamental principle of international law is sovereignty. States have nearly unassailable control over activities within their borders, including the use of natural resources. At the same time, however, legitimate actions within one country can create environmental problems for another. Usually, then, effective international policy requires limiting what a state does within its own borders. This conflict is embodied in Principle 21 from the 1972 Stockholm Declaration, often cited as one of the most important foundations of modern international environmental law. It reads, "States have, in accordance with the Charter of the United Nations and the principles of international law, the sovereign right to exploit their own resources pursuant to their own environmental policies, and the responsibility to ensure that activities within their jurisdiction or control do not cause damage to the environment of other states or of areas beyond the limits of national jurisdiction."[13]

Overcoming the inherent tension captured in this sentence is one of the most fundamental challenges of global environmental politics. Many states strongly resist regime provisions that, although beneficial to the environment, involve compromises to their national sovereignty. For example, many of the most controversial proposals during negotiation of the Biodiversity Convention involved potential restrictions on state control over genetic resources within their borders.[14] The debate over a forest convention has been strongly affected by states wanting to ensure that they maintain clear sovereignty over their forest resources. Concerns about potential infringements on national sovereignty led to the inclusion of veto clauses that allow each party to block third-party adjudication under the Basel Convention.[15] China, India, and the United States have argued that efforts to curtail GHG emissions should not hamper their right to economic growth or use of domestic coal reserves.

Some argue that elements of the international economic system also present a structural impediment to creating and implementing strong and effective global environmental regimes. Different discussions along these lines point to the system's emphasis on resource extraction, globalization, free trade, lowest-cost production, high levels of consumption and consumerism, and, especially, the failure to include the economic and other costs produced by environmental degradation in the cost of activities and products that cause the degradation.

Some aspects of these arguments seem well founded. For example, few of the economic costs associated with the environmental and human-health impacts of using toxic chemicals or burning coal or gasoline are included in their price. These costs are passed on to society as whole, rather than paid by the actors actually producing the pollution. Thus, there is little economic incentive for an individual company to reduce pollution when everyone pays its costs. There is an increasing consensus among a variety of theorists and politicians from across the political spectrum regarding the need to include the economic costs of environmental degradation into the larger economic system, although they often reach different conclusions about how to accomplish this.

Many also agree that the emphasis placed by certain international economic forces on developing countries to maximize resource extraction, pay off foreign debts, and industrialize as quickly as possible has produced serious environmental problems. The ultimate impact of free trade and economic integration on certain aspects of the environment also faces scrutiny, particularly when domestic environmental laws, such as the European Union (EU) ban on Canadian fur imports from animals caught in leghold traps, are overruled by free trade rules under the General Agreement on Tariffs and Trade and the World Trade Organization (WTO)[16] (see Chapter 7). Many also highlight what they view as negative impacts of globalization. For example, transnational corporations have played a large role in the globalization of the food system by pushing for and dominating mass production, large-scale processing and distribution systems, international trade, centralized retail, and, more recently, the patented seed and genetically modified organism sectors. Some argue that these processes and the role corporations play in globalization, including in the establishment of rules and regulations by which they themselves are governed, hold potentially negative consequences for the sustainability of the global food system.[17]

Yet, it is probably too simplistic to assert that the global economic system inhibits strong environmental regimes. Indeed, when properly harnessed, these same forces can support environmental regimes. For example, in the expansion of the ozone regime, the global economic system supported the introduction of more environmentally friendly technology into developing countries much more quickly than many had expected. The financial power amassed by the global insurance industry supports stronger action on climate change. Free trade rules and economic integration have likely improved overall energy efficiency in Europe. Thus, the key may be to examine, case by case, how dominant economic interests and systems run counter to the goals or operation of a particular environmental regime and how this relationship might be reversed—rather than reflexively accepting that such economic interests and systems necessarily inhibit stronger policy.

The Absence of Necessary Conditions: Concern, Contractual Environment, and Capacity

As discussed by Peter Haas, Robert Keohane, and Marc Levy, effective environmental regimes require three necessary, but not sufficient, conditions.[18] First, there must be sufficient concern within the government, and perhaps among the public at large, so that states decide to devote resources to examining and addressing the problem and implementing potential solutions. Environmental problems compete with many economic, security, and social issues for space on national and international agendas. Sufficient concern must exist for the issue-definition, fact-finding, bargaining, and regime-strengthening phases to occur and be completed successfully.

Second, there must be a hospitable contractual environment so that states can gather, negotiate with reasonable ease and costs, make credible commitments to each other, reach agreement on policies, and monitor each other's behavior in implementing those policies. In other words, if too many of the negative consequences of system structure—such as misperceptions or fears of cheating or free riding—are present or transaction costs (the time, money, and effort involved in negotiating a treaty) are too high, then creating strong agreements is difficult.

Third, states must possess the scientific, political, economic, and administrative capacity to understand the threat; participate in creating the global regime; and then implement and ensure compliance with the regime's principles, norms, and rules. Capacity is essentially a measure of the necessary scientific, administrative, economic, and political resources a country possesses to address a particular issue, as well as the physical and political ability to deploy those resources effectively.

Concern, contractual environment, and capacity are not obstacles themselves. The presence of each is a necessary but insufficient condition. Thus, it is their absence that significantly inhibits, if not prevents, the creation and implementation of strong environmental regimes. The concepts are easy to oversimplify, but concern, contractual environment, and capacity encapsulate important, even critical, causal factors and are interconnected with many of the other issues discussed in this chapter.

Procedural Obstacles

Once states begin the bargaining or negotiation phase, procedural problems can arise. Two stand out: the time-lag and lowest-common-denominator problems.[19] Each is a product of how international negotiations work, the structural obstacles outlined above, and varying levels of national concern for particular environmental issues.

It is neither an easy nor a speedy process to create and implement strong global environmental policy. The international agenda must be set, negotiations convened,

---

BOX 6.1   PROMINENT OBSTACLES TO CREATING STRONG AND EFFECTIVE ENVIRONMENTAL REGIMES

SYSTEMIC OBSTACLES

- Anarchical structure of the international political system
- Aspects of the structure of international economic systems
- Incongruence of global political and ecological systems
- Incongruence of fundamental principles of international law and fundamental requirements for effective environmental policy

THE ABSENCE OF NECESSARY CONDITIONS

- Inadequate concern
- Inhospitable contractual environments
- Insufficient capacity

PROCEDURAL OBSTACLES

- Slow-boat problem: time lags in regime development and implementation
- Lowest-common-denominator problem

CHARACTERISTICS OF GLOBAL ENVIRONMENTAL ISSUES

- Links to important economic and social activity and interests
- Unequal adjustment costs
- Significant scientific complexity and uncertainty
- Time-horizon conflicts
- Different core beliefs
- The large number of actors

INTERCONNECTIONS BETWEEN ENVIRONMENTAL ISSUES

- Solutions can require addressing multiple issues
- Solutions to one issue may exacerbate problems in another issue

REGIME DESIGN

- Other political and economic issues influence regime design
- Regimes are not created by environmental experts
- Effective regime design is difficult

---

appropriate policies identified, agreements reached, implementation strategies agreed to, treaties ratified, national and international policies implemented and reported upon, environmental problems monitored, and international policies revised in light of new data and lessons learned. The common practice of starting with a framework convention and adopting subsequent protocols adds even more time. Enough governments

PHOTO 6.1   The first Meeting of the Parties of the Cartagena Protocol on Biosafety in
February 2004.
Courtesy IISD/*Earth Negotiations Bulletin.*

must ratify the convention and protocols so that they can enter into force and be effective. To have an impact on the environmental problem, the implementation and revision phases must occur over a sufficient length of time.

Each step in this series can be time-consuming. As discussed in Chapter 3, the environmental problems posed by hazardous waste shipments were identified in the 1970s, but the Basel Convention did not come into effect until 1992, and the Ban Amendment still requires additional ratifications to take effect. The United Nations Convention on the Law of the Sea, a complex treaty that contains provisions on most aspects of maritime law, took nearly ten years to negotiate and another twelve to receive enough ratifications to enter into force. The International Convention for the Prevention of Pollution from Ships (MARPOL) experienced a ten-year time lag from its negotiation to its entry into force, despite the decades of collaborative efforts on oil pollution leading up to it.

Knowledge of the greenhouse effect goes back more than 180 years. Joseph Fourier, a French mathematician and physicist, discovered in 1824 that gases in the atmosphere likely increase the surface temperature of the earth. In 1859, John Tyndal, an Irish physicist, explained the ability of various gases, including carbon dioxide (CO_2) and water vapor, to absorb radiant heat, proving that the earth's atmosphere has a natural greenhouse effect. In 1896 Svante Arrhenius, a Swedish scientist, published an article suggesting that temperatures would rise 5 degrees Celsius if atmospheric CO_2 doubled. In 1960, Charles Keeling published data clearly showing that CO_2 levels were rising. Nevertheless, formal negotiations on the United Nations Framework Convention on Climate Change did not begin until 1991, and nearly twenty years later only modest controls exist for GHG emissions. Scientists discovered the threat to the ozone layer in 1974, but negotiations did not begin until 1982, the first binding controls did not come into force until 1988, developing countries did not have to phase out most uses of CFCs until 2010, and hydrochlorofluorocarbons (HCFCs) will not be phased out completely for another thirty years.

Yet, environmental issues do not wait for the policy process. As negotiations continue, more species become extinct, biodiversity declines, forests are cut down, land is degraded, GHGs are emitted into the atmosphere, toxic chemicals are released and accumulate, and hazardous wastes are not disposed of properly. As the process of regime creation and expansion drags on, environmental problems become worse, not better, making it even more difficult to create and implement effective regimes.

The second procedural obstacle, the lowest-common-denominator problem, is created by veto states. Because all states are sovereign entities, they can choose whether to join a global environmental agreement. However, because active participation by many countries is required to address a global environmental problem, the countries most interested in addressing a particular issue often need support from countries showing far less interest. Thus, an environmental treaty can be only as strong as its least cooperative state allows it to be. The regime's overall effectiveness is undermined by the compromises made in persuading these states, the veto states, to participate.

For example, as discussed in Chapter 3, during the Stockholm Convention negotiations, countries critical to its long-term success insisted on specific exemptions so that they could continue using small amounts of certain POPs, even though the convention called for eliminating all production and use of these substances. This process repeated itself when parties expanded the convention in 2009. Nearly all the new chemicals slated for "elimination" carry exemptions that allow countries to continue using them for at least four more years. During negotiation of the 1991 Protocol on Environmental Protection to the Antarctic Treaty, which protects Antarctica from possible mineral exploitation, opposition from the United States resulted in a fifty-year moratorium rather than the initially proposed permanent protection.[20] As discussed in Chapter 4, from 1977 to 1989, the European Community (EC) acted as a veto state and set the lowest common denominator for global ozone policy, forcing lead states to accept much weaker rules in the 1985 Vienna Convention and 1987 Montreal Protocol than they had sought.

The lowest-common-denominator problem severely limited the strength of the MARPOL agreement, even though the oil-pollution regime had a long history. Laggard states pushed for the cheapest methods of accommodating pollution complaints. Jurisdictional issues brought stronger proposals for the rejection of port-state inspection rights: States were relentless in their protection of exclusive flag-state sovereignty over ships, particularly Liberia for economic reasons and the Soviet Union for security.[21] Furthermore, the proposal that states provide onshore reception facilities for waste was agreed to only in its weakest form as states kept the rule legally nonbinding.[22]

The lowest-common-denominator problem has also impacted the climate regime for many years. As discussed in Chapter 4, all the major emitters of GHGs, but especially China, Europe, India and the United States, must cooperate for the regime to succeed. However, China, India, and the United States have been reluctant even to discuss substantive actions to curb their domestic emissions. This has limited the ability of Europe, the Alliance of Small Island States, and other lead states to move forward with aggressive global policies. They could create an agreement without Chinese, Indian, and U.S. participation, like the Kyoto Protocol, or act on their own domestically, as the EU has done, but effective global policy requires the eventual participation of the veto states—putting them in a position to continue to force a lowest-common-denominator agreement.

Characteristics of Global Environmental Issues

Another set of obstacles to creating strong regimes stems from common characteristics inherent in global environmental problems. Although they are certainly not unique to environmental issues and have impacts that are both interconnected and vary across countries and issue areas, these characteristics are important elements of global environmental politics and have the capacity to exacerbate many of the other obstacles outlined above.[23]

One of the most critical characteristics is that environmental issues are inextricably linked to important economic and political interests. Environmental issues, and therefore environmental negotiations, are not independent of other economic and political activities and interests; environmental issues exist because of these activities and interests. Environmental problems are produced as externalities of individuals, corporations, and nations pursuing other interests. They result from such important local, corporate, national, and international economic and political activities as energy production, mining, manufacturing, farming, fishing, transportation, resource consumption, livestock husbandry, urbanization, weapons production, territorial expansion, and military conflict.

Few, if any, individuals or organizations harm the environment as an end in itself. People do not get up in the morning, leave their homes, and announce, "I intend to pollute today." What people do say is, "I intend to manufacture. I intend to produce energy, to farm, to drive my car to work." Environmental degradation is a consequence

of these otherwise legitimate pursuits. It is the consequence of important local, corporate, national, and international economic and political activities. The fact that many
of these activities could be pursued successfully while doing less harm to the environment does not erase the links between the issues.

Creating strong international environmental regimes, therefore, often requires addressing economic, social, and even security interests that are important to certain
countries or interest groups. Regardless of whether these interests are justified, this
fact obviously creates obstacles to effective action. The presence of important economic
interests can lower relative concern, make veto states more determined, and bring powerful domestic economic actors to lobby for their views. They can enhance fears of
free riding, create more opportunities for positional bargaining, and otherwise harm
the contractual environment.

Examples of the obstacles posed by the links between environmental problems and
economic interests are common. Protecting the earth's remaining biodiversity requires
addressing the economic and political pressures that cause habitat destruction, something that has proved almost impossible to date. A strong regime to address climate
change will require significant changes in fossil fuel consumption, which currently remain out of reach. Complete protection of the ozone layer requires a near total phaseout of methyl bromide emissions, but major agricultural interests, particularly in the
United States, are hesitant to agree to this. Combating deforestation in some developing
countries would have a major impact on the timber industry and the national economy. Addressing the serious decline in fisheries will impact the economies of both distant-water fishing states and coastal states.

Sometimes the linkages are particularly difficult to argue against, even for strong
proponents of the environmental regime. For example, the total elimination of DDT
would prevent its use as an inexpensive tool in the battle against malaria in Africa and
Asia. Even those countries most committed to addressing POPs under the Stockholm
Convention agree that the use of DDT should continue (using methods that better prevent malaria and reduce the environmental impact of DDT) while alternative products
and processes are developed. Similarly, the toxic chemical perfluorooctane sulfonate
(PFOS) is used in certain medical devices. While strongly agreeing the substance should
be eliminated as part of the expansion of the Stockholm Convention in 2009, the United
States and Switzerland also successfully argued that given the interest in advancing
medical care, an exception should be granted so that very small amounts of the substance can be used in certain medical devices until replacements are developed.[24]

A second characteristic, and one closely linked to the first, is unequal adjustment
costs. Addressing an environmental problem means changing the economic, political,
and/or cultural activities that ultimately cause the problem. Making these changes, or
"adjustments," can produce many benefits, but they also carry different economic and

political costs in different countries. For example, the transition to using solar, wind, and geothermal energy to replace fossil fuels will clean the air of harmful pollutants, reduce CO_2 emissions, and create new, sustainable jobs in the alternative-energy industry, but countries, regions, companies, and individuals with strong connections to the old, polluting industries will experience higher costs during the transition than those that do not. Parts of the United States with significant solar or wind resources might find the transition relatively easy. Saudi Arabia or Russia, whose economies rely on fossil fuel exports, will incur significant costs. While the overall transition will likely produce far greater long-term benefits for nearly all countries and the planet as a whole, it will involve changes, or adjustment costs, that certain regions, countries, or businesses will find objectionable.

Countries face different adjustment costs depending on the environmental issue. These variations can reflect differences in their contribution to the problem, their level of economic development, and the political and economic influence of the relevant industry, as well as their enforcement capability, existing level of regulation, resource base, trade profile, method of energy production, transportation policy, and a host of other factors.

Large variations in adjustment costs in countries essential to a regime act as obstacles to creating a strong regime. Indeed, they are part of the reason that veto coalitions form. Large and unequal adjustment costs "accentuate the difficulties inherent in international cooperation and significantly impact the contractual environment. Because states can be concerned with relative or positional advantages, they may reject solutions that ask them to bear a relatively larger burden than other states. Alternatively they may demand special compensation for joining the regime,"[25] which, in turn, can weaken the regime.

Unequal adjustment costs exist in all the regimes outlined in chapters 3 to 5, and addressing their impact is a critical and difficult part of global environmental politics. During negotiation of the Kyoto Protocol, many governments argued that their different levels of industrialization, energy profile, transportation infrastructure, core industries, and even local temperatures made adhering to one set of mandatory reductions in CO_2 emissions inherently unfair. As a result, the Kyoto Protocol contains not only a relatively modest set of controls but no mandatory reductions of CO_2 emissions for developing countries and different targets for most developed countries. The prospect of unequal adjustment costs continues to pose huge problems for the climate regime, including efforts to craft successor agreements to the Kyoto Protocol. Strong controls on carbon emissions mean enormous adjustment for oil-exporting states, as demand for oil will fall, as well as for countries that depend on cheap coal for energy, such as Australia, China, India, and parts of the United States, as they will have to capture the CO_2 before it is released or turn to other energy sources. However, adjustment costs would be far less for countries such as France, which relies on nuclear power for most of its electricity, or Iceland, which uses geothermal energy. Developing countries as a whole also face the challenge of altering their energy future at a crucial point in their economic development, a prospect they believe carries far higher adjustment costs than those faced by the industrialized countries, which, in general, have greater technological and financial resources. Reconciling these positions remains a huge challenge for global climate policy, even with the progress made in the negotiations in recent years.

Similar problems exist in other regimes. Different governments consistently seek to exclude certain substances from the toxic chemicals regime or press for special exemptions, arguing that a particular industry using the substance would bear higher and unfair burdens if forced to comply with the same standards as companies in other countries that do not use the substance. Iceland, Japan, Norway, and other countries that permit whaling argue that the economic, cultural, or scientific adjustment costs of stopping all whaling would place unfair burdens on particular groups. Some developing countries express concern that future efforts to protect biodiversity or a future forest convention will include attempts to prevent their use of large forested areas for traditional types of economic development—costs most industrialized countries would not bear.

A third obstacle is that environmental issues often involve significant scientific complexity and uncertainty regarding their scope, severity, impact, or time frame. This can make it difficult to design possible solutions and create strong regimes. Lack of knowledge about an environmental problem can undermine concern. Large degrees of scientific uncertainty can allow other, more certain economic or political interests to be prioritized in the policy hierarchy. The scientific complexity of environmental issues can challenge the capacity of government bureaucracies to understand the problem or implement proper solutions. Uncertainty and complexity can lead different states to perceive the payoff differently, perhaps reducing incentives to risk cooperation and increasing incentives either to free ride or to ignore the problem altogether, thereby harming the contractual environment.[26]

For example, opponents of a strong regime for climate change emphasized not only the costs of such an agreement (including the links to important economic interests and unequal adjustment costs) but also what they argued were important uncertainties regarding the severity and perhaps even the existence of a problem (the vast majority of scientists and the Intergovernmental Panel on Climate Change do not share this view). Lack of certainty regarding the long-term impacts of low exposure to, and slow accumulation of, toxic chemicals inhibits the chemicals regime from expanding more quickly, despite increasing evidence that causes many experts to express significant concern. Biodiversity loss, biosafety, ozone depletion, and acid rain are some of the other issues for which scientific complexity and uncertainty slowed or prevented the creation of strong regimes.

A fourth characteristic that can act as an obstacle to creating and implementing strong regimes is time-horizon conflicts. Because the most serious consequences of many environmental problems will not occur for many years (or this appears to be the case, even if it is proven incorrect later), policy makers sometimes find it difficult to create strong regimes with significant short-term costs, even if such action would be less expensive and more successful in the long run. That some environmental issues do not develop in a linear, predictable pattern complicates matters.

In addition, the impacts of some environmental problems do not occur simultaneously in all regions and in all countries. This can mask their global impact or cause some actors to remain less concerned about addressing them. The time-horizon obstacle is enhanced if concern for the problem is low, the nature of the threat is not well defined, or the costs of acting are very high. Ozone depletion, biodiversity loss, and climate change are obvious examples of issues impacted by time-horizon conflicts. Efforts to add larger numbers of additional toxic chemicals to the POPs regime also face this problem. While thousands of chemical spills occur each year,[27] sometimes resulting in large short-term exposure to POPs and other toxic substances, the greatest long-term and most widespread threats posed by many chemicals, including potential impacts on reproductive health, could occur in the future as a result of long-term exposure from their slow accumulation in humans and the environment. Preventing these impacts requires preventing the buildup, and this means accepting certain current costs for likely, but future, benefits.

The time structures of environmental systems and those of political and corporate systems are not congruent. As noted, environmental problems can build up slowly over many years before very serious impacts emerge. Addressing them requires an informed, long-term perspective. Most political and corporate systems, however, operate on much shorter timescales. Major political figures in the United States, for example, face elections every two (members of the House of Representatives), four (president and governors), or six years (senators). Most corporations release reports on their revenues, costs, and profits every three months—reports that can significantly impact their stock price and executive compensation. Thus, even if every political figure and corporate leader wanted to address environmental issues, the time horizon for their most immediate approval processes (elections and quarterly reports) are not in tune with the long-term time horizons needed to address environmental issues.

Fifth, states and groups within states sometimes possess different core religious, cultural, or political beliefs and values relevant to environmental issues. Such conflicting core beliefs and values can play important roles in environmental negotiations. They can limit the creation of sufficient transnational concern, block potential policies, cause some actors not to participate or comply, and necessitate compromises that weaken the resulting regime. For example, as discussed in Chapter 5, some groups in Iceland, Japan, and Norway have strong cultural links to whaling. They do not view it as a moral issue and thus reject international attempts to curtail their whaling as inappropriate foreign intrusion on their rights and beliefs. Some individuals in Asia believe products from endangered animal species, such as rhino horn, have important medicinal, physical, or sexual properties. This creates a market for these animals and undercuts international controls designed to protect them. Many Catholics and Muslims oppose policies designed to control human population growth. Some political ideologies treat economic development and freedom from government regulations as higher priorities than environmental protection and thus resist cooperative solutions that involve what they view as additional restrictions on economic and personal freedom. Some nongovernmental organizations (NGOs) believe just the opposite.

Sixth, large numbers of actors must cooperate to create and implement an effective global environmental regime. Social science has long acknowledged the difficulties that a multiplicity of actors poses for cooperation. An increase in the number of actors often causes more heterogeneity of interests and perceptions as well as more uncertainty within each actor as to the preferences of others. Thus, the search for solutions to an environmental problem becomes more difficult as the number of parties increases. The larger the number of actors, the more likely it is that an agreement, if concluded at all, will be "partial" in at least one of three ways: (1) covering only some of the agenda topics, (2) leaving some disagreement latent in an ambiguous text, or (3) being signed and accepted only by some states. In addition, the risk of suboptimal outcomes, or lowest-common-denominator agreements, seems to increase as the number of actors increases.[28]

Large numbers can also increase incentives for noncompliance (because of reduced fears of detection), particularly if the benefits of cooperation are suspect or the adjustment costs are high or uneven. Large numbers can be particularly dangerous to the success of a regime that seeks to protect the commons, such as the oceans or atmosphere, which all can use but no one controls. If some states fear that others will cheat, they may believe they face a "use it or lose it" scenario that compels them to use the resource, leading to its more rapid degradation.[29] The situation is compounded in cases where many states need to control many private actors in order for the environmental policy to succeed. The Convention on International Trade in Endangered Species of Wild Fauna and Flora (CITES) faces obstacles with compliance because the number of potential violators is so large, especially with the advent of Internet sales of endangered species and their products. An immense number of ships can violate ocean pollution and fishing agreements. Thousands of companies in countries around the world work with toxic chemicals or create hazardous waste. The huge number of GHG emissions sources complicates global policy making.

Interconnections Between Environmental Issues

Environmental issues do not exist in isolation. Causes, impacts, consequences, and solutions are often interconnected in surprising ways. Sometimes these connections can inhibit successful action. This is the case when one environmental problem exacerbates another one. This makes the problem more difficult to solve because long-term success in that issue also requires successfully addressing both issues. For example, the problem of climate change makes solving ozone depletion more difficult. As the troposphere warms due to anthropogenic climate change, the stratosphere will cool. A colder stratosphere accelerates the chemical reactions that deplete ozone. So, even as we reduce the amount of ozone-depleting chemicals, those that remain do more damage. Climate change also threatens millions of species with extinction, making the preservation of biodiversity more difficult. Similarly, coral reefs face serious threats from warming seas, increased runoff from land degraded by deforestation, and pollution released by industrial facilities. Each of these harms the reefs, exacerbating the impact of the others. Solving one threat to a reef will not save it unless the others are solved as well. Deforestation and land degradation are major contributors to biodiversity loss, through habitat destruction, and to climate change, through the release of CO_2 into the atmosphere and because the forested lands can no longer act as carbon sinks by absorbing CO_2 from the air. Thus, global policies on biodiversity or climate change will also require action to combat the destruction of tropical forests and land degradation if they are to be successful.

Interconnections also create obstacles when the solution to one environmental problem causes another problem to worsen. For example, dams help address climate change because they produce electricity without burning fossil fuels, but they can also produce harmful environmental impacts such as riparian habitat loss, erosion, impacts on river animal and fish populations, and potential declines in water quality. Similarly, replacing coal-fired power plants with nuclear plants may decrease GHG emissions, but it creates the potential for immense environmental problems if radiation is released due to an accident at the plant, a terrorist attack, or a leak from the storage of the nuclear waste. Biofuels can be used to replace gasoline and reduce GHGs, but certain biofuels create equally serious problems. Biofuels made from corn, soybeans, or other crops requiring good soil divert land from food production and usually require significant quantities of water and fertilizer. Some biofuels require immense amounts of energy to gather, transport, and refine into fuel, negating their climate impact and adding to other problems. (Research continues on developing biofuels from plants that can grow on marginal land without fertilizer or from algae that can be grown in greenhouses with recycled water, alleviating many of these negative impacts). Similarly, cars that run on hydrogen do not burn fossil fuels, but producing hydrogen on an industrial scale can use a great deal of energy. If this energy comes from burning fossil fuels, then the climate benefits are greatly reduced.

Removing salt from sea water (desalination) is a potential solution to the increasing shortage of fresh water. Unfortunately, current methods require large amounts of energy, which in most parts of the world means more CO_2 emissions. In addition, in most cases, the salt is returned to the ocean. If desalination increases significantly, this process could actually increase the salt content of the ocean, with negative effects on marine life, while improper storage on land could lead to contaminated freshwater resources. Desalination can be done in an environmentally sound manner (e.g., using geothermal or solar power and storing the salt in depleted oil fields), but this example shows how even a seemingly benign solution to one environmental problem can cause another to worsen if careful consideration is not given.

Several chemicals developed to replace ozone-depleting substances, and thus safeguard the ozone layer, have had an impact on other environmental problems. As outlined in Chapter 4, companies developed HCFCs and hydrofluorocarbons (HFCs) as substitutes for ozone-depleting CFCs. These chemicals proved crucial to protecting the ozone layer while requiring relatively small changes to the huge refrigeration and air-conditioning industries. Unfortunately, like the CFCs they replaced, HCFCs and HFCs are potent GHGs. Thus, their invention and increased use, which occurred only as part of global attempts to protect the ozone layer, exacerbated climate change. HCFCs have been addressed under the amended Montreal Protocol, but HFCs, which do not deplete the ozone layer, have not and are being discussed in the climate regime. Similarly, when China eliminated the use of halons in 2008 (as noted in Chapter 4, halons are excellent fire-suppressants but powerful ozone-depleting gases), they did so with firefighting foam mixes that included PFOS (or a closely related chemical, PFOSF, a highly toxic POP). As outlined in Chapter 3, parties to the Stockholm Convention recently added PFOS to the list of chemicals slated for elimination, but China and others argued successfully that an exemption should be granted for use in firefighting foam as it would not be economical to phase out another method of fire control so soon after the elimination of halons.[30] Thus, one country's solution to the problem of halons as ozone-depleting chemicals resulted in the expanded use of a toxic chemical, which both exacerbated the problems of toxics in the environment and complicated policy discussions within the Stockholm Convention.

Regime Design

Another obstacle to strong effective global environmental regimes is sometimes the design of the regime itself. As Ron Mitchell puts it, "Regime design matters."[31] Regime rules inappropriate to an issue area are unlikely to work. Control measures and reporting requirements that are too complex or extremely vague might not be implemented correctly. Treaties without enough flexibility cannot be adjusted in response to new scientific findings. Treaties with too much flexibility might be changed so often that some governments and industries, frustrated with the inability to make long-term plans, may begin to leave or ignore the regime.

All the issues outlined in the previous sections can inhibit the design of an effective regime. Equally important is the fact that regimes are negotiated as much as they are designed. And they are negotiated by people whose instructions from their governments include concerns that might run counter to what may be required to create a perfectly crafted environmental regime.

Environmental treaties are not designed by a very small group of experts whose only goal is to eliminate a global environmental problem. In reality, treaties result from negotiations involving hundreds of government representatives from different types of ministries whose collective job is to address the environmental issue but whose individual instructions also reflect concerns for other national and international economic and political goals. Delegates operate within frameworks established by instructions and briefing books given to them by their government. People from different parts of the government, with different perspectives on the regime negotiations, often participate in creating these frameworks. In the United States, for example, while Environmental Protection Agency officials might see the negotiations as a means to address the environmental issue, trade officials might want to make sure a tough stand in the negotiations does not impact relations with a crucial trading partner or upset relationships important to an upcoming trade negotiation. State Department officials might object to a particular regime component, even if it would be very effective, for fear that it will set a precedent that could be demanded in negotiations on other issues. Congressional staff and White House domestic political advisors might not want policies that will upset key political allies or donors. Budget officials might insist on limiting provisions of FTA. None of this is improper—each person is simply attending to his or her government responsibility—but it does point out how the complexities underlying national positions can produce pressures that can influence national negotiation positions away from consensus on the optimal regime design for a given issue.

Thus, sometimes a government's goals in negotiations on a global environmental regime have little to do with the environmental issue under discussion. Some developing countries might try to use the negotiations to obtain general development assistance masked as environmental investments. Donor countries might try to limit financial obligations in general or to funnel all assistance through the Global Environment Facility (GEF) because they think they can control the GEF more easily, regardless of what might be best for a particular regime. Some governments might push against a particular principle, for example, the precautionary principle, because they do not want it to become acceptable as a general principle of international law. Some might try to build global scientific networks or increase scientific training in their countries. Some might push for a strong noncompliance regime because they support strong international adjudication procedures in general. Some countries might have disagreements with particular international organizations, NGOs, or other governments that could affect their negotiating positions in the regime.

Thus, environmental regime design should not be seen as the equivalent of blueprints drawn by a small group of brilliant architects who specialize in building hospitals and have been given the time and money to create an outstanding facility that will address one particular disease. They are more like blueprints drawn by a group of several hundred architects that specialize in different types of design who have been assigned the group task of designing an outstanding hospital to address one particular disease. Plus, many of the architects have other jobs and must make sure that parts of the planned hospital can also be used as a bank, training facility, research center, advertising agency, book publisher, school, police station, courthouse, travel agency, or construction company. Moreover, they do not agree on which of these other uses is the most important, they do not have enough land or money to construct a building that could do all these things as well as each of them would like, not all of them are particularly good architects, and they do not have a great deal of time before the disease spreads and many more people start to die.

Regime design is also simply difficult. It requires a nuanced understanding of the science of the environmental issue, including its causes and consequences, how it interacts with other issues, and how it will evolve over time; the economic and social activities that give rise to the problem and will be affected by it; how to address the issue so that a long-term solution is environmentally, economically, and politically possible; and how to design the solution in the form of an international regime that can be implemented effectively at the national level. This last point is often overlooked. No matter how well-meaning a treaty's intention or how strong its control provisions are, it will not yield measurable environmental benefits if states cannot implement it. Regimes will not succeed if they do not pay attention to the obstacles to effective implementation, to the relative costs of compliance, or to the need to address adjustment costs and FTA. The next section examines several of these issues.

OBSTACLES TO EFFECTIVE NATIONAL
IMPLEMENTATION AND COMPLIANCE
WITH GLOBAL ENVIRONMENTAL REGIMES

Treaties contain many different types of obligations. The most important are sometimes referred to as substantive obligations, particularly obligations to cease or limit a specific activity such as GHG emissions, CFC production, or the release of certain toxic chemicals. Also important are a variety of procedural obligations, such as monitoring and reporting requirements. Compliance refers to whether countries adhere to the mandatory provisions of an environmental convention and the extent to which they follow through on the steps they have taken to implement these provisions.[32]

Global environmental regimes and national governments employ a variety of mechanisms to promote compliance. These include regular reporting by the parties, independent evaluation and public availability of such reports, review of implementation at regular meetings of the parties, readiness of some parties to call noncomplying parties to account publicly, monitoring of compliance by NGOs, technical and financial assistance for building capacity, and otherwise assisting certain parties to fulfill their obligations under the regime.[33] Of course, not all regimes or countries employ each measure, and their success varies significantly across regimes and among parties.

Most countries that sign and ratify an international convention do so with the intention of complying with its provisions, and most comply to the best of their ability.[34] However, compliance sometimes turns out to be politically, technically, administratively, or financially impossible, even if a government remains committed to the regime. Sometimes compliance becomes sufficiently difficult that a state decides to focus time, effort, and resources in other areas; that is, compliance is still possible, but a state chooses not to comply because of other priorities. Only rarely does a state deliberately set out to sign and ratify a treaty with no intention of complying.

As attention turns from creating new global environmental regimes to implementing and strengthening existing ones, compliance has become an even more important issue in global environmental politics. In addition to the general obstacles outlined above, the growing literature on implementation and compliance with international environmental agreements suggests that noncompliance can be traced to several different types of factors, including inadequate translation of regime rules into domestic law, insufficient capacity to implement or administer relevant domestic policy, inability to monitor compliance and report on implementation, lack of respect for rule of law by particular groups within a country, the costs of compliance, misperception of the relevant costs and benefits, inadequate FTA, poorly designed regimes, and the large number of environmental conventions and the confusing and uncoordinated web of requirements they have produced.[35] As with the discussion of the obstacles to creating strong and effective regimes, these categories of implementation obstacles overlap significantly and are extremely interrelated. They are not listed in order of importance, as their impacts vary from country to country and issue to issue. Indeed, scholars and national officials have many different opinions about which obstacles are most important overall or most relevant to particular issue areas.

Inadequate Translation of Regime Rules into Domestic Law

Some states are unable to adopt the domestic legislation necessary to implement and fully comply with an international agreement. This can include failing to adopt any or all of the needed regulations or adopting poorly crafted regulations. For instance, Peter Sand has noted that "the main constraint on the implementation of CITES in each Party has been the need to create national legislation. Although this is an obligation under [CITES], several countries have not complied. . . . Others have only incomplete legislation, lacking . . . means for sanctions against offenders."[36]

The failure to enact domestic law can stem from a variety of factors. Sometimes domestic economic or political opposition that failed to block a country from negotiating or signing a particular treaty can nevertheless prevent the country from ratifying it. If national ratification depends on approval by a legislative branch, as in the United States, then treaty ratification, and consequently, the translation of international regime rules into domestic law, can be prevented by interest groups or lawmakers opposed to its goals or means, by politicians seeking leverage to achieve other political ends, by an overburdened legislative agenda, or by conflicts over resource allocations. For example, since the early 1990s, opposition from powerful interest groups and key senators has prevented the U.S. Senate even from holding formal ratification votes on several key treaties, including the Kyoto Protocol and the Biodiversity, Basel, Rotterdam, and Stockholm conventions.

Even when a treaty is ratified, interest groups or the political opposition might still manage to prevent or significantly weaken the necessary implementing legislation. Weak legislative and bureaucratic infrastructures or a lack of expertise on the issue can also prevent the most effective regulations from becoming law. Some of the chemical treaties, for example, require relatively high levels of knowledge about toxic chemicals and their management to enact all their provisions effectively into domestic law. Inefficient legislative procedures or political or economic instability also can keep states from fully or accurately enacting necessary domestic legislation. Finally, in democracies with nonintegrated federal structures, the federal government may not always have the jurisdiction to implement international environmental agreements completely at the state or provincial level. For example, in Belgium, each of the autonomous regions must separately adopt environmental legislation. In Canada, the provinces, not the federal government, control many aspects of environmental policy.[37]

Insufficient Capacity to Implement and Administer Domestic Policy

It is not enough simply to enact laws and regulations. They must also be effectively implemented, administered, and enforced. Doing so requires sufficient issue-specific skills, knowledge, technical know-how, legal authority, financial resources, and enforcement capacity at the individual and institutional levels. Therefore, a second reason for inadequate compliance is insufficient state capacity to implement, administer, or enforce the relevant domestic policies and regulations. Insufficient capacity is a particular problem for some developing countries, but it exists in all parts of the world and varies from issue to issue and country to county.

Examples of capacity problems inhibiting compliance are unfortunately common. CITES has provisions for trade measures to enforce its controls on wildlife trade, but many countries, including industrialized countries, lack the budgets or trained personnel needed to comply fully and effectively.[38] Compliance with the Convention on Biological Diversity (CBD) has been hindered by a lack of national capacity to manage protected-area systems and to analyze the impacts of development projects on biodiversity. Russia did not comply with its obligations under the ozone regime for several years because its government temporarily lacked the capacity to stop the black market production and export of CFCs. Full compliance (and effective implementation) of the Stockholm Convention includes locating, identifying, and destroying stockpiles of obsolete pesticides in an environmentally sound manner, something beyond the technical and financial ability of many countries. The central governments of Brazil, Indonesia, and some other countries have not demonstrated the consistent ability to prevent illegal logging and deforestation.[39] The Basel Convention contains no provision for international monitoring of the accuracy of hazardous waste labels or spot-checking shipments in the ports of receiving countries. Developing countries, whose inability to monitor and regulate trade led them to call for a ban on international waste shipments in the first place, often do not have the capacity to monitor this shipping themselves.[40] African countries continue to express concern that they are sometimes unable to prevent unwanted shipments of obsolete pesticides or other toxic chemicals and wastes into their countries.[41]

Inability to Monitor Compliance and Report on Implementation

Similarly, some states may be unable to monitor or can easily overlook violations of the national laws that implement an environmental regime. In fact, even states that want to comply can end up not doing so because they do not know what is happening domestically. Two principal sets of factors impact states' ability to monitor domestic compliance with environmental laws: (1) whether states have adequate feedback mechanisms, such as on-site monitoring by inspectors, reporting requirements, complaint

---

BOX 6.2   OBSTACLES TO EFFECTIVE
NATIONAL IMPLEMENTATION

- Inadequate translation of regime rules into domestic law
- Insufficient capacity to implement, administer, or enforce legislation
- Inability to monitor compliance and report on implementation
- Lack of respect for the rule of law
- Costs of compliance
- Misperception of relevant costs and benefits
- Inadequate financial and technical assistance
- Poorly designed regimes
- Many regimes, little coordination

---

mechanisms, or close working relationships with NGOs; and (2) the number and size of the potential violators whose conduct the government must monitor.[42] For example, the relatively high level of compliance with the Montreal Protocol results not only from the widely accepted science regarding the cause and potential impact of the problem but also from the manageable limits the regime places on the number of sources or sites that require monitoring. Monitoring long-term compliance with any post-Kyoto climate regime may prove far more difficult, however, because of the multitude of GHG emissions sources. Similarly, monitoring compliance with CITES remains difficult in part because the number of potential violators is so large.

Lack of Respect for the Rule of Law

A related obstacle is a lack of respect for the rule of law by particular groups within some countries. Merely passing legislation has no practical effect if the government, corporations, or the public then simply ignore it. This problem tends to arise more often in countries where severe economic pressures, political instability, and patterns of corruption lead particular groups, government officials, or the general public to ignore elements of the legal system.

For example, the Central African Republic, Democratic Republic of Congo, and sections of several other African countries are among the most lawless in the world,[43] making it difficult to preserve their significant biodiversity, forest, and ecosystem resources. Illegal deforestation in Brazil, Colombia, Indonesia, and other countries, which includes clearing land to grow drug crops in Colombia (and other countries), not only reflects lack of government capacity but also indifference to the law by those clearing the land. In Kenya during the rule of Daniel arap Moi, from 1978 to 2002, systematic corruption, extreme poverty, and the absence of a meaningful democratic process caused many people to feel alienated from the lawmaking apparatus, undermining their respect for the law, including regulations on wildlife conservation.[44] Similarly, the epidemic of illegal logging in national parks in Indonesia following the 1998 financial crisis resulted, at least in part, in a breakdown of law and order combined with economic pressures in the affected areas.[45]

Costs of Compliance

Domestic compliance with international environmental agreements is also affected by the costs of such compliance relative to the country's level of economic development, current economic situation, resource base, and budgetary preferences.[46] Affluent countries experiencing relatively high economic-growth rates are historically far more willing and able to comply with environmental regulations than poorer states or states with economies that are growing slowly or not at all. States with low per capita incomes are generally reluctant to commit significant funds to comply with commitments to reduce global threats, even if doing so is in the country's long-term interest, because such compliance would likely come at the expense of spending for economic and social development. Other competing budgetary preferences, such as military spending, can also inhibit compliance. On the other hand, if the costs of compliance are relatively modest, or if compliance produces a net economic gain, a state's current level of economic well-being may be less critical.

The United States did not ratify the Kyoto Protocol in part because a majority of senators and President George W. Bush believed implementing the agreement would prove too expensive (and did not place similar costs on China and other large developing countries). As it currently stands, several industrialized countries are unlikely to meet their individual mandated reductions in GHG emissions under the protocol, due in part to the perceived cost of complying. For example, Canada had a 6 percent reduction target in annual emissions from 1990 levels, but its emissions have actually increased. Norway, Slovenia, and Switzerland have increased their emissions by about 17 percent, 8 percent, and 10 percent, respectively. Australia's target permitted an 8 percent increase in emissions, but it has increased emissions by about 18 percent.[47]

Countries experiencing economic and financial crisis often refuse or become unable to comply fully with global environmental agreements. The Russian Federation, for example, could not immediately comply with the 1996 phaseout of CFCs because of its critical economic situation at the time. At different times, other countries have also failed to comply with particular aspects of the ozone regime because of what they perceived to be the relatively high costs of implementation relative to other immediate needs.[48] Structural adjustment programs instituted by the International Monetary Fund (IMF, see Chapter 2) have also had a negative impact on the relative cost of compliance because they usually involve budget cuts in the debtor countries and favor programs designed to promote exports rather than limit pollution, conserve resources, or protect biologically important areas.

Misperception of Relevant Cost and Benefits

A related obstacle is a lack of understanding regarding the full set of economic costs and benefits of complying with an environmental regime. Many analyses indicate that even if policy makers wish to ignore nonmonetary concepts relating to environmental and human-health protections, purely economic arguments exist that support implementing global environmental regimes. However, such arguments are not always included in policy discussions. For many environmental issues, the adjustment costs are well understood. Companies and other groups that would likely have to stop or change particular operations or practices make their case clearly to the government. Less clear, however, are the potential economic benefits of environmental protection. These are often obscured by the importance placed on short-term adjustment costs (which, in some issues, could be substantial for certain actors), insufficient analysis of economic changes that will occur if more environmentally benign technology or practices are required, and a failure to include the negative economic impacts of environmental degradation.

For example, arguments in the late 1970s that eliminating CFCs from aerosol spray cans would be extremely costly to consumers proved inaccurate when new processes and products actually saved money. A groundbreaking study estimated that the economic value of "ecosystem services" provided by natural ecosystems in the form of fresh water, cleaner air, pollination, food production, recreation, waste treatment, and other outputs at $16 to $54 trillion per year (compared with the total global gross national product in 2007 of around US$18 trillion per year).[49] In 2009, several studies by the United Nations concluded that investments in green infrastructure projects, while requiring short-term costs, would both stimulate national economies and pay for themselves in energy savings, new jobs, and reduced costs associated with the impacts of pollution.[50]

Global efforts to reduce GHG emissions and thus mitigate more extensive climate change carry significant costs, but these efforts would likely avoid far more significant economic costs associated with sea-level rise, changes in rainfall patterns, droughts, more extreme weather, and an increase in the range of tropical diseases.[51] Similarly, in the United States, while many understand the economic costs of reducing GHG emissions, less widely acknowledged are the potential economic benefits of significantly reduced oil and gas imports, fewer health problems from air pollution, increased energy efficiency, and the creation of new jobs in the solar, wind, and geothermal industries.

For example, a recent study by a consortium of researchers from the Global Environment Facility, European Commission, McKinsey & Company, Rockefeller Foundation, Standard Chartered Bank, Swiss Re, and the ClimateWorks Foundation estimates that without mitigation and adaptation efforts, the impacts of climate change will soon begin to carry significant economic costs and, under certain scenarios, could even cost some nations up to 19 percent of their gross domestic product (GDP) as early as 2030.[52] A 2008 study that examined thousands of policy simulations from twenty-five models used to predict the economic impacts of reducing U.S. carbon emissions concluded that even under pessimistic assumptions, reducing GHGs by 40 percent below the emissions path that would otherwise occur ("business as usual") by 2030 would still result in national GDP growth of 2.4 percent, if economic factors unrelated to climate change stayed constant.[53] A 2009 report revealed that the number of jobs in the United States associated with renewable and other clean energy activities grew nearly two and a half times more quickly than overall jobs between 1998 and 2007 and that this trend would accelerate, with positive net economic benefits, if additional policies to address climate change were enacted.[54] A narrower study on the well-publicized issue of auto fuel-economy standards estimated that even if new U.S. fuel-economy standards announced by President Barack Obama in May 2009 raise car prices as much as critics claim, New England states would still see a net economic benefit of $10 billion by 2025 due to the money saved through increased fuel efficiency and the economic multiplier effect, as the saved dollars are spent by consumers and businesses on other goods and services in local economies.[55] A 2008 UN-commissioned study estimated that concerted efforts to address climate change and sustainable development would increase the global market for environmental goods and services by $1.4 trillion by 2020. By 2030, 20 million additional jobs would be created in the renewable-energy sector, and a worldwide transition to make all buildings energy efficient would create 2 to 3.5 million more green jobs in Europe and the United States alone, with the potential much higher in developing countries.[56]

Inadequate Financial and Technical Assistance

Many global environmental regimes—including those for ozone, climate, biodiversity, desertification, and toxic chemicals—contain specific measures for providing financial and technical assistance (FTA) to developing countries and so help them fulfill their obligations. Developing countries consistently argue that implementation and compliance with specific environmental regimes, including, for example, the Montreal Protocol and Stockholm Convention, depend on the provision of adequate FTA. For some developing countries, such measures are indeed critical to their ability to comply with the regime; for others, they provide an important boost. Outside the ozone regime, however, one can argue that the provision of FTA has not reached levels that ensure compliance by many developing countries. Many negotiators believe it is the most important obstacle to improved compliance.[57] Areas of need highlighted in regime negotiations (which vary significantly from issue to issue and country to country) include environmental assessments, monitoring, reporting, capacity building, drafting of appropriate legislation, equipment, regulatory and administrative infrastructure, customs control, technology transfer, and affordable access to alternative products and processes and other environmentally friendly technologies.

Poorly Designed Regimes

A party's failure to comply with a regime sometimes reflects problems with the regime itself. As discussed above, regime design matters. Control measures and reporting requirements that are too complex or too vague allow states to make honest or intentional errors when translating them to domestic law. Regimes without flexibility leave states with little recourse but to violate regime rules when domestic circumstances change significantly. Regimes that do not pay attention to states' ability to enact necessary domestic legislation, to the relative costs of compliance, to the importance of reporting and monitoring, to the interconnections between environmental issues, or to the need to provide sufficient FTA are vulnerable to compliance problems and failure. Thus, implementation and compliance, to some extent, are also a function of regime design.

Several regimes with particularly vague requirements have encountered implementation problems. Vagueness can be due to simple mistakes, the consequence of a lowest-common-denominator compromise, or an intentional negotiating strategy designed to produce imprecise requirements that allow states significant choice regarding which, if any, concrete actions they wish to take. Regardless of the source, if a treaty does not contain clear, implementable requirements, parties often have trouble translating the vague language into domestic rules or regulations, or parties can choose to interpret the vague requirements in ways that produce few adjustment costs. The language in the biodiversity and desertification conventions and their related compliance challenges illustrate this point. In both cases, while countries are called upon to develop their own national plans, there is little guidance in how to enable these plans to actually be effective in combating desertification or conserving biodiversity.

Many Regimes, Little Coordination

Another obstacle to compliance is the sheer number of environmental conventions and the confusing and uncoordinated web of requirements they now include. Since all parties, particularly developing countries, have only limited financial, technical, and political resources available to implement environmental treaties, the more complex and confusing the total set of obligations, the more likely that compliance will suffer.

Each environmental regime has its own set of core control measures, reporting requirements, monitoring systems, assessment mechanisms, implementation procedures, meeting schedules, financing requirements, and review procedures. In addition, nearly all of these regimes exist independently of each other. As such, they sometimes place uncoordinated and confusing obligations on states that are difficult to fulfill. In some countries, particularly small states, more human and financial resources are spent on reporting to treaty bodies than on implementing the treaties themselves. This is compounded by mandatory reporting requirements that sometimes conflict, or at least remain uncoordinated, in their schedules, procedures, units of analysis, and required methods and formats.

In addition, some regime rules establish contrary rules or incentives. For example, HFCs are considered a replacement for CFCs under the ozone regime, but they are also a GHG subject to mandatory controls under the climate regime. Some closely related regimes have uncoordinated membership and regulatory gaps that potentially impede effectiveness. For example, as discussed in Chapter 3, several treaties exist to address hazardous waste and toxic chemicals, including the Basel, Rotterdam, and Stockholm conventions and the Aarhus POPs Protocol under the regional LRTAP convention. Although efforts are underway to increase coordination of the Basel, Rotterdam, and Stockholm conventions significantly, different ratification patterns exist, meaning that certain countries have pledged to fulfill obligations under some chemicals agreements but not others. This pattern could become more pronounced as new chemicals are added to the Stockholm regime and some countries opt out of the new controls. This could threaten the effective implementation of the agreements, individually and as a package, because each treaty focuses on different aspects of the chemical life cycle (production, use, emissions, trade, destruction, and disposal) and a slightly different set of chemicals and wastes. Parties that implement one convention but not another allow certain chemicals or certain parts of their life cycles to escape global control.

OPPORTUNITIES TO IMPROVE COMPLIANCE

Several options are available to strengthen compliance with global environmental agreements. None of these options can address all the obstacles discussed in the previous two sections. Furthermore, whether these options or incentives can actually lead a government to comply depends on the willingness of states and other actors to take action. However, existing experience with global environmental regimes, academic research, and deductive logic indicates that regime compliance and effectiveness can be improved.

Raise Awareness and Concern

One of the most important factors in improving compliance is elevating awareness, concern, and knowledge among government elites and the general public regarding environmental issues. For each issue discussed in chapters 3 to 5, sufficient expert knowledge exists on key aspects of the problem to demonstrate the scientific seriousness of the issue; the availability of technological, economic, and policy tools to address it; and the environmental, human-health, or, in many cases, long-term economic impacts. Many significant obstacles remain to implementing solutions, however, in part because concern for environmental issues remains relatively low compared to other economic or political interests. The effectiveness of, and compliance with, international environmental regimes likely cannot increase significantly until public and corporate officials decide to prioritize the issues—or until elevated public concern and concerted individual action causes them to do so. Political will is, in many cases, the missing ingredient.

Create Market Incentives

As discussed in Chapter 1, most economic forces at work today still reward rather than punish nonsustainable activity because the local and global costs of pollution and nonsustainable resource use carry no economic costs to those responsible. There is broad agreement that changing this situation so that market forces reward environmentally friendly activities would greatly assist implementation of major environmental regimes and the pursuit of sustainable development frameworks like Agenda 21 and the Millennium Development Goals (MDGs).

A variety of important technologies essential to global sustainable development become profitable if the environmental and health costs are included in the price of the nonsustainable option currently in use. Clean energy is the most obvious example. Wind, solar, and geothermal energy sources are all economically superior to fossil fuels if one includes the full costs of the health impacts of the air pollution from fossil fuels, the climate impacts of their CO_2 emissions, and the broader environmental and national security impacts of finding, extracting, and transporting them. Placing a price on CO_2 emissions, therefore, is widely seen as a critical step toward addressing the climate-change issue.[58] The same can be said for addressing most aspects of air and water pollution, rapacious resource use, and even some types of deforestation.

Establishing market prices (via tradable emission credits, permits, incentives, taxes, or other measures) for pollution and nonsustainable activity can reward efficiency and emission avoidance, encourage innovation, create a level playing field for nonpolluting and sustainable technology options, induce the use of low-and zero-emission technologies, and reduce the overall, systemwide cost of sustainable economic growth. Any negative, systemic economic impact of the additional costs could be offset by tax reductions in other areas, such as income taxes or sales taxes on particularly sustainable products or services.

Countries can utilize market forces on their own, through agreements with neighbors or trading partners or through international agreements. Individual regimes, the United Nations Environment Programme (UNEP), the United Nations Development Programme (UNDP), the World Bank, the IMF, and other institutions could expand efforts to raise awareness of the broad benefits of employing market mechanisms and perhaps provide incentives. However, efforts by a regime, a group of countries, or a single state to utilize market forces for environmental goods can run afoul of the WTO if they impact free trade. Broad agreement exists that the global trade regime need not stand in the way of more ambitious national and international environmental policy, including market mechanisms, to address climate change or other issues, but the precise frameworks need clarification.[59] Similarly, it is not entirely clear under which circumstances a country can exclude or tax certain imports for environmental reasons or when a country with a particular type of pollution tax relevant to the manufacture of certain products can introduce a tariff on the import of similar products that carry a price advantage because the country of its manufacture has no such tax. This could be particularly relevant to climate change as some political figures in the European Union and the United States have called for consideration of tariffs on goods imported from countries without GHG-reduction policies.[60]

Build Domestic Capacity

Improved compliance requires increased funding from donor countries and multilateral agencies for programs that strengthen the capacity of developing countries to implement environmental conventions. It also requires commitment and serious efforts on behalf of developing countries so that the assistance provided helps to develop permanent infrastructures. Governments and international organizations recognize this need. UNDP's Capacity 21 and Capacity 2015 programs seek to strengthen developing company capacities to meet their sustainable development goals under Agenda 21 and the MDGs. All GEF projects on biodiversity and climate change focus on capacity building or integrate capacity-building components into investment projects. Capacity-building activities also exist within particular regimes. For example, the CITES training strategy "trains the trainers" in a country by holding seminars and providing training materials.[61] The ozone regime supports significant capacity building through its Multilateral Fund. The Basel Convention and Stockholm regional centers act as

---

BOX 6.3   OPPORTUNITIES TO IMPROVE COMPLIANCE

- Raise awareness and concern.
- Create market incentives.
- Build domestic capacity.
- Develop more effective financial and technical assistance.
- Build secretariat stability and capacity.
- Augment coordination between regimes and conventions.
- Improve international and national reporting and monitoring.
- Consider trade sanctions.
- Generate publicity.

---

nodes for capacity-building programs on issues relating to hazardous wastes and, increasingly, toxic chemicals.

Despite these efforts, many of which are important and productive, results to date in most regimes indicate that additional, well-targeted capacity building can augment regime compliance and effectiveness. Areas of particular need include environmental assessment and analysis, monitoring, reporting, regulatory infrastructure, enforcement, science education, public education and communication, and the use and maintenance of a wide variety of environmentally friendly technologies. Capacity building can also increase government concern for an issue by expanding awareness of the issue within the bureaucracy and increasing the number, skills, and visibility of people working on the issue.

Develop More Effective Financial and Technical Assistance

In addition to building capacity, FTA is needed to augment compliance in other areas. The line between capacity building and other types of FTA is largely an artificial one; in general, however, capacity building refers to permanent improvements in the ability and self-sufficiency of a country to comply, whereas financial and technical assistance refers to help regarding specific instances or types of compliance. As noted above, the provision of effectively targeted FTA is one of the most important avenues toward improved compliance and regime effectiveness. The most important areas include obtaining access to new products and processes; technology transfer; developing new or expanded legislation and regulations; purchasing scientific, monitoring, administrative, and communications equipment; helping to develop and carry out national implementation plans; financing individual implementation projects; properly disposing of hazardous wastes and toxic chemicals; and introducing substitute technologies.

However, the mere availability of increased FTA should not be seen as a panacea. Increased compliance also requires more effective assistance—that is, assistance targeted toward the most important needs; monitored to avoid waste; provided conditionally in stages to promote real action; continually assessed and reviewed so that procedures can be improved; and coordinated within and across regimes to achieve potential synergies and to avoid duplication and unintended negative consequences.

Build Secretariat Stability and Capacity

Environmental regimes require treaty secretariats to fulfill a variety of key functions. Secretariats coordinate and facilitate day-to-day regime operations, organize meetings of the parties and subsidiary bodies, draft background documents on relevant policy issues, facilitate communication among parties, manage regime reporting, gather and disseminate information on treaty implementation, maintain clearinghouse mechanisms and websites, and support public education. Yet, secretariat staffs tend to be small and their budgets minuscule in comparison with formal international organizations and most national bureaucracies (the Climate Secretariat is an exception). Combined with problems caused by late payment of or defaults on financial pledges by some parties, their small staffs and limited budgets decrease the ability of many secretariats to perform these functions. For example, the use of short-term contracts (one to six months) for staff positions in some secretariats, a practice caused by budget uncertainties and funding constraints, negatively impacts secretariat productivity, reduces institutional memory, and limits the development of long-term working relationships with national officials so important to effective implementation.[62] Thus, efforts by donor countries and foundations to stabilize funding for secretariats of global environmental conventions and to end the practices of late payment and nonpayment of country pledges would allow secretariats to provide greater support to the regime. Another method is to augment coordination between regimes and their secretariats.

Augment Coordination Between Regimes and Conventions

The broadest issue areas in global environment politics now involve multiple, overlapping global and regional regimes, international organizations, and soft-law guidelines and procedures. Indicative examples include the atmosphere (ozone, climate, and LRTAP regimes); chemicals and wastes (the Basel, Rotterdam, and Stockholm conventions and various regional treaties); biodiversity, wildlife, and habitat protection (CBD, CITES, Ramsar Convention, the Convention on Migratory Species, and a host of wildlife-specific treaties); oceans (the Law of the Sea, the London Convention, and MARPOL); and fisheries (the Fish Stocks Agreement, the FAO Code of Conduct for Responsible Fisheries, and numerous regional fisheries agreements). The Desertification Convention contains provisions that address biodiversity, climate change, forests, and freshwater resources, as well as other issues that overlap with other regimes.

Improved coordination among treaties and organizations would improve regime implementation and compliance by (1) helping to remove the obstacles produced by the lack of such coordination (outlined above), (2) allowing for more effective use of limited resources, (3) avoiding unnecessary duplication of tasks, and (4) potentially creating unforeseen opportunities where efforts for joint initiatives could improve reporting, monitoring, environmental assessments, financing, and implementation.

The potential for such activity is broadly recognized. UNEP has repeatedly addressed the issue, and environmental ministers have discussed it in a variety of fora.[63] The United Nations Conference on Environment and Development and the World Summit on Sustainable Development both endorsed the concept. A variety of secretariats consult regularly. As noted in Chapter 3, a formal initiative to increase coordination in the chemicals sector is well under way.[64] But much more can be done. Donor countries in particular are pushing for enhanced coordination as a way to reduce duplicated bureaucratic costs so that available resources can be targeted at implementation programs that achieve measurable environmental results. Opportunities for enhanced coordination that have received particular attention and exhibit promise include examining and eliminating regulatory gaps or conflicts, coordinating reporting schedules and formats, co-locating more secretariats and relevant international organizations, coordinating the scheduling of the conferences of the parties (COPs) of related regimes, supporting ratification to remove membership gaps, integrating appropriately related implementation activities, and establishing common regional centers and other programs for capacity building and the provision of FTA.

Improve International and National Reporting and Monitoring

Reporting is an essential component of monitoring and an important tool for improving compliance and regime effectiveness. Without regular and accurate reporting by parties, it is difficult to assess the baseline, trends, and current status of an environmental problem, to assess current levels of regime implementation, to identify specific instances or patterns of noncompliance, and to develop potential solutions. Studies on institutional effectiveness indicate that regimes employing systems of regular reporting and monitoring of the relevant actions of parties have better levels of domestic implementation and compliance than those that do not.[65] Thus, efforts to emphasize and improve national reporting and associated monitoring, combined with the ability to review, publicize, and act on the information, will likely increase regime compliance and effectiveness.

Most environmental regimes require parties to submit data and reports on issues related to the environmental problem as well as on their implementation of the regime. Secretariats often compile this information and make it available to other parties and the public. Unfortunately, not all countries submit the required data and reports, and significant variations exist in the quality and timeliness of those that do. In addition, because most countries rely on existing national systems to gather information for regime reporting, the reports often define, estimate, and aggregate the required data in different ways, making comparisons and analyses difficult.

As a result of these problems, some regimes have large information gaps. For example, reporting from parties under the Basel Convention, while improving, has often been incomplete, late, and sometimes based on different standards of measuring (or estimating) the generation, management, and disposal of hazardous wastes.[66] Analysts believe that differences in national reporting systems under the LRTAP regime in Europe undercut the effectiveness of the data-reporting requirements and the secretariat's ability to analyze the relevant data.[67] Large data gaps exist regarding the production, use, trade, management, and potential environmental and human-health consequences of many known toxic chemicals and perhaps the majority of commercial chemicals.[68]

The CBD's fourth national reports were due on March 30, 2009. These reports are supposed to provide essential information to assess progress toward the 2010 biodiversity target at the national level and through their contributions to the third edition of the *Global Biodiversity Outlook* at the global level. The secretariat held several regional workshops to help developing countries prepare their reports in an effort to build national capacity. However, only 25 of 191 parties to the convention submitted their reports on time.

Emphasizing and providing support for regular and harmonized reporting from all parties is an effective and financially efficient opportunity to enhance regime compliance and effectiveness. This occurred when the CITES regime made a concerted effort to get parties to fulfill reporting requirements. CITES requires that countries provide annual reports, which include export and import permit data, as well as biennial reports on legislative, regulative, and administrative measures undertaken to improve implementation and enforcement. For many years, the secretariat repeatedly expressed frustration with the quality and quantity of reports it received from parties. In the 1990s, parties adopted a resolution that failure to file the required annual report on time constituted an infraction of the treaty. A list of countries committing infractions was compiled and circulated publicly. CITES also tried to streamline and clarify its reporting guidelines. Later, the secretariat sent a letter to countries telling them that failure to file reports would be considered a "major implementation problem" under the convention. The letter further offered the secretariat's assistance in preparing and filing the reports. In 2007, the COP decided that cases where parties failed to submit

PHOTO 6.2   Rifles and ivory tusks taken from poachers in Kenya with the assistance of the NGO TRAFFIC.
Photo by Rob Barnett/TRAFFIC.

their annual reports by October 31 of the following year would be referred to the Standing Committee for review.[69] As a result of these measures, the number of reports filed has begun to increase, and their timeliness and quality has improved.[70]

Looking ahead, observers believe that regular and harmonized reporting from parties to the Basel, Rotterdam, and Stockholm conventions (if this occurs as part of the effort to augment coordination) could allow for far more accurate assessments of global levels and trends in the production, use, generation, transport, management, and disposal of hazardous chemicals. It would also make it easier to monitor progress in implementing these conventions and improve the ability to direct international policies toward areas where they would have the most impact.[71] Furthermore, harmonized reporting could help reduce the overall volume of reporting requirements, which could free up human and financial resources to improve compliance.

However, even when parties submit reports on time and with the required information, some conventions fail to give the secretariat or another body the necessary authority or resources to evaluate and verify information properly. This limits the value that regular reporting can have, for example, in revealing areas in need of financial or technical assistance or in producing information relevant to placing public pressure on governments to comply with an agreement.

In the absence of formal mechanisms, some regimes, secretariats, and governments depend on cooperation with NGOs, intergovernmental organizations, academics, and industry to help monitor and enhance different aspects of compliance. For example, governments, the major industries in the private sector, and NGOs monitor compliance with the Montreal Protocol. International NGOs also work closely with the CITES Secretariat to monitor wildlife trade. The Trade Records Analysis of Flora and Fauna in Commerce (TRAFFIC)—the wildlife-trade-monitoring program of WWF and the International Union for the Conservation of Nature and Natural Resources—helps ensure that wildlife trade remains at sustainable levels and in accordance with domestic and international laws and agreements. Established in 1976, TRAFFIC is now a network of thirty offices organized in nine regional programs. TRAFFIC assists in official investigations and enforcement actions; provides expertise for formulation, review, and amendment of wildlife trade legislation; and liaises with key wildlife consumers, producers, and managers to determine how best to dissuade unsustainable and illegal trade and to advocate to stakeholders solutions to problems identified.[72]

Consider Trade Sanctions

Improving compliance may require additional sticks as well as more carrots. In some cases, sanctions, perhaps including trade sanctions, against parties found to be in willful noncompliance could be employed. Sanctions can also be used against countries that choose to remain outside of a particular regime in an effort to discourage or punish "free riders." The ozone regime includes such provisions, prohibiting parties from exporting or importing ozone-depleting chemicals or products that use them to or from nonparties.

To be effective, trade sanctions must be credible and potent. States in conscious violation of a treaty or measures adopted by a multilateral environmental agreement (MEA) must be convinced not only that they will face penalties for the violation but also that the costs of the violation will exceed the gains expected from it.[73] Trade sanctions could represent such a cost in some cases, but the larger the economy of the violating country, the less likely it is that sanctions will bite hard enough.

Although little support currently exists for expanding the use of sanctions as a remedy for treaty violations, some argue they would make sense in situations such as illegal, unreported, and unregulated fishing, where sanctions (in this example, curbs on fishing rights or imports) could be directly related to the failure to comply with the treaty. Many developing countries, however, oppose the potential use of sanctions, arguing that under the United Nations Charter and the Rio Declaration such sanctions violate national sovereignty and, equally importantly, could be used as a disguised form of trade protectionism.[74]

Although some treaties, such as the Montreal Protocol and CITES, include the possibility of sanctions as a potential punishment for noncompliance, the potential for broader use is the subject of much debate within MEAs and the WTO. The key question is under what conditions should national governments have policy space to pursue ecological goals by restricting international trade in certain goods to promote the conservation of environmental resources harmed by production of those goods?[75] (See Chapter 7 for more about this debate.) Resolving this issue requires balancing the principles, norms, and rules of the trade and environmental regimes.

Generate Publicity

Fear of negative publicity has sometimes proven a meaningful deterrent to treaty violations. Environmental conventions could create mechanisms through which negative publicity would become a more prominent consequence of refusal to participate in a global regime or failure to implement specific provisions.[76] The Internet, global television networks, and improved telecommunications make it easier, cheaper, and faster than ever to collect and distribute information, and evidence exists that such campaigns can work. Countries go to significant lengths to deny or explain implementation lapses during many COPs to avoid potential embarrassments in meeting reports, which shows they might be sensitive to systematic exposures. Norway lost money and public support when the European Union boycotted Norwegian fish products because of Norway's position on whaling. Iceland stopped whaling because of a public campaign of negative publicity and boycotts, although it resumed whaling after about two years. Negative publicity can also be used to expose and deter corporate noncompliance with national laws. In the United States, for example, environmental groups have been an important complement to the government's enforcement efforts, in particular, when they serve as watchdogs reporting violations to the appropriate authorities.

Positive publicity can also improve compliance and some diplomats argue that efforts should be made to publicize compliance more effectively.[77] In this case, regimes would create mechanisms through which positive publicity or other benefits would flow as the result of meeting particular standards. The intention would be to create competition to achieve certain levels of implementation and environmental status. Other mechanisms could reward special achievements. For example, in 2007, representatives from wildlife enforcement agencies in Cameroon and Hong Kong received Interpol's Ecomessage Award in recognition of the extraordinary level of cooperation that they provided in the investigation surrounding the 3,900-kilogram cache of ivory smuggled out of Cameroon and seized in Hong Kong. Interpol's Ecomessage Award comes with a prize sponsored by the International Fund for Animal Welfare valued at $30,000.[78]

Several broader efforts, such as the Environmental Sustainability Index,[79] rank countries according to various environmental and sustainability criteria. Supporters of such initiatives hope that such measures can replace, or at least augment, traditional gross national product rankings and that countries will take steps to attempt to rise in the rankings, or at least avoid being placed near the bottom.

INCREASING FINANCIAL RESOURCES FOR IMPLEMENTING GLOBAL ENVIRONMENTAL REGIMES

The issue of financial resources has been at the center of global environmental politics for many years and will continue to be for the foreseeable future. Providing developing countries with FTA to help them implement their obligations under environmental treaties and soft-law regimes such as Agenda 21 remains a crucial challenge.[80] For many developing countries, the major obstacle to effective implementation is the lack of adequate financial and technical resources to fulfill treaty obligations. These countries simply do not have the resources to comply effectively. For others it provides valuable economic assistance so that resources can flow to other social needs, as well as political assistance, to ease domestic objections regarding adjustment costs. In addition, regime provisions regarding technical and financial assistance are a crucial political issue for developing countries. Such measures fulfill the principle of common but differentiated responsibilities (discussed in detail in Chapter 7) and represent a prerequisite to their participation in global policies, especially those that address problems caused primarily by industrialized countries.

Most of the opportunities outlined in the previous section for improving compliance also require additional financial and technical resources. More broadly, the successful expansion and implementation of the newest generation of global environmental regimes, including those for climate, biodiversity, desertification, fisheries, and chemicals, require transitions to environmentally sound technologies and new strategies for natural resource management. Although they could yield long-term economic benefits, such transitions are costly in the short run and require significant investments to implement, to ease the transition for those hardest hit, and to overcome resistance from powerful economic and political interests in developing and industrialized countries alike.

Most treaties have no separate funding mechanism; the ozone regime is the exception. The Montreal Protocol was the first regime in which the financing mechanism was a central issue in the negotiations. It demonstrated that donor and recipient countries participating in a global environmental regime can devise a financial mechanism that equitably distributes power and effectively links financial assistance with compliance.

The GEF, which the biodiversity, climate, desertification, and chemicals regimes use as their financing mechanism, has developed a somewhat similar governance structure but faces more difficult issues in trying to link assistance with global environmental benefits. As discussed in Chapter 2, governments created the GEF in 1991 essentially as an arm of the World Bank, with UNEP and UNDP providing technical and scientific advice. The grants and concessional funds disbursed complement traditional development assistance by covering the additional costs (also known as agreed incremental costs) incurred when a national, regional, or global development project also targets global environmental objectives, for example, funds not for local pollution cleanup but for climate, oceans, biodiversity, and ozone depletion, from which other countries would benefit as well. Initially, the GEF provided funding only for four global environmental issues: ozone depletion, international waters, climate change, and biological diversity. Subsequently, land degradation/desertification and POPs were added to the GEF's portfolio. To date, the GEF has provided $8.3 billion in grants and leveraged $33.7 billion in cofinancing from other partners for over 2,200 projects in over 160 developing countries and countries with economies in transition.[81] At its replenishment in 2006, donor countries pledged $3.13 billion to fund GEF operations through 2010.

However, given the immense challenges ahead, the GEF is very unlikely to receive sufficient funds from donor countries to enable it to assist developing countries achieve full compliance with the biodiversity, climate change, desertification, and POPs conventions, particularly if their controls expand. As discussed in Chapter 7, official development assistance (ODA) levels rose in the last decade after falling in the 1990s. This included the significant expansion of assistance pledged for Africa by the Group of Eight (not all of which has been provided).[82] While certainly welcomed by its recipients, most of this money was directed toward traditional development activities, not toward implementing global environmental priorities. In addition, the severe global recession that started in 2008 has put tremendous pressure on national budgets in both developed and developing countries. Thus, industrialized-country ODA may decline even as regime-implementation and sustainable development needs grow in developing countries. Indeed, the total investment needed to fulfill current regime obligations, implement Agenda 21, and achieve the environmentally related MDGs is many times higher than total current ODA levels. Even if such funding is possible economically,[83] donor countries do not yet seem to have the political will to make such investments or provide adequate bilateral funding in support of global environmental objectives.

So what potential sources exist that could provide significant increases in financial resources for implementing global environmental regimes? This section outlines several possibilities, some possible in the near term, others farther down the road. They include refocusing existing bilateral and multilateral assistance toward projects supportive of environmental regimes; developing revenue from emissions trading; creating new revenue streams from coordinated taxes on air travel, energy, currency transactions, the arms trade, or pollutant emissions; canceling developing-country debt; and eliminating subsidies for natural resource extraction and shifting the money to conservation. Governments, NGOs, or other experts in different international fora have proposed each of these options, and each is theoretically possible. Yet, each faces significant obstacles before it can become international policy.

Focus Multilateral and Bilateral Assistance Toward Sustainable Development Goals

Existing ODA programs, which dwarf environmental funding in size, could apply more resources to programs that also enhance environmental goals. Overall ODA flows would not be reduced. Instead, governments would funnel greater levels of aid to programs with shared environmental and developmental goals. Thus, ODA programs focused on industrialization or energy production would support only projects that produce or use "green" energy (such as solar, wind, geothermal, or tidal power), employ significant energy-conservation measures, and emit low levels of air or water pollution. Many developing countries have tremendous renewable energy resources, including outstanding conditions for cost-efficient solar power plants in large sections of northern and southern Africa, the Arab states, and parts of Pakistan and India. Tremendous resources for constructing geothermal facilities exist in East Africa and the western Pacific—including Indonesia, the Philippines, and the west coasts of Mexico, Central America, and South America (see Figure 6.1). Significant wind-power resources exist in many places, including off the coasts of Brazil, China, India, South America, and southern Africa.

Similarly, cleaning and redeveloping "brownfields"—former industrial properties containing hazardous substances, pollutants, or contaminants—would enjoy priority over clearing land for construction or agriculture. Projects that would clear tropical forests or place roads into or near protected areas would not be funded; nor would products that use or produce toxic chemicals. Reuse and recycling projects would be emphasized over mining projects or production processes that require large amounts of raw materials. Funding would be increased to countries that followed these types of guidelines in their own policies and decreased to countries that continued "business as usual." Sustainable agriculture that produces food for local consumption on a regular basis would receive priority over boom-and-bust industrial export agriculture that consumes significant quantities of water and fertilizer and leaves many producing countries as net importers of food. Energy-efficiency projects that train people in this

FIGURE 6.1   Areas of the world with potential for producing electricity using geothermal energy

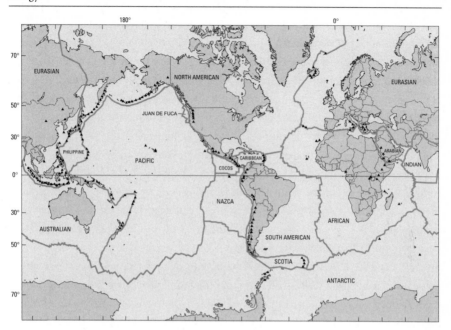

Source: The USGS Energy Resources Program website at
http://energy.usgs.gov/images/geothermal/geothermal_lithoplatesLG.gif.

profitable industry, save the target country money in energy savings, and reduce GHG emissions would be supported over other types of jobs programs with more limited reach.

Donors or recipients wishing to focus all or part of their ODA programs on health and social issues could effectively pursue these goals while also promoting the social bases of sustainable development, including basic health and nutrition, vaccinations, family planning, land preservation, and education—especially for women and girls. Indeed, better health and education are widely shown to contribute to smaller, healthier families, more productive agriculture, higher incomes, and less stress on the environment and natural resources. Many governments, international organizations, and foundations have efforts in these areas, but many observers agree that a broad-based commitment to make sustainable development a copriority in all ODA initiatives would significantly impact sustainable development.

Develop Revenue from Regime Mechanisms Such as Emissions Trading

A potential source of financing for greater energy efficiency, zero-GHG-emission energy sources, technological innovation, and technological diffusion is emissions trading, such as the mechanism under the Kyoto Protocol (see Chapter 4). By making emissions reduction a potential profit source, the competitive nature of market capitalism is employed to combat climate change.

Title IV of the U.S. Clean Air Act of 1990 established one of the first national systems for emissions trading for meeting sulfur dioxide emissions targets in the electric-power sector as a means to reduce acid rain in the United States. In Europe, the European Union Greenhouse Gas Emission Trading Scheme commenced operation in January 2005 as the world's largest multicountry, multisector GHG-emission-trading scheme worldwide. Regional GHG-trading schemes have been developed in the United States, and the U.S. House of Representatives approved a national system in June 2009 as part of its proposed landmark climate and energy legislation.

The difficulty lies in creating and then continually improving such systems so that they work at both the business and the environmental levels. It is still too early to tell whether the U.S. regional or proposed national systems will work. The EU system experienced difficulties for the first few years because an excess of permits drove prices too low. However, some of these problems have been fixed (the system is designed to be adjusted if needed), and the EU Greenhouse Gas Emissions Trading Scheme has expanded to cover emissions from more types of sources, and most analysts believe that in the long term the system will achieve its goals.[84] The success of emissions-trading programs in the United States for other pollutants, such as sulfur oxides, also argues that this is at least theoretically possible, although maintaining an effective and efficient trading system for CO_2 presents a more difficult challenge.

In the negotiations toward a successor agreement to the Kyoto Protocol, parties might seek to develop a more active trading system than they have to date. In such a system, countries or private corporations would be able to sell their excess rights to emit CO_2 if they significantly reduced their emissions through conservation or by using wind, solar, or geothermal power; cogeneration; or zero-CO_2-emission coal, oil, or gas power plants (currently under development). Including a provision that a small percentage of the transaction cost would go into a fund for clean-energy development would expand the resources available for developing countries to pursue clean-energy options. Should a robust global system not develop under the climate regime, major national and regional schemes could likely link together. The participating countries could then agree to a similar levy within their trading systems, for example, in the United States and the European Union, and then pool these resources. Indeed, proposals for the U.S. system included provisions for certain revenues going to international projects, and the EU is the world's largest provider of climate-related funding to developing countries.

The climate regime already includes another mechanism for raising revenues, and possibilities exist in other regimes. The Clean Development Mechanism allows indus-

> ### BOX 6.4 OPPORTUNITIES TO INCREASE FINANCIAL RESOURCES FOR IMPLEMENTING GLOBAL ENVIRONMENTAL REGIMES
>
> - Focus multilateral and bilateral assistance toward sustainable development.
> - Develop revenue from regime mechanisms such as emissions trading.
> - Create a new revenue stream from coordinated taxes.
> - Forgive debt obligations.
> - Eliminate counterproductive subsidies.

trialized countries to implement GHG-emissions-reduction projects in developing countries and receive saleable certified emissions-reduction credits, which can be counted toward meeting their Kyoto targets. The climate regime's Adaptation Fund will receive proceeds from the equivalent of a 2 percent tax on these credits. While this will not raise anything close to the amount of money required for climate adaptation, it may provide a dedicated revenue stream from a regime mechanism. Similar efforts might be possible in other pollution-control regimes should they adopt trading schemes, a Clean Development Mechanism, or analogous methods.

Create a New Revenue Stream from Coordinated Taxes on Air Travel, Energy, Currency Transactions, the Arms Trade, or Pollutant Emissions

Many ideas exist for global or coordinated national taxes to raise new revenue for sustainable development and protection of the environment.[85] In each, countries would impose similar taxes or user fees and then pool or use the money individually to finance sustainable development and environmental regimes. Taxes would be levied on activities harmful in their own right, and therefore reasonable to discourage through taxes.

The idea of taxing international air travel has been around since the early 1990s, when the European Union called for a tax on air fuel used for international flights to raise funds for environmental projects.[86] More recently, at the June 2009 climate talks in Bonn, the group of least-developed countries proposed that developed countries should accept a compulsory levy on international flight tickets and shipping fuel to raise billions of dollars to help the world's poorest countries adapt to combat climate change. The aviation levy, which proponents claim would increase the price of long-haul fares by less than 1 percent, could raise $10 billion a year.[87] Also in Bonn, Mexico proposed creation of a "green fund" plan, to which all countries would contribute according to a formula reflecting the size of their economy, GHG emissions, and population. This would ensure that rich countries, which have the longest history of fossil fuel use, pay the most into the fund. The money would then be used to help developing countries mitigate and adapt to climate change.[88]

A global energy tax of $1 per barrel of oil or its coal equivalent could raise more than $66 billion annually, while acting as a further incentive for conservation. Another well-known proposal is to tax large-scale speculative currency trading. A levy of just 0.005 percent could generate $15 billion a year for environmental projects if enacted in countries through which most of such trading takes place. Larger levies, which have been proposed, would raise even more and also act as a small brake on such speculation, which some argue presents an unnecessary threat to the stability of national currencies.[89] Taxes on arms sales could raise similar sums with appropriate ancillary benefits. Other possibilities include taxes on certain types of energy production, fossil fuel–powered transportation, transboundary shipments of hazardous waste, the production of particular substances, or emissions of toxic chemicals, heavy metals, or other types of air or water pollution. In addition to raising funds for implementing globally agreed-upon environmental goals, the taxes would create additional economic deterrents to unnecessary pollution. An analogous and successful domestic example is the excise tax on CFCs enacted by the United States to help implement its obligations under the ozone regime. The tax has raised several billion dollars for the U.S. Treasury and acted as a significant incentive for companies to speed their transition to alternatives.[90]

Many practical issues exist concerning the administration of such taxes, and the system would be subject to significant concerns about free riders. In addition, some national governments might fear that they will lose revenue, that the money raised in their countries will be wasted on inefficient international projects, or that the taxes will be used to create slush funds for international organizations. The U.S. Congress, for example, passed legislation in 1999 making it illegal for the United States to participate in global taxes.[91] Although a national tax, albeit one enacted in concert with other governments and administered domestically by the United States with proceeds distributed only by the United States, might pass muster against this legislation and meet at least some of the concern expressed by other countries, it would still face formidable political obstacles.

Forgive Debt Obligations of Developing Countries in Return for Sustainable Development Policy Reforms and Investments

Debt obligations can place huge burdens on developing countries. Sometimes they are forced to mine their natural resources for export and to use up budgetary resources at the expense of implementing environmental conventions or sustainable development programs. Implementing aggressive debt-relief programs in concert with agreements by the debtor country to use a specific amount of the savings for environmental programs offers potential to tap an additional source of funds for problems largely neglected by most assistance programs, such as programs needed to combat desertification in Africa.

Several initiatives in this direction have been developed in the past two decades. Under pressure from poor countries and NGOs in September 1996, the World Bank and the IMF launched the Initiative for Heavily Indebted Poor Countries (HIPC), which seeks to ensure that no poor country faces a debt burden it cannot manage.[92] The HIPC initiative is an agreement among official creditors designed to help the poorest and most heavily indebted countries escape from unsustainable debt. It enables poor countries to focus their energies on building the policy and institutional foundation for sustainable development and poverty reduction. The initiative is designed to reduce debts to sustainable levels for poor countries that pursue economic and social policy reforms and is used specifically where traditional debt-relief mechanisms are insufficient to help countries exit from the rescheduling process. Unlike earlier debt-relief mechanisms, it deals with debt in a comprehensive way and involves all creditors, including multilateral financial institutions.

In 2005, to help accelerate progress toward the UN MDGs, the HIPC was supplemented by the Multilateral Debt Relief Initiative, which allows for 100 percent relief on eligible debts from three multilateral institutions—the IMF, the World Bank, and the African Development Fund—for countries completing the HIPC initiative process. In 2007, the Inter-American Development Bank also decided to provide additional debt relief to the five HIPCs in the Western Hemisphere.

Under current rules, forty countries can potentially receive debt relief under HIPC. By July 2009, twenty-five of these countries had reached the final point in the process and were receiving irrevocable debt relief. Ten countries were in an interim stage and receiving debt-service relief. The remaining five suffer from persistent governance challenges, civil strife, cross-border armed conflict, substantial arrears, and other problems that prevent them from establishing the track record of government and macroeconomic performance required for participation in the program.[93] The process continues, with Haiti becoming one of the most recent countries to complete the process in 2009.

The 2005 Group of Eight (G-8) summit culminated an equally substantive process, when leaders of the world's eight leading industrialized countries agreed to cancel the debt of eighteen of the world's poorest nations and to increase overall aid to Africa to $50 billion by 2010.[94] This debt-cancellation pledge addressed the needs of some of the countries eligible for the HIPC or Multilateral Debt Relief initiatives but that could not participate because of the domestic exigencies and the structural adjustments required by the program. Several broad alliances of various religious, charitable, environmental, and labor groups (the best known being the Jubilee Network) continue to advocate for debt cancellation.[95] Although the HIPC, G-8, and other initiatives represent significant steps, debt levels remain an impediment to successful environmental protection and sustainable development in many developing countries.

Eliminate Counterproductive Subsidies

One direct method for increasing the sustainability of agriculture, forestry, and fisheries is to eliminate subsidies that contribute to the unsustainable use and long-term degradation of the affected land, forests, and fish. The period from the 1960s through the 1980s saw a rapid, worldwide expansion of subsidies for natural resource production. Although some reductions occurred in subsidies to agriculture and fisheries in the 1990s and early 2000s, the scale of environmentally harmful subsidies in the energy, road transport, water use, and agricultural sectors remains staggering[96] (see Chapter 7).

Despite the overall financial and environmental advantages of ending such subsidies, governments tend to keep such policies in place in response to political pressures and powerful economic elites. The WTO Agreement on Subsidies and Countervailing Measures attempts to discipline the use of subsidies, but it concentrates only on subsidized imports that hurt domestic producers. It will take a concerted effort to fashion the necessary national and international consensus needed to end, or even severely limit, subsidies impeding conservation. Doing so, however, would release billions of dollars that currently subsidize environmental degradation, perhaps allowing some to be used for environmental protection.

CONCLUSION

The effectiveness of an environmental regime, that is, the extent to which it produces measurable improvements in the environment, is a function of regime design, particularly the strength of the key control provisions aimed at addressing the environmental threat, as well as the level of implementation (the extent to which countries adopt domestic regulations to enact the agreement) and compliance (the degree to which countries conform to these regulations and other regime rules and procedures). Many factors can inhibit or promote the effectiveness of an environmental regime. Among the most fundamental are six broad sets of obstacles that can make it difficult to create regimes with strong and binding control measures: (1) structural or systemic obstacles that arise from the structure of the international system, the structure of international law, and the structure of the global economic system; (2) the lack of sufficient concern, a hospitable contractual environment, or necessary capacity; (3) the time lag and the lowest-common-denominator procedural obstacles; (4) obstacles that stem from the characteristics of global environmental issues themselves (including the inherent links between environmental issues and important economic and political issues, unequal adjustment costs, scientific complexity and uncertainty, time-horizon conflicts, the presence of different core values and beliefs, and the involvement of large numbers of actors); (5) obstacles that stem from the interconnections between environmental issues; and (6) regime-design difficulties.

Once regimes are created, certain factors can then negatively influence national compliance with their requirements. These include inadequate translation of regime rules into domestic law; insufficient capacity to enact, administer, or enforce the domestic regulations; inability to monitor compliance; lack of respect for the rule of law; the costs of compliance; misperception of relevant cost and benefits; inadequate FTA; poorly designed regimes; and the lack of coordination among the increasingly large number of environmental conventions.

Despite these obstacles, options exist to strengthen compliance with environmental agreements. Among the most important are elevating concern, creating market incentives, augmenting domestic capacity, increasing and more effectively targeting technical and financial assistance, enhancing secretariat capacity, emphasizing and supporting improved national reporting and monitoring, enhancing coordination between regimes and conventions, improving reporting and monitoring, applying trade sanctions, and utilizing positive and negative publicity.

Lack of financial resources is often cited as a key reason for many countries' failure to implement and comply with global environmental regimes. External financing for environmental agreements is closely linked to the economic and political interests and resources of industrialized countries. Given the current reluctance among donor countries to increase financing for environmental regimes, as well as the potentially large amounts needed to assure their effectiveness, it appears necessary for regimes to seek alternative sources for such resources. This chapter has outlined several ways to increase funding for global environmental regimes, including focusing existing bilateral and multilateral assistance on projects directly supportive of environmental regimes and sustainable development; developing revenue from regime mechanisms such as emissions trading; creating new revenue streams from coordinated taxes on energy, pollution, currency transactions, international travel, or arms sales; canceling debts owed by poor countries; and eliminating counterproductive subsidies and shifting some of the savings to conservation.

In spite of daunting obstacles that prevent the creation and effective implementation of international environmental agreements, successful conventions and protocols do exist. Examining the obstacles to creating strong agreements and options for increasing compliance provides insights into additional tools for creating effective global environmental policy. Although this chapter has outlined what leading experts see as policy prescriptions that could help solve these problems, the most important factor in meeting the challenge might be political will.

DISCUSSION QUESTIONS

1. Choose one of the regimes discussed in chapters 3 to 5. Which obstacles to effective environmental policy are most relevant to that case?
2. Which obstacles do you think are the most important and why? Which are most relevant to U.S. participation in global environmental policy and why?
3. Which obstacles might become less or more important in the future?
4. What are lowest-common-denominator agreements and why do they occur? Can you give an example of a provision in a treaty that results from such an agreement?
5. What are some of the problems regarding implementation and compliance by parties to a convention? How might some of these problems be overcome?
6. What options for strengthening compliance with an agreement do you think may be the most effective in the short term? Why?
7. Why has the proliferation of environmental conventions possibly had a negative impact on implementation? How do you think this might be overcome?
8. Which of the options available for generating additional financial support for the implementation of environmental conventions do you think would be the most effective? How would you overcome political resistance to this option?

7

Environmental Politics, Economics, and Development

In recent years, global environmental politics have become increasingly intertwined with core economic and social-development concerns of countries. Sustainable development, trade and environment, HIV/AIDS, and unsustainable consumption patterns were not on the international political agenda twenty years ago. But several developments converged to change all that: the emergence of environmental problems and regimes that require social and economic transitions in all societies, the recognition of these issues during the first global negotiations encompassing environmental and economic policies (the 1992 United Nations Conference on Environment and Development [UNCED]); the subsequent UN global conferences in the 1990s covering issues including women, population, social development, and human settlements; the United Nations Millennium Summit; and the growing influence of the World Trade Organization (WTO).

North-South economic issues have become a crucial element of the political context of global environmental politics. The perception held by many developing countries that global economic relations are fundamentally inequitable often shapes their policy responses to global environmental issues and their negotiating strategies on issues as different as elephants and climate. Moreover, unfavorable trends in North-South economic relations since the mid-1970s have not only have sharpened the inequalities between the North and South but also affected the bargaining position of the South on issues involving North-South economic relations, including environmental issues.

As linkages with economic and social development have multiplied, the boundaries of global environmental politics have broadened and sometimes been lost within the larger context of sustainable development. This chapter looks at three elements in this broadening debate: North-South economic relations and the environment, the role of environmental politics in the evolution of global economic and social-development policies, and the clash between the drive for free trade and environmental protection.

NORTH-SOUTH INEQUALITIES AND THE ENVIRONMENT

In 1974, encouraged by a surge in commodity prices and the Organization of Petroleum Exporting Countries' successful manipulation of oil supplies in the early 1970s, developing countries attempted to restructure the global economic system. The South called for a bold but largely unrealistic plan, the **New International Economic Order** (NIEO), a list of demands for the redistribution of wealth, which would include a new system of international commodity agreements, a unilateral reduction of barriers to imports from developing states into industrialized countries, the enhancement of developing countries' capabilities in science and technology, increased northern financing of technology transfer, and changes in patent laws to lower the cost of such transfers.[1]

After the late 1970s, however, the NIEO faded from the global political agenda as economic trends turned against the South; the North consequently felt even more strongly that it could disregard southern demands for change. Yet, although some northern observers might have considered the NIEO agenda "discredited,"[2] it remained unfinished business for much of the South and was still considered a goal "very much worth pursuing."[3] By the beginning of the 1990s, a sense of new vulnerabilities, the persisting pangs of an unfinished agenda, and the opportunity to renew a North-South dialogue under environmental auspices began to serve as a new rallying point and translated into a renewed southern assertiveness, especially around the broad issue of sustainable development.[4]

Economic Realities

Commodity prices, debt, and trade issues have shaped the economic picture in developing countries since the 1980s. Falling commodity prices devastated the economies of countries heavily dependent on commodity exports. Between 1980 and 1991, the weighted index for thirty-three primary commodities exported by developing countries, not including energy, declined by 46 percent.[5] Meanwhile, heavy debt burdens, taken on at a time when commodity prices were high and northern banks were freely lending dollars from Arab oil revenues, siphoned off much of the foreign exchange of many developing countries. By 1995, the total external debt of the least-developed countries was $136 billion, a sum that represented 112.7 percent of their gross national product that year.[6]

During the early 1990s, trade barriers erected by industrialized countries against imports of manufactured and processed goods from the developing countries continued to increase even as most developing countries (under pressure from international financial institutions) were lowering their own barriers to imports.[7] Tariffs on textiles and other products of particular importance to developing countries' exports tended to be the highest in industrialized countries, which often increase tariff rates on goods in proportion to the degree of processing involved, a process called "tariff escalation." New kinds of **nontariff barriers** to trade (such as antidumping and countervailing duty actions), export-restraint agreements (such as the Multi-Fiber Arrangement), and direct subsidies have been used to protect industries in the industrialized countries against imports from developing countries. To this day, developing countries are suspicious of anything called a nontariff barrier.

Negotiations on liberalization of world trade, known as the **Uruguay Round**, began in 1985 under the auspices of the General Agreement on Tariffs and Trade (GATT) and concluded in April 1994. The Uruguay Round reduced some of these barriers, but the overall impact was not as much as developing countries had hoped. A 2000 joint report by the United Nations Conference on Trade and Development and the WTO found that in spite of the substantial progress in trade liberalization resulting from the Uruguay Round, peak tariffs, relatively high effective protection, and significant tariff escalation persisted for an important number of products and sectors.[8]

Although the average level of protection in the industrialized countries is relatively low, serious barriers to entry exist in certain sectors of particular interest to developing countries, including agriculture, textiles, clothing, fish, and fish products.[9] With regard to the agricultural sector, developing countries complained that they had liberalized their agricultural markets only to face domestic competition from subsidized agricultural imports from developed economies. At the same time, they charge that developed countries' markets remain relatively closed to agricultural exports from developing countries through such nontariff barriers to trade as sanitary measures and country-of-origin labeling. Exacerbating the situation, depressed commodity prices and a subsequent decline in investment in agriculture hampered developing countries' attempts to modernize their agriculture infrastructures.

From 2000 to 2007, however, developing countries saw an improvement in their overall terms of trade as commodity prices hit record highs, sparked largely by growth in consumption in China.[10] The years preceding the 2008 global financial crisis saw the strongest economic growth in decades. Global economic output grew 4 percent per year from 2000 to 2007, led by record growth in low- and middle-income economies. Developing economies averaged 6.5 percent annual growth of gross domestic product, or GDP, from 2000 to 2007, and growth in every region was the highest in three decades. During this period, China and India emerged as drivers of global economic growth, accounting for 2.9 percentage points of the 5 percent growth in global output in 2007. By 2008, low- and middle-income economies contributed 43 percent of global output, up from 36 percent in 2000. China and India accounted for 5 percentage points of that increased share.[11]

However, despite the growth of economies in countries like Brazil, China, and India, the income gap between the industrialized world and the developing world has not narrowed. The richest 25 percent of countries of the world (the so-called North) control about 60 percent of the world's income (see Figure 7.1). Furthermore, the richest 10 percent of the world controls 85 percent of global assets.[12] A few countries are seeing median household incomes rise, but most are not, and the "cavernous divide" between the world's rich and poor is not closing.[13] In fact, most of the world's population earns an average annual income either below $1,500 or above $11,500, while only a small fraction makes up the global middle class.[14] This apparent lack of mobility in the global division of labor has reinforced the popular perception in the poorest countries in the global South that the world is divided into haves and have-nots and that they exist solely on the world's periphery.[15]

Northern and Southern Perspectives on the Global Environment

Historically, developing countries perceived global environmental issues as a distinctively North-South issue and, sometimes, as an effort to sabotage their development aspirations. This was exemplified in the 1971 Founex Report produced by a group of southern intellectuals as part of the preparatory process for the Stockholm Conference on the Human Environment.[16] The tone and substance of the report foreshadowed, nearly exactly, what soon became the South's rhetoric not only during the NIEO debates in the early 1970s but also during UNCED and subsequent global environmental conferences and regime negotiations. The Founex Report provides critical testimony that these interests (1) have remained unchanged over time, (2) are the same interests that informed the NIEO ideology, and (3) lie at the heart of today's global politics of sustainable development.[17] As the Founex Report puts it,

> The developing countries would clearly wish to avoid, as far as feasible, the [environmental] mistakes and distortions that have characterized the patterns of development of the industrialized societies. However, the major environmental problems of the developing countries are essentially of a different kind. They are predominantly problems that reflect the poverty and very lack of development in their societies. . . . These are problems, no less than those of industrial pollution, that clamor for attention in the context of the concern with human

FIGURE 7.1A   Global adult population distribution, 2000

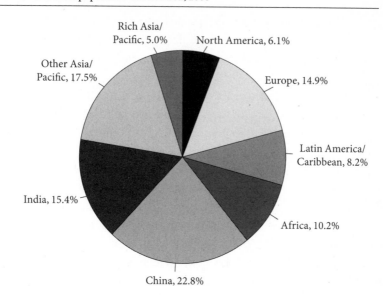

Rich Asia/
Pacific, 5.0%   North America, 6.1%

Other Asia/
Pacific, 17.5%

Europe, 14.9%

Latin America/
Caribbean, 8.2%

India, 15.4%

Africa, 10.2%

China, 22.8%

FIGURE 7.1B   Global wealth distribution, 2000

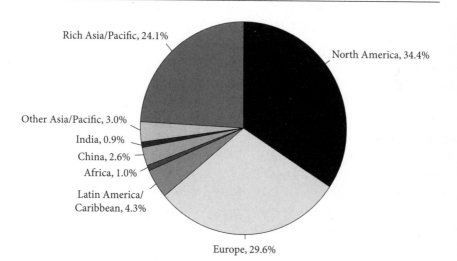

Rich Asia/Pacific, 24.1%

North America, 34.4%

Other Asia/Pacific, 3.0%

India, 0.9%

China, 2.6%

Africa, 1.0%

Latin America/
Caribbean, 4.3%

Europe, 29.6%

Data source: James B. Davies et al., *The World Distribution of Household Wealth*, Discussion Paper No. 2008/03 (Helsinki: United Nations University World Institute for Development Economics Research, 2008).

environment. They are problems which affect the greater mass of mankind. . . .
In [industrialized] countries, it is appropriate to view development as a cause
of environmental problems. . . . In [the southern] context, development becomes
essentially a cure for their major environmental problems.[18]

Although many developing country officials, particularly in environment ministries,
recognize the seriousness of local and global environmental degradation for their own
economic future, the viewpoints expressed in the Founex Report help to explain why
many also regard global environmental regimes as largely unrelated to their core concerns and even suspiciously—as a means by which industrialized countries will maintain, or even gain new, control over resources and technology located in the South.
For example, one developing-country delegate to the second Meeting of the Parties to
the Montreal Protocol in 1990 declared that for "some [industrialized] countries" the
protocol was a "pretext to place new obstacles in the way of efforts by developing countries to develop their economies."[19] And some officials of developing countries viewed
the efforts of industrialized countries to bring them into a new global climate regime
as a ploy to constrain economic development in the South so that the developed countries could dominate the world's remaining oil resources.[20]

Developing countries, many of which were already subject to macroeconomic policy conditions on loans from multilateral banks, reacted strongly anytime they believed
that an environmental regime, multilateral institution, or industrialized country policy
initiative would also impose environmental conditions on economic assistance or restrict their exports or internal economic development on environmental grounds. The
September 1998 Conference of the Non-Aligned Movement subscribed to the values
of environmental protection, labor standards, intellectual property protection, sound
macroeconomic management, and the promotion and protection of human rights, but
it rejected all attempts to use these issues as conditionalities and pretexts for restricting
market access or aid and technology flows to developing countries.[21] This tenet has
been reiterated at each Non-Aligned Movement meeting, including the July 2009 summit in Sharm el-Sheikh, Egypt: Each country has the sovereign right to determine its
own development priorities and strategies, and the international community should
categorically reject any conditionality in the provision of development assistance.

Developing countries share a largely common view of the relationship between
global environmental issues and North-South economic relations. This unanimity exists despite growing disparities between the rapidly industrializing developing countries (such as Brazil, China, India, and Malaysia) and the least-developed countries
(such as Haiti, Myanmar, and many countries in sub-Saharan Africa), which suffer
from profound poverty, structurally weak economies, limited capacity for growth and
development, and extreme vulnerability to external shocks.

Developing countries insist that the industrialized countries, because of their historical dominance in the production and consumption of chlorofluorocarbons (CFCs), combustion of fossil fuels, and production of toxic chemicals and hazardous wastes, are responsible for the thinning of the ozone layer, global warming, and international contaminations caused by toxic chemicals and wastes. More generally, they identify wasteful northern patterns of excessive consumption as a key cause of global environmental degradation. According to the United Nations Development Programme the 20 percent of the world's people in the highest-income countries account for about 80 percent of total private consumption expenditures; the poorest 20 percent, for a minuscule 1.3 percent. More specifically, the richest fifth:

- consumes about 45 percent of all meat and fish; the poorest fifth, 5 percent;
- consumes more than 50 percent of total energy; the poorest fifth, less than 4 percent;
- has about 75 percent of all telephone lines; the poorest fifth, 1.5 percent;
- consumes more than 80 percent of all paper; the poorest fifth, 1.1 percent; and
- owns more than 85 percent of the world's vehicle fleet; the poorest fifth, less than 1 percent.[22]

Based on such comparisons, developing-country officials and nongovernmental organizations (NGOs) began to demand in the early 1990s that industrialized countries reduce their share of what they call "environmental space"—the use of the earth's limited natural resources and environmental services—and permit developing countries to use more of that environmental space to raise their living standards.[23]

Southern concerns about environmental space and resource transfers led to the institutionalization of several principles that emerged at the Earth Summit in Rio and have become a feature of all post-Rio environmental negotiations, including the Convention to Combat Desertification, the Cartagena Protocol on Biosafety, and the climate-change and chemicals conventions. The first of these principles is "additionality," which arose out of the southern concern that environmental issues would attract international aid away from traditional developmental issues. Developing countries were concerned that instead of raising new funds for dealing with global environmental issues, the North and international finance institutions would simply divert resources previously targeted for development toward the environment. Thus, the principle of additionality sought to ensure that new monies would be made available to deal with global environmental issues.[24]

Despite assurances given to the South, however, this principle suffered a setback soon after UNCED, during the negotiation of the desertification convention. Early in these negotiations, it became clear that no new funds would be made available. This dismayed developing countries, particularly those in Africa, and became a major

CARTOON 7.1   "And may we continue to be worthy of consuming a disproportionate
share of this planet's resources."

source of contention during the negotiations. Ultimately, the Global Mechanism was
established under the United Nations Convention to Combat Desertification
(UNCCD), its role essentially being to use existing resources more efficiently to meet
the action needs of the convention.[25] Even though in 2002 the Global Environment
Facility (GEF) decided to include desertification activities in its funding, the fact that
the UNCCD regime began without new and additional financial resources to combat
desertification severely damaged the principle of additionality.[26]

Developing countries also believe that the North should bear the financial burden
of measures to reverse ecological damage. This is a key component of the principle of
"common but differentiated responsibilities." This principle states that global environmental problems are the common concern of all nations, and all nations should work
toward their solution (common responsibilities), but responsibility for action should
be differentiated in proportion to the responsibility for creating the problem and the
financial and technical resources available for taking effective action (differentiated
responsibilities). Since some nations have a greater and more direct responsibility for
creating environmental problems, they have a greater responsibility to address them.

The principle of "common but differentiated responsibilities" enjoys broad support
and has been explicitly acknowledged in nearly all international environmental agree-

ments since Rio. It is reflected in specific regime rules, such as the different requirements for industrialized and developing countries under the Montreal Protocol (as discussed in Chapter 4, developing countries are given additional years before they have to phase out particular chemicals), the absence of developing-country commitments to reduce greenhouse gas (GHG) emissions in the Kyoto Protocol, and provisions to provide developing countries with financial and technical assistance (FTA) to help them implement the ozone, climate, biodiversity, hazardous waste, and chemicals regimes.

At the same time, important differences exist regarding how countries believe the principle of common but differentiated responsibilities should impact global environmental policy both in general and on specific issues. Developing countries emphasize historical responsibilities for causing global environmental problems, the very large disparities in current per capita contributions (e.g., in per capita GHG emissions or resource consumption), and their need to devote resources to lifting billions of people out of stifling poverty and underdevelopment. It would be unfair, counterproductive, and perhaps immoral, they maintain, for developing countries to devote scarce resources to combating global environmental problems at the expense of addressing development. Thus, many southern states argue that the principle of common but differentiated responsibilities not only demands that industrialized countries should take far more significant action far earlier than developing countries and provide greatly increased FTA but also that developing countries should participate in a global regime only to the extent that they receive sufficient FTA to allow them to implement the regime without having a negative impact on their economic development. This means, for example, that the FTA must meet all the extra, or incremental, costs for using alternatives to the inexpensive ozone-depleting chemicals or coal-fire power plants that industrialized countries used during their economic development.

In contrast, while most industrialized countries allow that historical responsibility and current per capita emissions are relevant to policy discussions, they also emphasize the common responsibility of all countries to contribute to solving global environmental problems, which implies a need for developing countries to avoid duplicating the unsustainable historical development patterns of the industrialized world. They also point out that some developing countries are currently among the most important contributors to particular environmental problems and that it will be simply physically impossible to address these issues, in particular climate change and deforestation, if these developing countries do not act, and act soon. Thus, many industrialized countries maintain that while it is appropriate for them to act first and to provide FTA, developing countries must also take action; particular levels of FTA are not a precondition for developing countries to take responsible action; and those developing countries experiencing very rapid levels of economic growth or that have large impacts on particular environmental problems also have more responsibility to act than other developing countries with regard to those problems. These differences are on full display in the climate negotiations. The United States and some other countries believe that certain developing nations should agree to take significant action to reduce their GHG emissions from burning fossil fuels (e.g., China and India) and deforestation (e.g., Brazil and Indonesia). However, many developing countries reject these arguments, citing their low per capita emissions, their need for energy and economic development, inadequate FTA provisions, and especially the responsibility of industrialized countries for creating the problem and the implications this should have on commitments to emissions reductions. During the Kyoto Protocol negotiations, for example, Brazil presented an analysis that compared the relative responsibility of Annex I (industrialized) countries and non–Annex I (developing) countries for climate change, not just in carbon dioxide (CO_2) emissions in a given year but in CO_2 concentrations from historical emissions. It showed that the non–Annex I countries' responsibility for accumulated emissions would not equal that of Annex I countries until the middle of the twenty-second century.[27]

The principle of common but differentiated responsibilities is linked to southern demands for "new and additional" funding for developing countries' implementation of environmental agreements. However, a sharp reduction in official development assistance (ODA) levels in the 1990s and the failure of wealthy countries to amend trade policies that harm the interests of poor countries increasingly irritated developing countries. In response, developing countries started to use the threat of retreating from previous consensus agreements on global environmental issues as leverage against the donor countries. For example, at the Earth Summit +5 (the 1997 Special Session of the United Nations General Assembly [UNGA] to review the implementation of Agenda 21 and the other Rio agreements), the Group of 77 and China refused to oppose proposals by oil-exporting states to delete all references to reducing consumption of fossil fuels. This tactic failed, however, to shake the veto exercised by donor countries on targets for ODA.[28]

Commitments made at the March 2002 United Nations Conference on Financing for Development reversed the ODA decline in 2003 and 2004. In 2005, donors committed to increase ODA at the Group of Eight summit in Gleneagles, Scotland[29] and at the United Nations Millennium +5 Summit.[30] The pledges made at these summits, combined with other commitments, implied an increase in aid from $80 billion in 2004 to $130 billion in 2010, at constant 2004 prices. In 2008, total net ODA from members of the Development Assistance Committee of the Organization for Economic Cooperation and Development (OECD) rose by 10.2 percent in real terms to $119.8 billion. This is the highest dollar figure ever recorded (see Figure 7.2). It represents 0.30 percent of members' combined gross national income. Despite this increase,

FIGURE 7.2   Net official development assistance from OECD countries, 1992–2008

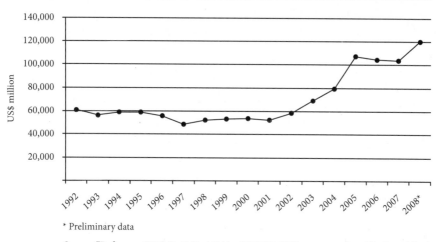

* Preliminary data

Source: "Reference DAC Statistical Tables," OECD, 2009, www.oecd.org/dac/stats/dac/reftables.

however, only five countries exceeded the UN target of 0.7 percent of gross national income: Denmark, Luxembourg, the Netherlands, Norway, and Sweden.[31] Nevertheless, environmental aid from both bilateral and multilateral aid agencies remains a small percentage of this figure. One study found that from 1980 until the end of the twentieth century, environmental aid increased from roughly $3 billion to about $10 billion a year.[32] To put this in perspective, the estimated cost of implementing Agenda 21 in 1992 was $561.5 billion a year, with the North bankrolling $141.9 billion (20 percent of the total cost) with low or no-interest lending. Of that, $15 billion a year of ODA was to be devoted to global environmental issues, with the rest targeting more localized sustainable development programs within developing countries.[33] So, while there has been "new and additional funding," the current and projected levels of ODA still fall far short of the estimates of what is necessary to achieve internationally agreed sustainable development goals.

The third principle is the "polluter pays principle," which seeks to ensure that the costs of environmental action, economic and other, will be borne by those who created the need for that action. As with other Rio principles, the South has argued that the polluter pays principle has been steadily diluted. They point to an increasing pattern of pushing treaty implementation steadily southwards, including in the climate, desertification, and biodiversity regimes, by seeking relatively fewer changes in behavior patterns in the North and relatively more in the South—even though northern behavior gave rise to many problems in the first place.[34]

Another consistent theme in developing-country views of global environmental issues is the inequality in governing structures of international organizations such as the World Bank, which allows a minority of donor countries to outvote the rest of the world. Developing countries have demanded that institutions making decisions on how to spend funds on the global environment should have a "democratic" structure, that is, one in which each country is equally represented. Thus, developing countries did some of their toughest bargaining in negotiations relating to the environment when they resisted the donor countries' proposed governance structure for the GEF.

The South also has demanded that transfer of environmental technologies on concessional or preferential terms be part of all agreements and treaties. In the Montreal Protocol negotiations, for instance, developing states requested a guarantee from the industrialized countries that corporations would provide them with patents and technical knowledge on substitutes for CFCs. In 1990, India tried unsuccessfully to have language included in the amended protocol that would subject the obligations of developing states to phase out CFCs to the private transfer of technology. This has also been a major issue in the climate-change negotiations.

Needless to say, developing countries remain frustrated with global environmental politics, an attitude clearly related to convictions that the global economic system remains unfairly skewed in favor of the advanced industrialized countries. On the one hand, one can argue that the concept of sustainable development has allowed developing countries to incorporate long-standing concerns about economic and social development into the environmental agendas; by doing so, they have influenced the nature of global environmental discourse.[35] On the other hand, the South claims that it has seen few benefits from its continuing involvement in global environmental politics. Much of North-South environmental relations in the more than seventeen years since Rio has focused on what the South sees as the North's failure to deliver what was promised or implied at Rio—new and additional financial resources, technology transfer, and capacity building. As the concept of sustainable development loses its policy edge, and as the key principles of additionality, common but differentiated responsibilities, and polluter pays are steadily eroded (at least in the South's view), developing countries have a diminishing interest in staying engaged in global environmental politics. Although southern disenchantment may not turn into total disengagement, it is certainly not conducive to meaningful North-South partnerships for what remain pressing global environmental challenges.[36]

ENVIRONMENT AND DEVELOPMENT

The North-South debate is one factor that has shaped global environmental politics since the 1970s. Increased awareness of environmental issues, improved scientific understanding of them, the increased number of countries involved in the negotiation of environmental treaties, and the relationships between trade and environment and particularly between environmental protection, economic development, and social development—the so-called three pillars of sustainable development—have also contributed to the current global environmental landscape.

Since the historic Stockholm Conference in 1972, the international community has framed environmental protection within the overall goal of sustainable development. The 1972 Stockholm Conference on the Human Environment was the first major event to address environmental deterioration. Fifteen years later, the 1987 Brundtland Report, *Our Common Future*, first brought the idea of sustainable development to the public's attention. Just five years later, UNCED achieved a pact, underpinned by a set of core principles, between countries of the North and South linking environmental and developmental concerns.

UNCED also launched a new round of global development conferences that would lead to the Millennium Assembly in 2000, where heads of state committed themselves to tackling poverty, malnutrition, and a host of other problems by 2015. The Millennium Assembly was soon followed by a second round of world conferences dealing with the difficulties faced by the world's least-developed countries as well as challenges in global trade and finance. The thirty-year process reached its culmination with the World Summit on Sustainable Development (WSSD) in Johannesburg, South Africa, in 2002. The Johannesburg summit marked a key juncture in the multilateral process initiated all those years ago in Stockholm. Johannesburg represented a crucial step in the efforts of the international community to deal with humankind's relationship with the natural environment. The WSSD was designed to bring the curtain down on a decade-long process aimed at establishing a global agenda for development. At Rio and the many meetings held subsequently, the multilateral agenda for achieving sustainable development emerged. At Johannesburg, the goal was to turn this agenda into something more.

Most interesting about this period of summits and world conferences is how the sustainable development agenda advanced. In the earlier years—up through Rio—the discussion was sectoral; that is, the environmental issues were discussed in parallel with issues of social and economic development, such as population, human settlements, education, health, poverty, trade, and finance. Agenda 21 illustrates this point; it contains eight chapters on social and economic issues and fourteen chapters on environmental issues. However, by the time delegates arrived in Johannesburg ten years after UNCED in Rio, the scope had changed, and the economic and social-development pillars received much greater emphasis, as can be seen in the structure of the Johannesburg Plan of Implementation, which contained one chapter on environmental issues and four chapters on economic and social development (see Table 7.1). This section will look at this trend and how it affects global environmental politics.

TABLE 7.1 The Evolving Three Pillars of Sustainable Development

AGENDA 21*

JOHANNESBURG PLAN
OF IMPLEMENTATION**

Chapters on Environmental Issues

- Protection of the atmosphere
- Planning and management of land resources
- Combating deforestation
- Combating desertification and drought
- Sustainable mountain development
- Sustainable agriculture and rural development
- Conservation of biological diversity
- Environmentally sound management of biotechnology
- Protection of the oceans and seas
- Protection of the quality and supply of freshwater resources
- Environmentally sound management of toxic chemicals
- Environmentally sound management of hazardous wastes
- Environmentally sound management of solid wastes and sewage
- Safe and environmentally sound management of radioactive wastes

Chapters on Social and Economic Issues

- Economic development and trade
- Combating poverty
- Changing consumption patterns
- Demographic dynamics
- Protecting and promoting human health
- Sustainable human-settlement development
- Integrating environment and development in decision making

Chapters on Environmental Issues

- Protecting and managing the natural resource base of economic and social development

Chapters on Social and Economic Issues

- Poverty eradication
- Changing unsustainable patterns of consumption and production
- Sustainable development in a globalizing world
- Health and sustainable development

Chapters on Regional Issues

- Sustainable development of small island developing states
- Sustainable development for Africa
- Other regional initiatives

* This does not reflect all forty chapters of Agenda 21, including chapters on means of implementation and major groups.

** This does not include the two chapters on means of implementation.

Agenda 21 was negotiated primarily by government delegates with expertise in environmental issues. Therefore, the one chapter on economic development and issues such as trade, debt, and macroeconomic policies did not receive as much attention during the negotiations. However, the changes in the global economy in the years following the Earth Summit—the rise of globalization being a dominant concern—characterized by rapidly increasing trade and capital flows, coupled with the revolution in information and communications technologies (such as the Internet), made countries more independent and more interconnected than ever before. Since 1990, the value of world trade has tripled, and the flows of foreign direct investment (companies investing in other countries) have increased fourteenfold.[37] Absolute priority has been given to expanding the scope for trade and investment in line with neoliberal economics (a political-economic movement, increasingly prominent since 1980, that deemphasizes or rejects government intervention in the economy and focuses on achieving progress, and even social justice, through promoting free market methods and emphasizing economic growth). For example, neoliberals argue that the best way to protect the environment is by overcoming poverty via increasing privatization, foreign direct investment, and free trade. As a result, the institutions governing the global economy have grown stronger, but those promoting social equity, poverty alleviation, and environmental cooperation remain weak. After 1990, the barriers to trade and investment began to fall, and the belief that poor countries could grow themselves out of poverty by boarding the liberalization express train took on almost a religious force in some rich countries.[38] If poorer countries supported trade liberalization, these people believed, many of their economic development problems would be solved.

Some viewed the trend toward globalization—the rapid growth and integration of markets, institutions, and cultures—as a threat; others saw it as an opportunity. Many policy makers and industrialists in the developed world were positive about the phenomenon. However, a majority of those living in developing countries or engaged in a variety of NGOs worried that environmental and labor standards were in a "race to the bottom" and that social and economic disparities were being exacerbated. Many NGOs were concerned that developing countries would eliminate or ignore environmental and labor standards in their efforts to attract foreign direct investment. There was a fear that if a host country demonstrated that it did not have strict pollution standards and did not condemn child labor or support an eight-hour work day, it would attract more corporate investment.[39]

In a speech delivered to the UNGA in April 2000 to launch the Millennium Report, former UN Secretary-General Kofi Annan tackled the globalization issue. Observing that the opportunities provided by this phenomenon were being distributed unequally, he called for a candid debate on the positive and negative consequences of globalization and for discussions about how to make globalization work for all people in all countries.

"How can we say that the half of the human race which has yet to make or receive a telephone call, let alone use a computer, is taking part in globalization?" he asked.[40]

In the first decade of the new millennium, a number of major international events focused on the various challenges to achieving sustainable development while taking into account the impact of globalization. Those organizing these events sought to provide a blueprint for global development through a new round of international obligations focusing on quantitative targets and means of implementation. This process started with, and has largely been shaped by, the Millennium Assembly.

The Millennium Assembly

To help prepare the United Nations to meet the challenges of the twenty-first century, the UNGA decided to designate its fifty-fifth session, starting on September 6, 2000, as the Millennium Assembly and to hold a Millennium Summit of world leaders to address the pressing challenges facing the world's people. At the Millennium Assembly, world leaders agreed to a far-reaching plan to support global development objectives for the new century. The world's leaders reaffirmed their commitment to work toward peace and security for all and a world in which sustainable development and poverty eradication would have the highest priority. The agreement, set out in the Millennium Declaration, addressed a wide range of core international issues relating to fundamental values and principles; peace, security, and disarmament; development and poverty eradication; the protection of the environment; human rights, democracy, and good governance; the needs of the most vulnerable; the special needs of Africa; and the strengthening of the United Nations. Set against a backdrop of widespread concern about the social and ecological implications of globalization, the Millennium Assembly placed the relationship between poverty, environmental decline, and economic development firmly in the international spotlight.[41]

The following year, Secretary-General Annan presented his report, titled *Road Map towards the Implementation of the United Nations Millennium Declaration* (UN document 56/326). The report contains, in an annex, eight development goals containing eighteen targets and forty-eight indicators, which are commonly known as the Millennium Development Goals (MDGs). The first seven goals are directed toward eradicating poverty in all its forms: halving extreme poverty and hunger, achieving universal primary education and gender equity, reducing the mortality of children under five by two-thirds and maternal mortality by three-quarters, reversing the spread of HIV/AIDS, halving the proportion of people without access to safe drinking water, and ensuring environmental sustainability. The final goal outlines measures for building a global partnership for development. The goals, targets, and indicators were developed following consultations held among members of the United Nations

Secretariat and representatives of the International Monetary Fund, the OECD, and the World Bank in order to harmonize reporting on the development goals in the Millennium Declaration and the international development goals (see Figure 7.3).

In a relatively short period, the MDGs gained tremendous currency, primarily in development circles, but increasingly in related trade and finance spheres. Many actors counted on the MDGs to galvanize disparate and sometimes competing development agendas. Increasingly, stakeholders viewed the MDGs as a powerful political tool to hold governments and international institutions accountable. A key reason for this is that the Millennium Declaration and its MDGs clarify the shared and individual roles and responsibilities of key stakeholders. The declaration sets out the responsibilities of governments to implement various specific goals and targets. It instructs the network of international organizations to marshal their resources and expertise in the most strategic and efficient way possible to support and sustain the efforts of partners at global and country levels. And it urges citizens, civil-society organizations, and the private sector to bring to the table their unique strengths for motivation, mobilization, and action.[42]

Over the next two years, other major international meetings reinforced the momentum achieved with the adoption of the MDGs. In Brussels at the third United Nations Conference on the Least Developed Countries in May 2001, governments addressed the needs of the least-developed countries, and in Doha at the fourth WTO ministerial conference in November 2001, they expressed the need to link sustainable development and trade. Meanwhile, in March 2002, the International Conference on Financing for Development in Monterrey, Mexico, supported the mobilization of resources to finance development; the June 2002 World Food Summit +5 in Rome confirmed the global commitment to eradicate hunger; and a series of special sessions of the UNGA promoted issues relating to women, social development, human settlements, and children.

The World Summit on Sustainable Development

All these issues came to a head at the WSSD in Johannesburg, South Africa, in 2002, held to map out a detailed course of action for the further implementation of Agenda 21. Once again, the issue of sustainable development was on the negotiating table, but the series of development-focused conferences over the previous two years definitely had an impact. The Johannesburg summit did not aim to renegotiate Agenda 21, but it did attempt to fill some key gaps that impeded its implementation and the shift to sustainable development.

The WSSD took place in a difficult international climate. The 1992 optimism about a large "peace dividend" that could be reallocated to sustainable development had deflated along with the rest of the world economy, especially in the year before the summit.

FIGURE 7.3   The Millennium Development Goals

BY 2015, ALL UN MEMBER STATES HAVE PLEDGED TO

Eradicate extreme poverty and hunger

- Reduce by half the proportion of people living on less than $1 per day
- Reduce by half the proportion of people who suffer from hunger

Achieve universal primary education

- Ensure that all boys and girls complete a full course of primary schooling

Promote gender equality and empower women

- Eliminate gender disparity in primary and secondary education, preferably by 2005, and at all levels of education no later than 2015

Reduce child mortality

- Reduce by two-thirds the mortality rate among children under five

Improve maternal health

- Reduce by three-quarters the maternal mortality ratio

Combat HIV/AIDS, malaria, and other diseases

- Halt and begin to reverse the spread of HIV/AIDS
- Halt and begin to reverse the incidence of malaria and other major diseases

Ensure environmental sustainability

- Integrate the principles of sustainable development into country policies and programs and reverse the loss of environmental resources
- Reduce by half the proportion of people without sustainable access to safe drinking water
- Achieve a significant improvement in the lives of at least 100 million slum dwellers by 2020

Develop a global partnership for development

- Develop further an open trading and financial system that is rule based, predictable, and nondiscriminatory (This target includes a commitment to good governance, development, and poverty reduction, both nationally and internationally.)
- Address the special needs of the least developed countries (This includes tariff- and quota-free access for their exports, enhanced debt relief for heavily indebted poor countries, cancellation of official bilateral debt, and more generous ODA for countries committed to poverty reduction.)
- Address the special needs of landlocked countries and small island developing states
- Deal comprehensively with the debt problems of developing countries through national and international measures in order to make debt sustainable in the long term
- In cooperation with developing countries, develop decent and productive work for youth
- In cooperation with pharmaceutical companies, provide access to affordable essential drugs in developing countries
- In cooperation with the private sector, make available the benefits of new technologies, especially information and communications technologies

Source: "Millennium Development Goals," United Nations, www.un.org/millenniumgoals.

One year after the September 11, 2001, terrorist attacks, the U.S. government, preoccupied with the war on terrorism and laying the groundwork for the war in Iraq, was generally indifferent and sometimes even hostile to environmental causes and multilateralism. The developing countries were wary of, and frustrated with, the industrialized countries. The failure to implement the Rio agreements effectively—especially the perceived lack of new and additional financial resources—had cast a long shadow and raised questions about the credibility and accountability of these large, multi-issue global conferences.[43]

The Johannesburg summit opened in August 2002, bringing together government representatives from more than 190 countries, including one hundred world leaders. An estimated 37,000 people attended either the summit or one of the many other gatherings held alongside the main event.[44] The difficult negotiations focused on an ambitious plan that would address poverty eradication, how to change unsustainable patterns of consumption and production, and the protection and management of natural resources. As in Stockholm and Rio, governments' views diverged on how to tackle issues ranging from water and sanitation to desertification, climate change, biodiversity, oceans, health, education, science and technology, trade, and finance. Indeed, at moments negotiations came to a standstill, and skeptics questioned the negotiators' commitment to sustainable development.

The summit produced three key outcomes: The first was the Johannesburg Declaration, a pledge by world leaders to commit their countries to the goal of sustainable development. The second was the Johannesburg Plan of Implementation, which sets out a comprehensive program of action for sustainable development and includes quantifiable goals and targets with fixed deadlines. Finally, the summit produced nearly three hundred voluntary partnerships and other initiatives to support sustainable development. Unlike the Johannesburg Declaration and the plan of implementation, this outcome was not the result of multilateral negotiations involving the entire community of nations. Instead, it involved numerous smaller partnerships comprising private-sector and civil-society groups, as well as governments, which committed themselves to a wide range of projects and activities.

Many of the commitments and partnerships agreed to in Johannesburg echoed the MDGs. For example, countries agreed to commit themselves to halving the proportion of people who lack clean water and proper sanitation by 2015. These commitments were backed up by a U.S. announcement of an investment of $970 million in water projects over the next three years and a European Union (EU) announcement to engage in partnerships to meet the new goals, primarily in Africa and Central Asia. The United Nations received twenty-one other partnership initiatives in this area and at least $20 million in extra resources.[45]

PHOTO 7.1   NGOs reminding governments about their responsibility to future generations in Bali, Indonesia, during the fourth meeting of the preparatory committee for the WSSD.
Courtesy IISD/*Earth Negotiations Bulletin.*

In energy, countries committed themselves to expanding access to the two billion people who do not have access to modern energy services. In addition, although countries did not agree on a target for phasing in renewable energy (e.g., a target of 15 percent of the global energy supply from renewable energy by 2010), which many observers said was a major shortcoming of the summit, they did commit to green energy and the phaseout of subsidies for types of energy inconsistent with sustainable development. And to bolster these commitments, a group of nine major electric companies signed agreements to undertake sustainable energy projects in developing countries. In addition, the EU announced a $700 million partnership initiative on energy, and the United States announced investments of up to $43 million for energy in 2003.[46]

On health issues, in addition to actions to fight HIV/AIDS and reduce water-borne diseases and the health risks caused by pollution, countries agreed to phase out, by 2020, the use and production of chemicals that harm human health and the environment. Many commitments were also made to protect biodiversity and improve ecosystem management. These include commitments to reduce biodiversity loss by 2010, to restore fisheries to their maximum sustainable yields by 2015, to establish a representative network of marine protected areas by 2012, and to improve developing countries' access to environmentally sound alternatives to ozone-depleting chemicals by 2010. These commitments were supported by thirty-two partnership initiatives submitted to the United Nations, with $100 million in additional resources, and a U.S. announcement of $53 million for forest management between 2002 and 2005.[47]

Yet, among all the targets, timetables, commitments, and partnerships agreed upon at Johannesburg, there were no silver-bullet solutions to aid the fight against poverty and a continually deteriorating natural environment. In fact, as an implementation-focused summit, Johannesburg did not produce a particularly dramatic outcome—no agreements emerged that will lead to new treaties, and many of the agreed targets had already been agreed upon at the Millennium Assembly and other meetings. As UN Secretary-General Kofi Annan told the press on the last day of the summit, "I think we have to be careful not to expect conferences like this to produce miracles. But we do expect conferences like this to generate political commitment, momentum and energy for the attainment of the goals."[48]

Among the summit's legacies was a shift in the balance of the three pillars of sustainable development. During the previous decade, sustainable development more often than not equaled protection of the environment. Johannesburg was the first true summit on sustainable development in the sense that advocates of all three pillars were under one roof arguing their cases, raising real issues, and confronting those with different interests and perspectives. It was not a social summit dealing only with poverty, exclusion, and human rights. It was not an economic and globalization summit addressing only trade and investment, finance, and the development and transfer of technology. And it was not an environmental summit focusing only on natural resource degradation, biodiversity loss, climate change, and pollution. Johannesburg was instead a summit about the intersections of all these issues.[49]

The Road to 2015: Challenges in Implementing the MDGs

In 2005, world leaders gathered once again in New York to reaffirm the MDGs and discuss related issues. Among the outcomes, the heads of state and government expressed their commitment to achieve the MDGs by 2015, pledged an additional $50 billion a year by 2010 to fight poverty, and addressed such issues as innovative financing for development, debt relief and restructuring, and trade liberalization.[50]

Developing countries and many international organizations have adopted the MDGs as their framework for international development cooperation. However, there have also been great contributions from the private sector and, critically, civil society in both developed and developing countries. This partnership has resulted in sound progress in some areas, and the UN fully expects a number of the targets to be reached by their target dates. *The Millennium Development Goals Report 2008* states the following:

- The overarching goal of reducing absolute poverty by half is within reach for the world as a whole.
- In all but two regions, primary school enrollment is at least 90 percent.
- Deaths from measles fell from over 750,000 in 2000 to less than 250,000 in 2006, and about 80 percent of children in developing countries now receive a measles vaccine.
- The number of deaths from AIDS fell from 2.2 million in 2005 to 2.0 million in 2007, and the number of people newly infected declined from 3 million in 2001 to 2.7 million in 2007.
- Malaria prevention is expanding, with widespread increases in insecticide-treated net use among children under five in sub-Saharan Africa. In sixteen out of twenty countries, use has at least tripled since around 2000.
- The incidence of tuberculosis is expected to be halted and begin to decline before the target date of 2015.
- Some 1.6 billion people have gained access to safe drinking water since 1990.
- The use of ozone-depleting substances (ODS) has nearly been eliminated, and this has contributed to the effort to reduce global warming.
- The share of developing countries' export earnings devoted to servicing external debt fell from 12.5 percent in 2000 to 6.6 percent in 2006, allowing them to allocate more resources to reducing poverty.
- The private sector has increased the availability of some critical essential drugs and rapidly spread mobile-phone technology throughout the developing world.[51]

In September 2009, the United Nations Children's Fund (UNICEF) reported that the child mortality rate has declined by more than a quarter in the last two decades— to 65 deaths per 1,000 live births last year from 90 in 1990. Yet, even with 10,000 fewer children dying per day, there is still a long way to go before we achieve the goal set by leaders of 189 nations in 2000: to cut the child mortality rate by two-thirds by 2015.[52] Thus, while these successes are encouraging, much more work remains to be done in certain areas to meet the 2015 targets. For example, the proportion of people in sub-Saharan Africa living on less than $1 per day is unlikely to be reduced by the target of one-half. Of the 113 countries that failed to achieve gender parity in both primary and secondary school enrollment by the target date of 2005, only 18 are likely to achieve the goal by 2015; in other words, girls are still not going to school in many countries. With regard to the empowerment of women, in one-third of developing countries, women still account for less than 10 percent of parliamentarians. In addition, more than 500,000 prospective mothers in developing countries die annually in childbirth or from complications due to pregnancy.[53]

On the environmental sustainability targets, approximately 2.5 billion people, almost half the developing world's population, still live without improved sanitation.

More than one-third of the growing urban population in developing countries lives in slum conditions. And CO_2 emissions have continued to increase, despite the Kyoto Protocol.[54]

Perspectives on the MDGs and their implementation differ. Some argue that the MDGs form just another set of international development goals in a long history of nations' setting and failing to achieve such goals. To name just two examples, in the 1960s the United Nations set its sights on universal primary education by 1980. In 1980 it committed to achieving 6.5 percent economic growth throughout the developing world by 1990. During the 1980s and 1990s, there was economic growth, poverty reduction, improved schooling, and much else to celebrate in the developing world, but these impossible goals were not met. Some believe that these types of broad global goals focus attention away from what was accomplished (through sound domestic policies, aid, and other forms of cooperation), creating an unnecessary impression of failure.[55]

The Center for Global Development, a Washington, D.C.–based think tank, argues that the vast majority of developing countries, especially in Africa, will probably miss most of the MDG targets in 2015. But this should not be taken as a sign that poor countries have failed or that aid has been a waste. Nor will it result from a lack of ODA. In fact, during the first decade of the millennium, many of the world's poorest countries have made great progress in improving the quality of life of their people. For example, in 2007 Burkina Faso in Africa had net primary school enrollment of 40 to 45 percent. Should it be considered a failure if a country achieves only 60 percent enrollment by 2015 instead of the MDG of 100 percent enrollment? Such a feat would be extraordinary by historical standards—but still a failure to achieve the MDG. By way of comparison, it took the United States over a century to transition from 40 percent enrollment to universal primary schooling.[56] As the Center for Global Development has argued, "development is a marathon, not a sprint."[57] From this perspective, failure to achieve the MDGs, provided that significant progress has been made, need not be seen as a failure in economic and social development.

Others argue that there needs to be a greater link between the MDGs and the environment. As noted earlier, there has been concern that the environmental pillar of sustainable development has been diminished in the context of the MDGs. Jeffrey Sachs and Walter Reid have noted that development goals cannot be achieved and sustained without sound environmental management. Similarly, environmental goals cannot be achieved without development. Yet the world underinvests in both, and developing and developed countries tend to overlook the policy link between poverty reduction and the environment.[58] For example, investing in environmental assets and management is vital to cost-effective and equitable strategies to achieve goals relating to poverty alleviation, hunger, and disease. Investments in improved agricultural practices to reduce water pollution by runoff, as well as the use of chemical fertilizers and pesticides, can also boost the coastal fishing industry. Wetlands protection can meet the needs of rural communities while avoiding the costs of expensive flood-control projects. Yet these investments are often overlooked.[59]

So what do the MDGs mean for global environmental politics? Some believe that the tide has turned away from the environment and toward the economic and social-development pillars of sustainable development. The MDGs, a large part of the overall UN agenda, and most bilateral and multilateral aid programs focus on these two areas. Seeing this, many environmental regimes have tried to show how their priorities are in fact aligned with the MDGs so that they will continue to receive attention within the larger development agenda that has overtaken much of the international community since the Millennium Summit. In some respects, "global environmental politics" have quite possibly become "global sustainable development politics." This trend, as well as the influence of the MDGs on how environmental issues are discussed, can be seen not only at the largest global conferences but also in regime negotiations and in the World Bank, the International Monetary Fund, the United Nations Development Programme, and even the Group of Eight (G-8). Does this represent a victory of sorts for developing countries? Does it present new obstacles to effective global environmental policy to address climate change, biodiversity loss, toxic chemicals, and other issues? Is it a new opportunity to mainstream environmental concerns into development discussions? Regardless of how the balance between the economic, social, and environmental pillars of sustainable development continues to evolve—along with the attention of policy makers—one thing is clear: Global environmental politics can no longer be examined in isolation from economic and social development issues.

TRADE AND THE ENVIRONMENT

Another issue that has had a significant impact on global environmental politics is the effects of trade policy on the environment. This is a bit ironic given the fact that the global trade system evolved for decades without a thought about its impact on the environment. When the GATT, the central pillar of the international trading system, was negotiated just after World War II, there was no mention of the word "environment." At that time, no one saw much connection between trade liberalization and environmental protection. In fact, for the next forty years, trade officials and their environmental counterparts pursued their respective agendas on nearly parallel tracks that rarely, if ever, intersected. The wake-up call for environmentalists was the U.S. ban on tuna from Mexico and Venezuela on the grounds that their fleets did not meet U.S. standards for minimizing dolphin kills in tuna fishing. In 1991, the GATT declared the U.S. ban illegal under the rules of international trade. U.S. environmentalists were alarmed that a national environmental law could be overturned by the GATT and began serious efforts to address the environmental implications of international trade policy.[60]

Concerned about by the potential impact of the proposed North American Free Trade Agreement (NAFTA) between the United States, Mexico, and Canada (negotiations on the treaty also began in 1991), U.S. environmentalists sought ways to influence the process. There was concern among environmentalists and organized labor that a trade agreement with Mexico might trigger a downward spiral in environmental and labor standards on both sides of the border as industry claims of competitive disadvantage induced governments to relax their environmental and labor regulations.[61] In response, U.S. environmentalists worked more closely than ever before with organized labor in the United States and with Mexican environmental groups and workers' organizations to build public concern and to lobby policy makers (especially the U.S. Congress, which needed to approve the trade pact for it to take effect) to incorporate their concerns into the treaty. The efforts succeeded, resulting in the first international trade agreement that included supplemental agreements on labor and environmental issues. This marked the beginning of a broader, mutual understanding and working relationship among some key labor, environmental, and consumer groups.

The GATT and the WTO constitute a regime that seeks to promote a common set of international trade rules, a reduction in tariffs and other trade barriers, and the elimination of discriminatory treatment in international trade relations.[62] The WTO, which was created in 1995, has the mandate to rule on a broad spectrum of issues from trade in goods and services to intellectual property rights, including issues affecting human health, the use of natural resources, and the protection of the environment.

The preamble to the 1994 treaty that established the WTO recognized that the organization should ensure "the optimal use of the world's resources in accordance with the objective of sustainable development."[63] This was a last-minute victory for environmentalists, although the statement is nonbinding. With this in mind, and with a desire to coordinate the policies in the field of trade and the environment, when trade ministers approved the results of the Uruguay Round negotiations in Marrakech, Morocco, in April 1994, they also decided to begin a work program on trade and environment in the WTO. Their decision, which established the WTO's Committee on Trade and Environment (CTE), ensured that the subject would be given a place on the WTO agenda. The CTE has been mandated to address key trade-and-environment issues, including ecolabeling, the WTO's relationship with multilateral environmental agreements, and the effects of environmental measures on market access. However, the CTE cannot make binding recommendations and has generally proven ineffective in making progress on substantive issues.

In November 2001, the WTO held its fourth ministerial conference in Doha, Qatar, and ministers agreed to set the current round of trade-liberalization negotiations in motion. They had attempted to start a new round of trade negotiations two years earlier at the third ministerial conference in Seattle, Washington, but were unable to agree on the agenda amid protests against the WTO and its policies by thousands of environmental, labor, and human rights activists. The Doha Ministerial Declaration launched a broad-based round of multilateral trade negotiations on nine topics—eight of which were supposed to be completed as a single undertaking by 2005: implementation, agriculture, services, industrial tariffs, subsidies, antidumping, regional trade agreements, and the environment. The declaration contained more language on both economic development and environmental issues, including fisheries subsidies, than any of its predecessors.

However, WTO member states failed to complete their negotiations in 2005, and while negotiations are likely to resume in 2010 or soon thereafter, controversy and lack of transparency still surround the WTO.[64] This section examines some of the key issues along the trade-and-environment nexus, specifically, the relationship between environmental treaties and the WTO, how environmental issues have been dealt with in the dispute-settlement process, ecolabeling, standards and certification, genetically modified organisms (GMOs), subsidies and the environment, and liberalizing trade in environmental goods and services.

Relationship Between Multilateral
Environmental Agreements and the WTO

More than twenty multilateral environmental agreements (MEAs) incorporate trade measures to help achieve their goals.[65] This means that the agreements use restraints on trade in particular substances or products, either between parties to the treaty or between parties and nonparties, or both. Although this includes a relatively small number of MEAs, they are some of the most important, including the Convention on International Trade in Endangered Species of Wild Fauna and Flora (CITES); the Montreal Protocol; the Basel, Rotterdam, and Stockholm conventions; and the Cartagena Protocol on Biosafety. Under all these treaties, trade in the specified products (endangered species, controlled ODS, hazardous wastes, toxic chemicals, and GMOs) is banned or restricted between parties or between parties and nonparties.

CITES, which was negotiated in the early 1970s before trade became an issue for environmentalists, uses a number of different trade measures to promote compliance. It invokes trade restrictions against parties and nonparties to protect listed species of animals and plants threatened with extinction and endangerment. CITES also uses a permit-and-listing system to prohibit the import or export of listed wildlife and wildlife products unless a scientific finding is made that the trade in question will not threaten the existence of the species. These trade provisions are designed to severely constrict the market demand for wildlife and wildlife products and, it is hoped, reduce the international market demand for the products, thereby discouraging the initial taking of the wildlife.

The Montreal Protocol prohibits trade in ODS with nonparties unless the nonparty has demonstrated its full compliance with the control measures under the protocol. The protocol seeks to restrict the global market in the consumption and production of ODS; it uses trade provisions to encourage the phaseout of these substances and to discourage the establishment of "pollution havens" in which parties shift their manufacturing capabilities to nonparties. In reducing market demand, the protocol reduces the release of these substances into the atmosphere and provides an incentive for the development of benign substitutes.

The Basel Convention uses trade measures to limit the market for the transboundary movement and disposal of hazardous waste between OECD and non-OECD countries. The agreement's trade provisions encourage the management of waste in an environmentally sound manner and with prior informed consent. The convention also provides that a party shall not permit hazardous waste or other wastes to be traded with a nonparty unless that party enters into a bilateral, multilateral, or regional agreement.[66]

Under the Rotterdam Convention, parties can decide, from the convention's agreed list of chemicals and pesticides, which ones they will not import. When trade in the controlled substances does take place, labeling and information requirements must be followed. Decisions taken by the parties must be trade neutral; if a party decides not to consent to imports of a specific chemical, it must also stop domestic production of the chemical for domestic use, as well as imports from nonparties.[67]

The Cartagena Protocol on Biosafety states that parties may restrict the import of some living GMOs as part of a carefully specified risk-management procedure. Living GMOs that will be intentionally released into the environment are subject to an advance informed-agreement procedure, and those destined for use as food, feed, or processing must be accompanied by identifying documents.[68]

Trade-restricting measures in an environmental agreement may serve one of two broad purposes. First, they may control a type of trade perceived to be a source of the environmental damage that the convention seeks to address. CITES, which requires import and export licenses for trade in endangered species, is a good example. The Basel Convention seeks to restrict or ban the movement and trade of hazardous waste, seeing such movement as a source of environmental harm. The Rotterdam Convention calls on parties to notify other parties before they make certain types of exports and allows parties to ban some imports, because the trade of toxic substances to countries unaware of their potential for harm can lead to environmental damage. Second, they may control trade as a means to ensure regime participation, compliance, and effectiveness. Some regimes use trade measure as an additional incentive to join and adhere to the MEA by barring nonparties from trading in restricted goods with parties. Nonparties to the Basel Convention, for example, cannot ship waste to any of the parties; nor can they import it from them. Some, like the Montreal Protocol, have provisions that would allow parties to impose trade sanctions on countries found to have significantly violated regimes rules (to date, this has not been used in the ozone regime). Some use trade restrictions as a means to enhance regime effectiveness, again by restricting trade in certain controlled substances (as a means to reinforce controls on production and use) or with nonparties. This prevents "leakage," that is, situations where nonparties or parties with exemptions simply increase production of a restricted good and ship it to the parties that have restricted their own production.[69]

The potential problem with using trade measures in MEAs is that they might conflict with WTO rules. An agreement that says parties can use trade restrictions against some countries (nonparties) but not against others (parties) could violate Articles I, III, and XI of the GATT (provisions addressing most-favored nations and national-treatment principles, as well as provisions on eliminating quantitative restrictions). Free trade advocates worry that countries might use trade-restricting measures in an MEA as a means to seek economic gain or to reward friends and punish enemies rather than protect the global environment. Environmentalists worry that countries impacted by MEA trade restrictions might challenge their legitimacy before the WTO, which could weaken the MEA.

Most analysts argue that the latter is not particularly a problem when both countries involved are parties to the MEA. In such cases both countries have voluntarily agreed to be bound by the MEA's rules, including the use of trade measures as spelled out in the agreement. However, problems can arise when the agreement spells out objectives only and leaves it to the parties to make domestic laws to achieve them. Parties to the Kyoto Protocol, for example, may fulfill their obligations (spelled out in the protocol) to lower GHG emissions by any number of trade-restrictive measures (not spelled out). Although WTO members have expressed hope that disputes between parties might be settled within the MEAs themselves, a party complaining about the use of such nonspecific trade measures would almost certainly choose to take its case to the WTO.[70]

The situation is further complicated if a party to an MEA uses trade measures in the agreement against a nonparty, but both countries are WTO members. Here, the nonparty has not voluntarily agreed to be subjected to the MEA's trade measures. As with party-to-party measures, the trade-restricting party may be violating the nonparty's rights under WTO rules, but here the nonparty might take the matter to the WTO even if the measures are spelled out specifically in the MEA.

This raises the crucial question of which regime, the MEA or the WTO, should be accorded primacy when they conflict. The relationship between the WTO and MEA trade measures has been part of the CTE's agenda within the WTO since its creation in 1995. However, its most recent discussions are taking place under the mandate of paragraphs 31 and 32 of the Doha Ministerial Declaration, which deal with the relationship between existing WTO rules and specific trade obligations set out in MEAs.[71] Thus far, parties have not made much progress, largely as a result of the overall state of the Doha round of trade negotiations. Continued efforts will be required to reach common ground on these aspects of the mandate, with the objective of achieving an outcome that will equally benefit trade, the environment, and development.

Environmental Issues and the WTO Dispute Settlement System

Given the explosive growth of environmental policy over the last three decades, to the extent that it increasingly affects economic policy, it is not surprising that disputes between trade liberalization and environmental protection have risen in prominence. Indeed, the first case heard by the WTO Dispute Settlement Body involved an environmental dispute.[72]

An increasing number of domestic and international policies seek to regulate or restrict trade as a tool to address environmental problems. Such laws have been called environmental trade measures (ETMs) and include import prohibitions, product standards, standards governing production of natural resource exports, and mandatory ecolabeling schemes.[73] But exporters disadvantaged by such environmental measures sometimes charge that they are intended to protect domestic producers from foreign competition. Sometimes, the governments of the exporting countries have brought such complaints to the WTO's dispute-resolution panels.

The United States has taken the lead in defending the right to use ETMs for domestic and international environmental objectives and has been the target of cases brought before WTO dispute panels. As the largest national market in world trade, the United States can exert pressure on the environmental and trade policies of other countries, and it has been pressured by U.S. environmental NGOs to do so, especially in marine-conservation issues. The United States used trade restrictions in conjunction with its leadership role to end commercial whaling, to protect dolphins from excessive killing by tuna fishermen, to improve protection of marine mammals from the use of destructive drift nets, and to support CITES. For example, the U.S. threatened to ban South Korean fish products from the U.S. market and prohibit Korean fishing operations in U.S. waters, persuading South Korea to give up whaling as well as drift-net operations in the Pacific Ocean.[74] The United States banned wildlife-related exports from Taiwan in 1994 after that country violated CITES by failing to control trade in rhino horn and tiger bone. Although environmentalists see these as justifiable protections, less powerful countries view the United States as throwing its weight around.

Environmental NGOs have long argued that basic trade rules and institutions have been systematically biased against the environment: When the GATT was created in the 1940s, the environment was not an issue. Trade rules and mechanisms that are used to handle disputes between trading partners have long been geared primarily to removing barriers to free trade. The deliberations of GATT/WTO dispute panels are carried out in secret with no opportunity for nongovernmental testimony or briefs. All this adds up to a secret trial (for that is what these deliberations are) without benefit of expert witnesses, observers, or the opportunity to appeal

GATT/WTO dispute-resolution panels have the authority to determine whether a particular trade measure is compatible with the GATT articles based on a complaint by a state alleging that the measure has restricted its market access unfairly. These panels consist of trade specialists from three or five contracting parties with no stake in the issue and who have been agreed to by both parties to the dispute. Dispute panel rulings are normally submitted to the WTO Council (which includes all parties to the agreement) for approval. Under the old GATT dispute-resolution rules, a ruling could be vetoed by one member of the GATT Council. However, the WTO provides for automatic acceptance of a dispute panel ruling by the WTO Council within sixty days unless there is a consensus within the council to reject it. Decisions carry real weight. If a country fails to bring its law into conformity with the decision, other states are allowed to implement retaliatory trade measures. This is more threatening to small countries than large trading countries such as the United States. Few small countries will risk taking significant retaliatory measures on their own against the United States or the EU, as these could prove counterproductive. One exception was when Ecuador sought WTO approval for retaliatory sanctions against the EU for the EU's failure to comply with the WTO ruling on its banana-import regime, which discriminated against a number of South and Central American banana-exporting countries. However, realizing that as a small country, imposing punitive tariffs on EU imports would have had little impact on the EU but a devastating effect on Ecuador's consumers, Ecuador said it would seek to target intellectual property rights and services for retaliation.[75]

U.S. laws that mandate trade measures to pursue environmental goals have been challenged before the GATT/WTO dispute-resolution panels on several occasions. The first panel decision, on the U.S.-Mexican tuna-dolphin dispute, helped to shape the politics of trade-and-environment issues.

In 1991 Mexico filed a complaint with the GATT charging that a U.S. embargo against Mexican yellowfin tuna was a protectionist measure on behalf of the U.S. tuna industry. The embargo had been imposed under an amendment to the 1972 Marine

Mammal Protection Act (MMPA), which included provisions to use trade sanctions against countries that killed too many dolphins while catching tuna (the Mexican fleet killed dolphins at twice the rate of the U.S. fleet). The complaint to the GATT claimed the amendment was simply a measure to protect the U.S. tuna fleet. It also argued that the U.S. measures should not be allowed to apply to activities in international waters, where most of the tuna was caught. More broadly, Mexico, supported by Venezuela, asked why they should forgo export earnings and a low-cost source of protein for their own people to reduce the incidental impact on a marine mammal that was not an endangered species.[76]

The GATT panel found that the U.S. ban was a violation of the GATT because it was concerned only with the process of tuna fishing rather than with the product. It also ruled that Article XX of the GATT, which allows trade restrictions for human health or the conservation of animal or plant life, cannot justify an exception to that rule because the article does not apply beyond U.S. jurisdiction. This was a historic decision. The GATT panel's ruling on the tuna-dolphin issue reflects the tendency of most trade specialists to view restrictions on trade for environmental purposes as setting dangerous precedents that could harm the world trade system. That eight governments or agencies spoke against the U.S. tuna ban before the panel and not one party spoke for it may also have had an influence.[77]

The decision came at an embarrassing moment, when the United States and Mexico were negotiating NAFTA. Because both governments really wanted the agreement, the United States was able to work out an agreement with Mexico that prevented the GATT panel decision from being presented to the GATT Council for formal approval and implementation. But in 1994, the European Union brought a second complaint against the U.S. tuna ban to a GATT dispute panel to secure resolution on the principle of extraterritorial unilateral actions. The EU charged that its exports of tuna were adversely affected by the MMPA's "secondary embargo" against imports of tuna from intermediary nations that fail to certify they do not buy tuna from nations embargoed under the law.

The GATT panel again found the U.S. ban incompatible with the GATT articles, but it accepted two key contentions of environmental critics of the GATT. It rejected the EU's arguments that dolphins are not an exhaustible natural resource and that Article XX applies only to the protection of resources located within the territory of the country applying the trade measure in question. But it held that such measures could be used only to conserve those resources directly and not to change the policy of another state—a distinction that is difficult, if not impossible, for policy makers to apply in practice—and thus found the U.S. MMPA incompatible with the GATT.[78]

Although Mexico won the case, the prospect that more refined versions of the MMPA's embargo would withstand WTO scrutiny made many developing countries even more determined to create international rules against what they regarded as unfair trade restrictions masquerading as environmental policy. Meanwhile, many environmental NGOs in the United States began to press even harder for changes in the GATT, including provisions that would give wider latitude for ETMs covering issues beyond the jurisdiction of the importing country.[79]

In two other cases, the EU challenged U.S. laws meant to increase fuel efficiency in automobiles sold in the United States—the 1978 gas guzzler tax and the **Corporate Average Fuel Economy (CAFE) standards**.[80] The gas guzzler tax levied taxes on cars with fuel efficiencies below 22.5 miles per gallon, with the size of the tax depending on how far it fell below the minimum. The EU argued that treatment of its cars under the measure was discriminatory since the tax fell disproportionately on cars of European origin and that the measure was not effective in conserving fuel because only a small proportion of cars in the U.S. market were subject to the tax. The GATT panel found that the gas guzzler tax did not unfairly protect U.S. auto manufacturers and that, although the measure may not be as effective in fuel conservation as a fuel tax, it has had the desired effect. While environmentalists applauded the decision to uphold the U.S. law, many were troubled that a GATT panel with essentially no environmental expertise was also making a judgment about what is the best conservation strategy.

On the CAFE standards, the GATT panel ruled slightly differently. The CAFE legislation, passed in 1975, sought to double the average fuel efficiency of the automobiles sold in the U.S. market within ten years. It requires that automakers' domestic fleets average at least 27.5 miles per gallon of gasoline and that the total fleet of foreign-made automobiles sold in the U.S. market must meet the same average. Failure to meet the fleet average results in a fine of $5 for every tenth of a mile per gallon below that average multiplied by the number of automobiles in the manufacturer's fleet. U.S. manufacturers could average their large fuel-consuming vehicles with smaller, more fuel-efficient models; European manufacturers, who sell almost entirely larger luxury automobiles in the U.S. market, could not. The EU argued that the law worked to the disadvantage of limited-line car producers concentrating on the top of the car market and that individual European cars were treated differently from domestic cars. The United States insisted that the CAFE legislation was based on objective criteria and was not aimed at affording protection to domestic production.

The panel found that CAFE was intended to promote fuel efficiency. But the requirement that foreign fleets must be accounted for separately, based on ownership and control relationships rather than characteristics of the products themselves, was found to give foreign cars less favorable conditions of competition than domestically produced cars and was also not aimed at conserving fuel. It concluded that the separate foreign-fleet accounting could not be justified under the exceptions in Article XX(g) and recommended that the United States be requested to amend the CAFE regulation to eliminate that requirement, which it did.[81]

Two other environmental complaints that have been brought under WTO dispute settlement rules are worth noting because of their precedent-setting nature. In the Venezuela reformulated-gasoline case, Venezuela and Brazil claimed they were discriminated against by a U.S. Environmental Protection Agency rule under the Clean Air Act that required all refineries to make cleaner gasoline using the 1990 U.S. industry standard as a baseline. Because fuel from foreign refineries was not as "clean" in 1990 as that from U.S. refineries, the importing countries were starting their cleanup efforts from a different starting point. The WTO panel ruled in 1997 for Venezuela and Brazil, and the Environmental Protection Agency revised its rules.[82]

In a second case, in January 1997, India, Malaysia, Pakistan, and Thailand charged that a U.S. ban on the importation of shrimp caught by vessels that kill endangered migratory sea turtles violated WTO rules that no nation can use trade restrictions to influence the (fishing) rules of other countries. The United States argued that relatively simple and inexpensive turtle-excluder devices (TEDs) can be placed on shrimp trawlers to save the turtles. To implement the U.S. Endangered Species Act, the U.S. Court of International Trade, in response to a lawsuit brought forth by an NGO, the Earth Island Institute, ruled in December 1995 that in order to export mechanically caught marine shrimp to the United States, countries that trawl for shrimp in waters where marine turtles live must, from June 1996, be certified by the U.S. government to have equipped their vessels with TEDs. TEDs have been mandatory on all U.S. shrimp trawlers since December 1994. If properly installed and operated, TEDs, while minimizing loss of the shrimp catch, permit most sea turtles to escape from shrimp trawling nets before they drown. The United States argued the trade measure was necessary because sea turtles were threatened with extinction and the use of TEDs on shrimp nets was the only way to effectively protect them from drowning in shrimp nets.

In April 1998, the WTO dispute settlement panel held that the U.S. import ban on shrimp was "clearly a threat to the multilateral trading system" and consequently was "not within the scope of measures permitted under the chapeau of Article XX." The United States appealed the decision, and in October 1998 the appellate body found that the U.S. ban legitimately related to the "protection of exhaustible natural resources" and thus qualified for provisional justification under Article XX(g). This decision represented a step forward for the use of unilateral trade measures for environmental purposes. But the decision also found that the U.S. import ban was applied in an unjustifiably or arbitrarily discriminatory manner and cited seven distinct flaws in the legislation. It found, for example, that the requirement that all exporters adopt "essentially the same policy" as that applied by the United States had an unjustifiably "coercive effect" on foreign countries. It also found that the United States had not seriously attempted to reach a multilateral solution with the four complaining countries and that the process for certification of turtle protection programs was not "transparent" or "predictable."[83]

The ruling thus left open the possibility that a unilaterally imposed trade ban in response to foreign environmental practices could be implemented in compliance with the GATT. But some trade law experts believed the procedural criteria in the ruling were unrealistic. The case once again underlined the question of whether a WTO panel, which lacks both environmental expertise and mandate, should pass judgment on trade measures for environmental purposes.

In response to the appellate body decision, the United States adjusted its policy. The new guidelines still prohibited the import of shrimp harvested with technology adversely affecting the relevant sea turtle species. But instead of requiring the use of TEDs by the exporting country, it allowed the exporting country to present evidence that its program to protect sea turtles in the course of shrimp trawling was comparable in effectiveness to the U.S. program. The guidelines noted, however, that the Department of State was not aware of technology as effective as the TED.[84]

Ecolabeling, Standards, and Certification

Ecolabels are labels indicating that certain products are better for the environment. They help consumers exercise preferences for environmentally sound production methods for products, such as wood harvested from sustainably managed forests rather than clear-cutting or tuna caught with methods that do not kill large numbers of dolphins. Although some ecolabels are conferred by product firms themselves or by trade associations, the ones with the most credibility are "third-party" ecolabels awarded by independent entities that use clear and consistent criteria to evaluate the process and production methods by which a product is made, grown, or caught. Some governments sponsor ecolabel programs but some of the most important are private, voluntary schemes. Third-party ecolabels have already demonstrated their potential for attracting the attention of producers where international policy making has failed, as shown by the case of the Forest Stewardship Council (FSC) and timber products.

Certification and labeling became an international issue after the establishment in 1993 of the FSC, an independent NGO that created the world's first third-party ecolabeling scheme for wood products. By 1995, the FSC had begun to set standards for sustainable forest management and criteria for potential certifiers to meet and had released a label that could be used to show that a product is certified by FSC standards. The FSC hoped to create a market for certified forest products among consumers and to use that market to leverage more sustainable forest management. Today, the FSC's governing body comprises more than 827 member organizations and individuals equally divided among environmental, social, and economic voting "chambers." FSC members include environmental organizations such as WWF, Greenpeace, and Friends of the Earth, as well as companies such as IKEA and Home Depot.

The FSC has the support of a large and growing number of companies that have united themselves in various countries into "buyers groups" committed to selling only independently certified timber and timber products. The FSC-labeling scheme is the preferred scheme for buyers groups in numerous countries, including Austria, Belgium, Brazil, Germany, Japan, the Netherlands, Switzerland, the United Kingdom, and the United States. This unprecedented alliance of major companies, NGOs, and other supporters has resulted in arguably greater levels of dialogue and progress than the formal international negotiations and has begun to change forest-management practices worldwide. In 2008, over 100 million hectares of forested land were FSC certified in over seventy-eight countries around the world—the equivalent of roughly 7 percent of the world's production forests. The value of FSC-labeled sales is estimated at over $20 billion, demonstrating that there is a demand for sustainably managed timber and timber products.[85]

Similarly, the London-based Marine Stewardship Council (MSC) has developed an environmental standard for sustainable and well-managed fisheries. It uses a product label to reward environmentally responsible management and practices. Consumers concerned about overfishing can choose seafood products that have been independently assessed against the MSC standard and labeled to prove it. The MSC, which was developed by Unilever, the world's largest buyer of seafood, and WWF in 1997, has operated independently since 1999 and succeeded in bringing together supporters from more than one hundred organizations in more than twenty countries. By the end of 2008, thirty-five fisheries had been certified, representing over 8 percent of global wild fisheries production for human consumption. Another seventy-five or so fisheries are currently undergoing assessment, and over one hundred major seafood buyers, including large supermarket chains in France, Germany, the Netherlands, Switzerland, the United Kingdom, and the United States, have pledged to purchase MSC-certified seafood products. Overall, there are approximately 1,900 MSC-certified fish products on sale in forty countries—ranging from fresh, frozen, smoked, and canned fish to fish-oil dietary supplements.[86]

In addition to the FSC and the MSC, there are over three hundred different types of ecolabels, which can get quite confusing for the consumer regarding which systems are the most valid (see Figure 7.4). Although the FSC, MSC, and some other initiatives have proven quite successful, ecolabeling systems do have the potential to be unfair and discriminatory. Consequently, while labeling and related issues had been discussed within several WTO bodies for some time, at Doha governments gave the CTE a formal mandate to address the issue and make recommendations, including possibly calling for new negotiations.[87]

FIGURE 7.4   **Examples of ecolabels**

Forest Stewardship
Council

WaterSense

Green Restaurant
Association

Energy Star

Marine Stewardship
Council

Fairtrade

Developed and developing countries have expressed justifiable concerns about some government-sponsored ecolabeling schemes that are skewed in favor of domestic producers and against foreign competitors. An ecolabeling scheme may convey an advantage to a domestic industry by virtually mandating a particular technology or production process, ignoring that another technology or process may be equally or more environmentally sound and more suitable in the country of origin. Some countries are also hostile to private ecolabeling schemes because they threaten to reduce markets for a domestic industry guilty of unsustainable practices. The transparency of official and private voluntary ecolabeling schemes and the ability of affected exporters to participate in their development thus emerged as an issue in the WTO.

The current discussions on environmental standards and certification requirements show areas of both consensus and divergence. There appears to be consensus that voluntary, participatory, market-based, and transparent environmental labeling schemes are potentially efficient economic instruments for informing consumers about environmentally friendly products. Almost all members agree on the need for transparency in developing and implementing ecolabeling schemes to avoid disadvantaging foreign producers. However, many developing—and some developed—countries remain wary of further discussion in this area because of concerns that stronger environmental standards and certification regimes could prove a barrier to their market access.[88]

Genetically Modified Organisms

The issue of genetically modified organisms has led to major trade conflicts between the United States and other major agricultural exporters and the European Union. People and governments in different parts of the world react to agricultural biotechnology in different ways. Countries' diverging attitudes on GMOs may reflect different approaches toward science, different levels of influence of the biotechnology industry, or the different levels of risk that governments and people in different parts of the world are willing to accept.

The WTO is not the only international organization to address trade in GMOs. International standards have also been established by the Cartagena Protocol on Biosafety as well as with the relevant guidelines adopted by the World Health Organization and United Nations Food and Agriculture Organization (FAO) Codex Alimentarius Commission in 2003 and by the International Convention on Plant Protection. The Cartagena Protocol takes a precautionary approach and establishes an advance informed-agreement procedure for ensuring that countries are provided with the information necessary to make informed decisions before agreeing to the import of such organisms into their territory.[89] The Codex Alimentarius Commission set forth a risk-analysis process for foods derived from modern biotechnology that is consistent with the Codex Working Principles for Risk Analysis.[90] The International Convention on Plant Protection set forth guidelines for National Plant Protection Organizations on the assessment of living modified organisms regarding pest risk.[91] Thus, all three of these approaches are based on the precautionary principle and feature the importance of risk analysis.

The WTO, on the other hand, bases its view largely on the perspective that restricting GMO imports could negatively impact global agricultural trade. When assessing the rationale behind a country's position on labeling genetically modified crops and derived products, it is important to place it within the context of that country's domestic agricultural policies and adoption of GMO technologies. Exporters of genetically modified crops, including the United States, believe that the European Union and countries that are opposed to, or do not have access to, the necessary technology are using GMO-labeling as an unjustified form of protectionism. Countries seeking to restrict imports of genetically modified crops say that concerns remain regarding the potential health and environmental impacts of the technology and that the scope of possible impacts justifies taking actions in the absence of conclusive scientific information. At the foundation of many of the differences in the GMO debate is this difference among national approaches to regulation.[92]

This issue came before the WTO in May 2003 when the United States, supported by Canada and Argentina, launched a case against the EU authorization regime for GMOs. Canada, Argentina, and the United States asserted that the moratorium applied by the European Community (EC) since October 1998 on the approval of biotech products had restricted imports of agricultural and food products from their countries. They also asserted that a number of EC member states maintain national marketing and import bans on biotech products even though the EC had already approved some of those products for import and marketing in the EC.[93] In an unusual move, the WTO panel stated that it would be unwise to rule on such a complex topic without hearing the views of scientists. The panel eventually decided to gather the views of independent and highly reputable scientists from different parts of the world, including Europe and the United States. The EU argued that this consultation process confirmed the legitimacy of the health and environmental issues addressed in EU regulations and procedures.[94] However, three years later, the WTO ruled that the EU's de facto ban on genetically modified food imports violated world trade rules.[95]

Implementation of the WTO ruling has been problematic, as EU member states each have their own regulations about genetically modified food and feed, and some regions within countries have declared themselves genetically modified–free zones. While some European officials have tried to emphasize risk-assessment criteria over political considerations in the approval process, they have not had much success. The main problem lies in implementing the EU's revised legislation under conditions of adverse public attitudes toward GMOs and the strong resistance of several EU member countries against lifting their unilateral bans on genetically modified crops. Six countries had such bans at the time of the WTO verdict—Austria, France, Germany, Greece, Italy, and Luxembourg. While Italy subsequently lifted its ban, Hungary adopted one. In late 2007 the EU Commission (the EU's executive branch based in Brussels) proposed that the unilateral bans must be lifted, but the Council of Ministers did not support the proposal. A reversal of the EU's GMO policy is unlikely because of low public acceptance of genetically modified food, low trust in regulators, pressure by NGOs, significant opposition to genetically modified crops among farmers, strong incentives for food processors and retailers to stay away or withdraw from the market for genetically modified foods, and institutional inertia in EU policy making.[96]

Subsidies and the Environment

Another issue on the trade-and-environment agenda is what the CTE calls "the environmental benefits of removing trade restrictions and distortions"—a diplomatic euphemism for eliminating subsidies that harm the environment. A **subsidy** may be defined as any government-directed intervention that, whether through budgeted programs or other means, transfers resources to a particular economic group. Subsidies distort markets by sending signals to producers and consumers that fail to reflect the true costs of production, thus misallocating financial and natural resources. And subsidies to goods traded internationally give unfair advantages to exports that are subsidized over others.

Subsidies can also have negative impacts on the environment, especially in the commodity sectors (agriculture, forests, and fisheries). They draw a higher level of investment into these sectors and exacerbate the overexploitation of land, forests, and fish.

They can also reduce the cost of particular practices, products, or technologies that harm the environment, such as flood irrigation, mining, or excessive use of pesticides.[97]

Eliminating environmentally harmful subsidies represents a rare win-win solution in which trade liberalization benefits the environment. The Uruguay Round represented the first substantial step toward subsidy removal in agriculture, and the United States and the Cairns Group, a coalition of industrialized and developing countries supportive of agricultural trade liberalization, persuaded the EU to accept a 20 percent reduction in agricultural subsidies. But subsidies to fisheries and forests remained outside the agreement.

Fisheries subsidies are one of the factors that have led to massive overfishing (see the fisheries case in Chapter 5). Fisheries subsidies total between $16 and $20 billion per year worldwide (roughly 25 percent of the value of global fish catches). This not only negatively impacts the world's fish stocks but also harms developing countries as they confront the excess capacity exported from the mostly depleted fisheries of richer countries. The global fishing fleet ballooned in the past forty years, and government subsidies worldwide contributed to this growth.[98] Since the establishment of the CTE, some members have focused on the elimination of fisheries subsidies as possibly the greatest contribution the multilateral trading system could make to sustainable development. In particular, the lead-state coalition known as the Friends of Fish (Australia, Chile, Ecuador, Iceland, New Zealand, Peru, the Philippines, and the United States) pointed to the "win-win-win" nature of such action: good for the environment, good for development, and good for trade. Their major argument is that subsidies are at least partly responsible for the alarming depletion of many fish stocks because much of the money is spent on commissioning new vessels or enhancing the efficiency of older boats.[99] But a veto coalition consisting of heavily subsidizing members (EU, Japan, and South Korea) argued that empirical evidence that subsidy elimination would benefit the environment was still weak. Japan and South Korea insisted that poor fisheries management, rather than subsidies, was the root cause of stock depletion.

Subsidy elimination was one of the most hotly contested issues in the preparations for the 1999 WTO ministerial conference in Seattle. The Friends of Fish pushed for the inclusion of a paragraph in the draft ministerial declaration for the Seattle WTO summit calling for a working group on fisheries subsidies. And a disputed paragraph in the draft called for "further substantial reductions in export subsidies, including commitments resulting in the elimination of such subsidies." While protestors were stealing the headlines, the EU and Japan agreed with the United States on language endorsing the aim of ending agricultural subsidies in return for U.S. concessions on other trade issues, but the two sides could not agree on a timetable for eliminating subsidies before the talks collapsed.

PHOTO 7.2   **Protests at the WTO ministerial conference in Seattle, Washington, in 1999.**
Photo by Al Crespo.

The Friends of Fish, however, didn't give up and were able to put the issue of fisheries subsidies firmly on the WTO agenda in Doha. The Doha Ministerial Declaration explicitly called for negotiations aimed at clarifying and improving WTO rules on fisheries subsidies. The mandate reflected the concerns of the potentially harmful trade, developmental and environmental effects of subsidies to the fisheries sector, and the benefits that stronger WTO rules would achieve. WTO negotiations on fisheries subsidies since Doha have taken place in the WTO's Rules Committee. After languishing for several years, the discussions took off in June 2004. It was then no longer a question of whether, but of how, international cooperation to reform fisheries subsidies should move forward. These developments—along with signs that leading developing countries would support a deal that included solid "special and differential treatment" language—paved the way for a breakthrough agreement at the December 2005 WTO ministerial conference in Hong Kong.[100]

The ministerial declaration from the Hong Kong meeting called on the Negotiating Group on Rules to "strengthen disciplines on subsidies in the fisheries sector, including through the prohibition of certain forms of fisheries subsidies that contribute to overcapacity and over-fishing."[101] In the two years following the Hong Kong ministerial, various WTO delegations submitted technical proposals on a range of fisheries subsidies topics. These submissions revealed convergence on some points and conflict on others. The first draft of a fisheries subsidies legal text was issued by the Negotiating Group on Rules chairman in November 2007. The draft's proposals include:

- prohibiting a broad range of directly capacity- or effort-enhancing fisheries subsidies, as well as any subsidies affecting fishing on "unequivocally overfished stocks";
- exempting several specific classes of subsidies from the prohibition (e.g., for vessel safety or reducing fishing capacity);
- subjecting most permitted fisheries subsidies to the condition that basic fisheries management systems be in place;
- allowing developing countries to use most prohibited subsidies, subject to fisheries management and other conditionalities;
- creating a mechanism for involving the FAO in the review of measures taken to fulfill fisheries management criteria;
- strengthening WTO notification rules for fisheries subsidies.[102]

While this text indicated great progress, it soon became clear that many governments considered the proposed disciplines too strict. The chair of the rules group, Ambassador Guillermo Valles Galmés of Uruguay, subsequently released a more general "road map" for the fisheries discussions in December 2008, hoping this would guide governments back toward an agreement. The chair indicated that the purpose of the road map was to allow delegates to take a step back from the most recent draft text—without abandoning it—and "reflect on the fundamental issues" of its mandate to "strengthen disciplines on subsidies in the fisheries sector" and establish "appropriate and effective" flexibilities for poorer countries.[103] Although the WTO has not yet finalized new rules on fisheries subsidies eight years after Doha—and no deadline was set for these negotiations—the agreement by each side that subsidies pose a threat to the environment, development, and trade is seen as a small step in the right direction.

Liberalizing Trade in Environmental Goods and Services

The final trade-environment issue to be discussed here is the issue of liberalizing trade in environmental goods and services. The 2001 Doha Ministerial Declaration instructs WTO members to negotiate the reduction or elimination of tariff and non-tariff barriers on environmental goods and services. The WTO emphasizes that these negotiations could yield a win-win-win situation for trade, the environment, and development. The negotiations will facilitate trade since domestic purchasers will be able to acquire environmental technologies from foreign companies at lower costs. The environment will benefit because of the wider availability of less expensive products and technologies, which in turn will improve the quality of life by providing better access to clean water, sanitation, and clean energy. Finally, the liberalization of

BOX 7.1   OECD CLASSIFICATION
OF ENVIRONMENTAL GOODS AND SERVICES

Pollution management: This group includes goods that help control air pollution; manage wastewater and solid waste; clean up soil, surface water, and groundwater; reduce noise and vibrations; and facilitate environmental monitoring, analysis, and assessment.

Cleaner technologies and products: These goods are intrinsically cleaner or more re-source efficient than available alternatives. For example, a solar photovoltaic power plant is fundamentally cleaner than a coal-fired one.

Resource management: Goods under this category are used to control indoor pollu-tion, supply water, or help manage farms, forests, or fisheries sustainably. This group also includes goods used to conserve energy (such as double-paned windows) and to prevent or reduce the environmental impacts of natural disasters, such as fire-fighting equipment.

Environmentally preferable products: The United Nations Conference on Trade and Development defines environmentally preferable products as "products that cause significantly less environmental harm at some stage of their life cycle than alterna-tive products that serve the same purpose." Examples include improved solid-fuel cooking stoves and reusable shopping bags made of canvas or jute rather than plastic or paper.

"Opening Markets for Environmental Goods and Services," OECD, September 2005, www.oecd.org/dataoecd/63/15/35415839.pdf.

trade in environmental goods and services will help developing countries obtain the tools they need to address key environmental priorities as part of their ongoing de-velopment strategies.[104]

So, what are environmental goods and services? And which ones should be the tar-gets for easing trade restrictions? These are not straightforward issues. According to the OECD, "The environmental goods and services industry consists of activities which produce goods and services to measure, prevent, limit, minimize or correct en-vironmental damage to water, air and soil, as well as problems related to waste, noise, and ecosystems. This includes cleaner technologies, products and services that reduce environmental risk and minimize pollution and resource use."[105]

When the OECD drew up a list of environmental goods for the purposes of study-ing trade and trade barriers, it classified them into four categories: pollution manage-ment, cleaner technologies and products, resource management, and environmentally preferable products (see Box 7.1). However, while it is useful to understand what these categories are, they have not been universally accepted by all WTO members.

In fact, the difficulty of defining environmental goods and services for the purposes of reducing trade barriers has plagued the negotiations since they began in 2002. So far, the WTO discussions have focused on two broad categories: traditional environmental goods, which have a main purpose of addressing or remedying an environmental problem (for example, carbon capture and storage technologies), and environmentally preferable products, which include any product with environmental benefits over a similar product arising during the production, use, or disposal stages.[106]

Prioritizing categories for discussion, however, does not address the core issue of agreeing on actual goods, services, products, or technologies on which trade barriers will be reduced. The so-called Friends of Environmental Goods, comprising Canada, Chinese Taipei (Taiwan), the European Union, Japan, New Zealand, Norway, Switzerland, South Korea, and the United States, favor the "list approach," which essentially entails identifying and submitting lists of what members regard as environmental goods of interest for accelerated and permanent liberalization by reducing or eliminating bound tariffs. India's "project approach" proposes liberalizing any good or service intended for a specific environmental project as approved by a designated national authority. Such liberalization would be temporary, lasting for the duration of the project, and domestic implementation of the criteria would be subject to WTO dispute settlement. The "integrated approach," proposed by Argentina, resembles the project approach but with further identification of goods used in the various approved projects. Brazil has proposed a fourth approach, the "request offer approach," whereby countries would request specific liberalization commitments from each other on products of interest to them and extend tariff cuts they deem appropriate equally to all WTO members. Some members have informally proposed combining various approaches. However, at the time of writing, there appears to be no resolution regarding which approach or combination of approaches that countries will use.[107]

These negotiations will have an impact on numerous MEAs. The outcome of the trade-liberalization discussions could have far-reaching effects on the availability of technologies to replace the use of ODS and persistent organic pollutants under the Montreal Protocol and Stockholm Convention, respectively. They could affect and improve the availability of technologies for the environmentally sound management of hazardous wastes under the Basel Convention. The potential for liberalization in the area of low-carbon goods could also lead to major gains in implementing the United Nations Framework Convention on Climate Change (UNFCCC), the Kyoto Protocol, and any successor agreement. According to the World Bank, removing tariffs on four basic clean-energy technologies (wind, solar, clean coal, and efficient lighting) in eighteen developing countries with high GHG emissions would result in trade gains of up to 7 percent.[108] Trade liberalization could also contribute toward fulfilling the technology-transfer mandates contained in the UNFCCC and similar provisions in other MEAs.

The Outlook for Trade and Environment

In September 2003, the Doha round of trade negotiations started to collapse at the fifth WTO ministerial conference in Cancún, Mexico. Developing countries viewed the EU-U.S. position on agricultural subsidies, put forward in their pre-Cancún proposal paper, as inadequate because it failed to address developing-country calls for the elimination of export subsidies and substantial reductions in domestic support and tariffs in the North—measures that would undercut local production in poor countries, suppress world prices, and prevent efficient exporters in poorer countries from selling their produce.[109] Developing countries reacted to the EU-U.S. proposal by forming a coalition, the Group of 20, including Brazil, China, India, South Africa, and others with significant agrarian populations and large growing markets of interest to the North.[110]

As negotiations on the Doha agenda continue to falter through the WTO's various committees and negotiating fora, several developments are likely to have an impact on the trade-environment nexus. First, as was demonstrated in Cancún, developing countries are no longer willing to go along with the demands made by the developed nations that have been running the show. This was the first time that developing countries led and maintained negotiating coalitions in the WTO, even though the specific national interests of coalition partners differed. This was a shift in the balance of power in the WTO and has had far-reaching implications in other fora, including in the negotiation of regional trade agreements, such as the proposed Free Trade Area of the Americas,[111] and in the environment and development arenas.

The relationship between governments and NGOs within the WTO is another evolving development. While protests of WTO policies continue outside the negotiating rooms, NGOs and civil-society groups have provided much needed technical analysis and political support on the inside, especially to small-staffed developing country delegations that face severe disadvantages during the multilateral negotiating process in keeping up with the blizzard of proposals and large number of meetings.[112]

Environmental, labor, and human rights groups' have continued to protest over a range of complaints about the WTO and globalization of the economy. One common theme is that the world's trade officials reach agreements without sufficient transparency to and participation by civil society. Environmental NGOs had been advocating greater WTO transparency, including dispute panels, since the early 1990s, but with little success. They called for meetings open to the press and the public, NGO input into the selection of experts on the dispute panels, and more NGO input into

WTO decisions, but these requests fell on deaf ears. The United States, under pressure from its own NGOs, has pushed for greater transparency in the WTO. But WTO delegations from developing countries and other industrialized countries alike rejected the participation of environmental NGOs generally because they perceived the worldwide NGO movement as being dominated by U.S. NGOs. They also rejected proposals to breach the confidentiality of the dispute-resolution process.

Many of the issues described in this chapter are likely to remain on the top of the trade-and-environment agenda in the coming years, particularly the relationship between trade rules and MEAs, labeling for environmental purposes, reducing fisheries and agricultural subsidies, and liberalizing trade in environmental goods and services. The roles that developing countries and NGOs play within the context of the WTO will continue to evolve, as will the emphasis given to the relationship between trade and environment.

CONCLUSION

The evolution of global environmental politics cannot be understood completely outside the context of North-South economic issues, the three pillars of sustainable development, and the important trade-environment nexus. Many developing countries' perception of global economic relations as fundamentally inequitable often shapes their policy responses to global environmental issues and their strategies for negotiating on issues as different as elephants and climate. Moreover, unfavorable trends in North-South economic relations since the mid-1970s have not only sharpened the inequalities between North and South but also affected southern bargaining positions on issues involving North-South economic relations, including environmental issues.

As linkages with economic and social development have multiplied, the boundaries of global environmental politics have broadened and, sometimes, been lost within the larger context of sustainable development. While this, in part, can be explained by the plethora of MEAs that address many environmental and natural resource management issues, there is still concern that the focus on the MDGs is siphoning potential funding away from the environment and toward social development. Some observers, including Walter Reid and Jeffrey Sachs,[113] make the case for sustainable development as envisioned in the Brundtland Report, arguing that environmental goals cannot be achieved without development, and development goals cannot be achieved without sound environmental management. This debate between environment and development priorities carries through to the trade arena, where it has been difficult to achieve a balance between free trade and environmental protection within the context of the

WTO on various issues, including endangered-species protection, genetically modified food and animal feed, and fisheries subsidies, to name a few.

Can the MDGs be achieved by 2015? Is the planet on a path to sustainable development or environmental disaster? Despite the apparent tension between economic, social, and ecological goals in both developed and developing countries, in the long run economic health depends on social and ecological health. The global economy cannot thrive in the face of the total devastation of our biospheric envelope; nor can it survive in the face of increasing poverty and disease. If the public and policy makers accept that fact, then there are two ways to resolve this tension: They can let it continue until the integrity of the ecology and the economy deteriorate and snap like old rubber bands, releasing all tension, or they can make the economic, social, and cultural changes that will support sustainable development at the community, national, and global levels. The challenge is for governments to have the political will to make this shift happen and for the people of the world to demand change.[114]

DISCUSSION QUESTIONS

1. In what ways are the interests of developing and industrialized countries at odds over global environmental issues? In what sense are they compatible?
2. Explain how developing countries' concerns about economic growth might affect their position on ozone depletion or climate change. Why would their position on the Basel Convention be different?
3. How has the concept of sustainable development evolved since the 1980s?
4. What changed in the world between the Earth Summit in 1992 and the World Summit on Sustainable Development in 2002? How did these changes affect the summit in Johannesburg?
5. How have the Millennium Development Goals affected global environmental politics?
6. Explain how trade and environmental issues affect each other. What is the nature of this relationship?
7. Compare the trade-environment issue with other global environmental issues in the regimes discussed in chapters 3 to 5. Is the WTO/GATT an environmental regime in any sense? Why or why not?
8. How might the liberalization of trade in environmental goods and services affect GHG reductions under the Kyoto Protocol and any successor agreement?

8

The Future of
Global Environmental Politics

"Getting action in the United Nations," a diplomat once complained, "is like the mating of elephants. It takes place at a very high level, with an enormous amount of huffing and puffing, raises a tremendous amount of dust and nothing happens for at least 23 months."[1] Many who see the need for urgent action on environmental problems are skeptical of entrusting complete responsibility to the slow and often cumbersome, "huffing-and-puffing" multilateral negotiating process within the United Nations. While not every multilateral environmental agreement (MEA) has been negotiated within the UN system (bilateral and trilateral agreements, for example, are usually negotiated directly among states, as are some multilateral agreements), since 1972 the United Nations or one of its specialized agencies—primarily the United Nations Environment Program (UNEP)—has been recognized as the main venue for addressing global and regional environmental issues. Although there are frustrations inherent in this process, as described throughout this book, governments are not ready to surrender environmental decision making and their own sovereignty to a supranational body with legislative and enforcement powers. As a result, the international community is forced to employ some method of intergovernmental cooperation—usually through the negotiation and implementation of MEAs.[2]

At the same time, the stakes in global environmental politics continue to increase. The costs of environmental degradation and measures to reverse it are growing. More and more global environmental regimes require greater changes in economic- and social-development strategies and production techniques to be effective. However, because the globalization of investment and the liberalization of trade have accelerated, global economic forces and the policies that support them can threaten the effectiveness of global environmental policy. Thus, the ambitious agenda of sustainable development is in danger of being overwhelmed by economic forces that, in their current form, threaten the health of the planet. This final chapter examines the challenges that the international community faces during the second decade of the twenty-first century and looks ahead at the future of global environmental politics.

GLOBALIZATION AND THE GLOBAL ENVIRONMENT

Everywhere you turn today, you see globalization. Your clothes, shoes, phone, and television could have been made nearly anywhere in the world. When we log onto our computers (perhaps with key parts manufactured in the United States and assembled in Mexico by a Japanese company) and surf the Internet, we can reach out and connect with anyone, anywhere, anytime around the world. You can walk down the street in any town in the United States and find restaurants selling burritos, sushi, or tandoori chicken. You can buy tuna harvested from the Pacific Ocean, furniture built from Amazon hardwoods, blueberries from Chile, and cell phones from South Korea. The tremendous expansion of international trade—the movement of capital, technology, products, and labor—allows you to buy low-cost clothing, electronics, food, and just about anything else at giant retail stores. You can listen to African music, watch Bollywood movies, read international newspapers on the Internet, travel to nearly any country, and watch news events from around the world as they happen on CNN. You are part of what geographers call cultural diffusion—the spread of items and ideas across boundaries.

Globalization is the accelerating and complex process by which governments, companies, individuals, information, and knowledge are integrated and interconnected on a global scale.[3] In some ways, there is nothing new about globalization. Human ideas and practices have been "globalized" for millennia; societies and civilizations have always learned from one another. The spread of agriculture was an ancient case of globalization; so was the Silk Road and colonization. In historical terms, therefore, the present phase of globalization is only the latest in a process of international economic extension, expansion, and integration.[4] Thomas Friedman describes three phases of globalization: Globalization 1.0 (1492 to 1800) shrank the world from a size large to a size medium, and the dynamic forces in that era were powerful countries searching globally for resources and imperial conquest. Globalization 2.0 (1800 to 2000) shrank the world from a size medium to a size small, and it was spearheaded by companies globalizing for markets and labor. Globalization 3.0 (which started around 2000) is shrinking the world from a size small to a size tiny and flattening the playing field at the same time. Friedman argues that Globalization 3.0 differs from the previous eras not only in how it is shrinking and flattening the world and empowering individuals but also in that Globalization 1.0 and 2.0 were driven primarily by European and American countries and companies. Globalization 3.0 is driven more by individuals and a much more diverse—non-Western, nonwhite—group of individuals.[5] Also new is the scale and volume of international movements of people, capital, and products; the expansion of capitalism to nearly all countries around the world; and the commodification of things never before exchanged in markets, such as genes, air pollution, and whale watching.[6]

So how does globalization have an impact on the environment and on global environmental politics? There are two primary sides to this debate. One argues that globalization is beneficial for the environment because it is an "engine of wealth creation" that will fund environmental improvements. As societies become richer, the initial process of industrialization results in greater pollution. This happened in Europe and the United States and is happening now in many developing countries. However, a point is eventually reached at which wealth creation is sufficient, at least for a majority of the population, and with it comes greater concern for pollution reduction and environmental protection. And because of the wealth creation, the society has the ability to implement the necessary measures to achieve these goals. Globalization, by delivering the "development" side of the sustainable development equation, will solve the social problems that contribute to environmental degradation. Along these lines, poverty is seen as a critical component of environmental degradation, and environmentalists who oppose globalization are sometimes condemned as "eco-imperialists" for trying to deny poor countries the right to develop.[7]

The contrary argument sees most aspects of globalization as bad for the environment. By extending the exclusionist paradigm into all aspects of international economic relations, globalization is responsible for rapidly accelerating the overconsumption of natural resources and overproduction of waste on a global scale. It has advanced the movement of capital, technology, goods, and labor to areas with high returns on investment without regard for the impact on the communities and people who live there. Globalization stretches the chains of production and consumption over great distances and across many locations, which increases the separation between sources of environmental problems and their impact. The division of labor associated with globalization results in the increased transport of raw materials, commodities, semiprocessed materials, parts, finished goods, and waste, as well as greater energy consumption and more pollution, including higher carbon emissions, and the risk of major environmental accidents.[8] Globalization also reinforces the sharp inequalities between North and South discussed in Chapter 7. For example, the ready availability of every vegetable or fruit in your supermarket throughout the year is the result of a shift from subsistence farming to intensive cash cropping in developing countries. In addition to the

BOX 8.1   COMMODITY CHAINS

The reorganization of production under globalization has led to the creation of extended "commodity chains" that spread environmental impacts over many countries. For example, the production of cotton T-shirts can involve as many as six different countries, creating different types of pollution and environmental impacts in each one.

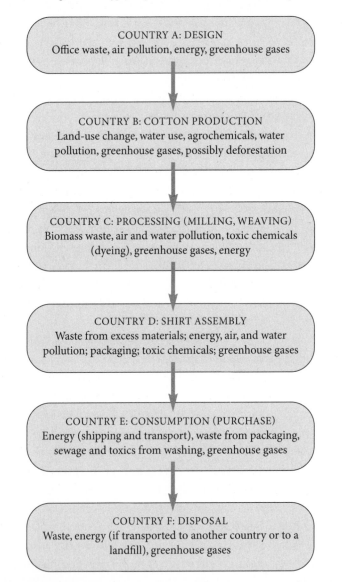

COUNTRY A: DESIGN
Office waste, air pollution, energy, greenhouse gases

COUNTRY B: COTTON PRODUCTION
Land-use change, water use, agrochemicals, water pollution, greenhouse gases, possibly deforestation

COUNTRY C: PROCESSING (MILLING, WEAVING)
Biomass waste, air and water pollution, toxic chemicals (dyeing), greenhouse gases, energy

COUNTRY D: SHIRT ASSEMBLY
Waste from excess materials; energy, air, and water pollution; packaging; toxic chemicals; greenhouse gases

COUNTRY E: CONSUMPTION (PURCHASE)
Energy (shipping and transport), waste from packaging, sewage and toxics from washing, greenhouse gases

COUNTRY F: DISPOSAL
Waste, energy (if transported to another country or to a landfill), greenhouse gases

Ronnie D. Lipschutz, *Global Environmental Politics: Power, Perspectives and Practice* (Washington, DC: Congressional Quarterly Press, 2004), 124.

significant **environmental externalities** of flying these products to northern markets, cash crops bring questionable benefits to developing countries. Agribusinesses, not farmers, often reap the benefits and own the best-quality land. Chemical fertilizers and pesticides are relied upon to produce uniform, high-export-quality produce. Poor farmers, on the other hand, are forced to cultivate low-quality, marginal land, contributing to soil erosion, habitat destruction, and desertification.[9] In addition, the reorganization of production under globalization has led to the creation of extended "commodity chains" that spread environmental impacts over many countries. For example, the production of cotton T-shirts can involve as many as six different countries, creating different types of pollution and environmental impacts in each one (see Box 8.1).

The exact relationship between the environment and globalization is likely more complex than either of these two archetypal arguments—and probably contains elements of both. The environment itself is inherently global, with life-sustaining ecosystems and watersheds frequently crossing national boundaries, air pollution moving across entire continents and oceans, and a single shared atmosphere providing a hospitable global climate and an ozone layer shielding us from harsh ultraviolet rays. As the cases in this book demonstrate, monitoring and responding to environmental issues frequently provokes a need for coordinated global or regional governance. Moreover, as was discussed in Chapter 7, the environment is intrinsically linked to economic development, providing natural resources that fuel growth and ecosystem services that underpin both life and livelihoods. While the importance of the relationship between globalization and the environment is obvious, our understanding of how these twin dynamics interact remains weak. Much of the literature on globalization and the environment is vague (discussing generalities), myopic (focused disproportionately only on trade-related connections), one-sided (examining the issue from only one of the perspectives outlined above), or partial (highlighting the impacts of globalization on the environment but not vice versa). It is important to highlight that not only does globalization impact the environment, but the environment impacts the pace, direction, and quality of globalization. At the very least, this happens because environmental resources provide the fuel for economic globalization, but it also happens because our social and policy responses to global environmental problems constrain and influence the context in which globalization happens.[10]

The dominant discourse on globalization has tended to highlight the promise of economic opportunity. This is the globalization paradigm discussed in Chapter 1. On the other hand, there is a parallel global discourse on environmental responsibility. We need to develop a more nuanced understanding or paradigm, one that understands that some aspects of globalization are inevitable and seeks to actualize the positive opportunities offered by globalization while fulfilling global ecological responsibilities and advancing equity. Such an understanding would make sustainable development a goal of globalization, rather than its victim.[11] So how do we get to this point? One option, to be explored in the next section, is better global governance.

GLOBAL ENVIRONMENTAL GOVERNANCE

Global governance, in essence, can be described as the political interaction of states, international organizations, and other transnational actors aimed at solving problems that affect more than one state or region. The current global governance architecture is largely based on institutions created at the end of World War II, which represent the world as it was in 1945—the United Nations, the World Bank, the International Monetary Fund (IMF), and the General Agreement on Tariffs and Trade/World Trade Organization (WTO). However, this architecture has not kept pace with fundamental changes in the international system, including, but not limited to, globalization. This book has focused largely on the system of global environmental governance, which includes the organizations, treaties, financing mechanisms, rules, procedures, and norms that regulate the processes of global environmental protection. Like the overarching global governance architecture, the global environmental-governance system has outgrown its original design.

Better global governance is the key to managing both globalization and the global environment. More importantly, it is also the key to managing the relationship between the two. Although they are both vast and complex systems, neither the environment nor globalization is immune to policy influence. Indeed, the international processes as we know them have been shaped by the policies that we have—or have not—put in place in the past, as demonstrated by the various environmental regimes discussed in this book. Equally important, the policy decisions of the future will shape the direction that globalization, the global environment, and the interaction of the two will take in the years to come. Governance, therefore, is the key avenue for action by decision makers today. However, at the same time it is clear that both globalization and the need to address global environmental issues challenge the architecture of the international system as it now exists. As noted in a report by the International Institute for Sustainable Development, both these dynamics limit a state's ability to make decisions about and control key issues affecting it. Globalization accomplishes this by design as states commit to liberalizing trade and embrace new technologies. The environment challenges the system, as discussed in Chapter 6, by default as ecosystem boundaries rarely overlap with national boundaries, pollution knows no boundaries, and the requirements of effective international environmental policy often run up against issues of state sovereignty. The role of the state in the management of the international system

CARTOON 8.1 "Ecological Ostriches."
© Andy Singer, 2009 and PoliticalCartoons.com.

has to evolve to respond to the evolution of the challenges facing it.[12] Needless to say, this process is not, and will not be, an easy one.

Yet, perhaps the biggest obstacle in changing the current system of global governance in general and global environmental governance in particular is political will. Changes in policy and practice have been urged in numerous internationally agreed declarations and documents. Some world leaders agree; others do not. Among leaders in disagreement are those who appear to believe they live on an isolated island of stability. They dismiss the idea that global warming, biodiversity loss, contamination by persistent organic pollutants (POPs), or ozone destruction are undermining the future of "their" country. Their narrow vision completely misses the seriousness of "our" circumstances.[13] Other world leaders agree that action is needed and aspects of the system need to be changed, but they either don't have the political will or the necessary resources to make this happen. Given these political constraints, how then can we improve global environmental governance in such a way that we can successfully manage the relationship between environmental responsibility and globalization?

There are two main camps among the scholars and writers starting to look deeply into the issue: institutional reformists who want to make the system of treaty regimes and international institutions work better and those who believe far deeper changes are necessary. Among the former, some have focused on strengthening key institutions in specific issue areas (e.g., UNEP for global environmental governance), negotiating stronger and more effective global regimes, and elevating the precautionary principle to an official guiding principle of international policy. Increasing coherence and coordination among the goals and processes of the major global environmental-governance, financial, trade, and development institutions and systems should also be a major priority.[14]

Among the latter, one reformist vision involves creating a World Environment Organization or a United Nations Environmental Organization. If we were writing on a clean slate—approaching afresh the question of which international regulatory organizations should be created—the case for it would be very strong. A World Environment Organization could be quite modest or quite powerful. In one model, UNEP would become a specialized agency of the United Nations, gaining in stature, size, and independence. This would increase its financial resources and provide a more efficient and effective structure for governance and leadership. Another model would bring the various environmental treaties together under the new World Environment Organization. The most ambitious idea would create a world environment agency that would counterbalance the WTO and operate as a type of global legislature, entrusted with setting international standards and enforcing them against laggard countries. In practice, some argue that it might be wise to begin at the modest end of the spectrum and gradually strengthen the new organization as trust and confidence build.[15]

Another vision conceives of opening the door for nonstate stakeholders to participate directly in global environmental governance. Supporters believe that effectively responding to the challenges of environment and globalization requires a concerted effort to find new and meaningful ways to engage nonstate actors from business and civil society. As described in Chapter 2, nonstate actors, including nongovernmental organizations (NGOs), multinational corporations, and large philanthropic organizations, like the Gates Foundation or the Ford Foundation, often clamor to take part in decision-making forums that have traditionally been the purview of states alone. How to integrate these new stakeholders into multilateral deliberations remains a major challenge for global governance.[16]

A third reformist vision is to take a major step outside the world of conventional regimes and explore the idea of "global issues networks" to reach an effective "global accord" on major environmental issues by a quite different path. Originally coined by former World Bank Vice President Jean-François Rischard, the global issues network approach realizes that, while the intergovernmental system is often bogged down in endless and ineffectual negotiations, there is enormous new potential in the world outside governments.[17] Rischard and others of this view argue that the greatest roadblock to dealing with global issues is the territorial and hierarchical institutions that are supposed to solve them: states. States, as described in Chapter 2, recognize the strength of their own self-interests and have acted to confine them through treaties and conventions, extensive intergovernmental conferences, Group of Eight (G-8)–type groupings, and the forty or so intergovernmental organizations (IGOs).[18]

Global issues networks would be composed of governments, NGOs, and corporations concerned about a particular global challenge. This concept has two generic characteristics that directly address the limitations of the current international system. First, bureaucracy and hierarchy must be minimized. Each global issue requires its own problem-solving vehicle so that the greater global issues challenge is unbundled. Second, start-up and delivery time must be fast. The world cannot afford to waste the time it takes to negotiate treaties, let alone ratify them by quorum. Global issues networks aim not for global legislation but for global action outside of the slow-moving traditional public arena. These vehicles must operate in a space that moves more quickly—one that produces norms and influences states' behavior by directly affecting their reputations. Moreover, existing institutions should be utilized so these vehicles might harness the expertise, knowledge, and legislative power of governments and get the best out of existing multilaterals. Time is insufficient to establish new institutions and waste the capabilities of old ones.[19] This potential would not be possible without the growing vitality and—thanks to the Internet—the growing connectivity of governments, the international NGO community, IGOs, and others. The potential result, according to Rischard, would be a new kind of legitimacy—a horizontal legitimacy—emerging from joint deliberations, both across borders and throughout government, business, and civil society, by a large group of people deeply concerned with, and knowledgeable about, one issue. Horizontal legitimacy would not replace, but rather would complement, the vertical legitimacy of the traditional local-to-global electoral processes of nation-states, which deal with all issues but within the confines of a defined territory.[20]

Another view, exemplified by the International Forum on Globalization, doubts that global environmental challenges can be addressed unless much is done to curb corporate power and reshape the present process of economic globalization. They believe that globalization is intrinsically harmful to the environment because it is based on ever-increasing consumption, exploitation of resources, and high energy use, and they argue that not much can be done about negative environmental trends without far-reaching changes in the economic and political distribution of power in modern society. They see the solution in assertive local control. Indeed, a surprisingly diverse array of local organizations and communities—taking the slogan "Think globally, act

locally" to heart—are impatient with international processes and believe the way forward is to "just do it" by working toward sustainability in everyday life and in local
communities. Individuals and communities can also exert influence as voters and citizens, as investors, as consumers, as association members, as workers, as activists, and
as educators. This is already beginning to happen in the United States, as described in
Chapter 2, where citizen initiatives and local action began to address the global problems of energy and climate change rather than continuing to wait for the federal government in Washington, D.C.[21]

Others believe that a much more fundamental change is needed—a change in basic
values, actions, and habits of thought. The transition they seek, the acceptance of a
broad new paradigm, is captured well in the *Earth Charter*, which urges us "to bring
forth a sustainable global society founded on respect for nature, universal human
rights, economic justice, and a culture of peace."[22] Not until human beings have abandoned the values and practices that produced today's global problems, this line of rea-
soning maintains, will we truly be able to solve them.

Today, efforts to strengthen key environmental institutions, negotiate more effective
regimes, and mainstream the principles of sustainable development and the precautionary principle appear to have the most support as practical ways forward. However,
elements of all these approaches are at play in global environmental politics. Which,
if any, of these initiatives will gather sufficient global support to increase the effectiveness of global environmental governance remains unclear.

CONCLUSION: THE PROSPECTS FOR GLOBAL
ENVIRONMENTAL POLITICS

Over the last forty years, the international community's quest for planetary stewardship
has encompassed a variety of intergovernmental, governmental, and civil-society initiatives. The results are mixed and, it is generally conceded, inadequate. Disturbing environmental trends continue.

Can the international community develop effective cooperative efforts to address
our major global environment problems successfully? The case studies presented in
this book show that, on some issues, states have taken collective actions that significantly reduced specific environmental threats, such as hunting endangered species of
whales and the poaching of African elephants. In the case of the ozone layer, states
have devised a regime that has been innovative in its rule making and effective in phasing out products responsible for the damage.

But the successful regimes have had favorable circumstances. The ozone case involved a relatively small number of interested economic actors and substitute tech-

nologies that turned out to be cost-effective. The initial whaling ban passed because only a few countries wanted to continue to hunt whales and there was no large world-wide market for whale products. The ivory ban has succeeded because a few major countries were able to shut down most of the market for elephant ivory. The European air-pollution regime has been successful because of the availability of cleaner technologies and the politics associated with European Union (EU) strengthening and expansion. At the same time, however, none of these regimes has completely solved the problems involved. The black market for ivory still exists; Iceland, Japan, and Norway still hunt whales; air pollution in parts of Europe still exceeds desired limits; and the ozone layer has not fully recovered.

In other cases we examined, the international community has not yet been able to reach an effective agreement, often because of the problem's links to major economic and social interests. The lack of progress toward a forest regime reflects the veto power wielded by a loose, ever-changing coalition of key developing and developed countries. Potential lead actors have failed to define the issue in a way that could contribute to an effective regime, in large part because they are unwilling to restrict the global trade in forest products. Slowing the hemorrhaging of the world's forests will require both wealthy countries and forest countries to consider what value the remaining forests have to present and future generations worldwide.

The climate regime faces another set of major economic and social interests, including requirements for major changes relating to energy production and use. Challenges to the science of global warming by one veto coalition, led by the United States under the George W. Bush administration, and a desire to uphold the principle of common but differentiated responsibilities by a second veto coalition, led by some of the larger developing countries, have delayed effective implementation of the Kyoto Protocol and seriously hampered discussion of emissions reductions beyond 2012.

This book has outlined the importance of continued efforts to improve the effectiveness of environmental regimes even after they are adopted. We have shown how parties can strengthen regimes by tightening the requirements for regulating activities that are causing the environmental disruption or resource depletion, by improving compliance with those requirements, or by broadening state participation in the regime. The regimes for biodiversity, desertification, and fisheries will need different kinds of strengthening in the next several years to become effective in reversing these environmental problems. Each of these issues is at a different stage of development and has a unique combination of political and economic dynamics. But for each threat, it will take unprecedented political commitments by major states to create a truly effective regime.

The biodiversity regime has initiated work on seven thematic work programs addressing marine and coastal biodiversity, agricultural biodiversity, forest biodiversity,

island biodiversity, the biodiversity of inland waters, dry and subhumid lands biodiversity, and mountain biodiversity. Work is also underway on protected areas; traditional knowledge; innovations (Article 8[j]); intellectual property rights; indicators;
taxonomy; public education and awareness; incentives; and alien species—not to mention the implementation of the Cartagena Protocol on Biosafety. There is a 2010 deadline for a new agreement on access and benefit-sharing. With so many working groups
and programs, many are concerned that the regime has become overextended, minimizing its effectiveness.

The desertification regime faces considerable administrative and financial problems
in fulfilling its mandate to combat desertification and mitigate the effects of drought.
Although nearly universal ratification of the convention can be seen as recognition of
the problem of land degradation in the drylands, the issue is complicated by the fact
that combating desertification has to work hand in hand with efforts to address poverty
eradication, water resources management, agriculture, deforestation, biodiversity conservation, climate change, and population growth. The success or failure of this regime
is a key indicator for the overall success or failure of sustainable development.

The regime for global fisheries management needs a stronger compliance system
and increased participation. It is more complex than any of the others discussed in
this book, consisting of a legally binding regime governing the management of straddling fish stocks and highly migratory fish stocks, as well as the nonbinding Food and
Agriculture Organization (FAO) Code of Conduct for Responsible Fisheries, the nonbinding FAO International Plan of Action on Managing Fishing Capacity, and numerous regional agreements. The Fish Stocks Agreement lacks a conference of the parties,
relying entirely on regional fisheries organizations to track compliance, and most of
the major fishing states have failed to ratify it. The code of conduct has strong and relatively concrete norms for sustainable fisheries management but a weak system of accountability. The FAO is responsible for reporting on progress in implementing the
norms in the agreement, but states feel little or no pressure to conform to them because
the FAO has no mandate to monitor and report on the implementation of the norms
by individual states. The FAO Plan of Action on Managing Fishing Capacity, which
could be the most important part of the regime for overfishing, has the same problems.
A new agreement under negotiation on port-state responsibility for combating illegal,
unregulated, and unreported fishing could, if properly designed and implemented,
contribute greatly to sustainable fisheries management.

But environmental regimes are not the only forces that influence the global environment. Multilateral institutions impact environmental politics and the development
of regimes, be it by helping to set the global agenda, in particular UNEP and the Commission on Sustainable Development (CSD); bringing states together to negotiate

(CSD, UNEP, FAO); monitoring global environment trends (UNEP); conducting comprehensive scientific assessments (IPCC); or providing financial support for environmental activities (Global Environment Facility, World Bank, United Nations Development Programme). But these institutions have generally lacked the resources and the mandate to promote strong regimes. The Global Environment Facility has funding that can accomplish only a small fraction of what is needed to support effective international cooperation in biodiversity, climate, ozone protection, international waters, land degradation, and POPs. UNEP and the CSD have both been subject to the veto power and weak political will of key states.

The world's global trade and financial institutions—the WTO, the IMF, and the World Bank—also play important roles. Historically, each has often pursued policies that run counter to the needs of effective global environmental regimes. WTO dispute panels have rendered decisions against unilateral trade measures for environmental purposes that seemed to rule out such measures even in cases of endangered species, not because these measures were protectionist but because they would restrict trade. The WTO's decision on the shrimp/turtle issue suggests the possibility of an accommodation between global trade rules and carefully crafted environmental trade measures, but the issue remains a potential conflict among states and between trade specialists and environmentalists. Also unresolved is whether the WTO will accommodate the use of trade measures by multilateral environmental agreements, how trade in environmental goods and services will be liberalized, and how this may affect the hazardous wastes, chemicals, ozone, and climate regimes, among others.

The IMF and the World Bank have similarly been driven by economic interests that often conflict with global cooperation on environmental threats. The global financial crisis has not helped the situation. These institutions cannot be expected to change their policies unless the finance ministries of the world's major industrialized countries instruct them to, something that will likely require domestic political pressure.

Some observers have argued that global environmental regimes will not be effective until the ability of individual states to veto action is finally overcome. Some have proposed creating a World Environment Organization, as described earlier in this chapter, to counterbalance the World Trade Organization. This new organization could develop global environmental policies that would be binding on member states and, like the WTO, sanction states that fail to comply with global policies. Such proposals appear to put the cart of effective global regimes ahead of the horse of adequate political will. Without the political will to make greater sacrifices to reverse global environmental degradation, the world's major states will clearly not agree to give up their power and sovereignty to choose which regulations or regimes to adopt. The real problem for those advocating much stronger global environmental governance is how to raise concern for the importance of effective international cooperation and generate the political and public commitment to create it. That cannot be accomplished by establishing a new international organization.

The leadership of the highly industrialized countries, beginning with the United States, is a key to effective regimes. The United States is the one state actor without whose leadership any environmental regime is certain to be much weaker. When the United States has actively engaged in trying to achieve consensus on stronger institutions or actions, it has often been able to overcome reluctance on the part of other industrialized countries, as in the negotiations on ozone depletion, African elephants, whaling, and fish stocks. When the United States has been a veto state, as in the case of climate change and the hazardous waste trade, or has played a much lower-profile role, as in cases of desertification, POPs, long-range transboundary air pollution, and biodiversity, the resulting regime is weaker. The U.S. executive branch wavered on these issues during the Bill Clinton and George W. Bush administrations, and Congress has remained a force for reducing U.S. leadership and enforcing a veto role, especially in the climate-change negotiations, the Cartagena Protocol on Biosafety, and the Stockholm and Rotterdam chemicals conventions. It is still too early to know what the legacy of Barack Obama's administration will be in this regard.

Developing-country governments, too, must move beyond simply demanding technology transfer and financial assistance and participate fully in global environmental regimes, particularly those for biodiversity, forests, climate change, chemicals, and fisheries. But this may be unrealistic. Developing countries need to take new initiatives for North-South bargains in which they accept new commitments in each of the major areas in return for financial or other forms of compensation. In the climate negotiations, for example, a successful regime requires a breakthrough in the discussions of developing-country commitments. As stated in Chapter 1, if present trends in energy and fossil fuel consumption continue, energy-related emissions of carbon dioxide are projected to increase by about 40 percent by 2030. More than two-thirds of this increase will come from developing countries, whose emissions are projected to exceed industrialized-country emissions by 77 percent by 2030.[23] If developing countries do not take on GHG-reduction commitments, there is little that developed countries alone can do to prevent significant climate change. In addition, it is unlikely that the United States will be able to support any new agreement that does not include developing-country commitments.

There is increasing awareness among business groups regarding the implications of global environmental threats and global environmental regimes for their interests. As a result, more and more corporations and trade associations are playing an active role in global environmental politics. Because treaties could impose significant new costs or open up new opportunities, depending on their details, corporations recognize that early involvement in the negotiating process will often bring long-term benefits once the regime is in place. Sometimes, this involvement is negative. Corporations and industry associations sometimes work to defeat strong international environmental measures. Exxon/Mobil reportedly once funded reports that minimized the seriousness and scientific proof of climate change. The agroindustrial complex in the United States, along with the chemical companies producing methyl bromide, worked to prevent the phaseout of methyl bromide under the Montreal Protocol. At other times, corporate interests can assist creation of strong environmental regimes. During the Montreal Protocol negotiations, U.S. chemical companies that manufactured chlorofluorocarbons realized significant regulations were on the way and started to develop chlorofluorocarbon alternatives. Their success enabled U.S. negotiators to take a stronger position and emerge as a lead state in the negotiations.

Domestic political support for new political commitments on global environmental issues likely will not happen without environmental movements and the engagement of civil society that can influence national public opinion and push governments into action. At the international levels, NGO networks on climate change, chemicals, biodiversity, and desertification are mapping strategies for monitoring treaty implementation in every country and encouraging public participation in national action programs and strategies. The Trade Records Analysis of Flora and Fauna in Commerce, or TRAFFIC, continues to monitor the international trade in endangered species. International NGOs such as Greenpeace and WWF are contributing substantial ideas on land-based sources of marine pollution, whales, and fisheries. Nevertheless, the most important challenge for NGOs will be to build political pressure on reluctant states to support participation in, or strengthening of, global environmental regimes. This has become increasingly challenging as fund-raising for global environmental activities has become more difficult for NGOs, forcing many to focus on domestic priorities rather than global environmental problems.

Global environmental politics has grown significantly more complex since the first global environmental meeting in Stockholm in 1972. Many more issues, treaties, institutions, and policy initiatives exist, and the environment is now integrated into a broad array of international economic, trade, and development issues. In some ways, this growth is a sign of the progress made in the last forty years by the international community in learning how to address global environmental issues.

However, caution is necessary. Most of the spirit of Rio from 1992 has dissipated. The enthusiasm for environmental issues expressed by many governments in the early 1990s has waned. Although recent MEAs have applied the precautionary principle and made genuine efforts to grapple with equity issues, many observes believe these steps are not enough to meet the significant challenges of the twenty-first century.[24] Many aspects of global politics are still subject to the dominant economic paradigm described in Chapter 1. Moreover, many MEAs have not been effectively implemented, largely due to a lack of financial resources, appropriate technology, capacity, and political will. In some areas, including the three Rio conventions (climate change, biodiversity, and desertification), the response to the problem has proven inadequate. Moreover, an increasing number of experts agree that these global environmental challenges cannot be dealt with by focusing solely on developing new environmental regimes. Because many sources of environmental degradation go beyond the reach of environmental diplomacy, these issues also must be addressed within the context of social and economic development, trade, and globalization.[25]

This book has examined the principle paradigms, actors, issues, and challenges in global environmental politics. What the future will bring is still unclear. There are reasons for both optimism and grave concern. We do know that today's environmental challenges are global in nature and unprecedented in scope, and they will require innovative and creative global solutions.

DISCUSSION QUESTIONS

1. How has globalization helped to protect the environment, and how has it harmed the environment? Provide some specific examples from your own knowledge or experience.

2. The relationship between globalization and environmental protection is complex at best. How might globalization be used to help improve implementation of one of environmental regimes described in this book?

3. How has globalization complicated the nature of commodity chains? What environmental impacts does the globalized commodity chain have, and how might they be reduced?

4. What are the different types of global environmental governance currently under discussion? Which do you think is the best solution and why?

5. The world has evolved significantly in the past forty years of global environmental politics and policy making. What do you see as the most significant advances? What still needs to be done?

Notes

Chapter 1

1. WWF, *Living Planet Report 2008* (Gland, Switzerland: WWF, 2008), 15.

2. Ibid., 14–15.

3. Peter Dauvergne, *The Shadows of Consumption* (Cambridge, MA: MIT Press, 2008), 4.

4. WWF, *Living Planet Report 2008*, 27.

5. Worldwatch, *State of the World 2004* (New York: W. W. Norton, 2004), 5.

6. Alex Wilson and Jessica Boehland, "Small Is Beautiful: U.S. House Size, Resource Use, and the Environment," *Journal of Industrial Ecology* 9 (winter/spring 2005), 277–287.

7. United Nations, *Millennium Development Goals Report 2008* (New York: United Nations, 2008), 4. Available at www.un.org/millenniumgoals/pdf/The%20Millennium%20Develop ment%20Goals%20Report%202008.pdf.

8. Worldwatch, *State of the World 2004*, 10.

9. UN Population Division, "World Population to Exceed 9 Billion by 2050," United Nations, March 11, 2009, www.un.org/esa/population/publications/wpp2008/pressrelease.pdf.

10. Ibid. Projections of future population growth depend on assumptions made about fertility trends, which actions undertaken in the coming years will affect strongly.

11. WWF, *Living Planet Report 2008*, 15. For more data on different countries' carbon footprints, see "Carbon Footprint of Nations," Norwegian University of Science and Technology, http://carbonfootprintofnations.com/index.php.

12. World Bank, *2009 World Development Indicators* (Washington, DC: World Bank, 2008), 128.

13. "Energy INFOcard," Energy Information Administration, August 2008, www.eia.doe.gov/ neic/brochure/infocard01.htm.

14. Energy Information Administration, *International Energy Outlook 2008* (Washington, DC: EIA, June 2008), www.eia.doe.gov/oiaf/ieo/world.html.

15. Energy Information Administration, *International Energy Outlook 2009: Highlights* (Washington, DC: EIA, June 2009), www.eia.doe.gov/oiaf/ieo/pdf/highlights.pdf.

16. Asbjørn Eide, *The Right to Food and the Impact of Liquid Biofuels (Agrofuels)* (Rome: FAO, 2008), 14.

17. Ibid.

18. Ibid.

19. A hectare is 10,000 square meters.

20. Millennium Ecosystem Assessment, *Ecosystems and Human Well-being: Biodiversity Synthesis* (Washington, DC: World Resources Institute, 2005), www.millenniumassessment.org/ documents/document.354.aspx.pdf.

21. FAO, *The State of World Fisheries and Aquaculture* (Rome: FAO, 2008).

22. Ibid.

23. Commission on Sustainable Development, *Comprehensive Assessment of the Freshwater Resources of the World: Report of the Secretary-General* (New York: UN Economic and Social Council, 1997); UN World Water Assessment Programme, *World Water Development Report: Water for People, Water for Life*, UNESCO.org, March 2003, www.unesco.org/water/wwap/wwdr/index.shtml, as cited in Peter Gleick, *The World's Water: 2008–2009* (Washington, DC: Island Press, 2008).

24. UNEP, *Global Environmental Outlook 4: Environment for Development* (Nairobi: UNEP, 2007), as cited in Peter Gleick, *The World's Water: 2008–2009* (Washington, DC: Island Press, 2008).

25. UNEP, *Vital Water Graphics: An Overview of the State of the World's Fresh and Marine Water*, 2nd ed. (Nairobi: UNEP, 2002).

26. UN Department of Economic and Social Affairs/Population Division, *World Urbanization Prospects: The 2007 Revision* (New York: United Nations, 2008), 1. Available at www.un.org/esa/population/publications/wup2007/2007wup.htm.

27. Ibid., 10.

28. UN Human Settlements Program, *State of the World's Cities 2004/2005: Globalization and Urban Culture* (Nairobi: UN-HABITAT/Earthscan, 2004). The United Nations Human Settlements Program, or UN-HABITAT, is the UN agency for human settlements. It is mandated by the UN General Assembly to promote socially and environmentally sustainable towns and cities with the goal of providing adequate shelter for all. As such it is also a key source of data on living conditions.

29. Andrew Hurrell and Benedict Kingsbury, *The International Politics of the Environment* (Oxford: Clarendon Press, 1992), 2; Pamela S. Chasek, *Earth Negotiations: Analyzing Thirty Years of Environmental Diplomacy* (Tokyo: United Nations University Press, 2001).

30. For an early effort to categorize the different types of international environmental problems, see Clifford S. Russell and Hans H. Landsberg, "International Environmental Problems: A Taxonomy," *Science* 172 (June 25, 1972): 1307–1314.

31. Robert Dorfman and Nancy S. Dorfman, eds., *Economics of the Environment* (New York: W. W. Norton, 1993), 75.

32. Garrett Hardin, "The Tragedy of the Commons," *Science* 162, no. 3859 (December 13, 1968): 1243–1248, as cited in Chasek, *Earth Negotiations*.

33. Oran R. Young, *International Governance* (Ithaca, NY: Cornell University Press, 1994), 19–26.

34. Ibid., 23.

35. Ibid., 25.

36. Agreement on the Cartagena Protocol on Biosafety was reached in Montreal in January 2000. See Chapter 5.

37. Susan Strange, "Cave! Hic Dragones: A Critique of Regime Analysis," *International Organization* 36 (spring 1982): 479–496.

38. Compare the definition and use of the term *regime* in John Gerard Ruggie, "International Responses to Technology: Concepts and Trends," *International Organization* 29 (1975): 557–583; Ernst Haas, "On Systems and International Regimes," *World Politics* 27 (1975): 147–174; Robert Keohane and Joseph Nye Jr., *Power and Interdependence: World Politics in Transition* (Boston: Little, Brown, 1977); Oran Young, "International Regimes: Problems of Concept For-

mation," *International Organization* 32 (1980): 331–356; Stephen Krasner, *International Regimes* (Ithaca, NY: Cornell University Press, 1983), which includes an earlier version of the definition used here; Robert Keohane, *After Hegemony* (Princeton, NJ: Princeton University Press, 1984); Jack Donnelly, "International Human Rights: A Regime Analysis," *International Organization* 40 (1986): 599–642; Stephan Haggard and Beth A. Simmons, "Theories of International Regimes," *International Organization* 41 (summer 1987): 491–517; Thomas Gehring, "International Environmental Regimes: Dynamic Sectoral Legal Systems," in *Yearbook of International Environmental Law*, vol. 1, ed. G. Handl (London: Graham and Trotman, 1990); David Downie, "Road Map or False Trail: Evaluating the Precedence of the Ozone Regime as Model and Strategy for Global Climate Change," *International Environmental Affairs* 7 (fall 1995): 321–345; and David Downie, "Global Environmental Policy: Governance through Regimes," in *Global Environmental Policy: Institutions, Law, and Policy*, ed. Regina Axelrod, David Downie, and Norman Vig, 2nd ed. (Washington, DC: Congressional Quarterly Press, 2005), 64–82.

39. For influential review discussions of this tradition, see and compare Friedrich Kratochwil and John Gerard Ruggie, "International Organization: A State of the Art on an Art of the State," *International Organization* 40 (1986): 753–776; James Dougherty and Robert Pfaltzgraff, *Contending Theories of International Relations*, 3rd ed. (New York: Harper and Row, 1990), ch. 10; and Joseph Grieco, "Anarchy and the Limits of Cooperation: A Realist Critique of the Newest Liberal Institutionalism," *International Organization* 42 (1988): 485–507.

40. Classic examples include Thucydides, Machiavelli, and Hobbes. Influential modern examples include Hans Morgenthau, *Politics among Nations*, 5th ed. (New York: Knopf, 1973); Robert Jervis, "Cooperation under the Security Dilemma," *World Politics* 30 (1978): 167–186; Kenneth Waltz, *Theory of International Politics* (Reading, MA: Addison-Wesley, 1979); and Glenn Snyder, "The Security Dilemma in Alliance Politics," *World Politics* 36 (1984): 461–495.

41. Constitutionalists believed "international governance is whatever international organizations do; and formal attributes of international organizations, such as their charters, voting procedures, committee structures and the like, account for what they do" (Kratochwil and Ruggie, "International Organization," 755). The institutional process approach examines influence, how information is produced and digested, who speaks to whom, how decisions are made, and so on. It argues that the outputs of international organizations do not always reflect their charters or official procedures. A classic example is Robert Cox and Harold Jacobson, eds., *The Anatomy of Influence* (New Haven, CT: Yale University Press, 1973).

42. For example, Richard Falk, *A Study of Future Worlds* (Princeton, NJ: Princeton University Press, 1975).

43. Important examples and discussions of functionalism include David Mitrany, *A Working Peace System* (Chicago: Quadrangle Books, 1943); David Mitrany, *The Functional Theory of Politics* (London: M. Robertson, 1975); and A. J. R. Groom and Paul Taylor, eds., *Functionalism: Theory and Practice in International Relations* (New York: Crane, Russak, 1975).

44. See and compare discussions in Kratochwil and Ruggie, "International Organization," 756–763; Dougherty and Pfaltzgraff, *Contending Theories of International Relations*, ch. 10; and Groom and Taylor, *Functionalism*, ch. 1.

45. Leading examples and discussion include Ernst Haas, *Beyond the Nation State* (Stanford, CA: Stanford University Press, 1964); Ernst Haas, "The Uniting of Europe and the Uniting of Latin America," *Journal of Common Market Studies* 5 (1967): 315–343; Philippe Schmitter, "Three Neo-functional Hypotheses about International Integration," *International Organization*

23 (1969): 161–166; Ernst Haas, "The Study of Regional Integration: Reflections on the Joy and Anguish of Pretheorizing," *International Organization* 24 (1970): 607–646; Joseph Nye, *Peace in Parts: Integration and Conflict in Regional Organization* (Boston: Little, Brown, 1977); Kratochwil and Ruggie, "International Organization," 757–759; and Dougherty and Pfaltzgraff, *Contending Theories of International Relations*, 431–447. Influential comparisons of functionalism and neofunctionalism include Haas, *Beyond the Nation State*, and Groom and Taylor, *Functionalism*, chs. 11–12.

46. An example is Ernst Haas, "On Systems and International Regimes," *World Politics* 27 (1975): 147–174; and Ernst Haas, *When Knowledge Is Power: Three Models of Change in International Organizations* (Berkeley: University of California Press, 1990).

47. Robert Keohane and Joseph Nye, *Transnational Relations and World Politics* (Cambridge, MA: Harvard University Press, 1972); Robert Keohane and Joseph Nye, "Transnational Relations and International Organizations," *World Politics* 27 (October 1974): 39–62.

48. Keohane and Nye, *Power and Interdependence*. Complex interdependence and turbulent fields share important concerns and insights.

49. John Gerard Ruggie, "International Responses to Technology: Concepts and Trends," *International Organization* 29 (1975): 570.

50. Haas, "On Systems and International Regimes," 147–174.

51. Keohane and Nye, *Power and Interdependence*, 5, 19.

52. Stephen Krasner, *International Regimes* (Ithaca, NY: Cornell University Press, 1983), 2.

53. This paragraph is adapted from I. William Zartman, *The 50% Solution* (New Haven, CT: Yale University Press, 1983), 9–10.

54. Oran Young, *International Cooperation* (Ithaca, NY: Cornell University Press, 1989), 13–14.

55. Michael M'Gonigle and Mark W. Zacher, *Pollution, Politics and International Law: Tankers at Sea* (Berkeley: University of California Press, 1979), 58–59, 84–85, 93–96; Jan Schneider, *World Public Order of the Environment: Toward an International Ecological Law and Organization* (Toronto: University of Toronto Press, 1979), 33, 92–93.

56. See Robert Keohane, *After Hegemony: Cooperation and Discord in the World Political Economy* (Princeton, NJ: Princeton University Press, 1984), for an influential discussion of why it is easier to change international regimes and other institutions to make them more effective than it is to create new ones.

57. For more information on the Convention on Migratory Species initiative on migratory sharks, see www.cms.int/bodies/meetings/regional/sharks/sharks_meetings.htm.

58. For an early analytical overview of these theoretical approaches, see Stephan Haggard and Beth A. Simmons, "Theories of International Regimes," *International Organization* 41 (summer 1987): 491–517.

59. Keohane and Nye, *Power and Interdependence*, 50–51.

60. For the former approach, see Robert Gilpin, *The Political Economy of International Relations* (Princeton, NJ: Princeton University Press, 1987); Grieco, "Anarchy and the Limits of Cooperation"; and Strange, "Cave! Hic Dragones," 337–343. Susan Strange, "The Persistent Myth of Lost Hegemony," *International Organization* 41 (summer 1987): 570, argues that inconsistency in U.S. policy rather than the loss of U.S. global hegemony has caused the erosion of international regimes.

61. Oran R. Young, "The Politics of International Regime Formation: Managing Natural Resources and the Environment," *International Organization* 43 (summer 1989): 355.

62. Fen Osler Hampson, "Climate Change: Building International Coalitions of the Like-minded," *International Journal* 45 (winter 1989–1990): 36–74.

63. See Peter M. Haas, "Do Regimes Matter? Epistemic Communities and Mediterranean Pollution Control," *International Organization* 43 (summer 1989): 378–403.

64. The issue of ocean dumping of radioactive wastes, in which scientific evidence was explicitly rejected as the primary basis for decision making by antidumping states, is analyzed in Judith Spiller and Cynthia Hayden, "Radwaste at Sea: A New Era of Polarization or a New Basis for Consensus?" *Ocean Development and International Law* 19 (1988): 345–366.

65. Robert Putnam, "Diplomacy and Domestic Politics: The Logic of Two-Level Games," *International Organization* 42, no. 3 (summer 1988): 427–460.

66. For an influential and accessible discussion of paradigm shifts, see Thomas Kuhn, *The Structure of Scientific Revolutions* (Chicago: University of Chicago Press, 1962). Our discussion of paradigm shifts in this section is not offered as a new theory to compete with existing theories of international regimes. Rather, this is supposed to represent a supplementary set of lenses through which to discuss environmental issues.

67. Harold and Margaret Sprout, *The Ecological Perspective in Human Affairs* (Princeton, NJ: Princeton University Press, 1965); Kenneth Boulding, "The Economics of the Coming Spaceship Earth," in *Environmental Quality in a Growing Economy*, ed. H. E. Jarrett (Baltimore: Johns Hopkins University Press, 1966).

68. For an analysis of neoclassical economic assumptions as they bear on environmental management, see Daniel A. Underwood and Paul G. King, "On the Ideological Foundations of Environmental Policy," *Ecological Economics* 1 (1989): 317–322.

69. See Michael E. Colby, *Environmental Management in Development: The Evolution of Paradigms* (Washington, DC: World Bank, 1990).

70. John McCormick, *Reclaiming Paradise: The Global Environmental Movement* (Bloomington: Indiana University Press, 1989), 67.

71. Lars-Göran Engfeldt, "The Road from Stockholm to Johannesburg," *UN Chronicle* 39, no. 3 (September–November 2002): 14–17.

72. See Clem Tisdell, "Sustainable Development: Differing Perspectives of Ecologists and Economists, and Relevance to LDCs," *World Development* 16 (1988): 377–378.

73. Donella H. Meadows et al. *The Limits to Growth* (New York: Universe Books, 1972); Council on Environmental Quality and Gerald O. Barney, *Global 2000: The Report to the President Entering the Twenty-first Century* (New York: Pergamon Press, 1980).

74. Julian Simon and Herman Kahn, eds. *The Resourceful Earth* (Oxford: Basil Blackwell, 1984).

75. For an account of the background of the sustainable development concept, see UN Center for Transnational Corporations, *Environmental Aspects of the Activities of Transnational Corporations: A Survey* (New York: United Nations, 1985).

76. See World Commission on Environment and Development, *Our Common Future* (Oxford: Oxford University Press, 1987).

77. Ibid.

78. See Jim MacNeill, "Sustainable Development, Economics and the Growth Imperative" (paper presented at the conference "The Economics of Sustainable Development," Smithsonian Institution, Washington, DC, January 23–26, 1990).

79. See Edith Brown Weiss, "In Fairness to Future Generations," *Environment* 32 (April 1990): 7ff. See similar arguments made in *Our Own Agenda*, report of the Latin American and Caribbean Commission on Development and Environment (Washington, DC, and New York: Inter-American Development Bank and UNDP, 1990).

80. See Alan Durning, "How Much Is Enough?" *Worldwatch* 3 (November–December 1990): 12–19.

81. See Yusuf J. Ahmad, Salah El Serafy, and Ernst Lutz, eds. *Environmental Accounting for Sustainable Development* (Washington, DC: World Bank, 1989). For a concrete example of how natural resources accounting would work, see Robert Repetto et al., *Accounts Overdue: Natural Resources Depreciation in Costa Rica* (Washington, DC: World Resources Institute, 1991).

82. See Partha Dasgupta and Karl Goran Maler, "The Environment and Emerging Development Issues" (paper presented at the World Bank Conference on Development Economics, April 26–27, 1990, Washington, DC), 14–20; Herman E. Daly, "Toward a Measure of Sustainable Social Net National Product," in Ahmad, Serafy, and Lutz, *Environmental Accounting for Sustainable Development*, 8–9; and Herman E. Daly and John B. Cobb Jr., *For the Common Good: Redirecting the Economy toward Community, the Environment and a Sustainable Future* (Boston: Beacon Press, 1989), 368–373, 401–455. A similar effort to rate the distributive effects of national policies is embodied in the UNDP's human development indicators in its annual Human Development Report available at www.undp.org/hdro.

83. Andrew Revkin, "A New Measure of Well-being from a Happy Little Kingdom," *New York Times*, October 10, 2005, F1. Nadia Mustafa, "What about Gross National Happiness?" *Time*, January 10, 2005, www.time.com/time/health/article/0,8599,1016266,00.html. For discussion, see Karma Ura and Karma Galay, eds., *Gross National Happiness and Development: Proceedings of the First International Seminar on Operationalization of Gross National Happiness* (Thimpu, Bhutan: Center for Bhutan Studies, 2004), www.bhutanstudies.org.bt. See also the website of the Third International Conference on Gross National Happiness, November 22–28, 2007, Bankok, Thailand, at www.gnh-movement.org.

84. For information on the Environmental Sustainability Index, see www.yale.edu/esi.

85. European Commission Eurostat, *Measuring Progress towards a More Sustainable Europe* (Brussels: Eurostat, 2007), http://ec.europa.eu/sustainable/docs/estat_2007_sds_en.pdf. The European Commission is the institution that acts as the administrative body, or executive branch, of the European Union (EU). Based in Brussels and employing about 25,000 civil servants, it is responsible for proposing legislation and policy, implementing decisions by the EU parliament and heads of state, and the general day-to-day operations of the EU.

86. See, e.g., Dasgupta and Maler, "The Environment and Emerging Issues," 22, and Sander G. Tideman, "Gross National Happiness: Towards a New Paradigm in Economics," in Ura and Galay, *Gross National Happiness and Development*, 222–246.

87. See Robert Repetto, *Promoting Environmentally Sound Economic Progress: What the North Can Do* (Washington, DC: World Resources Institute, 1990); and Daly, "Toward a Measure of Sustainable Social Net National Product."

88. "Economic Policies for Sustainable Development," ministerial brief, Conference on Environment and Development in Asia and the Pacific, October 10–16, 1990, Bangkok, Thailand (Manila: Asian Development Bank, October 1990); Latin American and Caribbean Commission on Development and Environment, *Our Own Agenda*; and Organization of American States,

Permanent Council, Status Report Submitted by the Chairman of the Special Working Group on the Environment (Washington, DC: General Secretariat of the OAS, February 6, 1991).

89. Al Gore, *Earth in the Balance: Ecology and the Human Spirit* (Boston: Houghton Mifflin, 1992), as cited in Gary C. Bryner, *From Promises to Performance: Achieving Global Environmental Goals* (New York: W. W. Norton, 1997), 329.

90. UN Conference on Environment and Development, *Agenda 21, Rio Declaration, Forest Principles* (New York: United Nations, 1992). All three documents are widely available online. See, for example, www.un.org/esa/sustdev/documents/agenda21/index.htm.

91. Ibid. See especially ch. 8 of Agenda 21.

92. See especially ch. 8 of Agenda 21.

93. The issue was woven through several chapters of Agenda 21 as well as the Rio Declaration and the Statement of Forest Principles.

94. Tideman, "Gross National Happiness," 229.

95. Martin Khor, "Globalisation and Sustainable Development: Challenges for Johannesburg," *Third World Resurgence* 139/140 (March–April 2002): www.twnside.org.sg/title/twr139a.htm.

96. Ibid.

97. James Gustave Speth, "Two Perspectives on Globalization and the Environment," in *Worlds Apart: Globalization and the Environment*, ed. James Gustave Speth (Washington, DC: Island Press, 2003), 12.

98. Ibid., 13.

99. For updated information on EU sustainable development policy, see the relevant official websites, including: http://ec.europa.eu/environment/eussd and http://ec.europa.eu/sustainable/welcome/index_en.htm.

100. "Top Legislature Endorses Climate Change Resolution," *China Daily*, August 28, 2009, www.chinadaily.com.cn/bizchina/2009-08/28/content_8629277.htm. Jonathan Watts, "Chinese Legislature Passes Its First Climate Change Resolution," *Guardian*, August 27, 2009, www.guardian.co.uk/environment/2009/aug/27/china-climate-change.

101. Paul Raskin et al., *Great Transition: The Promise and Lure of the Times Ahead* (Boston: Stockholm Environment Institute, 2002). Compare this analysis to Kuhn's analysis of paradigm shifts in science in Kuhn, *The Structure of Scientific Revolutions*.

102. Ibid., x.

103. Noted examples of his influential work include Thomas Homer-Dixon, "On the Threshold: Environmental Changes as Causes of Acute Conflict," *International Security* 16, no. 2 (1991): 76–116; Thomas Homer-Dixon, "Environmental Scarcities and Violent Conflict: Evidence from Cases," *International Security* 19, no. 1 (1994): 5–40; Thomas Homer-Dixon and Jessica Blitt, eds. *Ecoviolence: Links among Environment, Population and Security* (Lanham, MD: Rowman & Littlefield, 1998); and Thomas Homer-Dixon, *Environment, Scarcity and Violence* (Princeton, NJ: Princeton University Press, 1999). Recent discussions that review the field include Larry Swatuk, "Security, Cooperation, and the Environment," in *International Environmental Politics*, ed. Michelle Bestsill, Kathryn Hochesteltler, and Dimitri Stevis (New York: Palgrave, 2006); and Richard Matther, "Man, the State and Nature: Rethinking Environment Security," in *Handbook of Global Environmental Politics*, ed. Peter Dauvergne (Northampton: Edward Elgar, 2005). For current news, discussion, and reports, see the Environmental Change and Security Program website at www.wilsoncenter.org/index.cfm?fuseaction=topics.home&topic_id=1413.

104. The situation in Darfur is complex and tragic. The government and various rebel groups, which divide roughly on ethnic and religious lines in addition to their political differences, have opposed each other for many years. In Darfur, evidence indicates that government soldiers and allied militia groups have been responsible for significant atrocities. The Sudanese military and the Janjaweed, a Sudanese militia group recruited mostly from the Afro-Arab tribes, have been accused of genocide by several governments and human rights groups. In March 2005, the United Nations Security Council formally referred the situation in Darfur to the Prosecutor of the International Criminal Court (ICC). In 2007, the ICC issued arrest warrants for the former Sudanese Minister of State for the Interior, Ahmed Haroun, and a Janjaweed leader, Ali Kushayb, for crimes against humanity and war crimes. In March 2009, an arrest warrant was issued for the president of the Sudan, Omar al-Bashir. Sudan has rejected the ICC's jurisdiction in the case and all those accused of crimes remain in the Sudan.

105. Doug Hawley, "Drug Smugglers Curtail Scientists Work," *USA Today*, December 27, 2007, www.usatoday.com/tech/science/2007-12-26-border-scientists_N.htm

106. Colin H. Kahl, "Population Growth, Environmental Degradation, and State-Sponsored Violence: The Case of Kenya, 1991–93," *International Security* 23:2 (1998): 80–119.

107. Peter Goodspeed, "Poverty, Chaos Threaten Haiti, UN Envoy Warns," *National Post*, May 27, 2009, www.nationalpost.com/news/world/story.html?id=1636704.

108. Examples include Carolyn Pumphrey, ed. *Global Climate Change National Security Implications* (Carlisle, PA: Strategic Studies Institute, U.S. Army War College, 2008); Geoffrey Dabelko and P. J. Simmons, "Environment and Security: Core Ideas and U.S. Government Initiatives," *SAIS Review* (winter/spring 1997): 127–146; Gen. Gordon Sullivan (Ret.), et al. *National Security and the Threat of Climate Change* (Alexandria, VA: CAN Corporation, 2007); German Advisory Council on Global Change, "Climate Change as a Security Risk" (English translation), WBGU, May 11, 2007, www.wbgu.de/wbgu_jg2007_engl.pdf; and Simon Dalby, *Security and Environmental Change* (Cambridge, MA: Polity Press, 2009).

109. Oli Brown and Alec Crawford, *Rising Temperatures, Rising Tensions: Climate Change and the Risk of Violent Conflict in the Middle East* (Winnipeg: International Institute for Sustainable Development, 2009), 2. Available at www.iisd.org/security/es.

110. Oli Brown and Alec Crawford, *Climate Change and Security in Africa* (Winnipeg: International Institute for Sustainable Development, 2009), 2. Available at www.iisd.org/security/es.

111. For discussion, see J. Oglethorpe, J. Shambaugh, and R. Kormos, "Parks in the Crossfire: Strategies for Effective Conservation in Areas of Armed Conflict, *IUCN Protected Areas Programme: Parks* 14, no. 1 (2004): 2–8.

112. G. Debonnet and K. Hillman-Smith, "Supporting Protected Areas in a Time of Political Turmoil: The Case of World Heritage Sites in the Democratic Republic of Congo," *IUCN Protected Areas Programme: Parks* 14, no. 1 (2004): 11.

113. Ibid.

114. See, e.g., Talli Nauman, "Illegal Drugs Root of Evil for Conservation Community," *Herald Mexico*, August 1, 2006.

115. Hawley, "Drug Smugglers Curtail Scientists Work."

116. "Rio Declaration on Environment and Development," in *Report of the United Nations Conference on the Human Environment*, Stockholm, June 5–16, 1972, ch. 1. Available at www.un-documents.net/rio-dec.htm.

117. These concepts are adapted from David Kriebel et al., "The Precautionary Principle in Environmental Science," *Environmental Health Perspective* 109, no. 9 (September 2001): 871–876. See the article for a more complete discussion of these points.

118. Carolyn Raffensperger and Katherine Barrett, "In Defense of the Precautionary Principle," *Environmental Health Perspective* 109, no. 9 (September 2001): 811–812.

119. For a collection of examples, see Joel Tickner, Carolyn Raffensperger, and Nancy Myers, *The Precautionary Principle in Action: A Handbook*, Science and Environmental Health Network, www.sehn.org/rtfdocs/handbook-rtf.rtf.

120. Ibid.

121. Ministerial Declaration, Second International Conference on the Protection of the North Sea, London, November 24–25, 1987, seas-at-risk.org/1mages/1987%20London%20Declaration.pdf.

122. Preamble, Montreal Protocol, September 16, 1987, 26 ILM 1541. Text available from the Ozone Secretariat website at http://ozone.unep.org or directly at http://ozone.unep.org/Publications/MP_Handbook/Section_1.1_The_Montreal_Protocol/Preamble.shtml.

123. UN Framework Convention on Climate Change, United Nations, May 9, 1992, 31 ILM 849. Text available from the UNFCCC website at http://unfccc.int or directly at http://unfccc.int/essential_background/convention/background/items/1349.php.

124. See Article 10 and Article 11 at www.biodiv.org/biosafety/protocol.asp.

125. Article 1 of the Stockholm Convention on Persistent Organic Pollutants, May 22, 2001. Available online at http://chm.pops.int/Portals/0/Repository/convention_text/UNEP-POPS-COP-CONVTEXT-FULL.English.PDF.

126. Philippe Sand and Jacqueline Peel, "Environmental Protection in the Twenty-first Century: Sustainable Development and International Law," in *The Global Environment: Institutions, Law and Policy*, ed. Regina Axelrod, David Downie, and Norman Vig, 2nd ed. (Washington, DC: Congressional Quarterly Press, 2005), 56.

127. European Union, Communication from the commission on the precautionary principle COM 1. 1 final (Brussels: Commission of the European Communities, February 2, 2000), http://europa.eu.int/comm/off/health_consumer/precaution.htm.

128. See Tickner, Raffensperger, and Myers, *The Precautionary Principle in Action*, 16–17.

129. Ibid.

130. Ibid.

131. Kenneth R. Foster, Paolo Vecchia, and Michael H. Repacholi, "Science and the Precautionary Principle," *Science* 288, no. 5468 (May 12, 2000): 2.

132. For example, the appellate body of the WTO in the beef hormones case refused "to take a position on whether the principle amounts to customary international law, commenting that the international status of the principle is 'less than clear'" (Sand and Peel, "Environmental Protection the Twenty-first Century," 56).

133. These are personal observations by David Downie during negotiations related to the Montreal Protocol and Climate, Rotterdam, and Stockholm conventions.

134. Jon M. Van Dyke, "The Evolution and International Acceptance of the Precautionary Principle," in *Bringing New Law to Ocean Waters*, ed. David Caron and Harry Scheiber (Koninklijke, Netherlands: Martinus Nijhof, 2004), 357. Available at www.mmc.gov/sound/international wrkshp/pdf/vandyke.pdf.

Chapter 2

1. David Day, *The Whale War* (Vancouver and Toronto: Douglas and MacIntyre, 1987), 103–107.

2. Michael M'Gonigle and Mark W. Zacher, *Pollution, Politics and International Law: Tankers at Sea* (Berkeley: University of California Press, 1979).

3. See Peter Dauvergne, *Shadows in the Forest* (Cambridge, MA: MIT Press, 1997), 59–98; David W. Brown, *Addicted to Rent: Corporate and Spatial Distribution of Forest Resources in Indonesia: Implications for Forest Sustainability and Government Policy* (Jakarta: Indonesia-UK Tropical Forest Management Programme, 1999).

4. Richard Benedick, *Ozone Diplomacy* (Cambridge, MA: Harvard University Press, 1991), 59.

5. John McCormick, *Acid Earth: The Global Threat of Acid Pollution* (London: Earthscan, 1985), 88–90.

6. The German Green Party lost all of its parliamentary members in the first all-German elections since 1932 because it opposed reunification, but it had begun to rebound by mid-1991, when polls showed it had the support of 6 percent of the voters—above the 5 percent needed to achieve representation in the parliament. The Green Party won thirty-four seats in the German Parliament in 1998 and made history by becoming part of a coalition government with the Social Democratic Party. In 2002, the Green Party won fifty-five seats and continued its role in the coalition government with the Social Democratic Party, which lasted until 2005.

7. Brian Wynne, "Implementation of Greenhouse Gas Reductions in the European Community: Institutional and Cultural Factors," *Global Environmental Change Report* (March 1993): 113, 122.

8. With the 2008 election of Barack Obama to the U.S. presidency and the defeat of many antienvironmental Congressmen during the 2008 general election, many environmentalists were hopeful that they may have regained some influence in electoral politics.

9. *Earth Summit Update* 7 (March 1992): 3.

10. Detlev Sprinz and Tapani Vaahtoranta, "The Interest-based Explanation of International Environmental Policy," *International Organization* 48, no. 1 (1994): 77–105.

11. Carolyn Thomas, *The Environment in International Relations* (London: Royal Institute of International Affairs, 1992), 228.

12. For detailed information on this policy, see the European Commission's Climate Action website at http://ec.europa.eu/environment/climat/climate_action.htm.

13. On EU ambitions for global leadership on the environment, see Wynne, "Implementation of Greenhouse Gas Reductions," 102; Paleokrassas is quoted in *Energy, Economics and Climate Change* 4, no 7 (July 1994): 14.

14. Eugene Robinson and Michael Weisskopf, "Bonn Pushes Tough Stand on Warming; U.S. Puts Pressure on 3 Allies to Drop 2nd Stiff Initiative," *Washington Post*, June 9, 1992, A1.

15. Philippe Le Prestre and Evelyne Dufault, "Canada and the Kyoto Protocol on GHGs," *ISUMA* 2, no. 4 (winter 2001): 40.

16. For more information, see the "U.S. Conference of Mayors Climate Protection Agreement," Mayors Climate Protection Center website, at www.usmayors.org/climateprotection/agreement.htm.

17. Greg Nickels, "Keynote Address," Summit for American Prosperity: Washington and Metro Areas Working Together, Seattle.gov, June 12, 2008, www.seattle.gov/mayor/speeches/080612 proseritySummit.htm.

18. "Climate Action Plan," Salt Lake City Green, www.slcgreen.com/CAP/default.htm.

19. New York City, *Plan NYC Progress Report 2008* (New York: Mayor's Office of Long-Term Planning and Sustainability, 2008), 34. Available at www.nyc.gov/html/planyc2030/downloads/pdf/planyc_progress_report_2008.pdf.

20. "States with Renewable Portfolio Standards," U.S. Department of Energy, June 2007, http://apps1.eere.energy.gov/states/maps/renewable_portfolio_states.cfm. See also "Renewable and Alternative Energy Standards," Pew Center on Global Climate Change, www.pewclimate .org/what_s_being_done/in_the_states/rps.cfm.

21. Pew Center on Global Climate Change, *Learning from State Action on Climate Change: May 2008 Update* (Arlington, VA: Pew Center on Global Climate Change, 2008), 9. Available at www.pewclimate.org/docUploads/States%20Brief%20(May%202008).pdf. For updated information on the program, see information provided by the California Environmental Protection Agency, Air Resources Board, at www.arb.ca.gov/cc/capandtrade/capandtrade.htm.

22. See the Regional Greenhouse Gas Initiative website at www.rggi.org.

23. See the Western Climate Initiative website at www.westernclimateinitiative.org and the Midwestern Greenhouse Gas Reduction Accord website at www.midwesternaccord.org.

24. Ben Cubby, "Carbon Neutral NSW by 2020," *Sydney Morning Herald*, May 9, 2008, www.smh.com.au/news/environment/carbonneutral-nsw-by-2020/2008/05/08/1210131165892 .html.

25. Council of the Federation Secretariat, *Climate Change: Leading Practices by Provincial and Territorial Governments in Canada* (Ottawa: Council of the Federation Secretariat, 2007), 3. Available at www.councilofthefederation.ca/pdfs/CCInventoryAug3_EN.pdf.

26. See for example, the Clinton Climate Initiative at www.clintonfoundation.org/what-we-do/clinton-climate-initiative.

27. For a similar discussion that uses different terms, see David Downie, "UNEP and the Montreal Protocol: New Roles for International Organizations in Regime Creation and Change," in *International Organizations and Environmental Policy*, ed. Robert V. Bartlett, Priya A. Kurian, and Madhu Malik (Westport, CT: Greenwood Press, 1995).

28. Richard Elliott Benedick, "The Ozone Protocol: A New Global Diplomacy," *Conservation Foundation Letter* 4 (1989): 6–7; and Benedick, *Ozone Diplomacy*, 109–110.

29. For more details on the challenges that UNEP faced in the latter half of the 1990s, see David L. Downie and Marc A. Levy, "The United Nations Environment Programme at a Turning Point: Options for Change," in *The Global Environment in the Twenty-first Century: Prospects for International Cooperation*, ed. Pamela S. Chasek (Tokyo: United Nations University Press, 2000).

30. UNEP, "State of the Environment and Contribution of the United Nations Environment Programme to Addressing Substantive Environmental Challenges: Report of the Executive Director," UNEP/GC.23/3, October 21, 2004, www.unep.org/gc/gc23/working_docs.asp.

31. See UNEP, "United Nations Environment Programme Medium-Term Strategy 2010–2013," UNEP/GCSS.X/8, 2007, www.unep.org/PDF/FinalMTSGCSS-X-8.pdf.

32. Pamela S. Chasek, "The UN Commission on Sustainable Development: The First Five Years," in Chasek, *The Global Environment in the Twenty-first Century*, 385.

33. Stine Madland Kaasa, "The UN Commission on Sustainable Development: Which Mechanisms Explain Its Accomplishments?" *Global Environmental Politics* 7, no. 3 (August 2007): 114.

34. Ibid., 114–115. For more details on the consultative process, see www.un.org/Depts/los/consultative_process/consultative_process.htm.

35. Felix Dodds et al., "Post Johannesburg: The Future of the UN Commission on Sustainable Development," Stakeholder Forum for Our Common Future paper 9, November 2002, 5. Available at www.earthsummit2002.org/es/issues/governance/csdfuture.pdf.

36. Gunnar Sjöstedt and Bertram Spector, conclusion to *International Environmental Negotiation*, ed. Gunnar Sjöstedt (Newbury Park, CA: Sage, 1993), 306.

37. Pamela S. Chasek, "Scientific Uncertainty in Environmental Negotiations," in *Global Environmental Policies*, ed. Ho-Won Jeong (London: Palgrave, 2001).

38. Ibid.

39. For more information on the Millennium Ecosystem Assessment, see www.millenniumassessment.org.

40. "Summary of the First Special Session of the Committee on Science and Technology (CST S-1) and the Seventh Session of the Committee for the Review of the Implementation of the Convention (CRIC 7) of the UN Convention to Combat Desertification: 3–14 November 2008," *Earth Negotiations Bulletin* 4, no. 218 (November 17, 2008): 12. Available at www.iisd.ca/download/pdf/enb04218e.pdf.

41. Andrew Hurrell and Benedict Kingsbury, *The International Politics of the Environment* (Oxford: Clarendon Press, 1992), 2; Pamela S. Chasek, *Earth Negotiations: Analyzing Thirty Years of Environmental Diplomacy* (Tokyo: United Nations University Press, 2001).

42. See Khalil Sesmou, "The Food and Agriculture Organization of the United Nations: An Insider's View," *Ecologist* 21 (March–April 1991): 47–56, as well as other critical analyses in this special issue on the FAO.

43. See Richard Stone, "Researchers Score Victory over Pesticides—and Pests—in Asia," *Science* 256 (May 29, 1992): 1272–1273.

44. Michael Hansen, *Sustainable Agriculture and Rural Development: FAO at the Crossroads* (Yonkers, NY: Consumers Union of the United States, 1993), 16–18.

45. For example, the FAO has supported the Commission on Sustainable Development's Intergovernmental Panel on Forests and Intergovernmental Forum on Forests, as well as the United Nations Forum on Forests.

46. For more information about UNDP's Energy and Environment Group, see www.undp.org/energyandenvironment.

47. UNDP, *Evaluation of the Role and Contribution of UNDP in Environment and Energy* (New York: UNDP, 2008), www.undp.org/eo/documents/thematic/ee/EE-Full-Report.pdf.

48. This formulation is used in the context of a different conceptualization of the role of IGOs in global environmental policy making in Marc A. Levy, Robert O. Keohane, and Peter M. Haas, "Improving the Effectiveness of International Environmental Institutions," in *Institutions for the Earth: Sources of Effective International Environmental Protection*, ed. Peter M. Haas, Robert O. Keohane, and Marc A. Levy (Cambridge, MA: MIT Press, 1993), 400.

49. For a critical analysis of the environmental impacts of various multilateral development bank loans, see Bruce Rich, *Mortgaging the Earth: The World Bank, Environmental Impoverishment, and the Crisis of Development* (Boston: Beacon Press, 1994).

50. Jim Douglas, "World Bank Involvement in Sector Adjustment for Forests in Indonesia: The Issues" (unpublished paper, 1998).

51. World Bank/WWF, "WWF/World Bank Forest Alliance Launches Ambitious Program to Reduce Deforestation and Curb Illegal Logging," May 25, 2005, World Bank, http://web.world bank.org/WBSITE/EXTERNAL/NEWS/0,,contentMDK:20515080~pagePK:64257043~piPK:43 7376~theSitePK:4607,00.html, and World Bank/WWF, "WWF/World Bank Alliance: What We Do," WWF, www.worldwildlife.org/what/globalmarkets/forests/worldbankalliancetargets.html.

52. World Bank/WWF, "WWF/World Bank Forest Alliance Launches Ambitious Program."

53. Gareth Porter et al., *Study of GEF's Overall Performance* (Washington, DC: GEF, 1998), 44.

54. World Bank, *Biodiversity, Climate Change and Adaptation: Nature-based Solutions from the World Bank Portfolio* (Washington, DC: World Bank, 2008), 2. Available at http://sitere sources.worldbank.org/INTBIODIVERSITY/Resources/Biodiversity_10-1-08_final.pdf.

55. WWF, "The World Bank and Its Carbon Footprint: Why the World Bank Is Still Far from Being an Environment Bank," WWF-UK, June 23, 2008, 5. Available at http://assets.wwf .org.uk/downloads/world_bank_report.pdf.

56. World Bank, "World Bank Tells UN Earth Summit of New Action to Safeguard Environment," news release 97/1401/S, June 25, 1997.

57. Sustainable Energy and Economy Network/Institute for Policy Studies, "The World Bank and Fossil Fuels: A Clear and Present Danger," September 2002, 3. Available at www.seen.org/ PDFs/wb_brief_sept02.pdf.

58. World Bank Group, "Renewable Energy and Energy Efficiency," World Bank, http://go.worldbank.org/6XC42PKNI0.

59. WWF, "The World Bank and Its Carbon Footprint."

60. Janet Redman, *Dirty Is the New Clean: A Critique of the World Bank's Strategic Framework for Development and Climate Change* (Washington, DC: Institute for Policy Studies/Sustainable Energy and Economy Network, October 2008), 2. Available at www.ips-dc.org/reports/#770. This leap is due particularly to large increases in lending to coal projects by the International Finance Corporation (part of the World Bank group), effectively ending a bankwide informal moratorium on coal financing. Fossil fuel lending calculations are made by Oil Change International. Additional information compiled earlier in the year shows similar trends. See Heike Mainhardt-Gibbs, "World Bank Group Extractive Industries and Fossil Fuel Financing, FY05–FY08," Bank Information Center, July 23, 2008. Available at www.bicusa.org/en/Article .3840.aspx.

61. Redman, *Dirty Is the New Clean*, 7.

62. Mainhardt-Gibbs, "World Bank Group Extractive Industries and Fossil Fuel Financing."

63. "IMF Reviews Its Approach to Environmental Issues," *IMF Survey* (April 15, 1991): 124.

64. For more information about the HIPC initiative, see www.imf.org/external/np/ exr/facts/hipc.htm.

65. "Climate Change, Environment and the Work of the IMF," IMF, September 2008, www.imf.org/external/np/exr/facts/enviro.htm.

66. Ved P. Gandhi, *The IMF and the Environment* (Washington, DC: IMF, 1998).

67. The latter pledge referred to the clear-cutting of forests that had already been logged over but were still productive to plant oil palm and timber plantations; indeed, these plantations were rapidly becoming as important a source of logs as commercial logging concessions. Conversion of forests to oil palm plantations, usually accomplished by burning logging refuse after clear-cutting the forests, was the largest cause of the catastrophic forest fires that raged in Indonesia

in 1997 and 1998. See, for example, "Indonesia's Illegal Logging Crisis," Environmental Investigation Agency, September 12, 2005, www.eia-international.org/cgi/background/background .cgi?t=template&a=24.

68. Future conversion or change in forest land-use status was to be reviewed through a transparent and consultative process involving nongovernmental stakeholders and interdepartmental dialogue within the government. Finally, the agreement required that the government publish a list of applications received before the date of the agreement and "subject them to public review prior to final approval." This account of the adjustment loans to Indonesia in 1998 and 1999 is based on interviews by Gareth Porter in Jakarta in April 1999.

69. Ibid.

70. Ibid.

71. Macroeconomics Program Office, "Poverty Reduction for the Poor, Not the Privileged," Poverty Reduction Paper 1, WWF, May 30, 2003, www.panda.org/downloads/policy/poverty reductionpaper1.doc.

72. Ibid.

73. Belgium, West Germany, Luxembourg, France, Italy, and the Netherlands formed three organizations: the European Economic Community, the European Coal and Steel Community, and the European Atomic Energy Community.

74. The community has been a party to international conventions on environmental conservation since the 1970s. At present, it is a party to more than thirty conventions and agreements on the environment and takes an active part in the negotiations leading to the adoption of these instruments. The community also takes part, normally as an observer, in the activities and negotiations taking place within the context of international bodies or programs and in particular under the auspices of the United Nations.

75. For more information on EU environmental policy, see http://europa.eu/pol/env/ index_en.htm.

76. "European Parliament Seals Climate Change Package," European Parliament, December 12, 2008, www.europarl.europa.eu/pdfs/news/expert/infopress/20081216IPR44857/20081 216IPR44857_en.pdf.

77. Department of Sustainable Development, "Sustainable Development and the Organization of American States," Organization of American States, December 2006, 2. Available at www.oas.org/dsd/policy_series/dsd_eng.pdf.

78. UNEP, "Action Plan of the Environment Initiative of the New Partnership for Africa's Development," NEPAD, June 2003, www.nepad.org/2005/files/documents/113.pdf.

79. "APEC Economic Leaders' Declaration," APEC, November 18, 1998, www.apec.org/ apec/leaders__declarations/1998.html.

80. "Sydney APEC Leaders' Declaration on Climate Change, Energy Security and Clean Development," APEC, September 9, 2007, www.apec.org/etc/medialib/apec_media_library/ downloads/news_uploads/2007aelm.Par.0001.File.tmp/07_aelm_ClimateChangeEnergySec.pdf.

81. Adil Najam, "The View from the South: Developing Countries in Global Environmental Politics," in *The Global Environment: Institutions, Law and Policy*, ed. Regina S. Axelrod, David L. Downie, and Norman J. Vig, 2nd ed. (Washington, DC: Congressional Quarterly Press, 2005).

82. This description is based on "What Is the Group of 77?" Group of 77, www.g77.org/doc; and Najam, "The View from the South."

83. The organization was originally called the South Pacific Regional Environment Program. For more information on SPREP, see its official website at www.sprep.org.

84. For additional information about the Central American Commission on Environment and Development, see its website at www.ccad.ws.

85. See Michelle M. Betsill and Elisabeth Corell, eds., *NGO Diplomacy* (Cambridge, MA: MIT Press, 2008); Thomas Weiss and Leon Gordenker, eds., *NGOs, the UN and Global Governance* (Boulder, CO: Lynne Rienner, 1996); Paul Wapner, "Politics beyond the State: Environmental Actions and World Civic Politics," *World Politics* 47, no. 3 (April 1995): 311–340; Thomas Princen and Matthias Finger, eds., *Environmental NGOs in World Politics* (London and New York: Routledge, 1994); and Barbara J. Bramble and Gareth Porter, "Non-governmental Organizations and the Making of U.S. International Environmental Policy," in *The International Politics of the Environment*, ed. Andrew Hurrell and Benedict Kingsbury (Oxford: Clarendon Press, 1992).

86. "The History of Greenpeace," Greenpeace, www.greenpeace.org/international/about/history.

87. The National Environmental Directory lists more than 12,000 organizations in the United States concerned with the environment, but most of these are small local entities that do not attempt to work directly with international or national U.S. policy makers on international environmental issues (www.environmentaldirectory.net).

88. There has been much debate over the declining influence of the national U.S. environmental movement and the "death of environmentalism." For more information, see Robert Brulle and J. Craig Jenkins, "Fixing the Bungled U.S. Environmental Movement," *Contexts* 7, no. 2 (spring 2008): 14–19; Michael Shellenberger and Ted Nordhaus, "The Death of Environmentalism," Thebreakthrough.org, 2004, www.thebreakthrough.org/images/Death_of_Environmentalism.pdf; Christina Larson, "The Emerging Environmental Majority," *Washington Monthly*, May 2006, www.washingtonmonthly.com/features/2006/0605.larson.html; Dale Jamieson "The Heart of Environmentalism," in *Environmental Justice and Environmentalism: The Social Justice Challenge to the Environmental Movement*, ed. Ronald D. Sandler and Phaedra C. Pezzullo (Cambridge, MA: MIT Press, 2007), 85–104.

89. Ramachandra Guha, "The Environmentalism of the Poor," in *Varieties of Environmentalism*, ed. Ramachandra Guha and Juan Martinez-Alier (London: Earthscan, 1997), 15.

90. See Julie Fisher, *The Road from Rio: Sustainable Development and the Nongovernmental Movement in the Third World* (Westport, CT: Praeger, 1993), 123–128; and Monsiapile Kajimbwa, "NGOs and Their Role in the Global South," *International Journal of Not-for-Profit Law* 9, no. 1 (December 2006): 58–64.

91. Guha, "The Environmentalism of the Poor," 4.

92. Ibid.

93. See Third World Network, *The Battle for Sarawak's Forests* (Penang, Malaysia: World Rainforest Movement, 1989).

94. For representative press reports available online, see Sarah Stewart, "Malaysia's Penan Tribe Ups Anti-logging Campaign," Agence France-Presse, August 22, 2009, www.google.com/hostednews/afp/article/ALeqM5gC9ocrnNCQH_mjxYVgwQBarIH3nw; Stephen Then, "New Penan Blockages as Anti-loggers Protests Flare Up Again," *The Star* (Malaysia), July 22, 2009, http://thestar.com.my/news/story.asp?file=/2009/7/22/nation/4363112&sec=nation; "Logging Protests Spread in Borneo as Nomads Block Roads," *Survival*, August 24, 2009, www.survival-international.org/news/4889.

95. For more information about the Green Belt Movement, see its website at www.greenbelt movement.org.

96. For more information about Third World Network, see its website at www.twnside.org.sg.

97. For more information on the Center for Science and Environment, see its website at www.cseindia.org.

98. Interview with Barbara Bramble, National Wildlife Federation, March 1990; Stephen Schwartzman, "Deforestation and Popular Resistance in Acre: From Local Movement to Global Network" (paper presented to the Eighty-eighth Annual Meeting of the American Anthropological Association, Washington, DC, November 15–19, 1989).

99. David Malin Roodman, "Building a Sustainable Society," in State of the World 1999, ed. Lester R. Brown, Christopher Flavin, and Hilary French (New York: W. W. Norton, 1999), 183.

100. The NGOs started their campaign in 1997, and the OECD cancelled the talks in December 1998.

101. For more information on the International POPs Elimination Network, see its website at www.ipen.org.

102. Working with Merck and Genentech, the World Resources Institute, the World Wildlife Fund, and the Environmental and Energy Study Institute drafted an interpretive statement and persuaded President Clinton in 1993 to sign the treaty with such a statement attached.

103. For references to the boycott as well as broader discussion, see "Iceland," The Europa World Yearbook, 2004 (London: Taylor and Francis, 2004), 2049. Guillermo Herrera and Porter Hoagland, "Commercial Whaling, Tourism and Boycotts: An Economic Perspective," Marine Policy 30, no. 3 (May 2006): 261–269. Steinar Andresen, "Science and Politics in the International Management of Whales," Marine Policy 13, no. 2 (April 1989), 88–117. "Burger Chain Targeted," Los Angeles Times, June 19, 1988, http://articles.latimes.com/1988-06-19/news/mn-7670 _1_burger-king.

104. Scott Couder and Rob Harrison, "The Effectiveness of Ethical Consumer Behavior," in The Ethical Consumer, ed. Rob Harrison, Terry Newholm, and Diedre Shaw (London: Sage Publications, 2005), 89–104.

105. Robert Boardman, International Organization and the Conservation of Nature (Bloomington: Indiana University Press, 1981), 88–94.

106. Patricia Birnie, "The Role of International Law in Solving Certain Environmental Conflicts," in International Environmental Diplomacy: The Management and Resolution of Transfrontier Environmental Problems, ed. John E. Carroll (Cambridge: Cambridge University Press, 1988), 107–108.

107. Personal communication from a member of the U.S. delegation to the biodiversity negotiations, February 1994.

108. Kal Raustiala, "States, NGOs and International Environmental Institutions," International Studies Quarterly 41 (1997): 728.

109. The Earth Negotiations Bulletin was initially published as the Earth Summit Bulletin and was created by Johannah Bernstein, Pamela Chasek, and Langston James Goree VI. For more information, see www.iisd.ca/linkages.

110. Raustiala, "States, NGOs and International Environmental Institutions," 730. See also Pamela S. Chasek "Environmental Organizations and Multilateral Diplomacy: A Case Study of the Earth Negotiations Bulletin," in Multilateral Diplomacy and the United Nations Today, ed. James P. Muldoon Jr. et al., 3rd ed. (Boulder, CO: Westview, 2005).

111. Laura H. Kosloff and Mark C. Trexler, "The Convention on International Trade in Endangered Species: No Carrot, but Where's the Stick?" *Environmental Law Reporter* 17 (July 1987): 10225–10226.

112. Paul Lewis, "Rich Nations Plan $2 Billion for Environment," *New York Times*, March 17, 1994. Also see Zoe Young, "NGOs and the Global Environmental Facility: Friendly Foes?" *Environmental Politics* 8, no. 1 (1999): 243–267.

113. This discussion is based on Barbara J. Bramble and Gareth Porter, "Non-governmental Organizations and the Making of U.S. International Environmental Policy," in *The International Politics of the Environment*, ed. Andrew Hurrell and Benedict Kingsbury (Oxford: Clarendon Press, 1992), 325–346.

114. A. Enders, "Openness and the WTO" (working paper, International Institute for Sustainable Development, Winnipeg, Canada, 1996); Dan Esty, *Why the WTO Needs Environmental NGOs* (Geneva: International Centre for Trade and Sustainable Development, 1997).

115. Marc Williams and Lucy Ford, "The World Trade Organisation, Social Movements and Global Environmental Management," *Environmental Politics* 8, no. 1 (1999): 281.

116. Michael Margolik and Doug Russell, "Corporate Greenhouse Gas Reduction Targets," Pew Center on Global Climate Change, November 2001, www.pewclimate.org/docUploads/ghg_targets.pdf. See also the Business Environmental Leadership Council website at http://www.pewclimate.org/companies_leading_the_way_belc.

117. "States Taking Action on Climate," Environmental Defense, September 13, 2007, www.edf.org/article.cfm?contentID=4889.

118. See Gareth Porter, *The United States and the Biodiversity Convention: The Case for Participation* (Washington, DC: Environmental and Energy Study Institute, 1992). The Industrial Biotechnology Association merged with the Association of Biotechnology Companies in 1993 to form Biotechnology Industry Organization, or BIO.

119. *International Environment Reporter*, June 2, 1993, 416.

120. For example, in 2008, Munich Re announced that insured losses came in at $45 billion, up from nearly $30 billion in 2007. It said total economic losses, including losses not covered by insurance, leapt to some $200 billion from 2007's $82 billion. "Catastrophe Figures for 2008 Confirm That Climate Agreement Is Urgently Needed," Munich Re, December 29, 2008, www.munichre.com/en/press/press_releases/2008/2008_12_29_press_release.aspx.

121. For more information on the UNEP Finance Initiative, see www.unepfi.org.

122. "Proposal Outlines Steps Negotiators Should Take to Put Insurance in the Copenhagen Climate Change Agreement," Munich Climate Insurance Initiative, December 8, 2008, www.climate-insurance.org/upload/pdf/20081205_COP_14_MCII_press_release_final.pdf.

123. M'Gonigle and Zacher, *Pollution, Politics and International Law*, 58–62.

124. S. Res. 98, "A resolution expressing the sense of the Senate regarding the conditions for the United States becoming a signatory to any international agreement on greenhouse gas emissions under the United Nations Framework Convention on Climate Change." 105th Congress, 1st Session, http://thomas.loc.gov/cgi-bin/bdquery/z?d105:SE00098. It is widely known as the Byrd-Hagel Resolution.

125. Day, *The Whale War*, 103–107.

126. Laura Eggerton, "Giant Food Companies Control Standards," *Toronto Star,* April 28, 1999.

127. Aron Tal, *Pollution in the Promised Land: An Environmental History of Israel* (Berkeley, CA: University of California Press, 2002), 305.

128. Interview with William Nitze, Alliance to Save Energy, June 20, 1994.

129. Jennifer Clapp, "Transnational Corporate Interests and Global Environmental Governance: Negotiating Rules for Agricultural Biotechnology and Chemicals," *Environmental Politics* 12, no. 4 (2003): 1–23. Prominent industry groups at the negotiations included the Biotechnology Industry Organization (a U.S.-based biotechnology lobby group), BioteCanada, Japan Bioindustry Association, the International Chamber of Commerce, and the International Association of Plant Breeders for the Protection of Plant Varieties.

130. Alan S. Miller and Durwood Zaelke, "The NGO Perspective," *Climate Alert* 7, no. 3 (May–June 1994): 3.

131. *Daily Environment Reporter*, August 27, 1992, B2.

132. Examples include the companies that signed the Global Roundtable on Climate Change statement (http://grocc.ei.columbia.edu), participants in the United States Climate Action Partnership (www.us-cap.org) and Combat Climate Change initiatives (www.combatclimate change.org), and the companies profiled on the Pew Center on Global Climate Change website at www.pewclimate.org/companies_leading_the_way_belc/company_profiles.

133. Robert L. Paarlberg, "Managing Pesticide Use in Developing Countries," in *Institutions for the Earth: Sources of Effective International Environmental Protection*, ed. Peter M. Haas, Robert O. Keohane, and Marc A. Levy (Cambridge, MA: MIT Press, 1993), 319.

134. See Stephen Schmidheiny, with the Business Council for Sustainable Development, *Changing Course: A Global Business Perspective on Development and the Environment* (Cambridge, MA: MIT Press, 1992).

135. See the World Business Council for Sustainable Development website at www.wbcsd.org.

136. Steinar Andresen and Jon B. Skjærseth, "Can International Secretariats Promote Effective Co-operation?"—a background paper written for the United Nations University Conference on Synergies and Co-ordination between Multilateral Environmental Agreements, Tokyo, Japan, July 14–16, 1999. Available at www.geic.or.jp/interlinkages/docs/Andresen.PDF.

137. Rosemary Sandford, "International Environmental Treaty Secretariats: Stage-Hands or Actors," in *Green Globe Yearbook of International Cooperation on Environment and Development 1994*, ed. Helge Ole Bergesen and Georg Parmann (Oxford: Oxford University Press, 1994), 21.

138. Andresen and Skjaerseth, "Can International Secretariats Promote Effective Co-operation?" 15.

139. Discussion of these two topics has been based on the analysis presented in Steffen Bauer, Per-Olof Busch, and Bernd Siebenhüner, "Administering International Governance: What Role for Treaty Secretariats?" (Global Governance Working Paper 29, October 2007), www.glogov.org/images/doc/WP29.pdf.

140. This observation is supported by personal observations of the authors during attendance at various global environmental negotiations since 1990. For discussion, see Richard Elliot Benedick, "Perspectives of a Negotiation Practitioner," in *International Environmental Negotiation*, ed. Gunnar Sjöstedt (Newbury Park, CA: Sage Publication, 1993), 224.

141. Bauer, Busch, and Siebenhüner, "Administering International Governance," 5.

142. Ibid., 18–19.

143. Ibid., 10.

144. UNFCCC website statistics, cited March 17, 2009, available at http://unfccc.int/essential_background/about_the_website/items/3358.php.

145. Oran Young, *International Environmental Governance: Protecting the Environment in a Stateless Society* (Ithaca, NY: Cornell University Press, 1994), 170.

146. Bernd Siebenhüner and Jessica Suplie, "Implementing the Access and Benefit Sharing Provisions of the CBD: A Case for Institutional Learning," *Ecological Economics* 53 (2005): 507–522; Bauer, Busch, and Siebenhüner, "Administering International Governance," 19.

147. Johan Kaufmann, *Conference Diplomacy: An Introductory Analysis*, 3rd ed. (London: Macmillan, 1996), 93–94.

148. Benedick, "Perspectives of a Negotiation Practitioner," 225. Downie also observed this firsthand while attending the 1990 ozone negotiations in London.

149. Farhana Yamin and Joanna Depledge, *The International Climate Change Regime: A Guide to Rules, Institutions and Procedures* (Cambridge: Cambridge University Press, 2005); Bauer, Busch, and Siebenhüner, "Administering International Governance."

150. Bauer, Busch, and Siebenhüner, "Administering International Governance," 13.

151. This observation is supported by personal observations of the authors and conversations with secretariat and government officials during attendance at global environmental negotiations since 1990.

152. See, for example, Steffen Bauer, "The United Nations and the Fight against Desertification: What Role for the UNCCD Secretariat?" in *Governing Global Desertification*, ed. Pierre Marc Johnson, Karel Mayrand and Marc Paquin (Hampshire, UK: Ashgate Publishing, 2006), 83.

Chapter 3

1. For a more detailed discussion on this dilemma, see Richard Elliot Benedick, "Perspectives of a Negotiation Practitioner," in *International Environmental Negotiations*, ed. Gunnar Sjöstedt (Beverly Hills, CA: Sage, 1993), 240–243.

2. For an early discussion of decision-making procedures in global environmental regimes, see Glenn Wiser and Stephen Porter, "Effective Decision-Making: A Review of Options for Making Decisions to Conserve and Manage Pacific Fish Stocks" (Washington, DC: WWF–U.S., January 1999), www.ciel.org/Publications/effectivedecisionmaking.pdf.

3. Marc A. Levy, "European Acid Rain: The Power of Tote-Board Diplomacy," in *Institutions for the Earth*, ed. Peter M. Haas, Robert O. Keohane, and Marc A. Levy (Cambridge, MA: MIT Press, 1993), 81.

4. *Acid rain* is a broad term referring to wet or dry deposition from the atmosphere that contains higher than normal amounts of nitric and sulfuric acids. When sulfur dioxide and nitrogen oxide get released from coal-burning power plants and other sources, they mix with water vapor, oxygen, and other compounds in the atmosphere to form mild solutions of sulfuric acid and nitric acid, which then gets deposited on the ground, on trees, and in lakes and rivers either via rain, snow, and fog (wet deposition) or dust particles that stick to hard surfaces (dry deposition).

5. Lars Bjorkbom, "Resolution of Environmental Problems: The Use of Diplomacy," in *International Environmental Diplomacy: The Management and Resolution of Transfrontier Environmental Problems*, ed. John E. Carroll (Cambridge: Cambridge University Press, 1988), 128; Harald Dovland, "Monitoring European Transboundary Air Pollution," *Environment* 29 (December 1987): 12.

6. The Federal Republic of Germany (West Germany) and the German Democratic Republic (East Germany) merged in 1990. Germany had been split into two countries by the Allied powers following World War II. Federal Republic of Germany is the official name of the reunited state, although it is commonly called Germany.

7. Although the United States was not involved in transboundary air pollution in Europe, it was concerned about a similar situation whereby U.S. emissions were causing acid rain in Canada. See Don Munton, "Acid Rain and Transboundary Air Quality in Canadian-American Relations," *American Review of Canadian Studies* 27, no. 3 (fall 1997): 327–358.

8. Levy, "European Acid Rain," 83.

9. Don Hinrichsen, "Acid Indigestion in Stockholm," *ambio* 11, no. 5 (1982): 320–321.

10. Sten Nelson and Peter Druinker, "The Extent of Forest Decline in Europe," *Environment* 29, no. 9 (1987): 7–8.

11. The 1985 Helsinki Protocol on the Reduction of Sulfur Emissions or Their Transboundary Fluxes by at least 30 percent entered into force on September 2, 1987. See the official UNECE website for details and the convention text: www.unece.org/env/lrtap/sulf_h1.htm.

12. Seven states pledged to reduce their emissions by 40 to 50 percent by various dates. See John McCormick, *Acid Earth: The Global Threat of Acid Pollution* (London: Earthscan, 1985), 11 (especially figure 1).

13. The 1994 Oslo Protocol on Further Reduction of Sulfur Emissions entered into force on August 5, 1998. See the official UNECE website for details and the convention text: www.unece.org/env/lrtap/fsulf_h1.htm.

14. Henrik Selin and Stacy D. VanDeveer, "Mapping Institutional Linkages in European Air Pollution Politics," *Global Environmental Politics* 3, no. 3 (August 2003): 14–46.

15. The 1988 Protocol Concerning the Control of Nitrogen Oxides or Their Transboundary Fluxes entered into force on February 14, 1991. See the official UNECE website for details and the convention text: www.unece.org/env/lrtap/nitr_h1.htm.

16. See Levy, "European Acid Rain," 99–100.

17. The 1991 Geneva Protocol Concerning the Control of Emissions of Volatile Organic Compounds or Their Transboundary Fluxes entered into force on September 29, 1997. See the official UNECE website for details and the convention text: www.unece.org/env/lrtap/vola_h1.htm.

18. The 1998 Protocol on Heavy Metals entered into force on December 29, 2003. See the official UNECE website for details and the convention text: www.unece.org/env/lrtap/hm_h1.htm.

19. The 1998 Aarhus Protocol on Persistent Organic Pollutants (POPs) entered into force on 23 October 2003. See the official UNECE website for details and the convention text: www.unece.org/env/lrtap/pops_h1.htm.

20. See Henrik Selin, "Regional POPs Policy: The UNECE/CLRTAP POPs Agreement," in *Northern Lights against POPs: Combating Toxic Threats in the Arctic*, ed. David L. Downie and Terry Fenge (Montreal: McGill-Queens University Press, 2003); and Noelle Eckley and Henrik Selin, "Science, Politics, and Persistent Organic Pollutants: Scientific Assessments and Their Role in International Environmental Negotiations," *International Environmental Agreements: Politics, Law and Economics* 3, no. 1 (2003): 17–42.

21. Noelle Eckley, "Dependable Dynamism: Lessons for Designing Scientific Assessment Processes in Consensus Negotiations," *Global Environmental Change* 12 (2002): 15–23.

22. See the official UNECE LRTAP website for updated ratification information at www.unece.org/env/lrtap/multi_h1.htm.

23. See "Targets and Trends," *Acid News* 3 (October 1997): 11, as cited in Jørgen Wettestad, "The 1999 Multi-pollutant Protocol: A Neglected Break-Through in Solving Europe's Air Pollution Problems," in *Yearbook of International Co-operation on Environment and Development 2001/2002,* ed. Olav Schram Stokke and Øystein B. Thommessen (London: Earthscan Publications, 2001), 36.

24. Wettestad, "The 1999 Multi-pollutant Protocol," 36.

25. Ute Collier, "Windfall Emission Reduction in the UK," in *Cases in Climate Change Policy: Political Reality in the European Union*, ed. Ute Collier and Ragnar E. Löfstedt (London: Earthscan, 1997), 87–108, as cited in Wettestad, "The 1999 Multi-pollutant Protocol," 39.

26. Wettestad, "The 1999 Multi-pollutant Protocol," 39. In an overview of the total implementation costs for each country, Germany came out clearly at the top, with €2.15 billion per year, almost twice as much as number two on the list, the United Kingdom. See "European Union— Commission Proposes National Ceilings for Sulfur Dioxide, NOx, VOCs, Ammonia," *International Environmental Reporter* 22, no. 13 (1999): 519.

27. The 1999 Protocol to Abate Acidification, Eutrophication and Ground-Level Ozone entered into force on May 17, 2005. See the official UNECE website for details and the convention text: www.unece.org/env/lrtap/multi_h1.htm.

28. See the official UNECE LRTAP website for updated ratification information at www.unece.org/env/lrtap/multi_h1.htm.

29. Netherlands Environmental Assessment Agency, *Review of the Gothenburg Protocol: Report of the Task Force on Integrated Assessment Modeling and the Centre for Integrated Assessment Modeling* (Bilthoven: Netherlands Environmental Assessment Agency, December 31, 2007), www.pbl.nl/en/publications/2007/ReviewoftheGothenburgProtocol.html.

30. For information on the Non-Aligned Movement, see its website at http://espana.cubanoal.cu/ingles/index.html. The coalition has taken positions on hazardous waste trade for more than twenty years.

31. Carol Annette Petsonk, "The Role of the United Nations Environment Programme (UNEP) in the Development of International Environmental Law," *American University Journal of International Law and Policy* 5 (winter 1990): 374–377; *International Environment Reporter*, April 1989, 159–161.

32. For the text of the convention, meeting reports, official documents, updated lists of signatories and ratifications, and other information on the regime, see the Basel Convention website at www.basel.int.

33. See David P. Hackett, "An Assessment of the Basel Convention on the Control of Transboundary Movements of Hazardous Wastes and Their Disposal," *American University Journal of International Law and Policy* 5 (winter 1990): 313–322; Mark A. Montgomery, "Travelling Toxic Trash: An Analysis of the 1989 Basel Convention," *Fletcher Forum of World Affairs* 14 (summer 1990): 313–326.

34. *International Environment Reporter*, April 1989, 159–160.

35. *Greenpeace Waste Trade Update* 2 (July 15, 1989, and December 1989).

36. Party data is accurate as of September 9, 2009. For updated treaty information, see the African Union's official website at www.africa-union.org/root/au/Documents/Treaties/treaties.htm.

37. Two other regional conventions on hazardous wastes have been adopted since 1992. The Convention to Ban the Importation into Forum Island Countries of Hazardous and Radioactive Wastes and to Control the Transboundary Movement and Management of Hazardous Wastes within the South Pacific Region (Waigani Convention) was adopted on September 16, 1995, in Papua New Guinea. The Acuerdo Regional sobre Movimiento Transfronterizo de Desechos Peligrosas (Regional Convention on the Transboundary Movement of Hazardous Wastes) was adopted by Costa Rica, El Salvador, Guatemala, Honduras, Nicaragua, and Panama in December 1992.

38. *International Environment Reporter,* May 6, 1992, 275.

39. Only the republics of the former Soviet Union, desperate for foreign exchange and willing to disregard the health and environmental consequences, appeared willing to accept significant shipments of hazardous wastes. See Steven Coll, "Free Market Intensifies Waste Problem," *Washington Post,* March 23, 1994; Tamara Robinson, "Dirty Deals: Hazardous Waste Imports into Russia and Ukraine," *CIS Environmental Watch* (Monterey Institute of International Studies) 7, no. 5 (fall 1993).

40. Greenpeace, *The International Trade in Wastes: A Greenpeace Inventory,* 5th ed. (Washington, DC: Greenpeace, 1990); "Chemicals: Shipment to South Africa Draws Enviro Protests," *Greenwire,* February 18, 1994; and Michael Satchell, "Deadly Trade in Toxics," *U.S. News and World Report,* March 7, 1994, 64–67.

41. John H. Cushman Jr., "Clinton Seeks Ban on Export of Most Hazardous Waste," *New York Times,* March 1, 1994; "Basel Convention Partners Consider Ban on Exports of Hazardous Wastes," *International Environment Reporter,* March 22, 1994, A9.

42. Charles P. Wallace, "Asia Tires of Being the Toxic Waste Dumping Ground for Rest of World—Environment: A Global Conference in Geneva Could End Many Recycling Programs in Developing Nations." *Los Angeles Times,* March 23, 1994, cited in *Greenwire,* March 23, 1994. For a detailed account of the Geneva meeting, see Jim Puckett and Cathy Fogel, "A Victory for Environment and Justice: The Basel Ban and How It Happened," Basel Action Network, September 1994, www.ban.org/about_basel_ban/a_victory.html.

43. Greenpeace, *The International Trade in Wastes: Database of Known Hazardous Waste Exports from OECD to Non-OECD Countries: 1989–March 1994* (Washington, DC: Greenpeace, 1994.

44. Jim Puckett, "The Basel Ban: A Triumph over Business-as-Usual" (Amsterdam: Basel Action Network [Greenpeace], October 1997), www.ban.org/about_basel_ban/jims_article.html. In mid-2005, the Ban Amendment still needed five more instruments of ratification. For up-to-date information, see the Basel Convention website at www.basel.int.

45. For up-to-date information, see www.basel.int/ratif/protocol.htm.

46. See "Regional Centers," Basel Convention, www.basel.int/centers/centers.html.

47. David Downie, personal observation and discussion during COP-7. Other officials echoed these remarks at several subsequent meetings of the Basel and Stockholm conventions attended by Downie.

48. In February 2007, the company that had leased the tanker, Trafigura, settled with the government for the equivalent of US$198 million. As part of the agreement, the government released three jailed Trafigura executives, dropped all criminal charges against the company and its executives, and sealed the investigation results. International Network for Environmental Compliance and Enforcement, "Côte d'Ivoire Toxic Waste Scandal Triggers Legal Action in 3

Countries," *INECE Newsletter* 14 (April 2007): www.inece.org/newsletter/14/regional
_africa.html.

49. For more information on COP-8 and the issue discussed in this section, see official documents from the meeting, including the meeting report, available on the Basel Convention website at www.basel.int/meetings/meetings.html. See also "Summary of the Eighth Meeting of the Parties to the Basel Convention: 27 November–1 December 2006," *Earth Negotiation Bulletin* 20, no. 25 (December 4, 2006), www.iisd.ca/vol20/enb2025e.html.

50. The Nairobi Declaration on e-waste states that parties will work to promote awareness on e-waste, clean technology, and green design; encourage information exchange from developed to developing countries; improve waste management controls relevant to e-waste; and prevent and combat illegal traffic of e-wastes.

51. For more information on COP-9 and the issues discussed in this section, see official documents from the meeting, including the meeting report, available on the Basel Convention website at www.basel.int/meetings/meetings.html. See also "Summary of the Ninth Meeting of the Parties to the Basel Convention: 23–27 June 2008," *Earth Negotiation Bulletin* 20, no. 31 (June 30, 2008), www.iisd.ca/vol20/enb2031e.html.

52. UNEP/Basel Convention Press Release, "Basel Convention Launches New Initiative on Computing Equipment," Bali, Indonesia, June 27, 2008. See also relevant documents from COP-9.

53. The remainder of this section on the Basel Convention draws on the official report of the meeting with regard to the general views expressed by parties. It also relies heavily on the information, analysis, and insights found in the "Summary of the Ninth Meeting of the Parties to the Basel Convention."

54. "Summary of the Ninth Meeting of the Parties to the Basel Convention: 23–27 June 2008," www.iisd.ca/vol20/enb2031e.html.

55. As stated in the *Earth Negotiations Bulletin*, "It is not surprising that the COP was unable to resolve the issue of interpretation of Article 17(5) of the Basel Convention, which will determine how many ratifications are required for the Ban Amendment to enter into force. In essence, delegates are divided into two camps. The first supports the 'current time' approach, according to which the number of ratifications required for the Ban Amendment to enter into force should be based on the current number of parties to the Basel Convention, namely 170. The second camp defends the 'fixed time' approach, according to which the number of ratifications required should be calculated on the basis of the number of parties to the Convention when the Ban Amendment was adopted, namely 82. To complicate matters, two different views are held within the second camp. One claims that the number of ratifications required for the Ban to enter into force has been met, as 63 parties, more than three-quarters of 82, have ratified the Amendment. The other argues that the magic number has not yet been met, as it is only the ratifications of those parties 'who accepted' the amendment in 1995 that count, and not the ratifications of those who joined the Convention later on." "Summary of the Ninth Meeting of the Parties to the Basel Convention: 23–27 June 2008," www.iisd.ca/vol20/enb2031e.html.

56. Ibid.

57. Statistics in this paragraph, which are commonly used estimates, are from the International Labor Organization at www.ilo.org/public/english/protection/safework/papers/smechem/ch2.htm.

58. The Toxic Substances Control Act (TSCA) of 1976 provides the Environmental Protection Agency (EPA) with authority to impose reporting, record-keeping, and testing requirements,

as well as restrictions relating to chemical substances and/or mixtures. Certain substances are generally excluded from TSCA, including, among others, food, drugs, cosmetics, and pesticides; thus not all toxic products are included. It includes provisions that anyone making or importing a potentially harmful substance notify the EPA. The 2,000 to 3,000 number thus refers to annual notifications. For detailed information, see www.epa.gov/lawsregs/laws/tsca.html.

59. Thomas R. Dunlap, *DDT: Scientists, Citizens, and Public Policy* (Princeton, NJ: Princeton University Press, 1981); J. G. Koppe and J. Keys, "PCBs and the Precautionary Principle," in *The Precautionary Principle in the 20th Century*, ed. P. Harremoës et al. (London: Earthscan, 2002), 64–78.

60. The action plan produced at the conference called for improved international efforts to develop and harmonize procedures for assessing and managing hazardous substances and to make more resources available to developing countries for building domestic capacity.

61. Global agreements include the 1972 International Convention on the Prevention of Marine Pollution by Dumping of Wastes and Other Matter (London Convention) and the MARPOL Convention, which includes the 1973 International Convention for the Prevention of Pollution from Ships and its 1978 protocol. Early regional and river agreements that touched on hazardous chemicals include the 1972 Convention for the Prevention of Marine Pollution by Dumping from Ships and Aircraft (Oslo Convention); 1974 Convention for the Prevention of Marine Pollution from Land-Based Sources (Paris Convention); 1974 Convention on the Protection of the Marine Environment of the Baltic Sea Area (Helsinki Convention); 1976 Convention on the Protection of the Rhine against Chemical Pollution; 1976 Protocol for the Prevention of Pollution of the Mediterranean Sea by Dumping from Ships and Aircraft; and the 1978 Great Lakes Water Quality Agreement.

62. Jonathan Krueger and Henrik Selin, "Governance for Sound Chemicals Management: The Need for a More Comprehensive Global Strategy," *Global Governance* 8 (2002): 323–342.

63. David G. Victor, "Learning by Doing in the Nonbinding International Regime to Manage Trade in Hazardous Chemicals and Pesticides," in *The Implementation and Effectiveness of International Environmental Commitments: Theory and Practice*, ed. David G. Victor et al. (Cambridge, MA: MIT Press, 1998), 228.

64. The IOMC includes UNEP, FAO, the International Labor Organization (ILO), WHO, UNIDO, UNITAR, and OECD. Other global institutions active on chemicals include the GEF, UNDP, and the World Bank. Regional institutions active on chemicals include the Arctic Council, European Union, Great Lakes Program, Helsinki Commission (HELCOM), North American Agreement on Environmental Cooperation (NAAEC)/Sound Management of Chemicals Initiative, OECD, and the Oslo-Paris Commission for the Protection of the Marine Environment of the North-East Atlantic (OSPAR).

65. For the text of the convention, official documents from its negotiation, reports from the Conference of Parties, updated lists of parties, and other information, see the Rotterdam Convention website at www.pic.int. Leading analyses of the development and content of the Rotterdam Convention include Victor, "Learning by Doing in the Nonbinding International Regime to Manage Trade in Hazardous Chemicals and Pesticides," and Richard Emory Jr., "Probing the Protections in the Rotterdam Convention on Prior Informed Consent," *Colorado Journal of International Environmental Law and Policy* 23 (2001): 47–91.

66. Of course, extensive variations occur in substances, species, and exposures. For broader discussions of the science of POPs, see Downie and Fenge, *Northern Lights against POPs,* and

Theo Colborn, *Our Stolen Future: Are We Threatening Our Fertility, Intelligence, and Survival?* (New York: Dutton, 1996).

67. For a discussion of the science and politics of this point, see Downie and Fenge, *Northern Lights against POPs.*

68. Other initiatives also contributed to the process. For example, in November 1995, the Washington Declaration issued from the Intergovernmental Conference to Adopt a Global Programme of Action for Protection of the Marine Environment from Land-Based Activities (GPA) called for talks on a legally binding treaty targeting the dirty dozen.

69. For official proceedings of the workshops, see http://irptc.unep.ch/pops/newlayout/prodocas.htm. For background on the workshops, see http://irptc.unep.ch/pops/newlayout/wkshpintro.htm.

70. These are personal observations and discussions by David Downie with UNEP Chemicals and national government officials during this period and during the first negotiating session in 1998.

71. For official reports and other documents from the negotiations, see http://chm.pops .int/Convention/Negotiations/tabid/62/language/en-US/Default.aspx. For detailed secondary-source reports, see www.iisd.ca/linkages/chemical/index.html.

72. The World Health Organization estimated that about 250 million new cases of malaria cases occur each year and nearly 1 million deaths. People living in the poorest countries are the most vulnerable. Malaria is a serious problem especially in Africa, where its effects lead to 20 percent of childhood deaths. An African child has on average between 1.6 and 5.4 episodes of malaria fever each year. And every thirty seconds a child dies from malaria ("10 Facts on Malaria," WHO, www.who.int/features/factfiles/malaria/en/index.html). For detailed information and links, see www.who.int/topics/malaria/en.

73. For detailed analysis of the convention, see David Downie, "Global POPs Policy: The 2001 Stockholm Convention on Persistent Organic Pollutants," in *Northern Lights against POPs: Combating Toxic Threats in the Arctic*, ed. David L. Downie and Terry Fenge (Montreal: McGill-Queens University Press, 2003), 133–159.

74. Very small amounts of DDT can also be used as an intermediate in production of the chemical dicofol with the understanding that no DDT will be released into the environment.

75. Aspects of this debate and the resulting procedure are addressed in several chapters of Downie and Fenge, *Northern Lights against POPs.*

76. For a detailed discussion of this process, including the original version of Figure 3.3, see Downie, "Global POPs Policy," 140–142.

77. See, in particular paragraphs 7(a) and 9 of Article 8 of the Stockholm Convention.

78. This compromise followed the path set forth by both the climate-change and biodiversity conventions. The parties will review the GEF's performance and have the option of making a final decision to use or exclude the GEF.

79. Updated figures can be found in GEF documents, including its biannual report to the Stockholm Convention COP.

80. Updated information can be found on the Stockholm Convention's website at http://chm.pops.int.

81. Because the United States had already controlled the dirty dozen, its costs to implement the original treaty would be low. President Bush participated in a Rose Garden ceremony heralding the convention when it was signed in May 2001 and stating his intention to push

for ratification. In the absence of 9/11, it is logical that he would have done so, if for no other reason than to provide his administration with an environmental victory before the 2004 election. It is possible that President Barack Obama will submit the treaty for consideration when it likely has the votes for ratification, although this has been complicated by the regime's recent expansion.

82. For more information on Stockholm Convention COPs and meetings of the parties, including documents from the meeting and the official meeting reports, see the Stockholm Convention's website at http://chm.pops.int. For daily and summary reports, analyses, and photos of the COP and POPRC meetings, see the relevant issues of the *Earth Negotiation Bulletin* at www.iisd.ca/process/chemical_management.htm#pops.

83. For more information on POPRC, including documents from the meeting and the official meeting reports, see the Stockholm Convention's website at http://chm.pops.int. For summary reports, analyses, and photos, see the relevant issues of the *Earth Negotiation Bulletin* (ENB) at www.iisd.ca/process/chemical_management.htm#pops. This discussion of POPRC relies heavily on the official meeting reports and ENB analyses.

84. For example, nominations coming from a developing country might carry more influence with other developing countries or countries in a certain regime. Or a government, having considered all factors, may favor nomination but not want to be a lead state in order to avoid, or at least delay, conflict with certain domestic lobbying groups.

85. "Summary of the Fourth Meeting of the Persistent Organic Pollutants Review Committee of the Stockholm Convention: 13–17 October 2008," *Earth Negotiation Bulletin* 15, no. 161 (October 20, 2008).

86. Ibid.

87. "Summary of the Third Meeting of the Stockholm Convention on Persistent Organic Pollutants: 30 April–4 May 2007," *Earth Negotiation Bulletin* 15, no. 154 (May 7, 2007).

88. For details of the meeting, see background documents and the official meeting report on the Stockholm Convention's website at http://chm.pops.int and the daily and summary reports provided by the *Earth Negotiations Bulletin* at www.iisd.ca/chemical/pops/cop4. This section draws heavily on personal observations and notes made by David Downie while attending the meeting, the official report of the meeting, and "Summary of the Fourth Conference of Parties to Stockholm Convention on Persistent Organic Pollutants: 4–8 May 2009." *Earth Negotiations Bulletin* 15, no. 174 (May 11, 2009).

89. As noted above, the original twelve chemicals (the so called dirty dozen) included the pesticides aldrin, chlordane, DDT, dieldrin, endrin, heptachlor, mirex, and toxaphene; the industrial chemicals, PCBs and hexachlorobenzene (HBC), which is also a pesticide; and dioxins and furans—two unintentional byproducts of many industrial processes and combustion. The newly listed chemicals are the pesticides alpha and beta hexachlorocyclohexane (both added to Annex A—elimination)—once widely used as an insecticide and still a byproduct of lindane; Hexabromodiphenyl and Tetrabromodiphenyl ether (Annex A)—used as additives in flame retardants; Chlordecone (Annex A)—once widely used as an agricultural pesticide; Hexabromobiphenyl (Annex A)—an industrial chemical used as a flame retardant mainly in the 1970s; Lindane (Annex A)—a broad-spectrum insecticide for treating seeds, soils, plants, animals, and people whose production has decreased rapidly in recent years although a few countries still produce and use it; Pentachlorobenzene (Annexes A and C) used in PCB products and as a fungicide, flame retardant, and chemical intermediate and also produced unintentionally during

combustion and as an impurity in certain solvents and pesticides (hence the additional listing in Annex C); Perfluorooctane sulfonic acid, its salts, and perfluorooctane sulfonyl fluoride (PFOS) (Annex B)—PFOS is still produced and widely used in several countries and found in electric and electronic parts, firefighting foam, photo imaging, hydraulic fluids, and textiles.

90. Ireland and Italy are less of an issue because, as members of the EU, they follow internal EU chemicals policy, which exceeds the convention.

Chapter 4

1. At ground level ozone is a pollutant, a key component of urban smog produced by the interaction in bright sunlight of chemicals from factory emissions and automobiles that can contribute to respiratory problems and damage plants.

2. Mario Molina and F. Sherwood Rowland, "Stratospheric Sink for Chlorofluoromethanes: Chlorine Atomic Catalyzed Destruction of Ozone," *Nature* 249 (June 28, 1974): 810–812.

3. There are numerous detailed discussions of the creation and expansion of the ozone regime. This section draws on David Downie, "Understanding International Environmental Regimes: The Origin, Creation and Expansion of the Ozone Regime" (PhD diss., University of North Carolina, Chapel Hill, 1996); Richard Benedick, *Ozone Diplomacy*, 2nd ed. (Cambridge, MA: Harvard University Press, 1998); Karen Litfin, *Ozone Discourses* (New York: Columbia University Press, 1994); Stephen Anderson and K. Madhavea Sarma, *Protecting the Ozone Layer: The United Nations History* (London: Earthscan, 2002); David Downie, "UNEP and the Montreal Protocol: New Roles for International Organizations in Regime Creation and Change," in *International Organizations and Environmental Policy*, ed. Robert V. Bartlett, Priya A. Kurian, and Madhu Malik (Westport, CT: Greenwood Press, 1995).

4. See, in particular, Iwona Rummel-Bulska, "The Protection of the Ozone Layer under the Global Framework Convention," in *Transboundary Air Pollution*, ed. Cees Flinterman et al. (Dordrecht, Netherlands: Martinus Nijhoff, 1986), 281–296.

5. For detailed analysis of this point, see David Downie, "The Power to Destroy: Understanding Stratospheric Ozone Politics as a Common Pool Resource Problem," in *Anarchy and the Environment: The International Relations of Common Pool Resources*, ed. J. Samuel Barkin and George Shambaugh (Albany: State University of New York Press, 1999), and "An Analysis of the Montreal Protocol on Substances That Deplete the Ozone Layer" (staff paper prepared by the Oceans and Environment Program, Office of Technology Assessment, U.S. Congress, December 10, 1987), 9, table 1.

6. J. Farman et al., "Large Losses of Total Ozone in Antarctica Reveal Seasonal ClO_x/NO_x Interaction," *Nature* 315 (May 16, 1985): 207–210.

7. For discussion, see Downie, "Understanding International Environmental Regimes," ch. 6; Litfin, *Ozone Discourses*, 96–102, and Sharon Roan, *Ozone Crisis: The 15 Year Evolution of a Sudden Global Emergency* (New York: John Wiley & Sons, 1989), 125–141, 158–188.

8. Although a historic agreement, the protocol did permit the continued production of ozone-depleting chemicals, neglected to specify that alternatives must not damage the ozone layer, included no provisions for independent monitoring of production and consumption of ozone-destroying chemicals, and contained no real penalties for noncompliance.

9. See, for example, Anderson and Sarma, *Protecting the Ozone Layer: The United Nations History*, 93–94, as well as discussion of reactions to the 1987 Protocol in Benedick, *Ozone Diplomacy*; Roan, *Ozone Crisis*.

10. NASA, *Executive Summary of the Ozone Trends Panel* (Washington, DC: NASA, Office of Management, Scientific and Technical Information Division, March 1988). UNEP and WMO established the trends panel in 1986 as part of a new U.S. initiative, continuing efforts by UNEP. It included more than one hundred scientists from ten countries and examined satellite and ground-based data.

11. World Meteorological Organization et al., *Scientific Assessment of Stratospheric Ozone: 1989*, WMO Global Ozone Research and Monitoring Project, report no. 20 (Geneva: WMO for WMO, UNEP, NASA, NOAA, and UK DOE, 1989).

12. For example, at the first Meeting of the Parties (MOP-1) in Helsinki in May 1989, EC members were among eighty nations (along with the United States but not Japan or the Soviet Union) that supported a strong, but nonbinding, declaration calling for a complete CFC phase-out by 2000.

13. For the text of the ozone treaties, amendments, and adjustments, as well as official reports from each Meeting of the Parties, visit the Ozone Secretariat's website at www.unep.org/ozone.

14. Countries with economies in transition (CEITs) include the Communist countries in Eastern Europe formerly aligned with the Soviet Union, as well as Russia, Ukraine, and other countries created when the Soviet Union collapsed, which are transitioning from Communist to capitalist economies. The GEF later took over most of the responsibility for assisting CEITs on ozone issues.

15. The fund has been replenished seven times: $240 million (1991–1993), $455 million (1994–1996), $466 million (1997–1999), $440 million (2000–2002), $474 million (2003–2005), $400.4 million (2006–2008), and $400 million (2009–2011). The total budget for the 2009–2011 triennium is US$490 million. Of that budget $73.9 million is leftover funds from the 2006–2008 triennium, $16.1 million will be provided from interest during the 2009–2011 triennium, and the rest is new money provided by the industrialized countries. For these figures and details of the history and operation of the fund, see the Multilateral Fund homepage at www.multilateralfund.org.

16. Ibid. The implementation of these projects will result in the phaseout of the consumption of more than 254,687 tons and the production of about 176,439 tons of ozone-depleting substances. Of this total, about 230,786 tons of consumption and 175,864 of production have already been phased out from projects approved as of December 2007.

17. The tiny amount allowed over the last ten years is a known as a "servicing tail" that allows for the continued use and servicing of equipment that uses HCFCs during this period.

18. The "Implementation Committee under the Non-compliance Procedure for the Montreal Protocol" and the MOP have considered many cases of potential noncompliance. Most of these involved countries with economies in transition, although more developing-country cases could occur in the future as their controls intensify. Although it has the ability to impose trade sanctions for severe cases of intentional noncompliance, the committee and MOP decided that each instance fell below such a threshold and opted for consultation and targeted technical assistance to remove barriers to implementation and, on occasion, the equivalent of a public rebuke to try harder.

19. HCFCs have shorter atmospheric lifetimes, and one HCFC molecule destroys far fewer ozone molecules than one CFC molecule. But ozone destruction by HCFCs takes place sooner. Opponents of HCFCs, therefore, point to their relatively high impact over five years, and supporters highlight their low five-hundred-year impact.

20. "Summary of the Sixteenth Meeting of the Parties to the Montreal Protocol: 22–26 November 2004," *Earth Negotiation Bulletin* 19, no. 40 (November 29, 2004), www.iisd.ca/download/pdf/enb1940e.pdf.

21. For detailed summaries of the HCFC debate and other developments at the nineteenth MOP, see "Summary of the Nineteenth Meeting of the Parties to the Montreal Protocol: 17–21 September 2007," *Earth Negotiation Bulletin* 19, no. 60 (September 24, 2007), www.iisd.ca/download/pdf/enb1960e.pdf; "Report of the Nineteenth Meeting of the Parties to the Montreal Protocol on Substances that Deplete the Ozone Layer," UN Document UNEP/OzL.Pro.19/7 of September 21, 2007, www.unep.ch/ozone/Meeting_Documents/mop/19mop/MOP-19-7E.pdf; Keith Bradsher, "Push to Fix Ozone Layer and Slow Global Warming," *New York Times*, March 15, 2007, www.nytimes.com/2007/03/15/business/worldbusiness/15warming.html; David Ljunggren, "Ozone Deal Hailed as Blow against Climate Change," Reuters Newswire, September 22, 2007, www.reuters.com/article/topNews/idUSN2142304520070922?feedType=RSS&feedName=topNews.

22. "Summary of the Nineteenth Meeting of the Parties to the Montreal Protocol: 17–21 September 2007."

23. Delegates still brought paper documents to the meeting. Eliminating most of the paper documents reduced the cost and environmental footprint of the meeting but depends on the meeting facility's having installed the appropriate technology.

24. "Decision XIX/6: Adjustments to the Montreal Protocol with Regard to Annex C, Group I, Substances (Hydrochlorofluorocarbons)," Report of the Nineteenth Meeting of the Parties to the Montreal Protocol, Montreal, September 17–21, 2007, UN Document UNEP/OzL.Pro.19/7, 33.

25. For a report on the meeting that also makes this point, see "Summary of the Twentieth Meeting of the Parties to the Montreal Protocol and Eighth Meeting of the Conference of Parties to the Vienna Convention: 16–20 November 2008," *Earth Negotiation Bulletin* 19, no. 66 (November 24, 2008). For the official meeting report, see the report of the Eighth Meeting of the Conference of the Parties to the Vienna Convention and the Twentieth Meeting of the Parties to the Montreal Protocol on Substances That Deplete the Ozone Layer, UN Document UNEP/OzL.Conv.8/7-UNEP/OzL.Pro.20/9.

26. "Press Backgrounder," Ozone Secretariat, November 2008, www.unep.ch/ozone/Events/ozone_day_2008/press_backgrounder.pdf.

27. Ozone Secretariat, "Press Backgrounder."

28. Ibid.

29. Ibid.

30. For a representative and detailed discussion, see Guus Velders et al., "The Importance of the Montreal Protocol in Protecting Climate," *Proceedings of the National Academy of Science* 104, no. 12 (March 20, 2007): 4814–4819.

31. See, e.g., Guus Velders, "The Importance of the Montreal Protocol in Protecting Climate," (presentation to the WMO/UNEP Ozone Research Managers, Geneva, Switzerland, May 19, 2008), http://ozone.unep.org/Meeting_Documents/research-mgrs/7orm/Velders_Montreal Protocol.ppt.

32. United Nations Environment Programme, *Climate Change Science Compendium* Nairobi: UNEP, 2009.

33. For an overview of the state of the science of climate change, see IPCC, "Summary for Policymakers," in *Climate Change 2007: The Physical Science Basis*, Contribution of Working

Group I to the Fourth Assessment Report of the Intergovernmental Panel on Climate Change, ed. S. Solomon et al. (Cambridge: Cambridge University Press, 2007), www.ipcc.ch/pdf/assessment -report/ar4/wg1/ar4-wg1-spm.pdf.

34. On the importance of perceptions of cost to early climate policies and the absence of accurate cost estimates for the Netherlands, Germany, Japan, and the United States, see Yasuko Kawashima, "A Comparative Analysis of the Decision Making Processes of Developed Countries toward CO$_2$ Emissions Reduction Targets," *International Environmental Affairs* 9 (spring 1997): 95–126.

35. See Matthew Paterson, *Global Warming and Global Politics* (London: Routledge, 1996), 77–82.

36. Richard A. Houghton and George M. Woodwell, "Global Climatic Change," *Scientific American* 260 (April 1989): 42–43.

37. Lamont C. Hempel and Matthias Kaelberer, "The Changing Climate in Greenhouse Policy: Obstacles to International Cooperation in Agenda Setting and Policy Formulation" (unpublished paper, April 1990), 6; and Daniel Bodansky, "The United Nations Framework Convention on Climate Change: A Commentary," *Yale Journal of International Law* 18, no. 2 (summer 1993): 461.

38. The IPCC is organized into three working groups: Working Group I on the climate system, Working Group II on impacts and response options, and Working Group III on economic and social dimensions. For more information, see the IPCC website at www.ipcc.ch.

39. Japan subsequently backtracked by proposing a process of "pledge and review" in place of binding commitments. Individual countries, it suggested, would set for themselves appropriate targets that would be publicly reviewed. Most EC member states and NGOs were cool to the idea. Bodansky, "The United Nations Framework Convention on Climate Change," 486.

40. For country GHG emissions, contributions to total emissions, and rankings at the time of the negotiations, see World Resources Institute, *World Resources, 1992–1993* (New York: Oxford University Press, 1992), 205–213, 345–355. For a good early discussion of different methods of greenhouse gas accounting, see Peter M. Morrisette and Andrew J. Plantinga, "The Global Warming Issue: Viewpoints of Different Countries," *Resources* 103 (Washington, DC: Resources for the Future) (spring 1991): 2–6.

41. *Earth Summit Update* 9 (May 1992): 1; *Wall Street Journal,* May 22, 1992, 1.

42. "Global Warming Basics: Glossary," Pew Center on Global Climate Change, www.pew climate.org/global-warming-basics/full_glossary/glossary.php.

43. As of 2009, 192 countries had ratified the convention. "Status of Ratification," UN Framework Convention on Climate Change, August 22, 2007, www.unfccc.int.

44. For a complete summary and analysis of the Kyoto Protocol, see Herman E. Ott, "The Kyoto Protocol: Unfinished Business," *Environment* 40, no. 6 (1998): 16ff.; Clare Breidenrich et al., "The Kyoto Protocol to the United Nations Framework Convention on Climate Change," *American Journal of International Law* 92, no. 2 (1998): 315.

45. See "The Mechanisms under the Kyoto Protocol: Joint Implementation, the Clean Development Mechanism and Emissions Trading," UNFCCC, www.unfccc.int/kyoto_mechanisms/ items/1673.php.

46. Subsequently, the White House revealed that the United States planned to achieve up to 75 percent of the U.S. reduction requirement by purchasing allowances from the Russian

Federation and Ukraine. See Christopher Flavin, "Last Tango in Buenos Aires," *WorldWatch* (November–December 1998): 13.

47. International Centre for Trade and Sustainable Development, "COP 6: US-EU Differences Blamed for Failure of Climate Change Negotiations," *Bridges Weekly Trade News Digest* 4 (November 28, 2000): www.ictsd.org/html/weekly/story2.28-11-00.htm.

48. For more information on the agreements reached at COP-7 in Marrakesh, see "Summary of the Seventh Conference of the Parties to the UN Framework Convention on Climate Change: 29 October–10 November 2001," *Earth Negotiations Bulletin* 12, no. 189 (November 12, 2001): www.iisd.ca/vol12/enb12189e.html.

49. International Centre for Trade and Sustainable Development, "EU Attacks Bush's U-turn on Climate Change," *Bridges Weekly Trade News Digest* 5, no. 11 (March 27, 2001): www.ictsd .org/html/weekly/27-03-01/story3.htm.

50. For a variety of different ratification scenarios, see Greenpeace, "How the Kyoto Protocol Can Come into Force without the U.S.A.," Climate Action Network Europe, 2001, www.climnet.org/ EUenergy/ratification/GP-rat_without_usa.pdf.

51. Australia had previously been the remaining nonparty, but it ratified the protocol following the election of Prime Minister Kevin Rudd in December 2007.

52. Jonathan Boston, "Post-2012: Towards a New Global Climate Treaty," *Towards a New Global Climate Treaty: Looking Beyond 2012*, ed. Jonathan Boston (Wellington, New Zealand: Institute for Policy Studies, 2007), 8.

53. By tradition, conventions usually have "Conferences of the Parties," or COPs. Protocols usually have "Meetings of the Parties," or MOPs. The meetings serve the same function—to bring all parties together to conduct treaty business as specified by the treaty.

54. UNFCCC Secretariat, "Decisions Adopted by the Conference of the Parties," in *Report of the Conference of the Parties on Its Eleventh Session*, Montreal, November 28—December 10, 2005, Addendum, Part Two (FCCC/CP/2005/5/Add.1), Decision 1/CP.11.

55. UNFCCC Secretariat, "Decisions Adopted by the Conference of the Parties Serving as the Meeting of the Parties to the Kyoto Protocol," in *Report of the Conference of the Parties Serving as the Meeting of the Parties to the Kyoto Protocol on its First Session*, Montreal, November 28—December 10, 2005, Addendum, Part Two (FCCC/KP/CMP/2005/8/Add.1), Decision 1/CMP.1.

56. This section draws heavily on conversations had by Pamela Chasek and David Downie with participants and observers to the Bali negotiations before, during, and after the meetings; observations by David Downie while attending the Bali meetings; daily and summary reports on the negotiations by the *Earth Negotiation Bulletin*, available at www.iisd.ca/climate/cop13 (see, in particular, "Summary of the Thirteenth Conference of the Parties to the UN Framework Convention on Climate Change and the Third Meeting of Parties to the Kyoto Protocol: 3–15 December 2007," *Earth Negotiations Bulletin* 12: 354 (December 18, 2007), www.iisd.ca/vol12/ enb12354e.html); and official meeting documents, including the official UNFCCC conference report available at http://unfccc.int or directly at http://unfccc.int/meetings/cop_13/items/ 4049.php.

57. "Summary of the Fourteenth Conference of the Parties to the UN Framework Convention on Climate Change: 1–12 December 2008," *Earth Negotiations Bulletin* 12, no. 395 (December 15, 2008): 17. Available at www.iisd.ca/download/pdf/enb12395e.pdf.

58. Ibid. For more information on the EU climate-change policy, see European Commission, *EU Action against Climate Change: Leading Global Action to 2020 and Beyond* (Luxembourg: Office for Official Publications of the European Communities, 2009), http://ec.europa.eu/environment/climat/pdf/brochures/post_2012_en.pdf.

59. Ibid., 18.

60. Group of Eight, "Responsible Leadership for a Sustainable Future," Group of Eight Summit 2009, July 8, 2009, www.g8italia2009.it/static/G8_Allegato/G8_Declaration_08_07_09_final,2.pdf.

61. Indeed, it is difficult to overstate the impact on the environment or human health were stratospheric ozone completely destroyed or the current climate system very significantly altered.

Chapter 5

1. Oran Young, *International Environmental Governance: Protecting the Environment in a Stateless Society* (Ithaca, NY: Cornell University Press, 1994), 21.

2. Ibid., 21–22.

3. Ibid., 23.

4. A revised version of the 1973 Endangered Species Conservation Act banned whaling in U.S. waters or by U.S. citizens, outlawed the import of whale products, and required that the United States initiate bilateral and multilateral negotiations on an agreement to protect and conserve whales.

5. The effort to build an IWC majority to ban whaling was stymied in the latter half of the 1970s because otherwise antiwhaling states such as Canada, Mexico, and other Latin American states were primarily concerned about protecting rights to regulate economic activities within their own 200-mile (320-kilometer) economic zones and opposed the jurisdiction of an international body over whaling.

6. Statement by Craig Van Note, Monitor Consortium, before the Subcommittee on Human Rights and International Organizations, Committee on Foreign Affairs, U.S. House of Representatives, September 28, 1989.

7. "Whaling: Soviet Kills Could Affect Sanctuary Decision," *Greenwire*, February 22, 1994.

8. Teresa Watanabe, "Japan Is Set for a Whale of a Fight," *Los Angeles Times*, April 20, 1993.

9. Paul Brown, "Playing Football with the Whales," *Guardian* (London), May 1, 1993. The Caribbean states cooperating with Japan were Grenada, St. Lucia, St. Kitts and Nevis, Antigua and Barbuda, Dominica, and St. Vincent.

10. "During Clinton's Watch Global Whaling Triples," Greenpeace, May 20, 1997, http://archive.greenpeace.org/majordomo/index-press-releases/1997/msg00126.html.

11. *Greenwire,* May 28, 1999; "IWC Steps Back from the Brink," WWF, May 28, 1999, www.wwfno.panda.org/what_we_do/endangered_species/news/?1952/IWC-steps-back-from-the-brink.

12. Kieran Mulvaney, *The Whaling Effect* (Washington, DC: WWF, 1999). International Whaling Commission, "Catches Taken: Under Scientific Permit," August 10, 2008, www.iwcoffice.org/conservation/table_permit.htm.

13. WWF, "Total Whales Killed in Whaling Operations Since the IWF Whaling Moratorium Went into Effect," May 2006, http://assets.panda.org/downloads/totalwhaleskilled2006.pdf.

14. Fisheries Agency head Masayuki Komatsu in an Australian Broadcasting Corporation radio interview. See "Japan 'Buys' Pro-whaling Votes," CNN.com, July 18, 2001, http://edition.cnn.com/2001/TECH/science/07/18/japan.whale/index.html, and "Japan Denies Aid-for-

Whaling Report," CNN.com, July 18, 2001, http://edition.cnn.com/2001/WORLD/asiapcf/east/07/19/japan.whaling. See also Andrew R. Miller and Nives Dolšak, "Issue Linkages in International Environmental Policy: The International Whaling Commission and Japanese Development Aid," *Global Environmental Politics* 7, no. 1 (February 2007): 69–96.

15. In an interview with BBC News Online, Japanese parliament member Mr. Yoshimasa Hayashi said, "If we do get a simple majority here, that would be a very good sign. It would let us either abolish the conservation committee, or change it to embrace both conservation and the sustainable use of whales." See Alex Kirby, "Japan Sets 2006 Whaling Ultimatum," BBC News Online, July 19, 2004, http://news.bbc.co.uk/2/hi/science/nature/3907415.stm.

16. For example, see Dennis Normile, "Japan's Whaling Program Carries Heavy Baggage," *Science* 289, no. 5488 (September 29, 2000): 2264–2265.

17. WWF, "Report from the Third Day of the 51st IWC Meeting—26 May 1999"; UNEP, "CITES Maintains Trade Bans on High-Profile Species, Revises Rules for Other Plants and Animals," news release 2000/48, UNEP, April 20, 2000, www.unep.org/Documents.Multilingual/Default.asp?documentid=121&articleid=2061; "Thirteenth Conference of the Parties to the Convention on International Trade of Endangered Species of Wild Fauna and Flora: 2–14 October 2004," *Earth Negotiations Bulletin* 21, no. 35 (October 3, 2004): www.iisd.ca/vol21/enb2135e.html.

18. See www.cites.org/eng/res/11/11-04.shtml.

19. International Whaling Commission, "Resolution 2006–1: St. Kitts and Nevis Declaration," Fifty-eighth Annual Meeting, St. Kitts and Nevis, June 16–20, 2006, www.iwcoffice.org/_documents/commission/IWC58docs/Resolution2006-1.pdf.

20. Calestous Juma, a Kenyan national, is professor of the practice of international development and director of the Science, Technology, and Globalization Project at Harvard University's Kennedy School. A former executive secretary of the UN Convention on Biological Diversity and founding director of the African Centre for Technology Studies in Nairobi, he served as chancellor of the University of Guyana. Ambassador Raúl Estrada-Oyuela has been a major player, in particular, with climate-change discussions and the Kyoto Protocol and its implementation, chairing sessions to finalize the negotiations on the Kyoto Protocol. Ambassador Alvaro de Soto recently concluded twenty-five years' service at the United Nations, where he was deeply involved in a range of peace negotiations, his last role being the UN special coordinator for the Middle East Peace Process. "Chair's Report of the Intersessional Meeting on the Future of IWC, Renaissance London Heathrow Hotel, UK, 6–8 March 2008," International Whaling Commission, www.iwcoffice.org/_documents/commission/future/60-7.pdf.

21. Media release by Dr. William Hogarth, chair of the International Whaling Commission, March 11, 2009, Rome, www.iwcoffice.org/_documents/commission/future/PressRelease Mar09.pdf.

22. "Too Much to Whalers and Not Enough to Conservation in IWC Proposals on Japanese Whaling," WWF, February 2, 2009, www.panda.org/who_we_are/wwf_offices/japan/?155502/Too-much-to-whalers-and-not-enough-to-conservation—in-IWC-proposals-on-Japanese-whaling-WWF.

23. The newest members were Estonia, Lithuania, and Poland. The list of member countries can be found on the IWF website at www.iwcoffice.org/commission/members.htm.

24. International Whaling Commission, "Press Release—Day 1—Monday 22 June," IWC, www.iwcoffice.org/meetings/meeting2009.htm#one.

25. "Media Statement on the Future of the IWC by the Chair of the IWC, Cristian Maquieira," IWC, June 26 2009, http://www.iwcoffice.org/_documents/commission/IWC61docs/Media%20 statement%20on%20the%20future%20of%20the%20IWC.pdf.

26. "Too Much To Whalers," WWF.

27. Ronald B. Mitchell, "Discourse and Sovereignty: Interests, Science and Morality in the Regulation of Whaling," *Global Governance* 4 (1998): 277.

28. Rebecca Goldman, "Notes from the IWC/60—Will Comity Save the Whales?" *Whales Alive* 17, no. 3 (July 2008): 3. Available at http://csiwhalesalive.org/csi2008_07.pdf.

29. Ibid.

30. Detailed and updated information on CITES, including its history, operation, species covered, current parties, and other issues, can be found on the regime's official website at www.cites.org.

31. Ed Stoddard, "CITES Does Not Follow Standard U.N. Divisions," Environmental News Network, October 14, 2004, www.enn.com/today_PF.html?id=180.

32. For detailed and updated information on these figures see the TRAFFIC website at www.traffic.org and TRAFFIC, *Annual Report 1997–98* (London: TRAFFIC, 1998), 1, and subsequent annual reports.

33. IISD, "Summary of the Fourteenth Conference of the Parties to the Convention on International Trade in Endangered Species of Wild Fauna and Flora: 3–15 June 2007," *Earth Negotiations Bulletin* 21, no. 61 (June 18, 2007): 21. Available at www.iisd.ca/download/pdf/enb2161e.pdf.

34. See Sarah Fitzgerald, *Whose Business Is It?* (Washington, DC: WWF, 1989), 3–8, 13–14.

35. World Resources Institute, *World Resources 1990–1991* (New York: Oxford University Press, 1990), 135.

36. For updated lists and other information concerning the species listed in each appendix, see the Convention on International Trade of Endangered Species website at www.cites.org.

37. Liana Sun Wyler and Pervaze A. Sheikh, *International Illegal Trade in Wildlife: Threats and U.S. Policy* (Washington, DC: Congressional Research Service, March 3, 2008), 1. Available at http://fpc.state.gov/documents/organization/102621.pdf.

38. See, e.g., Greg Warchol, Linda Zupan, and Willie Clack, "Transnational Criminality: An Analysis of the Illegal Wildlife Market in Southern Africa," *International Criminal Justice Review* 13, no. 1 (2003): 7; Jolene Lin, "Tackling Southeast Asia's Illegal Wildlife Trade," *Singapore Year Book of International Law and Contributors* 9 (2005): 198; and Gavin Hayman and Duncan Brack, "International Environmental Crime: The Nature and Control of Environmental Black Markets" (paper prepared for the Royal Institute of International Affairs, London, May 2002): 114. Available at http://www.isn.ethz.ch/isn/Current-Affairs/Policy-Briefs/Detail/?lng=en&id=23688.

39. Wyler and Sheikh, *International Illegal Trade in Wildlife*, 7.

40. Ibid., 8.

41. International Fund for Animal Welfare, *Killing with Keystrokes* (Yarmouth Port, MA.: IFAW, 2008), 4. Available at www.ifaw.org/Publications/Program_Publications/Wildlife_Trade/Campaign_Scientific_Publications/asset_upload_file848_49629.pdf.

42. See Sarah Fitzgerald, *Whose Business Is It?* (Washington, DC: WWF, 1989), 3–8, 13–14.

43. David Harland, "Jumping on the 'Ban' Wagon: Efforts to Save the African Elephant," *Fletcher Forum on World Affairs* 14 (summer 1990): 284–300.

44. "CITES 1989: The African Elephant and More," *TRAFFIC* 9 (December 1989): 1–3.

45. See World Resources Institute, *World Resources 1990–1991* (New York: Oxford University Press, 1990), 135.

46. "U.S. Ivory Market Collapses after Import Ban" *New York Times*, June 5, 1990, C2. Available at www.nytimes.com/1990/06/05/science/us-ivory-market-collapses-after-import-ban.html; Raymond Bonner, *At the Hand of Man: Peril and Hope for Africa's Wildlife* (New York: Vintage Books, 1994), 157.

47. In each case the proposals were withdrawn prior to a formal vote. WWF, "The Challenge of African Elephant Conservation," *Conservation Issues*, April 1997.

48. "CITES and the African Elephants: The Decisions and the Next Steps Explained," *TRAFFIC Dispatches* (April 1998): 5–6.

49. CITES, "Verification of Compliance with the Precautionary Undertakings for the Sale and Shipment of Raw Ivory," Doc. SC.42.10.2.1, Forty-second Meeting of the Standing Committee, Lisbon, Portugal, September 28–October 1, 1999.

50. IISD, "Summary of the Thirteenth Conference of the Parties to the Convention on International Trade in Endangered Species of Wild Fauna and Flora: 2–14 October 2004," *Earth Negotiations Bulletin*, 21, no. 45 (October 18, 2004): 16. Available at www.iisd.ca/download/pdf/enb2145e.pdf.

51. Julie Gray, "TRAFFIC Report of the 14th meeting of the Conference of the Parties to CITES," TRAFFIC, 2007, www.traffic.org/cop-papers.

52. IISD, "Summary of the Fourteenth Conference of the Parties to the Convention on International Trade in Endangered Species of Wild Fauna and Flora: 3–15 June 2007," *Earth Negotiations Bulletin* 21, no. 61 (June 18, 2007): 21. Available at www.iisd.ca/download/pdf/enb2161e.pdf.

53. CITES, "Ivory Sales Get the Go-ahead," CITES, June 2, 2007, www.cites.org/eng/news/press/2007/070602_ivory.shtml.

54. CITES, "Report on the One-Off Ivory Sale in Southern African Countries," SC58 Doc. 36.3 Fifty-eighth Meeting of the Standing Committee, Geneva, Switzerland, July 6–10, 2009, www.cites.org/eng/com/SC/58/E58-36-3.pdf.

55. Arthur Blundell, "A Review of the CITES Listing of Big-leaf Mahogany," *Oryx* 38, no. 1 (2004): 84–90.

56. Guatemala Official Delegation to CITES COP-12, "Presentation by Guatemala on the Inclusion of Big Leaf Mahogany in CITES Appendix II," CITES, November 2002, www.cites.org/eng/cop/12/inf/E12i-33.PDF.

57. "Mahogany-Swietenia macrophylla," TRAFFIC Network Briefing, June 1998.

58. Guatemala Official Delegation in CITES COP-12, "Presentation by Guatemala on the Inclusion of Big Leaf Mahogany in CITES Appendix II."

59. "Big-Leafed Mahogany and CITES," TRAFFIC Network briefing, October 2001.

60. It is difficult to say, however, whether the difference in the position of the major consumer states resulted from differences in approach (assuring that products were legally obtained versus protecting commercial interests) or in the listing itself (an Appendix I listing places much more stringent restrictions on trade than does an Appendix II listing).

61. Arthur G. Blundell and Bruce D. Rodan, "Mahogany and CITES: Moving beyond the Veneer of Legality," *Oryx* 37, no. 1 (January 2003): 85–90.

62. For discussion and examples of this argument, see Philippe Le Prestre and Peter Stoett, "International Initiatives, Commitments, and Disappointments: Canada, CITES, and the CBD,"

in *Politics of the Wild: Canada's Endangered Species*, ed. Karen Beazley and Robert Boardman (Toronto: Oxford University Press, 2001), 190–216; and Joshua Ginsberg, "Enhancement of Survival or Abandonment of the Endangered Species Act?" *BioScience* 54, no. 3 (2004): 180–181. However, neither work nor any other of which we are aware provides clear empirical evidence to support this view.

63. Millennium Ecosystem Assessment, *Ecosystems and Human Well-being: Synthesis Report* (Washington, DC: Island Press, 2005).

64. National sovereignty over natural resources implies that a government has control over its resources, such as oil, minerals, and timber. Common heritage implies that no one can be excluded from using natural resources, except by lack of economic and technological capacity; conversely, everyone has a right to benefit from the exploitation of the resources. This concept has been used for fisheries and mineral resources found in the high seas and more recently in the debate about genetic resources. See G. Kristin Rosendal, "The Convention on Biological Diversity: A Viable Instrument for Conservation and Sustainable Use," in *Green Globe Yearbook of International Cooperation on Environment and Development 1995*, ed. Helge Ole Bergesen, Georg Parmann, and Øystein B. Thommessen (Oxford: Oxford University Press, 1995), 69–81.

65. Kenton R. Miller et al., "Issues on the Preservation of Biological Diversity," in *The Global Possible: Resources, Development and the New Century*, ed. Robert Repetto (New Haven, CT: Yale University Press, 1985), 341–342; IUCN, "Explanatory Notes to Draft Articles Prepared by IUCN for Inclusion in a Proposed Convention on the Conservation of Biological Diversity and the Establishment of a Fund for That Purpose," pt. 1: General Comments, 1.

66. The main interest of the Reagan administration in making this proposal was to create financial and logistical synergies by bringing the multiplicity of species-specific or region-specific conservation conventions already in existence under one convention so that there could be a single secretariat instead of several. Personal communication from E. U. Curtis Bohlen, former assistant secretary of state for oceans, environment, and science, Washington, DC, February 2, 1994.

67. "Report of the Ad Hoc Working Group on the Work of Its Second Session in Preparation for a Legal Instrument on Biological Diversity of the Planet," UNEP/Bio.Div2/3, February 23, 1990, 7.

68. Personal communication from a member of the U.S. delegation to the biodiversity convention negotiations, April 12, 1994.

69. For contrasting analyses of the text of the convention regarding intellectual property rights, see Melinda Chandler, "The Biodiversity Convention: Selected Issues of Interest to the International Lawyer," *Colorado Journal of International Environmental Law and Policy* 4, no. 1 (winter 1993): 161–165; and Gareth Porter, *The United States and the Biodiversity Convention: The Case for Participation* (Washington, DC: Environmental and Energy Study Institute, 1992), 13–21.

70. Personal communication from a member of the U.S. delegation to the biodiversity convention negotiations, October 21, 1994. See also Fiona McConnell, *The Biodiversity Convention: A Negotiating History* (London: Kluwer Law International, 1996).

71. A coalition of NGOs with major interests in biodiversity got together with several companies to pressure the Clinton administration into signing the treaty. The Clinton administration dealt with the objections to the text that had been raised by the Bush administration by announcing that it would issue a statement asserting that it interpreted the treaty's provisions on

intellectual property rights and the financial mechanism to be compatible with U.S. interests. See U.S. Senate, "Convention on Biological Diversity: Message from the President of the United States," November 20, 1993, Treaty Document 103-120 (Washington, DC: U.S. Government Printing Office, 1993).

72. The Senate Foreign Relations Committee approved the ratification of the Convention on Biological Diversity by a vote of 16 to 3 on June 29, 1994. However, in a dramatic move in September 1994, CBD ratification was removed from the Senate's agenda, and since then the ratification issue has never come up for voting. As soon as he was elected, President Obama faced pressure from U.S. environmental groups to push for ratification.

73. For updated information on the status of signatures and ratifications, see the official Convention on Biological Diversity website at www.cbd.int/convention/parties/list.

74. "Thematic Programmes," Convention on Biological Diversity, www.cbd.int/programmes.

75. For more details on this case (WTO Dispute DS291), see "European Communities—Measures Affecting the Approval and Marketing of Biotech Products," WTO, 2006, www.wto.org/english/tratop_e/dispu_e/cases_e/ds291_e.htm.

76. "The Cartagena Protocol on Biosafety," Australian Wheat Board, 2005, www.awb.com.au/aboutawb/factsandindustryinformation/publicpositionpapers/cartagenaprotocol/GM+Crop+Trials.htm.

77. For a summary of the negotiations and a synopsis of the protocol, see "Report of the Resumed Session of the Extraordinary Meeting of the Conference of the Parties for the Adoption of the Protocol on Biodiversity to the Convention on Biological Diversity: 24–28 January 2000," *Earth Negotiations Bulletin* 9, no. 137 (January 31, 2000): www.iisd.ca/biodiv/excop.

78. "Summary of the Third Meeting of the Parties to the Cartagena Protocol on Biosafety: 13–17 March 2006," *Earth Negotiations Bulletin* 9, no. 351 (March 20, 2006): www.iisd.ca/download/pdf/enb09351e.pdf.

79. Ibid.

80. Ibid.

81. Article 1 of the CBD states, "The objectives of this Convention, to be pursued in accordance with its relevant provisions, are the conservation of biological diversity, the sustainable use of its components and the fair and equitable sharing of the benefits arising out of the utilization of genetic resources, including by appropriate access to genetic resources and by appropriate transfer of relevant technologies, taking into account all rights over those resources and to technologies, and by appropriate funding."

82. For more information, see "The Calophyllum Story," Forest Department of Sarawak, Malaysia, www.forestry.sarawak.gov.my/forweb/research/fr/ip/eco/calophys.htm.

83. See Kabir Bavikatte, Harry Jonas, and Johanna von Braun, "Shifting Sands of ABS Best Practice: Hoodia from the Community Perspective," United Nations University Institute of Advanced Studies, March 31, 2009, www.unutki.org/default.php?doc_id=137.

84. "Access and Benefit-sharing," Convention on Biological Diversity, 2008, https://www.cbd.int/doc/programmes/abs/factsheets/ABS-factsheet-general-en.pdf.

85. While the phrase "facilitated access" generally implies that providers will make genetic resources available to other parties consistent with Article 15, it can also be interpreted as an obligation to minimize regulatory burden and transaction costs. There has not been agreement on a comprehensive definition of facilitated access.

86. "Summary of the Third Meeting of the Ad Hoc Open-ended Working Group on Access and Benefit-Sharing: 14–18 February 2005," *Earth Negotiations Bulletin* 9, no. 311 (February 21, 2005): www.iisd.ca/download/pdf/enb09311e.pdf.

87. For up-to-date information on the access-and-benefit-sharing negotiations, you can check the *Earth Negotiations Bulletin* at www.iisd.ca and the convention's website at www.cbd.int.

88. According to the CBD website, "There is ample evidence that climate change affects biodiversity. According to the Millennium Ecosystem Assessment, climate change is likely to become the dominant direct driver of biodiversity loss by the end of the century. Climate change is already forcing biodiversity to adapt either through shifting habitat, changing life cycles, or the development of new physical traits. At the same time, biodiversity has a role to play in climate change adaptation and mitigation. For example, the conservation of habitats can reduce the amount of carbon dioxide released into the atmosphere. Currently, deforestation is estimated to be responsible for 20 percent of human-induced carbon dioxide emissions. Moreover, conserving mangroves and drought-resistant crops, for example, can reduce the disastrous impacts of climate change such as flooding and famine." For more information, see www .cbd.int/climate.

89. For more information on the 2010 target, see www.cbd.int/2010-target.

90. FAO, *The State of World Fisheries and Aquaculture* (Rome: FAO, 2008), 30. Available at ftp://ftp.fao.org/docrep/fao/011/i0250e/i0250e01.pdf.

91. FAO, *Review of the State of World Marine Fishery Resources* (Rome: FAO, 2005), 2–3.

92. FAO, *The State of World Fisheries and Aquaculture,* 10.

93. See Gareth Porter, *Estimating Overcapacity in the Global Fishing Fleet* (Washington, DC: WWF, 1998).

94. FAO, *The State of World Fisheries and Aquaculture,* 10–11.

95. According to European law, the European Commission, on behalf of the EU, negotiates fisheries agreements with third countries.

96. See, e.g., Commission of the European Communities, "Fishing on the High Seas: A Community Approach," Communication from the Commission to the Council and the European Parliament, SEC (92) 565, April 2, 1992, 5.

97. On Canadian mismanagement, see Raymond Rogers, *The Oceans Are Emptying* (Montreal: Black Rose Books, 1995), 96–147; on EU allocations and Spanish and Portuguese catch, see background document by Bruce Atkinson, Canadian Department of Fisheries and Oceans, Northwest Atlantic Fisheries Centre St. Johns, Newfoundland.

98. "Canada Hits EU's Atlantic Overfishing," *Washington Times,* February 19, 1995, A11.

99. Marvin Soroos, "The Turbot War: Resolution of an International Fishery Dispute," in *Conflict and the Environment,* ed. Nils Petter Gleditsch (Dordrecht, Netherlands: Kluwer Academic Publishers, 1997), 248.

100. "Summary of the Fifth Substantive Session of the UN Conference on Straddling Fish Stocks and Highly Migratory Fish Stocks: 24 July–4 August 1995," *Earth Negotiations Bulletin* 7, no. 54 (August 7, 1995): www.iisd.ca/vol07/0754000e.html.

101. To date there are twelve technical guidelines relevant to data in fisheries management: #1—Fisheries operations (1996); #2—Precautionary approach to capture fisheries and species introductions (1996); #3—Integration of fisheries into coastal-area management (1996); #4—Fisheries management (1997); #5—Aquaculture development (1997); #6—Inland fisheries (1997); #7—Responsible fish utilization (1998); #8—Indicators for sustainable development

of marine capture fisheries (1999); #9—Implementation of the International Plan of Action to deter, prevent, and eliminate illegal, unreported, and unregulated fishing (2002); #10—Increasing the contribution of small-scale fisheries to poverty alleviation and food security (2005); #11—Responsible fish trade (2009); and #12—Information and knowledge sharing (2009). For more information and any updates, see Fisheries and Aquaculture Department, "Technical Guidelines for Responsible Fisheries," FAO, www.fao.org/fishery/publications/technical-guide lines/en.

102. The other international plans of action are the 1999 International Plan of Action for Reducing Incidental Catch of Seabirds in Longline Fisheries and the 1999 International Plan of Action for the Conservation and Management of Sharks. For more details, see FAO Fisheries and Aquaculture Department, Implementation of the 1995 FAO Code of Conduct for Responsible Fisheries at www.fao.org/fishery/ccrf/2,3/en.

103. Committee on Fisheries, "Progress in the Implementation of the Code of Conduct for Responsible Fisheries, Related International Plans of Action and Strategy (COFI/2009/2)," FAO, November 2008, ftp://ftp.fao.org/docrep/fao/meeting/015/k3833e.pdf.

104. "Summary of the UN Fish Stocks Agreement Review Conference: 22–26 May 2006," *Earth Negotiations Bulletin* 7 no. 61 (May 29, 2006), www.iisd.ca/download/pdf/enb0761e.pdf.

105. Ibid.

106. For up-to-date information on the resumed review conference, see the UN Division for Oceans Affairs and the Law of the Sea at www.un.org/Depts/los/index.htm and the *Earth Negotiations Bulletin* at www.iisd.ca.

107. UNEP, *Desertification: The Problem That Won't Go Away* (Nairobi: UNEP, 1992); Ridley Nelson, "Dryland Management: The 'Desertification' Problem" (working paper 8, World Bank Policy Planning and Research Staff, Environment Department, September 1988), 2.

108. For a news report on these findings see William K. Stevens, "Threat of Encroaching Deserts May Be More Myth Than Fact," *New York Times,* January 18, 1994, C1, 10.

109. UN Governmental Liaison Service, "Second Session of Desertification Negotiations, Geneva, 13–24 September 1993," *E and D File* 2, no. 13 (October 1993).

110. "A Convention for Africans," *Impact* (Nairobi) 6 (September 1992): 3.

111. UNEP, *Desertification Control Bulletin* (Nairobi) 20 (1991); Dr. Mostafa K. Tolba, "Desertification and the Economics of Survival" (statement to the International Conference on the Economics of Dryland Degradation and Rehabilitation, Canberra, Australia, March 10–11, 1986).

112. *World Bank News* (May 27, 1993): 4; *Crosscurrents* 5 (March 16, 1992): 13.

113. E. U. Curtis Bohlen, deputy chief of the U.S. delegation, recalls that he made the decision personally without consulting with higher U.S. officials. Private communication from Bohlen, August 15, 1994. On the earlier suggestion by African countries of a possible bargain linking African support for a forest convention with U.S. support for a desertification convention, see *Crosscurrents* 5 (March 16, 1992): 13.

114. *Earth Summit Bulletin* 2, no. 13 (June 16, 1992): 3, www.iisd.ca/vol02/0213000e.html.

115. "Summary of the First Session of the INC for the Elaboration of an International Convention to Combat Desertification, 24 May–3 June 1993," *Earth Negotiations Bulletin* 4, no. 11 (June 11, 1993): 2–6, www.iisd.ca/linkages/vol04/0411000e.html.

116. "Summary of the Fifth Session of the INC for the Elaboration of an International Convention to Combat Desertification, 6–17 June 1994," *Earth Negotiations Bulletin* 4, no. 55 (June 20, 1994): 7–8, www.iisd.ca/linkages/vol04/0455000e.html.

117. "Summary of the Second Session of the INC for the Elaboration of an International Convention to Combat Desertification, 13–24 September 1993," *Earth Negotiations Bulletin* 4, no. 22 (September 30, 1993): 11, www.iiisd.ca/linkages/vol04/0422000e.html.

118. "Summary of the Fifth Session of the INC," 9–10.

119. For more information on the challenges the convention faced, see "Summary of the Second Conference of the Parties to the Convention to Combat Desertification, 30 November–11 December 1998," *Earth Negotiations Bulletin* 4, no. 127 (December 14, 1998), www.iisd.ca/download/pdf/enb04127e.pdf.

120. "Summary of the Seventh Conference of the Parties to the Convention to Combat Desertification, 17–28 October 2005," *Earth Negotiations Bulletin* 4, no. 186 (October 31, 2005): 16, www.iisd.ca/download/pdf/enb04186e.pdf.

121. Ibid.

122. Even Fontaine Ortiz and Guangting Tang, *Review of the Management, Administration and Activities of the Secretariat of the United Nations Convention to Combat Desertification (UNCCD)* (Geneva: UN Joint Inspection Unit, 2005), 7, www.unjiu.org/data/reports/2005/en2005_5.pdf.

123. Ibid.

124. Ibid.

125. UNCCD, "Ten-Year Strategic Plan and Framework to Enhance the Implementation of the Convention (2008–2018)," document ICCD/COP(8)/16/Add.1, October 23, 2007, www.unccd.int/cop/officialdocs/cop8/pdf/16add1eng.pdf.

126. At COP-6, the general discontent over the budget, the elections of officers, and financing the participation of only NGOs known to be supportive of the secretariat came to the fore. These concerns, strongly articulated by Canada during the closing session, provided food for thought for the secretariat. In her statement, the Canadian delegate expressed regret that the budget negotiations put accountability, transparency, and effectiveness into doubt. She warned that her country would not hesitate to redirect its funds into processes that combat desertification more efficiently if these three principles remained neglected at COP-7. For more information on this, see "Summary of the Sixth Conference of the Parties to the Convention to Combat Desertification, 25 August–6 September 2003," *Earth Negotiations Bulletin* 4, no. 173 (September 8, 2003), www.iisd.ca/download/pdf/enb04173e.pdf.

127. For more information about the role of the UNCCD Secretariat in treaty implementation, see Steffen Bauer, "Does Bureaucracy Really Matter? The Authority of Intergovernmental Treaty Secretariats," *Global Environmental Politics* 6, no. 1 (February 2006): 23–49.

128. For more information on the relationship between the UNCCD Secretariat and the Global Mechanism, see Wagaki Mwangi and Lynn Wagner, "Institutional Design by Compromise and Its Consequences" (paper presented at the annual meeting of the ISA's Fiftieth Annual Convention, New York, New York, February 15, 2009).

129. Steffen Bauer and Lindsay C. Stringer, "Science and Policy in the Global Governance of Desertification: An Analysis of Institutional Interplay under the United Nations Convention to Combat Desertification" (working paper 35, Global Governance Project, Amsterdam, Netherlands, 2008), 5. Available at www.glogov.org.

130. Ibid., 5–6.

131. Bauer and Stringer, "Science and Policy in the Global Governance of Desertification," 3.

132. Marc Debois and Marco Morettini, "Meeting on Desertification in Cuba," *ACP-EU Courier* 200 (September–October 2003): 5.

133. UNEP, *Global Environmental Outlook 4: Environment for Development* (Nairobi: UNEP, 2007), 88, www.unep.org/geo/geo4/media.

134. "UN Adopts New International Agreement to Protect World's Forests," United Nations, April 28, 2007, www.un.org/apps/news/story.asp?NewsID=22389&Cr=forests&Cr1=.

135. FAO, *State of the World's Forests 2009* (Rome: FAO, 2009), 109–115.

136. FAO, *The Challenge of Sustainable Forest Management* (Rome: FAO, 1993), 9.

137. Even prior to the formation of the United Nations, forests had been discussed as an international issue between Canada and the United States as early as the late nineteenth century. See Peter Gillis and Thomas Rich, *Lost Initiatives* (Westport, CT: Greenwood Press, 1986). There is also a long history of international conferences on forestry convened by the British under the banner of "Empire Forestry." See Gregory Barton, *Empire Forestry and the Origins of Environmentalism* (Cambridge: Cambridge University Press, 2002).

138. FAO, "History of the Committee on Forestry," COFO/2005/INF/8, 2005, www.fao.org/docrep/meeting/009/J4566e.htm.

139. David Humphreys, "The Elusive Quest for a Global Forests Convention," *Review of European Community and International Environmental Law* 14, no. 1 (April 2005): 1–10.

140. This is a non–legally binding authoritative statement of principles for a global consensus on the management, conservation, and sustainable development of all types of forests (Rio de Janeiro, June 13, 1992).

141. Agenda 21, 1992 report of the UNCED, I (1992), UN Doc. A/CONF.151/26/Rev. 1, ch. 11.

142. David Humphreys, "The UNCED Process and International Responses to Deforestation" (paper presented to the Inaugural Pan-European Conference on International Studies, Heidelberg, Germany, September 16–20, 1992), 34–35.

143. Malaysia openly charged that industrialized countries were using the issue of conserving tropical forests to prevent rapidly industrializing countries from achieving developed-country status. Claude Smadja, "Malaysia: Objective 2020," *World Link* (Geneva) 3 (1991): 26–29.

144. *Earth Summit Update* 8 (April 1992): 7.

145. These initiatives included the Conference on Global Partnerships on Forests organized by Indonesia, the India–United Kingdom initiative to establish reporting guidelines for forests to the Commission on Sustainable Development, and the Intergovernmental Working Group on Global Forests, convened jointly by Malaysia and Canada, which met twice in 1994.

146. Jag Maini, introduction to *The World's Forests—Rio +5: International Initiatives towards Sustainable Management* by A. J. Grayson and W. B. Maynard (Oxford: Commonwealth Forestry Association, 1997), ix. Also see David Humphreys, "The Global Politics of Forest Conservation Since the UNCED," *Environmental Politics* 5, no. 2 (summer 1996): 231–256.

147. Ans Kolk, *Forests in International Politics: International Organisations, NGOs and the Brazilian Amazon* (Amsterdam: International Books, 1996), 162.

148. H. C. Thang, "Need for a Global Forests Convention?" (paper presented to the GTZ Kick-off Workshop on Knowledge Management, Pulau Pangkor, Malaysia, October 26–29, 2003), and Humphreys, "The Elusive Quest."

149. For a summary of the international initiatives in support of the IPF process, see Grayson and Maynard, *The World's Forests—Rio +5*, 29–46.

150. The IPF's report to the Commission on Sustainable Development (E/CN.17/1997/12) can be found at www.un.org/documents/ecosoc/cn17/ipf/1997/ecn17ipf1997-12.htm.

151. *Practitioner's Guide to the Implementation of the IPF Proposals for Action,* prepared by the Six Country Initiative in Support of the UN Ad Hoc Intergovernmental Forum on Forests, 2nd rev. ed., May 1999.

152. See "Americans, Canadians at Odds over 'Sustainable Forestry' Plan," *Ottawa Citizen,* February 1, 1997.

153. NGO briefings on developments in IPF and the Convention on Biological Diversity at BIONET, January 26, 1996, and December 5, 1996.

154. Humphreys, "The Elusive Quest."

155. Ibid.

156. Interview with William Mankin, Global Forest Policy Project, fourth session of the UN Forum on Forests, Geneva, Switzerland, May 11, 2004, as cited in Humphreys, "The Elusive Quest."

157. "Summary of the Nineteenth United Nations General Assembly Special Session to Review Implementation of Agenda 21: 23–27 June 1997," *Earth Negotiations Bulletin* 5, no. 88 (June 30, 1997): 5–6, www.iisd.ca/download/pdf/enb0588e.pdf/; David Humphreys, "The Report of the Intergovernmental Panel on Forests," *Environmental Politics* 7, no. 1 (spring 1998): 219–220.

158. United Nations Economic and Social Council Resolution E/2000/3, Economic and Social Council Official Records (2000), Supplement No. 1, para. 11.

159. The Collaborative Partnership on Forests currently comprises fourteen international organization members: Centre for International Forestry Research (CIFOR); Food and Agriculture Organization of the United Nations (FAO); International Tropical Timber Organization (ITTO); International Union of Forestry Research Organizations (IUFRO); Secretariat of the Convention on Biological Diversity (CBD); Secretariat of the Global Environment Facility (GEF); Secretariat of the United Nations Convention to Combat Desertification (UNCCD); Secretariat of the United Nations Forum on Forests (UNFF); Secretariat of the United Nations Framework Convention on Climate Change (UNFCCC); United Nations Development Program (UNDP); United Nations Environment Programme (UNEP); World Agroforestry Centre (ICRAF); World Bank; and World Conservation Union (IUCN).

160. Deborah S. Davenport and Peter Wood, "Finding the Way Forward for the International Arrangement on Forests: UNFF-5, -6 and -7," *Review of European Community and International Environmental Law* 15, no. 3 (2006): 317.

161. Ibid.

162. For more information on UNFF-5, see "Summary of the Fifth Session of the United Nations Forum on Forests: 16–17 May 2005," *Earth Negotiations Bulletin,* 13, no. 133 (May 30, 2005), www.iisd.ca/download/pdf/enb13133e.pdf.

163. ECOSOC Resolution E/2006/49, Economic and Social Council Official Records (2006), E/2006/INF/2/Add.1, www.un.org/esa/forests/pdf/2006_49_E.pdf.

164. See General Assembly Resolution 62/98, "Non–Legally Binding Instrument on All Types of Forests," www.un.org/esa/forests/about-resolutions.html.

165. Economic and Social Council, *United Nations Forum on Forests: Report of the Seventh Session, 24 February 2006 and 16 to 27 April 2007* (E/2007/42) (New York: United Nations, 2007), 13.

166. UK Office on Climate Change Eliasch Review, *Climate Change: Financing Global Forests* (London: Crown Copyright, 2008), www.occ.gov.uk/activities/eliasch/Full_report_eliasch_review(1).pdf, as cited in "Summary of the Eighth Session of the United Nations Forum on

Forests: 20 April–1 May 2009," *Earth Negotiations Bulletin* 13, no. 174 (May 4, 2009): 9, www.iisd.ca/download/pdf/enb13174e.pdf.

167. "Summary of the Eighth Session of the United Nations Forum on Forests: 20 April–1 May 2009."

168. Ibid.

169. Ibid.

170. Ibid.

171. See, e.g., Wynet Smith, "Undercutting Sustainability: The Global Problem of Illegal Logging and Trade," *Journal of Sustainable Forestry* 19, nos. 1–3 (2004): 7.

172. For more information about the Forest Law Enforcement and Governance initiatives, see the World Bank's Forest Governance Program's website at http://go.worldbank.org/FMKUFABJ80.

173. "Forest Law Enforcement and Governance," World Bank, June 3, 2009, http://go.worldbank.org/FMKUFABJ80.

174. UN Department for Economic and Social Affairs, "Forests: The Green and REDD of Climate Change," Policy Brief No. 16, United Nations, April 2009, www.un.org/esa/policy/policybriefs/policybrief16.pdf.

Chapter 6

1. The commonly cited figure of about 150 multilateral environmental agreements is taken from UNEP data and includes only multilateral agreements totally directed to environmental issues. See Harold K. Jacobson and Edith Brown Weiss, "A Framework for Analysis," in *Engaging Countries: Strengthening Compliance with International Environmental Accords*, ed. Edith Brown Weiss and Harold K. Jacobson (Cambridge, MA: MIT Press, 1998), 1, 18. The 950 number is compiled from the International Environmental Agreements Database Project (http://iea.uoregon.edu), directed by Ronald Mitchell. The International Environmental Agreements statistics page is at http://iea.uoregon.edu/page.php?query=home-contents.php.

2. Broader discussions of issues related to implementation and compliance include Weiss and Jacobson, *Engaging Countries*; Edward Miles et al., *Environmental Regime Effectiveness* (Cambridge, MA: MIT Press, 2001); Michael Faure and Jurgen Lefevere, "Compliance with Global Environmental Policy," in *Global Environmental Policy: Institutions, Law and Policy*, ed. Regina Axelrod, David Downie, and Norman Vig, 2nd ed. (Washington, DC: Congressional Quarterly Press, 2005); "The Oslo-Potsdam Solution to Measuring Regime Effectiveness: Critique, Response, and the Road Ahead." *Global Environmental Politics* 3, no. 3 (August 2003): 74–96; and Ronald Mitchell, "Problem Structure, Institutional Design, and the Relative Effectiveness of International Environmental Agreements," *Global Environmental Politics* 6, no. 3 (August 2006); 72–89.

3. The discussion of the first four sets of factors draws explicitly on research and publications by one of the coauthors. See particularly, David Downie, *Understanding International Environmental Regimes: Lessons of the Ozone* (PhD diss., University of North Carolina, 1996), which the publications below and this chapter follow closely with regard to these four sets of factors; David Downie, "Opportunities and Obstacles to Effective International Environmental Cooperation" (paper presented to Institute for Defense Analysis Conference on Environmental Issues, Washington, DC, July 28, 1995); David Downie, "Road Map or False Trail: Evaluating the Precedence of the Ozone Regime as Model and Strategy for Global Climate Change," *International Environmental Affairs* 7 (fall 1995): 321–345; David Downie, "Global Environmental Policy:

Governance through Regimes," in *Global Environmental Policy: Institutions, Law and Policy*, ed. Regina Axelrod, David Downie, and Norman Vig, 2nd ed. (Washington, DC: Congressional Quarterly Press, 2005).

4. Classic examples include Thucydides, Niccolò Machiavelli, Thomas Hobbes, and Barthold Niebuhr. Influential modern examples include Henry Kissinger; Hans Morgenthau, *Politics among Nations*, 5th ed. (New York: Knopf, 1973); Robert Jervis, "Cooperation under the Security Dilemma," *World Politics* 30 (1978): 167–186; Kenneth Waltz, *Theory of International Politics* (Reading, MA: Addison-Wesley, 1979); and Glenn Snyder, "The Security Dilemma in Alliance Politics," *World Politics* 36 (1984): 461–495.

5. For an excellent discussion of the impact of positional concerns on cooperation, see Joseph M. Grieco, "Anarchy and the Limits of Cooperation: A Realist Critique of the Newest Liberal Institutionalism," *International Organization* 42 (summer 1988): 485–507. Subsequent references in this subsection also refer to theoretical discussions of the structural obstacle, not a specific discussion of its impact on environmental cooperation.

6. Jervis, "Cooperation under the Security Dilemma," and Kenneth Oye, ed., *Cooperation under Anarchy* (Princeton, NJ: Princeton University Press, 1986), 1–22.

7. Mancur Olson, *The Logic of Collective Action* (Cambridge, MA: Harvard University Press, 1965).

8. Garrett Hardin, "The Tragedy of the Commons," *Science* 162, no. 3859 (December 13, 1968): 1243–1248. J. Samuel Barkin and George Shambaugh, eds., *Anarchy and the Environment: The International Relations of Common Pool Resources* (Albany: State University of New York Press, 1999).

9. Robert Keohane, *After Hegemony* (Princeton, NJ: Princeton University Press, 1984).

10. Robert Jervis, *Perception and Misperception in International Politics* (Princeton, NJ: Princeton University Press, 1976).

11. M. A. Giordano and A. T. Wolf, "Sharing Waters: Post-Rio International Water Management," *Natural Resources Forum* 27 (2003): 163–171 (information on 163–164).

12. Elli Louka, *International Environmental Law: Fairness, Effectiveness and World Order*, 5th ed. (New York: Cambridge University Press, 2006).

13. UN Document A/CONF.48/14, 118. This principle later became Principle 2 of the Rio Declaration, but with the words "and developmental" inserted before "policies," thus making it even more self-contradictory.

14. Gary C. Bryner, *From Promises to Performance: Achieving Global Environmental Goals* (New York: W. W. Norton, 1997), 59.

15. Peter Sand, *Lessons Learned in Global Environmental Governance* (Washington, DC: World Resources Institute, 1990), 21.

16. Representative discussions of the trade and environment issue include Kevin Gallagher, *Handbook on Trade and the Environment* (Northampton: Edward Elgar, 2009); Jeffrey Frankel and Andrew Rose, "Is Trade Good or Bad for the Environment? Sorting Out the Causality," *Review of Economics and Statistics* 87, no. 1 (February 2005): 85–91; and Brian Copeland and M. Scott Taylor, *Trade and the Environment: Theory and Evidence* (Princeton, NJ: Princeton University Press, 2003).

17. For a comprehensive discussion of these issues, see Jennifer Clapp and Doris Fuchs, eds. *Corporate Power in Global Agrifood Governance* (Cambridge, MA: MIT Press, 2009).

18. Peter Haas, Robert Keohane, and Marc Levy, eds., *Institutions for the Earth: Sources of Effective International Environmental Protection* (Cambridge, MA: MIT Press, 1993).

19. For extended discussion of these two obstacles, see Lawrence E. Susskind, *Environmental Diplomacy: Negotiating More Effective Global Agreements* (New York: Oxford University Press, 1994); and Sand, *Lessons Learned in Global Environmental Governance.*

20. This point is also made by Susskind, *Environmental Diplomacy*, 156.

21. Elaine M. Carlin, "Oil Pollution from Ships at Sea," in Miles et al., *Environmental Regime Effectiveness*, 336.

22. Ibid., 345.

23. As with similar discussions in this book, the categories presented in this subsection should also be seen as indicative and heuristic rather and exhaustive and exclusive.

24. This conclusion is based on personal observations by David Downie during the fourth Conference of the Parties to the Stockholm Convention on Persistent Organic Pollutants, Geneva, Switzerland, May 4–8, 2009.

25. Downie, "Global Environmental Policy," 76.

26. Ibid., 74.

27. Most spills occur in industrial facilities and laboratories and are relatively contained but can expose particular individuals to high doses. However, very large spills and area contaminations also occur as a result of industrial accidents; fires; accidents involving trains, ships, or trucks transporting chemicals; illegal bumping; and inadequate production facilities that allow substances to contaminate the surrounding area. Some of the most famous chemical spills in history provide examples. In August 2008 a series of explosions at a large chemical plant in Guangxi Province, China, released toxic gas into the air and contaminated the Longjiang River, forcing evacuation of the nearby town. In November 2005, about one hundred tons of toxic pollutants flooded into the Songhua River in China after an explosion at another chemical plant. In 1991, seven train cars carrying the pesticide metam sodium fell off the tracks in California, broke apart, and released the chemicals into the Sacramento River. Plant and aquatic life for forty-three miles downriver died as a result. In 1986, the chemical company Ciba-Geigy accidentally discharged large amounts of toxic agricultural chemicals into the Rhine River in Europe. The next day a fire at a chemical warehouse in Basel, Switzerland, caused thirty tons of mercury-laden toxic waste to be sluiced into the Rhine. In December 1984, a cloud of poisonous gas escaped from a Union Carbide chemical plant in Bhopal, India, that produced the pesticide Sevin. Hundreds of thousands of people were exposed. In 1983, the U.S. government purchased the entire town of Times Beach, Missouri, and relocated more than 2,200 residents because the land was so badly contaminated with highly toxic dioxins that came from nearby plants. The town of Love Canal in New York was essentially closed after the discovery of widespread toxic contamination from illegal dumping.

28. See Knut Midgaard and Arild Underdal, "Multiparty Conferences," in *Negotiations: Social-Psychological Perspectives*, ed. Daniel Druckman (Beverly Hills, CA: Sage Publications, 1977), 339; and Pamela S. Chasek, *Earth Negotiations: Analyzing Thirty Years of Environmental Diplomacy* (Tokyo: United Nations University Press, 2001), ch. 3.

29. Barkin and Shambaugh, *Anarchy and the Environment.*

30. Personal observation by David Downie during the fourth Conference of the Parties to the Stockholm Convention on Persistent Organic Pollutants, Geneva, Switzerland, May 4–8, 2009.

31. Ronald B. Mitchell, "Regime Design Matters: Intentional Oil Pollution and Treaty Compliance," *International Organization* 48, no. 3 (summer 1994): 425–458. Ronald B. Mitchell,

"Problem Structure, Institutional Design, and the Relative Effectiveness of International Environmental Agreements," *Global Environmental Politics* 6, no. 3 (August 2006): 72–89.

32. Jacobson and Weiss, "A Framework for Analysis," 4.

33. Edith Brown Weiss, Daniel B. Magraw, and Paul C. Szasz, *International Environmental Law: Basic Instruments and References* (Dobbs Ferry, NY: Transnational, 1992), 696.

34. Abram Chayes and Antonia H. Chayes, "Compliance without Enforcement: State Behavior under Regulatory Treaties," *Negotiation Journal* 7 (1991): 311–330; J. Timmons Roberts, Bradley C. Parks, and Alexis A. Vásquez, "Who Ratifies Environmental Treaties and Why? Institutionalism, Structuralism and Participation by 192 Nations in 22 Treaties," *Global Environmental Politics* 4, no. 3 (August 2004): 22–64.

35. In addition to those already cited, prominent examples of this literature include Peter H. Sand, ed., *The Effectiveness of International Environmental Agreements* (Cambridge, MA: Grotius Publications, 1992); Ronald B. Mitchell, *Intentional Oil Pollution at Sea* (Cambridge, MA: MIT Press, 1994); Weiss and Jacobson, *Engaging Countries*; David G. Victor, Kal Raustiala, and Eugene Skolnikof, eds., *The Implementation and Effectiveness of International Environmental Commitments: Theory and Practice* (Cambridge, MA: MIT Press, 1998); Michael J. Kelly, "Overcoming Obstacles to the Effective Implementation of International Environmental Agreements," *Georgetown International Environmental Law Review* 9, no. 2 (1997); Michael Faure and Jurgen Lefevere, "Compliance with Global Environmental Policy," in *Global Environmental Policy: Institutions, Law and Policy*, ed. Regina Axelrod, David Downie, and Norman Vig, 2nd ed. (Washington, DC: Congressional Quarterly Press, 2005); Ronald B. Mitchell, "Compliance Theory: A Synthesis," *Review of European Community and International Environmental Law*, 2 no. 4 (1993): 327–334.

36. Sand, *The Effectiveness of International Environmental Agreements*, 82.

37. Kelly, "Overcoming Obstacles," 462–463.

38. For example, in an experiment conducted by WWF, volunteers declared or displayed a cactus to customs officials in several countries, including the United Kingdom, Switzerland, Germany, Sweden, Denmark, and the United States. Although virtually all cacti are protected under the CITES agreement, no questions were asked by officials in any of these countries about the species of the plant or its origins. See Bill Padgett, "The African Elephant, Africa and CITES: The Next Step," *Indiana Journal of Global Legal Studies* 2 (1995): 529, 538–540, as cited in Kelly, "Overcoming Obstacles," 469–470.

39. See, e.g., Duncan Brack, "Combating International Environmental Crime," *Global Environmental Change* 12, no 2 (July 2002): 79–147; William F. Laurance et al., "Deforestation in Amazonia" *Science* 304, no. 5674 (May 21, 2004): 1109–1111; and Richard Dudley, "Dynamics of Illegal Logging in Indonesia," in *Way Forward? People, Forests, and Policymaking in Indonesia*, ed. Carol Pierse Colfer and Aju Pradnja Resosudarmo (Washington, DC: RFF Press, 2002).

40. David Mulenex, "Improving Compliance Provisions in International Environmental Agreements," in *International Environmental Treaty-Making*, ed. Lawrence E. Susskind, Eric Jay Dolin, and J. William Breslin (Cambridge, MA: Program on Negotiation at Harvard Law School, 1992), 174.

41. Personal observations by David Downie during meetings of the Stockholm, Rotterdam, and Basel conventions between 2005 and 2009 and personal communications from very senior environmental officials from several African countries during the Fourth Conference of the Parties to the Stockholm Convention on Persistent Organic Pollutants, Geneva, Switzerland, May 4–8, 2009.

42. David Vogel and Timothy Kessler, "How Compliance Happens and Doesn't Happen Domestically," in *Engaging Countries: Strengthening Compliance with International Environmental Accords*, ed. Edith Brown Weiss and Harold K. Jacobson (Cambridge, MA: MIT Press, 1998), 24.

43. Caroline Gammell, "Somalia Named the Most Volatile Place in the World," Telegraph.co.uk, December 17, 2008, www.telegraph.co.uk/news/worldnews/africaandindian ocean/somalia/3814571/Somalia-named-the-most-volatile-place-in-the-world.html. This article cites a report by Jane's Country Risk.

44. Andrew J. Heimert, "How the Elephant Lost His Tusks," *Yale Law Journal* 104 (1995): 1473, as cited in Kelly, "Overcoming Obstacles," 465.

45. Environmental Investigation Agency and Telepak, *The Final Cut: Illegal Logging in Indonesia's Orangutan Parks* (Washington, DC: Environmental Investigation Agency, 1999); David W. Brown, *Addicted to Rent: Corporate and Spatial Distribution of Forest Resources in Indonesia: Implications for Forest Sustainability and Government Policy* (Jakarta: Indonesia-UK Tropical Forest Management Programme, 1999).

46. Vogel and Kessler, "How Compliance Happens," 35.

47. Netherlands Environmental Assessment Agency, "Industrialised Countries Will Collectively Meet 2010 Kyoto Target," Government Dossier, Planbureau voor de Leefomgeving, February 17, 2009, www.pbl.nl/en/dossiers/COP13Bali/moreinfo/Industrialised-countries-will -collectively-meet-2010-Kyoto-target.html. See also data in the "GHG Data" section of the UNFCCC website at http://unfccc.int.

48. For specific and numerous examples, see reports of the ozone regime's Implementation Committee, available at the Ozone Secretariat's website at www.unep.org/ozone.

49. Robert Costanse et al., "The Value of the World's Ecosystem Services and Natural Capital," *Nature* 387 (May 15, 1997): 253–260.

50. *UNEP Year Book 2009* (Nairobi: UNEP, March 2009), available at www.unep.org/geo/ yearbook, and UNEP, *Global Green New Deal: Policy Brief* (Nairobi: UNEP, March 2009), available at www.unep.org/pdf/A_Global_Green_New_Deal_Policy_Brief.pdf.

51. Nicholas Stern, *The Economics of Climate Change: The Stern Review* (Cambridge: Cambridge University Press, January 15, 2007). Frank Ackerman and Elizabeth A. Stanton, *The Cost of Climate Change: What We'll Pay if Global Warming Continues Unchecked* (Washington, DC: NRDC, 2008), www.nrdc.org/globalwarming/cost/cost.pdf. Economics of Climate Change Adaptation Working Group, *Shaping Climate Resilient Development: A Framework for Decision-Making* (Washington, DC: ECA, 2009), www.gefweb.org/uploadedFiles/Publications/ECA_Shaping _Climate%20Resilent_Development.pdf (see also, www.gefweb.org/interior_right.aspx?id=26782).

52. Economics of Climate Change Adaptation Working Group, *Shaping Climate Resilient Development: A Framework for Decision-Making*, www.gefweb.org/uploadedFiles/Publications/ ECA_Shaping_Climate%20Resilent_Development.pdf.

53. To use the meta-analysis tool, see www.climate.yale.edu/seeforyourself/index.php.

54. The Pew Charitable Trusts, *The Clean Energy Economy*. (Washington, DC: Pew Charitable Trusts, 2009), www.pewcenteronthestates.org/uploadedFiles/Clean_Economy_Report_Web.pdf.

55. Matt Magnusson et al., "Economic and Greenhouse Gas Impacts of the New 2009 Fuel Economy (CAFE) Standards in New England," Carbon Solutions New England, June 2009, http://carbonsolutionsne.org/resources/reports/2009_CAFE_report.

56. Michael Renner et al. *Green Jobs: Towards Decent Work in a Sustainable, Low-Carbon World* (Nairobi: UNEP 2008), www.unep.org/labour_environment/features/greenjobs-report.asp.

57. Delegates from developing countries consistently make this argument during meetings of the parties to most global environmental regimes (personal observations by the authors). For specific examples, see the official reports from such meetings, which can be found on the relevant secretariat websites or in reports by the *Earth Negotiations Bulletin* at www.iisd.ca.

58. For extensive discussion of this point, see Nicholas Stern, *The Economics of Climate Change: The Stern Review* (Cambridge: Cambridge University Press, January 15, 2007), xvii and chs. 14 to 17.

59. For discussion, see the 2009 WTO and UNEP report "Trade and Climate Change," UNEP, www.unep.ch/etb/index.php.

60. Such provisions were even included as part of the climate-change legislation that passed the U.S. House of Representatives in 2009, HR 2454: American Clean Energy and Security Act of 2009. As of September 14, 2009, it was unknown if a climate bill would also pass the U.S. Senate and if it would contain similar provisions.

61. Edith Brown Weiss, "The Five International Treaties: A Living History," in *Engaging Countries: Strengthening Compliance with International Environmental Accords*, ed. Edith Brown Weiss and Harold K. Jacobson (Cambridge, MA: MIT Press, 1998), 115–116.

62. Ibid., 162. This conclusion is also supported by the personal observations of the authors and communications with secretariat and government officials.

63. Including, for example, the UNEP Governing Council, Open-ended Intergovernmental Group of Ministers or Their Representatives on International Environmental Governance, and Global Ministerial Environment Forum.

64. The Strategic Approach to International Chemicals Management, or SAICM, seeks to integrate better chemicals management into all aspects of development activity. One part of this is to increase coordination among chemical-related institutions. For more information see the SAICM website at www.chem.unep.ch/saicm.

65. See, e.g., Victor, Raustiala, and Skolnikoff, *The Implementation and Effectiveness of International Environmental Commitments.*

66. For a full discussion, see Basel Convention Secretariat, *Global Trends in Generation and Transboundary Movement of Hazardous Wastes and Other Wastes: Analysis of the Data Provided by Parties to the Secretariat of the Basel Convention*, UN Publication Series, Basel Convention on the Control of Transboundary Movements on Hazardous Wastes and Their Disposal 14 (Geneva: Basel Convention Secretariat, 2004).

67. Juan Carlos di Primio, "Data Quality and Compliance Control," in Victor, Raustiala, and Skolnikoff, *The Implementation and Effectiveness of International Environmental Commitments*, 283–299.

68. European Environment Agency and UNEP, "Chemicals in the European Environment: Low Doses, High Stakes?" in *The EEA and UNEP Annual Message 2 on the State of Europe's Environment* (Copenhagen: European Commission, 2001).

69. See Decision Conf. 11.17 (Rev. COP-14) at www.cites.org/eng/res/11/11–17R14.shtml.

70. Weiss, "The Five International Treaties," 112. This progress has been slow, however. As of July 2009, only 42 percent of parties had submitted their 2007 national reports by the October 31, 2008, deadline, and 42 percent of parties had still not submitted their 2007 national reports. See "Annual Reports of CITES Parties," CITES, www.cites.org/common/resources/annual_reports.pdf.

71. Jonathan Krueger and Henrik Selin, "Governance for Sound Chemicals Management: The Need for a More Comprehensive Global Strategy," *Global Governance* 8 (2002): 323–342;

Jonathan Krueger, Henrik Selin, and David Downie, "Global Policy for Hazardous Chemicals," in *Global Environmental Policy: Institutions, Law and Policy*, ed. Regina Axelrod, David Downie, and Norman Vig, 2nd ed. (Washington, DC: Congressional Quarterly Press, 2005).

72. For additional information, see the TRAFFIC website at www.traffic.org.

73. Mitchell, *Intentional Oil Pollution at Sea*, 47–48.

74. For more information, see Martin Khor, *The Proposed New Issues in the WTO and the Interests of Developing Countries*, Trade and Development Series 14 (Penang, Malaysia: Third World Network, 2001).

75. There are many good discussions of this problem. See, e.g., Sanford Gaines, "The WTO's Reading of the GATT Article XX Chapeau: A Disguised Restriction on Environmental Measures," *University of Pennsylvania Journal of International Economic Law* 22, no. 4 (winter 2001): 739–858; Steve Charnovitz, "Exploring the Environmental Exceptions in GATT Article XX," *Journal of World Trade* 25 (1991); and Beatrice Chaytor and James Cameron, "The Treatment of Environmental Considerations in the World Trade Organization," in *Yearbook of International Co-operation on Environment and Development 1999/2000*, ed. Helge Ole Bergesen, Georg Parmann, and Øystein B. Thommessen (London: Earthscan Publications, 1999), 55–64.

76. See, e.g., Susskind, *Environmental Diplomacy*.

77. Personal communications.

78. Ecomessage was created by Interpol in the 1990s as a reporting system to improve sharing of wildlife-crime information among international wildlife law enforcement agencies. It was designed to facilitate the efficient transmission of critical data to the Interpol General Secretariat in Lyon, France. The International Fund for Animal Welfare's sponsorship of the Ecomessage Award and its collaboration with Interpol on the development of a guidebook on Ecomessage are provided in recognition of the costs of compliance with the reporting system as well as its significant benefits. For more information on this award, see www.ifaw.org/ifaw_international/ join_campaigns/fight_illegal_wildlife_trade/protecting_animals_with_international_treaties/eco message_award/index.php.

79. "2008 Environmental Performance Index," Socioeconomic Data and Applications Center, http://sedac.ciesin.columbia.edu/es/epi.

80. Harold K. Jacobson and Edith Brown Weiss, "Assessing the Record and Designing Strategies to Engage Countries," in *Engaging Countries: Strengthening Compliance with International Environmental Accords*, ed. Edith Brown Weiss and Harold K. Jacobson (Cambridge, MA: MIT Press, 1998), 527.

81. For updated information, see the GEF website at www.gefweb.org.

82. Jim VandeHei, "G-8 Leaders Agree on $50B in Africa Aid," *Washington Post*, July 9, 2005. Karen Travers, "G-8's Broken Promises to Africa: Some Leaders Have Failed to Deliver Fully on Their 2005 Pledge of Aid to Africa, Making Many Wary of New Commitments," *ABC News*, June 10, 2009, http://abcnews.go.com/Politics/story?id=8055007&page=1.

83. See particularly Jeffrey Sachs, *The End of Poverty: Economic Possibilities for Our Time* (New York: Penguin, 2005); and Jeffrey Sachs, *Common Wealth: Economics for a Crowded Planet* (New York: Penguin, 2008).

84. For official, detailed information on the EU Emissions Trading Scheme, see http://ec .europa.eu/environment/climat/emission/index_en.htm.

85. For example, see IISD, "Financing Climate Change: Global Environmental Tax?" *Developing Ideas* 15 (September–October 1998).

86. UN Commission on Sustainable Development, "Financial Resources and Mechanisms for Sustainable Development: Overview of Current Issues and Developments, Report of the Secretary-General" E/CN.17/ISWG.II/1994/2, February 22, 1994, 24.

87. "Levy on International Air Travel Could Fund Climate Change Fight," *Guardian,* June 8, 2009, 13. Available at www.guardian.co.uk/environment/2009/jun/07/international-flight-levy-un-climate-change.

88. Alister Doyle, "Mexico Sees Support for UN Climate Finance Plan," Reuters, June 3, 2009, www.reuters.com/article/latestCrisis/idUSL3730686.

89. The original proposal, by Nobel Prize–winning economist James Tobin, was for a 0.5 percent tax on speculative currency transactions that would raise $1.5 trillion annually and was aimed at deterring such transactions. The UNDP proposed reducing the tax to 10 percent of the original level. See UNDP, *Human Development Report 1994* (New York: Oxford University Press, 1994), 69–70; Martin Walker, "Global Taxation: Paying for Peace," *World Policy Journal* 10, no. 2 (summer 1993): 7–12.

90. Stephen R. Seidel and Daniel Blank, "Closing an Ozone Loophole," *Environmental Forum* 7 (1990): 18–20; "Effect of Ozone-Depleting Chemicals Tax Could Be Wide-Ranging, IRS Attorney Says," *Environment Reporter* 21 (November 2, 1990): 1257.

91. See section 921 of the United Nations Reform Act of 1999 (Chapter 2 of Title IX of the Admiral James W. Nance and Meg Donovan Foreign Relations Authorization Act for Fiscal Years 2000 and 2001 [as enacted into law by section 1000(a)(7) of Public Law 106-113 and contained in appendix G of that act; 113 Stat. 1501A-478] [commonly referred to as "Helms-Biden"]).

92. Updated information on HIPC can be found on the World Bank and IMF websites at www.worldbank.org/debt and www.imf.org/external/np/exr/facts/hipc.htm.

93. Ibid.

94. Jim VandeHei, "G-8 Leaders Agree on $50B in Africa Aid," *Washington Post,* July 9, 2005.

95. See www.jubileeusa.org.

96. Institute for European Environmental Policy, "Reforming Environmentally Harmful Subsidies" (final report to the European Commission's DG Environment, March 2007), www.ieep.eu/publications/publications.php?pub=68382; "Energy Subsidies Distorting Trade and Harming the Environment/Stop Harmful Fishing Subsidies/WTO Focuses on Trade in Forest Products," UNEP, March 25, 1999, www.grida.no/news/press/1920.aspx; A. De Moor and P. Calamai, *Subsidizing Unsustainable Development: Undermining the Earth with Public Funds* (San Jose, Costa Rica: Earth Council, 1997); V. P. Gadhi, D. Gray, and R. McMorran, "A Comprehensive Approach to Domestic Resources for Sustainable Development," in *Finance for Sustainable Development: The Road Ahead* (New York: United Nations, 1997).

Chapter 7

1. See Karl P. Sauvant and Hajo Hasenpflug, eds., *The New International Economic Order: Confrontation or Cooperation between North and South?* (Boulder, CO: Westview Press, 1977).

2. James K. Sebenius, "Negotiating a Regime to Control Global Warming," in *Greenhouse Warming: Negotiating a Global Regime,* ed. Jessica Tuchman Mathews (Washington, DC: World Resources Institute, 1991), 87.

3. South Commission, *The Challenge to the South: The Report of the South Commission* (Oxford: Oxford University Press, 1990); Mohammed Ayoob, "The New-Old Disorder in the Third World," *Global Governance* 1, no. 1 (1995): 59–77; Adil Najam, "An Environmental Ne-

gotiation Strategy for the South," *International Environmental Affairs* 7, no. 3 (1995): 249–287; Adil Najam, "The View from the South: Developing Countries in Global Environmental Politics," in *The Global Environment: Institutions, Law and Policy*, ed. Regina S. Axelrod, David L. Downie, and Norman J. Vig 2nd ed. (Washington, DC: Congressional Quarterly Press, 2005), 224–243.

4. Dennis Pirages, *Global Ecopolitics: The New Context for International Relations* (North Scituate, RI: Duxbury Press, 1978); Hayward R. Alker Jr. and Peter M. Haas, "The Rise of Global Ecopolitics," in *Global Accord: Environmental Challenges and International Responses*, ed. Nazli Choucri (Cambridge, MA: MIT Press, 1993), 133–171; Najam, "An Environmental Negotiation Strategy for the South"; Najam, "The View from the South."

5. This was part of a longer-term decline in the real prices of primary products in the world market, caused by slow growth in demand, the development of cheaper substitutes, and overproduction. See UNDP, *Human Development Report 1992* (New York: UNDP, 1992), 59.

6. UNDP, "Financial Inflows and Outflows," *Human Development Report 1998* (New York: Oxford University Press, 1998). The term least developed countries (LDCs) was originally used at the United Nations in 1971 to describe the "poorest and most economically weak of the developing countries, with formidable economic, institutional and human resources problems, which are often compounded by geographical handicaps and natural and man-made disasters." There are currently fifty LDCs.

7. World Bank, *Global Economic Prospects and the Developing Countries* (Washington, DC: World Bank, 1992), 13.

8. United Nations Conference on Trade and Development (UNCTAD), "The Post-Uruguay Round Tariff Environment for Developing Country Exports: Tariff Peaks and Tariff Escalation: A UNCTAD/WTO Joint Study," TD/B/COM.1/14/Rev.1, January 20, 2000, www.unctad .org/en/docs/c1d14r1.en.pdf.

9. "Barriers to entry" are any obstacle that impedes a potential new entrant (a company or country) from entering a market to produce or sell goods or services. Barriers to entry shelter incumbent companies against new entrants. They can include government regulations, subsidies, intellectual property rules, restrictive practices, preexisting supplier or distributer agreements, control of resources, economies of scale, advantages independent of scale, consumer preferences, and other factors.

10. See Oli Brown and Jason Gibson, *Boom or Bust: Developing Countries' Rough Ride on the Commodity Price Rollercoaster* (Winnipeg: IISD, 2006), www.iisd.org/pdf/2006/security _boom_or_bust.pdf.

11. World Bank, *World Development Indicators 2009* (Washington, DC: World Bank, 2009), 2.

12. James B. Davies et al., *The World Distribution of Household Wealth, Discussion Paper 2008/03* (Helsinki: United Nations University World Institute for Development Economics Research, 2008).

13. J. Timmons Roberts and Bradley C. Parks, *A Climate of Injustice: Global Inequality, North-South Politics, and Climate Policy* (Cambridge, MA: The MIT Press, 2007), 12.

14. Ibid.

15. Roberts and Parks, *A Climate of Injustice*; Najam, "The View from the South."

16. Development and Environment (Paris: Mouton, 1971), report and working papers of experts convened by the secretary-general of the UN Conference on the Human Environment, Founex, Switzerland, June 4–12, 1971.

17. Najam, "The View from the South."

18. *Development and Environment*, 5–6, as cited in Adil Najam, "Why Environmental Politics Looks Different from the South," in Peter Dauvergne, *Handbook of Global Environmental Politics* (Cheltenham, UK: Edward Elgar Press, 2005), 111–126.

19. Statement by H. E. Datuk Amar Stephen K. T. Yong, leader of the Malaysian delegation, at the second Meeting of the Parties to the Montreal Protocol, London, June 27–29, 1990.

20. Talk by Mohammed El-Ashry, then vice president of the World Resources Institute, at the Egyptian Embassy, Washington, DC, March 9, 1990.

21. "Final Document of the XIIth Summit of the Non-Aligned Movement," September 2–3, 1998, Durban, South Africa, www.nam.gov.za/xiisummit/index.html.

22. UNDP, *Human Development Report* 1998 (New York: Oxford University Press, 1998). These figures have remained largely stable over the last decade. For details and illustrations of the developing-country point of view, see also Anil Agarwal, Sunita Narain, and Anju Sharma, eds., *Green Politics: Global Negotiations*, vol. 1 (New Delhi: Center for Science and Environment, 1999).

23. Friends of the Earth Netherlands developed the environmental space concept as part of its 1992 Sustainable Netherlands Action Plan. Environmental space is the total amount of pollution, nonrenewable resources, agricultural land, and forests that can be used globally without impinging on access by future generations to the same resources. For additional information, see the report of the Oslo Ministerial Roundtable on Sustainable Production and Consumption, February 6–10, 1995, www.iisd.ca/linkages/consume/oslo000.html.

24. Najam, "The View from the South."

25. Pamela S. Chasek, "The Convention to Combat Desertification: Lessons Learned for Sustainable Development," *Journal of Environment and Development* 6, no. 2 (1997): 147–169.

26. Najam, "The View from the South."

27. "Proposed Elements of a Protocol to the United Nations Framework Convention on Climate Change, Presented by Brazil in Response to the Berlin Mandate," Ad Hoc Group on the Berlin Mandate, seventh session, Bonn, July 31–August 7, 1997, 22.

28. See *Outreach* 1997 1, no. 24 (April 22, 1997).

29. See the final communiqué from the Gleneagles Summit at www.g7.utoronto.ca/summit/2005gleneagles/communique.pdf.

30. See the outcome document from the 2005 UN summit at www.un.org/summit2005.

31. "Development Aid at Its Highest Level Ever in 2008," OECD, March 30, 2009, www.oecd.org/document/35/0,3343,en_2649_34487_42458595_1_1_1_1,00.html.

32. Robert L. Hicks et al., *Greening Aid? Understanding the Environmental Impact of Development Assistance* (New York: Oxford, 2008), 247.

33. Ibid., 2.

34. Najam, "The View from the South." See also Anil Agarwal and Sunita Narain, *Global Warming in an Unequal World: A Case of Environmental Colonialism* (New Delhi: Center for Science and Environment, 1991); Agarwal, Narain, and Sharma, *Green Politics*.

35. Najam, "The View from the South."

36. Ibid.

37. Kevin P. Gallagher, "The Economics of Globalization and Sustainable Development," in "Trade, Environment and Investment: Cancún and Beyond," *Policy Matters* 11 (September 2003).

38. Mark Halle, "Sustainable Development Cools Off—Globalization Demands Summit Take New Approach to Meeting Ecological, Social Goals," *Winnipeg Free Press*, July 29, 2002.

39. Pamela S. Chasek, "Sustainable Development in the Twenty-first Century," in *Introducing Global Issues*, ed. Michael T. Snarr and D. Neil Snarr, 4th ed. (Boulder, CO: Lynne Rienner, 2008), 243–264.

40. "Addressing Inequities of Globalization 'Overarching Challenge' of Times Says Secretary-General, Presenting Millennium Report to General Assembly," Press Release SG/SM/7343, United Nations, April 3, 2000, www.un.org/News/Press/docs/2000/20000403.sgsm7343.doc.html.

41. Pamela S. Chasek and Richard Sherman, *Ten Days in Johannesburg: A Negotiation of Hope* (Cape Town: Struik Publishers, 2004); and IISD, *Millennium Review Meeting Bulletin* 104, no. 2 (March 16, 2005): www.iisd.ca/sd/ecosocprep1/sdvol104num2e.html.

42. Ibid.

43. James Gustave Speth, "Perspectives on the Johannesburg Summit," *Environment* 45, no. 1 (2003).

44. United Nations, *Report of the World Summit on Sustainable Development* (A/CONF.199/20) (New York: United Nations, 2002), www.un.org/esa/sustdev/documents/WSSD_POI_PD/English/WSSD_PlanImpl.pdf.

45. Department of Economic and Social Affairs, "The Johannesburg Summit Test: What Will Change," United Nations, September 25, 2002, www.un.org/jsummit/html/whats_new/feature_story.html.

46. Ibid.

47. Ibid.

48. Ibid.

49. Speth, "Perspectives on the Johannesburg Summit," 24–29.

50. See the 2005 World Summit website at www.un.org/summit2005.

51. United Nations, *Millennium Development Goals Report 2008* (New York: United Nations, 2008), 4. Available at www.un.org/millenniumgoals/pdf/The%20Millennium%20Development%20Goals%20Report%202008.pdf.

52. Celia W. Dugger, "Child Mortality Rate Declines Globally," *New York Times*, September 10, 2009, A6.

53. United Nations, *Millennium Development Goals Report 2008*.

54. Ibid.

55. Michael Clemens and Todd Moss, "What's Wrong with the Millennium Development Goals?" *CGD Policy Brief* (Washington, DC: Center for Global Development, 2005), 3. Available at www.cgdev.org/content/publications/detail/3940.

56. Ibid.

57. Ibid., 4.

58. Jeffrey D. Sachs and Walter V. Reid, "Investments toward Sustainable Development," *Science* 312 (May 19, 2006): 1002.

59. Ibid.

60. Steve Charnovitz, "Environmentalism Confronts GATT Rules," *Journal of World Trade* 28 (January 1993): 37; Daniel C. Esty, "Economic Integration and the Environment," in *The Global Environment: Institutions, Law, and Policy*, ed. Norman J. Vig and Regina S. Axelrod (Washington, DC: Congressional Quarterly Press, 1999), 192.

61. John J. Audley, *Green Politics and Global Trade: NAFTA and the Future of Environmental Politics* (Washington, DC: Georgetown University Press, 1997).

62. GATT/WTO, preamble to "Agreement Establishing the World Trade Organization," WTO, 1994, www.wto.org/english/docs_e/legal_e/04-wto.pdf.

63. Ibid.

64. For more information on the Doha Ministerial Declaration, see "Ministerial Declaration," WT/MIN(01)/DEC/1, WTO, November 20, 2001, www.wto.org/english/thewto_e/minist_e/min01_e/mindecl_e.htm. A good analysis of the declaration can be found at International Center for Trade and Sustainable Development, "The Doha Declaration's Meaning Depends on the Reader," *Bridges* 5, no. 9 (November–December 2001): www.netamericas.net/Researchpapers/Documents/Charnovitz/Charnovitz1.pdf. For updates on the Doha Development Round of Negotiations, see www.wto.org/english/news_e/archive_e/dda_arc_e.htm.

65. For a matrix of selected MEAs and their trade provisions, see WTO, "Matrix on Trade Measures Pursuant to Selected Multilateral Environmental Agreements," WT/CTE/W/160/Rev.4, March 14, 2007.

66. The description of the trade provisions of CITES, the Montreal Protocol, and the Basel Convention is excerpted from Douglas J. Caldwell, *Multilateral Environmental Agreements and the GATT/WTO Regime* (Cambridge, MA: Harvard University Trade, Health, and Environment Program, 1998).

67. UNEP and IISD, *Environment and Trade: A Handbook* (Winnipeg: IISD/UNEP, 2000).

68. Ibid.

69. Ibid.

70. Ibid.

71. "Doha Ministerial Declaration," WT/MIN(01)/DEC/1, WTO, November 20, 2001, www.wto.org/english/thewto_e/minist_e/min01_e/mindecl_e.htm.

72. Richard Tarasofsky, "Trade, Environment, and the WTO Dispute Settlement Mechanism" (report commissioned by the European Commission, June 2005), 4. Available at http://ecologic.eu/download/projekte/1800-1849/1800/4_1800_cate_wto_dispute_settlement.pdf.

73. The term "environmental trade measures" is used in Steve Charnowitz, "The Environment vs. Trade Rules: Defogging the Debate," *Environmental Law* (Northwestern School of Law of Lewis and Clark College) 23 (1993): 490. Charnowitz lists all these forms of ETMs except mandatory ecolabeling.

74. Sang Don Lee, "The Effect of Environmental Regulations on Trade: Cases of Korea's New Environmental Laws," *Georgetown International Environmental Law Review* 5, no. 3 (summer 1993): 659.

75. International Centre for Trade and Sustainable Development, "Ecuador, U.S. Reject EU Banana Proposal; Ecuador to Cross-retaliate," *Bridges Weekly Trade News Digest* 3, no. 45 (November 15, 1999).

76. Daniel C. Esty, *Greening the GATT: Trade, Environment and the Future* (Washington, DC: Institute for International Economics, 1994), 188. In an ironic twist, research undertaken by the Inter-American Tropical Tuna Commission found that "dolphin-safe" tuna fishing results in catching tuna at least thirty-five times more immature (because young tuna do not school beneath groups of dolphins as mature tuna do) and thus threatens to deplete tuna fisheries. See Richard Parker, "The Use and Abuse of Trade Leverage to Protect the Global Commons: What We Can Learn from the Tuna-Dolphin Conflict," *Georgetown International Environmental Law Review* 12, no. 1 (1999): 37–38.

77. For environmental critiques of the decision, see Steve Charnovitz, "GATT and the Environment: Examining the Issues," *International Environmental Affairs* 4, no. 3 (summer 1992): 203–233; Robert Repetto, "Trade and Environment Policies: Achieving Complementarities and

Avoiding Conflict," *WRI Issues and Ideas* (July 1993): 6–10. For an alternative view of the decision, see John H. Jackson, "World Trade Rules and Environmental Policies: Congruence or Conflict?" *Washington and Lee Law Review* 49 (fall 1992): 1242–1243.

78. For an excellent summary, see Donald M. Goldberg, "GATT Tuna-Dolphin II: Environmental Protection Continues to Clash with Free Trade," *CIEL* 2 (June 1994).

79. It was widely believed among NGOs that more such disputes over unilateral actions in the future would ultimately force the negotiation of new GATT rules on the issue. See Bruce Stokes, "The Road from Rio," *National Journal* (May 30, 1992): 1288.

80. The panel's conclusions were released in GATT, "United States Taxes on Automobiles: Report of the Panel," restricted, DS31/R, September 29, 1994.

81. Ibid.

82. Janet Welsh Brown, "Trade and the Environment," *Encyclopedia of Violence, Peace and Conflict*, vol. 3 (San Diego, CA: Academic Press, 1999), T12–14.

83. The appellate body also noted that the United States had failed to sign the Convention on Migratory Species or the United Nations Convention on the Law of the Sea; nor had it ratified the Convention on Biological Diversity or raised the issue of sea turtles during recent CITES conferences. These inconsistencies in the U.S. record on protection of endangered species do not prove, of course, that the U.S. intention in the shrimp/turtle case was not to protect endangered sea turtles.

84. See "Revised Guidelines for the Implementation of Section 609 of Public Law 101-162 Relating to the Protection of Sea Turtles in Shrimp Trawl Fishing Operations," Public Notice 3086, Federal Register, July 1999.

85. For additional information about the Forest Stewardship Council, see www.fsc.org.

86. For more information, see the Marine Stewardship Council's website at www.msc.org and "Sustainable Fishing: Sustainable Seafood," WWF, www.panda.org/what_we_do/how_we_work/conservation/marine/our_solutions/sustainable_fishing/sustainable_seafood.

87. Since 1994, labeling and related issues have been discussed in the WTO's Committee on Trade and Environment, the Committee on Technical Barriers to Trade (TBT), and the Committee on Sanitary and Phytosanitary Measures, as well as during two triennial reviews of the TBT agreement, at various informal WTO symposia, in external conferences attended by WTO Secretariat staff, and in dispute-settlement panels and appellate bodies. For more information on this debate, see Tom Rotherham, *Labelling for Environmental Purposes: A Review of the State of the Debate in the World Trade Organization* (Winnipeg: IISD, 2003), www.tradeknowledgenetwork.net/pdf/tkn_labelling.pdf.

88. International Centre for Trade and Sustainable Development and IISD, "Trade and Environment," *Doha Round Briefing Series* 3, no. 9 (December 2004): http://ictsd.net/downloads/2008/06/v3_09.pdf.

89. For more details, see the Cartagena Protocol on Biosafety at www.cbd.int/biosafety.

90. For more details, see the "Principles for the Risk Analysis of Foods Derived from Modern Biotechnology," CAC/GL 44-2003, FAO, 2003, amended 2008, www.codexalimentarius.net/download/standards/10007/CXG_044e.pdf.

91. For more details, see the "Pest Risk Analysis for Quarantine Pests Including Analysis of Environmental Risks and Living Modified Organisms," ISPM No. 11, International Plant Protection Convention, 2004, https://www.ippc.int/id/34163?language=en.

92. Rotherham, *Labelling for Environmental Purposes*, 4.

93. "Dispute DS291: European Communities—Measures Affecting the Approval and Marketing of Biotech Products," WTO, January 21, 2009 www.wto.org/english/tratop_e/dispu_e/cases_e/ds291_e.htm.

94. European Union, *Europe's Rules on GMOs and the WTO* (Brussels: European Commission, 2006), www.europa-eu-un.org/articles/en/article_5661_en.htm.

95. For an analysis of the WTO ruling, see ITCSD, "A Preliminary Analysis of the WTO Biotech Ruling," *Bridges* 10, no. 7 (November 2006): http://ictsd.net/i/news/bridges/11680.

96. Thomas Bernauer and Philipp Aerni, "Trade Conflict over Genetically Modified Organisms," in *Handbook on Trade and the Environment*, ed. Kevin Gallagher (Northampton, MA: Edward Elgar Publishers, 2008), 188–189.

97. See WTO, Committee on Trade and Environment, *Environmental Benefits of Removing Trade Restrictions and Distortions: Note by the Secretariat* (Geneva: WTO, 1997); Gareth Porter, Fisheries Subsidies, Overfishing and Trade (Geneva: UNEP, 1998).

98. ITCSD, "Trade Leaders Call for Fisheries Subsidies Reform on World Oceans Day," Bridges Weekly Trade News Digest 13, no. 21 (June 10, 2009): http://ictsd.net/i/news/bridgesweekly/48339.

99. International Centre for Trade and Sustainable Development and IISD, "Trade and Environment."

100. UNEP, *Fisheries Subsidies: A Critical Issue for Trade and Sustainable Development at the WTO: An Introductory Guide* (Geneva: UNEP, 2008), 4–5. Available at www.unep.ch/etb/areas/pdf/UNEP-ETB%20Brochure%20on%20Fisheries%20Subsidies_May2008.pdf.

101. "Ministerial Declaration," WT/MIN(05)/DEC, Annex D, WTO, December 22, 2005 www.wto.org/english/theWTO_e/minist_e/min05_e/final_text_e.pdf.

102. WTO Negotiating Group on Rules, "Draft Consolidated Chair Texts of the Ad and Scm Agreements," Tn/Rl/W/213, Annex VIII, WTO, November 30, 2007, www.wto.org/english/news_e/news07_e/rules_nov07_e.doc.

103. ITCSD, "Trade Leaders Call for Fisheries Subsidies Reform on World Oceans Day," *Bridges Weekly Trade News Digest* 13, no. 21 (June 10, 2009): http://ictsd.net/i/news/bridgesweekly/48339.

104. "Eliminating Trade Barriers on Environmental Goods and Services," WTO, www.wto.org/english/tratop_e/envir_e/envir_neg_serv_e.htm.

105. "Opening Markets for Environmental Goods and Services," OECD, September 2005, www.oecd.org/dataoecd/63/15/35415839.pdf.

106. International Center for Trade and Sustainable Development, "Liberalization of Trade in Environmental Goods for Climate Change Mitigation: The Sustainable Development Context" (paper prepared for the Seminar on Trade and Climate Change, Copenhagen, Denmark, June 18–20, 2008), www.gmfus.org/doc/economics/GMF-EGS.pdf.

107. Ibid., 5.

108. World Bank, *International Trade and Climate Change* (Washington, DC: World Bank, 2007). For additional information on trade and climate change, see Peter Wooders, *Greenhouse Gas Emission Impacts of Liberalising Trade in Environmental Goods and Services* (Winnipeg: IISD, April 2009), www.iisd.org/pdf/2009/bali_2_copenhagen_egs.pdf.

109. Maria Pia Hernandez, "From Cancún to Hong Kong: WTO Update," *Center Focus* 166 (March 2005).

110. The members of the G-20 developing countries with special interest in agriculture as of 2009 are Argentina, Bolivia, Brazil, Chile, China, Cuba, Ecuador, Egypt, Guatemala, India, In-

donesia, Mexico, Nigeria, Pakistan, Paraguay, Peru, Philippines, South Africa, Tanzania, Thailand, Uruguay, Venezuela, and Zimbabwe. See also www.g-20.mre.gov.br.

111. For information on the Free Trade Area of the Americas proposal, see www.ftaa-alca.org/Alca_e.asp.

112. Ritchie and Dawkins, "A New Beginning for WTO after Cancún."

113. Sachs and Reid, "Investments toward Sustainable Development," 1002.

114. This paragraph has been adapted from Pamela S. Chasek, "Sustainable Development in the Twenty-first Century," in *Introducing Global Issues*, ed. Michael T. Snarr and D. Neil Snarr, 4th ed. (Boulder, CO: Lynne Rienner, 2008), 243–264.

Chapter 8

1. Richard N. Gardner, "The Role of the UN in Environmental Problems," in *World Eco-crisis*, ed. David A Kay and Eugene B. Skolnikoff (Madison: University of Wisconsin Press).

2. Pamela S. Chasek, *Earth Negotiations: Analyzing Thirty Years of Environmental Diplomacy* (Tokyo: United Nations University Press, 2001), 1–2.

3. Rosa Gomez Dierks, *Introduction to Globalization* (Chicago: Burnham Publishers, 2001), 2.

4. Ronnie D. Lipschutz, *Global Environmental Politics: Power, Perspectives and Practice* (Washington, DC: Congressional Quarterly Press, 2004), 122.

5. Thomas Friedman, "It's a Flat World, After All," *New York Times Magazine*, April 3, 2005.

6. Lipschutz, *Global Environmental Politics*, 122.

7. Neil Carter, *The Politics of the Environment*, 2nd ed. (Cambridge: Cambridge University Press, 2007), 272–273. For additional views on this argument, see Jagdish Bhagwati, *In Defense of Globalization* (Oxford: Oxford University Press, 2004); and Jennifer Clapp and Peter Dauvergne, *Paths to a Green World: The Political Economy of the Global Environment* (Cambridge, MA: MIT Press, 2005).

8. Carter, *The Politics of the Environment*, 273, and Lipschutz, *Global Environmental Politics*, 121.

9. Carter, *The Politics of the Environment*, 273, and Arthur Mol, *Globalization and Environmental Reform* (Cambridge, MA: MIT Press, 2003), 71–72, 126.

10. Adil Najam, David Runnalls, and Mark Halle, *Environment and Globalization: Five Propositions* (Winnipeg: IISD, 2007), 6–7. Available at www.iisd.org/pdf/2007/trade_environment_globalization.pdf.

11. Ibid., 7.

12. Ibid., 29.

13. Massoumeh Ebtekar, "Market Messengers," *Our Planet* (February 2007): 15. Available at www.unep.org/pdf/OurPlanet/OP_Feb07_GC24_en.pdf.

14. Najam, Runnalls and Halle, *Environment and Globalization*, 32. See also Adil Najam, Mihaela Papa, and Nadaa Taiyab, *Global Environmental Governance: A Reform Agenda* (Winnipeg: IISD, 2006).

15. James Gustave Speth, "Beyond Reform," *Our Planet* (February 2007): 16. Available at www.unep.org/pdf/OurPlanet/OP_Feb07_GC24_en.pdf. For more on the World Environmental Organization proposal, see Daniel Esty, "The Case for a Global Environmental Organization," in *Managing the World Economy: Fifty Years after Bretton Woods*, ed. P. Kenen (Washington, DC: Institute for International Economics, 2004), 287–307; Frank Biermann, "The Rationale for a World Environment Organization," in *A World Environmental Organization: Solution or Threat for Effective Environmental Governance*, ed. Frank Biermann and Steffen Bauer (Aldershot, UK: Ashgate, 2005), 117–144.

16. Speth, "Beyond Reform," 16; Najam, Runnalls and Halle, *Environment and Globalization*, 32; "International Institutions and Global Governance Program: World Order in the 21st Century: A New Initiative of the Council on Foreign Relations," Council on Foreign Relations, May 1, 2008, www.cfr.org/content/thinktank/CFR_Global%20_Governance_%20Program.pdf.

17. See Jean-François Rischard, "Global Issues Networks: Desperate Times Deserve Innovative Measures," *Washington Quarterly* 26, no. 1 (winter 2002–2003): 17–33.

18. Ibid., 20.

19. Ibid., 24.

20. Ibid., 30.

21. Speth, "Beyond Reform," 16.

22. Speth, "Beyond Reform," 16, and "The Earth Charter [2000]," Earth Charter Initiative, www.earthcharterinaction.org/content/pages/Read-the-Charter.html.

23. Energy Information Administration, *International Energy Outlook 2009: Highlights* (Washington, DC: EIA. June 2009), www.eia.doe.gov/oiaf/ieo/pdf/highlights.pdf.

24. Carter, *The Politics of the Environment*, 268.

25. Ibid.

Suggested Readings

This section provides an indicative list of additional readings on core issues addressed in this volume. Any such list, especially one so short, must necessarily omit many important and informative works. Thus, we have striven to create a list of accessible, easily obtainable, and recent works, not a comprehensive bibliography. Please also note that many of the works cited in the footnotes are not listed again here. Finally, many of the edited volumes in the first section of the list include detailed case studies of the regimes introduced in Chapters 3 to 5.

Global Environmental Politics, Law, and Institutions

Andresen, Steinar, "The Effectiveness of UN Environmental Institutions." *International Environmental Agreements: Politics, Law and Economics* 7, no. 4 (December 2007): 317–336.

———. "Key Actors in UN Environmental Governance: Influence, Reform and Leadership." *International Environmental Agreements: Politics, Law and Economics* 7, no. 4 (December 2007): 457–468.

Baber, Walter F., and Robert V. Bartlett. *Global Democracy and Sustainable Jurisprudence: Deliberative Environmental Law.* Cambridge, MA: MIT Press, 2009.

Betsill, Michele, Kathryn Hochstetler, and Dimitris Stevis. *International Environmental Politics.* New York: Palgrave, 2006.

Biermann, Frank, and Steffen Bauer, eds. *A World Environment Organization: Solution or Threat for Effective International Environmental Governance?* London: Ashgate, 2004.

Breitmeier, Helmut, Oran R. Young, and Michael Zürn. *Analyzing International Environmental Regimes: From Case Study to Database.* Cambridge, MA: MIT Press, 2006.

Chasek, Pamela S. *Earth Negotiations: Analyzing Thirty Years of Environmental Diplomacy.* Tokyo: United Nations University Press, 2001.

———, ed. *The Global Environment in the Twenty-first Century: Prospects for International Cooperation.* Tokyo: United Nations University Press, 2000.

Clapp, Jennifer, and Peter Dauvergne. *Paths to a Green World: The Political Economy of the Global Environment.* Cambridge, MA: MIT Press, 2005.

Conca, Ken, and Geoffrey D. Dabelko, eds. *Green Planet Blues: Environmental Politics from Stockholm to Johannesburg.* 4th ed. Boulder, CO: Westview Press: 2010.

Dauvergne, Peter. *Handbook of Global Environmental Politics.* Northampton, MA: Edward Elgar, 2005.

DeSombre, Elizabeth R. *The Global Environment and World Politics: International Relations in the 21st Century.* 2nd ed. London: Continuum Publishing Group, 2007.

Harris, Paul, ed. *Environmental Change and Foreign Policy: Theory and Practice.* London: Routledge, 2009.

Ivanova, Maria. "Designing the United Nations Environment Programme: A Story of Compromise and Confrontation." *International Environmental Agreements: Politics, Law and Economics* 7, no. 4 (December 2007): 337–361.

Kanie, Norichika, and Peter M. Haas. *Emerging Forces in Environmental Governance.* Tokyo, New York: United Nations University Press, 2004.

Kjellén, Bo. *A New Diplomacy for Sustainable Development: The Challenge of Global Change.* New York: Routledge, 2008.

Lipschutz, Ronnie D. *Global Environmental Politics: Power, Perspectives and Practice.* Washington, DC: Congressional Quarterly Press, 2004.

Litfin, Karen, ed. *The Greening of Sovereignty in World Politics.* Cambridge, MA: MIT Press, 1998.

Miles, Edward, Arild Underdal, Steiner Andresen, Jorgen Wettestad, Jon Birger Skjaerseth, and Elain Carlin. *Environmental Regime Effectiveness.* Cambridge, MA: MIT Press, 2002.

Mitchell, Ronald B. *International Politics and the Environment.* New York: Sage Publications, 2009.

Najam, Adil, Ioli Christopoulou, and William R. Moomaw. "The Emergent 'System' of Global Environmental Governance." *Global Environmental Politics* 4, no. 4 (2004): 23–35.

Najam, Adil, Mihaela Papa, and Nadaa Taiyab. *Global Environmental Governance: A Reform Agenda* (Winnipeg, Canada: International Institute for Sustainable Development, 2006).

O'Neill, Kate. *The Environment and International Relations.* Cambridge: Cambridge University Press, 2009.

Sands, Philippe, ed. *Principles of International Environmental Law.* 2nd ed. Cambridge: Cambridge University Press, 2003.

Schreurs, Miranda A. *Environmental Politics in Japan, Germany, and the United States.* Cambridge: Cambridge University Press, 2002.

Schreurs, Miranda, Henrik Selin, and Stacy D. VanDeveer, eds. *Transatlantic Environment and Energy Politics: Comparative and International Perspectives.* Burlington, VT: Ashgate, 2009.

Tolba, Mostafa K. *Global Environmental Diplomacy: Negotiating Environmental Agreements for the World, 1973–1992.* Cambridge, MA: MIT Press, 1998.

Young, Oran R., Leslie A. King, and Heike Schroeder. *Institutions and Environmental Change.* Cambridge, MA: MIT Press, 2008.

International Organizations

Barkin, J. Samuel. *International Organization: Theories and Institutions.* New York: Palgrave, 2006.

Barnett, Michael, and Martha Finnemore. *Rules for the World: International Organizations in Global Politics.* Ithaca, NY: Cornell University Press, 2004.

Biermann, Frank, and Steffen Bauer. *A World Environment Organization: Solution or Threat for Effective International Environmental Governance?* Burlington, VT: Ashgate Publishing, 2005.

Biermann, Frank, Bernd Siebenhuener, and Anna Schreyögg. *International Organizations in Global Environmental Governance.* New York: Routledge, 2009.

DeSombre, Elizabeth R. *Global Environmental Institutions.* New York: Routledge, 2006.

Franceschet, Antonio, ed. *The Ethics of Global Governance.* Boulder, CO: Lynne Rienner, 2009.

Jørgensen, Knud Erik. *European Union and International Organizations.* New York: Routledge, 2009.

Karns, Margaret P., and Karen A. Mingst. *International Organizations: The Politics and Processes of Global Governance*, 2nd ed. Boulder, CO: Lynne Rienner, 2009.

Developing Countries and Global Environmental Politics

Adams, W. M. *Green Development: Environment and Sustainability in a Developing World*. 3rd ed. London: Taylor and Francis Books UK, 2008.

Chasek, Pamela S., and Lavanya Rajamani. "Steps toward Enhanced Parity: Negotiating Capacity and Strategies of Developing Countries." In *Providing Global Public Goods: Making Globalization Work for All*, edited by Inge Kaul. New York: Oxford University Press, 2002.

DeSombre, Elizabeth R. "Developing Country Influence in Global Environmental Negotiations." *Environmental Politics* 9, no. 3 (autumn 2000): 23–42.

Espach, Ralph H. *Private Environmental Regimes in Developing Countries: Globally Sown, Locally Grown*. New York: Palgrave Macmillan, 2009.

Gupta, Avijit. *Ecology and Development in the Third World*. London: Francis & Taylor, 2007.

Najam, Adil. "The View from the South: Developing Countries in Global Environmental Politics." In *The Global Environment: Institutions Law and Policy*, edited by Regina Axelrod, David Downie, and Norman Vig. 2nd ed. Washington, DC: Congressional Quarterly Press, 2004.

———. "Why Environmental Politics Looks Different from the South." In *Handbook of Global Environmental Politics*, edited by Peter Dauvergne. Cheltenham, UK: Edward Elgar Press, 2005.

Roberts, J. Timmons, and Bradley C. Parks. *A Climate of Injustice: Global Inequality, North-South Politics and Climate Policy*. Cambridge, MA: MIT Press, 2007.

Nongovernmental Organizations

Bebbington, Anthony, Samuel Hickey, and Diana C. Mitlin. *Can NGOs Make a Difference? The Challenge of Development Alternatives*. London: Zed Books, 2008.

Betsill, Michele. "Environmental NGOs Meet the Sovereign State: The Kyoto Protocol Negotiations on Global Climate Change." *Colorado Journal of International Environmental Law and Policy* 13, no. 1 (winter 2002): 49–64.

Betsill, Michele, and Elisabeth Corell, eds. *NGO Diplomacy: The Influence of Nongovernmental Organizations in International Environmental Negotiations*. Cambridge, MA: MIT Press, 2008

Breitmeier, Helmut, and Volker Rittberger. "Environmental NGOs in an Emerging Global Civil Society." In *The Global Environment in the Twenty-first Century: Prospects for International Cooperation*, edited by Pamela S. Chasek. Tokyo: United Nations University Press, 2000.

Chasek, Pamela S. "Environmental Organizations and Multilateral Diplomacy: A Case Study of the *Earth Negotiations Bulletin*." In *Multilateral Diplomacy and the United Nations Today*, edited by James P. Muldoon Jr. et al. 3rd ed. Boulder, CO: Westview Press, 2005.

Charnowitz, Steve. "Two Centuries of Participation: NGOs and International Governance." *Michigan Journal of International Law* 18, no. 2 (1997): 183–286.

Doh, Jonathan, and Michael Yaziji. *NGOs and Corporations: Conflict and Collaboration: Business, Value Creation and Society*. Cambridge: Cambridge University Press, 2009.

Esty, Daniel C. "Non-governmental Organizations at the World Trade Organization: Cooperation, Competition or Exclusion." *Journal of International Economic Law* 1 (1998): 123–148.

Raustiala, Kal. "States, NGOs and International Environmental Institutions." *International Studies Quarterly* 41 (1997): 719–740.

Transnational Corporations

Clapp, Jennifer, and Doris Fuchs, eds. *Corporate Power in Global Agrifood Governance.* Cambridge, MA: MIT Press, 2009.

Fuchs, Doris. *Business Power in Global Governance.* Boulder, CO: Lynne Rienner Publishers, 2007.

Morgera, Elisa. *Corporate Accountability in International Environmental Law.* Oxford: Oxford University Press, 2009.

Sustainable Development

Blewitt, John. *Understanding Sustainable Development.* London: Earthscan Publications, 2008.

Chasek, Pamela S. "Sustainable Development in the Twenty-first Century." In *Introducing Global Issues,* edited by Michael Snarr and D. Neil Snarr. 4th ed. Boulder, CO: Lynne Rienner, 2008.

Chiappori, Pierre-André, Jean-Michel Lasry, and Damien Fessler. *Finance and Sustainable Development: Opposition or Partnership?* London: Economica, 2009.

Hettne, Björn. *Sustainable Development in a Globalized World: Studies in Development, Security and Culture.* New York: Palgrave Macmillan, 2008.

Kallhauge, Angela Churie, Gunnar Sjostedt, and Elisabeth Corell, eds. *Global Challenges: Furthering the Multilateral Process for Sustainable Development.* Sheffield, UK: Greenleaf Publishing, 2005.

Meadows, Donella H., Dennis L. Meadows, Jørgen Randers, and William W. Behrens III. *The Limits to Growth.* New York: Universe Books, 1972.

Munasinghe, Mohan. *Sustainable Development in Practice: Sustainomics Methodology and Applications.* Cambridge: Cambridge University Press, 2009.

Park, Jacob. *The Crisis of Global Environmental Governance: Towards a New Political Economy of Sustainability.* Hoboken, NJ: Taylor & Francis, 2008.

Revesz, Richard L., Philippe Sands, and Richard B. Stewart. *Environmental Law, the Economy and Sustainable Development: The United States, the European Union and the International Community.* Cambridge: Cambridge University Press, 2008.

Rogers, Peter P., Kazi F. Jalal, and John A. Boyd. *An Introduction to Sustainable Development.* London: Earthscan Publications, 2007.

World Commission on Environment and Development. *Our Common Future.* New York: Oxford University Press, 1987.

Earth Summit and World Summit on Sustainable Development

Chasek, Pamela S., and Richard Sherman. *Ten Days in Johannesburg: A Negotiation of Hope.* Cape Town: Struik Publishers, 2004.

Grubb, Michael, et al. *The "Earth Summit" Agreements: A Guide and Assessment.* London: Earthscan, 1993.

Haas, Peter M. "UN Conferences and Constructivist Governance of the Environment." *Global Governance* 8, no. 1 (2002): 73–92.

Hens, Luc, and Bhaskar Nath. *The World Summit on Sustainable Development: The Johannesburg Conference.* New York: Springer Publishing, 2005.

Najam, Adil, Janice M. Poling, Naoyuki Yamagishi, Daniel G. Straub, Jillian Sarno, Sara M. De Ritter, Eonjeong Michelle Kim. "From Rio to Johannesburg: Progress and Prospects." *Environment* 44, no. 7 (September 1, 2002): 26–38.

Sjöstedt, Gunnar, Bertram Spector, and I. William Zartman, eds. *Negotiating International Regimes: Lessons Learned from the United Nations Conference on Environment and Development.* London: Graham and Trotman, 1994.

Speth, James Gustave. "Perspectives on the Johannesburg Summit." *Environment* 45, no. 1 (2003): 24–29.

Wapner, Paul. "World Summit on Sustainable Development: Toward a Post-Jo'burg Environmentalism." *Global Environmental Politics* 3, no. 1 (2003): 1–10.

Air Pollution

Casper, Julie Kerr. *Fossil Fuels and Pollution: The Future of Air Quality.* New York: Facts on File, 2009.

Selin, Henrik, and Stacy D. VanDeveer. "Mapping Institutional Linkages in European Air Pollution Politics." *Global Environmental Politics* 3, no. 3 (August 2003): 14–46.

UN Economic Commission for Europe. *Strategies and Policies for Air Pollution Abatement.* Geneva: United Nations, 2004.

Biodiversity

Bagnoli, Philip, Timo Goeschl, and Eszter Kovács. *People and Biodiversity Policies: Impacts, Issues and Strategies for Policy Action.* Paris: OECD, 2008.

Epstein, Charlotte. "The Making of Global Environmental Norms: Endangered Species Protection." *Global Environmental Politics* 6, no. 2 (2006): 32–55.

Kontoleon, Andreas, Unai Pascual, and Timothy Swanson. *Biodiversity Economics: Principles, Methods and Applications.* Cambridge: Cambridge University Press, 2008.

Le Prestre, Philippe G., ed. *Governing Global Biodiversity: The Evolution and Implementation of the Convention on Biological Diversity.* London: Ashgate, 2002.

Lefroy, Ted. *Biodiversity: Integrating Conservation and Production.* Melbourne: CSIRO Publishing, 2008.

Maclaurin, James, and Kim Sterelny. *What Is Biodiversity?* Chicago: University of Chicago Press, 2008.

McConnell, Fiona. *The Biodiversity Convention: A Negotiating History.* London: Kluwer, 1996.

Millennium Ecosystem Assessment. *Ecosystems and Human Well-being: Synthesis Report.* Washington, DC: Island Press, 2005.

Sala, Osvaldo E., Laura A. Meyerson, and Camille Parmesan. *Biodiversity Change and Human Health: From Ecosystem Services to Spread of Disease.* Washington, DC: Island Press, 2009.

Chemicals and Hazardous Wastes

Ackerman, Frank. *Poisoned for Pennies: The Economics of Toxics and Precaution.* Washington, DC: Island Press, 2008.

Carson, Rachel. *Silent Spring.* Boston: Houghton Mifflin, 1962.

Downie, David, and Terry Fenge, eds. *Northern Lights against POPs: Combating Toxic Threats in the Arctic.* Montreal: McGill-Queens University Press, 2003.

O'Neill, Kate. *Waste Trading among Rich Nations: Building a New Theory of Environmental Regulation.* Cambridge, MA: MIT Press, 2000.

Pellow, David Naguib. *Resisting Global Toxics: Transnational Movements for Environmental Justice.* Cambridge, MA: MIT Press, 2007.

Selin, Henrik. *Global Governance of Hazardous Chemicals: Challenges of Multilevel Management,* Cambridge, MA: MIT Press 2009.

Swanson, Timothy M. *Regulating Chemical Accumulation in the Environment: The Integration of Toxicology and Economics in Environmental Policy-making.* Cambridge: Cambridge University Press, 2008.

Thornton, Joe. *Pandora's Poison: On Chlorine, Health and a New Environmental Strategy.* Cambridge, MA: MIT Press, 2000.

Wargo, John. *Green Intelligence: Creating Environments That Protect Human Health.* New Haven, CT: Yale University Press, 2009.

Climate Change

Aldy, Joseph, and Robert Stavins. *Architectures for Agreement: Addressing Global Climate Change in the Post-Kyoto World.* Cambridge: Cambridge University Press, 2007.

Andersen, Stephen O., K. Madhava Sarma, and Kristen N. Taddenio. *Technology Transfer for the Ozone Layer: Lessons for Climate Change.* London: Earthscan, 2007.

Blockstein, David E., and Leo Wiegman for the National Council for Science and the Environment. *The Climate Solutions Consensus.* Washington, DC: Island Press, 2009.

Bodansky, Daniel. "The United Nations Framework Convention on Climate Change: A Commentary." *Yale Journal of International Law* 18, no. 2 (summer 1993): 451–558.

Burroughs, William James. *Climate Change: A Multidisciplinary Approach.* 2nd ed. Cambridge: Cambridge University Press, 2007.

Dalby, Simon. *Security and Environmental Change.* Cambridge: Polity Press, 2009.

Downie, David, Kate Brash, and Catherine Vaughan. *Climate Change: A Reference Handbook.* Santa Barbara, CA: ABC Clio, 2009.

Harris, Paul G., eds. *The Politics of Climate Change: Environmental Dynamics in International Affairs.* London: Routledge, 2009.

Kolbert, Elizabeth. *Field Notes for Catastrophe: Man, Nature and Climate Change.* New York: Bloomsbury Publishers, 2006.

Letcher, Trevor M. *Climate Change: Observed Impacts on Planet Earth.* San Diego, CA: Elsevier, 2009.

Mintzer, Irving M., and J. A. Leonard, eds. *Negotiating Climate Change: The Inside Story of the Rio Convention.* Cambridge: Cambridge University Press, 1994.

Schmidt, Gavin, and Joshua Wolfe, eds., *Climate Change: Picturing the Science.* New York: W. W. Norton, 2009.

Schneider, Stephen H., Armin Rosencranz, Michael D. Mastrandrea, and Kristin Kuntz-Duriseti. *Climate Change Science and Policy.* Washington, DC: Island Press, 2009.

Selin, Henrik, and Stacy D. VanDeveer, eds. *Changing Climates in North American Politics: Institutions, Policymaking and Multilevel Governance.* Cambridge, MA: MIT Press 2009.

Spence, Chris. *Global Warming: Personal Solutions for a Healthy Planet.* New York: Palgrave, 2005.

Vanderheiden, Steve. *Atmospheric Justice: A Political Theory of Climate Change.* Oxford: Oxford University Press, 2009.

Desertification

Chasek, Pamela S. "Negotiations on the Convention to Combat Desertification." In *Professional Cultures in International Negotiation: Bridge or Rift?* ed. Gunnar Sjöstedt. Lanham, MD: Lexington Books, 2003.

Chasek, Pamela S., and Elisabeth Corell. "Addressing Desertification at the International Level: The Institutional System." In *Global Desertification: Do Humans Cause Deserts?* eds. James Reynolds and Mark Stafford Smith. Berlin: Dahlem University Press, 2002.

Corell, Elisabeth. "North-South Financial Tensions: Desertification after UNGASS." *Environmental Politics* 7, no. 1 (1998): 222–226.

Geist, Helmut. *The Causes and Progression of Desertification.* Burlington, VT: Ashgate Publishing, 2005.

Johnson, Pierre Marc, Karel Mayrand, and Marc Paquin. *Governing Global Desertification.* Burlington, VT: Ashgate, 2006.

Najam, Adil. "Dynamics of the Southern Collective: Developing Countries in Desertification Negotiations." *Global Environmental Politics* 4, no. 3 (August 2004): 128–154.

Fisheries

Clark, Colin W. *The Worldwide Crisis in Fisheries: Economic Models and Human Behavior.* Cambridge: Cambridge University Press, 2007.

Food and Agriculture Organization. *The State of World Fisheries and Aquaculture 2008.* Rome: FAO, 2009.

Pitcher, Tony J. *Seamounts: Ecology, Fisheries and Conservation.* Chichester, UK: John Wiley and Sons, 2008.

Taylor, William W., Michael G. Schechter, and Lois G. Wolfson. *Globalization: Effects on Fisheries Resources.* Cambridge: Cambridge University Press, 2007.

Forests

Cashore, Benjamin, Graeme Auld, and Deanna Newsom. *Governing through Markets: Forest Certification and the Emergence of Non-state Authority.* New Haven, CT: Yale University Press, 2004.

Dauvergne, Peter. *Shadows in the Forest: Japan and the Politics of Timber in Southeast Asia.* Cambridge, MA: MIT Press, 1997.

———. "Globalisation and Deforestation in the Asia-Pacific." *Environmental Politics* 7, no. 4 (winter 1998): 114–135.

Davenport, Deborah S. "An Alternative Explanation for the Failure of the UNCED Forest Negotiations." *Global Environmental Politics* 5, no. 1 (2005): 105–130.

Davenport, Deborah S., and Peter Wood. "Finding the Way Forward for the International Arrangement on Forests: UNFF-5, -6 and -7." *Review of European Community and International Environmental Law* 15, no. 3 (November 2006): 316–326.

Humphreys, David. *Logjam: Deforestation and the Crisis of Global Governance.* London: Earthscan, 2008.

———. "Redefining the Issues: NGO Influence on International Forest Negotiations." *Global Environmental Politics* 4, no. 2 (2004): 51–74.

Oceans, Seas, and International Rivers

Conca, Ken. *Governing Water: Contentious Transnational Politics and Global Institution Building.* Cambridge, MA: MIT Press, 2005.

DeSombre, Elizabeth R. *Flagging Standards: Globalization and Environmental, Safety, and Labor Regulations at Sea.* Cambridge, MA: MIT Press, 2006.

Haas, Peter M. *Saving the Mediterranean: The Politics of International Environmental Cooperation.* New York: Columbia University Press, 1990.

Hamblin, Jacob Darwin. *Poison in the Well: Radioactive Waste in the Oceans at the Dawn of the Nuclear Age.* Piscataway, NJ: Rutgers University Press, 2008.

Mitchell, Ronald B. *Intentional Oil Pollution at Sea: Environmental Policy and Treaty Compliance.* Cambridge, MA: MIT Press, 1994.

Ozone Depletion

Anderson, Stephan, and Madhava Sarma, eds. *Protecting the Ozone Layer: The United Nations History.* London: Earthscan, 2002.

Benedick, Richard Elliott. *Ozone Diplomacy.* Cambridge, MA: Harvard University Press, 1998.

Chasek, Pamela S. "The Ozone Depletion Regime." In *Getting It Done: Post-agreement Negotiations and International Regimes,* edited by Bertram Specter and I. William Zartman. Washington, DC: U.S. Institute of Peace Press, 2003.

Downie, David. "UNEP and the Montreal Protocol: New Roles for International Organizations in Regime Creation and Change." In *International Organizations and Environmental Policy,* edited by Robert V. Bartlett, Priya A. Kurian, and Madhu Malik. Westport, CT: Greenwood Press, 1995.

Litfin, Karen. *Ozone Discourses: Science and Politics in International Environmental Cooperation.* New York: Columbia University Press, 1994.

Parson, Edward A. *Protecting the Ozone Layer.* Oxford: Oxford University Press, 2003.

Whaling

Baker, C. S., G. M. Lento, F. Cipriano, M. L. Dalebout, S. R. Palumbi, Mutsuo Goto, and Seiji Ohsumi. "Scientific Whaling: Source of Illegal Products for Market?" (Letter). *Science* 290, no. 5497 (2000): 1695–1696.

Birnie, Patricia. *International Regulation of Whaling: From Conservation of Whaling to Conservation of Whales and Regulation of Whale-Watching.* New York: Oceana Publications, 1985.

Epstein, Charlotte. *The Power of Words in International Relations: Birth of an Anti-whaling Discourse.* Cambridge, MA: MIT Press, 2008.

Francis, Daniel. *A History of World Whaling.* New York: Viking, 1990.

Friedheim, Robert L. *Toward a Sustainable Whaling Regime.* Seattle: University of Washington Press, 2001.

Economics and Trade

Copeland, Brian R., and M. Scott Taylor. *Trade and the Environment: Theory and Evidence.* Princeton, NJ: Princeton University Press, 2003.

Dauvergne, Peter. *The Shadows of Consumption: Consequences for the Global Environment.* Cambridge, MA: MIT Press, 2008.

Esty, Daniel C. "The World Trade Organization's Legitimacy Crisis." *World Trade Review* 1, no. 1 (2002): 7–22.

Esty, Daniel C., and Andrew S. Winston. *Green to Gold: How Smart Companies Use Environmental Strategy to Innovate, Create Value, and Build Competitive Advantage.* New Haven, CT: Yale University Press, 2006.

Hicks, Robert L., Bradley C. Parks, J. Timmons Roberts, and Michael J. Tierney. *Greening Aid? Understanding the Environmental Impact of Development Assistance.* New York: Oxford University Press, 2008.

Najam, Adil, Mark Halle, and Ricardo Melendez-Ortiz. *Trade and Environment: A Resource Book.* Winnipeg: International Institute of Sustainable Development, 2007.

Park, Susan. *The World Bank Group and Environmentalists: Changing International Organisation Identities.* London: Manchester University Press, 2009.

Parker, Richard. "The Use and Abuse of Trade Leverage to Protect the Global Commons: What We Can Learn from the Tuna-Dolphin Conflict." *Georgetown Environmental Law Review* 12 (1999): 1–123.

Repetto, Robert. *Mortgaging the Earth: The World Bank, Environmental Impoverishment, and the Crisis of Development.* Boston: Beacon Press, 1994.

Weiss, Edith Brown, John Jackson, and Nathalie Bernasconi-Osterwalder, eds. *Reconciling Environment and Trade.* 2nd ed. Leiden, Netherlands: Martinus Nijhoff Publishers/Koninklijke Brill, 2008.

Annual Publications

Science Magazine's State of the Planet 2008–2009. Washington, DC: Island Press, 2008 (published biannually).

United Nations Development Programme. *Human Development Report 2009.* New York: Oxford University Press, 2009, http://hdr.undp.org/en (published annually).

United Nations Environment Programme. *GEO Yearbook 2008.* Nairobi: UNEP, 2008, www.unep.org/GEO/GEO_Products/Yearbook (published annually).

United Nations Population Fund. *The State of World Population, 2008.* New York: UNFPA, 2009, http://unfpa.org/swp (published annually).

Wildlife Conservation Society. *State of the Wild 2008–2009: A Global Portrait of Wildlife, Wildlands, and Oceans.* Washington, DC: Island Press, 2008 (published biannually).

World Bank. *World Development Report 2010.* Washington, DC: World Bank, 2009, http://go.worldbank.org/LOTTGBE9I0 (published annually).

World Resources Institute. *World Resources, 2008.* Washington, DC: World Resources Institute, 2008 (published biennially).

Worldwatch Institute. *State of the World 2009.* New York: W. W. Norton, 2009 (published annually).

Internet Resources

The following list of Internet resources does not represent a comprehensive list of all resources related to global environmental politics. Instead, it consists primarily of organizations mentioned in this book and their Internet addresses as of the date of publication. All Internet addresses are subject to change at any time.

Alliance of Small Island States: www.sidsnet.org/aosis

Arctic Monitoring and Assessment Program: www.amap.no

Asian Development Bank: www.adb.org

Asia-Pacific Economic Cooperation: www.apec.org

Basel Convention on the Control of Transboundary Movements of Hazardous Wastes and Their Disposal: www.basel.int

Carbon Dioxide Information Analysis Center: http://cdiac.esd.ornl.gov

Cartagena Protocol on Biosafety (at the Convention on Biological Diversity website): www.cbd.int/biosafety

Center for International Earth Science Information Network: http://ciesin.columbia.edu

Climate Action Network: www.climatenetwork.org

Commission for Environmental Cooperation, North America: www.cec.org

Conservation International: www.conservation.org

Convention on Biological Diversity: www.cbd.int

Convention on International Trade in Endangered Species of Wild Fauna and Flora: www.cites.org

Convention on Long-Range Transboundary Air Pollution: www.unece.org/env/lrtap

Convention on the Conservation of Migratory Species of Wild Animals: www.cms.int

Convention on the Prevention of Marine Pollution by Dumping of Wastes and Other Matter: www.londonconvention.org

Coordinator of the Indigenous Organizations of the Amazon Basin: www.coica.org

Earth Negotiations Bulletin: http://www.iisd.ca

Environmental Defense: www.edf.org

Environmental Protection Agency (U.S.): www.epa.gov

Environmental Treaties and Resource Indicators: http://sedac.ciesin.columbia.edu/entri

European Environmental Bureau: www.eeb.org

European Union: http://europa.eu

Food and Agriculture Organization: www.fao.org

Foundation for International Environmental Law and Development: www.field.org.uk

Friends of the Earth (U.S.): www.foe.org

Friends of the Earth International: www.foei.org

Global Environment Facility: www.gefweb.org

Greenpeace International: www.greenpeace.org

Group of 77: www.g77.org

Inter-American Development Bank: www.iadb.org

Intergovernmental Forum on Chemical Safety: www.who.int/ifcs

Intergovernmental Panel on Climate Change: www.ipcc.ch

International Atomic Energy Agency: www.iaea.org

International Chamber of Commerce: www.iccwbo.org

International Council for Science: www.icsu.org

International Institute for Environment and Development: www.iied.org

International Institute for Sustainable Development Reporting Services (*Earth Negotiations Bulletin, Linkages,* and so forth): www.iisd.ca

450   *Internet Resources*

International Institute for Sustainable
 Development: www.iisd.org
International Maritime Organization:
 www.imo.org
International Monetary Fund: www.imf.org
International POPs Elimination Network:
 http://ipen.org
International Programme on Chemical Safety:
 www.who.int/ipcs
International Tropical Timber Organization:
 www.itto.int
International Whaling Commission:
 www.iwcoffice.org
Inter-organization Programme for the Sound
 Management of Chemicals:
 www.who.int/iomc
International Union for the Conservation of
 Nature and Natural Resources/World
 Conservation Union: www.iucn.org
Mediterranean Action Plan: www.unepmap.org
Montreal Protocol on Substances That Deplete
 the Ozone Layer/Ozone Secretariat:
 http://ozone.unep.org or www.unep.ch/ozone
Multilateral Fund for the Implementation of
 the Montreal Protocol:
 www.multilateralfund.org
National Wildlife Federation: www.nwf.org
Natural Resources Defense Council:
 www.nrdc.org
New Partnership for Africa's Development:
 www.nepad.org
Organization for Economic Cooperation and
 Development: www.oecd.org
Organization of American States: www.oas.org
Pacific Regional Environment Programme:
 www.sprep.org
Pesticide Action Network: www.pan-
 international.org
Ramsar Convention on Wetlands of
 International Importance: www.ramsar.org
Rotterdam Convention on the Prior Informed
 Consent Procedure for Certain Hazardous
 Chemicals and Pesticides in International
 Trade: www.pic.int
Sierra Club: www.sierraclub.org
Stockholm Convention on Persistent Organic
 Pollutants: http://chm.pops.int
Stockholm Environment Institute: www.sei.se
Strategic Approach to International Chemicals
 Management: www.chem.unep.ch/saicm
Third World Network: www.twnside.org.sg

TRAFFIC: www.traffic.org
UNEP, Geneva Office: www.unep.ch
UNEP Chemicals: www.chem.unep.ch
United Nations: www.un.org
United Nations Commission on Sustainable
 Development: www.un.org/esa/sustdev/csd
United Nations Conference on Trade and
 Development: www.unctad.org
United Nations Convention to Combat
 Desertification: www.unccd.int
United Nations Development Programme:
 www.undp.org
United Nations Development Programme,
 Energy and Environment for Sustainable
 Development:
 www.undp.org/energyandenvironment
United Nations Division for Ocean Affairs and
 the Law of the Sea: www.un.org/Depts/los
United Nations Division for Sustainable
 Development: www.un.org/esa/dsd
United Nations Economic and Social Council:
 www.un.org/ecosoc
United Nations Environment Programme:
 www.unep.org
United Nations Fish Stocks Agreement:
 www.un.org/Depts/los/convention_agreem
 ents/convention_overview_fish_stocks.htm
United Nations Forum on Forests:
 www.un.org/esa/forests/
United Nations Framework Convention on
 Climate Change: http://unfccc.int
United Nations Human Settlements
 Programme: www.unhabitat.org
United Nations Industrial Development
 Organization: www.unido.org
United Nations Population Fund:
 www.unfpa.org
U.S. Department of State: www.state.gov
Women's Environment and Development
 Organization: www.wedo.org
World Bank: www.worldbank.org
World Business Council for Sustainable
 Development: www.wbcsd.ch
World Health Organization: www.who.int
World Meteorological Organization:
 www.wmo.int
World Resources Institute: www.wri.org
World Trade Organization: www.wto.org
World Wildlife Fund (U.S.):
 www.worldwildlife.org
Worldwide Fund for Nature: www.panda.org

Glossary

Acid rain is precipitation that deposits nitric or sulfuric acids on the earth, buildings, and vegetation.

Biodiversity (or biological diversity) is the variety of organisms, including species of plants and animals, genetic variation within individual species, and diversity of ecosystems.

Biofuels are liquid, solid, or gaseous fuel produced by conversion of biomass. Examples include bioethanol from sugar cane, corn, charcoal, or woodchips and biogas from anaerobic decomposition of wastes.

Biosafety refers to a set of precautionary practices to ensure the safe transfer, handling, use, and disposal of living modified organisms derived from modern biotechnology.

Biosphere refers to the earth's land, water, atmosphere, and living things or to a particular zone of the whole.

Biotechnology is the branch of molecular biology that studies the use of microorganisms to perform specific industrial processes.

A **blocking** or **veto state** is one that by virtue of its importance on a particular environmental issue is able to block or weaken international agreement.

The **Bretton Woods institutions** are the international financial institutions, such as the World Bank, the International Monetary Fund, and the International Finance Corporation, named after the New Hampshire resort at which they were negotiated.

Bycatch is unintentionally caught fish, seabirds, sea turtles, marine mammals, and other ocean life.

Certification and labeling is the process of inspecting particular forests or fisheries to see if they are being managed according to an agreed-on set of principles and criteria and labeling them as such.

Civil society refers to an array of non-governmental institutions, such as trade unions, business associations, environmental and development organizations, women's and youth groups, cooperatives, and religious groups having an interest in public policy issues and decisions.

The **Clean Development Mechanism** (CDM) is a procedure under the Kyoto Protocol by which developed countries may finance greenhouse-gas-emissions-avoiding projects in developing countries and receive credits for doing so, which they may apply toward meeting mandatory limits on their own emissions.

Climate change refers to the likelihood of increased change in the average weather over a period of time (usually thirty or more years) from natural causes (e.g., ice ages brought on by changes in the earth's orbit around the sun) or as the result of human intervention (e.g., through the release of carbon dioxide and other greenhouse gases).

The **commons** are the natural resources and vital life-support services that belong to all humankind rather than to any one country.

A **Conference of the Parties** (COP) is an annual or otherwise regularly scheduled gathering of all parties to a convention as well as interested observers where decisions are taken about the implementation of the convention.

Consensus decision making is a group decision-making process that avoids voting or majority rule by seeking the agreement of all participants as well as the resolution or mitigation of minority objections.

A **convention** is a multilateral legal agreement and the most common form of legal instrument used in agreements on international environmental issues.

The **Corporate Average Fuel Economy (CAFE) standards** are a measure of fuel efficiency imposed on U.S. auto manufacturers and importers of cars since 1975.

Deforestation occurs when forests are converted permanently to nonforest uses such as agriculture, highways, or urban settlements.

Desertification is the deterioration of the biological potential of land from a combination of adverse climate and excessive human exploitation, leading ultimately to desertlike conditions.

E-waste, or electronic waste, includes discarded, broken, or obsolete electronic devices, including computers, printers, and monitors; televisions; CD, DVD, and MP3 players; phones; and their parts and components.

An **ecosystem** is a system in which the interaction between different organisms (plants, animals, bacteria) and their environment generates a cyclic interchange of materials and energy.

Emissions trading is a mechanism under the Kyoto Protocol by which parties with emissions commitments may trade units of their emissions allowances with other parties. The aim is to improve the overall flexibility and economic efficiency of making emissions cuts.

Environmental externalities are third party (or spillover) effects arising from the production and/or consumption of goods and services for which no appropriate compensation is paid.

Environmental services are the conserving or restorative functions of nature, for example, the ability of plants to convert carbon dioxide to oxygen, the ability of marshlands to cleanse polluted waters, or the capacity of a vegetation-covered floodplain to dissipate the destructive power of a river in flood.

Eutrophication is a process whereby water bodies, such as lakes, estuaries, or slow-moving streams, receive excess nutrients that stimulate excessive plant growth (algae, periphyton attached to algae, and nuisance plants and weeds). This enhanced plant growth, often called an algal bloom, reduces dissolved oxygen in the water when dead plant material decomposes and can cause other organisms to die.

The **exclusionist paradigm** (also known as frontier economics) is the dominant social paradigm in contemporary societies and holds that humans are not subject to natural laws in their use of natural resources and systems for economic purposes.

Exclusive economic zones (EEZs) are the 200-mile-wide (320-kilometer-wide) territorial waters under the jurisdiction of individual nations.

A **framework convention** is a multilateral agreement that establishes common principles but does not include binding commitments to specific actions.

Genetically modified organisms (GMOs) are like living modified organisms (see below) except that they include any living (capable of growing) or dead organism that possesses a novel combination of genetic material obtained through the use of modern biotechnology.

Germplasm is the genetic material that carries the inherited characteristics of an organism.

Global commons are the natural resources and vital life-support services, such as the earth's climate system, ozone layer, and oceans and seas, that belong to all humankind rather than to any one country or private enterprise.

Global warming refers to the trend toward increasing temperatures on the world's surface and in the lower atmosphere, caused by the entrapment of heat due to the buildup of certain gases (see greenhouse gases).

Globalization is a term used to describe the changes in societies and the world economy that result from dramatically increased trade and cultural exchange. In the economic context, it refers almost exclusively to the effects of trade, particularly trade liberalization or "free trade."

Green taxes include a variety of measures that would penalize practices that pollute or degrade the environment or encourage excessive use or waste of a valuable natural resource or service.

Greenhouse gases (GHGs) are certain gases—mainly carbon dioxide, methane, nitrous oxide, and water vapor—that trap heat in the lower atmosphere. This process, called the greenhouse effect, naturally warms the earth, providing a relatively stable and hospitable climate. Increasing emissions of GHGs from human activities—especially carbon dioxide (CO_2), methane, nitrous oxide (NO_x), and a number of man-made gases such as chlorofluorocarbons (CFCs), hydrochlorofluorocarbons (HCFCs), hydrofluorocarbons (HFCs), and halons—are raising the amount of GHGs in the atmosphere. This is warming the earth, a process often called global warming, which, in turn, produces climate change.

The **Group of Eight** industrialized nations includes the United States, Canada, the United Kingdom, Japan, Germany, France, Italy, and Russia. It used to be referred to as the Group of Seven before 1998 when Russia was invited to join.

The **Group of 77** (G-77) is a coalition of developing countries (numbering more than 130) that has pressed for reform of North-South economic structures since the mid-1970s.

A **hegemonic** power, or **hegemon**, is a state able to set the primary rules of an international system, usually through a combination of military and economic power.

Integrated pest management is an effective and environmentally sensitive approach to pest management that uses comprehensive current information about pests' life cycles and their interaction with the environment. This information, in combination with available pest-control methods, is used to manage pest damage using the most economical means with the least possible hazard to people, property, and the environment.

Intellectual property rights (IPR) are the rights of businesses, individuals, or states to legal protection of their discoveries and inventions.

Intergenerational equity is a norm of state behavior that calls for giving adequate consideration to the interests of future generations, including the enjoyment of a healthy environment and natural resources.

An **international regime** is a set of principles, norms, rules, operating procedures, and institutions usually centered on one or more international agreements that govern particular issues in world politics.

Joint implementation is a mechanism under the Kyoto Protocol by which a developed country can receive "emissions-reduction units" when it helps to finance projects that reduce net greenhouse gas emissions in another developed country (in practice, the recipient state is likely to be a country with an "economy in transition").

The **Law of the Sea** was adopted in December 1982 by the third United Nations Conference on the Law of the Sea. The convention comprises 320 articles and nine annexes governing all aspects of ocean space, such as delimitation, environmental control, marine scientific research, economic and commercial activities, transfer of technology, and the settlement of disputes relating to ocean matters. The convention entered into force on November 16, 1994.

A **lead state** is one that sponsors and asserts leadership on behalf of the most advanced proposal for international regulation on an environmental issue.

Living modified organisms (LMOs) include any living organism that possesses a novel combination of genetic material obtained through the use of modern biotechnology.

Mangroves are forests that grow in saline (brackish) coastal areas in the tropics and subtropics.

A **Meeting of the Parties** (MOP) is an annual or otherwise regularly scheduled gathering of all parties to a protocol, as well as interested observers, where decisions are taken about the implementation of the protocol.

The **Millennium Development Goals** (MDGs) are eight goals to be achieved by 2015 that respond to the world's main development challenges. The MDGs are drawn from the actions and targets contained in the Millennium Declaration adopted by 189 nations and signed by 147 heads of state and governments during the United Nations Millennium Summit in September 2000.

Neoclassical economics is a school of economic theory maintaining that free markets will allocate resources so that the greatest number of people will be satisfied.

The **New International Economic Order** (NIEO) is the list of demands made in the 1970s by the Group of 77 (developing nations) for changes in the structure of North-South economic relations.

The **Non-Aligned Movement** is a group of 118 members representing the interests and priorities of developing countries. The movement has its origin in the Asia-Africa Conference held in Bandung, Indonesia, in 1955, where Third World leaders shared their similar problems of resisting the pressures of the major powers, maintaining their independence, and opposing colonialism and neocolonialism, especially Western domination.

Nontariff barriers are trade barriers, other than tariffs, erected by a government to discourage imports, for example, quotas (both formal and "voluntary"), outright prohibition of specific imports (such as the Japanese refusal to import rice), discriminatory restrictions, or licensing requirements.

Official development assistance (ODA), or foreign aid, consists of loans, grants, technical assistance, and other forms of cooperation extended by developed-country governments to developing countries.

The **ozone layer** is the concentration of ozone in the stratosphere, between 15 and 50 kilometers (9.3 and 31 miles) above the earth's surface, depending on latitude, season, and other factors.

Paradigm refers to a set of assumptions about reality that define and often limit the scope of inquiry in a field of knowledge.

Persistent organic pollutants (POPs) are a set of toxic chemicals that remain intact in the environment for long periods, can become widely distributed geographically, and accumulate in the fatty tissue of living organisms.

Plantation forests, or seminatural forests, are forests created usually for commercial benefit. Trees are selected for their wood properties, planted (usually as a single species), and encouraged to grow to a useful size as quickly as possible.

Polychlorinated biphenyls (PCBs) are a set of synthetic organic chemicals suspected of causing cancer, endocrine disruption, and other adverse impacts on organisms. Because of their nonflammability, chemical stability, high boiling point, and electrical insulating properties, PCBs were used in hundreds of industrial and commercial applications, including electrical, heat transfer, and hydraulic equipment; as plasticizers in paints, plastics, and rubber products; and in pigments, dyes, and carbonless copy paper; as well as many in other applications. More than 1.5 billion pounds of PCBs were manufactured in the United States prior to cessation of production in 1977.

The **precautionary principle** states that where there are threats of serious or irreversible damage, lack of full scientific certainty shall not be used as a reason for postponing cost-effective measures to prevent environmental degradation.

Primary forest refers to untouched, pristine forest that exists in its original condition. This forest has been relatively unaffected by human activities.

The **prior informed consent (PIC) procedure** is a means of formally obtaining and disseminating importing countries' decisions about whether they wish to receive future shipments of a certain chemical and of ensuring exporting countries' compliance with these decisions. The aim is to promote a shared responsibility between exporting and importing countries in protecting human health and the environment from the harmful effects of such chemicals.

A **protocol** is a multilateral agreement providing detailed, specific commitments attached to a convention.

Salinization occurs in warm and dry locations where water-soluble salts accumulate in the soil.

Soft law refers to nonbinding documents drawn up by international bodies that establish norms; these documents can take on the force of law through customary practice.

The **stratosphere** is the upper part of the atmosphere, approximately six to thirty miles above the earth's surface.

A **subsidy** is a government-directed intervention, whether through budgeted programs or other means, that transfers resources to a particular economic group.

A **supporting state** is one that is willing to publicly support and work for the farthest-reaching proposal for international regulation on an environmental issue.

Sustainable development is a perspective on environmental management that emphasizes the need to reconcile present and future economic needs through environmental conservation.

Sustainable forest management is a process rather than a prescribed system of forest management. Elements may include participatory and equitable approaches to decision making geared toward maintaining ecosystem and landscape functions while also meeting economic, social, and cultural needs.

A **swing state** is one that attempts to bargain for major concessions in return for acceding to a global environmental agreement.

Technology transfer is the transfer, usually from highly industrialized to less industrialized, developing countries, of the means of producing scientifically or technically advanced goods in the form of patents, machinery and equipment, or necessary scientific-technical knowledge.

Transboundary air pollution is the emission of pollutants, such as nitric and sulfuric acids, across national boundaries.

A **unitary actor model** is an explanatory concept based on the assumption that state actors can be treated as though they are a single entity with a single, internally consistent set of values and attitudes.

The **Uruguay Round** refers to the negotiations under the auspices of the General Agreement on Tariffs and Trade on liberalization of world trade that began in 1985 in Uruguay and ended in 1994 with the establishment of the World Trade Organization.

A **veto coalition** is a group of veto states that forms around a given issue.

A **veto (or blocking) state** is one that by virtue of its importance on a particular environmental issue is able to block or weaken international agreement.

Volatile organic compounds (VOCs) are organic gases emitted from certain solids or liquids. Examples include paints, lacquers, and paint strippers; cleaning supplies; pesticides; building materials and furnishings; office equipment such as copiers and printers; and graphics and craft materials, including glues and adhesives, permanent markers, and photographic solutions. VOCs are a major contributor to ground-level ozone pollution.

Index